PURPOSES OF ART

Second Edition

PURPOSES OF ART

An Introduction to the History and Appreciation of Art

ALBERT E. ELSEN

Indiana University

HOLT, RINEHART AND WINSTON, INC.

New York   Chicago   San Francisco   Toronto   London

DEDICATIONS LIKE REVISIONS NEED ADDITIONS:
TO MATTHEW, NANCY, AND KATHERINE

Library of Congress Catalogue Card Number: 67–10266.
All rights reserved. No part of the contents of this book may
be reproduced without the written permission of the publishers,
Holt, Rinehart and Winston, Inc., New York.
A Helvetica Press production: Printed in black-and-white gravure
and bound by the Héliogravure Centrale, Lausanne, Switzerland;
color offset by Joh. Enschedé en Zonen, Haarlem, Holland,
printed by the Imprimeries Réunies, Lausanne, Switzerland.
2594851

PREFACE

The purpose of this book is to increase the reader's awareness, understanding, and tolerance of art. The appreciation of art presupposes these conditions of mind, and they are best achieved by a familiarity with art's history. Art is not for every man, and this is not a book that tries to bring art to the public by diluting its complexity or by ignoring its mysteries. The public that *cares* should be encouraged to come to art seriously and openly, and it is for such readers that *Purposes of Art* has been written.

The plan of *Purposes of Art* has been conceived as an alternative to the linear, chronological history of art, and also to the art appreciation book that dissects works of art into "elements," thereby giving a piecemeal exposure to what was intended as a unified expression of a complete experience. Consequently, this book is not structured according to a strict historical chronology, and in it art's history is presented as a type of mosaic composed of both themes and chronological evolution. Each work of art is treated as an integrated whole of meaning and form, set within the various historical and topical contexts illustrative of the book's essential premise: *art's great purpose has been to assist men in mastering their environments and liberating themselves.* Thus, art takes its place along with science in the civilizing of humanity.

The various chapters include many environments that overlap each other and influence men's artistic expression—the religious and spiritual, the political and economic, the natural and man made, the intellectual and esthetic, and the social and psychological. The working definition of art used for this book is that art is the skillful and imaginative creation of objects which interpret human experience and produce an esthetic response. As ego-gratification or extensions and metaphors of human experience, painting, sculpture, and architecture can be shown to have been effective means of achieving harmony with the visible and invisible world.

Historians attempt to answer the questions of what, where, when, how, and why. The why, or purpose of art, is here brought into special focus in the search for answers to a question commonly posed by the public before works of art. While seeking a representative and interesting sampling of world art with which to pursue this question and its answers, the author has continued the book's imbalance, in its new edition, between East and West, and among painting, sculpture, and architecture. The final selection of works illustrated reflects the author's ideas about their appropriateness for an introductory book of this type as well as his competence to comment on them. In a real sense, art history is the record of how individual historians react to their subject.

The late critic and connoisseur, Bernard Berenson, reportedly was once asked whether he had changed the views he expressed about a Renaissance artist in a book written fifty years earlier. Berenson answered that he had. When asked if he would include this change of attitude in a revision, he is said to have replied, "No! One does not tamper with a classic." This preface to the second edition of *Purposes of Art* should reassure the reader of the author's more modest estimate of his book and his willingness to modify its original, unclassical plan. A principal change has been in the enlargement of chapters, which makes possible fuller commentary upon more works of art. There has been an improvement in the number and quality of illustrations, more than sixty of which are now in color. New chapters include those on the artist—his training and status throughout history—the architecture of secular authority, the art of the nineteenth century, imaginative art, and abstraction.

There is also a new sequence for certain parts of the book. The chapters on Michelangelo and Rembrandt are now preceded and followed by topics representative of the artistic and intellectual milieu in which these artists work. The reader should in this edition obtain a more specific sense of the chronology of Western art from the Middle Ages to the twentieth century. The art of our time is either partially or entirely the subject of the last seven chapters.

Today it appears harder than five years ago to interest students and the general reader in art produced before 1900. This is partly the result of the greater familiarity with modern art made possible by the mass media and countless exhibitions in museums and galleries throughout the country. While in this revision additions have been made to the material on modern art, still more have been made to the sections on older art. The purpose of this and other changes is one the author hopes will appeal to his readers. Mary Renault expressed it in *The Bull from the Sea:* "It is the mark of little men that they like what they know." The quality and productive character of the research done by the author's colleagues in art history are constant reminders of that irritating but wonderful discontent that advances knowledge and makes imperative the rewriting of what has been written.

ACKNOWLEDGMENTS

The bibliography at the end of the book suggests the many historians to whom I am indebted for ideas and information. Not always thus acknowledged but deserving of gratitude are the teachers at Columbia University under whom I studied many years ago—among them Professors Meyer Schapiro, William Bell Dinsmoor, Julius Held, Emerson Swift, Millard Meiss, and Howard Davis. My present colleagues Henry R. Hope, Roy Sieber, Bertrand Davezac, Diether Thimme, and John Jacobus have been generous in helping me reduce errors of fact and in supplying sources of information. For reviews and criticisms of the original edition and this revision I want to thank Alfred Moir and Corlette Walker of the art faculty at the University of California, Santa Barbara. Year in and year out the development of *Purposes of Art* has received considerable impetus from the many good art history graduate students at Indiana University who have taught from it. Among those whose contributions I am able to recall are Peggy Gilfoy, Mazelle Kirkpatrick, Jan and Gerald C. Maddox, Ellen Bauer, Millard Hearn, David Rogers, Wilma Stern, now teaching at Pennsylvania State University, Bradley Nickels, now on the faculty of Lawrence University, and George Bauer of Northwestern's French Department. This revised edition was midwifed by former research assistants Arthur Stevens of Scripps College and Harry Gaugh, now at Skidmore College. Their good humor matched their research abilities, and the revision has been all the more enjoyable to write because of them.

London, England   Albert E. Elsen
March, 1967

CONTENTS

CHRONOLOGY OF TEXT REFERENCES TO WESTERN AND EASTERN ART

(All dates are approximate)

PREHISTORY				
AURIGNACIAN	40,000–20,000 B.C.			
MAGDALENIAN	16,000–10,000			
LATE NEOLITHIC: EARLY BRONZE AGE IN BRITAIN	1800–1400			
EGYPT				
OLD KINGDOM	3200–2160 B.C.			
MIDDLE KINGDOM	2160–1590			
NEW KINGDOM	1590–525	**CHINA**		
MESOPOTAMIA		SHANG-YIN DYNASTY	1500–1000 B.C.	
ASSYRIA	884–626 B.C.	CHOU DYNASTY	1000–221	
GREECE				
ARCHAIC	600–500 B.C.	**INDIA**		
TRANSITIONAL	500–450	MAURYA	322–185 B.C.	
CLASSICAL	450–400	SUNGA	185–80	
TRANSITIONAL	400–350	**CHINA**		
HELLENISTIC	350 B.C.–300 A.D.	HAN DYNASTY	220 B.C.–225 A.D.	
ROME		**JAPAN**		
REPUBLIC	700–31 B.C.	PROTOHISTORIC	250–550 A.D.	
WESTERN EMPIRE	31 B.C.–400 A.D.	**INDIA**		
EASTERN OR BYZANTINE EMPIRE	323–1453	KUSHAN, LATER ANDHRA PERIOD	50–230 A.D.	
EARLY CHRISTIAN ART IN ITALY	3rd–8th CENTURIES	GUPTA AND SUCCESSORS	320–650	
HIBERNO-SAXON	7th–8th			
CAROLINGIAN EMPIRE	8th–9th			
ANGLO-SAXON; OTTONIAN	10th–11th	**CHINA**		
		SUNG DYNASTY: NORTH	960–1126	
ROMANESQUE	1000–1200	SOUTH	960–1280	
GOTHIC		**JAPAN**		
NORTH	12th–16th CENTURIES	FUJIWARA	1185–1392	
SOUTH	13th–15th	ASHIGAKA	1392–1593	
FLEMISH	15th	**CHINA**		
RENAISSANCE (ITALY)	1420–1515	MING DYNASTY	1368–1644	
MANNERISM (COUNTER-RENAISSANCE)	1515–1600			
BAROQUE	1600–1780			
NINETEENTH CENTURY				
ROMANTICISM	1815–1850			
REALISM	1850–1875			
IMPRESSIONISM	1865–1885			
COUNTER-IMPRESSIONISM	1885–1900			
TWENTIETH CENTURY				
FAUVISM	1900–1910			
EXPRESSIONISM	1905–1920			
CUBISM	1907–			
FUTURISM	1910–1914			
DADA	1916–1922			
SURREALISM	1924–1940			
ABSTRACT ART	1910–			

1

INTRODUCTION: THE ARTIST'S PAST TRAINING AND STATUS

A true and thorough study of art and its historical development necessarily calls for an examination of the artist and his work from many points of view. Beginning with the work itself and taking account of all the available relevant information, the student of art should recognize that an intelligent appreciation of creative activity must proceed from varied sources: biographical data, knowledge of the historical situation and social context, philosophical and esthetic premises of the time, and particular considerations such as working methods, patronage systems, and immediate purposes.

The first thing to be conceded about the purposes of art is that historians are without information in many historical areas of this subject. A mica hand made by an American Indian (Fig. 1), for example, confronts the viewer like a stop sign. This object is a many-sided sign, however, for it directs one to the past, to a distinctive culture and possibly to religious beliefs, to an excellent craft tradition that allowed beautiful work in such unlikely material, and to a creator of considerable artistic intelligence. Although the hand was found in a burial mound in Ohio, experience with similar burial finds in other cultures, such as those in the southeastern United States, does not allow us to say with certainty whether this object was identified

with a funerary cult, a god, or simply the deceased, or whether it was a ritual object or talisman, a sign of prestige or an occupational symbol. There is no suggestion that the hand is broken off from a wrist, so that it has a curious and mysterious look of completeness and self-

Figure 1. *Hand*, from Ross County, Ohio. Hopewell Culture, 300 B.C.–500 A.D. Mica, $11^{1}/_{5} \times 6''$. The Ohio Historical Society, Columbus.

sufficiency. Yet, without a convincing explanation of the actual burial, social, or religious context, can we even be sure of this impression? The hand may have been traced from that of the artist. The fingers, long and tapered, are not those which would testify to hard manual exercise; but is this perhaps a convention of style rather than a symbol of elevated rank? We cannot be sure of whether or not it was intended to be seen from a given direction, or that it is some symbolic gesture. What *is* sure is its existence, and the reminder it provides that such a presentation of the human hand by itself still has the power to move us, to provoke thought and wonder. Whatever the motive behind its creation, we can assume that the hand was important to its maker and his patron, whether living or deceased.

Some of the oldest known wall paintings give abundant testimony of the importance that the leaving of a visible trace of one's hand had for some prehistoric men. On the walls of the northern Spanish caves of Altamira, Stone Age men are presumed to have blown colored pigments through a hollow bone, like a rudimentary spray gun, on and around their hands placed against the wall so that the outlines would thus be traced on the surface (Fig. 2). There is no evidence of the handprints being arranged in any kind of sequence; nor is there any discernible relation to the bison depicted with them. Moreover, they are not always found in conjunction with painted animals, so that one becomes cautious about their identification as the artist's "signature." We must also be guarded in attributing the frequency of such handprints merely to a childlike delight in

Figure 2. *Polychrome Bison*, with hands superimposed. Magdalenian period, c. 15,000–9000 B.C. Cave painting. Length of bison c. 36″. Altamira, Spain.

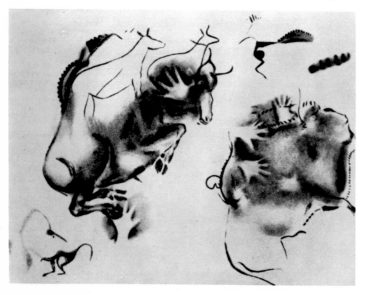

discovering how to leave marks of one's presence, for these animal paintings show signs of a certain sophistication.

That a man's individuality could be expressed through his hand has been known for centuries; even in ancient times, it was customary to refer to a work of art as "coming from the hand of" some artist. To our knowledge, not until the twentieth century did an artist actually affirm his identity in his work by means of his handprint. The American abstract painter Jackson Pollock not only applied his paint-covered hand to the upper right corner of his canvas, but he repeated the gesture several times—perhaps in view of the absence of any other single readily comparable shape in his entire painting (Fig. 3). Rarely used by Pollock, the handprint was, needless to say, the best possible guarantee against forgery of his abstractions.

The absence of evidence other than the works themselves confounds us when we try to discover why the Indian and Altamira artists made their objects and chose their motifs. Despite the fact that Pollock, who died relatively recently, had many friends and made personal statements about his art, modern research methods still cannot disentangle and decide the psychological motives or the purposes that impelled his response to life through his art. Every serious artist has, in a sense, been the pupil and rival of artists who came before him, and the twin motives of continuing and surpassing art of the past were certainly not unknown to Pollock. More surprisingly, perhaps, present-day studies of Stone Age peoples suggest that these same incentives, though tied in with religion, magic, and other purposes, may have obtained from the earliest periods of human history in which art was made.

Despite the similar feature of the handprint included in both, between the Paleolithic and Pollock paintings there is a difference that, in order to be accounted for, involves citing the whole history of Western and, to some extent, Eastern art. Not only the character and location of their paintings, their styles and media, but also the differences in the very relationship of the artists to their societies and the occasion for making their paintings are factors that required thousands of years to evolve. Rather than write in generalities about art in this introduction, the author feels that it may be more helpful for the reader to learn something of the history of the Western artist's profession

Figure 3. JACKSON POLLOCK. *Number 1*. 1948. Oil on canvas, 5′8″ × 8′8″. The Museum of Modern Art, New York (Purchase). (See detail in Fig. 531).

in terms of his training, his social status, and those for whom he worked. In this way, the implications of Pollock's handprint may become more understandable, as part of the evidence of what men have created through coordination of mind, feelings, eye, and hand throughout the history of art.

THE ARTIST IN ANTIQUITY

The manual effort required for the creation of art was throughout much of history the principal reason for the artist's low social status. Physical labor of any sort was looked down upon by the ruling classes in the ancient Near East, Greece, and Rome, and it was not until the coming of Christianity and the making

of religious art by monks—many of whom had been noblemen—that there was a significant change in attitude toward the manual activity required by art. There is circumstantial evidence that some form of art training existed even in prehistoric times, if one is to judge on the basis of cave drawings that appear to have been done by apprentices and then corrected by more skilled hands. There is abundant evidence that art shools existed in ancient Egypt over 5,000 years ago. Many models of sculpture and painting from which students were trained to imitate have survived. Egyptian wall paintings show craftsmen, artists' assistants, and master artists at work on projects for the royal palaces, temples, and tombs (Fig. 4). Since "high" art, as distinguished from village handicrafts, was the prerogative of the pharaohs and priests

Figure 4. *Egyptian Craftsmen at Work*. c. 1400 B.C. Wall painting. Tomb of the Sculptors Nebamun and Ipuki, Thebes.

of Egypt, the best artists were in their service. With some few exceptions, basic formulas and styles of Egyptian art hardened at an early date and persisted for almost three millenniums. Artists were enjoined to repeat the art that already existed, and originality was unheard of and uncalled for as a quality of art. The perpetuation of a relatively constant art was intimately linked with the preservation of the pharaoh's political authority and the power of the priests; the art schools ensured this continuity. While certain Egyptian architects achieved distinction, and even divinity (not being required to use their hands), there was no such official or social recognition for painters and sculptors.

In ancient Greece, well before the time of Alexander the Great (fourth century B.C.), painters and sculptors of distinction were known by name. From scenes on Greek vases we obtain an idea of what the activity in a sculptor's shop was like: assistants are shown working at various tasks amid the tools and products of their craft (Figs. 5, 6). Classical Greek literature before the fourth century B.C., however, tells us nothing about important artists and their training, a fact which suggests that although great visual art was appreciated, its makers were either scorned or considered unworthy of mention in poetry and drama. A sixth-century Greek sculptor named Theodorus of Samos is known to have cast a bronze sculpture of himself holding a file, and the fifth-century sculptor Polyclitus wrote a celebrated "canon" of ideal proportions in sculpture, both of which works were lost. The activity of these men indicates that some artists were interested in recognition and were concerned with passing on their ideas and work to later generations. It is thus from the fifth century B.C. that we have the first record of writing by artists on art. Manual labor in ancient Greece was reserved for slaves, and although

painters and sculptors were mostly freemen, their engaging in work with their hands and for monetary reward combined to keep their social status down in pre-Classical and Classical times. From the time of Alexander the Great, there arises in Greek literature the celebration of the godlike attributes of great painters such as Apelles. For centuries after, even into the Renaissance, stories were told of the favors that Alexander bestowed upon his favorite painters, such as that of his giving one of his mistresses to Apelles. During and after Alexander's time, famous artists were known to have dressed well, lived in luxury, and made magnanimous civic gestures: Polygnotus, for instance, painted public walls without recompense. Working for money was a social stigma in Greece and Rome. In the late fourth century B.C., Douris of Samos wrote the first biographical book on artists, composed largely of traditional stories or anecdotes concerning artists who had died long before. Although this book survives only in a fragment, it is important historically for inaugurating the biographical literature on artists. One does not find in Greek literature, however, any appreciation or commentary on the imaginative or esthetic aspect of art, simply references to its technical aspects.

Roman writers such as Seneca and Plutarch were repeating Greek prejudices when they commented that works of art might be enjoyed but their makers were to be disdained. What drew the ire of Roman writers upon their artist contemporaries was, more usually, the high prices affixed to their works. Roman emperors such as Nero were dilettante painters (none were sculptors, probably explainable by the less physical effort demanded of the painter than of the sculptor), but even this circumstance did not elevate the painters socially. Despite the great importance of artists for the Romans—their use by generals to record military cam-

Left : Figure 5. The Foundry Painter. *Bronze Foundry* (detail of an Attic kylix). c. 470 B.C. Full height 4¾". Staatliche Museen, Berlin.   *Right :* Figure 6.   Opposite side of kylix in Fig. 5.

paigns, by emperors to establish their authoritative image throughout the empire and to decorate whole cities, and by the priests to give tangible form to the gods—Roman literature shows no interest in the personalities or life histories of Rome's artists. In consequence of the great interest the Romans had in Classical Greek art of the fifth century B.C., as expressed in their avid collecting and their commissioning of copies, Roman artists were unfavorably compared with their Greek predecessors in the quality of sincerity. It is not surprising that, other than a few painted vases, there has not come down to us from Greece and Rome any significant body of painting or sculpture having artists and their work as the subject matter. When it was suspected that the great Greek sculptor Phidias had carved his own portrait on the shield of the *Athena Parthenos*, housed in the illustrious temple on the Acropolis, he was publicly criticized for his vanity. This over-all absence of self-portraits or other visual evidence of the making of art should not be construed as proof that important ancient artists were but anonymous, or humble workmen; yet the nature of their paid physical work did link them with the craftsmen assigned a low rung on the social ladder despite the flamboyant and zealous efforts of a few great Greek artists. Not until the fifteenth century, when certain Italian artists began to concern themselves with theoretical knowledge, was art ranked with the liberal arts and thus given greater dignity than mere craft or artisanship.

THE MONASTIC ARTIST

From the fourth to the twelfth century, Christian monasteries in Western Europe were the great schools and production centers of art. In the early Middle Ages the chief task of the monastic libraries was the preservation and duplication of books, many of which had come down from antiquity. In the monastic writing rooms, where there was often a division of artistic labor, scribes and illuminators reproduced and decorated Christian texts and, to a lesser extent, ancient secular books (see Chapter 5, "The Sacred Book"). As part of the monastic routine, the artistic work of the monks was viewed as the proper service of God and the Church, and some of the social stigma attached to the physical labor involved was removed.

Figure 7. *Two Scribes at Work* and *Presentation of the Manuscript to the Emperor*, from *The Book of Pericopes of Henry III*. 1039–40. Manuscript illumination. Staatsbibliothek, Bremen.

From the time of Charlemagne, at the end of the seventh and the beginning of the eighth century, many monasteries had imperial support and undertook important royal commissions for making sumptuous books. An eleventh-century German manuscript illustrates such officially sponsored monastic activity (Fig. 7). Book adornment was not the only artistic form engaged in by the monasteries, however; sculpture, goldsmithing, enamel work, weaving, and building also enlisted the talents of the monks and lay brethren who were brought into the monasteries because of their special skills. Secular artists and architects so employed were often itinerant, and they formed a mobile labor supply that journeyed about Europe, and worked in various monasteries on painting, sculpture, or architectural projects. Until the rise of the large cities of Western Europe in the eleventh and twelfth centuries, monasteries were unrivaled in the training of artists and for their artistic production. Through the centuries many monasteries had accumulated great wealth along with their religious and artistic prestige. By the eleventh and twelfth centuries, in the large monastic centers much of the actual art was made by laymen, inside and outside the walls, and the monks were often cast in the role of organizers or overseers of secular artistic labor. All through the Middle Ages, the monasteries provided the artistic schooling for those employed in the manors, courts, and gradually in the cities, until by the twelfth and thirteenth centuries, the cities themselves began to rival and then surpass the monasteries in the training of artists and in the production of art.

LODGE, GUILD, AND WORKSHOP

Of great importance in the history of art is the transition, during the twelfth and thirteenth centuries, from the making of art by monks in monasteries to secular artists working in cities. During this period the "lodge" form of artist's organization and artisan's cooperative came into being in conjunction with the building and decorating of the great cathedrals. The lodge hierarchy consisted of the supervising master architect, who directed the general artistic program, other master artists, and journeymen masons and carvers. Members were free to come and go, but usually a nucleus of lodge members remained to finish an assignment and then often moved on as a group to a new project. The activities of the lodge were all coordinated by one supervisor, who in turn was following specifications set down by the Church. The lodge organization was thus intended to facilitate and harmonize the various special tasks of these great undertakings.

In the eleventh and twelfth centuries, the decorative carving and painting were actually executed directly on the building, with artists working from scaffolds. Gradually, in the twelfth and thirteenth centuries, the painters and sculptors quite literally "detached" themselves from the architecture and began to make the sculpture and paintings in workshops located near the site or elsewhere in the town. This was reflected in and eventually changed the character of the relationship of painting and sculpture to the architecture (with the first two becoming more independent). The craftsmen who worked in the lodge proper, which was usually a building attached to or near the cathedral, were committed to live on the premises as well and were subject to strict regulations regarding their pay and standards of workmanship.

It was not until the fourteenth and fifteenth centuries, when a broad middle class first had enough money and the incentive to commission painting and sculpture on its own, that it became economically feasible for an artist to set up his own workshop in a city. With the growing wealth and the increasing demand of the urban populace for both religious and secular art, the lodge organization gave way to the guilds of painters and sculptors. Other professions had, in general, organized into guilds even earlier than the artists. In Italy, one finds artists associated in guilds as early as the thirteenth century. In northern Europe, the artist guilds became numerous in the fourteenth and fifteenth centuries, with some of the earlier ones being formed in Ghent (1339), Tournai (1341), and Bruges (1351).

The purposes of the guilds were to protect members from outside competition and to instill and ensure pride, respectability, skill, and loyalty by providing and enforcing standards for the professional and personal welfare of the members. With the exception of royal commissions, which were outside such regulation, in many cities only guild members were allowed to work at painting and sculpture. The organization of the guild was hierarchical, consisting of a board of overseers responsible for the observance of rules, the master artists, journeymen (or paid assistants), and apprentices, and each group had its own spokesmen. Regulations for training, for performance, and for promotion to the different grades were set forth in writing. The guild often solicited customers, determined the just price of a finished work, and decided whether or not its quality met required standards. Defective work could be confiscated, and delinquent members fined or expelled. Prices were largely determined on the basis of the cost of materials and the time involved. Artists were expected to be able to do an accepted amount in a given period of time, and they could be paid on the basis of the size of the area painted.

The guilds' emphasis was placed not on artistic theory but on the more matter-of-fact technical considerations, such as the making of tools and the employment of high-quality materials. The guilds also occupied themselves with providing codes of morality for members and ensuring fair labor practices, such as the proper housing of apprentices. In addition, they were responsible for burial insurance, widows' pensions, and the saying of Masses for deceased members. Organized artists also participated effectively in local political affairs and were found in civic posts such as town councilmen or tax-collecting officials. Both in Italy and the Netherlands, guilds were themselves important patrons of art and commissioned paintings and sculpture for their guild halls and chapels. As an attempt by artists to achieve some measure of collective security, the medieval guilds had no counterpart in antiquity.

Plate 1.   ROGIER VAN DER WEYDEN. *St. Luke Drawing the Virgin.* C. 1435.
Oil on panel, 4′6¼″ × 3′7⅞″. The Museum of Fine Arts, Boston.

Plate 2. DIEGO VELÁZQUEZ. *The Maids of Honor (Las Meninas).*
1651. Oil on canvas, 10′5″ × 9′. Prado, Madrid.

Plate 3. Cave Paintings. c. 15,000-9000 B.C. Lascaux (Dordogne), France.

Plate 4. Movable Mask, from Cape Mudge, British Columbia. 1850–75. Painted wood, height 21 ½ ". The Museum of the American Indian, Heye Foundation, New York.

The guilds were not always confined to painters and sculptors, but often included other professionals and artisans such as saddle makers, pharmacists, and glass blowers. Artists were also called upon to decorate banners, armor, ships, furniture, and other household objects. Such alliance with the crafts did not help to raise the social status of artists as a whole, but there were outstanding individual painters and sculptors who did achieve public recognition and played important roles in their city's history. At the height of the guild system, nonetheless, the honor of the guild was to be placed above all by its members.

The patron saint of many artists' guilds throughout Europe was St. Luke the Evangelist, who it was believed had been an artist and had actually drawn the Virgin and Christ. A fifteenth-century panel painting by the Flemish artist Rogier van der Weyden (Pl. 1) depicts the Evangelist sketching the Virgin and the Christ child; in the light of its subject, this painting may have been a guild commission. Of particular interest to the history of the artist himself is the fact that there is a strong likelihood that van der Weyden painted himself as St. Luke. Since the fourteenth century, artists and their secular patrons have left their own image in religious works of art, whereas formerly a monk or abbot would have at most signed a work as being by his hand or through his commission.

Van der Weyden's painting, and conceivably even his likeness, would have passed guild inspection and approval primarily in these respects: the preparation and quality of the wood of the panel; the priming coat of a plasterlike substance; the quality of the pigments purchased and then ground either by the artist himself or by an apprentice; the clarity and purity of the glazes laid over the paint; the appropriateness and decorum of his symbols and figure types, as well as their setting. From the guild, an artist would learn of the lives of the saints and their symbols, in other words, all the suitable elements for a religious painting. When an artist inherited his profession, as was often the case, the guild served to school him from childhood in many areas directly and indirectly connected with his profession.

ARTISTIC GENIUS AND OFFICIAL PATRONAGE

It was during the fifteenth century in Italy that the most important steps were taken to elevate art from the lower, craft status of the mechanical arts to that of the liberal and theoretical arts. What impeded a general improvement of the artists' social status in Italy during this century were the age-old considerations of their low birth—with the exception of a very few artists such as Alberti and Leonardo—and their training in a workshop as craftsmen, for until the end of the century, with the advent of the art of Michelangelo, large painting and sculpture commissions were expected to be collaborative efforts (Fig. 8). This does not mean that individual artists failed to gain handsome financial reward and great civic admiration; but when this was the case, it was often because the artist had been able to resist the guild monopoly by undertaking important commissions for the Church or official court circles, enterprises that permitted mobility from town to town and at least temporary exemption from guild membership and regulations. (It was not until 1571 that Italian artists could legitimize their independence from the guild as legally recognized supported individual professionals.)

In 1455, the sculptor Lorenzo Ghiberti published the first artist's autobiography. It appeared after the successful completion of his second great

Figure 8. Nanni di Banco. *Sculptor's Workshop*, from the base of the *Tabernacle of the Four Saints*. c. 1410–14. Marble. Or San Michele, Florence.

Figure 9. LORENZO GHIBERTI. *Self-portrait*, detail of the "Gates of Paradise." c. 1435. Gilded bronze. Baptistery, Florence.

pair of bronze doors for the Baptistery of Florence, the "Gates of Paradise" (Fig. 9), on which Ghiberti had the temerity to include his own portrait. In his autobiography, not only does he proudly or boastfully proclaim all that he has accomplished and that he is an inventive rather than an imitative artist, but he also writes what he feels the education of the new artist of his day should include. His insistence upon the liberal arts, still acquired in the context of a workshop such as he himself operated, is symptomatic of the changing status of the artist. Ghiberti wrote: "The sculptor—and the painter also—should be trained in all these liberal arts: Grammar, Geometry, Philosophy, Medicine, Astronomy, Perspective, History, Anatomy, Theory of Design, Arithmetic." Ghiberti was thus equating the artist with the scholar, and the idea of the artist as a man of learning was taking shape. It was Leonardo, Michelangelo, and Raphael who were most responsible for putting Ghiberti's admonition into practice, and by working independently, they achieved great respect for themselves and new recognition for their profession in the early sixteenth century. Leonardo established nature, rather than a workshop master, as the true source and guide of artistic inspiration.

10   Purposes of Art

Albrecht Dürer's engraving of 1514 entitled *Melencolia I* is a spiritual self-portrait that illustrates, in an appropriately esoteric way, the new concept of the artist as a genius, albeit a melancholy one (Fig. 10). By means of symbol and allegory, in keeping with the practice and intellectual taste of his time, he shows genius or the creative gift in terms of a superior feminine winged being who is reduced to a state of inaction amid the symbols of the arts and sciences. In Dürer's time, people of melancholy disposition (hence of unpleasant and unstable nature) were considered superior to other men. Born under Saturn, they were thought to have the gift of imagination but to be limited in attainment in such higher fields as metaphysics. Dürer used the inactive, despondent pose and the varied array of objects to indicate that, although inspired by transcendent visions, his own limitations as a human prevented him from realizing his hopes. Having mastered the skills and the geometry required in his art, he was in turn trapped by their very inadequacies. It was in the sixteenth century that the concept of artistic "genius" achieved widespread acceptance, when important artists such as Dürer, Michelangelo, and Titian gained intellectual recognition and helped substantially to upgrade their profession. It was also from the time of Dürer that collectors

Figure 10. ALBRECHT DÜRER. *Melencolia I.* 1514. Engraving, 9¼ × 6⅝". The National Gallery of Art, Washington, D.C. (Rosenwald Collection).

came to value drawings as finished and valuable works of art in themselves, important especially in that they intimately reflect the hand of the artist who made them.

In the annals of the sixteenth century it is not uncommon to read of the great artists accepted in the company of intellectuals as well as royalty. Pieter Bruegel the Elder, for example, kept company with some of the most learned men in Europe. His drawing of the 1560s (Fig. 11), in which he had the self-confidence and courage to satirize those who purchase art, may have been a spiritual self-portrait in the manner of the Dürer engraving. Bruegel shows an artist intent upon his work, as a bespectacled buyer fumbles for the money to buy the painting. The drawing is a calculated contrast in human types and in vision. The artist frowns at that which clearly pleases the foolish patron. (The Flemish word for spectacles also signified "fool.") The strong, sure hand of the artist emphasizes the awkward gesture of the patron. Both Bruegel and Dürer tell us that the artist's vision is inaccessible to us, and that the making of art involves problems the layman cannot recognize.

The homely dress of Bruegel's artist is deceptive in regard to the way the successful artist of his century and thereafter might be expected to appear in public. From the sixteenth and seventeenth centuries there have survived innumerable prints and paintings in which artists pay homage to other artists and affirm that in dress and manners they could be gentlemen. Upon the death of the Flemish artist Hans Bol, his friend Hendrik Goltzius did an engraving (Fig. 12) in which the dead man was accorded symbolic funerary honors of an important person. Bol is shown as a well-groomed and handsomely attired gentleman, his effigy surrounded by attributes of his profession as well as those of death.

During the seventeenth century, Peter Paul Rubens attained not only great artistic fame in northern Europe but also renown as a diplomat in the service of the Spanish king. Amassing great wealth as a consequence of the quality and productivity of his large workshop (run not unlike that of a medieval artist), he acquired a palatial house in Antwerp, filled it with works of art and antiquities, and on their wedding day painted himself and his bride in their beautiful rose garden (Fig. 13). Rubens

Figure 11. PIETER BRUEGEL THE ELDER. *The Painter and the Connoisseur.* c. 1565. Brown ink on paper, 9⅝ × 8½". Albertina, Vienna.

Figure 12. HENDRIK GOLTZIUS. *Portrait of Hans Bol.* c. 1593. Engraving, 10¼ × 7". Private Collection.

Figure 13. PETER PAUL RUBENS. *Self-portrait with Isabella Brandt.* 1609–10. Oil on canvas, 5′9½″ × 4′5½″. Alte Pinakothek, Munich.

and his wife are seen dressed in the height of fashion, and their good looks and personal bearing help to create what might well be an aristocratic image.

Artists had served kings since the time of the pharaohs, usually being attached to the court but assigned an inferior status. By the sixteenth century, however, famous artists who had made their reputations as independent figures were often honored by kings by being given titles and special prerogatives. One of the great paintings in the history of art involving the work of the artist at court was done by Diego Velazquez, who in the seventeenth century was chamberlain to Philip IV, King of Spain. Velazquez' painting, originally titled *The Royal Family*, later came to be called *Las Meninas* because of the young ladies-in-waiting grouped around the Infanta Marguerita, the king's blond daughter (Pl. 2). The scene is in a high-ceilinged, sparsely furnished room of the royal palace, with paintings from the king's collection filling the walls. A mirror on the far wall reflects the

images of the King and Queen as if they are in the position of a viewer looking at the scene. Velazquez, standing at the left before a tall canvas seen from the back, is attired in court dress and wears at his belt the key of his office. The foreground focus is shared by the Infanta, her attendants, a dwarf, and a dog. Mindful of his station and prerogatives, Velazquez discreetly portrays himself in a position that is logical both in the context of the painting and for the courtly world of rank. The ingenuity and brilliance of the conception of this painting, as well as its virtuoso execution, help us to understand why such exceptional painters were favored by seventeenth-century rulers for projecting their official public image and for capturing the more private scenes of court life.

FROM ART CLUBS TO THE ACADEMIES

Leonardo protested in his writings against the guild method of education, in which children would begin at about twelve years of age as apprentices learning their craft by cleaning and repairing brushes, grinding pigments, preparing the canvas, and then imitating the drawing and painting of the master until the novice could complete a work from a sketch given to him. During this period, which might last for as long as six years, the apprentice would perform a variety of other, nonartistic services for the master. His journeyman period involved working for other artists in various locations, until he could show by his proficiency that he was ready to join a guild or company in some city, where he then settled down. Leonardo wanted aspiring artists to study science, especially perspective, and by such theoretical learning, painting as a creative effort might be divorced from mere craft. Michelangelo avoided the rigors of the guild system, since he was given the opportunity instead to study ancient works of art under the guidance of an old sculptor in the court of Lorenzo de' Medici. His later refusal to take pupils or to use assistants for his important work exemplified a new ideal of individuality.

In the first half of the sixteenth century, several artists' clubs were formed in Italy. An engraving by Eneas Vico from a drawing by Baccio Bandinelli, a sculptor and rival of

Michelangelo, shows a group of artists of various ages gathered in a room, where they have come to draw or watch others draw and to discuss theories and what was being done (Fig. 14). Not an art school in the sense of students executing a problem under the direction of a teacher, this group was rather an informal gathering of apprentices and artists, in order to practice drawing in a room of the Vatican provided for Bandinelli by the Pope.

One of the earliest art academies was founded in Florence in 1561 by the artist Giorgio Vasari, celebrated for his *Lives of the Artists*, which is the foundation of art historical writing. His Accademia del Disegno, which brought together outstanding artists in an organization under the patronage of the Grand Duke of Florence, Cosimo I de' Medici, provided an alternative to the guilds. Vasari's academy planned a more enlightened education of young artists, which was to include lectures on such subjects as geometry. Students were encouraged to learn from studying artists such as Michelangelo by imitating his figures or whole compositions. In reality, however, Vasari's academy did little more than create a new artists' guild, and it made some contribution to elevating the social status of the profession.

The most important and influential of the early academies was that called the Accademia di San Luca, founded in Rome in 1593. It received papal encouragement because of concern over the poor quality of art produced for the Church by inadequately trained young artists. Although there seems to have been a substantial emphasis on abstract theory, guided by the artist Federigo Zuccari, a definite educational program was outlined whereby students would be taught to draw from plaster casts of ancient sculpture and from life. Their work was to be corrected by instructors, and

prizes were occasionally to be awarded. While the academy was not a great success—and, in fact, did not finally rival the guilds or sustain a system of course instruction—its ideas, like those of Leonardo and Vasari, were to influence the future training of artists. At the beginning of the seventeenth century, small groups of artists in various Italian cities such as Genoa and Bologna often assembled in one of their own studios or a room provided by a patron for purposes of studying together and drawing from a live model. It was from Italy that this idea was exported to northern Europe, at first on a small scale in the Netherlands at the end of the sixteenth and into the seventeenth century. Rembrandt, for example, taught his pupils to draw from life, as well as to study older art for its lessons.

The most famous and influential of all art academies was that founded in France in 1648, which under Louis XIV came to be known as the Académie Royale of painting and sculpture. In the preceding century, the idea of an academy had been developed to allow artists greater freedom from the guilds; but under the King and his prime minister Colbert, the royal academy was closely tied to the absolutist centralization of government and culture in France. As a consequence, while the artists or academicians attained greater social security and prestige, they sacrificed their independence. The leading French artists were obliged to become members, and a definite schedule of teaching and courses was established —even to a timetable for each week's instruction held in a wing of the Louvre. An elaborate hierarchy of graded membership was established, and assigned duties included attendance at worship services and business meetings, selecting and posing the model, providing examples of art to be drawn from, and correcting student

Figure 14. ENEAS VICO (after BACCIO BANDINELLI). *Artists and Apprentices*. c. 1550. Engraving, 12¼ × 19″. Private Collection.

13

work. The chief aim of the Académie Royale was to teach students to draw, model, and paint in the officially approved court style. Drawing from a live model was a right reserved for the royal academy, and its artistic monopoly extended even to the area of print making, so that engravings had to carry the notice *cum privilège du roi*. This inscription is found in Sebastien Le Clerc's engraving of 1700 (Fig. 15), in which he shows an ideal academy of fine arts and sciences. Colbert had seen that through such officially sponsored academies all forms of culture could be harnessed to the aims of the king. The Le Clerc vision is an enactment of the ideals of Leonardo, Alberti, Ghiberti, and other earlier artists who were concerned with joining visual arts with the liberal arts. In the engraving, small groups of teachers and students are disposed throughout a courtyard and arcades of an academically approved style of architecture based upon precepts of the Renaissance and antiquity. In this splendid setting, students are being instructed in natural science, perspective, astronomy, geography, palm reading, heraldry, architecture, painting, drawing from ancient sculpture, measuring buildings, mechanics, and theology. The students and instructors are shown in ancient costume, as if Le Clerc were reconstructing some mythical academy from antiquity, but very likely he was also showing an academician's distaste for contemporary costume. The art of antiquity set the norm for subjects, postures, figure type, and dress.

In actuality, students at the Académie Royale did listen to lectures on art theory, particularly with regard to perspective, anatomy, proportion, decorum (the proper appearance and conduct of painted figures), drawing, and composition. Canons, or definite rules, of art were established and taught. Often the lectures were based upon analysis of officially approved paintings and sculpture, thereby anticipating the modern teaching of art history. After four years of schooling in the academy and successful passage of examinations, the more promising students were allowed to work in Rome for four years and to send back to France copies of Roman art. When by satisfactorily completing various tests a student finally achieved the rank of academician, he could still choose to ally himself with some company of painters in a town, and he was assured of royal patronage. Art continued in the seventeenth and eighteenth centuries to be a hereditary profession, and the sons of academicians were given preferential treatment of various kinds when they entered upon their formal schooling.

In the eighteenth century the authoritarian rule of the Académie Royale by the king was relaxed. Despite a subsequent decline in power, after 1750 the French academy became the basis for similar academies sponsored by royalty throughout Europe, as a means of bringing art into its service and improving the economy. Craftsmen as well as artists could benefit from the same artistic training, based on the French model of drawing from other drawings, then from casts, and finally from the live model. Business interests saw a greater accessibility of art education as a means of improving their products and stimulating trade. Free-tuition art schools and other schools dedicated only to the crafts emerged in the eighteenth century. The French royal academy did not undergo serious alteration in its make-up until the time of the Revolution, when its concept of art in the service of the state was challenged. From the time of the academy's founding and in its subsequent history, young artists continued, in medieval fashion, to learn much of their profession from master artists, from whom a letter was required as part of the academic admission requirements.

Figure. 15. SEBASTIEN LE CLERC. *Academy of the Fine Arts and Sciences.* 1700. Engraving, 9½ × 14⅞″. Private Collection.

14

As had taken place in sixteenth-century Italy, English art academies were started from private artists' studios in the eighteenth century. In contrast to the official auspices of the European royal academies, those in England were private schools, with studies centered upon drawing from the live model. Artists in Holland, though allied to the old guilds, had the greatest independence—and the least financial security—of any European artists. Unlike French academicians who worked for lucrative and often grandiose, but circumscribed, commissions issuing from a narrow patronage base in the court, Dutch painters sold small-scale easel paintings either out of their studios or to dealers who served a broad middle-class clientele. (The first art dealers appeared in the sixteenth century, but as a profession they became more numerous and international in the seventeenth century.) Thus, the precedent for—that is, conditions encouraging the rise of—the modern artist who works on an independent basis is to be found in the wider sources of patronage in seventeenth-century Holland.

The nineteenth century saw the greatest proliferation and enrollment in art academies throughout Europe; yet this was also the century of their decline in importance. There were many reasons for this change: the large size of many academies, such as the Ecole des Beaux-Arts in Paris (which continues today, as successor to the Académie Royale); the routine and methods of instruction, which were felt to be too impersonal, too old-fashioned, or inimical to the development of young artists with talent and originality. Moreover, the alliance of the academies, be it formal or indirect, with conservative political forces aroused the antipathy of many artists. Academic training and its apparatus for exhibiting and selling works of art did not change with the new ideals of individualism that were sweeping Europe in nineteenth-century art, nor did it make effective provision for exhibition and sale of work by thousands of painters and sculptors to the newly expanding middle-class market.

INDEPENDENCE

In a series of nineteenth-century French paintings, one can see some of the significant changes in the history and status of the artist.

Figure 16. Massé. *The Studio of Baron Gros.* 1830. Oil on canvas, 33½ × 39¼". Musée Marmottan, Paris.

The first, by an artist named Massé (Fig. 16), depicts a scene in the private art school of Baron Gros, in which a group of students are shown drawing from a female model posed in the manner of an ancient sculpture or drawing of Venus. On the wall are displayed the palette and plaster bust of the painter Jacques Louis David, whose school Baron Gros had taken over when David was forced to flee France for political reasons. During the French Revolution David, though a product of the Académie, had attacked its leadership, drastically curbed its powers, and liberalized the opportunities for artists to exhibit under its auspices. David and Baron Gros, like other important nineteenth-century artist-teachers, in reality continued the long-established master artist-pupil relationship but introduced into their studio schools teaching methods they derived from the academies, such as courses in drawing from master drawings, casts, and the live model. Instead of a faculty of several instructors, as found in the academies, the artist himself guided his pupils. The private art school was the source of many important nineteenth- and early-twentieth-century painters, such as Manet, Degas, Toulouse-Lautrec, and Matisse.

A possible self-portrait by the French painter Théodore Géricault (Fig. 17) shows the artist alone in his studio, flanked by a plaster model of a figure used for studying anatomy, his palette, and a skull. The inactive, reflective pose of the artist suggests, like Dürer's *Melencolia*, the dilemma of the artist who must work alone, guided by his own genius, achieving freedom but also suffering from indecision, doubt, or unattainable visions. In France as well as

Figure 17. THÉODORE GÉRICAULT. *Portrait of an Artist in His Studio (Self-portrait?)*. c. 1810–12. Oil on canvas, 4'9⅛"×3'8⅛". Louvre, Paris.

Germany, the new Romantic concept of artistic genius and the need for its free expression meant that the artist had to work outside the academic tradition, whereas for Dürer the artist of genius could still work effectively within the guild system.

In 1855, Gustave Courbet painted a large picture entitled *The Studio, A Real Allegory of the Last Seven Years of My Life* (Fig. 18). Because this work was not accepted by the official jury that determined who would show in the great annual exhibitions, or Salons, Courbet borrowed money to present the first one-man exhibit in art history. His painting is not only a manifesto of what type of art he had given up and of how he worked, but it also conveyed the artist's place in society. Unlike Velázquez, Courbet does not show himself at court or even in the home of a patron; representatives of society come to his studio, to seek out the artist and his work. He divides them into two groups— at the left, those who are mercenary or gain

from others, often through their suffering, and at the right, those who support the artist, including writers such as the poet Baudelaire, his patron, and other friends. Literally and symbolically, the artist situates himself in the middle of his world; he is the fulcrum, the heart and creative center of modern society. As a young student, he had studied at a provincial branch of the academy, and in the background of the studio can be seen hanging a figure of St. Sebastian, indicative of the art-school milieu and problems. For several years he had worked under the inspiration of literature and from his imagination, in the tradition of older artists. But in this painting he shows himself painting a landscape from memory, with nature, like the nude model standing behind him, serving as his inspiration. In a letter to some prospective students, Courbet voiced the feelings of many artists of his century and of our own:

> I cannot teach my art, nor the art of any school, since I deny that art can be taught . . . art is completely individual, and that talent of each artist is but the result of his own inspiration and his own study of past tradition. . . [1861].

For many of the important independent nineteenth-century artists, personal study in the museum, where they freely chose the works they would copy, replaced the academic insistence upon a steadfast focus on the antique. They could not accept the definitions, laws, or regulations of the academy but insisted instead upon personal empirical experience in art. Some older independent artists, such as Delacroix and Ingres, had large groups of formal students; others, such as Corot and Pissarro, had quite informal but intimate teaching relationships with younger painters. (Pissarro learned from Corot, and Cézanne from Pissarro, for example.) In France the old guild or master-apprentice instruction in craft had died out with the

Figure 18. GUSTAVE COURBET. *The Studio, A Real Allegory of the Last Seven Years of My Life*. 1855. Oil on canvas, 11'9¾"×19'6⅝". Louvre, Paris.

Revolution and with the dissolution of the Compagnie de St-Luc. Thereafter, artists had to learn craft techniques from each other or by themselves, and Degas spent a lifetime regretting the absence of this older tradition yet constantly experimenting with various media on his own. With the Impressionists, mutual stimulation by the artists in the form of informal café discussions, studio visits, and joint painting outings served to further the artist's education and were, in fact, continuations of practices among artists that go back at least to the time of Baccio Bandinelli and his evening drawing sessions. Renoir's picture of Monet painting in a garden (Fig. 19) is but one record of how serious independent artists worked together and directly from nature, rather than through the intermediary of academic theories and plaster casts.

In the nineteenth century, especially in France, the art critic and the art dealer did much to fill the breach caused by the separation of the serious artist from the academy and from state patronage. Writers such as Baudelaire not only commented on exhibitions of academic work but they also criticized or praised the younger and independent artists. The critic's role has continued and increased in the twentieth century, as an influence not only on the buying public but on the work of the artists themselves. The great market for paintings that developed with the prosperity of the middle class in nineteenth-century France, England, Germany, and the United States led to a revival of art dealing in the late 1850s, and through this development artists such as the Impressionists were able to reach the public and eventually support themselves. The emergence of nonacademically trained artists who supported themselves and achieved personal freedom through their art is related to another modern phenomenon, that of young men relinquishing their training or practice in law, medicine, and business professions to convert themselves into artists. (Monet, Manet, Degas, Gauguin, and van Gogh are, of course, the most notable examples.)

The art dealer, museum official, and critic have replaced the old guilds in determining the market, quality, and price of a work of art in modern times. The public's recognition that paintings and sculpture by good artists can increase in monetary value and the example of artists such as van Gogh who were neglected

Figure 19.   PIERRE AUGUSTE RENOIR. *Monet Painting in His Garden at Argenteuil.* 1873. Oil on canvas, 19¾ × 42″. Wadsworth Atheneum, Hartford, Connecticut.

in their own lifetime by the general public have led to speculation and to widespread and avid purchasing of the works of both known and unknown artists. Acquisition of art today constitutes a large-scale international business and presents a great lure for both the young artist and the neophyte collector.

It was in the late eighteenth and early nineteenth century that writers and artists began to proclaim the sovereignty of the artist over his art, the absence of any obligation to create his work for the public welfare. Down to the time of the French Revolution and David, it was taken for granted that artists would work on commission and serve the Church or the state, a prince or a cardinal, when called upon. In the Renaissance, only those on the craftsmen level produced or reproduced their work for the general public; even the greatest figures such as Michelangelo and Raphael worked only on commission. In the seventeenth century only the Neapolitan painter Salvator Rosa declared for artistic independence in Italy. Dutch artists produced paintings in large quantity for unknown or potential buyers, but they geared to the market by specializing in portraits, still lifes, landscapes, genre, or animal pictures. The last great artist who willingly devoted his talents to the service of his government on a large scale was Delacroix, who died in 1863.

(At the end of this book, more will be said about the sociological position of the artist in the recent past.)

2

ART AS A MATTER OF
LIFE AND DEATH

Throughout the world, from the beginnings of civilization to the present, men have made art for many social and religious purposes, but it has always satisfied some need and desire for beauty as well. Magical and symbolic purposes of art have not, however, required beauty for their efficacy. Nonliterate peoples as well as those with rudimentary written languages may not have had specific words for beauty and art, but both are virtually universal as concepts. Field research among nonliterate Stone Age peoples in Africa and the South Pacific in recent years has shown that, contrary to long-standing Western views, these societies do have a strong appreciation of artistic quality and of the importance of the artist. Even in cultures of which only the art survives, as with the pre-Columbian art of Mexico and Latin America, the practical purposes for which sculpture was made, for example, cannot alone explain the rich variety and sophisticated form of the works. Contemporary views of creativity—which for many has come to mean individuality and originality—make it difficult to understand that in the societies which encouraged the making of the art discussed in this chapter the artist was recognized and esteemed as a creator, despite the absence of such a word

or of a wide range of style and subject matter in a particular region, social group, and period. In societies strongly committed to tradition, adherence to the conventions of ritual or of previous forms of art was not felt as a restriction on creativity by the artists whose work is illustrated in this chapter. While we cannot fully re-create the cultural context that brought these works of art to life, the fact that we are moved by their quality and beauty links us, if only superficially, with the past and the peoples from whom they came. Thus the timeless purpose of unification is in some ways still served by art.

What distinguishes the art in this chapter from that of our own day is that it was seriously involved with life and death. Whether magical or symbolic, this art was intended to secure for men well-being in this life and hereafter. (Contrary to popular conception, most magic is "white," not "black," and is intended for good.) In early as well as late phases of many societies, art performed the vital function of assisting men to control their environment, whether human or natural, and to intervene in the course of events. Magical art was and is primitive man's science. Anthropologists and art historians have found in African and Oceanic cultures that this

Figure 20.   Paleolithic Cave Painting. c. 30,000–10,000 B.C. Lascaux (Dordogne), France.

type of art was an agent of control over those things men could not govern fully by themselves, such things as rain, the growth of crops, the fecundity of animal supply, health, childbirth, or what might in general be termed "success" in life.

From history and art we learn that there are no absolutes for beauty and reality; both are man-made and susceptible to change. A visit to a museum is sufficient to remind the reader of this. Our commonly held notion that the real is what is familiar or verifiable by the senses is constantly shaken by modern science, for example. In art we tend to equate the literal imitation of nature's appearance with reality. But art history, like the vicissitudes of philosophy and science, is in itself a reminder that reality in the past and present depends upon intellectual models or concepts which men form for themselves. *Art gives us a history of how men have interacted with their environment.*

To approach art of the past with tolerance and understanding involves a suspension of disbelief. Just as when we are absorbed in a book or film about the past, to confront sympathetically an art deriving from religious beliefs or social customs different from one's own involves setting the latter aside. The initial

confrontation of African, Oceanic, Aztec, or Chinese art can be a shock. But, in the words of the late distinguished anthropologist Melville Herskovits, "In art, familiarity breeds appreciation, which is to say that it takes time and experience to perceive, internalize and respond to the aesthetic values of peoples whose culture differs from one's own."

FERTILITY ART

The known art of the prehistoric period was created between 30,000 and 10,000 years ago. The paintings in the French cave at Lascaux (Fig. 20; Pl. 3), for instance, are estimated to be about 15,000 years old. The difficulties in providing exact dates for cave paintings are matched by the problems of interpreting the art itself. Because there are no written records to assist the archaeologist, he must rely to some extent upon cautious study of those primitive tribes of today among whom art has a religious or magical basis. More direct data are supplied by archaeological investigations of the floor strata near the cave paintings, of the location of art within underground chambers, of what the paintings themselves depict, and of whether or not anything had been done to the images as part of tribal rituals. The poor ventilation, absence of light, and dampness of the deepest caves in which art such as that at Lascaux is found are all factors that immediately suggest a prehistoric purpose as sanctuaries devoted not to daily human habitation but to special rites and perhaps to worship.

Even a casual glance at the walls of Lascaux indicates that esthetic ornamentation was not the primary intent of their artists. Many of the painted animals, such as the bison, deer, horses, and cows that constituted the principal staple of the artist's repertory and of his tribe's food supply, are to be found in both accessible and nearly inaccessible places within the caves. Some locations are remote from the entrance and require arduous climbing, crawling, and squeezing through narrow apertures to obtain uncomfortable glimpses of the paintings and rock engravings. On some of the ceilings of these subterranean grottoes, hundreds of painted and engraved images have been superimposed in the same area—a practice suggesting that there were privileged or sacred spots in which to locate art.

There is general agreement that the purpose of prehistoric art was magical, in that the representation of the animals in some way partook of the reality of the beasts themselves. Further definition of the type of magic or the use of the images remains a matter of controversy among archaeologists. Found in sites other than Lascaux are images that show unmistakable signs of having been defaced by pointed instruments, as if by sympathetic magic the hunters' rituals in the sacred cave were meant to ensure their power over the quarry. Most of the animals, however, are intact and healthy, and all the females are gravid. The painting of pregnant animals may have been designed to assure the tribe's food supply.

It is impossible to look at these cave paintings without being impressed by their intrinsic esthetic value and with the skill of the hands that realized them on the rough living rock of the cave walls. They suggest a mature artistic tradition in which the artist gained part of his training from his experience as a hunter, an activity in which he had to rely upon keenness of eye and hand to provide his food. Many of the polychrome paintings at Lascaux reflect a great

sensitivity not only to the configuration of the animals but also to their color and modeling. The paint, made from ground minerals and charcoal and bound with gummy substances, may have been either scraped on with shredded bone or blown on through a hollow bone. Animals were repainted from time to time, and in certain epochs the prevailing taste was for red or brown. A characteristic of the cave paintings is the predominance of the side view of the animals. Foreshortening was a difficult concept for the artist, and the frontal view would also have meant the visual, and perhaps magical, loss of the main body and hind legs of the animal. It was from the side that the most distinctive features of the animal—so important for magical purposes—were to be seen and rendered.

A wall from Lascaux may at first seem to have been painted with no plan or consistency, but a closer examination brings into focus several series, such as those of the reindeer and horses, which suggest that the artist may have been attempting to show more than one animal in the same area simultaneously. The confrontation of large bulls or the back-to-back arrangement of different animals seemingly painted in the same style and at the same time suggests that prehistoric painting may have known, at least in rudimentary form, devices such as groupings and episodes, even if the latter were emblematic or ritualistic in character. The location of each animal and the over-all dispersal of groups depended to some extent upon the surface quality of the wall. Ground lines were never drawn. It is possible that a certain rock formation evoked an animal image in the mind of the artist which he then drew, or that an outcrop or shelf served as a natural base for the figures. Again, it should be stressed, we may only conjecture about the presence of esthetic intent at Lascaux and other caves.

Stone Age figure sculpture is rare. The famous *Venus of Willendorf* (Fig. 21), an object less than 5 inches in height, is probably one of the oldest sculptures made to promote fertility. Support for this conjecture must come wholly from the suggestive proportions of the feminine figure, which exaggerate the reproductive areas of the body and minimize the face and arms. (The thin arms rest across the breasts.) Judged against anthropological reconstructions of what women may have looked

Figure 21. *Venus of Willendorf*. Upper Paleolithic period, c. 30,000–10,000 B.C. Limestone, height 4⅜″. Naturhistorisches Museum, Vienna.

Figure 22. Idol, from the Cyclades Islands. Early Helladic period, c. 2600–1100 B.C. Marble, height 15⁵⁄₁₆″. The City Art Museum, St. Louis, Missouri.

like anywhere from 12,000 to 15,000 years ago, the sculptor's bodily emphasis may not seem too great, and the natural configuration of the small stone may have aided or suggested the final shaping of the figure. The small scale allows it to be held in the hand; but this is about all that can be said concerning its original use.

The making of fertility images has been a global phenomenon, which should not be surprising in view of the fundamental importance of reproduction to all peoples. In some civilizations lacking written records, we must rely upon the location in which the art object is found to give us some clue to its use. On the Cyclades Islands, north of Crete in the Mediterranean, all that survives of their inhabitants from 2600 to 1100 B.C. are stone tombs, from which archaeologists have obtained marble

sculptures varying in size from a few inches to several feet in height (Fig. 22). The Cyclades finds provide the oldest known life-size nudes. The female figures, usually represented with arms folded across the abdomen, are possibly to be identified with a fertility and mother goddess known throughout the eastern Mediterranean world at this time. As many as a dozen such sculptures were found in a single grave. The placing of a fertility image in a grave is not surprising or uncommon in many parts of the world. While we now admire and exhibit these Cycladic figures for their sculptural beauty, in the third and second millenniums their efficacy for the needs of the deceased caused their burial underground.

Cycladic figures, usually referred to as idols, are uniformly frontal presentations of the body,

Art as a Matter of Life and Death   21

Above: Figure 23. *Tlazoltéotl*, Aztec Goddess of Childbirth. c. 1500 A.D. Aplite with garnets, height 8⅛". Dumbarton Oaks, Washington, D.C.

Right: Figure 24. *Tangaroa*, Polynesian God of the Ocean (sea god creating other gods and man). 18th or 19th century. Hollow wood closed at back with lid, height 44⅛". The British Museum, London.

and their surfaces show sophisticated shaping by scraping and rubbing, probably by hand as well as with tools. Portions of the body which protrude, such as the nose, breasts, and abdomen, were shaped in relief, and a knife blade was used to etch the outlines of other parts of the body. On the basis of certain of the finds, it is evident that at least some of these white-marble figure sculptures were painted in various colors on both the face and the body, thus supplying certain features omitted by the sculptor in his modeling. The fact that the sculptures cannot stand by themselves probably means that they were laid on their backs like the dead, a pose that makes the folded arms appropriate.

One of the most powerful sculptures of birth, probably made in the great Valley of Mexico about 1500 A.D., served the Aztec religion. Tlazoltéotl, the goddess of childbirth and "Mother of God," squats in the manner of Aztec Indian women as she brings forth the god of maize (Fig. 23). The sculptor of this small green-stone figure has chosen to show the goddess as baring her teeth at the moment the male child emerges, so that the pain or violence of birth is not concealed. The Aztecs were a particularly violent people, whose priests wore the skins of sacrificial victims to perform the rites of this mother goddess. The sculpture may also have signified a calendar change, indicating the birth of a special time period that the emerging male figure perhaps personified.

The concept of an all-powerful creator god or spirit arose long before the Judaeo-Christian God was first worshiped. Some religions forbade the making of an image of their most important god; this proscription has been generally true in African cults and, variously, according to Jewish, Moslem, and Christian religious beliefs. One of the most unusual works of art giving form to a supreme deity is also a unique sculpture from its geographical area. Carved sometime in the eighteenth or nineteenth century on one of the Austral Islands in the South Pacific was the pale hardwood figure of Tangaroa, a Polynesian sea god (Fig. 24). According to tradition, at the time when the world was

Left: Figure 25. Nimba Dance Headdress with Carrying Yoke, from Guinea (Baga, Simo Society). 19th century (?). Wood, height 46½″. The Museum of Primitive Art, New York.

Above: Figure 26. *Akua'ba*, Ashanti-style Doll. Wood, height 10″. Pepease Village, Kwanu, Ghana.

in chaos, Tangaroa created gods and men. Although committed to a human figure for his god, the unknown artist made of the head a great flat circular form, which like the smooth expanses of the rest of the body may have evoked associations with the sea. The god is shown giving birth to creatures that seem to rise out of his body through its surface. Just as they take their form from Tangaroa, by their own placement they seem to define his features, being located where the god's eyes, nose, and mouth would be. The sculpture is hollow, and not only are there figures carved on its back, but other small figures are found inside. The male genitals are attributes of the Polynesian supreme god's creative power. What is amazing about this sculpture is that it was made in a geographical area where the figural tradition was not strong. Until some precedent for it is discovered, this work apparently contradicts the generalization in primitive art that the sculptor invariably worked from some prototype.

Along the Atlantic west coast of Africa in French Guinea, the Baga peoples employ a

large shoulder mask known as a *nimba* as protection for pregnant women (Fig. 25). When the mask is being worn, the body of the wearer is covered by a raffia dress, and the carved headpiece itself rests on the shoulders. Members of a secret society known as the Simo society are entrusted with carrying the mask in ceremonies while the women dance around it. The raised ridge on the head probably relates to the tribal hairdress. The large, protruding nose is a fertility symbol. When not being worn on ceremonial occasions, the *nimba* is placed in a hut at a crossroads and set off by trees, where it serves as protection for the village. It is possible that the *nimba* represents the wife of Simo, the great spirit from whom the cult takes its name. Along with the nose, the swelling profile of the *nimba* in general may also allude to ripeness and fecundity.

As protection for the pregnant mother, to ensure a good birth and a perfect child, the Ashanti peoples of Ghana use a small wooden figure that is constant in type but variable in details (Fig. 26). The lower part of the sculpture is formed like a hand grip, and it was carried as a charm. The face is in the form of a disk, with stylized hair rendered around the edge and on the back, and indications of the eyes and nose are carved in relief. The mouth is marked by a thin incision, and below there may be a nob for the chin. There is a vague formal resemblance to Cycladic sculptured heads, which are more pointedly oval, but no possible stylistic connection. The ringed neck is attached to the back of the head so that the disk of the face is allowed to slant slightly forward. The body, reduced to minimal indications of the breasts and torso, ends just below the navel. Studies of the Ashanti peoples help us to account for the rings of the neck, which are schematizations of the rolls of fat considered desirable among them. The Ashanti also shape the heads of their newborn children artificially to develop broad receding foreheads, thereby enhancing, in their eyes, beauty.

THE MYRIAD FACES OF THE MASK

Halloween and other masquerade parties remind us of what happens when a face mask is worn. It permits us to assume a new identity emanating from the character of the mask itself. For some wearers, this is the occasion for casting off inhibitions and social responsibility. These possibilities of having fun, of becoming another being and playing a new role, are in some ways related to the various purposes served by the mask throughout the world in Stone Age cultures. Among tribal societies in Africa, the Northwest Coast Indians, and peoples of the South Pacific, the mask became and still becomes the symbol or locus of supernatural forces. The acts performed by the mask or directives attributed to it carry the authority of a particular spirit or power. That a face mask alone can embody supernatural power, without presenting the entire figure, is explainable because of the widespread belief that the head is the prime residence of such power. When movement is necessary for the mask to fulfill its proper function, it is worn by a dancer as part of a ritual. Therefore, to see masks hanging on museum walls is a distortion of their original purpose. In most societies

important masks, when not in use, were enshrined as cult objects, kept out of sight, or often destroyed. Although we tend to think of the variety possible in human features as depending upon individual differences evident in living persons, primitive masks that are not likenesses of the living manifest a comparable rich variety. In addition, they demonstrate the strong emotion and imagination called upon to make these supernatural forces tangible and impressive in the eyes of their tribes.

More so than in our society of today, masks have had long and notable histories of fulfilling serious and varied functions for the living. Besides dealing specifically with religious life, they have been regarded as important agents for good by helping to guarantee social order, fertility of crops and herds, health, victory in battle, and desirable solutions to various other crises in life, as well as to maintain a general equilibrium among the living and the dead and the spirit world. Despite the great number of masks in museums and private collections and the appreciable study and writing done on their purposes, there is still a great deal that we do not know about their important and complex usages. Research in the field, among groups where masks are still being made and put to genuine ritual use, depends on the memories and interpretations of tribe members and on how

Figure 27. Owl Mask, from Baining, New Britain. Cane and bark cloth, height 31¼″. Museum für Völkerkunde, Basel.

Plate 5. *Christ Enthroned, with Saints Vitale and Ecclesius.* c. 530. Mosaic. San Vitale, Ravenna.

Plate 6. MATTHIAS GRÜNEWALD. Isenheim Altarpiece (closed). c. 1512–15.
Oil on panel, center 8'10" × 10'1"; sides 7'3⁄4" × 3'6". Musée d'Unterlinden, Colmar, France.

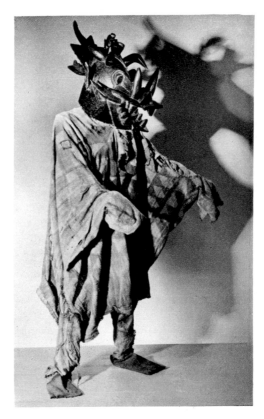

Above: Figure 28. Senufo "Fire Spitter" Helmet Mask, from the Ivory Coast. Wood, length 35⅝". The Museum of Primitive Art, New York.

Right: Figure 29. Man Wearing Double Helmet Mask with Costume, from central Senufo region (Nebunyonkaa Village), Ivory Coast. The Ethnographic Museum, Antwerp.

much information must be kept secret. Aside from the vital religious and social role they continue to play in many parts of the world, generalizations about masks are extremely difficult to formulate. The following selection of masks offers a meager sampling not only of the manifold purposes they serve but also of the infinite ways in which they have been made and decorated. Tribal peoples know full well that masks are paid for, what they are made of, and that they are carved and worn by members of their own tribes. This knowledge would seem likely to weaken the drama or potency of the masks; yet this is not the case. Mask making is usually done in secret, the rituals attended with respect, and the mask bearer generally considered to have cast off his previous identity. Wearing a mask is not a license to shed social responsibility, however, and dancers or other performers in the rites are carefully trained to observe conventions governing their movements and general mien. By wearing a mask, a tribal member takes on a different and more important social responsibility, and he shares magically in the power of the spirit or force he represents.

There are many types of masks having a protective function. On the island of New Britain, off the coast of New Guinea, an owl

mask made from cane and bark cloth is used to give supernatural protection to children (Fig. 27). Only the eyes obviously relate to our real experience of an owl, but learning to recognize all that is meaningful in the art of this tribal society would mean learning their formal (visual) language in the same way that one would try to master their verbal language. The owl of the natural world has been assimilated into, or transmuted by, certain artistic and tribal conventions compounded of symbols and decoration. (Children must be *taught* that this is an owl.) The radically asymmetrical structure of the face is most disturbing in the light of our acquaintance with any type of head; nor are we accustomed to art in which only a minimal resemblance to features or structure is sufficient to conjure effectively the presence of an animal or a human.

The "Fire Spitter" helmet masks made by the Senufo tribes of the Ivory Coast have several animal derivations, none of which relates to their actual purpose. The long-horned, open-jawed head with tusks (Fig. 28) comes from the water buffalo, the wart hog, the antelope, and the crocodile. Hornbill birds symbolizing fertility perch between the horns. The open jaws generously fitted with teeth help to create a

Figure 30. Egu Orumamu Mask, from northern Nigeria (eastern Igala Tribe). Carved c. 1940. Wood, height 23″. Museum Jos, Nigeria.

Figure 31. Bambara Ancestor Figure, from Mali (Bougouni District). Wood, height 4'⅝″. The Museum of Primitive Art, New York.

ferocious apparition, for the mask is intented to inspire fear. The "Fire Spitter" performs the function of driving off or destroying "soul eating" spirits. Its sacred character is enforced by the scrupulous treatment given it by the secret-society member who wears it and who is hidden behind a sacklike garment (Fig. 29). Brought forth at night, the mask is worn horizontally on top of the head so that the jaws and horns are parallel to the ground. Sacrifices are made to it by the villagers to ensure its good will. The mask wearer calls out incantations and also blows sparks through the jaws of the mask, or brandishes them about his person. Believed to have superhuman powers, because he has fused his being with the demon of the mask, the mask wearer can also walk or sit on burning coals. As in many other areas of Africa, the "Fire Spitter" is used for varied functions, such as initiation rites for secret societies, funerals, and agricultural ceremonies.

The widespread conversion of African tribes to the religions and legal systems of the modern Western world has created serious problems, some of which arise from loss of the power

previously invested in sculpture. This transition can be understood more easily from an example of a mask that had played a dominant role in the civil procedures of a Nigerian tribe presently undergoing Westernization. On one of many field trips to Nigeria, the art historian Roy Sieber studied the purposes of Egu Orumamu, or the "chief of masks," among the eastern Igala peoples (Fig. 30). In his studies showing its extensive use as an agent of social control, he wrote:

> Its power apparently is derived from the ancestors and it oversees the general well-being of the village. Certain of its appearances, for instance, are related to agriculture. More pertinent... is its judicial role in cases of murder and petty civil offenses... Orumamu (hidden in a hut) arbitrated complaints and arguments of the women... usually of a financial nature... Orumamu could send his minions to punish children who had gotten in trouble or to supervise the water supply in times of shortage .

The Orumamu mask illustrated is not one of the more beautiful African masks by our standards— or even among others of its tribe— but questions of beauty were secondary to the guardian functions described above.

Some of the most striking African animal carvings used as headdresses in rites for ensuring fertility of the soil, ample rain, and good crops are those made in the western Sudan by Bambara people (Fig. 31). Prior to the rainy season, men belonging to agricultural societies have prepared the carved antelope headpieces and then begin their rites in the dried fields. Their faces are covered with red masks, their bodies with fiber costumes. Upon their return to the villages, offerings and dances are conducted around the privileged performers, who imitate the movements of antelopes. The carvings represent both the male and the female antelope and are distinguished by curved horns for the former and straight horns for the latter. Intended to be seen from all sides and from some distance, the masks are given horns that extend extravagantly into space, and the mane is carved in an elaborate openwork pattern. Both the combative nature and the elegant grace of the animal are preserved. What seems an artibrary schematizing of the antelope into a succession of repeated rhythmic curves results from modeling sculpture more after other sculpture than after nature.

In many areas of Africa, there are secret societies that, within themselves, comprise miniature versions of tribal life itself. These societies perform various functions, which range from maintaining the social order to protecting the tribe against unfriendly demons. Both are roles of the Ekpo secret society of the Ibibio in southwestern Nigeria (Fig. 32). In one of the finest Ekpo masks the face is reconstructed in a menacing form, as a reminder to nonmembers of the hostile character of the spirits with which the society is concerned. If this head is looked at as sculpture, we can see how the artist conceived the various shapes not only as eyes, nose, and mouth but as variations and echoes of one another's form, or of a basic form. Their configuration—protrusion and recession—and vertical alignment guided their proportion and carving and produced an emphatic rhythmic sequence within the compactness of the head. The menacing quality of the mask comes in part from its battery of sharp teeth, which are visible because the jaw portion is hinged to permit movement during rituals.

The most spectacular examples of masks with moving parts were made by the Northwest Coast Indians of North America. The Kwakiutl and other tribes particularly delighted in fashioning masks within masks, which during ceremonial performances and dances were opened by strings pulled by their wearers, thus creating a type of dramatic revelation (Pl. 4). In some masks three or four such revelations were possible, ranging from various animal or bird heads to human representations. These masks were beautifully carved and painted, and exceptional craft went into their hinging. The designs were part of a clan and tribal repertory, with motifs often derived from animals and birds. The colors are strong and the color areas cleanly shaped, changing with each successive revelation within a single movable mask. The Kwakiutl mask illustrated belonged to a shaman, an equivalent of a witch doctor, who was believed to possess supernatural powers to heal or to perform feats of magic. By means of the mask he impersonated a demon or spirit.

Figure 32. Ibibio Mask (worn by member of the Ekpo secret society), from southwestern Nigeria. Wood, hinged jaw, height 12″. Lindenmuseum, Stuttgart.

Figure 33. Wall Painting, from Tomb of Nakht (view of south walls). C. 1422–1411 B.C. Thebes.

Figure 34. Wall Painting, from Tomb 261. C. 1500 B.C. 29½ × 41¼". Thebes.

Figure 35. *A Priest at Memphis Seated Before a Table of Offerings*, from Tomb of Ra-hetep at Meydum. Fourth dynasty, c. 2600 B.C. Wall relief. The British Museum, London.

28

The nonnaturalistic color and drastic reshaping of the facial features were calculated to evoke these supernatural forces. Art for these Northwest Coast tribes was a conscious form of competitive social ostentation, an attitude that accounts for their elaborate design and visual brilliance.

ART FOR THE DEAD

Created thousands of years after the execution of the cave paintings at Lascaux, the tomb paintings of ancient Egypt present a very different kind of wall painting—one that, despite its situation, was nevertheless employed for purposes of sustaining life. The function of Egyptian tomb painting and wall reliefs was to serve the wants of the deceased in the hereafter, to prevent his second death from starvation or thirst and to ensure his comfort and link him with the living (Figs. 33–35). In a wall painting from Thebes, we see a well-run estate being surveyed, or else the crops measured or harvested, and food production being recorded; at the far left are the standing figures of the deceased and his wife, for whose benefit these activities were undertaken. The deceased is always inactive, a passive observer of typical earthly pursuits. Depiction of unique events is rare in Egyptian art. In all the cultures mentioned in this chapter, death meant a change of status, not oblivion. In Egypt over 5,000 years ago, the change to the use of painting and sculpture —or of models of objects, animate beings, and crops, instead of burying servants and animals with the deceased and taking badly needed food from the living for his wants, was a tremendous step in civilization's advance. Through their murals, we gain an insight into the differences between the tribal food-hunting societies of the cave era and the hierarchical food-gathering cultures of the Nile Valley.

Setting aside its illuminating subject matter for the moment, we see that the formal organization of the Egyptian wall into clear, accurately divided zones, terminating at the sides, top, and bottom of the wall in strong borders, is in itself a sign of a highly organized society. Moreover, ground lines support the figures. The surface on which the painting has been done was artificially made and carefully prepared. The artists worked faithfully from preexisting art and codes to ensure the efficacy of their work.

Figure 36. Shang Ceremonial Vessel of the Yu Type (two horned owls back to back). Chinese, 14th–12th centuries B.C. Bronze, height 9½". The Freer Gallery of Art, Washington, D.C.

As in the cave paintings, the human figures, objects, and animals are disposed in such a way as to preserve their most recognizable and useful features. The human figures, as is also seen in the reliefs, combine a frontal eye in a profile head, a frontal view of the shoulders, a three-quarter view of the midriff, and a profile view of the legs. Except for some occasional overlapping, Egyptian art furthers no illusion of depth. To render a larger scene that would normally be perceived as existing in depth, the Egyptians and most ancient artists used vertical zones, so that no action, figure, or object would be diminished through overlap or because of its greater distance from the viewer. Egyptian funerary art was not intended for the critical eye of the living, however, but solely for the welfare of the dead in the afterlife.

Chinese Ritual Bronzes. In ancient China, if one is to judge by the art that has survived, greater attention may have been paid to the dead than to the living. As in Africa, Egypt, and Rome, veneration of departed ancestors was considered important for the successful conduct of life. Sacred rituals using special objects were performed to ensure rain and good harvests. Ornamented bronze ceremonial vessels (Fig. 36) dating from the Shang period in the second millennium B.C. held offerings of food and drink for ancestral spirits and were used in sacrifices performed by the king and aristocracy. These vessels, as ritual accessories the equivalent of communion plates, rank with the most beautiful and finished bronze castings in the history of civilization. When used to propitiate an ancestor, the vessel might bear the inscribed name of the deceased or his clan, along with that of the donor. More than fifty types of bronze ritual objects were employed for such functions as the preparation and serving of food offerings. Besides their ceremonial function of linking the ruler and aristocracy, these objects found in tombs may be considered as ex-votos, or fulfillments of a vow in the form of gifts to the departed.

Although they lasted for a thousand years, practically nothing is known of the Shang rituals. Their intent seems to have included assuring the resurrection of the deceased and the vitality and fertility of the donor and his tribe. Bronze was looked upon as a semiprecious material, and the ritual vessels were aristocratic objects. After many centuries they have acquired a beautiful patina, a surface film resulting from exposure, in hues ranging from green, yellow, and blue to red. Both their shape and complex ornamentation were probably symbolic of concepts and powers that are now unknown. Their motifs frequently derive from mythical and real animals and birds—dragons, bulls, tigers, elephants, water buffaloes, snakes, deer, rams, owls, and cicadas, to name a few. Each motif had various associations or potencies that contributed to the total magical force of the vessel: the more ferocious or terrifying the design, the more effective the protective force. For instance, the owl seems to have been connected with the sun and heavenly fire, while the pheasant was related to mother earth. Used in combinations, symbols were employed to meet different needs. When we search the ritual vessels for these motifs, we often find only vestiges of the whole or individual distinguishing features incorporated into the elaborate designs. The bronzeworker broke up bodies into parts, or fused them, or had forms growing out of one another in a highly imaginative manner. As in African art, the original motifs were greatly transformed but did not necessarily lose their potency. The decorators seemed to have filled compulsively every inch of surface, often using for filler areas an abstract spiral form referred to as the

"thunder pattern." Parts of the vessel, such as the handle or lip, were at times converted into animal or masklike forms, heightening the mystical nature of the object. The shape of the Shang vessel illustrated here is derived from the appearance of two eagle owls set back to back. Frequently, as in this vessel, there appears to be a hierarchical disposition of forms in size and relief, which may have alluded to the structure of the myths or beliefs from which they came.

Japanese Haniwa Funerary Sculpture. In the so-called "Great Burial" (or Yamato) period, from the third to the seventh century of our era, protohistoric Japanese society placed small-scale clay funerary sculpture in the tumuli, or burial mounds, in which were buried clan lords and emperors. These mounds, few of which remain with their sculpture content intact, were surrounded by moats; from an aerial view, they are seen to have a keyhole shape. It seems possible that the humane, economically prudent use of ceramic "stand-ins" for human beings and animals to serve the needs of the deceased ruler may have come from China, where, as in Egypt, human immolation had at one time been practiced.

Far from being gloomy and funereal in mood, this Japanese *haniwa* sculpture shows a broad range of lively expressions and gestures despite its purpose. Lacking are the dense formal designs and involved cryptic symbols of the Chinese ritual objects. Little is known of the religious beliefs of the "Great Burial" period, which ended with the seventh-century advent of Buddhism and cremation practices. The art styles that produced the *haniwa* objects and the Shang ritual vessel impress upon us, however, their makers' divergent tastes and attitudes toward life and death.

In the third and fourth centuries, low-fired unglazed hollow clay cylinders—from which *haniwa* comes—were set into the ground around the tumulus and filled with offerings for the dead. By about the sixth century, human, animal, object, and architectural representations were set atop many of these cylinders and arranged in elaborate groupings on and near the mounds. These objects were the property of the dead, placed near their burials to serve them eternally. At the top of the mound, directly above the burial chamber and the sarcophagus, was placed a *haniwa* replica of the

naïve to us, but for the viewer of the sixth and seventh centuries, unacquainted with detailed naturalistic art, the *haniwa* sculptors provided the information essential to establishing the horse's identity. The living horse was then looked at in terms of art, rather than the reverse, as old Japanese legends testify.

Zapotec Funerary Urns. Ceramics in the service of the dead from the same period as the *haniwa* can be found in the Zapotec culture of southern Mexico. The Zapotec peoples had important burial sites in the religious center and fortified city of Monte Alban, near present-day Oaxaca. From graves in this vicinity have come fired clay urns whose original contents are not known (Fig. 38). Some of these urns are adorned with elaborately molded figures, probably gods, who wear magnificent feathered headdresses and elaborate ornaments. Unlike the relatively

Figure 37. Haniwa Horse (tomb figure). Japanese, 300–600 A.D. Terra cotta, height 38″. Indiana University, Bloomington.

Figure 38. Zapotec Funerary Urn. c. 1000 A.D. Clay, height 25½″. Collection Sra. Machida Armila, Mexico City.

deceased's house, thus providing him with a permanent dwelling place. Gradually, around the house, there were added in successive periods and mounds, clay replicas of other houses, granaries, livestock, weapons, human attendants, and guardian figures, all recalling the ruler's earthly estates.

The horse (Fig. 37) was a favored subject as an aristocratic status symbol, and it was most frequently shown saddled and ready to be mounted. The horse's legs are frankly shaped as cylinders. Detail was kept to a minimum in these clay objects, and the design of the horse and other objects was intentionally simple, clear, and strong so as to be recognizable from an appreciable distance. In part because the sculptors worked quickly, this art has a fresh and varied quality. The eyes of the horse, like those of human beings in *haniwa* sculpture, were simply punched out of the clay. Legends grew up about the awesome and lifelike character of such horses. Such credulity may seem merely

simple *haniwa* figures, the Zapotec urn such as that which is illustrated stresses rank and ceremony, probably as a reflection of a powerful priesthood and monarchy. A large bird surmounts the headdress. With great skill and sensitivity to the pliability of clay and its capacity to withstand firing, the artist was able to suggest such accouterments as jade earrings, bells, beads, and thongs. The enthroned god holds an incense bag in his left hand. Building up these small forms into an aggregate that is widest at the top and yet without added support from the back was a notable feat. The rigidly frontal and symmetrical pose of the seated figure is a quite universal treatment for the deity, found in many religions having a highly dogmatic and authoritarian character.

Bakota Skull Guardians. The use of sculpture as guardians of the dead was as widespread as the making of ritual funerary objects. Tomb guardians in the form of human or supernatural figures and animals have been found as far east as China. In Africa, the Bakota tribes have for

Left: Figure 39. Bakota Skull Guardian, from French Equatorial Africa. 19th–20th centuries. Wood covered with copper and brass, height 30″. The Ethnographic Collection, University of Zurich.

Figure 40. Cult House with *Malanggan* Style Masks, from Medina, northwestern New Ireland. House of wood, bamboo, palm, and croton leaves, 8′ × 16′; figures representing ancestors, totem birds, and fish, of wood painted with oil and earth color. Museum für Völkerkunde, Basel.

Figure 41. *Malanggan* Pole (memorial festival figure, ancestor with shark), from New Ireland. 19th century (?). Wood, paint, sea-snail shell opercula, height 6′3¾″. The Museum of Primitive Art, New York.

centuries been remaking variations on a basic design of a figure that is literally tied to a container of human skulls (Fig. 39). Just as the configuration of this skull guardian has been altered within general limits by successive generations, so the oral tradition from which its meaning is known has undergone change. One interpretation is that this is a mother goddess who reigns over the dead; another, that the figure defends the living from an evil spirit.

There is also a question of whether or not the lower part of the figure is a schematic representation of the arms or is a contraction for the torso and legs. (The part below the face is intended to be buried in the ground along with the container of skulls, but in ceremonial dances it is sometimes carried by the performers.) The guardian figure is made of brass attached to a wooden frame—an indication of its importance, since metal is not a common material in this area. The many surviving Bakota grave guardians show a decided variation in the treatment of the face, with the older examples being more naturalistic. Some Bakotas refer to the horizontal crescent surmounting the head as a moon, while others call it a headdress; the panels flanking the central oval have been described as cheeks or as continuations of the face. Archaeologists have pointed out, however, that tribal hairdos and ornaments may have inspired these lateral shapes. While the original meaning of the guardian figure may be lost or obscure to the present-day tribe and its artists, what is significant is the value given to continuity with the past through repetition of what has proved to be an effective protection for the dead. Tolerance of deviation from a norm in this Bakota art allows a gifted artist to impart his own interpretation to the conventional theme as long as an accepted resemblance to its tribal model is preserved.

New Ireland Funerary Art. The islands of New Ireland lie east of New Guinea, which in turn is just north of Australia. Every year from May to July, the rites for the recently deceased and for ancestors long dead are performed in New Ireland. These rituals and the accompanying dances and art forms are known, collectively, as *malanggan* (Figs. 40–42). Every year the art

Figure 42. *Malanggan* Spirit Boat (figures representing deceased ancestors), from New Ireland. Wood painted, length 19′6″. Lindenmuseum, Stuttgart.

Left: Figure 43. Ancestral Skull, from Melanesia, Middle Sepik River, New Guinea. Face modeled in clay, eyes of cypraea shells. Ubersee-Museum, Bremen.

Right: Figure 44. *Ife King*, from Wunmonije, Nigeria. c. 12th–14th centuries. Bronze, crown partly painted to represent carnelian beads, height 14½". The British Museum, London.

must be renewed, for when the *malanggan* rites are completed the masks, poles, reliefs, and statues of dead kings that were used are all destroyed or sold. The purpose of the rites is ostensibly to offer memorials to ancestors, but it does not appear that the sculpture employed is intended to influence or even please the dead. As a matter of pride and prestige, clans made up of men from different villages who have a common ancestry take it upon themselves to re-create these ritual objects, which are so elaborate as to require months of preparation. The *malanggan* rites furnish annual occasions for achieving unity among the clan members, both living and dead. To prevent a loss of face in the eyes of other clans, each tries to outdo the other in the skill and beauty of the objects, and there is no exact repetition of motifs from one year to the next. Each clan has its own symbols and designs, and the artists are urged to elaborate upon or re-create their works within these traditions.

Although the repertory from which the artist works is general (sea life, snakes, birds, the human form, and decorative patterns) and there are no set meanings, many of the *malanggan* works do commemorate specific individuals, and generalized biographies of them are summarized on the poles and reliefs. (With their appearance during the ritual, the name of the deceased is called out, and he is mourned.) Clan members who are specialists at making these objects work under the scrutiny of elders in secret places or areas fenced off to keep out women and children.

New Ireland artists employ a wider variety of materials than probably any other group of artists in Africa or Oceania. Characteristic of their style is a desire for splendor, which is achieved largely by brilliant polychrome applied in small, clearly delimited areas and in strong juxtaposition. Often the sculptures are carved from logs, but some are constructed of small pieces of wood, shells, bark, roots, fruit rind, feathers, or bits of cloth. Great care and precision goes into the joinery of the parts. Many of the sculptures have a solid core that appears to be suspended within a cage or open framework. The great ornamental poles were probably intended to be seen from all sides, since every square inch of surface is given over to patterning, much of which may have lost its original symbolic meaning. As public testimony to his skill, the *malanggan* ritual objects are as much a tribute to the living artist as to the honored deceased—a fact that has been confirmed by anthropologists. The appearance of *malanggan* in the rituals has strong psychological effects and stimulates emotional participation by the audience. Nonetheless, while serving religious ends, they also evoke strong esthetic response.

New Guinea Ancestor Skulls. In New Guinea, along the Sepik River, certain tribes employ actual skulls of the deceased for ancestor spirit abodes (Fig. 43). Over the skull, after it has been cleaned and dried, clay is applied and modeled to resemble the dead man as closely as possible. Ornamentation is added, in designs appropriate to his social rank and similar to what was worn by the deceased while alive. Shells are sometimes used to replace the eyes. These embellished skulls are often set atop mannequins and manipulated like puppets before the women of the tribe during fertility rituals. Both in Oceania and Africa, ancestor worship is linked with fertility rites, on the premise that the dead members are sympathetic to the tribe's increase. Since it is believed that the dead still need sustenance, offerings of food are also made to the ancestor skull.

African Ancestor Sculpture. In Africa as in Oceania, there is the belief that the living are surrounded by the dead and that ancestors can play a significant role in the continuing life of the tribe. African ancestor figures are symbols and spirit abodes of the deceased. It is the hope of the carver and his patrons that the sculpture made for an ancestor will please him by its fine quality ("good" and "beautiful" are synonymous in many tribes) and that the markings, coiffure, and other tribal and individual attributes will be recognized by the ancestor as appropriate for his dwelling place. The ancestor can make his power accessible through his effigy, and thence passed on to those attending it during ceremonies that seek to evoke this power. Not only does ancestor sculpture express veneration or respect for the dead, but it also constitutes a surrogate for the living with the forces or powers controlling life. Sieber refers to these ancestral statues as "lobbyists," by means of which the living call upon their ancestors to intervene on their behalf with the appropriate spirits. Because the ancestor dwelling within is believed able to see, the eyes of these carved figures may have slits. Stress is often placed on the head, as the seat of power both in life and death, and the faces are characterized as benign rather than aggressive, because ancestors are considered friendly.

To Africans their art is intensely real, even when it seems to bear little resemblance to human or animal forms in nature. However, from the high culture of Ife, in Nigeria, which knew a monarchical system and pyramidal social structure, there have survived magnificent bronze heads and figures of royalty that have a naturalistic appearance and an ideal of classical composure (Fig. 44). Probably dating from between the twelfth and fourteenth centuries (or the equivalent of the medieval period in Europe preceding the Renaissance in Italy), heads such as that of an Oni, or supreme chief, were cast in bronze and presumably served as commemorations of the dead ruler. There is strong doubt, expressed by experts such as

Bernard Fagg of the British Museum, that these were actual portrait likenesses of specific individuals. (This degree of idealization within a context of naturalism has its counterpart in European ruler portraits, discussed in Chapter 12, "Images of Authority.") The Ife king is shown wearing the appropriate plumed and beaded crown, and the perforations around the mouth and chin may have been for insertion of beads or hair. Whether or not the vertical striations covering the face are related to actual scarification practice is not known. We can only speculate that these bronze effigies, too, served as spirit dwellings and were to be placed in shrines or honored locations.

The Ife heads readily draw our appreciation of their beauty because the physical subject naturalistically rendered is in itself handsome. Ancestor figures such as those of the Baoule tribe, on the other hand, derive their beauty in the eyes of those sympathetic with African art from the visual rightness of the rhythms and proportions of the parts as seen in relation to the whole work (Fig. 45). In the eyes of the Baoule themselves, however, the large head and elongated torso, the emphasis upon the navel, and the short squat legs all correspond to ideals of correctness and beauty prescribed for an ancestor figure. Again, the head is stressed as

Figure 45. Baoule Ancestor Figure, from the Ivory Coast. Early 20th century. Wood, height 16½". The University Museum, Philadelphia.

Figure 46. Cult Statues, from the Abu Temple, Tell Asmar. c. 2700–2500 B.C. Marble, height of tallest figure c. 30″. The Oriental Institute, University of Chicago.

Below: Figure 47. Mayan Stone Relief, from Guatemala (lintel from house "G," ancient Maya ceremonial center at Menche [Yaxchilan]; worshiper kneeling before double-headed serpent deity). c. 680 A.D. Height 4′2½″. The British Museum, London.

the seat of power both in life and in death; and emphasizing the navel and phallus confirms powers of fertility. Studies of ethnic physical types in Africa show not only that they are tremendously varied but also that there is often some correspondence between sculptural and human proportion in various regions. The Baoule figure bears the stylized headdress and scarification marks appropriate to this tribe. The immobility of the figure is conditioned as much by the irrelevance of motion to the ancestor portrayal as by the fact that it was carved directly from a round log, with perhaps some thought to preserving its natural quality. Connoisseurship, or the discrimination of excellence, in African sculpture is similar to that for any other art. Only when hundreds of sculptures from a given region are patiently examined can an outsider begin to grasp why tribal members esteem the work of certain carvers above others.

THE GODS' EPIPHANY

In contrast to the widespread utilization of sculpture for the well-being of the dead, as already discussed, a third-millennium group of cult statues (Fig. 46) from the site of Tell Asmar shows the early Mesopotamian concern with the living. These statues were found buried near the altar of a shrine and originally were undoubtedly arranged on the altar itself. Of what this original disposition consisted is not

Figure 48. Stonehenge (aerial view from the northeast), Salisbury Plain, Wiltshire, England. c. 1800–1400 B.C. Diameter of circle 97'; height of monoliths 13½'.

known. What is unique to Mesopotamia in the ancient world is that these statues include, on the one hand, a god and goddess and, on the other, a priest and human worshipers, with the two groups presented in mutual confrontation. In ways such as this, art magically enacted the gods' epiphany to man, probably at the great New Year's festival when the human and the divine were believed to be in closest communion. (The ritual cups in the hands of the gods and some of the worshipers suggest this.)

The tallest figure, about 30 inches high, is Abu, the Lord of Vegetation, from whom men, plants, and animals obtain their life force. The second tallest figure, to his left, is the mother goddess. In front and slightly to the right of Abu is the priest, and the congregation comprises the remaining figures. As alter-images of the real congregation and priest, these figures attest to their subjects' devotion and worthiness to confront their gods. The awesome, mystical nature of Abu is starkly realized by the sculptor's magnification of his eyes and by his bituminous black beard and immobile frontal posture. The versatility and expressiveness of the sculptor is shown in his treatment of the quiet ecstasy suggested in the priest's face. The vividness of the sculptures as a whole and their strength of design come from a forceful schematization of the human form into geometrical shapes. The assemblage of the body parts is additive in principle and does not show organic integration. (Try to visualize the figures in movement.) Such inorganic structur-

ing of the body was suited to the spiritual, trancelike state of the figures.

Carved on a stone block above a doorway in Central America during the seventh century of our era was a Mayan relief showing a human-headed serpent god appearing to a worshiper (Fig. 47). In this visionary conception, the serpent rises from a throne or altar before which, arms outstretched with offerings, the mortal figure kneels. He is bent backward, looking up at the menacing spear held by the god. The reference to impending blood-letting is specific and is related to Mayan religious rituals. The intricately carved blocks at the top are segments of the Mayan calendar, thus possibly linking the epiphany of the god to a certain time of year. The dense, shallow carving, in its elaborate style and symbolic content, indicates that both the religious rites and the tradition of stone carving had a long previous existence among the Maya; and both were later to influence Aztec priests and artists.

SACRED PRECINCTS

Another example of how a now extinct culture manifested, or accommodated, the epiphany of its gods in relation to its calendar is perhaps the most spectacular. One of civilization's earliest surviving sacred precincts was built between about 1800 and 1400 B.C. at Stonehenge, near Salisbury, England (Figs. 48, 49). The sacred enclosure is ringed by a 320-foot

Figure 49. Conjectural Reconstruction of Stonehenge after the Final Rebuilding, c. 1400 B.C. (Drawing by Alan Sorell.)

quarry ditch and embankment, within which are set two large concentric circles of upright stones and ritual pits, or stone holes. Within these are two horseshoe-shaped series of upright stones. These rings, which were built over a long period, may have at one time surrounded a wooden shrine. A few of the trilithons—two vertical stones topped by a horizontal stone cut to fit the curve of the circle—remain in place. To the northeast (lower right in the aerial photograph), over 250 feet from the center of the circle and connected to it by a causeway, is the so-called "sunstone." Originally, a wooden gate stood between the sunstone and the circle, thereby creating a formal approach and entrance. In the center of the innermost horseshoe is a thin stone slab that is conjecturally referred to as the "altar stone." The ring of white patches seen near the surrounding embankment consists of fifty-six shallow pits, whose use is also a matter of conjecture. In ancient times, holes in the ground were often considered openings to the underworld and were used as depositaries for offerings to spirits of the netherworld.

The orientation of Stonehenge probably gives a clue to its symbolic purpose. Recently a Boston University astronomer, Professor Hawkins, with the use of computers, was able to show that Stonehenge was an astronomical observatory. The fifty-six holes in the outer ring are equated with the three eclipses of the moon every fifty-six years. The lunar eclipse takes place exactly over the sunstone. The layout of Stonehenge was computed on the basis of certain annual risings and settings of the sun and moon, and conceivably it served religious purposes. The years could be charted by means of posts in the outer-ring holes, the days of the month by the intervals between the inner stone uprights. On the first day of the summer solstice, the sun rises directly above the sunstone for someone standing in the exact center of Stonehenge. On a straight line running southwest from the sunstone, through the no longer existing gate and the precinct's center, is the great central trilithon. On December 22, the first day of the winter solstice, the setting sun is framed by this trilithon. On this date, the congregation and priests may have entered the precinct through the northeast gate and then faced the spectacle of the fading sun. This may have been the great occasion for ceremonial funerary rites. In certain ancient cultures the door had connotations of life and death, and the winter solstice was identified with the death of the sun. What tribe or people built Stonehenge is not known. The astonishing exactness with which the massive stones are oriented (it is possible that in their original complete state they divided the year into four parts), coupled with the skill and organization needed for quarrying, transporting, cutting, and erecting them, indicates a high level of intelligence and social organization.

Thus, early in human history a plot of earth was marked off and endowed with a special order that set it apart from wilderness. The symbolic orientation strongly intimates that man used this sacred area as a link between himself and the spirit world, and Stonehenge is in this sense consistent with the continuing practice of setting aside holy ground for religious buildings and rituals in East and West.

We have often attributed ignorance and "savagery" to societies of which we ourselves are largely ignorant. But modern science, scholarship, and growing awareness of the ramifications of art are causing us to reevaluate Stone and Bronze Age man, whose works are represented in this chapter. While archaeologists can excavate bones and stones, to comprehend the mind that created and made use of art is a far more complex and difficult task. Through rediscovery and study of their art, we can meaningfully begin to perceive the humanity, the good and evil, of entire civilizations that are remote from us in time, place, and attitudes.

3

IMAGES OF GODS

The history of religion tells us that gods have made men in their own likeness, but the history of art tells us that by sculpture and painting men have remade the gods into their own image. No more important purpose has been served by art than its giving of a visible presence to gods. For millenniums, art provided the visual reminders of celestial authority and, in the eyes and minds of men, made more intelligible the nature of their deities. The sculptured or painted presence of the god was the focus of worship and ritual, and it also gave to the faithful a feeling of protection. Ancient Greek cities, for example, placed a statue of their tutelary god on the battlements to ensure their defense. Investing the god with material form also satisfied mortal curiosity and men's desire for familiarity with and recourse to their gods. The act of making a sculpture or painting of a god was both an honorific gesture and a means of coming to terms with the supernatural. The finished work of religious art also provided man with a visible ethic upon which to base or guide the conduct of his life. Today we need not believe in the religions that inspired the images of Apollo, Buddha, and Christ to be impressed and moved by them. Their greatness as works of art transcends time and the boundaries of religious belief. Still, unless we can to some extent share in or sympathize with the original concepts and emotions that produced this sacred imagery, we cannot fully appreciate the awe, wonder, and gratification with which they were received at the time of their creation. To content oneself with considering only the visual or esthetic value of religious art is to miss the equally rewarding experience of learning about significant human attempts to find out and give form to the truth of existence. Furthermore, we learn how elastic in its potential is the human body, which has been represented in so many ways to accommodate such divergent concepts, and how flexible is the human mind that has accepted the religious art which follows as being real, or full of conviction and sincerity.

APOLLO

On the temple of his sacred precinct at Delphi were inscribed the precepts of Apollo:

> Curb thy spirit.
> Observe the limit.
> Hate hybris.
> Keep a reverent tongue.

39

Fear authority.
Bow before the divine.
Glory not in strength.
Keep woman under rule.

In his study *The Greeks and Their Gods*, W. K. D. Guthrie has summarized Apollo's value to the Greeks by observing that Apollo is the very embodiment of the Hellenic spirit. Everything that marks off the Greek outlook from that of other peoples, and in particular from the barbarians who surrounded them—beauty of every sort, whether it lay in art, music, or poetry or in the qualities of youth, sanity, and moderation—is summed up in Apollo. Above all, he was the averter of evil, the god of purification and of prophecy. Any good Greek could see in Apollo the preacher of "Nothing too much" and "Know thyself." Under his most important and influential aspect may be included everything that connects him with principles of law and order. Primarily, he represents the Greek preference for the intelligible, the determinate and mensurable, as opposed to the fantastic, the vague, and the formless. Apollo was also looked to as a god of nature and was known as "keeper of the flocks." He was the god of the palaestra, or gymnasium, having been the first Olympic victor. He presided over the transition from boyhood to manhood and was also a warlike god who carried a silver bow. Concomitantly, he was thought of as the god of both physical and spiritual healing, capable of purifying the guilty and cleansing sin.

That any sculptor could somehow interpret all these attributes in a single human form seems impossible. In fact, the sculptor had to rely not only on his skill but on a sympathetic audience who would be inclined to read many of these traits into the sculpture. That such was the case, and that the artist's skill was of secondary importance, is borne out by such stories from ancient Greece as that of the father who enjoined his son to be like Apollo, but not like the sculptor who made his statue. When we look at the earliest surviving sculpture of the god (Fig. 50) and compare it with similar works of other subjects also from the first half of the seventh century B.C., there seem to be no apparent attributes of Apollo's deity. But inscribed on the thighs of the small figure are the following words: "Mantiklos dedicated me to the

god with the silver bow who strikes from afar." This votive sculpture, a gesture of homage to the god, may strike us as unreal in appearance; however, history teaches us that throughout time reality has been determined for the beholder by art itself, rather than measuring art against actual life. (In the seventh century B.C. the spirit of Apollo was probably thought to be truly present in this sculpture.) Down to the last century, the credibility of a sculpture or painting was most often determined by comparison with other works of art. Thus, when the various sculptures of Apollo illustrated here are compared with one another, the reader makes certain judgments about which of them is most lifelike, yet without necessarily relating the works to his own body. After the seventh century, there is a gradual change not only in the image of Apollo in art but also in the human image in general. His slow but perceptible assuming of more human aspect, his increasingly lifelike quality, depends first upon the sculptors' mastery of new skills with which to respond to and satisfy—and, in turn, to influence—changing tastes and conceptions of the god's nature.

In the *Tenea Apollo* (Fig. 51), of the mid-sixth century B.C., the god is still represented standing erect, rigidly vertical and frontal; with his body

Figure 50. *Apollo*, from Thebes (Boetia). c. 675 B.C. Bronze, height 8″. The Museum of Fine Arts, Boston.

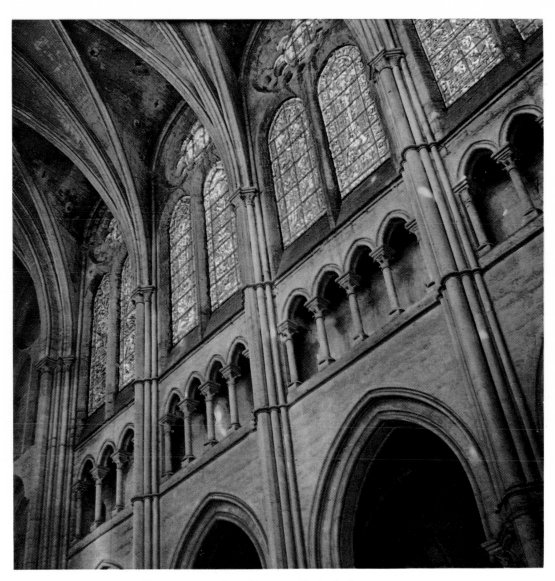

Plate 7.   Interior, Chartres Cathedral. 1194–1220.

Plate 8. LE CORBUSIER. Notre Dame du Haut (interior south wall). 1950–55. Ronchamp, France.

Plate 9. *The Crucifixion*, upper cover of the binding of the *Lindau Gospels*. Reims or St. Denis. c. 870.
Gold and jewels, 13¾″ × 10½″. The Pierpont Morgan Library, New York.

Plate 10. *St. Erhard Celebrating the Mass,* from the *Gospel Book of Abbess Uota.* Regensburg. 1002–25. Manuscript illumination. Staatsbibliothek, Munich.

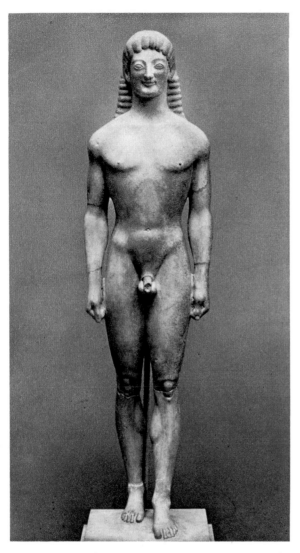

Figure 51. *Tenea Apollo.* c. 550 B.C. Marble, height 5′. Glyptothek, Munich.

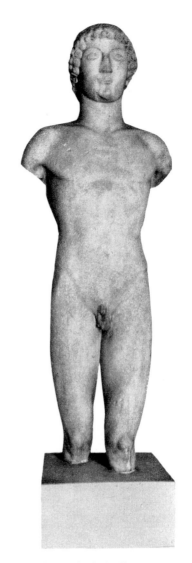

Figure 52. *Strangford Apollo.* c. 490 B.C. Marble, height 30⅜″. The British Museum, London.

forms a perfectly symmetrical composition, with the arms hanging at his sides and one leg extended forward, but with the body weight equally distributed on both legs. The figure has taken on more convincing musculature and proportions. All these characteristics are Egyptian in origin but are appropriate to the interpretation of Apollo as an authoritarian deity, in line with the Greek view of him as the giver of laws. His complete nudity relates to his role as a supreme athlete. Unlike Egyptian figures, he is not flatfooted, and his feet have a more resilient contact with the ground. Nudity in early Greek art was generally reserved for commemorative sculptures honoring athletes victorious in the Olympic games. The sixth-

century standing sculptures of Apollo were thus almost indistinguishable from the trophy sculptures erected for mortal, contemporary athletes. This ambiguity was caused by the customary idealization of the athlete, rather than the creation of a portrait likeness. It is often only through the dedicatory inscriptions on the base that the identity of the standing figure may be ascertained. (It is through these inscriptions, also, that the god speaks.) From his first appearance in art, Apollo was interpreted anthropomorphically, that is, in terms of man, and was depicted in perfect physical form.

The *Strangford Apollo* (Fig. 52) is not identified with certainty as this god, and it may simply have been an athletic, aristocratic youth

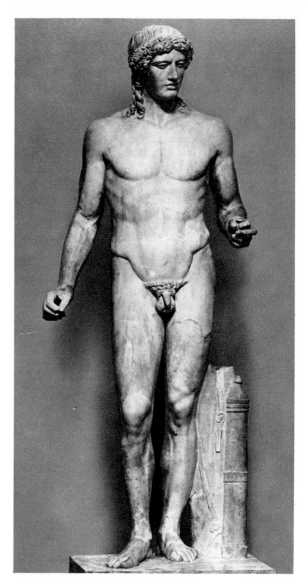

Figure 53. *Apollo*, detail from the west pediment of the Temple of Zeus, Olympia. c. 460 B.C. Marble, height of entire figure 10′4″. Olympia Museum.

Figure 54. *Apollo*. Roman copy after Phidias' original, of c. 460 B.C. Marble, height 6′5½″. Landesmuseum, Kassel.

celebrated for a victory in religious games. Although the statue is reduced by mutilation to a partial figure, there is clear evidence in such Greek sculpture of the fifth century B.C. that there was a greater softening and a more sensuous modeling of the body, which muted the separation of the body parts and resulted in a more subtle joining of the limbs to the torso. The treatment of the muscular fold of the pelvis was a Greek sculptural invention affirming the perfect fit of the thighs into the socket of the torso, like the modulated juncture of a column capital with a lintel above. The stiff, stylized facial expression of the *Tenea Apollo* has here been relaxed, and the sculptor has begun to be more

attentive to a full-round conception, to the successive and varied silhouettes of the body, rather than to merely the simple front and side views. With this increased physical perfection, there is no diminution in the subject's dignity or divine identity. In place of a loss in mystical remoteness, the *Strangford Apollo* has acquired new qualities of grace and physical self-confidence. By the fifth century B.C., however, the Athenian public is known to have voiced the opinion that her best sculptors could portray beautiful men, but not beautiful gods. (Polyclitus was the butt of such criticism, and one of his works is discussed in Chapter 18, "The Figure in Sculpture.")

The pediment of the Temple of Zeus at Olympia shows Apollo (Fig. 53) intervening in a legendary nuptial ceremony that has been disrupted by the drunkenness of the centaurs. It represents a developing idea of Apollo that parallels other changes in Greek art. The rigid frontal symmetry of the previous Apollo figures is broken by the profile position of the god's head and by the extension of his right arm, a gesture intended to restore order to the scene. This statue of Apollo, done toward the middle of the fifth century B.C., also departs from the preceding one in its even less severe modeling; emphasis upon the corporeality of the god does not, however, obscure his great self-control in a situation of emotional and mental stress. This portrayal thus epitomizes the faculty of rational conduct and restraint, as well as the sustaining of law and order through his presence and gesture. The face and body of the statue have become more beautiful in terms of the actual human body. The ideal proportions and bodily development, as well as the facial features, immediately set the god apart from the mortals and centaurs who surround him. His large scale and centrality in the composition are vestiges of older devices for presenting an authoritarian conception.

Although close in date to the Olympia *Apollo*, the Classical *Apollo* (Fig. 54) of the sculptor Phidias carries even further the sensual possibilities of the body. The rigid central body axis of the earlier figures has been eliminated, and the weight is placed on the right leg in a hipshot pose that creates a more active balancing of the body—one of the great achievements of Classical Greek sculpture. In this system of counterpoise, the movement of each portion of the body is an ideal compositional counterpart to the Apolline tradition of harmony between spirit and body. The strength of the still-idealized visage and the impressive physique, coupled with the resilient pose, assist in conveying a feeling of authority that has now become more humane than in the sixth-century model. The perfect proportioning of the torso is a striking lesson in moderation, in avoidance of physical or sensual excess.

The Hellenistic *Apollo Belvedere* (Fig. 55) depicts the god in decided movement, with his draped left arm extended. It is believed that originally his left hand held the silver bow, his military attribute. (Other statues of Apollo show him with a lyre, signifying his patronage of the arts.) The controlled movement permits illustration of Apollo's supreme physical grace and, by implication, of his intellectual discipline. While retaining obvious idealized traits in face and body, the *Apollo Belvedere* is the most lifelike, and hence the most nonsacred, of the Apolline sculpture we have discussed, and this change corresponds to religious and sculptural developments in Greece as a whole. This last figure also suggests why the religion of Greece declined in power. The gods are almost totally conceived and presented in terms of man, an attitude that permits a fatal familiarity and identifiableness between god and worshiper. This possibility of identity is apparent in spite of the fact that many of Apollo's attributes are beautifully incorporated within the sculpture. This handsome figure, with its athletic and dancerlike grace, retains a suggestion of the purity of mind and body and of the faculty of wisdom so cherished by the Greeks. In all

Figure 55. *The Apollo Belvedere*. Roman copy, probably after Leochares' bronze original of c. 330 B.C. Marble, height 7′4″. Musei Vaticani, Rome.

these images of Apollo, the Greeks sought to present the beauty of his mind and morality through the medium of a beautiful human body. And the mastery of sculptural mobility achieved by the artists, while powerfully evoking the personality or temper of the god, may ultimately have caused the weakening of his divine efficacy.

BUDDHA

Buddhism is composed of two main sects. The Mahayana ("Great Vehicle") or "pious" sect looks upon the Buddha as a god possessing the power of miracles and protecting the faithful from harm. He is lord of the universe. This sect developed strongly in China and Japan from its origins in India. The Hinayana ("Lesser Vehicle") or "rationalist" sect looks upon the Buddha as a great, but human, sage who provided a code of ethics that could deliver humanity from the sources of misery. His image in art was a reminder and not an actual presence, similar to images of Christ in Western art. The Hinayana sect was strongest in Southeast Asia, in Burma, Cambodia, Ceylon, and Thailand.

The history of the images of the Buddha goes back to the first centuries before our era, when he was not shown in human form but was represented by symbols—his footprints, the Wheel of Learning, the tree under which he achieved Enlightenment, an altar, or an honorific parasol recalling his princely origin. The faithful could achieve communion with Buddha by means of meditation on the symbols that induced his presence. One of the early sculptures that does not show the actual form of the Buddha (Fig. 56) is one in which an evil spirit menaces the divine throne. Although he is physically absent, attributes of the Buddha such as the throne and his footprints, as well as the reverent attitude of the court, are indicative of his sacred presence. This initial unwillingness to give tangible form to the Buddha has parallels in the history of Christian art, and there are no images of the Buddha or Christ dating from their own lifetimes. To have given tangible form to either of the gods may have seemed at first a contradiction of their divine being. An incentive for Buddhist artists to change was the growing competition with Hinduism and their exposure to Roman and Late Greek art. When the Buddha was finally given human form by the

Figure 56. *Cushioned Throne, with the Assault of Mara*, from Ghantasala (detail). School of Amaravati, late Andhra period, late 2nd century A.D. Grey marble, height 5′9¾″. Musée Guimet, Paris.

Gandhara artists, in the first or second centuries of our era, roughly eight centuries after his death, his body was to be a materialization of concepts similar to those the symbols had conveyed. The tasks facing the early sculptors of the Buddha included the incorporation of thirty-two mystic signs of his superhuman perfection: among these, the cranial protuberance, symbolic of wisdom; elongated ear lobes, indicative of royal birth; a tuft of hair on his forehead, which like the sundial halo signified his emission of light; spoked wheels on the soles of his feet to symbolize the progress of his doctrine and the power of the sun; and a series of ritual hand gestures, or mudras. The Buddha's right hand pointed downward meant his calling of the earth to witness his triumph over evil and his Enlightenment or dispensation of favors; his right hand raised was to dispel fear and give blessings. By joining his thumb and forefinger, the Buddha set the wheel of his doctrine in motion.

Of greater challenge to the sculptor was the metaphorical endowment of the Buddha's body with the strength of the lion and his legs with the grace of a gazelle. The sculpture had to embody the sacred flame or fiery energy of the Buddha and his preterhuman anatomy. Finally, the sculptor had to impart to the statue that ultimate state of serenity, perfect release, and deliverance from desire which the Buddha achieved in nirvana. According to his teachings, inward tranquillity was to be gained by first appeasing the senses, for only then could the mind become well balanced and capable of concentrated meditation. The sensuousness of Indian art is partly explained by this attitude that the senses should not be denied but should be used as the first stage in a spiritual ascent, whereby the faithful could ultimately be purged of attachment to the self and the world's ephemeral delights and could thus achieve a more perfect spiritual union with their gods and ideals. This confidence in the need for and mastery of the sensual suggests that Greek art such as the Apolline sculptures would have appealed to the early Buddhists.

Without question, the seated Buddha statue is indigenous to India and is a native solution to the artistic incarnation of the Great Teacher and god. The seated position was favored, for in the life of the Buddha it is recorded that after six years of penance he at last came to the Tree of Wisdom, where the ground was carpeted with green grass, and there vowed that he would attain his Enlightenment. Taking up the seated, cross-legged position with his limbs brought together, he said, "I will not rise from this position until I have achieved the completion of my task." The model or prototype for the seated Buddha seems likely to have been the earlier Hindu mystical system of yoga, which was constantly before the eyes of the early Indian artists and which was recorded as having been the means of the Buddha's achievement of nirvana (a release from pain in a state of blissful nonexistence.) The objective of yoga is enlightenment and emancipation, to be attained by concentration of thought upon a single point, carried so far that the duality of subject and object is resolved into a perfect unity. The Hindu philosophical poem the *Bhagavad-Gita* described the practice of yoga:

Abiding alone in a secret place, without craving and without possessions, he shall take his seat upon a firm seat, neither over-high nor over-low, and with the working of the mind and of the senses held in check, with body, head, and neck maintained in perfect equilibrium, looking not round about him, so let him meditate, and thereby reach the peace of the Abyss; and the likeness of one such, who knows the boundless joy that lies beyond the senses and is grasped by intuition, and who swerves not from the truth, is that of a lamp in a windless place that does not flicker.

Through yoga may be obtained the highest state of self-oblivion. It involves highly developed discipline in muscular and breath control and the ability to clear one's mind of all superficial sensory preoccupation in order to concentrate upon a single object or idea. The discipline of yoga seeks not only control of the physical body but a cleansing and rebuilding of the whole living being. The human body transformed by yoga is shown free not only from defects but also from its actual physical nature. The sensation of lightness, or release from the bondage of the body, induced by the practice of yoga produces the "subtle body."

It is often difficult to distinguish between the sculpture of the Mahayana and Hinayana sects. One of the most beautiful of the seated Mahayana Buddha sculptures, an example from Sarnath (Fig. 57), was made in the fourth

Figure 57. *Buddha Preaching in the Deer Park.* Gupta period, 320–600 A.D. Chunar sandstone, height 5'3". The Archaeological Museum, Sarnath (Copyright, Archaeological Survey of India).

Figure 58. *Seated Buddha*, Anuradhapura, Ceylon. 6th–7th centuries A.D. Dolomite, height 6′7″.

or fifth century of our era. It shows the Buddha seated upon the lotus throne, making the mudra of the wheel-turning as he preaches his first sermon in the Deer Park, where he first achieved his Enlightenment and to which he had returned. Below his throne (in a segment not shown in the illustration) are a group of his followers and the symbolic wheel. The back of the throne is ornamented with the winged lions of royalty and the foliate ornamentation of the sun disk. This decoration is an assimilation of earlier fertility and vegetative symbols which preceded Buddhism. Air-borne minor deities flank the Buddha in reverent attitudes, not unlike the angels in medieval Christian imagery. The hierarchic formality of the whole composition indicates that the sculptor is no longer dealing with a specific event; the sermon has been solemnized into a more abstract sacred symbol. The earlier, more individualized and human interpretations of the Buddha have been replaced by the idealized figure that was to be the basis of later imagery.

46   Purposes of Art

In the Deer Park Buddha, there is no reference to skeletal or even muscular substructure; the body appears to be inflated by breath alone. There is no trace of bodily strain caused by the posture. The seated attitude is firm and easy, indicating the Buddha's mastery of yoga. The proportions of the Buddha were almost canonical at this time, being based on a basic unit called the *thalam*, equivalent to the distance between the top of the forehead and the chin. The symmetrical arrangement of the body makes of it a triangle, with the head at the apex and the crossed legs as the base. The face, wearing the "subtle smile," is marked by the symbolic lotus-form eyes and ripe lips. The downcast eyes shut off his thoughts from the visible world.

In contrast to the Sarnath Buddha, symbolic of the regal and mystical beliefs of Mahayana Buddhism, is a more austere and unadorned seated Buddha from Ceylon, exemplifying the Hinayana view of the Great Teacher (Fig. 58). Notwithstanding the severe weathering of its

stone, the Ceylon Buddha has a less sensual, yet still firm aspect; the hermitlike figure has an appearance of complete absorption in meditation, indicative of the Buddha's renunciation of worldly concerns. It lacks the strongly stylized and pretty, or even effeminate, character of some later Buddha images in Southeast Asia.

Early standing sculptures of the Buddha (Fig. 59), created in the late first through the third centuries at Gandhara, display an obvious relationship to early sculptures of Christ—and both types of imagery were indebted to Hellenistic and Roman freestanding figures. (The Buddha is shown in monastic robes as the Great Teacher.) This indebtedness resulted from the invasions of India by Mediterranean cultures and the subsequent occupation of some of its territories by the Romans. Indian artists, working perhaps from Roman models, early produced a standing Buddha whose drapery and balance recall some of the first-century B.C. Roman imperial sculpture, such as the statues of the emperor Augustus. The toga-

Above left: Figure 59. *Buddha*, from Gandhara. 3rd century A.D. Stone.

Above: Figure 60. *Buddha*, from Mathura. 5th century A.D. Red sandstone, height 5'3". The National Museum, New Delhi.

like robe is cut in naturalistic channeled folds, so that we are aware of a counterpoised body structure beneath it. (It appears that Indian sculptures of royal personages also provided an early influence on the freestanding Buddha image.) Further late Greek influence can be seen in the face of the Buddha, which is a variant of the Apolline or Hellenistic ruler portrait type, with the addition of the mystic signs.

In succeeding centuries, notably in a fifth-century standing Buddha from Mathura (Fig. 60), Indian artists eventually departed more radically from Greek and Roman influence and developed a monumental standing Buddha more consistent with their own religious ideals. The Mathura standing Buddha is a sophis-

Images of Gods   47

ticated study in opposites. Against the vertical and immobile frontality of the body, the sculptor has designed an undulating sequence of drapery folds that prevent the eye from fastening on the boneless grace of the torso beneath. The transparency of the monastic robe suggests the shining forth of the Buddha's radiance. The hypnotic sequence of concentric disks leading into the ovoid head culminates in the downcast eyes that intimate the Buddha's withdrawal from earthly vision. The flat disk background, with its ornamental foliate motifs, is a foil for the sensual smooth volume of the head, while the rings of the halo and the outlines of the face and neck area play against the drapery rhythms. There is no abrupt transition or single detail to jar the eye or feelings; the totality of the design holds the eye soothingly within its borders and constantly returns it to the head of Buddha. The image is one of quiet authority that invokes love and respect without fear.

While repetition among the images of Apollo and Christ is frequent, Buddhist art exhibited far greater adherence to a prototype for almost 1500 years. Part of the explanation for successive replication in Buddhist imagery stems from a belief in the magical efficacy of certain prized statues; and copies were thought to partake of the original's power. Furthermore, the Buddhist artist was not encouraged to work from a living model or rely on natural perception. With the help of fixed canons, it was his obligation to study the great older images, meditate on them, and then work from his inspired memory. Because the Buddha's beauty defied apprehension by the outward senses, the artist worked from a mental conception in a way that has interesting parallels, as we shall see, in the art of Michelangelo.

CHRIST

Despite the many great paintings and sculptures devoted to Christ, in the last century he has been the subject of some of the worst art in history. Children are shown long-haired effeminate images of Christ that have often been based on nineteenth-century German or French art of the least inspired type. Banal commercial religious wares have been responsible for the cheap Sunday-school image of Christ so often

purveyed as art. Religious sentiment has, unfortunately, made most people and clergy uncritical of this debasement both of Christ and of art.

The first known paintings of Christ, dated no earlier than the third century, are found in the Christian catacombs on the outskirts of ancient Rome. Rather than being secret refuges from persecution or underground churches where large congregations would assemble, as many people formerly believed, these catacombs, burial chambers connected by long passages, were known to and inspected periodically by the Roman government. Moreover, their lack of ventilation and restricted size precluded their use for large worship services. The Christ of catacomb painting, a humble, rustic type lacking in distinct portraitlike features, is shown performing miracles (Fig. 61), in the guise of a teacher or a shepherd. The scenes from Christ's life, limited in number before the fourth century, were intended to encourage the hopes of the faithful with a promise of afterlife. Their optimistic message was that if one had faith, he too would achieve resurrection and salvation. The style of these small-scale images painted on plastered walls, many of which may have been done by non-Christian Roman house painters, is not new—any more than the beliefs of Christianity were completely new. The stress in the *Raising of Lazarus* is upon the Saviour's hand, not his body. The scene has a highly synoptic character, like the recitation of a litany of the divine miracles, as if the artist were painting essentially a reminder of a story known by heart to those who saw it.

Among the first images of Christ, found in the catacombs and in funerary sculpture, are those showing him as the "Good Shepherd," which was a familiar image in Greek art. There is ample evidence to confirm that the Christians recognized and valued the similarity between Christ as the shepherd and Orpheus. The Greek mythological figure had much in common with both Apollo and Christ, since he was associated with salvation, sacrifice, love, and protection. The shepherd image was an ideal expression of the Early Christian community, which was characterized by a close relationship between priest and congregation: the priest was seen as the shepherd, the congregation as the flock. The artistic presentation of the shepherd amid nature was also fitting,

Figure 61. *Raising of Lazarus*, fresco from the Sacrament Chapel, Catacomb of S. Callistus, Rome. Early 3rd century.

Figure 62. *Christ as the Good Shepherd*, detail from Lateran Sarcophagus. Late 4th century. Marble. Rome.

for the Early Christian view of paradise was comparable to the Roman poet Vergil's descriptions of a new sylvan paradise, a beautiful nature in which the soul could repose, ruled over by a gentle shepherd. Christ as the shepherd, whose coming Christian theologians saw prophesied in Vergil's writings, thus ruled over a bucolic world as if in a Golden Age. Second-century Christian saints also describe the paradise in which the soul can find rest with the image of a magnificent garden.

In a fourth-century sarcophagus (Fig. 62), the shepherd is surrounded by small winged figures harvesting grapes. Both the angels and the vineyard derive directly from pagan sources in which the grape harvest and wine alluded to premature death and regeneration. This explains the choice of theme for the sarcophagus

Images of Gods   49

of a deceased Christian who was well-to-do. Christian art that dates from before the fifth century mostly interprets the Jesus of the Gospels, or "the historic Jesus"—Jesus as the Messiah and not as a divinity. In the Lateran Sarcophagus, Jesus as the shepherd stands upon an altar, suggesting his death and sacrifice for mankind. His resurrection provided hope and a spirit of optimism for the Early Christian community and its converts. There is no stress on Christ's militant or royal nature before the fourth century. In general, the artistic prototype of this aspect of Christ seems to have been late Greek and Roman statues of seated or standing philosophers, a type associated with the contemplative or passive life. It was common for late Roman artists to work at depicting pagan figures at the same time they were fulfilling Christian commissions. Sometimes carved sarcophagi were completed except for the symbols or faces; thus they could be purchased by either pagan or Christian clients and then finished to suit their purpose.

In the fourth century Christianity received imperial support and was no longer the private religion it had been in its earlier phases. The Church as a body was reorganized along the lines of the Roman Empire, and the priesthood became an autocracy. Theology and art were subjected to radical transformation and formalization. The external forms and the cult aspect of religion that had been criticized by the historical Jesus became prominent. In the sixth century, the Byzantine emperor Justinian ordered an ambitious mosaic series for the apse of the Church of S. Vitale in the city of Ravenna, which he had just conquered from the Goths. The mosaic of the enthroned Christ flanked by angels and SS. Ecclesius and Vitalis (Pl. 5), in the half-dome of the apse, reflects the transition from the historical Jesus to the theological Jesus. The incarnate Messiah has been replaced by the Son of God, the humanity and humility of the shepherd by the impersonality of a celestial ruler over the hierarchy of religious government. The doctrines that lay behind this mosaic were not those which had been taught by Jesus himself; in S. Vitale the theology of the Incarnation and the Second Coming is the essential subject of the mosaic.

Like a Roman or Byzantine emperor, Christ holds an audience in which he grants and receives honors. Bishop Ecclesius donates the Church of S. Vitale to Christ, and Christ gives the crown of mercy and martyrdom to St. Vitalis. This is preeminently sacred art; the more mundane attitudes of earlier Christian imagery have been replaced. The event transpires outside a specific time and place, an intention affirmed by the fact that these saints lived in different centuries. Also, in the mosaic a replica of the exterior of the church is seen and, at the same time, the mosaic showing the donation is inside this very edifice. Christ sits upon the heavens, yet mystically he is also within the heavens, and beneath his feet flow the four rivers of paradise. This mosaic demonstrates how theologians had reconciled the divinity and authority of Christ with that of the earthly emperors who acknowledged obedience to him. Christ rules the heavens, while the emperor Justinian, shown in an adjacent but lower mosaic, rules the earth. The relative informality of earlier Christian imagery has been replaced by a complex series of artistic devices to convey the concept of Christ as the Second Person of the Holy Trinity. (In Chapter 12, "Images of Authority," Roman imperial sources of these devices are discussed). Against the gold background of the heavens, symbolizing the ineffable light of God, the youthful, beardless Christ sits attired in the imperial purple and gold. Contrasting with the attendant figures who must stand in his presence, Christ is frontal and larger; he appears oblivious to those around him. His ritual gestures of investiture and acceptance make a cross shape of his body, accentuating his centrality in the image and in Christian dogma. Although the mosaicists may have been inspired by St. John's descriptions of the radiance of Heaven, like the Evangelist they based the attributes and qualities of divinity on their experience of the highest form of earthly authority known to them, the magnificent court ceremonies of the temporal monarchs.

Esthetics changed in accordance with developments in theology. The S. Vitale mosaic embodies changed esthetic forms as well as dogma. Each figure, for example, is sharply outlined, with every detail clearly shown as if the viewer were standing close to each subject. The figures do not overlap, and they are all seen as being near the surface of the mosaic, which accounts for their great size. There is only a limited depth to the scene and no attempt to

Figure 63. *Buddha in Majesty*, fresco from Cave 9, Ajanta. Gupta period, 5th century A.D.

re-create atmospheric effects or the light and shadow of earthly perception. Positive identification of the role and status of each figure had to be achieved. The colors are rich and varied, but are governed in their use over large areas by symbolism. The composition is closed, or strongly self-contained, so that there is no suggestion that the frame cuts off any significant area or action. The figures display, at most, a limited mobility, for their static quality is meant to reflect a transcendent nature and to induce a meditative effect on the reverent viewer. Thus artist and theologian combined to give a physical presence to dogma by creating imagery of an invisible, divine world.

More than a century before the S. Vitale mosaics were executed, there was painted on a wall of one of the Ajanta caves of northern India a scene of the Buddha in Majesty (Fig. 63) that bears a striking similarity in its use of formal devices such as centrality, frontality, and pose and gesture for showing authority. It is possible that both the Ravenna mosaic and

the Ajanta fresco may have been influenced by Eastern sources such as Persian art, which, along with Roman art, provided models for the representation of rank in the late-antique world. The Buddha is enthroned between the sinuous figures of bodhisattvas (exceptional beings who renounce the possibility of nirvana in order to teach others of its attainment) and two of his disciples. Courtiers are seen in the background. Buddha's gesture of teaching and his robe and posture are as ritualistic as those of the Christ image. Lions guard his throne, and he and the disciples have halos shown under ceremonial parasols, further symbols of royalty. The flower-strewn background and wall suggest the garden of a palace, a special place that only the faithful are privileged to see and comprehend.

The great Byzantine images of Christ and those in the Early Christian basilicas of Italy were found within the churches. By the beginning of the twelfth century, however, French Romanesque sculptors had transferred sacred

Above: Figure 64. *Christ Enthroned,* tympanum of the west portal, St-Pierre, Moissac. 12th century.

Right: Figure 65. *Last Judgment: Separating the Sheep from the Goats,* mosaic from S. Apollinare Nuovo, Ravenna. c. 493–526 A.D.

Below: Figure 66. *Last Judgment,* tympanum, St-Foy, Conques. 12th century.

images to the exterior of the edifices, as seen, for instance, in the great relief carved over the doorway of the Church of St-Pierre, in Moissac (Fig. 64). But this did not as yet result in a conception of Christ as being of the world of the living. While adopting the ceremonial and sacred traits of the S. Vitale image, the Moissac sculptor forcefully added new ideas to the conception of the lordly Christ. Wearing a crown, Christ is a feudal king of kings, surrounded by elders who are his vassals. His remoteness is reinforced by the great difference in scale between his figure and the representatives of humanity. All glances are directed toward Christ as to a magnetic pole. From his immobile frontal figure, the composition moves outward in waves. Angels and evangelical symbols, intermediate in scale between Christ and the elders but more closely proportioned to Christ, serve to impress upon the onlooker the hierarchical nature of the universe and to bridge the figures in motion with that of the motionless Christ. Here Christ is like the awesome Old Testament God, commanding and completely aloof. He is thus shown as the Redeemer and God of judgment at the Second Coming. His beauty does not derive from the comely proportions with which Apollo was endowed; rather it is of an entirely impersonal and unsensual nature, appealing to thought and faith.

In neither the Apolline nor Buddhist religions is there an analogy to Christ's Second Coming and the Last Judgment, taken as themes for many of the most dramatic and interesting Christian works of art. The earliest Christian image of a Last Judgment is believed to be a scene from the sixth-century mosaic cycle in S. Apollinare Nuovo in Ravenna (Fig. 65). In this small work Christ is shown seated in the center and clad in a purple robe; he gestures to his right toward three sheep. Christ is flanked, on his right, by an angel in red and, on his left, by one in blue. The angel in blue stands directly behind three goats that, like the sheep, are facing toward the center. The episode is the fifth stage of the Apocalypse of St. John, in which Christ symbolically separates the sheep, or the elect, from the goats, the damned. The figure of Christ is almost completely frontal, and he expresses no emotion. It is an extremely simple but formal composition relying upon a knowledge of the scriptures, color, and gesticular symbolism, as well as the significance of left

and right. The artist, in illustrating literally St. John's metaphor, sought to give the event an almost sacramental dignity and transcendence.

An early-twelfth-century French Last Judgment tympanum on the Church of St-Foy in Conques (Fig. 66) represents a tremendous change in interpretation of the judgment theme. This is one of many exciting apocalyptic sculptures done in southern France during the first half of the twelfth century. In the St-Foy version, much more of the apocalyptic account has been encompassed by the artist, who relies far less upon metaphor and prefers to give a more tangible realization of the concrete details and mechanics of the Last Judgment that medieval man believed inevitable. His art was a vivid memento, in its brilliantly modulated carved surfaces and abundance of human, divine, and demonic forms, of that fateful event, the day and hour of which "no man knoweth" (Matt. 24:36).

The large tympanum is set above the main doorway of the church, through which the worshipers must pass every day and, hence, serves as an ever-present reminder of their obligations. Moreover, to enrich his subject, the St-Foy sculptor and his theological adviser drew upon sources outside the Bible; the writings of such Fathers of the Church as St. Augustine were absorbed into the work. As an example, the weighing of souls, which is not in the biblical accounts of the Last Judgment, is perhaps borrowed from Augustine, who wrote, "Good and evil actions shall be as if hanging in the scales, and if the evil preponderate, the guilty shall be dragged away to Hell." The motif of the scales may also have come from Near Eastern art and indirectly from Egyptian sources in the Book of the Dead. The Egyptian funerary god Anubis, as watcher of the "weighing in," has been replaced by St. Michael. Contrary to the inviolable conduct of the Egyptian ritual, a devil here seeks to tip the scales in his favor as he sees that a soul on the side of Michael (the right side of Christ) has outweighed one on his side. This attempt at judicial corruption on the part of an agent of Satan would have been amusing even in the twelfth century, particularly in southern France, where law had become so important as a result of the feudal system and the rise of the Church.

The ordered and legal aspect of the final judgment is stressed by the artist at Conques in both his composition and his disposition of figures. Each zone and compartment of the scene is strongly separated by a thick stone border, on which are written the virtuous phrases, the teachings of the Church, and so on, appropriate to the location. This composition reflects a view of the universe as strongly ordered, so that everyone has a definite area to which he will eventually be consigned, just as the living at the time had little difficulty in defining their own status in the feudal system. Thus the image of the universe on the last day becomes a projection of the real world as it was involved in the social, economic, and political structures of the time. The authority and absolute dominance of Christ over the scene is achieved by his centrality and great scale. He sits immobile and frontal as a symbol of power, gesturing upward with his right hand toward Heaven on his right side; with his left hand he points downward to Hell.

The upper zone of the scene contains angels carrying the Cross, the symbol of the Passion and the Second Coming on the day of justice. The central position of the Cross and the downward movement of the angels draw the eye centripetally to the Supreme Judge. On the right of Christ, in the largest zone, is a procession of the saved, who proceed in homage toward the ruler of Heaven. They are led by SS. Peter, Anthony, and Benedict, who symbolize the origins and rule of the Church. The saints lead a royal figure, believed to be Charlemagne, who had been a benefactor of the Abbey of St-Foy. The moral implied by this arrangement is that Charlemagne got into Heaven not by force of the crown which he carries but through the prayers and efforts of the holy men. (This is an unsubtle admonition to the secular rulers of the time to support the Church.) To the left of Christ, in another zone, are those consigned to Hell, nude and cramped in awkward poses, experiencing all sorts of painful indignities inflicted with enthusiasm by demons.

The lowest zone is divided into two large porticoes known as "basilican castrum." Between these, literally on the roofs at the point where the buildings come together, the weighing of souls takes place. (Thus it is also on the principal axis of the Cross and Christ.) Next to the weighing-in on the left, armed angels are rousing the dead from their coffins, and on the right demons are pummeling the resur-

Figure 67. *Christ*, detail of dome mosaic, Monastery Church, Daphne, Greece. c. 1100.

rected. In the center of the left portico (that on Christ's right) sits Abraham, who receives the souls of the deceased into his bosom. Entrance to Heaven is through a heavy open door, which reveals a fine medieval lock and set of strong metal hinges. The entrance to Hell is through the horrible jaws of the Leviathan, whose head protrudes through the door to Hell. The Book of Daniel (7:7) describes the terrifying Leviathan that God has created. Hell is ruled over by the seated Devil, surrounded by his squirming subjects. In the treatment of Hell and the Devil the medieval artist had his greatest freedom and could give vent to his fantasies, repressions, and humor. Here as elsewhere, by far the more interesting of the two sides is that dealing with the damned.

The twelfth-century Byzantine mosaic of Christ the Pantocrator (Fig. 67) in the dome of the monastery church of Daphne, outside Athens, focuses attention on the face of Christ, his gesture of benediction, and the Bible held by him. It is an image calculated to evoke awe, reverence, and fear in the beholder. The severe expression is climaxed by the hypnotic glance, giving the effect of watchfulness. The celestial countenance is that of an immutable, stern judge who is both giver and enforcer of the law. An impressive face, it is not beautiful in the classical sense, for it denies the importance of the flesh, of naturalistic rendering, and instead stresses the power of the divine will. There is an unclassical imbalance in the Byzantine stress upon the eyes and in the intensity of expression. No Greek sculpture of Zeus hurling his thunderbolt conveys the wrath of which the Daphne Christ seems capable.

The judicial and authoritarian aspects of the Byzantine Christ are continued but somewhat relaxed in the thirteenth-century French sculpture of the Beau Dieu (Fig. 68) from the Cathedral of Amiens. The figure of Christ stands between the main doors of the Cathedral and below the scene of the Last Judgment. Beneath Christ's feet are the lion and serpent symbolic of the evil he conquers. Both in his location and in his appearance, Christ has been made more accessible to the congregation. He stands before the doors to his house not as guard but as host, like a gallant feudal lord. This humanizing of Christ into an aristocratic ideal is reflected in his new familiar name, "the Handsome God," a title in many ways unthinkable at Moissac and Daphne. This investing of Christ with a more physically attractive, a more tender aspect accompanies his reentrance into the world of the living and the reduction of the sacrosanct nature of the art itself. The transition has been from the Byzantine Pantocrator, Lord of All the Universe, to the more human dignity of the Gothic lord of men.

The Beau Dieu has an idealized countenance that bears instructive comparison with the head of Apollo from Olympia (Fig. 69). The Gothic head is noticeable for its sharp features and subdued sensuality, indicating an essentially Christian attitude toward the body. This is particularly marked in the treatment of the mouth. The more pronounced ovoid outline of the Christ image, enhanced by the long tightly massed hair, and the axial alignment of the symmetrical beard, the nose, and the part of the hair give the deity an ascetic and spiritualized mien. Despite the generalized treatment of the forehead, cheeks, and hair, the Amiens Christ possesses a more individualistic character than does the Olympian Apollo, who is totally unblemished by the vicissitudes of mortal existence. The eyes of the Gothic Christ are worked

Above: Figure 68. *Beau Dieu,* detail of the west portal, Amiens Cathedral. 13th century.

Below: Figure 69. *Apollo,* detail of Fig. 53.

in greater detail in the area of the eyelid, and they have a more pointed upper arch than does the simplified perfect arc of the Apollo's upper lids. (Both sculptures originally had the iris painted in.) The Gothic Christ lacks the masklike calm of the Classical Apollo.

Comparison of a Buddha sculpture with a thirteenth-century head of Christ from the French Gothic cathedral of Reims provides us with a summation of two radically divergent tendencies in the respective art forms of Buddhism and Christianity (Figs. 70 and 71). The Buddhist head reveals the development toward anonymity in the celestial countenance, a refusal to glorify a specific individual. It seeks a pure incarnation of that spirit of Buddhism conceiving of the Buddha as representing the incorporeal essence of a religious attitude. The smile on the Buddha's lips recalls his wisdom and sublimity, which he attains in the abyss or sphere beyond nirvana. The Reims Christ wears the marks of his passionate earthly sojourn in the worn and wrinkled surface of his face, and we sense that this deity has a unique and dramatic biography. There is no intimation of past experience, of trial and pathos, in the images of Apollo and Buddha. The Christian face, however, speaks to us of a tragic personal drama; it displays or infers a far

subtler range of feeling than the faces of the other two deities. The Gothic sculptor wished the viewer to read tenderness, compassion, pain, and wisdom in the lines of the divine face. The Reims sculptor may even have taken a French king—perhaps Louis IX (St. Louis)—for his model, so that Christ was now literally presented in terms of man, or *a* man. The Reims Christ represents the second half of the cycle begun in the catacombs when Christ emerged first as a humble man, then as an emperor and ruler of Heaven. Now the cycle moved in the other direction, to terminate in the images of Christ discussed in the section on Rembrandt (Chapter 11).

Western Christian art, like its theology, is dominated by the execution of its God. Buddha's death came tranquilly: for three days he lay on his right side, with his head resting on his hand, until he passed into the final nirvana (Fig. 72), in which he was freed from reincarnation. Buddhist art as a consequence does not know the pathos of such Christian images as the great fifteenth-century French panel painting known as the *Villeneuve* (or *Avignon*) *Pietà*, depicting the lamentation over the dead Christ (Fig. 73). Used as a backdrop for the altar and thus seen in conjunction with the service, this large painting is a brilliant blending

Figure 70. *Head of Buddha*, from Gandhara. 5th century A.D. The Victoria & Albert Museum, London (Crown Copyright Reserved).

Figure 71. *Head of Christ*, detail from the *Coronation of the Virgin*, Reims Cathedral. 13th century.

Plate 11.   *Symbol of St. Mark*, from the *Echternach Gospels*. Anglo-Irish. c. 700.
Manuscript illumination. Bibliothèque Nationale, Paris.

Plate 12.   *St. Luke the Evangelist,* from the *Gospel Book of Otto III*. Reichenau. c. 1000.
Manuscript illumination. Staatsbibliothek, Munich.

Figure 72. *Ananda Attending the Parinirvana of the Buddha*, from Gal Vihara, near Polonnaruva. 12th century. Granulite, height 23'.

Figure 73. Avignon Master. *Villeneuve Pietà*. c. 1470. Oil on panel, 5'3½" × 7'1¾". Louvre, Paris.

of the actual and the symbolic. The radiant gold background establishes the celestial nature of the theme, and the dark reddish brown of the earth reflects the somber mood. The arrangement, which has the Virgin both supporting and displaying the wounded and distended body of Christ, is not an attempt to show literally the events after the Crucifixion, but rather to represent the symbolical nature of the death of Christ and the Virgin's sacrifice of her son for mankind. The words stamped into the gold leaf at the top of the painting ("Oh, all ye who pass along the way, stop and see what is my grief") are from the Good Friday Mass. Within the formal deployment of the starkly outlined and self-contained figures, the unknown artist has created strong characterizations so that each, by a differing psychological response to the event, has a humanity which shines through his symbolic function. The donor at the left, whose powerfully modeled head is juxtaposed with the flat reddish profile of the Heavenly Jerusalem, is not an actual participant in or witness to the scene, but he meditates prayerfully upon its significance in a way that was intended to inspire the beholder. As Christ's body achieved an increasingly mortal form toward the end of the Middle Ages, so did those of his followers, and the artist's challenge became one of reminding us that the Redeemer who died was greater than a man.

Christ's physical and spiritual anguish on the Cross has no counterpart in Buddhist or Greek

Figure 74. *The Crucifixion*. Early 5th century. Panel from an ivory box, length 3⅞". The British Museum, London.

art. It was not until the fifth century, however, that the first Crucifixion scenes appeared, and these were in sculpture. Prior to that, there had been symbolic references in the form of an empty cross. One reason for the early absence of this subject, so central to Christianity and its art, is that crucifixion was an undignified punishment meted out by the Romans to criminals, their bodies often left to be devoured by wolves. In Christ's time the cross was usually T-shaped, and the condemned man was roped to the crossbar he himself had carried on the way to execution. At the site of execution the victim was nailed through his hands to the crossbar, and while he was still on the ground, a single spike was driven through the left foot placed over the right and then into the wood. Next the executioners raised the dying man and joined the crossbar to the upright post. Prisoners wore an undergarment across their loins, and the plaque announcing their crimes was removed from around their necks and hung above them when the two parts of the cross were joined.

A small ivory relief carving from the beginning of the fifth century shows Christ on the Cross, with head erect and eyes open, fastened by four nails (Fig. 74). In this presentation, the sagging head and shoulders and the bent knees common in this type of death were avoided. There is no evidence of physical suffering, thus stressing Christ's divinity. At the right, below the crucified figure, is Longinus, the centurion who lanced his side; to the left, St. John and the Virgin, and at the far left, the hanged Judas. It was not until almost six centuries later that artists had the sanction of the Church to begin to show the pathetic tortured form of the crucified Christ and to close his eyes in death. On a reliquary made in the Rhineland in the twelfth century (Figs. 75, 76), an ivory inset shows the body of the crucified Christ, with his head slumped to the right, perhaps according to the sculptor's conception of what this form of death involved but more likely because of the tradition saying that in the last moment Christ's head bowed to his right. (From medical evidence, it would seem that a dead man on a cross would have his head slumped straight downward, in line with the median of his torso, which would have been vertical.) A more modest covering for the loins has replaced the simple fifth-century

Below: Figure 75. Reliquary in the Form of a Church Surmounted by a Dome. Cologne School. c. 1180. Gilt copper, champlevé enamel, with ivory figures and panels. The Guelph Treasure, Berlin.

Right: Figure 76. *Crucifixion*, detail of Fig. 75.

breechcloth. Even earlier than this example of 1180, the figures of Mary and St. John had taken up their familiar positions flanking the Cross, with Mary on Christ's left, and for centuries to come this became the fixed format. This panel is part of the gold and ivory decoration of a reliquary in the shape of a small enameled Byzantine cruciform church, made to receive the head of St. Gregory, brought to Braunschweig from Constantinople by Richard the Lionhearted in 1170. Reverence for the deceased saint and belief in the miraculous power of his remains account for the expenditure of substantial treasure on this small casket. The Crucifixion, also a theme of martyrdom, was an appropriate subject to honor the holy man on his reliquary.

All that remains from a large sculptured Crucifixion scene done about 1400 by Claus Sluter for a monastery is a bust of Christ crowned with thorns (Fig. 77). The true Crown of Thorns had found its way to Notre-Dame in Paris from Byzantium and Venice in the thirteenth century, and thence into Western medieval sculpture. Sluter avoided melodra-

Below: Figure 77. CLAUS SLUTER. *Head of Christ.* c. 1400. Stone, height 24″. The Archaeological Museum, Dijon.

matic expression and relied for effect instead upon the painful associations of the thorns seen against a still, dignified bearded face. The slight inclination of the head and the taut, finely modeled chest area, giving evidence of the sculptor's perceptive study from life, constituted important traits through which the monks could identify with an agonizing death; these qualities personalized Christ in ways that were artistically and spiritually unthinkable in Early Christian art.

One of the most impressive and personal interpretations of the theme of the Crucifixion is that by Matthias Grünewald, which occupies one of the main panels of the *Isenheim Altarpiece* (Pl. 6). Painted probably between 1513 and 1515, the altarpiece was intended for the monastery church of the hospital order of St. Anthony in Isenheim, Alsace. The monastery's hospital treated patients with skin diseases such as leprosy and syphilitic lesions. The first step in a new patient's treatment was to be taken before the painting of the Crucifixion and to have prayers said at the altar for his healing. It was thought that skin disease was the outward manifestation of sin and a corrupted soul. The patient was confronted with the larger-than-life-sized painting of the dead Christ, whose soulless body was host to such horrible afflictions of the flesh. Only the Son of God had the power to heal the sinner, for Christ had borne all the sorrows of the flesh that garbed the Word. The previous regal, authoritarian, and beautiful incarnations of Christ were replaced by the image of the compassionate martyr. The vivid depiction of the eruptions, lacerations, and gangrene of the body were intended to encourage the patient's identification with Christ, thereby giving solace and hope. From the late Middle Ages, partly because of the widespread pestilence, there are countless examples in the art and literature of northern Europe of the faithful being enjoined to identify themselves emotionally with the Passion of Christ. Grünewald probably drew upon the vision of the fourteenth-century Swedish saint Brigitta, who wrote:

> The crown of thorns was impressed on His head; it covered one half of the forehead. The blood ran in many rills...then the color of death spread....

After He had expired the mouth gaped, so that the spectators could see the tongue, the teeth, and the blood in the mouth. The eyes were cast down. The knees were bent to one side, the feet were twisted around the nails as if they were on hinges...the cramped arms and fingers were stretched.

Grünewald's image of Christ goes beyond this description in exteriorizing the body's final inner states of feeling. The extreme distension of the limbs, the contorted extremities, and the convulsive contraction of the torso are grim and eloquent testimony of Grünewald's obsession with the union of suffering and violence in Christ. He focused on the final rigidifying death throes so convincingly that the feet, a single hand, or the overwhelming face alone suffices to convey the expiration of the entire body. The brutal stripping of the living wood of the Cross is symbolically in accord with the flagellation of Christ. Cedar, used for the vertical member of the Cross, was also employed in the cure for leprosy. The hopeful message of the painting can be seen in the contrast between the light illuminating the foreground and the murky, desolate landscape behind—a device signifying Christ's triumph over death. Miraculously present for this Crucifixion, John the Baptist intones, "I shall decrease as He shall increase." Men are enjoined to humble themselves in order to renew their lives in God. The static doctrinal and symbolic right half of the painting contrasts with the extreme human suffering and emotion to the left, seen in the grieving figures of St. John and the Virgin and Mary Magdalen. Grünewald's painting and views of religion seem to have stressed a communal response to tragic but elevating religious experience. Psychologically and esthetically, each figure, like the composition as a whole, is asymmetrical and formed of an uneasy synthesis of polarities.

In subsequent chapters there will be many examples of the ways in which Christ was interpreted during the same century and in the centuries that followed Grünewald's altarpiece. In the twentieth century the finest painting and sculpture are no longer primarily in the service of religion, and the most important art has been secular. Nevertheless, in 1948 two enlightened Catholic priests approached the painter Henri Matisse, a non-Catholic, to decorate a convent chapel at Vence, in southern France. Matisse's

Figure 78. HENRI MATISSE. *Ave* (left) and *le Chemin de la Croix* (end wall). Murals, 1951. Rosary Chapel, Vence.

previous art had been entirely concerned with subjects that were sensual and delighted the eye, such as beautiful women and colorful interiors. The possessor of great gifts as a decorator and draftsman, Matisse accepted this commission. Part of his chapel decoration consisted of two linear black-and-white ceramic murals that received soft changing color reflected from adjacent windows of yellow, green, and blue glass. One mural shows the Virgin and the Christ child, and the other the Stations of the Cross (Fig. 78). The first subject is drawn in a soft, lyrical curvilinear style that, with the full blossom designs surrounding it, evokes a joyful mood. What initially astounds visitors to the Rosary Chapel is the absence of facial features for the Virgin and Child. It is as if Matisse had decided that each viewer could project into the mural a face of his own creation, but the brilliantly economical outlines of the figures suffice to identify them. In the Stations of the Cross, Matisse consciously changed his style: he avoided the graceful silhouettes and allowed a more harsh, angular drawing—rather than gestures and facial expression—to express the tragic theme. The events are numbered and follow one another abruptly, consisting of the most rudimentary indication of the action and no concern with background. Realizing that the worshiper knows the episodes

by heart, like the catacomb artist Matisse turned to a symbolical or synoptic rendering, but in a personal style only possible in his time. He exemplifies the sincere modern artist who feels he cannot, as the medieval artist willingly did, repeat the conventions, types, and styles of his predecessors.

Art helps to trace the changing conceptions of Christ, from those which saw in him a humble messianic shepherd, through the king-like God to be revered from afar, to the Godlike king who could be loved as a benevolent ruler, and finally to the Man of Sorrows, whose own compassion evoked the pity of suffering humanity. The transformation of sacred art proceeded differently for Apollo and the Buddha. Apollo's effigy began as sacred art and terminated in the profane imagery of a beautiful youth. The Buddha's early interpretation progressed from a humane individuality toward the sacrosanct impersonality of the sixth and seventh centuries. To comprehend the effectiveness of Greek, Indian, and Christian artists in uniting form and idea, one may interchange in the mind's eye the head of the Reims Christ with that of the Apollo at Olympia, the Lotus throne of Buddha with Christ's role in the Moissac relief, the nude figure of Apollo with the Beau Dieu of Amiens Cathedral, or finally, transfer the S. Vitale Christ to the Grünewald altar painting.

Images of Gods   61

4

RELIGIOUS ARCHITECTURE

The history of religious architecture is more than a record of styles and engineering achievements. Throughout history the construction of a temple or church has been an act of faith and gratitude by its builders—a gift to a god from the living in return for his manifold gifts. Until the nineteenth and twentieth centuries, we can speak of such architecture as in many ways being a collective social endeavor by which architects have expressed or symbolized the most sacred values of their cultures. Thereafter, proportionately the architect has had greater opportunity for self-expression. In a variety of ways, public conceptions of the nature of the deity, heaven, and the universe have been incorporated into the designs of religious structures. Religious architecture, like images of gods, is intended to make manifest to the senses and the intellect, and to evoke feelings of what lies beyond the visible world and this life. Thus far in this century there are few sacred buildings of lasting distinction, and these have been created by gifted individuals who relied less on a consensus of congregational attitudes and conventional symbols than on their own artistic intuition and personal interpretation of the faith for which they were working. Today as in the past, the architect can be as much the

teacher as the pupil, and while he has learned from the past, the views he expresses in architecture cannot help but influence the ensuing religious experience of those who worship in his church or temple. From antiquity to the present, there have been basic demands that the architect has had to meet in designing religious architecture: for instance, the structure's suitability as a house of God; its effectiveness for the performance of the liturgy; its conduciveness to prayer or communion with the god; its purpose as a meaningful expression of the beliefs of the clergy and worshipers. This chapter discusses how these constant demands and other special requirements have been met in differing ways by a few great architects in various epochs.

THE PARTHENON

The spiritual meaning of the Parthenon (Fig. 79), the celebrated Greek temple built on the Acropolis of Athens during the fifth century B.C., does not lie in its formation with cosmic symbols. Although the Parthenon's architecture does not literally represent the forms of myth and religion, it is nonetheless an inspired expression of the higher values of Classical

Figure 79. IcTINUS and CALLICRATES. The Parthenon (view from the northwest), the Acropolis, Athens. 447–432 B.C.

Greece. Through analogies and through the circumstantial evidence of culture, the Parthenon reflects the world view of Periclean Athens and is a type of idealized spiritual self-portrait of that city. The reason for and date of its building (447–438 B.C.; the sculptural decoration was finished by 432 B.C.) and its location on the sacred hill of the Acropolis in the city's center are important considerations. Athena was known as the protector of heights and goddess of fortified places. During the Persian invasions of the 480s, a partially constructed temple dedicated to Athena, tutelary goddess of Athens, was burned and largely destroyed. After what seemed the miraculous defeat of the Persians, the Athenian Senate tardily authorized construction of a new temple dedicated to the goddess. The building of the Parthenon occurred in the flush of Greek confidence in the Athenian gods, Athenian moral values, Athenian mer-

cantile success on the seas, and, above all, in Athenian culture. Ironically, construction of the great temple also coincided with the beginning of the fateful decline of Athens' political power and of what several historians have felt was her moral corruption. Many in Athens protested the great cost of the temple and were offended as well at Pericles' impatient offer to pay for it himself. To prevent that the glory accrue solely to Pericles, the Senate approved the project at public expense; these expenses were covered by contributions from the Athenian League, comprised of allies of that city-state, by loot from Athenian piracy and military campaigns, and by contributions from free citizens, who with their slaves donated work on a daily basis. The small size of the Parthenon compared with the immense Egyptian temples reflects a marked difference in respective resources and, to some extent, the absence of a

Above: Figure 80. The Parthenon: The Panathenaic Frieze above the Western Entrance to the Cella.

Right: Figure 81. The Parthenon (from the west; reconstruction by Gorham P. Stevens, The American School of Classical Studies, Athens).

powerful priestly caste in Greece. Nevertheless, for a city of 100,000 people, the Parthenon was an ambitious undertaking. The Parthenon was a gift to the goddess of war and wisdom from free men who willingly submitted to her. Moreover, it was a votive offering in return for past naval and commercial success, for Athena was also the protectress of the navy.

The extent of community participation in honoring Athena is commemorated in the 525-foot frieze running from west to east around the outside of the sanctuary walls at the top and above the entrances to the cella (see Fig. 80). The subject of this continuous relief is the Panathenaic ceremonies that took place every four years to honor Athena's birthday. A procession of representatives of all Athens escorted the wheeled model of a ship, from the mast of which there hung a newly woven purple woolen sail, or peplos; on this peplos were embroidered in gold mementos of legendary battles in which Athena triumphed. When the procession reached the Parthenon, the sail was lowered, folded, and turned over to a priest, who draped it on the statue of the goddess in the sanctuary. In the relief, also, the gods are shown seated as guests at the ceremonial banquet in the sanctuary. The relief depicts the sequence and the organizing of the procession, which began in the city and which included the marshals, magistrates, sacrificial animals, libation-bearing maidens, elderly citizens, youthful musicians, charioteers, and armed cavalry. The location of the relief, about 40 feet above the base, and the consequent poor illumination and partial obstruction by the columns indicate that it was primarily intended for the eyes of Athena. To accommodate the mortal viewers on ground level, the sculpture is in higher relief at the top of the frieze.

The Panathenaic procession recalls the spirit in which the temple was built. Art was interwoven with the civic ceremonies accompanying dramatic performances, athletic games, and religious offerings and rites (Fig. 81). Public expenditure for art was conceded as necessary to enrich the lives of Athenian citizens. The ideal citizen of Athens was an active contributor to the affairs of the city. Within half a century this ideal was realized by, among others, Pericles, Sophocles, Aeschylus, Euripides, Anaxagoras, Socrates, Thucydides, and the sculptor Phidias, overseer of the sculptural decoration of the Parthenon. In conjunction with Pericles, it may have been Phidias who assigned the architectural design to Ictinus and an assistant named Callicrates. Many artists were recruited for the project, and according to Plutarch, who wrote centuries later, such was the spirited rivalry among the workers and artists to excel in quality and speed that, to the amazement of subsequent generations, the Parthenon was finished within the lifetime of those who inaugurated it.

The prime purpose of the Parthenon was to provide a worthy house of Athena. The temple form is the descendant of the megarons, or dwellings of Mycenaean kings, built on the Acropolis long before the time of the Parthenon. This temple was not designed as an interior space in which a congregation worshiped; for this purpose an altar was placed outside, in front of the eastern entrance. The cella of the temple housed the gigantic 40-foot effigy of Athena Parthenos, garbed in military costume. The statue's great size therefore required an unusually wide plan to satisfy the necessary

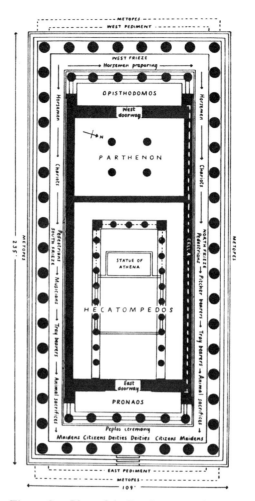

Figure 82. Plan of the Parthenon and Panathenaic Procession (after N. Yalouris).

height. Although the original is lost, we know that Phidias made this sculpture using gold for the dress and armor and ivory for the flesh. A ship's mast was used for the interior armature. Entrance to the sanctuary was reserved for the priests and for privileged laymen on certain occasions. The laity were permitted to look into the sanctuary through the enormous eastern doors.

The orientation of the temple was worked out with painstaking care, as was true for all ancient sacred architecture. The temple has a roughly east-west orientation. The central axis is slightly south of due east, so that on Athena's birthday the rising sun shone directly through the doors onto her effigy. The location of the temple on the Acropolis was also calculated to permit the widest view from the city below, and from various points the Parthenon may be seen against the sky, the sea, or the mountains.

The form of the Parthenon (Fig. 82) is basically that of the traditional Greek temple,

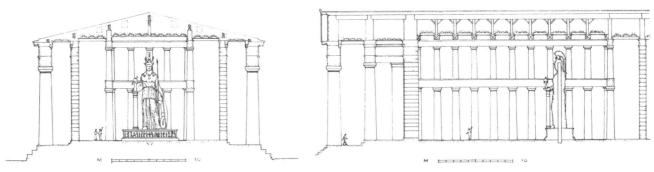

Figure 83. The Parthenon: Cross Section (left) and Detail of Longitudinal View of the Sanctuary (right), Omitting the Storage Chamber (reconstruction by Gorham P. Stevens, The American School of Classical Studies, Athens).

with its walled interior divided into two parts. The windowless eastern chamber housing the cult statue was known as the "*Hecatompedos*" (100 feet), because of its 100-foot length. As seen in the plan and section (Figs. 82, 83), there was an inner two-tier open colonnade that continued from the doorway to behind the statue, where it formed an aisle that permitted a view of the image from the rear. Natural illumination was provided by the huge doorway (32 feet high, 13 feet wide). Beneath the double-pitched tiled roof was a flat ceiling of wooden beams. The sanctuaries of the Greek temples are of substantial interest historically because they are among the first large enclosed interiors, even though the space within was not so expressively shaped as in other edifices of later periods, such as Imperial Rome and Gothic France. The statue of Athena completely dominated, if it did not crowd, the sanctuary. The second, and smaller, western chamber was the storage space for ritual objects, important votive offerings, and the treasury of the Athenian League and the state. This was known as the Parthenon ("Chamber of the Virgin"), from which the whole temple took its name.

Since the Classical Greek architects believed that the splendor of a temple should not be confined to its interior, perhaps the most inspired part of the Parthenon's design is its exterior. This emphasis may be explained by the fact that the public ritual was conducted out of doors, and visually the temple was intended to appear accessible. Worship of the Greek gods did not entail the secretive ceremonial of ancient Egypt. The presence of important sculptural programs outside in the pediments and metopes also suggests that the temple was more "extro-

verted" than interiorized in its address to the community. The exterior Pentelic marble columns were a shimmering white, and the triglyphs were painted blue; the horizontal architrave blocks above the columns were hung with military trophies.

The temple was mounted on a three-stepped base that set it apart from the earth and the viewer, much as a pedestal does for sculpture. The height of the individual steps was intended to discourage their being climbed. The sanctuary's outer wall and entrances were surrounded by a handsome range of columns. These columns and the horizontal elements above them belong to the Classical order known as Doric. The masculine severity of this order was appropriate to a war goddess. (The names and precise location of Classical architectural elements and decoration are shown in Fig. 84).

The Parthenon tells us more about the human than the metaphysical nature of the Greeks. Even in its ruined state it reminds us of the power of human intellect and of the Greeks' reverence for Athena as the goddess of wisdom, as well as an inclusive symbol of victory. The words of the fifth-century Athenian philosopher Anaxagoras could well have been inscribed on the Parthenon: "All things were in chaos when mind arose and made order." The temple, affirming its makers' belief in a rational unity of reality, is a visual analogy of the Greek idea of the world as ultimately knowable, static, and symmetrical; after its completion Athena's attributes were extended to include perfect equilibrium. A little over a century before, temple sculpture had been used to express the demonic and the common apprehension, if not fear, of the unknown. The Parthenon and its sculptural decoration, instead, expresses man's confidence in himself, in his place in the world, and in the dignity of his gods, who had human as well as divine qualities. To translate these religious and philosophical generalities into the specific components of the temple, it is important that we visualize the whole architectural ensemble, even though we can still perceive its radiant design from the ruins and appreciate how this accorded with Athenian speculation on the goddess' nature.

The Parthenon, like Classical sculpture, was designed according to the Greek ideal of eurythmy, or the well-proportioned, harmonious, and pleasing appearance of the whole. It gave the immediate impression of compactness and completeness, and its beauty lay in the impossibility of adding, subtracting, or altering any part without disrupting the whole. Its ideal rhythm consisted of a lucid repetition of similar elements, such as the columns, which within themselves have a harmonious stability. Oswald Spengler has described the Classical as that which can be taken in at a single glance. While this seems an oversimplification, the Parthenon's major design does give itself thus readily to the eye. We are immediately aware of certain individual parts, then of their tidy and disciplined relation to other parts and to the whole—not unlike the relationships making up the polis, or Greek city-state, of which Athena was the embodiment. Each component has its own identity, as seen in the nomenclature of the Doric order; if separated from the totality, the part and its location could be quickly identified. Parts with similar identity have a like measure and proportion to the whole, constituting the Greek ideal of symmetry. Given one half of a Greek temple, it would be possible to predict or reconstruct the other half with maximum certainty.

Beauty and nature were interpretable to the Classical Greeks in terms of an ideal, or conceptually perfect, human body. Such a body, composed of harmoniously disposed and interrelated parts, was symmetrical and lucidly manifested its weight and support. The temple columns and their capitals are like legs easily supporting a torso. The taste for a round, tapered, and fluted column is indicative of a preference for the animate and sensitive proportion found in the best fifth-century figure sculpture. Each groove or flute can contain a

man's back. As further evidence of the application of human scale, the intervals between the column axes can be expressed in terms of a column diameter and the width of a man's shoulders. The over-all size of the Parthenon is itself more humanly oriented than is that of the mammoth Egyptian temples. Like the perfect idealized human form, the form of the Parthenon is based upon a mathematical module and a consistent set of ratios. There was an Athenian foot unit, and Professor William Dinsmoor's meticulous measuring of the Parthenon has revealed Ictinus' use of mathematics rather than impulse to achieve the structure's perfect and unprecedented visual harmony. The ratio of the temple's height to its width on the east and west faces is 4 to 9; that of its width to its length is also 4 to 9, and that of the column diameter to the interval between columns (intercolumniation) is 9 to 4. The seventeen columns on the long sides are twice plus one the eight columns on the east and west, which again reduces to a 9 to 4 relation. With but a single module and ratio, the architect could calculate mentally all the proportions and dimensions of

Figure 84. Sectional Drawing of the Parthenon (after N. Yalouris).

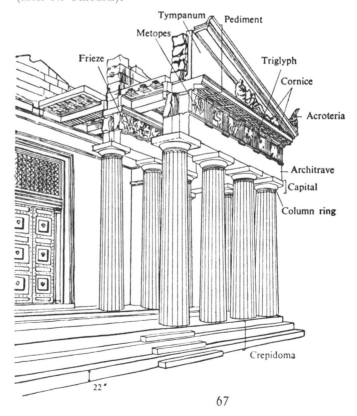

67

his building. (Reflect for a moment that one sheet of parchment cost an entire day's wage.) It is likely that Pythagoras' work with numbers and his belief that everything could be expressed in terms of them influenced Ictinus. Numbers were believed eternal and incorruptible values because they existed outside the senses. Looking patiently at the Parthenon permits both the visualization and the intuition of its proportional system, which induces a strong sense of equanimity and of the structure's rightness.

Further separating Ictinus' Parthenon from earlier Greek temples are the excellence and thoroughness of its optical refinements. There is not a perfectly straight line in the entire building. The purpose of every subtly curving edge may have been to correct the optical distortion of sagging that one experiences when looking at a long straight line or may have been to give a more sculptural appearance or a certain springiness to activate the temple's relation to the ground, and also that of its supporting columns to their load. Each step is convexly curved, with this almost imperceptible curvature forming the perimeter of a tremendous circle having a diameter, according to Dinsmoor, of 3½ miles. The entire upper portion of the temple above the column level

had a similar curve, and even the great door frames were curved. The columns near the corners have been placed closer together in order to provide a visual arrest for the eye as it moves along the peripheral colonnades. (It also serves to align the triglyphs and metopes with the columns in such a fashion that two triglyphs are made to meet at the corner.) The four corner columns have been slightly thickened so as not to appear spindly or thinner than the others since, because of their position, they are seen against the sky. The column shafts, which have been given a slight swelling (entasis) as they rise from the base, also are tilted back slightly to prevent the illusion that the building is falling forward. Use of such optical refinements, which required a consummate knowledge of mathematics and extremely difficult labor, augmented the beauty of the temple immeasurably, though such devices are not all or immediately apparent to the eye but impress themselves subtly on the mind and feelings. The brilliant execution of these refinements in the Parthenon surpasses any previous occasional but unsystematic use, thereby assisting Ictinus to bring the Greek temple form to perfection.

The Parthenon was further enhanced by superb sculpture (Figs. 85–87), in the form of

Below: Figure 85. *Hermes and Dionysus* (seated left) and *Magistrate with Boy Folding Peplos* (extreme right), from the east frieze of the Parthenon. Marble relief, height 3′7″. The British Museum, London.

Bottom: Figure 86. *Hermes and Dionysus,* detail of Fig. 85.

the above-described continuous frieze, metopes, two tympanum groups on the pediments, and decorative acroteria, or roof sculptures. (These last-named included lion heads and a sculpture group at the apex of the pediment, all of which have been lost.) The metope sculptures, which dealt not with the historically recent Persian Wars but with legendary victories won by the ancestors of the Athenians over the Lapiths, Centaurs, and Trojans, lent animation to the horizontal and vertical lines of the temple. The metope figures are carved in strong relief and in a wide variety of movements at variance with the axes of their frames. The tympanums contained sculptural representations of, on the east, the birth of Athena from the brow of Zeus and, on the west, the victory of Athena over Poseidon. These sculptures were supervised by Phidias. Many of them were painted and were carved in the round. Isolated, each figure has an autonomous beauty, and yet it fits harmoniously into a larger group. Despite the magnificence of these sculptures, as decoration they did not overbalance the temple as a whole but served as a crowning religious and esthetic element.

Just as the Parthenon pays tribute to the high civilizing ideals and the ordering instinct of the Classical Greek mind, so does it also recall some of the limitations of that culture and its art. Ictinus was respectful of tradition, though not a slave to it. Within definite limits he refined and improved what had come before, but he did not revolutionize Greek temple architecture. The engineering of the Parthenon is extremely conservative; its post-and-lintel system was thousands of years old. The Greeks knew the principles of the arch and the dome but continued to associate certain traditional forms with their sacred buildings, and there was no such structural adventurousness as was found in later Rome or the medieval period of Western Europe. It is recorded that Ictinus, like other great artists of his age, wrote a book about his work. Typical of Classical art is a desire to codify what is perfect, and there is no esthetic or engineering advance beyond the Parthenon in Greek architecture. The Greek ordering impulse found it hard to adapt to the tensions and changing times that followed. The cool aloofness and exquisite closed perfection of the Parthenon, like Classical sculpture, do not partake of the qualities of variety, the

Figure 87. Triglyphs and Metope on the Parthenon. Metope 4'8" × 4'2".

unexpected, emotional warmth, and psychological range encountered in ancient daily living. Herbert Muller has pointed out that the Classical Greeks had no respect for empirical knowledge, no sense of history (as shown by the metope mythical reliefs). In Classical art time is suspended. There are many links missing between the Parthenon and life in fifth-century Athens.

Perhaps it is coincidental, but part of the downfall of Athens was her inability to sustain successful alliances with other countries. Political misfortune and disunity caused the initiators of the Parthenon, Pericles and Phidias, to fall from power, the latter ironically and falsely accused of stealing gold intended for Athena's statue. Longer than the city-state that produced it, the Parthenon and its noble but restricted ideals have endured as a beautiful abstraction. Before we move on to the Gothic cathedral, it might be well to recall Spengler's observation that the Greeks' mode of worship was a pious observation of form, not soaring aspiration.

Figure 88. Chartres Cathedral (view from the city). c. 1194–1260.

THE GOTHIC CATHEDRAL

The best approach to the Gothic cathedral in France is that which was taken by the medieval pilgrim, who, traveling on foot to a city such as Chartres, first saw the distant cathedral spires across the open fields. Physically, esthetically, and spiritually, the Cathedral still dominates the town of Chartres (Fig. 88). The cathedrals that rose above the medieval houses glorified not only Christ and the Virgin but also the cities that erected them. The cathedrals symbolized man's awareness of the divine as well as his own self-consciousness. The Gothic was basically an urban style, for the very phenomenon of cathedral building presupposed the extensive development of cities in the eleventh and twelfth centuries. The growth of these cities in turn reflected important stages in European socio-economic growth: the accumulation of wealth, organization of labor, administrative efficiency, transportation and communications improvements, the establishment of relative political stability, and specific developments and techniques such as horseshoe nails and pulleys in mechanics. There also began to emerge significant intellectual resources and activity outside the monasteries.

During the twelfth and thirteenth centuries, the hundred-mile area around Paris was covered with what one medieval writer called a "snowfall of cathedrals." Cathedral building was at that time an economic expenditure surpassed only by war. Today it staggers the imagination that a city such as Chartres, having a probable population of 10,000 in the twelfth century, should undertake to erect, within a period of less than thirty years, a single structure that would now cost in excess of seventy-five million dollars. While to some extent satisfying civic pride, the Gothic cathedral was above all a gift to God. The rivalry between French cities to outdo one another in the size and magnificence of their cathedrals was undoubtedly motivated in part by secular concerns, such as economic benefits, but the deep and measureless religious faith and optimism of the builders were truly the prime movers. Like their cities, no two Gothic cathedrals are the same. In addition to great variations in their size, the sheer variety and complexity of Gothic cathedral architecture prohibits us from writing about a fixed type as we could about the Greek temple. This variety in itself furnishes evidence against the stereotype view of the essential unity, conservatism, and lethargy of medieval society. There was only one Church, however, and the cathedral does symbolize a basic spiritual unification. The so-called Gothic period was a time of continuing change; its architectural styles seemed constantly in process, their evolution reminding us of the vitality and discord of the Middle Ages.

The word "cathedral," derived from the Latin *cathedra*, signifies that the bishop's seat is within. The bishops and their urban dioceses represented, in a sense, a rivalry with the Cistercian monasteries and their ascetic world-denying doctrines. The richly ornamented and elaborately designed exteriors of the cathedrals reflect a more affirmative attitude toward life on earth and a more explicit recognition of the civil community than do the austere introverted monastic churches. From no matter which prospect within the town one views or approaches the cathedral, the forcefulness and rich variety of its design make themselves felt. There was no prescribed approach, no one sacred way by which the worshiper was to proceed to the front of this house of God. In their original state, the cathedrals were not isolated with the open spaces or plazas that girdle many of them in their present condition (Fig. 89). A cathedral might have had some sort of squares on the west and north or south, but usually the city's secular buildings encroached directly upon the church walls, on its complex of chapterhouse, cemetery, school, prison, and bishop's residence. This tight proximity of the secular and the sacred parallels the role that the cathedral played in the community.

The Gothic cathedral was more than the religious focus of its society. Its bells regulated the day's secular activities, just as the significant events in the life of Christ, the Virgin, and the saints provided the calendar for great fairs, festivals, and performances of the mystery plays. The cathedral met the public's needs and love for splendor and spectacle, serving as the backdrop and stage not only for its daily religious drama but also for public festivities that often were irreverent in nature. Public explosions that occurred at the Feast of the Fools were accepted by churchmen as safety valves against the rigors, the severe proscriptions of Christian dogma. For this reason, on specific occasions, gambling and sausage-eating at the high altar were permitted, donkeys were worshiped in the sanctuary amid the incense of burning shoe leather, or the laity might elect a mock pope, dress up as monks, and parody the church service. The house of the Heavenly Father served at times as a playground for his children. During the important fairs that brought wealth to the city and funds for the cathedral's construction, the Church-owned and tax-free property was used by the merchants. The city of Chartres was able to build its cathedral because of income from secular fairs that attracted people from all over France, and also because of the wealth attracted through the sale of indulgences, gifts to enshrine the sacred relic of the Virgin's cloak, and the enormous sums accruing to the bishop and deacons from land holdings and tithes. It was not unusual to have business transactions conducted within the nave of the cathedral, and on occasion, wine was sold in the crypt of Chartres.

The silence encountered today in the cathedrals is in great contrast to the clatter of voices about which the priests complained in medieval

Figure 89. Amiens Cathedral (aerial view). c. 1220–88.

Figure 90. *Left:* Tombstone of Hugh Libergier of Reims (died 1263). Photo courtesy Carl F. Barnes, Jr.

Below: Drawing of the Labyrinth, Reims Cathedral (begun 1211).

times. The building of the rood screen between the nave and eastern portion of the church in the sixteenth century was partly because of the need for privacy of the priests while they celebrated the Mass. The cathedral nave served variously as a lecture and concert hall, as a repository for important civic documents and for commemorative monuments, as an arsenal, a municipal museum, and a trysting place. In many instances the bishop or deacons owned only the eastern portion of the church and not the nave, which belonged to the city.

ARCHITECTS

The fact that we do not know the names of many architects who worked on the Gothic cathedrals—such as the principal one for Chartres—does not substantiate the view that they were anonymous in their own time or were simply of the "folk" or the priesthood. In reality, the names of many medieval architects have survived because of the medieval distaste

for anonymity, the great esteem in which master builders were held, and the means by which they were honored. (Jean d'Orbais and Hugh Libergier of Reims and Robert de Luzarches of Amiens are examples.) For instance, some builders were given such degrees as a doctorate in stonemasonry. Certain notable architects, such as Robert de Luzarches and Hugh Libergier, were entombed in churches they built, and their effigies were engraved on the burial slab; moreover, the names of the architects or "masters of the work" were inscribed in a floor medallion at the end of a labyrinth incised on the nave pavement (Fig. 90). The labyrinth was the architect's mark because it was associated with Daedalus, designer of the famous labyrinth in the ancient Cretan palace of Cnossos, who was honored as the ancestor of medieval architects. By crawling along the labyrinth on their knees, those who could not make the pilgrimage to Jerusalem were able to make the journey symbolically and, not coincidentally, pay their respects to the builder. The master builders of the cathedrals, the equivalents of

Plate 13.   ROBERT CAMPIN, or the MASTER OF FLÉMALLE. *Merode Altarpiece.* c. 1425–28.
Oil on panel, center 25³/₁₆ × 24⁷/₈″; wings 25³/₈ × 10³/₄″.
The Metropolitan Museum of Art, New York (The Cloisters Collection, Purchase).

Plate 14. JAN VAN EYCK. *St. Jerome in His Study.* C. 1432–41.
Oil on panel, $8\frac{1}{16} \times 5\frac{1}{4}''$. The Detroit Institute of Arts.

Plate 15. HUGO VAN DER GOES. *Adoration of the Shepherds*, center panel of the *Portinari Altarpiece*. c. 1476. Oil on panel, 8'3½" × 10'. Uffizi, Florence.

Plate 16. MASACCIO. *The Tribute Money.* c. 1427. Fresco, 8′4″ × 19′8″. Brancacci Chapel, Sta. Maria del Carmine, Florence.

present-day architects, frequently came from distinguished lay families, were trained by their fathers, and had roughly a middle-class and free professional status. They seemed to have been pious men of good moral character and education who were quite well off financially. They had opportunity for travel, since their services were often vied for on an international basis. Their education was in the craft of masonry or carpentry, Euclidean geometry, drafting, Latin and French, and various techniques and secrets of building that were passed on from one generation to the next. Much of their education was empirical, being based on what worked, and for centuries Gothic architecture developed by trial and error. The notebook of the thirteenth-century architect Villard de Honnecourt reveals a broad curiosity, encompassing machines, sculpture, furniture, details of buildings, and animals. The master builder might well be versed in the making of objects and ornaments, furniture, and fortifications, as well as churches and castles. He looked to established successful prototypes rather than to originality as a basis for design.

The function of the master builder was to conceive the plan in consultation with a priest or the cathedral canons, or even the bishop, and to decide how to go about building the edifice; thereafter he usually relied on a foreman to oversee its actual construction. Managing the business aspect per se was not the architect's job, and his tasks were more specific. Often responsible for selecting materials, he also procured the labor, estimated costs and quantities, settled labor disputes, and saw to the welfare of his artisans. A permanent workshop and planning office was established during a cathedral's building. By the thirteenth century the master builder needed only to give orders and, in turn, achieved a social status superior to that of earlier medieval architects.

Because of its prohibitive cost, plans were not drawn on parchment until the fourteenth century. Earlier, drafting of details or sections had usually been done on plaster slabs or wood panels, and these were not saved. Not until the fifteenth century, with the erection of Brunelleschi's Pazzi Chapel, was the whole building meticulously planned in advance. Many of the details of building and ornament were left to experienced and trusted masons, carpenters, and sculptors. When an architect on one of these great projects died, his successor respected what had already been constructed; still, while he might continue work on unfinished sections according to the original plans, he might also choose to introduce new ideas. The Cathedral of Chartres lacks a homogeneous style, for its sponsors did not insist upon any standard of architectural consistency other than excellence. It is a peculiarity, even a distinction, of the Gothic style that it is able to absorb such a heterogeneity of modes.

Although the Gothic cathedral impresses the modern viewer with its rich symbolism, the basic problems confronting the master builder were practical. His various considerations included adapting his plan to the demands of the liturgy and the performance of the canonical offices; providing for the proper disposition of relics and subsidiary altars; facilitating the movement of the congregation and of processions; and making provision for delivery of the sermon.

THE MEANING AND ORGANIZATION OF THE GOTHIC CATHEDRAL

The extent to which conscious symbolism entered directly into the form of the Gothic cathedral is difficult to assess. In the period of great cathedral building, there was a strong interest in symbolic interpretation, allegories, and metaphors. The cathedrals lent themselves to a wealth of allusions, to such views as the material form of the church structure symbolizing the spiritual church. Since Early Christian times the church was viewed as a metaphor of man's soul, and also as representing the Kingdom of Heaven and the mystical body of Christ (present in the altar and choir area). Both externally and internally, the cathedral served as a kind of sacred theater: its west façade provided a backdrop for mystery plays, and its altar area was where the mysteries of the ritual were performed and the holy objects displayed. The architects were literate, educated townsmen in contact with the intellectual leaders, spiritual and lay, of the community. They consulted with canons, bishops, theologians, and priests on the theological program for the sculpture. The meanings of measure and light as interpreted by great theologians of the past were also available as references, but that these abstruse interpretations were consistently and systematically translated into medieval architectural design is conjectural. Of great influence were the already existing religious buildings, as well as the practical problems posed, after 1200, by the erecting and supporting of enormous vaults more than a hundred feet from the floor of the nave. (The height of the nave at Chartres is 120 feet; Reims, 125 feet; Amiens, 138 feet.)

Official handbooks of Church symbolism did not exist for the artist to consult. While there were important twelfth- and thirteenth-century writings by such men as Durandus, these were not dogma, and the literary symbols contained within the treatises gave no assistance in matters of style or, in many cases, for evolving the shapes of parts. The cathedrals inspired reverent fantasies in many writers who worshiped within them, and their various interpretations of the same architectural features were formulated after the fact and were not consistent. What adds to the wonder of the cathedrals, and their intellectual greatness in history, is that their architects did give—in one way or another—symbolic form to the highest ideals and much of the spirit of their age. Acquaintance with the Gothic cathedrals makes us aware of their profound and sometimes elusive connection with the societies which produced the Crusades, the feudal system, and universities and which enriched the history of science and philosophy, contributed significantly to jurisprudence, and fashioned the poetry of the troubadours. To comprehend the meaning of the Gothic cathedral in its broadest and deepest sense, all these diversified activities must be explored, as modern scholarship has progressively undertaken to do.

By its great size and ornateness alone, the Gothic cathedral was truly acknowledged the house of God, but unlike a temple of Athena, the deity in tangible form did not dwell within. The cathedral was an ambivalent symbol of Christ, the heavenly Jerusalem, and the universe. Its magnificence, in terms of the treasure expended on it, was deemed appropriate to its function as an offering from the faithful and as the spiritual residence of Christ or the Virgin. It was through the cathedral that man was made aware of the invisible and infinite, that the divine became immanent. The master builder sought to devise a setting which would so stimulate the thoughts and feelings of the worshiper that he could realize the most important event of his life, the soul's communion with God.

The West Façade. All the major parts of the cathedral have a history extending back into the Middle Ages or, in some cases, even to antiquity. Their assimilation into the cathedral structure was a process involving not only formal adaptation and modification but also symbolic meaning. The "Gateway to Heaven," as the west façade was called, may trace its history back to Syrian churches of the sixth and seventh centuries and to certain Roman Imperial palaces fronted with twin-towered portals. As Baldwin Smith has shown in a brilliant study, towered gateways were used as entrances to royal cities and abbeys in Carolingian times and were the scene of impressive ceremonial receptions upon a king's arrival. The transformation of the Early Christian basilica into a twin-towered edifice must be seen in the light of Charlemagne's revival of Roman political symbolism and his desire to show his ascendancy over the Church as well as the state. The emperor's symbolic participation in the religious service and his exalted authority were indicated in the towered façades of Carolingian and certain Romanesque churches by a solarium, or balcony, on which was located his throne and behind which was placed a large circular window. Sun symbolism was in that epoch equated with the authority of the king as well as of Christ. By the late thirteenth century, however, the symbolism of the west façade alluded entirely to Christ. Nevertheless, the façades of such Gothic cathedrals as Chartres (Fig. 91), with their recessed portals that had evolved in Carolingian times, their "galleries of kings," their circular windows, and their double towers, still bear the impress of earthly royalty.

The Circular Window. The origin and significance of the great circular window of the west façade has been explored by Helen Dow, who has shown that circular windows go back to Babylonian times and had been known in Europe since Roman times. Unlike the well-known but misnamed Gothic "rose window," the circular window, with few exceptions, lacked stone tracery until the building of the Abbey Church of St-Denis, about 1140. The basic form of the rose window (Fig. 92), as found at Chartres, may have originated in old schemata of the symbolic wheel. The great Byzantine chandeliers composed of pierced metal disks were in use in France by the twelfth century, either as hanging or as standing lamps. Lamps lent themselves to expression of the sun and light symbolism that had become associated with Christ in the Middle Ages. The circular form was rich in meaning, for it might signify virtue, eternity, God, or the Church. The great circular window also echoed the form and associations of the wheel of fortune, through which Christian virtue and its reward could be contrasted with the vicissitudes and transient nature of earthly existence. Ezekiel's vision of the wheel made the window form an appropriate allusion to the Scriptures. The prominence of the window as well as its form symbolized the eternal and righteous eye of God. (The word *nave* means "ship" in Latin, the window being, thus, the ship's guiding eye.) Divine light and justice seem to have been two of the most important meanings of the window. As it had in its use by Charlemagne, the circular window in combination with the many sculptures of saints surrounding it conveyed the notion of a king surrounded by his armies. The full significance of this interpretation becomes apparent when the sculptural program of the west façade of Chartres is examined.

The Sculptural Program of the Chartres West Façade.
The great main doors represented the Gates of Paradise. The purpose of the programs worked out with theologians for the sculpture occupying the honored positions around and immediately above the doors and for the imagery in the stained-glass windows was to manifest Church doctrine. That these sculptures were directly intended to be didactic or self-evidently symbolic is a questionable aim, for it would appear that the faithful relied upon the spoken word for their instruction in dogma, and hence in the meaning of art. That elaborate theological programs were actually planned and carried

Above right: Figure 91. West Façade, Chartres Cathedral. Width 157′; south tower (right), height 344′; north tower (left), height 377′. Façade c. 1194–1260 (portals and lancet windows c. 1145); south tower c. 1180; north spire 1507–13.

Right: Figure 92. Rose Window, West Façade, Chartres Cathedral.

out for cathedral imagery has long been known. In this connection, Adolph Katzenellenbogen contributed an outstanding study of the sculptural program of the west façade of Chartres (Fig. 93), which explained that the figures of the three tympanums, or semicircular relief panels over the doors, present Christ in his dual nature of God and Man, as well as the source of divine wisdom.

At the far right, the Christ child is shown seated on the lap of the enthroned Virgin, indicating her role in his Incarnation. In the pointed vaults bordering the tympanum are representations of the seven liberal arts (grammar, dialectic, rhetoric, arithmetic, music, geometry, and astronomy), the intellectual means by which to attain awareness of divine wisdom. The Virgin, esteemed for her wisdom, became the inspiration and guide of these arts— an indication of the growth of humanistic studies within the medieval Church. The left tympanum depicts the Ascension of Christ. Its peripheral vaults contain symbols of the zodiac and of diverse manual labor. The concepts illustrated here are Christ's transcendence of and rule over time, and the value of active physical labor, which, balanced with the contemplative life of learning, led the faithful toward knowledge of God. The central tympanum shows the Second Coming of Christ and the Last Judgment. Immediately below the central tympanum, on the rectangular lintel panel, are arrayed the twelve prophets who foretold Christ's Incarnation and who are to assist at the Last Judgment.

Flanking the doors of the Royal Portal are the jamb figures, whose purpose it is to proclaim the sympathetic concord existing between Church and state and between the Old and the New Testament and to publicize the illustrious lineage of the French monarchy. It was common practice in the Middle Ages to portray past or present kings and queens of France as important personages from the Old and New Testament; this custom emphasized that the royal line was a defender of the Church and enhanced it in the public esteem. The implication was that the virtuous qualities of the Old Testament kings were continued in the monarchs of France. This was all part of the medieval preoccupation with searching for parallels between the present and the past, the old and the new, the visible and the invisible. The elongated jamb figures, which date from about the mid-twelfth century, have a columnar aspect, and their form and purpose suggest that they comprise a second wall by which the Church is strengthened and defended. One must pass between the predecessors of Christ on the jambs before reaching him; this sequence

Figure 93.   West Portals, Chartres Cathedral. c. 1145–70.

signified the old leading to the new. To pass through the door was to move toward God through Christ, for Christ had said, "I am the door. Whoever enters me will be saved." The gallery above the circular window contains effigies of French kings, hence the familiar name "gallery of kings" (see Fig. 91). The gallery itself may have derived from the earlier medieval and ancient palace "window of appearances," from which the ruler presented himself to the public. While the effigies of the kings protected the western front of the church, the bishops' images were presented as defenders of its sides.

The Bay System. Bays are the rectangular cubelike compartments formed by each vault and its four piers. Professor Walter Horn has traced the origin of the bay system in medieval churches to early medieval secular wooden architecture as used in all-purpose structures, episcopal tithe barns, and houses (Figs. 94, 95). A few timber churches subdivided into bays have survived from the Middle Ages. In many sections of medieval Europe, residences, markets, and barns were structurally interchangeable. Tithe barns, which stored the one-tenth of a crop given to the Church by the faithful, were often of tremendous dimensions, since their being built up of regular units permitted

structures of great length. The Early Christian basilicas were not composed of bays, and the entrance of this technique into religious architecture, probably during the ninth century, is another important example of drawing upon secular sources for religious architecture. (The Early Christian basilica had itself been derived

Above: Figure 94. Market Hall at Mereville, France. 15th century.

Below: Figure 95. Nave (looking east toward the apse), Chartres Cathedral. c. 1194–1221.

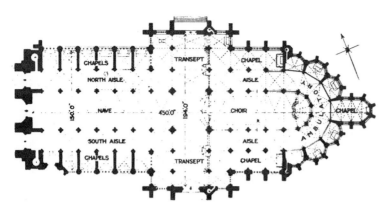

Figure 96. Plan of Amiens Cathedral.

from Roman public buildings.) The introduction of the bay into the basilican form skeletalized and partitioned the interior into similar units, thereby opening up great possibilities for expressive articulation of the space and for the use of geometrical or arithmetical premises in organizing the interior. The bay system was valued by the cathedral builders because of its familiarity and ease of handling. It met the Gothic need for a multiplicity of parts and satisfied a feudal (hierarchical) intent with the implications of the bay order. The Scriptures may not have provided sources for specific architectural shapes, but the Wisdom of Solomon (2: 20) might be quoted as comfort to the successful architect: "Thou hast ordered all things in measure and number and weight."

The Plan and Measure. As had been formerly practiced in ancient and early medieval times, the orientation of the Gothic cathedral was meant to place the building in harmony with the universe (Fig. 96). The apse, containing the altar that symbolized Christ's tomb, was oriented consistently toward the east, the direction signifying rebirth. The western end was traditionally associated with death and evil; hence it was on this entrance that the Last Judgment was carved. The north was identified with cold and darkness, the world of the old order. The south signified the new dispensation. In addition to its symbolic value as a form, the demands of the liturgy caused the retention of the long-established cross plan; it facilitated procession through the nave, provided a large area for the choir east of the transept and ample space for the altar, and made feasible side aisles for accommodating the pilgrims who came to venerate the relics in the chapels. The basic

plan of the Gothic cathedral had already emerged in Carolingian times, with the addition to the standard basilican elements (nave, aisles, apse, and an occasional transept) of a crypt, choir, and radiating chapels. The marked internal divisions of the church's plan signified the hierarchical order and authority of the clergy and its relation to the laity, who were prohibited access to the choir and altar areas.

Scholars who have taken pains to draw accurate ground plans of medieval churches have found that in certain cases it is possible to discover a kind of scientific organization. One of the trade secrets of the master builder was a module on which he established both the scale and the proportions of his building. It seems doubtful, however, that entire Gothic buildings were organized according to a single or consistent geometrical or arithmetical progression.

Using any polygon, the master builder worked out the problem of building a tower and effecting the transition from a square base to a round spire. While all builders recognized the use of geometry as an aid to building, there were undoubtedly some who by temperament sought to use it extensively in a way that guaranteed them "true measure" and thereby heightened the cathedral's symbolic analogy to the measure that unified the universe. Otto von Simson argued strongly for the incidence of the latter attitude in his study of Chartres. His findings showed that a basic ratio of 5 to 8 was utilized in the plan and elevation of the Cathedral. Von Simson found further support for his argument in the fact that God was frequently referred to and even depicted as a geometer (Fig. 97). Church literature before and during the time of the cathedrals is rich in religious interpretation of numbers and geometry: to cite but two examples, the triangle symbolized the Trinity, and the square the relation of God the Father to the Son. In mystical numerology, almost any number could be interpreted as revealing some aspect of divinity or dogma. Numbers and geometry were thought to be important means through which the intellect and workings of God could be made intelligible to human understanding. The Gothic designer's taste for numerology is displayed in towers, fenestration patterns, piers, balustrades, arcades, statues, and doors. The parts of the cathedral do lend themselves to counting in numerical sequences, but not to a single grand program of interpretation as numerical symbolism. Selectively, rather than in a literal quantitative way, the master builder again realized a vital preoccupation of his time.

The Interior and Light. The dedicatory services performed in the sanctuary of the cathedral drew principally upon three Biblical sources to link the building to the past. The first was the account of the Temple of Solomon (II Chron., 2–6), the second was the Temple of Ezekiel, and the third was the description of the Heavenly Jerusalem by St. John. While the Bible does not describe in detail what Solomon's temple looked like, it does record a facing of gold and precious gems, and this description may have influenced St. John, who presents the most striking reference for the celestial city:

> And the building of the wall of it was of jasper; and the city was pure gold, like unto clear glass. And the foundation of the wall of the city was garnished with all manner of precious stones.... And the city had no need of the sun, neither of the moon, to shine in it; for the glory of God did lighten it.

Other Biblical sources speak of glass walls, and the increased use of stained glass in the twelfth and thirteenth centuries may have been an attempt to strengthen the analogy between the church structure and the Heavenly Jerusalem. The design of the cathedral's exterior reflected much of the religious and secular history of life on earth; the interior was considered the mystical heart of the cathedral, where God's epiphany takes place.

Figure 97. *Christ as Geometer*, from the *Bible Moralisée*. 13th century.

To enter into the initial darkness of the cathedral from the sunlit exterior is to experience once more the medieval worshiper's sense of proceeding from the material to the celestial world (Pl. 7). Perhaps the most exalted efforts of imagination, the most inspired creations, of the Gothic builders are the internal colored light and the idealized space of the cathedral. Light and color are both form and symbol, the style and content of Gothic religious architecture. When the churches had their original complement of windows, the suffused polychrome glow never permitted total revelation of the space and detail or, significantly, of the measure of the interior. There was no comparable spatial or lighting effect in any other type of medieval building. The ranges of windows became luminous walls, and their deep and shifting reddish violet hues dematerialized the interior stonework, as if abstractly signifying spiritual triumph over material things. The space, lighting, and music of the cathedral interior transported the worshiper from an environment of familiar sounds, illumination, scale, textures, and dimensions into a world of intricate melodies of sound and color, changing vistas, elusive surfaces, and heights not determined by his own measure. The quick change from sunlight to darkness impelled the visitor to slow his pace in order to penetrate what initially seemed veiled from the eyes. The stained-glass windows were intended to keep out almost all external light and all reminders of the earthly world. Their task was to elevate and enlighten the mind and soul. Seen from the floor of the nave, windows 60 feet away did not lend themselves to easy reading, and details of the rose window were undecipherable. Within the relative obscurity of the interior, the sonorous reds and blues could be fully apprehended by the eye, and the gold of the altar achieved a finer luminosity.

The brilliance of the original cathedrals, however, was not confined to their stained-glass windows alone. In the thirteenth century, Durandus wrote:

> The ornaments of the nave consist of dorsals, tapestry, mattings, and cushions of silk, purple and the like. The ornaments of the choir consist of dorsals, tapestry, carpets and cushions. Dorsals are hangings of cloth at the back of the clergy. Mattings, for their feet. Tapestry is likewise strewed under the feet, particularly under the feet of Bishops, who ought to trample worldly things under their feet. Cushions are placed on the seats or benches of the choir.

But it was the light from the windows that inspired the greatest awe and inspired praise by Church theologians of the cathedral's "bright" and "lucid" structure. God was perfect light into which no mortal eye could look, and the light that man could see was but a pale reflection of God. Light was the source and requirement of beauty, the means by which God manifested his presence and his Creation to man. Light passing through the windows symbolized the Incarnation of Christ. Light symbolism, inherited from earlier Christian churches, was also known and used in ancient times. The power and uniqueness of its use in the Gothic cathedral inspired the great Abbot Suger, builder of St-Denis, to record his mystical ascension to God by means of meditation on the light of his cathedral:

Thus when—out of my delight in the beauty of the house of God—the loveliness of the many-colored gems has called me away from external cares, and worthy meditation has induced me to reflect, transferring that which is material to that which is immaterial, on the diversity of sacred virtues; then it seems to me that I see myself dwelling, as it were, in some strange region of the universe which neither exists entirely in the slime of the earth nor entirely in the purity of Heaven; and that, by the grace of God, I can be transported from this inferior to that higher world in an anagogical manner.

GOTHIC STYLE

The Gothic style had its highest expression in the cathedrals, and by 1400 it was to become an international style and be extended to secular buildings. In addition to the colored light, soaring spaces, and complex perspectives within the cathedral, other distinguishing features of the Gothic cathedral style include the pointed (occasionally rounded) arch, ribbed vault, and flying buttress, all of which had in some form been known or developed during previous architectural periods. These elements are usually combined in rhythmic numerical sequences. The subordination of components to larger parts and of larger parts to the whole has a strong feudal and hierarchical character. (Unlike the organization of the Parthenon, there are no fixed numbers or proportions of the parts.) Like elements and sequences recur in different scales and combinations with other motifs. It is difficult to separate individual parts from their contexts because of their sequential arrangement and the density of the sequential groups; the viewer, nevertheless, is always conscious of looking at the parts of a greater but incomplete whole. Unlike the Parthenon again, no single prospect permits comprehension of the cathedral's total design. Like Gothic sacred music, the composition of a cathedral is polyphonic— the simultaneous combination of a number of parts, each constituting an individual theme that harmonizes with the others. There is evidence to suggest further analogy in the use of mathematics to proportion musical and architectural structures. Surveys indicate, however, that many builders did not feel obliged to perpetuate older traditions and devised their own variant proportions to achieve more impressive visual harmonies.

Figure 98. Structural Diagram of a Gothic Cathedral (left buttress from Amiens Cathedral; right buttress from Reims Cathedral).

Above: Figure 99. Buttresses from the South Side, Chartres Cathedral.

Below: Figure 100. VILLARD DE HONNECOURT. Drawing of Exterior and Interior Elevations, Nave of Reims Cathedral. c. 1240.

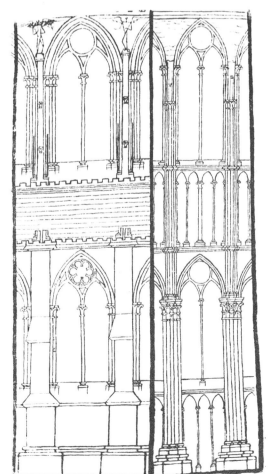

To a greater extent than early medieval architecture, the Gothic cathedral reveals its skeletal framework, the multiple play of its vector forces, and the resolution of its thrusts and weight (Figs. 98, 99). The massive walls of the militant-looking Romanesque churches were largely dematerialized by an increased replacement of stone by glass between the main piers supporting the vaults. The cradling action of the flying buttresses involves the external structure in a new way, lending what might be characterized as a muscular appearance to the exterior.

The plan of a Gothic cathedral (Fig. 96) shows the enclosure of the nave and aisles to be a continuous series of points, a regular constellation of piers, which are connected by thin, parallel wall sections. While the medieval architect may not have used the word or even thought of space in the terms of a modern architect, he had a great sensitivity for the effectiveness of certain distances between walls. Villard de Honnecourt's notebook shows a primary concern with graphically designed screenlike walls (Fig. 100). Much of the physical character of the cathedral was undoudtebly determined by the engineering functions of load and support; the width of the building was probably fixed by what the builder felt he could safely vault and buttress. It is too limited a judgment, however, to look upon the architect's intent as being only to raise a structural tour de force. Many design decisions—such as the addition of pinnacles to buttresses, the clustering of slender shafts against the main piers, the use of pointed arches, and probably the ribbing of the

Figure 101. Vaults at the Crossing of Nave and Transepts, Chartres Cathedral.

vaults—were not purely structural and were intended to enhance the whole and increase its visual expressiveness (Fig. 101). There is, for instance, greater articulation and sculptural treatment of the piers than is necessary for their physical function as support. The proportions of the nave arcade, triforium, and clerestory resulted from esthetic, and perhaps symbolic, decisions intended to bring the building closer to a visual and intellectual perfection. Only in part emotional and subjective, much of the experience of entering a Gothic cathedral derives from a rational and an intuitive awareness of the builder's logic, which he took pains to

make perceptible to the senses. The master builder's rich inventiveness with three-dimensional form and the various adjustments, alterations, and additions he made beyond a concern for structural necessity have occasioned the opinion that in the Gothic cathedral it is function which follows form.

LE CORBUSIER'S CHAPEL AT RONCHAMP

The Parthenon and Gothic cathedrals such as Chartres came out of definite established traditions of religious architecture, and their architects sought neither novelty nor original self-expression. In fifth-century Greece and in medieval Europe, the most advanced architecture in terms of design and engineering was in the service of religion. The builders had, in architectural precedent and from scriptural sources, a preestablished public basis for symbolic meaning or religious associations with their architectural forms. In the nineteenth and twentieth centuries, the finest and most advanced buildings in terms of design and structural techniques have been secular enterprises. The problem confronting twentieth-century architects has been to evolve, from this generally nonreligious background, an architecture suited to religious purposes, one that would capture the feeling and tone of the sacred. The best modern architects have utilized a personal, empirical approach to each problem rather than a dependence upon conventional formulas. The result has been an avoidance of imitating medieval church architecture—or that of any other period—for those enlightened congregations and clergy who would allow a gifted architect the freedom to create churches and synagogues appropriate to their time, place, and particular religious beliefs, thereby inspiring rather than inhibiting good architecture. Modern architecture has often proved that a fine religious structure (as has also been seen for certain painting commissions of Matisse) need not presuppose that the architect and his patron be of the same faith. Common to Phidias, Hugh Libergier, and the modern Swiss-born architect Le Corbusier (Charles-Edouard Jeanneret) has been their inspiration by noble ideals as communicated for their own time.

Ironically, Le Corbusier's pilgrimage chapel of Notre-Dame-du-Haut (Pl. 8; Fig. 102), located at Ronchamp in the Vosges Mountains of western France, near Switzerland, was inspired many years before when as a young architect he visited the Parthenon. In his notebook the youthful Le Corbusier set down his thoughts on what constitutes architecture and wherein for him lay the secret of the Parthenon's power, and these ideas were later to have a strong influence on the Ronchamp chapel. Architecture, he felt, is an art of sensation, affecting our visual responses, inciting emotion through the senses, and bringing joy to the mind: "Architecture is the skillful, accurate and magnificent play of masses seen in light." The Chapel of Notre-Dame-du-Haut can be profitably analyzed on this basis.

Le Corbusier's assignment was to crown a hill with a new Catholic chapel to replace an undistinguished building destroyed in the war, on a site where for as long as men could remember had been pagan and Christian places of worship. Surrounded by extensive hills and valleys, the elevated site had no accessible road. A specialist in residences and city planning, the architect had never before designed a place of worship, and he was not a Catholic. He was nevertheless given a free hand in the project by the Archbishop of Besançon—one can assume on the premise that architectural genius was nonsectarian. In a letter to the Archbishop when the chapel was finished in 1955, after five years of planning and construction, Le Corbusier wrote:

I wished to create a place of silence, of prayer, of peace, of spiritual joy. A sense of the sacred animated our effort. Our workmen...calculators... are those who brought this project into being, a difficult project, meticulous, primitive, made strong by the resources brought into play, but sensitive and informed by all-embracing mathematics, which is the creator of that space which cannot be described in words. A few scattered symbols, a few written words telling the praises of the Virgin. The cross—the true cross of suffering—is raised up in this space; the drama of Christianity has taken possession of the place from this time forwards....

In 1910, Le Corbusier had written, "The Parthenon is drama...." That special quality which unites the three religious edifices in this chapter, which set them apart from secular structures in their vicinities, is the dramatic. In what ways Le Corbusier was to achieve the dramatic is apparent from the moment the pilgrim or traveler first sights the Ronchamp chapel. Like the silhouettes of its Greek and Gothic predecessors, the silolike towers and sweeping roof line of the modern chapel reveal their general character from a considerable distance; but as one comes closer and mounts the hill, they become partially obscured and are then lost from sight—reminiscent of ascending the Sacred Way to the Acropolis or wending along toward the Cathedral through the streets of Chartres or Amiens. As one approaches the crest of the hill, the chapel slowly reemerges, like a ship rising above the swelling ground formation the architect had landscaped; and as noted by Le Corbusier himself, its crescent roof also echoes a wave. The distant view of Ronchamp, as is true also of the Acropolis, prepares us for the brilliant rough whitewashed exterior with the dark raw-concrete roof fold hovering above. (The Parthenon's brilliance served to recall the radiant wisdom and beauty of Athena; further, it was Le Corbusier who reminded us that the cathedral was once white.) When the summit is reached, the first view of the chapel is that opposite the huge, brilliantly enameled processional door and the nonuniform and randomly placed splayed openings, suggesting the gun ports of a fortress, on the sloping south wall.

When first seen from the hill's crown, the chapel's form creates a dramatic sensation that evades comparison. Le Corbusier wanted no possible association with any previous architectural style, and although interesting attempts have been made to liken the conjuncture of sloping roof with battened walls to forms found in crude Stone Age architecture, Ronchamp's architectural uniqueness prevails. Its qualities of a massive and militant aspect, the secretive darkened interior, and the prowlike juncture of the south and east walls evoke quick analogies with fortresses, sacred grottoes, and ships—none of which were consciously sought or intended by the architect as symbolic allusions or design sources. (The soaring prowlike form seems to combine imaginatively the heavenward sweep of the spire, roof, and towers of the Gothic cathedral.) Le Corbusier relied on the control

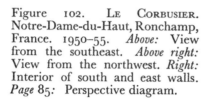

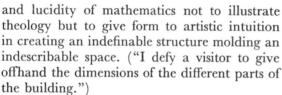

Figure 102. LE CORBUSIER. Notre-Dame-du-Haut, Ronchamp, France. 1950–55. *Above:* View from the southeast. *Above right:* View from the northwest. *Right:* Interior of south and east walls. *Page 85:* Perspective diagram.

and lucidity of mathematics not to illustrate theology but to give form to artistic intuition in creating an indefinable structure molding an indescribable space. ("I defy a visitor to give offhand the dimensions of the different parts of the building.")

This ingrained resistance to paraphrase and a succession of devices in the structure calculated to astonish the beholder are crucial to the architectural drama. As one instance of this, the massive walls do not bear the load of the roof, actually supported by triangularly shaped reinforced-concrete piers imbedded within the rubble-filled walls, which thereby allow an almost 4-inch space between the two elements, through which light penetrates the interior and imparts the sense of a floating roof. Like the Gothic architect, Le Corbusier does not wish to emphasize the engineering aspect of the construction. The dramatic visual and emotional effects devised to induce a meditative and awed mood were most important. The great roof, which seems as if cradled by the towers, bows downward near its center like an

enormous trough or sail catching the rain or wind; this covering is hollow and has external shell layers only about 2 inches thick but 7 feet apart. (An airplane wing is a comparable structure.) The architect claims that the inspiration for the shape and construction came from a crab shell picked up on a Long Island beach in 1946, which when inverted gave the idea for the roof.

When first asked to design the chapel. Le Corbusier refused. Only after several hours had been spent on the actual site and he had felt the impact of the sweeping natural panorama did the first ideas come and reverse his decision. He has written of his building "echoing" nature, as if it were some great sounding board for the natural forms around it. The metaphor and the relation to its site are poetical and imaginative, for the building does not literally illustrate by its formation the architect's comparison.

The spontaneous movement of the pilgrim once the hill is ascended is in a clockwise direction around the structure, and its various curving sides are more unpredictable in character than those of Gothic cathedrals. (One uses the great enameled door only for processions on special occasions; the north side contains the door for daily ingress, so that the newcomer usually walks one and a half times around before entering.) On the west the wall is not pierced with apertures, and its bulges reflect small interior chapels and the confessionals. From the roof parapet, there issues an omega-shaped waterspout or abstract gargoyle, from which the rainwater descends and splashes off geometrical shapes imbedded in a concrete pool below. The towers mark the interior chapels, and their vertical concrete louvers, giving texture and rhythmic variety, are permanently fixed. The north wall, though curved to a degree also, has a more markedly squarish character than the south, but its apertures are irregularly disposed in similar fashion, defying Greek and Gothic ideals of alignment and repetition.

The east wall is like a large open-air amphitheater or, with its upswept overhang, like a great acoustical backdrop for the Word that is given from the external pulpit and for the sounds of the choir and of the Mass performed at the nearby altar. As many as 10,000 pilgrims have assembled for Mass at this external church, for services not unlike those held before the Parthenon's west façade and analogous to the use of the cathedral façades as a backdrop for medieval religious plays.

Unlike the sculptural riches of the Parthenon and the cathedrals, at Ronchamp there is but one piece of sculpture, a nineteenth-century statue of the Virgin of indifferent artistic quality, which survived the bombardment during World War II and which is housed in a glass case high up on the western wall. The image can pivot so that, whatever the location of the service, it overlooks the congregation. Despite the absence of specially executed sculpture, the Ronchamp chapel is in itself the most sculptural or molded in appearance of the religious buildings here considered, and its forms often refute or disguise their structural function. Le Corbusier consciously sought to avoid a building that seemed the product of a technological age, with the rigid rectilinear, repetitive, and invertible forms that have become so familiar in the steel-and-glass boxes of modern commercial architecture. He regarded

this chapel as "a modern tool to open up fresh roads in a mechanistic society."

The actual building of Ronchamp was a curious blend of hand labor and modern practice, of traditional and new materials and tools, of intuition and sophisticated scientific calculation. With the efforts of a small group of versatile laborers of different nationalities under an excellent foreman, the building took shape from materials at hand such as the ruins of the previous stone church and with wood, sand, and cement hauled to the hilltop. In the great variety of materials and techniques represented in its construction, there is a parallel to the building of the cathedrals. Both inside and out, Le Corbusier viewed this work as "sculpture in the round." Pulpits, altars, stairways, and wall recesses and projections were all sensitively shaped and proportioned to catch the light or to cast striking shadows: "Observe the play of shadows...precise shadows, clear cut or dissolving. Projected shadows, precisely delineated, but what enchanting arabesques and frets. Counterpoint and fugue. Great music...."

Many modern architects, observing what they feel to be "truth to the medium," refuse to disguise the materials or conceal the structural system employed, thus usually producing a starkly skeletal building. Le Corbusier, however, did not hesitate to cover the rubble and steel reinforcing frames inside the walls with concrete, which in turn was given a rough stucco finish and whitewashed. As he once wrote of the poet, the architect must give us more than "an exercise in grammar."

Within the church there is more to astonish. The chapel does not symbolize a rational, finite world, expressible in numbers or geometry in

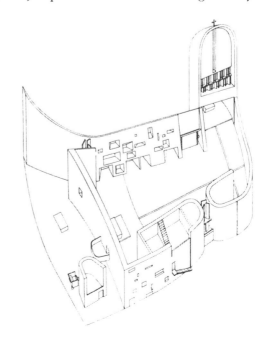

the way that Greek temples were microcosms of their universe; nor is it an evocation of the Heavenly Jerusalem of medieval society. Neither the north or south door is on the axis of the altar, and part of the dramatic effect of the interior scale results from entering on the building's narrow axis. Reversing the tendency on the exterior, inside one must turn on one's own axis. At first, standing in the darkened interior, one has the feeling of being within a fortress or cave, a citadel against death and a secret place for the enactment of religious mystery. Built to accommodate at most three hundred people, the acoustically fine nave brings to mind Le Corbusier's words, "Inside alone with yourself, outside ten thousand pilgrims in front of the altar." Silence and wonder are evoked by the relative darkness, the slope of the concave ceiling and the floor, which diverge upward and downward toward the altar, the absence of familiar right-angle corners or easily recognizable wall designs, and the unfocused illumination that filters in under the roof and down through the deep reveals of the windows, some of which have colored glass.

Outside, the structure is so conceived as to appear to rival the power and grandeur of its natural setting; within, one is struck by its intimate, human scale, unlike the cathedral's vastness. Le Corbusier and his associates, years before, had devised a proportional system based on a standing figure with arm upraised, equaling a height of about 7½ feet. By using this measure and its subdivisions, called the "modulor," in his designs the architect felt that he assured a human scale of reference. (Thus he comes closer to Ictinus, whose intervals between the Parthenon's columns were a column diameter and the width of a man's shoulders, than he does to Hugh Libergier.) Despite its massiveness, the south wall of Ronchamp, one of the great wall surfaces in the history of architecture, does not overwhelm the worshiper in scale. Its beauty and expressiveness depend upon an inspired and subtle coordination of apertures that all differ in scale, proportion, and angle of their reveals, as well as on the paradox of such a massive wall serving as a kind of sculptural quarry. Within each niche the windows differ in size, color, or decoration. (Often Le Corbusier painted a few words of praise of the Virgin on the glass: "Je vous salue Marie," "pleine de grâce.") The south wall, like the church as a whole, resists memorization or easy comprehension, and this adds to its richness in design and appropriateness for its function: to provide a suitable atmosphere for spiritual communion and to enhance the performance of the liturgy, with its attendant mysteries.

Le Corbusier cast off the obvious Euclidean geometric vocabulary and envelope of his earlier work and the symbolic axial symmetry customary in religious structures since the Parthenon and the cathedrals. Both in its parts and the whole, the chapel at Ronchamp demonstrates a decided asymmetry. Its most dramatic manifestation on the interior is the daring arrangement of the eastern end of the church. The Virgin's statue is set off to the upper right and balanced to the left by a concentration of perforations in the wall that looks like a constellation of lights. At first a great wooden freestanding cross was stationed directly on axis with and behind the main altar. Subsequent transfer of the large cross off to the right of the altar was a type of stage direction not licensed by tradition or Scripture, but the change was sincerely motivated by a desire to animate more effectively and dramatize the otherwise quiescent religious symbols. Perhaps mindful of future criticism aimed at this rearrangement, Le Corbusier wrote: "This focusing is an act of architecture, an act having a real relation to architecture... architecture which puts all in order and regulates." The large cross is actually movable and during religious processions can be carried outside to be placed before the second altar. A second cross at Ronchamp is located atop the south tower. ("Breaking the silence of the walls it proclaims the great tragedy that took place on a hilltop long ago in the East.")

Unlike the reception accorded many other modern churches, the chapel at Ronchamp has been well received by pilgrims and by those living in the area. It continues to function successfully as a religious structure. Le Corbusier has produced one of few modern religious structures that has the dignity, power, and beauty which bear comparison with the best of the past. He is a rare reminder that a modern architect, drawing from his own inspired imagination, can meaningfully symbolize the Virgin as well as the dynamo. In his own words, "I have worked for what men today most need: silence and peace."

5

THE SACRED BOOK

From the fall of Rome until the fourteenth- and fifteenth-century development of easel painting and the printing press, the handmade illuminated and miniature-filled book was the carrier of much of the most important painting and literary content in Western Christian art. The historical worth and intrinsic beauty of the medieval manuscript are insufficiently recognized by the general public today. We have come to associate great painting with that done on walls and easels, both executed on a fairly large scale. Excellence in art does not depend upon sheer physical size nor on the medium the painter chooses. Furthermore, the concept of a literally sacred art—in which the work of art mystically partakes of the liturgy—which includes many medieval manuscripts, is also alien to present-day thinking and experience.

Illuminated medieval manuscripts, precious records of the cultural and civilizing interests of society during the so-called "Dark Ages," reveal the varied development in art that prepared the way for Renaissance painting. They evidence the imagination and skill with which medieval men came to terms with their religious concerns. Far from being merely a public record of medieval man, this form of painting also furnishes a valuable reflection of his private nature.

SIGNIFICANCE OF THE SACRED BOOK

Christ is the only god who has the book as one of his principal artistic attributes, and in some respects Christianity is itself a book-oriented religion. Early Christian art includes images of a bejeweled throne on which sacred writings have replaced the figure of Christ. Many medieval Christian images show Christ holding a gem-encrusted Bible; a late-tenth-century manuscript from Trier depicts Christ giving the benediction with his right hand and holding the sacred book with his left (Fig. 103). Christ is shown seated upon the heavens with the earth as his footstool. The extreme formality of the arc alignments and the axial symmetry of Christ comprise a mystical and formal epiphany for the viewer. Although of great importance, the book is secondary to the conspicuous vortex design in the navel area, possibly a symbolic reference to Christ's divine birth.

The sumptuous type of medieval illuminated manuscript, that used for liturgical purposes, often possessed magnificent book covers on which were set precious stones, pearls, carved ivory panels, enamels, and elaborate gold and silver work. These covers, treasures in themselves, were often donated by kings or

Figure 103. *Christ Seated Upon the Heavens*, from the *Gospels of St. Maxim*. Trier. Late 10th century.

possess magical powers; the color and luster of gold were the most appropriate light symbolism of the period. Legends sometimes grew up about the miraculous powers of these richly adorned books, particularly those which had been the property of saints.

A superb example of these magnificent book covers is that of the *Lindau Gospels* (Pl. 9), which was made about 870, possibly in or near Reims. Within a carefully composed geometrical format, reliefs in bossed gold show Christ on the Cross, grieving angels, and above Christ's head, the contracted forms (head, shoulders, and arms) of Mary and St. John. The thinness and malleability of gold permitted the working of intricate details on the agitated angels and a handsome relief modeling of the figure volumes. The quiescent image of Christ contrasts both with the movement of the attendant figures and with the densely set, variegated gems and their setting. The precious stones and pearls are mounted on decorative motifs of arcades and lions' feet, which allow light to pass behind them, and are set off by filigree borders.

The key to understanding the reverence accorded the medieval illuminated Bible lies in the meaning of the phrase "the Word." The Gospel of St. John begins thus: "In the beginning was the Word, and the Word was with God, and the Word was God." The words of the Bible were therefore sacred, and it was the task of the artist, when commissioned by royalty, to "clothe" the word in the richest and finest manner of which he was capable. Many manuscripts contained gold or silver writing on purple-dyed parchment. In a German book written at the end of the tenth century are the words, "May the Lord clothe your heart with this book." The precious nature of the materials and the care lavished on the book were in a real sense gifts to God from the faithful.

The profound significance of the word in Christianity helps to explain why illuminated manuscripts made of it a cultural and imaginative object to a much greater extent than had the ancient scrolls and pagan books. No earlier writings demonstrate ornamentation of the letter (specifically, of the initial) of a comparable calligraphic beauty. While many ancient books were written in handsome script, the manuscripts themselves were not made the object of imaginative or fantastic treatment as were medieval Christian manuscripts. Ancient writing

queens. The precious materials were not intended primarily to delight the eyes but rather to create a binding appropriate for the sacred text and to symbolize mystical truths found in the Bible. The color, luminosity, and perfection of precious stones were interpreted as divine attributes or as symbolic of the blood of the martyrs, the Virgin's purity, the radiant presence of God, and so on. In some cases, medieval Christian patrons supplied pagan gems carved in antiquity. The gems were suitably baptized, the pagan spirits exorcised and made Christian.

Medieval artists and patrons did have an esthetic, or concept of beauty, but it was predominantly religious: beauty was equated with God. We know from medieval churchmen as well as alchemists that gold was thought to recognized no "privileged" words, except for the names of Roman emperors, and the task of writing was considered to be menial and fit only for slaves. With Christianity, the practice of writing passed from slaves to the priesthood, and down through the twelfth century the development of the book is bound to the history of the monks. Certain words and letters did have special value or emphasis to the medieval monastic scribe, who gloried in the task of transcribing the Gospel that was from and for God. For the Christian, the act of writing was in itself sacred.

A medieval Bible was not produced for the private pleasure of a wealthy secular patron. The layman, in fact, did not own hand-illuminated books until the late Middle Ages. Even the royalty who commissioned the most elaborate manuscripts seldom kept possession of the book or appreciated all its intricate beauty. The book was meant not for the eyes of the public but for God and for his servants in the Church. (There are many instances in art, such as the sculpture and painting in Egyptian temples or sculpture and stained glass in the Gothic cathedrals, of works that are inaccessible to the view of the public but exposed to the sight of God.)

The sacred book was a privileged object generally owned by a priest, abbot, or bishop, as the representative of the Church of God. The congregation was separated from the book, just as it was remote from the sacred objects on the altar. They submitted to it for their religious instruction, and the gospels along with the sacraments assumed a central position in medieval Christian life. It is difficult for us to comprehend the dramatic experience of the congregation when the sacred book was revealed during the Mass, at coronations, or for special blessings. The Gothic cathedrals make manifest the complex religious ordering of life and the universe, and the sacred book presents the source and basis of that order. More than a collection of sacred stories, for its medieval public *the book was Christ*.

In some medieval churches the Bible was suspended from the ceiling above the altar by gold chains. It was carried in religious processions, and in Eastern churches it was placed upon a throne. Usually the Bible stood on the altar, flanked by candles and incense burners; the candles symbolized the light shed by the

Gospels. A sumptuously decorated page of an early-eleventh-century manuscript made in Regensburg shows St. Erhard with an assistant celebrating the Mass (Pl. 10; Fig. 104), under a canopy symbolic of heaven; the saint is dressed in robes meant to be those of an Old Testament priest; to his right can be seen the sacred book, painted in gold, resting on the altar below a suspended gold crown and next to the Eucharistic objects. When the book was used during the Mass, it was kissed by the bishop, and when it was read from, the knights drew their swords as a gesture of their defense of the Scriptures and the people put down their staffs. During investiture ceremonies, the sacred book was laid on the neck of the candidate, indicating that Christ was the head (source of authority) of the bishop, who was about to assume leadership of the Church.

Figure 104. *St. Erhard Celebrating the Mass* (detail), from the *Gospel Book of Abbess Uota*. Regensburg. 1002–25. (See Plate 10).

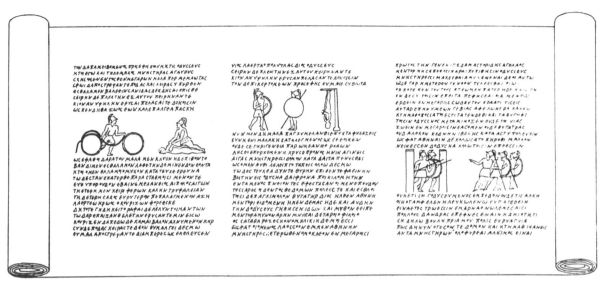

Figure 105. Reconstruction of an Odyssey Roll of the 3rd century B.C.

Clearly, the art within the decorated book is also sacred. (The chief exceptions are certain nonreligious themes appearing in the margins of the texts.) The miniatures and the figure rendering in medieval manuscripts give a first impression of unreality and naïveté. Nevertheless, it should be remembered that the artist was making images of sacred subjects, that is, of mystical themes, that were as vivid and real in his mind and the minds of the congregation as was actual life on earth.

PRODUCTION OF MANUSCRIPTS

Sometime between the second and fourth centuries the book form, or codex, evolved and replaced the papyrus scroll, a single horizontal sheet having its ends attached to rods and with columns of writing. The ancients had occasionally included text illustrations or technical diagrams in their scrolls; those found in the Egyptian *Book of the Dead* and in Greek and Roman scrolls dealt with medicine, science, and mythology (Fig. 105). Roman illustrations were primarily wall or panel paintings reduced to miniature size. Between the first and fourth centuries vellum, or lambskin, gradually replaced the more expensive and less durable papyrus. With the development of the vellum book that, unlike a scroll, opened from the side, the artist was offered an entire page, more or less a framed picture; the composition could be as elaborate as he desired. Painting on papyrus had consisted of ink and watercolor, whereas the qualities of vellum encouraged the use of gouache and richer coloring. Vellum also permitted painting on both sides of the page without the dangers of flaking experienced with scrolls.

Acquaintance with ancient books was essentially a matter of hearing the text, whereas the Christian book was intended to be appreciated both aurally and visually. The sustained imaginative development of the illuminated book stemmed from decorated initials made by Irish monks in the sixth century and from illustrations made by Byzantine artists of Constantinople and Syria. (Bibles had been brought to Ireland by Roman missionaries.) The earliest West European development of book illumination took place in England during the seventh and eighth centuries, principally in Northumbria (the border region between England and Scotland). During the reign of Charlemagne, at the beginning of the ninth century, illuminated book production accelerated beyond the rate of the preceding two centuries in France and England. Christianity and the book were essential to each other's growth. The Carolingian Renaissance, the efforts of Charlemagne about 800 A.D. to revive aspects of Roman culture, gave the great impetus to illuminated book production in Western Europe. In the eighth, ninth, and even the tenth centuries, there were specific, clearly defined locales and geographical sources for book production—most frequently in monasteries. Thereafter, production became widespread throughout Europe, and during the eleventh and twelfth centuries an enormous quantity of manuscripts was produced. After the thirteenth century, urban centers such as Paris began to rival or surpass the monastic production of decorated books. The mobility of artists as well as of the books themselves during this later period makes tracing their origins more difficult.

A great variety of illuminated books was produced during the Middle Ages. Sacred books fabricated consisted not only of the Bible but also of limited excerpts from the Bible, such as the Gospels or the Psalms, calendars of the religious feasts, prayers, blessings, commentaries, sermons, and lives of the saints. Generally these books had ornamented covers, frontispieces, canon tables, or tables of concordances for the Gospels; less frequently they contained a full page devoted to the cross, portraits of the Evangelists or saints, illuminated initials, and miniatures illustrating the particular text. The examples we shall use to illustrate most of the foregoing types are drawn from various manuscripts produced at different times and places; yet these represent but a slight sampling of the inexhaustible wealth of imagery that emerged from medieval writing rooms or scriptoria.

The notion of the medieval artist as a self-effacing craftsman resigned to oblivion is a glib one. At the end of books, there exist hundreds of signatures of artists—many of these accompanied by short prayers, in which the artist asks for praise, avows his reverence, and curses his arduous labor and the obdurate nature of his tools. "I've come to the end, curse this pen and damn this ink.")

PARTS OF SACRED BOOKS

Frontispiece. From a great Bible made during the first half of the ninth century at the Monastery of St-Martin in Tours, France, comes a painting of the Abbot Vivian presenting the finished manuscript to the Carolingian king (Fig. 106). The depiction of an actual historical event is the exception rather than the rule in medieval manuscript painting. The king is

shown enthroned in a space that suggests an apse of a church. Abbot Vivian and the other monks are shown in a semicircle before the king, and the artist ingeniously managed to show the faces as well as the backs of some figures. The frontispiece commemorates the king's patronage and the purpose of the Bible as a gift, inferring the supremacy of the Emperor over the Church. The artists of the Tours school were deeply imbued with an awareness of the world of rank and protocol and evolved important devices to interpret these themes. Rather than putting the spectator on the level with the monks, for instance, and thus obscuring part of the Emperor's person, the artist chose an elevated viewpoint that freely discloses the entire scene. The disposition of the figures and their gestures, as well as the pose of the ruler and his central placement, are governed by the conduct of the ceremony itself.

Figure 106. *Abbot Vivian Presenting the Bible to Charles the Bold*, from *Count Vivian's Bible*. Tours. 843–51. Bibliothèque Nationale, Paris.

Left: Figure 107. *Scribe Presenting the Bible to St. Peter*, from the *Gero Codex*, Reichenau (?). c. 970. Landesbibliothek, Darmstadt.

Below: Figure 108. *Christ Crowning King Henry II*, from the *Sacramentary of King Henry II*. Regensburg. 1002–14. Staatsbibliothek, Munich.

Another donation scene is in a German manuscript of the late tenth century known as the *Gero Codex* (Fig. 107). The scribe is seen presenting the Bible he has copied and embellished to his patron saint, the apostle Peter. Peter is shown enthroned, larger in scale than the scribe, and placed exactly beneath an arch of a simple structure symbolizing a church; the saint's gesture is made without any accompanying sign of recognition of the monk's presence in his facial expression. The head of St. Peter may have been copied from a late Roman sculpture of a pagan subject. The separation of the monk's feet from any ground line does not signify that he is "jumping for joy." In European art, painting had by this time ceased to attempt any suggestion of spatial depth. The visible world was reduced to symbols, and there was no need to preserve its three-dimensional qualities. Text and image shaped a common reality. With the absence of a convincing spatial setting, the figures acquired a relative flatness and weightlessness. Medieval painting was a symbolic and mystical art, whose power did not depend upon duplication of the world of appearances. The fact that the figures overlap the same architecture under which they at first seem to stand or sit is thus justified on the basis of a desirable clarity and an avoidance of cutting or segmenting the figure, gesture, or movement.

Some of the great German manuscripts made for eleventh-century Ottonian emperors possess magnificent coronation images for frontispieces, commemorating events in which the book itself played an important part. When Charlemagne's tomb was opened in the tenth century, the body was found seated on a throne, with the coronation Bible open on its lap. This Bible was used, in turn, by Ottonian kings at their coronation. A page showing the divine coronation of the German king Henry II, from an early-eleventh-century sacramentary painted in Regensburg (Fig. 108), depicts the arms of the king being supported by representatives of the Church. Seated above the ruler is the figure of Christ, who blesses the new king and places the crown upon his head. The use of gold and brilliantly colored patterns in the background and the robes, as well as the geometric composition and careful ordering of right and left, upper and lower zones, and center and subsidiary areas makes this page exciting testimony to the power, wealth, and tastes of the court. It also demonstrates the successful alliance of the Ottonian kings with the Church of Rome, an alliance that greatly influenced the course of medieval history.

Cross Page. During the seventh and eighth centuries, some English and French manuscripts included elaborate pages devoted to the Cross. In the cruciform page of the *Lindisfarne Gospels* (Fig. 109), the form of the Cross is seen against a dense field of interlaces. The conjunction of flowing lines and strict geometry may have been symbolic of the bringing of law to the lawless, for the interlacing has been subordinated to the limits and shapes of each area by strong linear boundaries and the right angles provided by the Cross and its frame, a Roman Christian heritage. This idea is only conjectural, however, for while the monks had converted the Saxons and Celts to the Cross, they themselves had been won to pagan art. Old barbaric notions of magic may have been carried over into manuscript painting, combined with the artist's desire to make the richest and most powerful presentation of the Cross.

The Cross page died out in the eighth century, but a painting of some two hundred years later (Fig. 110) seems to continue ideas that were implicit in the earlier works. In a state of mystical trance, St. Valerian makes his gesture of blessing in such a way that his whole body becomes a cross fixed centrally within the frame. Behind the saint, symbolically rendered in dark colors against his light form, are menacing bestial forms. The all-consuming faith and trancelike withdrawal of the saint ensure his survival and final glory in a world of evil. This moving image illustrates the medieval conception of the holy man who must live in a dark and hostile world.

Images of Evangelists. In many medieval Gospel books, the Evangelists were portrayed at the beginning of the scriptures for which they were responsible. Generally, the Evangelist was shown seated, usually in a side view; his symbol (the lion for Mark, eagle for John, ox for Luke, and winged man for Matthew) was often shown above him. (The Biblical source for these symbols was Ezekiel's vision.) In the *Echternach*

Above: Figure 109. Cross Page, from the *Lindisfarne Gospels.* Late 7th century. British Museum, London.

Below: Figure 110. *St. Valerian,* from the *Codex Gertrudianus.* Reichenau. c. 980. Cividale, Italy.

The Sacred Book   93

Above: Figure 111. *St. Sebastian,* mosaic from S. Pietro in Vincoli, Rome. 7th century.

Below: Figure 112. Purse Lid, from the Ship Burial at Sutton Hoo, southeastern England (Suffolk). Gold plaque inset with garnets and glass; ground (restored) in original probably of ivory or bone. 7th century. The British Museum, London.

Gospels, a late-seventh-century Irish manuscript, the Evangelist Mark is not shown in person but is represented by his lion symbol (Pl. 10). Remote from a literal image, this leonine figure presents a strongly imaginative equivalent. The sharpness of the lines that compose the body suggests that the painter may have been influenced by metal work. While the artist may have been unaware of true anatomy, he imparted a lively movement and ferocity to the beast. The design of the entire page is one of the most forceful in manuscript art. The geometric frame has an active life of its own, intruding into the central area and being played off against the lion. Since the writing also partakes of the color and calligraphic qualities of the lion, the whole takes on a powerful consistency and discipline.

Of great importance to Western medieval art was the coming together in manuscript painting of the figure-oriented Mediterranean tradition and the nonfigurative style of the North.

A mosaic from Rome and a purse lid from a ship burial found in southeastern England, both of the seventh century, illustrate these divergent traditions (Figs. 111, 112). The mosaic figure of St. Sebastian, which comes from a Roman church, shows the robed saint holding a martyr's crown. His body is largely concealed, but the pattern of folds suggests the correct location and general proportion of the limbs beneath, and the position of the feet suggests that they still carry weight. The face, while lacking in individuality, is nevertheless convincingly human. The origin of the purse lid, with its garnet and gold plaques, is not known for sure, but it came from somewhere in Northern Europe, possibly Scandinavia. Among the plaques are two showing a figure flanked by two rampant animals, which may or may not represent Daniel in the lion's den. Figures and animals are greatly schematized into flat, strongly outlined compartments, with no attempt to convince us of the corporeality of the subjects. The beautiful filigree and enamel work and the sureness of the outlining warn us that artistic skill need not presuppose naturalistic anatomical knowledge, and these jeweled images were no doubt intensely real to their owner.

The human figure was exceptional in this Northern non-Christian art, and abstract or animal ornament was more common. It was in the manuscript art of Irish monks, who had access to illustrated books from Rome and to barbaric art both in England and on the Continent, that these powerful artistic tendencies were joined. The Evangelist portraits provided the initiative for this synthesis in the seventh and eighth centuries. A page of an Irish Gospel book of the eighth century, the *Golden Codex of St. Gall*, gives evidence of the assimilation of the two traditions (Fig. 113). In the frame are found the motifs from Northern pagan art—knotted forms, spirals, fantastic four-legged animals, geometric shapes, rows of dots. The figure of the saint, still of paramount importance on the page, has had imposed upon it the Northern taste for incisive curvilinear outlining, flatness, and arbitrary proportion. There is no impression of a body existing beneath the drapery. Despite the rigid frontality and symmetry of the figure, and also the lack of flesh color and portrait features, the synthesized saint evokes a powerful presence. Later, before the end of the eighth century, as a result of the Carolingian Renaissance, the Mediterranean and Classical figure style gained ascendancy.

The artistic origin of the prototypes for the Carolingian Evangelist portraits probably goes back to third- and fourth-century Greek and Roman sculptures and paintings of seated philosophers (Fig. 114). The seated posture had, in antiquity, acquired connotations of the contemplative life, as opposed to the active life. Further sources may have been certain sixth-century Ravenna mosaics that depicted all four

Evangelists seated and accompanied by their symbols. Unlike the representations of ancient philosophers, who were shown dictating but never actually engaged in the inferior activity of writing, the images created by medieval artists included that of the inspired, pensive,

Above: Figure 113. *St. John the Evangelist*, from the *Golden Codex of St. Gall* (*51*), 8th century. Stiftsbibliothek, St. Gall.

Left: Figure 114. *Seated Philosopher*, sarcophagus from Sidamara. The German Archaeological Institute, Istanbul.

Left: Figure 115. *St. Matthew the Evangelist,* from the *Gospel Book of Archbishop Ebbo.* Hautvillers, near Reims. Before 823. Bibliothèque de la Ville, Epernay.

Below: Figure 116. *St. Matthew the Evangelist,* from the *Gospels of Judith of Flanders.* England. Early 11th century. The Pierpont Morgan Library, New York.

puzzled, aloof writer, clearly identified with his profession. The artist could associate himself with the Evangelist, since both were involved in conveying the words of God.

One of the most exciting Evangelist portraits in medieval art is from the so-called *Ebbo Gospels* (Fig. 115), produced near the city of Reims in the early ninth century. Nowhere in ancient art does one find so emotional an image. In an almost expressionistic manner, St. Matthew is shown as a deeply inspired figure. His inner agitation, as well as the artist's own passionate enthusiasm, can be seen in the energetic drawing and nervous rhythms of the garment—qualities that overflow into the landscape background and the frame. The reserve or detachment of Classical philosopher portraits is unknown to this artist, who charges with excitement his color, composition, and the frame itself.

In contrast, an Evangelist figure (Fig. 116) from an English manuscript of the early eleventh century, the *Gospels of Judith of Flanders,* presents a cool and elegant appearance. The elongated figure of St. Matthew and his gold-edged garment convey dignity and a restrained spirituality. The intricate, active qualities of the garment and frame are more expressive than the man's features or gestures in themselves. Expressiveness in medieval painting was not

confined to gestures and facial expressions, for emotional tone was frequently conveyed in the drawing of the entire composition.

An early-eleventh-century artist working on the island of Reichenau, situated in Lake Constance, Switzerland, produced an image of St. Luke in which the Evangelist is shown in an ecstatic and hypnotic trance (Pl. 12). In the Evangelist's lap are the five books of the Old Testament, and the prophets of these books are grouped about the Evangelist's symbol. The symbolic meaning of the image lies in the belief that the Old Testament prophesied the coming of Christ and that the Evangelists were the new heralds of his Incarnation. The trancelike state of the saint is appropriate to the time and place in which the image was painted. Monastic reform under the Ottonians called for an attitude of more intense piety and a renuncia-

tion of worldly pleasures. St. Luke is presented as a model of mysticism. Seen simultaneously are the saint and his vision, the image he appears to support, not unlike Hercules holding up the world. The miniature itself has a mesmerizing effect, with its rigid symmetry extending even to the enormous eyes and fixed gaze of the saint. The arch overhead is a symbol of heaven, the drinking animals refer to those who are nourished by the Scriptures, and the brilliant gold background transports the scene outside time and place.

Illuminated Initials. Writing was a privileged art in medieval Christianity. The written word came to have great personal value for the scribe, and between the two there evolved an intimate relationship unlike that between the ancient scribe and his text. St. Augustine, writing of the advantages of the priestly life, spoke of the opportunity to participate in the creation of the book and the meditation upon the Word. The results of this relationship between scribe and letters can be seen in the great changes in the appearance of writing and the structure of the written page that took place from the sixth through ninth centuries. The increased beauty and intricacy of the writing indicates that the scribes did not always worry about a ready legibility of the text, which was usually known by heart. The variety of scripts, the scale differences of the lettering on the opening page of a Gospel, the variety of colors, and the addition of elaborate decoration to certain initials created a hierarchical structure based on increased valuation of words stressed in prayers, the liturgy, and chants or stressed because of their location. In contrast to the uniformity of Greek and Roman writing (the latter did use capitals), no two pages of medieval text look the same, as can be seen in illustrations from the *Book of Kells* and the *Lindisfarne Gospels* (Figs. 117, 118). About the end of the sixth century, the initial was separated from the main body of the text by being enlarged, set out into the margin, and formed with different kinds of lines and colors. The illuminated initial gradually took over the margin of the page and began to intrude upon the text itself, as in the page from the *Lindisfarne Gospels,* until about 800, when the initial began to occupy an entire page. The illuminated initial opened to the artist an entirely new world of

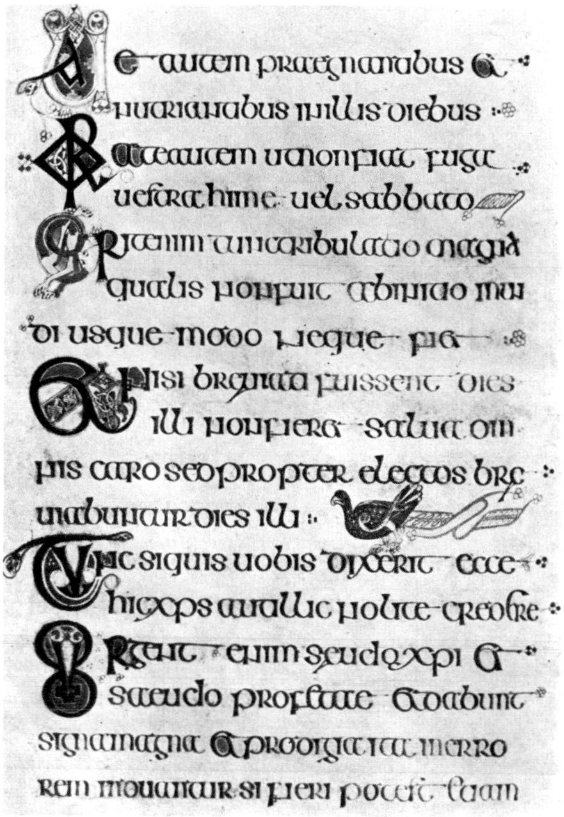

Figure 117. Page for Mark 13:17–22, from the *Book of Kells*. Northumbria. c. 800. The Trinity College Library, Dublin.

Figure 118. Page from the *Lindisfarne Gospels*. Late 7th century. The British Museum, London.

Figure 119. Two Initials for Psalm 1, from the *Winchester Bible*. England. 12th century. The Cathedral Library, Winchester.

meaning. The ornament or imagery enhancing the initial is not ordinarily illustrative of the text, but is the product of pure fantasy. Its justification probably lay in the belief that the magical power of the Word required commensurate visual garb.

During the Romanesque phase of manuscript art, the initial became the outlet for private sentiments of the monk illustrator and for themes that also reflected his immediate environment. Scenes of sadism, masochism, brutality, and conduct not generally associated with Christianity overflow initials and margins. The great *Winchester Bible*, produced in England during the twelfth century, contains a rich deposit of this type of imagery (Fig. 119). The two versions of the first Psalm are presented jointly, with the initial B filled with episodes from the Old Testament that prefigure those of the New Testament. At the upper left, David is about to slay a bear and rescue a lamb from its jaws. The antitype at the right shows Christ exorcising a demon through the mouth of an afflicted man. At the lower left, David is shown pulling open a lion's mouth to release a lamb, while at the lower right Christ, accompanied by the Archangel, harrows Hell by binding the hands of the devil and prying open the leviathan's jaws with the end of his cruciform staff. The initial has itself become the field for illustration, with the figures and action so composed as to move energetically within and over its curved frame. All the scenes stress the open jaws. The juncture of the two arcs of the B is an animal mask, from the jaws of which emerges intertwined ornament that in turn refers us to the very linear rendering of the entanglement of David and the beasts. Violent in theme, the jaws are identified with salvation and evil. This oral fascination has been traced to Anglo-Saxon literature such as *Beowulf*, with its detailed descriptions of monsters. The illustration from the *Winchester Bible* is but one of many instances in medieval religous painting and sculpture in which such mordant themes are encountered.

The initial had become a kind of safety valve for the artist of a religion that had a strongly prohibitive cast. It gave free play to demonic instincts, tastes for rapacious energy, and the convolutions of labyrinthine forms and processes. This type of art gives us an insight into the private torment and uncertainties of medieval religious life, as well as into the delight of the artist in the movement and freedom found in secular life. (The acrobatic figures in English initials may have been inspired by actual performances of *jongleurs*.) Comparable license was taken in the work of medieval sculptors who carved the capitals for monasteries and cathedrals, bringing to life an otherwise proscribed world of monsters and phantoms of irreligious imagination. It must be remembered that there was no artistic outlet for secular fantasy other than religious art. This intimate dialogue between the artist and his work, the personal conflicts and choices expressed in it—marginal to be sure in medieval art—was to become central in later periods.

STORYTELLING MINIATURES

Beginning with the ninth century, there was a revival of storytelling miniatures, a genre found in late Roman art. Frequently the artist had older manuscripts or copies of late Roman work from which he worked. Copying in manuscript art was not considered a dishonorable method but was, on the contrary, an important and accepted practice; originality was not the aim of the artists. Copying, however, did not preclude some display of individuality, and Carolingian copies of now lost Greek and Roman prototypes display important differences from what is known of the original styles.

Not all the decoration of medieval manuscripts was painted; many manuscripts contain outstanding drawings. Such manuscripts were not intended for royalty or for use in great public ceremonies but were what might be called nonofficial art, made for the private contemplation of the monks. The most notable medieval manuscript decorated with drawings is the *Utrecht Psalter*, produced in or near Reims about 833–835. It contains some 166 illustrations of the Psalms and thousands of figures and objects, drawn in brown ink on the text pages without the separation of a picture frame. The source of the *Utrecht Psalter* was probably a lost Greek manuscript made centuries earlier. There was great freedom in the copying of the earlier manuscript, and the artists of the *Utrecht Psalter* felt free to infuse their drawing with an energy and impulsiveness not characteristic of the original. The drawings contrast strongly with the uniformity of the script, and the narrative compositions are more loosely structured than are the columns of text. The artists did not interpret the Psalms literally, but often added to them or contrived fanciful metaphors. These drawn figures are much more animated and freely rendered than those found in the painting of the time. The *Utrecht Psalter* comes close to being encyclopedic in its manipulation of figures and groups, and one can perceive the artist's enthusiasm for landscape forms, notwithstanding the absence of the total integration of figure and background that has come to be associated with landscape painting. The psalter contains many images of the Mouth of Hell, as seen in the illustration for Psalm 102 (Fig. 120), which were to bear significant influence on later art. The manuscript as a whole was one of the most influential in medieval times because of the quality of execution and rich variety of subject matter.

Figure 120. Illustration for Psalm 102, with Hell Mouth, from the *Utrecht Psalter*. Reims. c. 833–35. The University Library, Utrecht, Netherlands.

Eleventh-century German artists such as those who produced the *Golden Codex of Echternach* (Fig. 121) rank among the finest storytellers in the history of art. Unlike Roman artists, the Ottonian painters conceived of the entire page as possessing an integral design. The placement of the figures or groups in each zone was carefully thought out in terms of the whole page. The climactic moments of the Adoration of the Magi and the Presentation in the Temple take place on the right side of the page, with the most important figures located beneath symbolic arches. The chronology of the events is rearranged in order to give the most important events privileged locations in the codex. Medieval art permits us to see simultaneously the inside and outside of a building; open doors signify that the action or location of the figures is indoors. The Ottonian artists created strong rhythmic designs and broad gestures played off against single-color backgrounds. While color is used symbolically in connection with the principal figures, it is also skillfully balanced against the background colors of the three zones. There is a distinctness and terseness in Ottonian miniatures that recall the actual narrative style of the Bible.

Versatility and great imagination went into manuscript miniatures such as an eleventh-century painting of Christ on the Sea of Galilee (Fig. 122). Through the precarious tilt of the dragonlike ship that seems about to swoop out of the frame, the undulating composition of sail and ship played against the agitated sea, and the anxious looks of the disciples, the painter has realized a spirited image of individuals in distress. The sleeping figure of Christ is the one stable element in the entire work. Even the frame has received impulsively flecked touches of gold.

To the modern viewer both of the preceding paintings perhaps seem lacking in truthfulness because they do not accord with our views of reality. Medieval painting had its own decided system and logic of conception, which contradicted perception; truthfulness in painting was based on *fidelity to the Scriptures*. (The visual world was only a reflection of a higher spiritual reality.) For example, in such a painting as *Christ on the Sea of Galilee*, the scriptural passage against which it would have been measured reads: "And behold, there arose a great tempest in the sea, in so much that the ship was covered with the waves: but He was asleep." No mention

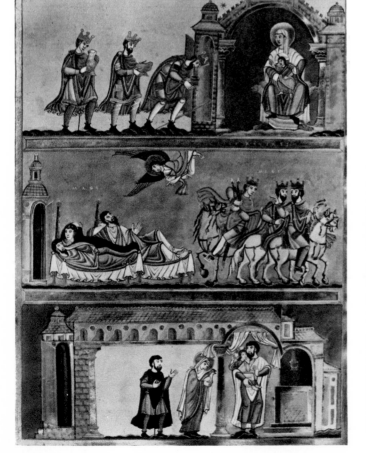

Left: Figure 121. *Adoration of the Magi; Divine Warning and Departure; Presentation in the Temple,* from the *Golden Codex of Echternach.* 962–1056. Germanisches Nationalmuseum, Nuremberg.

Below: Figure 122. *Christ on the Sea of Galilee,* from the *Gospels of the Abbess Hitda of Meschede.* Cologne. 978–1042. Landesbibliothek, Darmstadt.

Figure 123. *Noah's Ark*, from the *Psalter of St. Louis*. c. 1256. Bibliothèque Nationale, Paris.

is made of what the ship looked like; hence the artist had license to work from his own idea of an appropriate vessel. There is no horizon line to give depth, and the sea is rendered from above to ensure its identity, just as the boat is viewed from the more distinguishing side view. Clear identification, or readability, of forms precluded consistent or convincing perspective at this time. Textual brevity and abrupt changes of events have their visual counterpart in these terse images. The medieval idea of truthful representation of scriptural episodes was to scale the participants large relative to the picture area, give them simple declarative movements, and establish a minimal suggestion of surroundings when necessary. There is no shadow in these images because there is no reference to the sun or natural lighting conditions, and the brightly colored figures are flat because they move in a two-dimensional world.

A mid-thirteenth-century painting of Noah's Ark (Fig. 123) lacks the geometric perspective rendering employed by the Italian Renaissance painter Uccello, who also depicted Noah releasing the dove (Fig. 157); the medieval painter, instead, satisfies curiosity both as to the outside and inside of the crowded but tidy ark.

The elaborate Gothic architectural frame indicates how popular and pervasive was this style and its appropriateness as embellishment for a theme from Holy Scripture. In the thirteenth century the figures were still tightly bound to the picture surface. When in succeeding centuries, as evidenced in numerous illustrations that follow, the human form acquires volume, there is a gradual accompanying introduction of shallow depth until the Renaissance, when the space of the painting is made to appear to be a continuation of that enveloping the viewer. In the eleventh, twelfth, and thirteenth centuries, however, the medieval painter had neither the intention nor the capacity to imitate the visual appearance of the everyday world.

Like the sculpture of the Gothic cathedrals, medieval manuscripts were not entirely devoted to illustrating the Bible. Concern with inevitable death and moralizing about human vanity produced many images that were known as *memento mori*, or reminders of death. A late-thirteenth-century collection of French poems contains a painting of three living nobles who are confronting with apprehension their skeletal counterparts (Fig. 124). Although there is occasional evidence of observation from life and of death, the figures still straddle the picture frame and exist in a world apart from the natural environment of the viewer. That medieval artists did develop certain devices and skills to make their images more natural can be seen in one of the most powerful and morbid images from the early fifteenth century in which a dead man is confronted by the Lord (Fig. 125). The Rohan Master, as this

Figure 124. *Three Living Nobles and Their Dead Counterparts*, from the *Recueil de Poésies Françaises*. c. 1285. Bibliothèque de l'Arsenal, Paris.

The Sacred Book   101

painter is called today, convincingly depicts the emaciated naked mortal stretched out on a bone-strewn ground behind the picture frame. From his mouth, in medieval fashion, there issue the words with which he pleads for mercy. The Lord answers that the sinful must be punished and that on the Day of Judgment he will be with the Lord. The dead man's soul is fought over by a devil and an angel against a tapestrylike background of blue and gold angels. The Lord's countenance and sword are not comforting, and the painting was intended to evoke awe and fear in the viewer. The devices of simulating withered flesh and bone through modeling and tinted colors and the receding tilted ground plane encourage an emotional

identification with the subject and a projection of the spectator into the painting in ways that were not possible in the thirteenth-century *memento mori*. New demands were being placed on the artist at the end of the medieval period, partially inspired by his acquisition of new artistic devices by which the visible world could be plausibly rendered, but the break from medieval symbolism and style was slow. The Rohan Master skillfully joins symbol and fact, the visible and the invisible, mortal and God.

The development of naturalism in medieval art was to bring about the destruction of that which gave conviction to its greatest manuscript art—the visual and textual consistency, the superb coordination of the written word and the image existing on a common two-dimensional surface. Changes in patronage and ownership of books were also influential. From the thirteenth century on, private persons

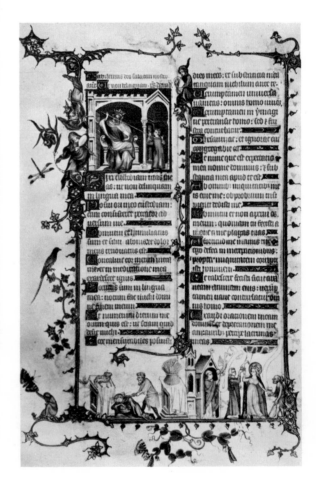

Above: Figure 125. THE ROHAN MASTER. *Dead Man Confronted by the Lord*, from the *Grandes Heures de la Famille de Rohan*. Early 15th century. Bibliothèque Nationale, Paris.

Right: Figure 126. JEAN PUCELLE. *David and Saul*, from the *Belleville Breviary*. c. 1323–26. Bibliothèque Nationale, Paris.

commissioned and collected beautiful books; urban workshops directed by a master painter catered to luxurious secular tastes.

A fourteenth-century page painted or supervised by Jean Pucelle (Fig. 126), whose workshop was in Paris, attests the persistence of the medieval coordination of text and decoration on a common surface, but in the new receding spatial box where Saul is threatening David with a spear, one sees the beginnings of the breakup of this unity of surface. The rudimentary spatial recession of the architectural setting punches a hole in the flatness of the page. Pucelle also influenced the development of elegant and amusing margins. Some of the strongly modeled playful figures in the margins seem to exist in front of the page surface. (The dragonfly at the left was a pun on his name and served as Pucelle's signature.) The amusing marginal byplay between animals and insects is symptomatic of the increasing interest of artist and patron in introducing elements from nature—a development paralleled in the increasing natural reference of the cathedral sculpture of the time. The development of volume and articulation of figures in fourteenth-century painting derived from imitation of sculpture. The close textual ties of earlier illustrations were gradually being weakened, and a split was developing between the reality of the words and the images.

About a century later, in a private prayer-book (the so-called *Turin-Milan Hours*) decorated probably by the Flemish painters Jan and Hubert van Eyck (Fig. 127), one reaches a point similar to that from which early medieval painting had departed: namely, manuscript illustration based on the style or actual example of panel painting. One of the oldest manuscripts surviving from antiquity with a similar character is the *Vatican Vergil*, dated about 400 A.D. (Fig. 128); though of lesser quality, one of its illustrations gives us an idea of how far Roman artists had gone in achieving illusionism—but how short that route seems next to the mastery of Hubert and Jan van Eyck's paintings of a bedroom and landscape. The ancient Romans had never achieved a spatial organization such as that of the van Eycks, in which the scene is rendered as if from the position of a theoretical observer standing at a fixed point.

In the Roman painting the parallel alignment of figures and setting makes the surface of

Above: Figure 127. JAN and HUBERT VAN EYCK. *Birth of St. John the Baptist,* from the *Très Belles Heures de Notre Dame (The Turin-Milan Hours).* 1416–20. Museo Civico, Turin.

Below: Figure 128. *Seated Philosopher with Figures Paying Homage,* from the *Vatican Vergil.* c. 400. Biblioteca Vaticana, Rome.

Figure 129. MICHEL WOLGEMUT. *Nuremberg Chronicle*. 1493. Woodcut. Private collection.

the page perceptible and prevents the picture space from advancing any farther in our direction. A thousand years later the van Eyck brothers were to transform the picture surface into a transparency, so that the bedroom of the miniature seems to be larger than the portion shown through the frame, and its space might conceivably extend into our own. Contrasting the Flemish and Roman landscapes, one sees that to achieve depth the earlier artist resorted to a raised viewpoint, whereas the van Eycks constructed a space from the ground. Eye-level projection gradually supplanted elevation in spatial perspective of the fifteenth century.

In earlier medieval art, one might say that the subject of the painting, not the viewpoint of the onlooker, determined the scale and location of the figures, as was appropriate to the sacred eminence and superiority of the subject over the viewer. Part of the democratiza-

tion of art at the end of the Middle Ages consisted not only of making it increasingly available to more people outside the privileged classes but also in rendering the world of the painting through the eyes of the living artist and his viewer. Thus medieval painting, once a cross section of the heavenly order, became "a slice of life." The *Turin-Milan Hours* shows the awkward conjunction of the new illusionism and older manuscript decoration. The bedroom scene can be viewed by itself, out of the context of the decorated page, with no loss of interest or completeness. The stylized vines of the margins are of a different reality than the flora of the Baptism landscape, just as the highly naturalistic and sculptural seated figure of the Lord is of a different style and character than the flat linear outlining of the initial within which he appears. The text paragraph no longer lies on a flat page but seems to intrude into the unframed sky over the Baptism. The calligraphy of the letters is not of the same spirit in which the midwives and objects of the room are outlined.

These and other developments eventually made the book dispensable to serious painting in the fifteenth century. A changing conception of reality, new criteria for truth to the natural world, the loss of mystical associations between the Word and the written text, the great demand for more books and the ultimate response in the printing press and movable type all brought to an end more than a thousand years of great contributions to art by the hand-decorated book. Easel painting and murals were soon to preempt the attention of the best artists and patrons. Van Eyck's rendering of the baptismal scene—a sacrament which itself means rebirth—prophesies the new life, the new direction, for painting as it began to centralize what had been the marginal medieval concerns for celebrating the time, places, persons, and events of earthly life. But the development of the woodcut in the fifteenth century brought a new and viable synthesis of text and illustration to the printed book toward the end of the fifteenth century (Fig. 129). The lines of wooden type and the carved wooden block illustration seen against the white page restored some of the beauty and unity of the earlier painted and calligraphic manuscripts—but not the sumptuous effects, grace, and power that had emanated from the hands which manipulated pen and brush.

Plate 17.   DOMENICO VENEZIANO. *Madonna and Child with Saints,* from the *St. Lucy Altarpiece.* c. 1445.
Oil on panel, 6'7½" × 6'11⅞". Uffizi, Florence.

Plate 18. GIOVANNI BELLINI.
St. Francis in Ecstasy. c. 1485.
Oil on panel, 4'1½ × 4'7". The
Frick Collection, New York
(copyright).

Plate 19. PETER PAUL RUBENS. *Descent from the Cross.* c. 1611–14.
Oil on panel, 13′10″ × 10′1″. Cathedral, Antwerp.

Plate 20.   PETER PAUL RUBENS. Detail of Pl. 19.

6

THE SYNTHESIS
OF HEAVEN AND EARTH
IN FIFTEENTH-CENTURY
FLEMISH ART

In the thirteenth and fourteenth centuries, medieval art gave evidence of an absorption of secular values and an increasing awareness of human worth. At the end of the Middle Ages, in fifteenth-century northern France and Flanders (what is present-day Belgium), there was a rapid development of illusionistic, or naturalistic, painting that displayed, to an unprecedented degree, a close correspondence between sensory experience and what was painted. This development began in book art, as discussed in the previous chapter, but received its greatest impetus in painting on wooden panels that were to be hung in churches, guild halls, and private homes. Flemish panel painting grew into a trend toward abandoning many medieval attitudes and artistic devices for the interpretation of religious subjects. No longer in consistent use were such symbolic attributes as halos and abbreviated settings. Also abandoned was the conventional surface adherence of figures caused by emphasis on strong linear contours and flat, bright colors, which resulted in an absence of depth and bodies apparently without weight or volume. Use of generic facial types was replaced by strong characterization and individual portraiture. Fifteenth-century Northern art rejected depictions of a remote mystical world which the viewer could not penetrate and which barred any identification with himself and his values. The celestial sphere of earlier manuscript painting was replaced by what appeared to be a spotless mirror of fifteenth-century Flemish life. Nonetheless, this art did not abandon religious subject matter but continued to affirm the attachment of artist and patron to the Christian beliefs, for essentially the objective of the Flemish artists was to garb mystical religious content with the appearance of the visible, material world.

The motives for this shift in Northern European art included the desire of the artist to present the real world as he saw, touched, and walked through it, as he experienced its beauty with all his senses. The affluent Flemish cities such as Bruges, Tournai, Ypres, and Ghent seemed appropriate incarnations of the Heavenly City, as well as means through which to express sentiments previously excluded from art. Rather than resist the new realism, the Church sought to utilize it for its own purposes. Because of the vivid and familiar aspect naturalism could lend to invisible holy personages, the new art seemed a strong instrument for the exposition and support of religious dogma, which itself had become more tolerant of the facts of earthly existence. Unforeseen by the Church was the possibility that the artist could not negate his private and nonreligious feelings when he painted religious figures and the interiors and landscapes in which they moved. Thus the new art of the late Middle Ages was an uneasy synthesis of religious and secular values —carrying, in fact, an undertone of conflict that was eventually settled in favor of the latter. This synthesis was the beginning of the disengagement of art and ideas of beauty from religion.

The key to this synthesis was the *symbol*, or the tangible sign of the invisible. One of the most brilliant scholars to study this period, Erwin Panofsky, has pointed out that the artists' and theologians' problem was to disguise religious symbolism under the cloak of real things, reconciling the idea of the symbol with empirical probability. Over a thousand years of Christian tradition had to be reconciled with the new naturalism and made into "corporeal metaphors of things spiritual." Use of the symbol was abetted by the fact that all reality came to be thought of as permeated with meaning. The process of looking discerningly at a Flemish painting becomes one of gradual penetration beyond the externals into submerged layers of meaning. The works of art discussed below have been chosen to illustrate the forms taken by the Flemish synthesis of heaven and earth.

One of the earliest and most important fifteenth-century Flemish paintings to illustrate the symbolic synthesis of the mundane and theological is the *Merode Altarpiece* (Pl. 13), assigned to the Master of Flémalle, who was probably the Tournai painter Robert Campin. In the left panel the donor, a businessman named Ingelbrecht, and his betrothed kneel in a walled garden. Through the open gate can be glimpsed a street like those of Tournai, where the painting was done. The figure standing behind the open gate has been variously interpreted as the painter himself, a servant, or the marriage broker who arranged the betrothal of the patron and his wife. (The figure of the wife was added after the original completion of the painting.) The garden and its flowers were, simultaneously, traditional symbols of the Virgin and familiar adjuncts to Flemish urban middle-class houses. The partially open door serves to link the left and center panels, but its rendering creates an ambiguous relationship between the donor and the scene to his

right. As a result, one does not know if he is intended as an actual eyewitness to the event. The Annunciation scene of the central panel is depicted, for the first time in art, in a fully appointed middle-class parlor. Only the presence of the angel and the small child carrying a cross hovering overhead on rays of light overtly announce a supernatural event. The child and cross, replacing the more customary dove in this Annunciation scene, signify Christ's Incarnation and Passion. In her physical appearance, posture, and surroundings, the Virgin is a middle-class type of the era. Her virtues are those esteemed in both the Virgin and the ideal Flemish housewife. Her sitting on the floor evokes her humility; the immaculate orderliness of the room and its contents alludes to her purity; the reading of the Bible and theological literature signifies her piety and awareness of her role. Meyer Schapiro has observed that what is seen in the room is a metaphor of what takes place within the Virgin's body. The handsome bronze utensil hanging in the niche above the angel's head refers to the Virgin's body as an immaculate vessel, and the lilies also are associated with her purity. The candle's wax and wick become the flesh and soul of Christ. The absence of flame from the candle and the fireplace is explicable on the basis of the divine light entering the room through the closed window; light had been the mystical metaphor of Virgin birth for centuries prior to this painting. In the words of St. Bernard, "Just as the brilliance of the sun fills and penetrates a glass window without damaging it, and pierces its solid form with imperceptible subtlety, neither hurting it when entering nor destroying it when emerging: thus the word of God, the splendor of the Father, entered the virgin chamber and then came forth from the closed womb." If extended, the rays of light would meet the side of the Virgin's head, consonant with the traditional view that she conceived through the ear.

The symbolic presence of the tiny infant carrying the cross links the middle panel to the third panel, in which Joseph is shown steadfastly at work in his carpenter's shop (Fig. 130). On the table before Joseph is a mousetrap, which is plausibly present as a household object of cleanliness. Its theological significance, as Schapiro has shown, pertains to Joseph's role as earthly husband of Mary and the meaning of Christ's Incarnation. Medieval theologians explained Christ's assumption of the flesh as a plan to redeem humanity from the devil: "The Deity was hidden under the veil of our nature, and so as is done by greedy fish, the hook of Deity might be gulped down along with the bait of the flesh" [Gregory of Nyassa]. Joseph was used in a ruse to conceal the birth of Christ from the devil, and the painter has shown him as neither too old to have fathered a son nor too young to disturb the attitudes of the faithful, but at the right age to deceive the devil. The mousetrap was a theological symbol explained by St. Augustine: "The devil exulted when Christ died, but by this very death of Christ the devil is vanquished, as if he had swallowed the bait in a mousetrap. He rejoiced in Christ's death like a bailiff of death. What he rejoiced in was his undoing. The Cross of the Lord was the devil's mousetrap; the bait by which he was caught was the Lord's death." The block into which Joseph is boring holes may correspond to contemporary fishing-bait box lids and to spike boards attached to the ankles of Christ in fifteenth-century Netherlandish paintings of the Carrying of the Cross.

To look at the *Merode Altarpiece* only in terms of its complex symbolism is to neglect Robert Campin's ability as a painter. The panels are marvels of lucidity, in the way in which figures and objects impress themselves upon the eye. The composition, like the painting's meaning, is a synthesis of medieval and new devices. The elevated viewpoint and careful alignment of shapes tend to orient them toward the old surface pattern, even while creating the illusion of spaces and objects seen in depth. The objects strewn on Joseph's workbench and the table between the angel and the Virgin manifest this double character. The inconsistency of scale permits complete re-creation and visibility of objects shown in depth—for example, the window lattice and shutters and the second trap seen through the window over Joseph's right shoulder. The rightness of the artist's compositional sensibility is perceived by trying to comprehend the whole of the Annunciation panel at one time and then mentally moving any object slightly out of position. The creator of this work seems to have conceived of the painter's purpose as being both a reconstitution and a more perfect ordering of reality.

Figure 130. ROBERT CAMPIN, or THE MASTER OF FLÉMALLE. *Joseph in His Carpenter's Shop*, right wing of *Merode Altarpiece*. c. 1420–30. Oil on panel, $25\frac{3}{8} \times 10\frac{15}{16}$". The Metropolitan Museum of Art, New York (The Cloisters Collection, Purchase).

Both the Joseph panel of the *Merode Altarpiece* and Jan van Eyck's small painting of *St. Jerome in His Study* (Pl. 14) might easily be taken for secular subjects. It is such painting that inaugurated the secular art of genre subjects. Van Eyck, asked by a Roman cardinal to paint St. Jerome, surrounded the translator of the Scriptures with all the accessories that would be found in a scholar's study. The result was a work in which the Cardinal could identify himself with the saint as a leader of the Church, while van Eyck, a man of substantial learning, could pay homage to Jerome's intellectual achievements. Among the objects associated with scholarship are books, writing materials, and the astrolabe, an instrument used in astronomical study. The two superimposed disks of the astrolabe were inscribed with drawings of the constellations and earth, so that the relations of the two at any time could be established. Van Eyck was a mapmaker and—judging by the wealth of meaning in his painting—an avid reader of books. The painter's task was also that of being a translator of the Scriptures into the vernacular of his society.

By contrast, medieval manuscript portraits of the Evangelists indicate how van Eyck humanized the saint he portrayed, who is shown neither in a trance nor in a moment of ecstatic inspiration, but in an attitude of quiet concentration, with the heavy weight of his head felt in the wrist of the supporting hand. A soft light illuminates the casual pile of books on the shelf and the clutter on the writing desk. The meticulous reproduction of objects contrasts with the naïve rendering of the lion, St. Jerome's attribute. The clumsy leonine body, which lacks the vitality of the Echternach lion, was no doubt a result of van Eyck's never having seen the live animal and working instead from inaccurate models. Van Eyck could accurately render anything with which he was familiar—light reflections, textural qualities, or craftsman objects.

The miniature size of the painting ($8^{1}/_{16}$ by $5^{1}/_{4}$ inches) attests to the origin of Flemish panel painting in manuscript art. Rarely did Flemish artists paint on the scale of the Italians, who created sizable mural art with great frequence. Painting such as van Eyck's gains much of its effect from its modest scale, which demands close viewing of its microscopic detail. The compositions do not consist of large, easily graspable relations between shapes. The sense

of a precious object imparted by the St. Jerome panel resides in its small, concentrated areas of saturate luminous colors and in the hard brilliancy of surface stressed in both technique and contents. Only by looking long and closely at the painting can one savor the sophisticated scale modulations of the forms. Van Eyck's painting permits focus on the smallest metal bolt without blurring of the adjacent areas. Proceeding from the most minute forms, one may take in the increasingly larger forms of the books, the hour glass and lectern, the strong box that serves for a desk, the Cardinal, his chair, and the draped shelves. The largest form is never completely contained within the painting, perhaps to remind us of the infinite variety and size of God's creation. Flemish painting reverses the intent of the earlier manuscript art by revealing God in worldly terms.

When van Eyck took up the motif of the human figure with a background of architecture and landscape, he was able to adapt the medieval habit of showing the principal figure on a large scale, in conjunction with its symbol or attribute, without forsaking his explorations of illusionism (Fig. 131). St. Barbara is shown before the tower in which she was to be imprisoned by her pagan father for her Christian beliefs. The plausibility of her size is achieved by seating the saint on a rocky ledge in the foreground, where she reads from a book in her lap. The middle ground falls away sharply, and to her right and left can be seen workmen bringing materials or shaping them for the churchlike tower under construction. Both the panel itself and its subject instruct us in how works of artistic projects were carried out in the fifteenth century. The tower's construction is being supervised by a foreman who stands on a block at the right and is perhaps arguing with a workman atop the edifice standing with arms akimbo near a hoist. The shed near the foreman is where the stonecutters or sculptors worked, protecjed from sun and rain. The logistics of quarrying, transport, cutting, carving, stonemasonry, and mechanics of construction are presented in detail against a gently swelling landscape to the right and a distant city to the left. It was a modern reminder of the medieval view that every Christian was a builder.

In this brush drawing van Eyck has also given us wonderful evidence of how his paintings were begun, even though in this St. Barbara panel his delineation is far more detailed than would normally have been the case—which suggests that he did not intend carrying the work further. Panel paintings were begun by carefully preparing and joining the wood segments together. Plaster or gesso was then applied to the surface and carefully smoothed. Upon this prepared surface the artist would then make his drawing, which served as the guide for the later building up of layers of color and glaze. In this small panel, color was applied only to the sky area. Desire to re-create the brilliance as well as detail of the visible world was probably the strongest incentive for van Eyck's improving on the old medieval technique of superposing layers of linseed oil over tempera painting; van Eyck and Robert Campin combined their pigment with oil rather than egg as in tempera painting. The glazes intensified the color and, because the medium dried slowly, permitted reworking and admixture of colors. This technique was ideal for the simulation of light and its reflection. The oil-treated surface was semitransparent, and natural light that fell on it was partly repelled and partly absorbed, further adding to the jewellike quality of Flemish art. As is apparent in a painting such as van Eyck's *Madonna with Chancellor Rolin* (Fig. 132), and also in the St. Barbara

Above: Figure 131. JAN VAN EYCK. *St. Barbara.* 1437. Brush drawing on panel, 12¾ × 7¼". Musée des Beaux-Arts, Antwerp.

Left: Figure 132. JAN VAN EYCK. *Madonna with Chancellor Rolin.* c. 1436. Oil on panel, 26 × 24½". Louvre, Paris.

109

panel, all the shapes were first drawn on a plaster ground. Tints of hand-ground mineral or earth color were applied directly to the gesso and then in layer after layer of glazes, so that the color acquired depth and volume as well as luminosity. Color became less separable as a property from the figures, and objects seen in depth tended to lie less consistently on the painting's surface than in earlier manuscript art. Van Eyck sought the illusion of three-dimensional sculptural roundness to increase his painting's verisimilitude to nature. He had also been a painter of stone and wood sculpture, which at the time was more naturalistic than painting.

Van Eyck's passion for exactitude and the virtuosity of his painted illusions may provoke the criticism that his is an unimaginative art. Such criticism does not take into account that an exact transposition of a three-dimensional object onto a two-dimensional surface, along with the convincing representation of space and light, requires more than manual dexterity. To begin to comprehend the nature of van Eyck's imagination, let us consider for a moment the subject and the whole composition of the *Madonna with Chancellor Rolin*. Van Eyck has created a spacious and luxurious interior inhabited by imposing figures, behind which there extends a seemingly infinite panorama. Every detail is empirically verifiable, and yet the totality is a scene that had never been beheld by van Eyck or anyone else before this painting was finished. As a gesture of self-confidence in his spiritual merit (or as wish-fulfillment), the chancellor of the Burgundian dukes commissioned for himself an audience in the heavenly chateau of Christ and the Virgin. Although inspired in its sculptural and architectural detail by archaeological sources that van Eyck mistakenly believed were from the time of Christ's stay on earth, the final design of the interior has no definite earthly counterpart. Through the colonnade is seen an enclosed flowering garden, a metaphorical reference to the Virgin and her purity. Two unknown and intriguing figures with their backs to the spectator look out over a crystal-clear river that divides an earthly city on the left (identified as Maastricht in Belgium) from the heavenly metropolis on the right. It is no accident that Christ's fingers which give the benediction are tangent to the symbolically seven-pillared bridge between the two cities,

Figure 133. JAN VAN EYCK. *Madonna with Chancellor Rolin*, detail from Fig. 132.

for the Christ child was the divine link between heaven and earth (Fig. 133).

Van Eyck's making of his art was activity in sympathy with God's creation of the world. The reality created in the painting is at once based on, yet remote from, his own. The painter has established himself as its sole arbiter—selecting, rejecting, refashioning what is to enter it. All material substance has been painstakingly and lovingly explored, has been given a heightened surface materiality and fixed into a complex order. The painting contains a thousand glittering points to be discovered and enjoyed. To be shared with the painter is his wonder at the traits of optical perception, as seen, for instance, in the fact that small objects near the eye may block out distant objects of far greater magnitude behind them or in the fact that the eye cannot take in at once all that exists within the sweep of its gaze. Thus, the wealth of a lifetime's accumulated visual and intellectual experience is given a new imaginative cohesion and existence on a rectangular surface measuring but 26 by 24½ inches.

Figure 134.   Rogier van der Weyden. *The Descent from the Cross.* c. 1435. Oil on panel, 86½ × 103 ″. Prado, Madrid.

To comprehend van Eyck's re-created world, the viewer is always obliged to commence with or return to the most minute detail. The face of the seventy-six-year-old chancellor, for example, betrays his hard and perhaps questionable career; and van Eyck has reconstructed the man beginning from the pores. There is a hint of visual wit in the painter's having made the distant obdurate hill adjacent to the chancellor's brow, while above the head of Christ are placed the spires of the Heavenly Jerusalem, forming a kind of halo. Although van Eyck was doubtlessly aware of the fallibility of his patron, his painting—like all of his art—is a radiant expression of optimism for the order of life, of faith that because of Christ's sacrifice the earth will again know paradise. He respects earthly rank as a counterpart of celestial authority, and his imagery is aristocratic in form and content. Van Eyck and the Master of Flémalle reflect the divergent tastes and conflicting attitudes that existed among the aristocracy and the middle class of their time. The domestic Virgin in the *Merode Altarpiece*, for example, cannot be interchanged with the regal Madonna of Chancellor Rolin.

More man-centered in the expression of his religious sentiments than the Master of Flémalle and van Eyck was the Flemish painter Rogier van der Weyden. He opposed their shared, more or less equal focus on figures and objects, and in particular van Eyck's pantheism. Van der Weyden's *Descent from the Cross* (Fig. 134) is unusual in Flemish painting because of its assigning the entire weight of expression and composition to the figures alone. To ensure its powerful and immediate impact upon the viewer, the painter compressed the action within a shallow boxlike space much like the sculptured altarpieces of the period. His intent was to provide an image for pious meditation through which the worshiper could empathize with the suffering of Christ and his anguished followers. The subject is the lowering of Christ's body from the Cross, and the theme is one of passion and compassion. The artist's purpose has been best summarized by Otto von Simson in a fine study of this painting: "The Christian artist must seek to approach God through the affect of compassionate love. He must seek to awaken these affects in others in order to help

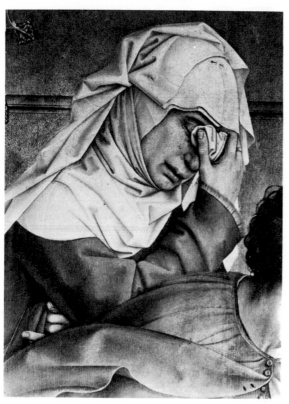

establish the bond of similitude between God and the contemplator of His image. This is the religious mission of the emotionalism of all Gothic art."

The van der Weyden painting grows out of the compassionate emphasis and concern with the tragic in Christianity that had arisen at the end of the Middle Ages. The critical response of the worshiper's self-identification with the grief-stricken followers of Christ hinged upon lifelike rendering. It is not only their outward physical appearance that the painter conveyed with such power but also the refined range of emotional states that they manifest. This range includes varying degrees of active and contemplative participation in the moment —from the deathlike swoon of the Virgin, who mystically shares the death of Christ in her role as intercessor for mankind, through the levels of awakening comprehension of the event seen in the figures supporting Christ, to the full capitulation to grief of the Marys, and finally St. John's calm resignation as he seems to foresee the consequences of Christ's death. The bodies as well as the faces make transparent the protagonists' inner state (Fig. 135). At the right, for instance, Mary Magdalen is caught in a suspended movement that is clearly the result of a total loss of self-consciousness. The emotional and psychological unity of the participants is marvelously embodied in the composition itself; the placement of and alliteration in the limbs join the whole in forceful rhythms. This complex unity was essential to the intent of van der Weyden—to induce the whole congregation to share in the mournful experience.

More intimate in scale and character is a drawing by Simon Marmion (one of the relatively few fifteenth-century Flemish drawings to have survived), in which the kneeling Virgin supports the body of the dead Christ (Fig. 136). This drawing, though perhaps a preparatory study for a painting, may also have been valued by the artist and its owner as a finished work, for by 1500 in Northern Europe drawings were known to have been sought by collectors and were no longer considered of secondary value. The pathetic expression and posture of the Virgin and the stiffened angularity of Christ's body were solicitations to share in the grief of the subjects. The studied care with which the drapery folds have been arranged and played against the lines of the

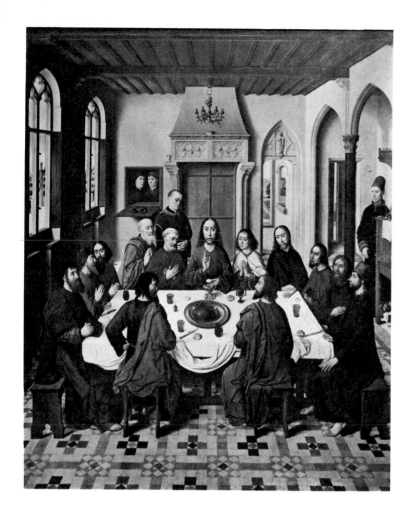

Figure 137. DIRK BOUTS. *The Last Supper*. c. 1464. Oil on panel, 71 × 59″. Church of St. Peter, Louvain.

torso demonstrates the calm, lucid control that Flemish artstis were wont to impose even on the most emotional subject. Part of the drawing's beauty comes from its medium: first the paper was covered with glue or some adhesive, over which an ivory-colored sizing was brushed; then silver was inserted into a stylus, like graphite in a pencil, and when the artist drew on the slightly roughened surfaces, the silver left its trace, in delicate silver tonalities and expressive drawing of exquisite craft.

The strongly meditative character of many Flemish paintings is witnessed in Dirk Bouts' *Last Supper* (Fig. 137). The altarpiece was commissioned and the subject chosen by the Brotherhood of the Blessed Sacrament of Louvain in 1464. In this gathering of the disciples, assembled for the solemn and sacred moment when Christ blessed the bread and wine, Bouts painted not only the origin of the sacred rite but also a humane ethic by which the contemporary brethren could imitate Christ and the disciples. The supper is set in a large Flemish hall, modest but dignified and immaculate in appearance. No obvious attempt was made to refer to Judas' betrayal. According to tradition, Judas sits diagonally across from Christ and is otherwise distinguishable only by his dark complexion and markedly downward gaze away from Christ. The painting's expressive tone comes from a cumulative build-up of the parts and the complex interrelation of figures and environment. Bouts has managed masterfully the subtle contrasts between the formal and the informal that enrich his style: the random appearance of the table's objects and the geometric regularity of the floor tiles; the isolation of the figures and the continuity of the architecture; the judicious spacings between shapes and the frequent tangencies uniting them as if on a common surface.

Behind the airless, measurable space of the room, segmented by the windows and doorways, are seen earthly vistas of infinite dimension. In contrast to earlier religious painting, Bouts' large-scale setting slightly dominates the figures.

The Synthesis of Heaven and Earth in Fifteenth-Century Flemish Art   113

The quiet mood evoked by the sunlit hall is consonant with the weighted stillness of the disciples that is their basic means of unification. Linkages between the figures and architecture have been thoughtfully calculated in order to make the composition cohesive and, perhaps, to intimate some invisible rapport between the animate and the inanimate. The curve of the disciple's back at the lower right, for instance, repeats that of the hood of the fireplace behind Christ. The pantry opening serves as the frame for a double portrait, possibly of Bouts' sons. The disposition of the figures around the table is related to the sequence of windows, arcades, and the divisions of the end wall. Nowhere is this integration stronger than between the slightly enlarged figure of Christ and the objects behind him. He is joined with the axis made by the panels that close off the fireplace, and their suggestive pattern replaces the former device of halo and cross. The lintel and chandelier extend this strong central axis upward. (As has been noted, the chandelier was a metaphor of Christ.) The central axis also marks the convergence points of the diagonals of the floor, table, and ceiling, so that the rationalization of space partakes of mystical symbolism. Christ's head, his gestures, and the bread and wine complete the axis. With familiar secular accessories, Bouts was able to symbolize the theological centrality of the Eucharistic rite. The figure of Christ shows the least mobility of all, and his fixed forward gaze is the most abstract of the expressions; despite the worldly context, Bouts has presented him as belonging to a higher spiritual order.

At first glance, Bouts' figures appear puppetlike, in their awkward, peculiarly human angularity. Their grace is spiritual, not physical, and each of them manifests a profound inner concentration. They are models of simplicity and purity, in the later Middle Ages adjudged to be the virtues necessary to emulate Christ.

It is likely that the figure standing to the far right is the painter himself (Fig. 138). This was not an unprecedented inclusion, as was seen before in the illustration from the *Gero Codex*. Also, Rogier van der Weyden had earlier portrayed himself as St. Luke drawing the Virgin (Pl. 1). Bouts was affirming the esteem in which the painter was held by Flemish ecclesiastical and secular patrons. While his inclusion was to some extent prideful, the painter present-

Figure 138. DIRK BOUTS. *Self-Portrait* (?), detail from Fig. 137.

ed himself as an attendant at the scene, respectfully apart from the sacred meal. He thus becomes a servant of Christ in a double sense.

Even when the artist did not actually show himself, his painting might constitute a self-portrait of his nature. Hugo van der Goes' *Adoration of the Shepherds* (Pl. 15) is characterized by explosive tensions and alternate strains of serenity and turbulence that are revealing in the light of the artist's withdrawal to a monastery and his eventual depressions and suicidal tendencies. The painting's large scale and ambitious panoramic composition rivaled the greatest works of such predecessors as Jan van Eyck and Rogier van der Weyden. Van Eyck's amplitude of setting and particularization of detail are present in the *Adoration*, as is van der Weyden's insistence upon strong emotive qualities. Van der Goes' painting is, in fact, a magnificent summation of Flemish achievements, climaxed by the bold intrusion of the painter's personality.

Van der Goes mined the symbolism of his painting from the rich deposits of theological literature. Joseph is given prominence by being placed in the left foreground in front of a large pillar that is part of a ruined stone edifice. His representing stability both in the painting and in his place in Christ's earthly family make his connection with the sturdy pillar appropriate. He kneels and pays homage to the scrawny newborn babe, lying on a few bits of straw in the center of a circle formed by attendant angels, shepherds, and the Virgin. The pillar may relate to the apocryphal tradition that had the Virgin leaning against it during the night when she gave birth to Christ, a description analogous to that of the birth of Buddha, whose mother stood beneath a tree and grasped it for support during childbirth. Van der Goes used the medieval device of scale discrepancies between the figures to set the angels apart from the mortals.

There is no shed for the Christ child, but the ruined stone setting relates to the decay of the Synagogue and the changing of the old order for the new that is signaled by the Nativity. Panofsky has shown that a vacant-looking building in the background bears the insignia of David, indicating that it is his house. The sheaf of wheat in the center foreground alludes to Bethlehem, "the house of bread," and the words of Christ, "I am the bread which came down from Heaven." The flowers (lily, iris, and columbine) refer to the blood of the Passion, the pain that pierced the Virgin's heart, and her grief and sorrow.

The presence of the ox and ass, standing behind the manger in the stone building, had a far different meaning than it does today. In medieval times the two animals had radically different connotations, partly because of a sentence in Isaiah, "The ox knoweth his owner, and the ass his master's crib." This was taken to mean that the ox recognized the Saviour, while the ass did not. The ass was often used as an anti-Semitic symbol referring to the Synagogue, which was at times personified as a woman riding an ass. In older images the ass was sometimes shown as eating, biting its tail, or tearing at the swaddling clothes, indicating its own stupidity and, by implication, that of the Jews for failing to recognize the Saviour. Van der Goes has shown the ass eating the straw of the manger. The ox is sometimes shown as engaged in a tug-of-war with the ass for the swaddling clothes, protecting the babe with its horns, or even reverently down on all fours before the child, identifying the event as a full epiphany.

Van der Goes has given the shepherds great importance in his painting, paralleling the magnified roles they began to play in the mystery plays, in which the authors had to fabricate dialogue for them because of their popularity with the audience. Van der Goes treats the annunciation of the Nativity to the shepherds and their appearance at the child's side in synoptic fashion (Fig. 139). (The annunciation is simultaneously represented as taking place on a hill in the right-hand corner of the panel.) The faces of the shepherds are a striking contrast in excitement and ascending levels of comprehension as they realize what they are witnessing. They are given an intensity of expression that borders on the fanatic. This study in psychological reactions to a situation, while occurring in a religious context and as a more or less marginal concern within the broad composition, holds the seeds for later art, which extracted such moments from Biblical incidents and described them in purely secular situations. Sent to Italy after its completion, the *Adoration* (commonly known as the *Portinari Altarpiece*)

Figure 139. HUGO VAN DER GOES. *The Adoration of the Shepherds*, detail from center panel of *Portinari Altarpiece*. c. 1476. Uffizi, Florence.

Left: Figure 140. HUGO VAN DER GOES. *The Death of the Virgin.* c. 1478–80. Oil on panel, 4'10"×4'. Musée Communal, Bruges.

Above: Figure 141. Parade Shield. 15th century. Paint and gilt, height 32". The British Museum, London.

elicited great interest and proved influential in subsequent Italian art.

In what may have been his last painting before his death in 1482, van der Goes further developed his characterization of those participating in great moments of emotional stress. In the *Death of the Virgin* (Fig. 140), the assembled disciples are shown in the pathetic attitudes of a shared human grief, and yet distinguished in ways appropriate to the nature invested in each of them by the painter. Compressed within the confines of a small room are not only the mourners and the deceased but also, penetrating the darkened interior, the brilliant glow issuing from Christ as he descends with angels to receive the Virgin's soul. Van der Goes was among the first to elevate the humble and ugly in art by showing them as possessing of true faith and enlightenment. Such dedication to the lowly perhaps accounts in part for his renunciation of early personal success and the pleasures of secular life for a monastic brotherhood. Deep feelings of guilt concerning the adequacy of his devotion and conflict of

his worldly interests as a painter with those of a strongly ascetic man were thereafter to cause severe mental problems and illness. The intensity of feeling displayed by his subjects and a rigorous pictorial construction from which we, as onlookers, cannot detach ourselves convey van der Goes' obsession for overwhelming the beholder's senses and reason with the emotional stress of witnessing the miraculous. (An open space is left for the viewer at the Virgin's bedside.) Van der Goes' condition was a case where the synthesis of heavenly and earthly values could not be easily or finally achieved—an affliction by conscience that was known to many at the end of the Middle Ages.

Before his retreat from public life, van der Goes had worked for royalty and, like many other important Flemish artists, had been employed in such commissions as the decoration of the sails of a ship. There are few such nonreligious paintings on objects left, and among these is a hand-painted shield used on parade occasions done by an unknown artist (Fig. 141). On the shield of gilt and paint is depicted a

Figure 142. PETRUS CHRISTUS. *St. Eligius.* 1449. Oil on panel. 38½ × 33⅝". Collection Robert Lehman, New York.

knight kneeling before a beautiful lady. Behind the knight, in the position of a second or a benefactor of his profession, is the figure of Death. The heraldic emblems used in like contexts in the earlier Middle Ages had by then given way to chivalric scene painting. For an artist of repute and social stature to undertake the painting of a utilitarian object was not considered demeaning in the fifteenth century, for by training and social status he was still a craftsman.

The Flemish veneration for the craftsman, joined with the purpose of homage to a saint, is seen in Petrus Christus' depiction of St. Eligius, patron saint of goldsmiths, in his shop as he waits upon a young couple about to be married (Fig. 142). The materials of his craft are displayed on shelves; and among the other objects, the mirror, which permits us to see the street and passers-by, may also have been a device to thwart the devil, who feared losing his image. In one of the earliest significant paintings devoted to the subject of business, Christus ingeniously created a type of marriage and professional portrait, and also treated a

whole wall as a still life. Moreover, it is a forerunner of the numerous paintings concerned with events enacted at or near a table, to be discussed in a later chapter.

Just how important jewelers and metal sculptors were to secular Flemish society is recorded by contemporary chronicles. The finest painters and craftsmen were employed by Charles the Bold for extravagant secular undertakings. One of the most famous spectacles was the wedding of Charles to Marguerite of York, the sister of the English king, in July of 1468, described by Baron van der Elst on the basis of chronicles of the event:

A forty-foot tower was set up, painted with heraldic devices and adorned with mechanical boars, wolves, and donkeys, to be operated by puppeteers so that they danced and sang.... Inside the hall was lighted by bronze chandeliers shaped like castles. They were surrounded by artificial forests, where wandered extravagant Gothic monsters.... A table was set for the bride and groom and for the most important guests under one canopy. Down the center

The Synthesis of Heaven and Earth in Fifteenth-Century Flemish Art 117

stretched a huge lake framed in silver. In its waters floated thirty ships, each so marked as to represent a territory of the Duke's domain. Some of them were seven feet long and rigged like the galleons that dropped anchor... before the port of Bruges and Damme. This marvelous fleet of carriers brought food to the guests seated around the table. Small boats were loaded with lemons, olives, rare fruits, and spices. After the main course dessert was brought in, borne aloft on the shoulders of the retinue of servants. The sweets were pastries in the shape of castles with very real bastions and battlements. Cooks and chefs had to be as skillful architects as the designers of the chandeliers.... From one of the huge pies emerged a whole band of musicians vigorously playing their instruments.

We can appreciate the dazzling banquet display despite the loss of all the works of art because of the survival of a small but magnificent silver ship built in the late fifteenth century by a Paris goldsmith named Pierre the Fleming (Fig. 143). Such ships were known as "nefs," and one of their uses was as a status symbol for the host, who had it set by his place at the dining table. That the *Burghley Nef* served such a practical purpose

is confirmed by the saltcellar in its poop. The ship has a nautilus shell for its hull and is mounted on a recumbent siren. Despite the fantastic design below its gunwales, the upper part of the three-masted ship corresponds to the latest in ship design of the period. Tiny figures of crewmen mount its silver-wire rigging to set its silver sails and stand by its many silver guns. At the foot of the main mast, two small figures playing chess represent Tristan and Isolde.

Not all sculpture of precious materials was meant to grace the secular table, for there is a spectacular example of a similar work serving to restore a nobleman to grace with the Church. A reliquary for Charles the Bold (Fig. 144) was made by a gifted goldsmith whose name may have been Gerard Loyet. The records of the Church of St. Lambert in Liége show that it was given by the Burgundian duke as atonement for extensive damage he had inflicted on the church building. A good likeness of the Duke shows him kneeling and holding his gift of a reliquary in which is housed St. Lambert's finger. The Duke's sponsor, St. George, backs him up and doffs his helmet in a courtly gesture of courtesy, as if presenting himself and his charge to the saint. The entire work, less than 22 inches high, was made of gold with inlaid enamel on a silver-gilt base, inscribed with the Duke's motto, " I undertook it."

The Flemish concern for law and punishment touched art in many ways. Convicted prisoners in some cities were forced to pay the expense of having bronze sculptures made of a hand or head by which to advertise to the public the nature of their guilt. At the very end of the fifteenth century, the city of Bruges commissioned the painter Gerard David to paint two pictures on the theme of justice taken from the writings of Herodotus. In the *Punishment of Sisamnes* (Fig. 145), David shows the corrupt Persian royal judge being punished by flaying; the victim is stretched out on a table before witnesses who watch him being skinned alive. Afterward, Sisamnes' son was made a judge in his father's place and forced to sit on a chair covered with the skin of his father. (The son's appointment is shown in the scene in the background.) This painting was hung in the town hall of Bruges as an admonition to that city's justices. The moralizing purpose of medieval art thus continues, but it is treated in mundane terms and deals with civil behavior. While it is David's Italian counterparts of the Renaissance who are most famous for reviving subjects from antiquity and for making studies of dissection, this painting shows a Flemish artist's interest in both concerns. Curious is the noticeable restraint in the expressions of the witnesses, and only a small boy at the right shows any sign of repugnance. (Skin-tingling pictures such as this remind us that the common view of art's purpose as being pleasing to the eye has many historical contradictions.)

Having briefly noted various changes in painting occurring since the twelfth century,

Figure 145. GERARD DAVID. *The Punishment of Sisamnes.* 1498. Oil on panel, 5′11⅝″ × 5′2⅝″. Musée Communal, Bruges.

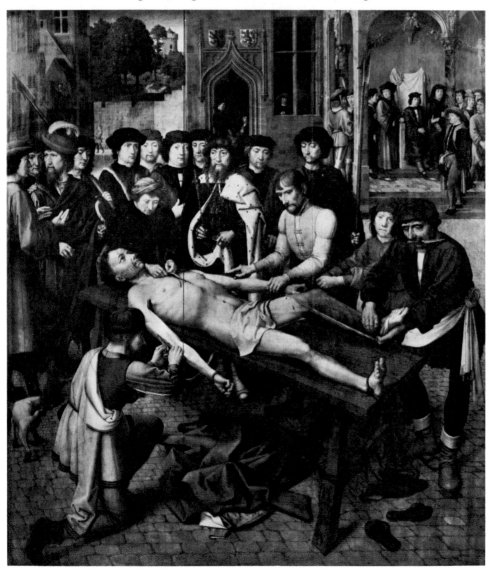

Figure 146.　Hans Memling. *The Last Judgment.* c. 1471. Oil on panel, center 7′3⅜″ × 5′3″; wings 7′3⅜″ × 2′9½″ each. Marienkirche, Danzig.

we shall turn again to the theme of the Last Judgment, discussed earlier in terms of cathedral sculpture. The Flemish artist Hans Memling created a version of this theme (Fig. 146) which provides a valuable illustration of significant differences in conception and execution from what was seen earlier, for instance, in the twelfth-century tympanum at Conques (Fig. 66). One of the most obvious developments in apocalyptic imagery of the fifteenth century, as exemplified by Memling, was the increased naturalism that gave great emphasis to the geographical locale and to the details of the physical action of the resurrected. Through its stark naturalism, the judgment scene has become increasingly more familiar, thereby permitting the viewer to identify with the fate of those in the painting. The central figure of St. Michael weighing the souls has assumed an importance equal if not superior to Christ, who sits enthroned upon the rainbow described by St. John. The weigher of

souls and the divine judge no longer seem so uncompromising or inaccessible as in earlier medieval versions of the scene. From the mouth of Christ there radiate the sword and the lily emblematic of his justice and mercy. At the sides of the rainbow and in heaven kneel John the Baptist and the Virgin, whose prayers intercede on behalf of mankind. The spectator has the impression that in Memling's view man has greater hope for clemency than he did at St-Foy.

The left wing of the triptych shows St. Peter herding the naked elect up a golden staircase where they are robed prior to entering the Gothic portals of the heavenly chateau. The right wing shows the infernal cascade of souls plummeting into the bowels of hell, where they are greeted by demons who exercise their punitive office with enthusiasm. The plausibility of the miraculous second advent of Christ and his judgment is achieved by couching the entire

Below: Figure 147. Rogier van der Weyden. *The Last Judgment* (center panel of a polyptych). 1443. Oil on panel, height 7'. Hôtel-Dieu, Beaune.

Right: Figure 148. Rogier van der Weyden. *The Damned*, detail of a side panel from *The Last Judgment*.

scene in as natural a setting and with accessories as realistic as was possible for the time. Christ and the citizens of heaven seem to be suspended just above the earth (a barren Flemish landscape), in a real sky that fades in color until it becomes almost white at the distant horizon.

Rogier van der Weyden's *Last Judgment* at Beaune (Fig. 147), done in 1443, provides an interesting variant on this theme in Flemish art. The scales held by the resplendent St. Michael (garbed in a costly Flemish robe of consummate workmanship) are tipped in inverse fashion from the position seen in Memling's and older judgment scenes: the saved soul is lighter than that of the damned. The painter was reverting to older traditions, going back to Greek times, in which the goodness of the spirit (or the merit of the ancient hero in the valence of the Greek gods) was outweighed by the lesser virtues of his adversary or counterpart. This restores to the weighing ceremony the traditional connotations of up and down, right and left, which we see carried out in the organization of heaven around Christ and in the elevated situation of heaven as contrasted with hell. Van der Weyden also deviated from his contemporary by not having demons inflict corporeal punishment upon the damned (Fig. 148); their

Figure 149. HIERONYMUS BOSCH. *The Adoration of the Magi* (center panel of a triptych). c. 1499. Oil on panel, 4'6⅜" × 2'4⅜". Prado, Madrid.

Netherlandish artist's cynicism about man, the Church, and the materialistic interests of society, which had found a glorification in art itself.

In the central panel of the triptych, Bosch has placed a decaying hut in the foreground, with a broad landscape above and behind it. Before the hut are grouped the three Magi, who are clearly differentiated ethnic types come from the far corners of the world. In the doorway of the hut stands a half-nude figure wearing golden chains, a crown of thorns over a metal hat, a crimson robe, a bell, and a frog. His leg displays leprous sores. This is the Antichrist, whom Bosch depicted from his acquaintance with Jewish tradition. An openly anti-Semitic act on his part, it presented a critiscim of the Jews for not recognizing the true Messiah and for worshiping a false deity. The bell relates to the Antichrist as a bad shepherd, the crown of thorns and robe to his attempt at imitating Christ, and the chain and sores to Jewish traditions citing these as signs of the Messiah. The Antichrist holds an object known to Bosch's contemporaries as an oven, which was a symbol or prop for hell. (Comparable to the funnel-shape structure of Dante's hell, it was carried by the Antichrist in the mystery plays). Behind the Antichrist can be seen the head of a donkey, referring to the Christian belief that the Jews worshiped the head of an ass. The decaying hut again refers to the fallen Synagogue. The shepherds who have climbed onto the roof and peer at the Virgin through a hole in the shed are the foolish shepherds or lost souls. The Magi who bring gifts represent humanity, which while longing for salvation is also foolish. (This is borne out by the expression of the kneeling king, the heretical symbols on their cloaks, and their warring armies in the distant fields.) The placement of the Antichrist between the Magi, as well as the position of the Virgin and Child to the right, signifies the poles of choice open to mankind. Their ultimate seduction by the devil is represented by the wars which take place on the fields behind. The city in the distance perhaps refers to the New Jerusalem after the wars and the advent of a truly Messianic era. It is almost as if Bosch were prophesying the Europe-shaking Reformation that was soon to come with such dramatic force.

punishment is inward, the result of conscience. With masterful skill and insight, the artist transcribed the anguished expressions of figures in varying states of mental distress.

Van der Weyden's pessimism about mankind was not only shared but surpassed in the thought and painting of Hieronymus Bosch. His painting of the *Adoration of the Magi* (Fig. 149), done at the very end of the fifteenth century, does not at first strike the modern viewer as being characterized by unpleasant associations. Nor is the painting technically an advance on the illusionism of van Eyck and van der Weyden from the first half of the century. Bosch's style is somewhat archaic, yet admirably suited to his moralizing imagination. This painting is a grim reflection of the

7

THE SYNTHESIS
OF HEAVEN AND EARTH
IN FIFTEENTH-CENTURY
ITALIAN ART

Although he painted early in the fourteenth century, the Florentine artist Giotto exerted great influence on the efforts of fifteenth-century Italian artists to unite in perfect harmony the divine and earthly aspects of existence. Giotto was able to project Biblical subjects into his paintings in ways that made the supernatural plausible and intelligible to all. He divested religious art of its aristocratic aloofness and theological abstraction, and he reduced reliance upon symbolic accessories and gestures. What his contemporary Dante was to literature, Giotto was to painting. They translated the divine into a new vernacular to facilitate simple devotion. To his own age, Giotto's great achievement was the more lifelike appearance of his subjects, in contrast to the art of his contemporaries. The criterion was not the direct matching of Giotto's paintings with the real world, but with the art that had gone before. While it may be difficult today to appreciate this difference, Giotto remains a brilliant interpreter of the Bible, whose mastery of composition was indivisible from his abilities as a narrator. *The Raising of Lazarus* (Fig. 150) is one of a great series of mural paintings adorning the Arena Chapel in Padua; it was painted about a thousand years after the cata-

comb painting of the same theme (Fig. 61). Dead for three days, the putrefying Lazarus was brought to life by Christ. To those who first looked upon this painting, it seemed that Giotto equally had brought new life to art.

To read the story within the painting is to retrace the major compositional movements. At the left, as if having turned from the disciples, Christ effects the miracle through the magnetism of his gaze and a gesture of his hand. There is no distracting object behind him. The gold background traditionally used in most art of this time has been replaced by blue sky, which returns the action to earth. So powerful is the eye of Giotto's Christ that it impels the viewer across half the painting to the figure of Lazarus. A second bridge between the Resurrector and the resurrected man is formed by the gestures of two intervening figures. The arm movements of the two figures on the center axis who serve as intermediaries are not symbolic but are instinctive, showing Giotto's relaxation of the figure's adherence to stereotype. Even when Giotto's people are motionless, they impress us as sentient beings. Gesture is precious coin for the artist who expends it judiciously; Giotto never squanders it. It must build the action and forcibly link or pace the composition, never

Figure 150. GIOTTO. *The Raising of Lazarus.* 1305–06. Fresco. Arena Chapel, Padua.

distract by trivial movement or ostentatious detail. Not only the arm movements of the principals lead from Christ to Lazarus, but also the powerful but simple directional arrangements of the draperies, which retain a medieval quasi-independence of the body. Those of the figure behind Lazarus, whose face is veiled to ward off the smell of putrefaction, slow the eye's drive to the right and refocus its attention on Lazarus. The small bending figure of the man who has removed the lid of the tomb is so placed as to guide our attention to the kneeling figures of the women, who return the elliptical movement of the action to Christ. The figures are bonded together by ties that reflect both a deep inward awareness and simple physical grace.

Figure 151. AMBROGIO LORENZETTI. *Effects on Good Government* (detail from scenes in the city). 1337–39. Fresco. Sala dei Nove, Palazzo Pubblico, Siena.

At all times the viewer's concentration is held within the frame. The painting's frame is like that of a window through which we look into a clear shallow space, sufficient for the firm sculpturesque volumes that displace it. Giotto develops a way of constructing a painting that is new. It is as if the viewer's eye were the apex of an imaginary pyramid or cone whose base is the rear plane, or blue sky, in the painting. The painting's surface is like a transparent plane intersecting the pyramid parallel to its apex and base. This form of visual cone allows Giotto to project his figures in depth with fair consistency, on the basis of their distance from the viewer—a way of seeing that was to be systematized mathematically in the next century. The frame works with the figures, serving as a measure and foil for their large scale, erectness, and resulting dignity.

As seen in this painting, Giotto's was a man-centered world in which Christ appeared as a man among men. His art fostered hope both in the humane vision of Christ and in the temperance, humility, and dignity assigned to man, who is shown as worthy of redemption. Giotto's rendering of the figure is integral with the spiritual values he assigned to his ideal of humanity. The painter made a historically influential equation between the weighty mass of his figures and their moral worth. The stability of their movements and disposition within the scene convey the impression that men have a meaningful part in a larger order.

In Italy as in Northern Europe, the artist's conquest of the visual world was a slow process attended by timid or hesitant efforts as well as bold advances. After Giotto, the fourteenth-century artist who strikes out in the most venturesome way to open up the space of his fresco and create a more natural environment, thereby representing the abundance of earthly life, is the Siennese Ambrogio Lorenzetti. Commissioned by the city-state of Siena to decorate its town hall, Lorenzetti filled the walls of a room with allegories and commentary on the subject of good and bad government. Visually and historically, the fresco containing the effects of good government on the city and the country is the most exciting (Figs. 151, 152). Both views are original panoramic vistas, which depend not upon conventions or memory but on actual visual experience, based on the hill city of Siena and its natural surroundings. The spatial construction of city and country is from the viewpoint of someone near the center foreground in the city, about the point

Figure 152. AMBROGIO LORENZETTI. *Effects of Good Government* (detail from scenes in the countryside). 1337–39. Fresco. Sala dei Nove, Palazzo Pubblico, Siena.

The Synthesis of Heaven and Earth in Fifteenth-Century Italian Art   125

at which the women dance as evidence of happiness under just rule. The architecture, figures, and landscape diminish in scale both in depth and laterally in relation to this vantage point within the city itself; the reference is not to and not based on their distance from us. The entire city is rendered in focus, as if to accommodate the movement of the eyes as one searches through the fresco outward from the city's center. Lorenzetti was not working with scientific perspective or photographlike naturalism, since his was an empirical effort based on trial and error. The obliqueness of the streets is convincing, for example. There are minor inconsistencies, such as his failure to make figures in the landscape smaller in proportion to their setting, but the painter took the artist's license of bending a rule for purposes of clarity and vividness.

Not since antiquity and the Roman wall paintings had a Western artist attempted such a sweeping embrace of the visual world. (Nor had the Romans been so topographically specific.) The light of the entire scene is strongest in the area of the principal viewpoint, and it diminishes as it moves outward. Lorenzetti caught the continuity of light and natural space, and the kind of roving focus of the traveler (not dissimilar to what was happening in Chinese painting of the time, as will be seen in Chapter 15, "Themes from Nature").

More than a hundred years after the creation of Giotto's Arena Chapel frescoes, the Florentine artist Masaccio contributed to a fresco cycle of St. Peter in a chapel newly built by a silk merchant named Brancacci. No artist in the intervening period had grasped the full import or extended the ideas of Giotto as did Masaccio in his fresco *The Tribute Money* (Pl. 16). The Brancacci Chapel became a fountainhead of ideas and inspiration for many artists who followed, including Michelangelo (who supposedly had his nose broken there during a quarrel). The events depicted by Masaccio are those attending the arrival of Christ and the disciples before the gates of Capernaum, where a toll was asked of them. (In 1427, the city of Florence imposed an income tax, but its relevance to this painting, if any, is not clear, although it is known that Brancacci opposed the tax.) St. Augustine interpreted this event as foretelling the toll that Christ was to pay upon the Cross for mankind. At this moment, for the first time Christ singled out a disciple, Peter, to participate in a miracle (a prophecy perhaps of Peter's role in founding the Church and his aid in the redemption of mankind). Following Christ's instructions to him, the episode in the center, Peter takes the coin out of a fish's mouth (far left), and then he pays the publican (extreme right). As in the work of Giotto, the main group is assembled in the center and close to the lower edge of the painting. Although the fresco was high up on the wall, the viewpoint of its construction is about on a level with the heads of the group. The intense illusion of reality Masaccio achieved is contingent upon the fresco's construction from a fixed viewpoint. As defined by John White: "One of the most significant characteristics of artificial perspective is that it assumes an observer with his eye in one particular position at a fixed distance and direction from the scene before him." But this viewpoint may not always coincide with where the beholder finds it possible to stand, as is the case in the Brancacci Chapel.

The setting is new. The scene takes place on a broad plain before an extensive mountain range, seen in atmospheric depth; and though small in relation to the figure scale, the entrance to the city is drawn in correct linear perspective. The vanishing point of its diagonals is coincident with Christ's head, thus uniting the structural with the theological focus. Dramatic emphasis as well as structural clarity was furthered by the new perspective. While the human form still dominates in the painting—a requirement of Florentine art in this century—it has been set into a natural context. As if affirming this relationship, Masaccio's figures cast shadows upon the ground, conveying a marked sense of their relation to the surrounding world and their exposure to natural light. The artist's building blocks were the study of such qualities as the reflection of light and shadow by broadly treated volumes, the relation of solids to voids, and the rhythmic interplay of the human body with the forms of nature and architecture. The figures around Christ belong to an impersonal ordering and do not display spontaneous volitional movement.

Masaccio modernized but did not basically alter Giotto's ideal of a stable world governed by powerful laws. This modernization took the form of a greater awareness of and skill in rendering the anatomical makeup and coordination of the human figure. The corporeal body asserts itself even when sheathed in draped folds. Masaccio utilized newly discovered gestures and postures modestly but tellingly in enriching the human role in religious drama. This release of the human body from a kind of limbo of inertia was as important for the future secularization of art as was the Flemish celebration of the man-made object. Subsequent artists with greater anatomical and physiological knowledge nonetheless came to copy Masaccio's figures, recognizing their durable expressivity, though not always sensing their coordination with the total design of his compositions.

The strength of Masaccio's treatment of the faces of the disciples heightens the intrusion of the human into what had been exclusively the domain of the divine. (There are good grounds for believing that Masaccio did not paint the face of Christ and that this weaker conception was executed by Masolino.) Like many who followed, Masaccio drew strength from empirical as well as from theoretical inspiration, and while the faces of his human characters gained in intensity and plausibility, that of the adult Christ—because of his divine nature—became a troublesome problem. This dilemma is a sign of the transitional nature of the fifteenth century, which stood with one foot in the medieval period and one in the modern. Noteworthy are the great fifteenth-century portraits of secular subjects and a few faces of saints (perhaps because of their humanization), but renderings of Christ's face as eloquent as that at Daphne (Fig. 67) are rare.

Masaccio literally and figuratively brought a new shudder to painting. The theme of baptism in which a figure is immersed in water or, as in Masaccio's fresco of *St. Peter Baptizing the Neophyte*, has it poured over him from a bowl was an old one (Fig. 153). But for the first time the Florentine painter gives us the reaction of trembling flesh under the touch of cold water, and the instinctive but futile warming gesture of the man who has disrobed while awaiting his own baptism in the icy stream underlines this sensation. What may well have brought a shiver to Masaccio's contemporaries was his power to bring home to them in this performance of a sacrament their all too human and familiar frailty during such an ordeal. With Masaccio, the senses of his subject come alive, and flesh and temperature become tangible—

Figure 153. MASACCIO. *St. Peter Baptizing the Neophyte*. c. 1427. Fresco. Brancacci Chapel, Sta. Maria del Carmine, Florence.

the viewer and the viewed are brothers in the same skin.

What imparts excitement to the developments of the fifteenth century is the artists' pursuit of objective correspondences to nature, which released tremendous energies, gave rise to a pervasive spirit of free inquiry that in turn nourished venturesome ideas, and produced brilliant individual styles. A galaxy of talents crowned Italian art before the century was half spent. Masaccio and Veneziano, the sculptors Donatello and Ghiberti, and the architects Brunelleschi and Alberti—the latter being primarily a theorist—evolved, both theoretically and empirically, scientific bases for the means of representation. For most of the century these discoveries did not dogmatically circumscribe the artist. Furthermore, these abstract devices for rendering and ordering— perspective, proportion, anatomy, and the study of light—were not the sole prerogative of

Figure 154. LORENZO GHIBERTI. *The Sacrifice of Isaac.* c. 1401. Bronze, 18 × 16″. Museo Nazionale, Florence.

Figure 155. FILIPPO BRUNELLESCHI. *The Sacrifice of Isaac.* c. 1401. Bronze, 18 × 16″. Museo Nazionale, Florence.

either sculpture or painting. Secular criteria were established for the making and judgment of all art. The rationalization of the means by which the artist could master the representation of the visible world coincided with the aggressive urban middle-class drive to systematize business conduct, explore the earth's surface in successful mercantile enterprises, and exalt man-made goods. Body and mind were to be in felicitous coordination, and this ideal enhanced the attraction of the ancient Roman sculpture known in that century. The supernatural was still respected; however, priority was given in art to the sensorily verifiable experiences, like the clear, measurable shaping of space and vital energetic bodies, as well as the convincing re-creation of familiar settings of home, city, and landscape. The artist continued to rely upon imagination for his basic conception, but he was now armed with new constructive and expressive means to suit his own taste and that of his time for emulation, but not literal imitation, of all that was material and measurable.

The promise of the fifteenth century in Florence was evident during its first years, when, between 1401 and 1403, two artists in their twenties competed for that city's greatest artistic honor: designing and casting in bronze the east doors of the Baptistery, which faced

the Cathedral. Finalists from among seven competitors, Filippo Brunelleschi, a goldsmith, and Lorenzo Ghiberti, a goldsmith and painter, still ranked as apprentices in the guild system. They presented their bronze relief panels depicting the Sacrifice of Isaac as prescribed by the large jury of businessmen, artists, and theologians (Figs. 154, 155). The competition, the focus and pride of and the source of argument for the entire city, was carried out despite a recent devastating plague that had wiped out 30,000 inhabitants. But Florence had also successfully withstood the military threat of the Duke of Milan, who died suddenly in 1402. The artistic enhancement of a holy building was a gesture both of thanks for divine protection and of civic pride. Both entries showed combinations of medieval and new ideas and forecast the vigor and creative imagination of Florentine sculpture.

Brunelleschi's was the more obviously dramatic of the two interpretations; his every figure (even the animals) was involved in strenuous movement. Cast in the round and then attached to the panel, Brunelleschi's energetic figures lean or twist into the viewer's space, overlapping the medieval frame. Their actions, however, lack the synchronized mutual integration of Ghiberti's design, which also divides the attendants from those of the sacrifice by a diagonal landscape device rather than in horizontal layers. Despite its high relief, Brunelleschi's design still clings to an over-all surface disposition of elements. The technical qualities of fine finish, down to the smallest detail of features, hair, and drapery, drew greater admiration for Ghiberti, but he may also have been supported over his competitor by achieving a more natural and graceful suggestion of depth. Cast in one piece except for the figure of Isaac, Ghiberti's panel may thus have seemed to the artists as being better grounded in conservative standards of craftsmanship. Brunelleschi's impetuous Abraham, also, may have appealed less to the theologian who might have admired Ghiberti's interpretation of reticence and thoughtfulness. The businessmen, anticipating the costs of twenty-eight such panels on the future door, would have appreciated the lighter weight of Ghiberti's relief. Both artists included paraphrases from Hellenistic-Roman art: Brunelleschi in the attendant pulling a thorn from his foot, and Ghiberti in the torso of the young Isaac and the decoration of the altar. Even before the painters, it was the sculptors and, above all, the architects who saw in ancient Roman art the basis for a new, beautiful, and expressive art.

Ghiberti won the competition and went on to design two great doors for the Baptistery. Brunelleschi became the greatest and most influential architect of the century, forsaking his great talents as a sculptor. The bitterness between the two that began with the competition never abated, for neither was a modest man. In his autobiography Ghiberti, the older of the two, wrote: "To me the palm of victory was conceded by all the experts and by all those who competed with me." There is some evidence of a split decision and no evidence that Brunelleschi admitted his rival's superiority.

Almost contemporaneous with Masaccio's *Tribute Money* is Donatello's relief sculpture *The Feast of Herod* (Fig. 156), made for the font in the Baptistery of S. Giovanni, Siena. Donatello drew upon Brunelleschi's newly discovered device of systematic linear perspective to create the appearance of the relief's orderly recession into depth. In the oldest extant example of a composition based on this system for transposing the three-dimensional world on to a flat surface with all distances measurable, the diagonals of the steeply sloping floor converge to a point marked by the elbow of the seated figure who gestures toward the severed head of John the Baptist. The diagonals of the upper part of the relief meet at a point slightly above, on the cornice of the wall behind the banquet table. Both points correspond roughly to a theoretical viewer's eye level. Thus in its actual location on the font, the visitor must bend or stoop to see the panel as Donatello wanted it viewed. Although influenced by Brunelleschi's new architecture, with its rounded arches, Donatello designed an ambitious imaginary architectural background consisting of three separate halls to extend the illusion of a palatial setting. It permitted him to expand the action to include the deliverance of John's head to Herod's servants in the most remote hall. In the foreground, Donatello left the center of the scene empty except for a few objects on the table. Seemingly, the action has been divided into two areas. At the left around the head of John is the explosive radial grouping climaxed by the horrified figure of Herod. No artist of his century surpassed Donatello's ability to dramatize the workings of the human mind in situations of great excitement. He brought to art a great awareness of crowd psychology that vivified and united his figures with a range and depth of feeling unequaled at the time. These qualities were suited to the subject, which shows not the sacred moment of martyrdom but the animated group response to a sadistic murder. The reactions of the figures to the

Figure 156. DONATELLO. *The Feast of Herod*. 1425–27. Gilt bronze, 23½" square. S. Giovanni. Siena.

sudden appearance of John's head polarize around expressions of attraction and repulsion. Donatello bridged the gap between the two foreground groups partially by means of the triple arches and the table but also, and most important, by the fanatical stare of Salome suspended in her dance.

The Venetian painter Domenico Veneziano, who came to Florence in 1439, drew insight and inspiration from Donatello and the insurgent art of his time to produce his masterwork, the *Madonna and Child with Saints* (Pl. 17). Flanking the enthroned Madonna and Child at the left are Saints Francis and John the Baptist, while at the right are Saints Zenobius and Lucy. This is a devotional and honorific painting of a type frequently found in later Italian art, called the "Sacred Conversation," implying the possibility of discourse between the figures. The formal symmetry by which divinity is honored is tempered by the forceful individualization of the saints. They belong at once to a timeless hierarchy, but have acquired personalities and states of feeling that prohibit their total submission to an impersonal order. We may speak of the saints' heads as portraits in an even more exact sense than in discussing the work of Masaccio or Giotto.

St. Lucy is shown in profile, a favored view both because of its ancestry in ancient numismatics and medallions and because of its use in secular portraits of the time. To St. Lucy is given serene elegance and contemplative composure. Her profile serves to draw the glance back into the painting and toward the masculine, rugged, and pensive head of St. Zenobius. No attempt was made to flatter the saint; the extent of the minute articulation of his features and strong modeling of the robes suggests that Veneziano was influenced by sculpture and Flemish painting. Both the pose and facial conception of St. Francis convey the painter's feelings about his arduous self-denial and humility. The figure of Francis is strong enough to be seen by itself as a moving image. It possesses the quality of strong inner piety the Italians admired in Flemish art. Within the larger painting, however, it serves as a counterweight to Veneziano's most inspired characterization, John the Baptist. Ironically, the saint has been used as an interlocutor between the viewer and the Mother and Child. He himself is the most magnetic figure in the painting.

Much may be read in his face—suffering, compassion, the gift of clairvoyance, and obliviousness to self. Taken as a whole, John has a late medieval head and the firm body of a Hellenistic athlete.

So strong is Veneziano's over-all design that it does not disintegrate under the weight of the attention given to the heads. His color lacks the detailed, sumptuous radiance of the Flemings, but is more obviously constructive in its broader application, as in the greens and pinks of the loggia. The airiness and clarity of the scene depends upon many light, delicate tones with strong accents, such as yellow and red, discretely allied to the principal figures. The severe clarity and simplicity of the architecture never conflicts with the gestures of the saints but serves to underscore their slightest movement. Veneziano's painting is a graphic demonstration of architectonic design, by which the figures are consistently related to the axes of the frame and architectural content of the scene, thus ensuring stability and immediate legibility of the whole design. Building on Masaccio's work, Veneziano introduced a convincing representation of brilliant sunlight, which shines from a single source on the rear wall just to the left of the Virgin and Christ. The light provides not only warm illumination of the background but a contrast with the cool foreground area.

Today it is possible for almost anyone to be taught in a single lesson simple perspective tricks and to suggest convincingly three-dimensional space on a flat surface. But in the fifteenth century the development of perspective devices was still a challenge and could produce great emotional excitement in the artist who discovered that, through these techniques, it was possible for him to explore a new artistic world. Consider for a moment that such artists as Masaccio, Donatello, and Veneziano were faced with the opportunity of depicting stories they had never actually witnessed but which could be painted or modeled as if they were happening before one's very eyes. At their disposal were the new scientific as well as optical perspectives to achieve this illusion. Artists most interested in the former had access to Florentine mathematicians interested in Euclidean geometry. One such artist was the energetic and inventive Paolo Uccello, who passionately loved the possible geometry of objects and the unifying space of scientific perspective but who would not submit totally or blindly to its use to dictate the form of an entire painting. As Paolo Uccello painted his fresco of *The Flood* (Figs. 157, 158) in a cloister of a Florentine church, he was weighing in his mind the effects of linear perspective against actual optical experience and making adjustments between the two. Thus in the perspective construction of the two views of the Ark, its length at the left, and width at the right, each has its own point toward which the diagonal lines of the ship converge, rather than a common vanishing point, which would be the case if the entire scene were constructed from a single, frozen viewpoint. As Giotto had done, Uccello was partly accommodating the shifting gaze of actual visual experience and the needs of pictorial organization, which could well differ from those of science and sight. Uccello recognized that linear perspective was not something toward which the beholder is neutral, and he exploited the

sensational possibilities of this system through the deep dramatic funneling space created by the sides of the Arks. He then proceeded to populate this deep space, thereby varying the scale and postures of his figures. Shown in the same fresco are the beginning of the Flood, at the left, and Noah's awaiting of the dove and the recession of the waters forty days later, at the right. (The present battered condition of the fresco explains our use of an old engraving to assist the reader.) The folly of men and women when faced with disaster is shown by the figures who continue personal quarrels and physical combat in the left foreground, of the futility of resisting the onslaught of the elements, as seen in the man who tries to climb into a barrel, or those who try to cling to the sides of the sealed Ark. The arched, bloated body of a drowned child lies in the right foreground. The identity of the tall standing figure who looks to heaven and whose ankles are clasped

Figure 157. PAOLO UCCELLO. *The Flood*. 1446–48. Fresco. Chiostro Verde, Sta. Maria Novella, Florence.

Figure 158. ROSSI. Engraving after *The Flood* by Uccello, from Rosini, *Storia della Pittura Italiana* (Pisa, 1848).

131

by a half-submerged figure is not known. (That he is Noah is doubtful; perhaps he is a priest who recognizes the truth of Noah's warning from God too late.) Here was a subject in which Uccello could indulge his curiosity and wonder about the appearance of the elements, the naked exposure of the body and human psychology, the shapes of objects such as the checkered collar around the neck of a struggling figure in the left foreground (which was a personal caprice or like a signature)—life and death in their most violent manifestations. His ego as an artist was gratified by proving he could convincingly render clouds, a windblown tree, drapery, animals, and the figure in unconventional ways.

Too often called a scientist rather than an artist, Uccello saw geometry and linear perspective as surveying tools for mapping what had in painting been unknown territory. Empirical study and intuition made him believe that there were certain geometric shapes common to men and animals which should serve truth and beauty as the artistic substructure of their re-creation. When he painted a fresco in the Cathedral as a memorial to a mercenary knight who had fought for Florence in the fourteenth century, both the horse and figure of Sir John Hawkwood were rationalized in comparison to perspective space (Fig. 159). The flanks and bowed neck of the horse and the shapes of the armor are easily discernible in terms of arcs, circles, demispheres, and various repeated simple curved silhouettes. Florentine painting such as this was nourished not alone by science and history, but also by sculpture; for the memorial is patterned after sculptural equestrian monuments. (The knight's horse is based on one of the famous bronze horses on St. Mark's in Venice.) Economically, fresco was cheaper than bronze. The elaborate architectural base is correctly rendered as if seen from below, but the horse and rider are as if seen from a higher viewpoint, thereby permitting the appropriate honor of a strong profile portrait of Sir John rather than merely the belly of his horse and the soles of his boots. Art and science, sight and reason, were not enemy faculties for Uccello—any more than celebrating a secular hero in a cathedral was felt to be contradictory in Florence at the time. Earthly heroes literally invaded the house of God in fifteenth-century Italy.

132   Purposes of Art

It is not in "high painting" such as that of Masaccio, Veneziano, and Uccello, however, that we can see what daily secular life in Florence looked like; ironically, this new subject matter in the history of art is best exemplified in the work of decorative painters whose styles show little awareness of the technical and stylistic innovations of the masters. Paintings in Florence were found not only in churches, chapels, and cloisters but also inside and occasionally outside private buildings, not merely on walls or panels but on plates and storage chests as well. It is this last form, *cassone* painting, that reveals (along with a wealth of images dealing with historical and literary themes) the everyday customs of Florence. Most of the evidence of the frequent and lavish pageantry with which the rulers of Florence satisfied their subjects and fellow citizens has been lost, but one surviving *cassone* painting shows a tournament of arms held periodically in Piazza Sta. Croce (Figs. 160–162). On such festive occasions the city itself became a work of art, with the decorations rivaling the ceremonies for attention. The

Figure 159.   PAOLO UCCELLO. *Sir John Hawkwood.* 1433. Fresco transferred to canvas. The Cathedral, Florence.

Figure 160.   Left section.

Figure 161.   Center section.

Figure 162.   Right section.

Figures 160–162.   Shop of the Vergil Master. *Tournament in the Piazza Sta. Croce, Florence.* 15th century. Tempera on *cassone* panel, 1′5⅞″ × 5′1¼″. The Yale Art Gallery, New Haven, Connecticut.

painter of this Florentine *cassone* gives us the tangle of combat as well as distinct multiple focus on the conduct of the bystanders. The over-all dispersal of bright, rather flat colors gives the work a decorative tone. For such tournaments or merely for parade display, in Florence as in Flanders, the best artists such as Leonardo would be called upon to design ornament for their patron's armor.

Fortunately preserved is a parade shield bearing the figure of David by Andrea del Castagno (Fig. 163). Instead of decorating the shield with a coat of arms, Castagno has staged David's triumph against a natural backdrop. The vital figure of David is shown as if first confronting Goliath with loaded sling, and at his feet is the grisly evidence of the story's end. David was one of the great heroes of Florence, as well as a symbol of freedom, and on the shield Castagno shows him as vigorous and vigilant, ready to repel his enemy and, by implication, those of Florence. In his figure of David, Castagno joined the posture of an ancient Greek statue and the results of his studies of human anatomy, for he was one of the first

Figure 163. ANDREA DEL CASTAGNO. *David.* c. 1450–57. Parade shield, tempera on leather, height 45½″. The National Gallery of Art, Washington, D.C. (Widener Collection).

artists to study the body by dissection. This practical knowledge of musculature imparted energy, strength, and new expressiveness to his figures but, in the case of David, created an awkward synthesis with the archaic or conventionalized landscape. Castagno was more effective in scenes where his figural studies could be complemented by architectural perspective.

Shortly after Veneziano's *Madonna and Child with Saints* was completed, Castagno painted his fresco *The Last Supper* (Fig. 164), which was the prototype for several later fifteenth-century versions of the same theme. Although the subject is Biblical and the fresco's location was in the refectory of a Florentine church, Castagno's interpretation is in human and mundane terms. The disciples and Christ are shown seated at a long table in a severely beautiful pavilion, whose design is based on contemporary architectural tastes. Castagno sought the appearance of complete orderliness and composure between the figures and their setting, and between the whole composition and the great dining room in which the fresco was located.

Marginal evidences of the increased interest in ancient art in the fresco are the bronze sphinxes at the ends of the bench and certain details of the architecture. As had their Flemish counterparts, painters such as Castagno often reconstructed or designed with the brush their own architecture and furnishings. Through linear perspective, Castagno created the forceful illusion of the pavilion's recession behind the end wall of the refectory. Within the resulting space of the room and seen against its coordinate system of verticals and horizontals are the impressive figures of Christ and the disciples. The initial appearance of the group resembles what might have been a social gathering, common to both Castagno's society and that of the ancient Hebrews, whose principal evening meal was an almost public occasion for the assembling of friends and a speaker. Castagno selected the moment when Christ has prophesied his betrayal. Judas is singled out by his placement across from Christ and by the absence of a halo. Because of Castagno's adherence to laws of perspective, Judas is actually larger in scale than Christ, who sits farther in depth—a relation of scale never seen in medieval art.

Christ has not, in fact, received the same emphasis given to the disciples who flank him and ponder the significance of his announce-

Figure 164. ANDREA DEL CASTAGNO. *The Last Supper.* c. 1445–50. Fresco, S. Apollonia, Florence.

ment. The group of Peter, Judas, and Christ is set off slightly by the accentuation of the marble pattern in the wall above their heads. The natural light entering the room through the windows at the right falls equally on all present. The individualization and humanization of the disciples is accomplished by their rugged countenances, the variety of their rhetorical postures, and the lack of restriction by the architectural framework. Despite the relative passivity of the figures, Castagno's ideals of latent muscular energy and cool hard-edge sculptural surfaces assert themselves. Painting such as this, in its time, was said to bring the dead and the past to life by giving them a vivid physical presence.

It was the locating of figures in architectural settings in the fourteenth and fifteenth centuries that accelerated developments in perspective. These settings acquired a beauty and interest of their own, competitive with the figures, as seen in the Castagno fresco and in Piero della Francesca's *Flagellation* (Fig. 165). One can conceive of the setting as existing prior to the presence of the figures, unlike medieval painting before the fourteenth century; indeed, there were drawings and paintings of architectural vistas without humans in fifteenth-century art. Piero was as devoted to geometry and perspective as Uccello had been, believing that its Euclidean shapes were the purest form of beauty. Pilate's palace invited an elegant

conception; using a basic unit of measurement and geometry, the artist carefully constructed a handsome open edifice in which the flagellation takes place. Christ is located against the traditional pillar—here surmounted by a bronze statue symbolizing paganism—and he stands in the center of a strongly foreshortened circle inscribed on the pavement. Conceivably, Piero was symbolically signifying his divinity and central place in the universe. The entire pavement design and the careful measurement of the building's elevation coordinated with it may have had richer esoteric symbolism, known to very few other than the artist. Piero's *Flagellation* has been the subject of much serious inquiry by scholars, who have yet to reveal all its meaning or reach agreement on its content. Why is Christ upstaged by the three large foreground figures at the right? Who are these three men? It has been conjectured that they may symbolize conspiracies against Christ (Acts 4: 27), a contemporary political assassination, the trials of Constantinople at the time, or just three anonymous bystanders relatable to many others in Florentine painting. Regardless of their identity, the important historical innovation here is the recession of the focus on the divine, for previously Christ had always enjoyed the center of the stage or foreground prominence. By placing three well-dressed and possibly contemporary Florentine types nearer to the spectator, the painter further humanizes the action and the immediacy of viewpoint, encouraging the onlooker to identify with the mortals in the foreground. In the next century the possibilities and ramifications of this recessive focus were to be more extensively explored.

Piero's style of drama avoids strong physical movement. Every figure has a gravity of appearance and action. The meditative or withdrawn mood of each individual eliminates the use of the glance as a unifying device. (In Pilate's aspect, Piero may have been interpreting the Biblical account of his misgivings about the execution because of his wife's dream.) By tracing the silhouettes of the figures, it can be seen that compositional cohesiveness came partly from their continuity of edge.

The solid, stable appearance of Piero's figures comes in part from a viewpoint slightly lower than the eye level of the subjects—a view that stresses the length and firmness of the leg. (This device was commented on by Piero in one of his two treatises on perspective.) Piero also situated his vanishing points in the area of Christ, noticeably off center, thereby creating an interesting visual pull between Christ and the foreground figures at the right. The fifteenth century knew no more thoughtful and gifted composer of pictures than Piero. None could so provocatively suggest to the viewer comparison of the beauty of architecture with that of the human form.

In view of their preoccupation with reason and physical laws, the most challenging religious subject for Italian artists was the miracle of the Resurrection. The *Resurrection of Christ* painted by Piero della Francesca (Fig. 166), one-time assistant of Veneziano, demonstrates how faith and reason joined to produce what may be the most profound painting of its age. Under a cool matinal light, Christ is risen, while at his feet lie the soldiers in deep slumber. The supernatural conversion is expressed in such subtle and diverse ways as to reflect the concentrated effort of a superior intelligence. Much of the shock immediately induced by the painting comes from the unexpected appearance of hieratic symmetry in a natural setting. Piero's passion for geometry as form and symbol explains the arrangement of the base of the tomb and the head of Christ into an isosceles triangle; and at its apex Piero painted the most powerful head of Christ of the entire fifteenth century. In this head, and specifically in the hypnotic area of the eyes, is condensed the most crucial mystery of the Christian religion. Through the eyes, Piero conveys the concept of the risen Christ awakening into a world beyond mortal vision. The rigidity of Christ's face and pose and his obliviousness to the surroundings suggest a spiritual or psychological rather than physical transformation. True to the account of the Resurrection, Piero shows Christ in human

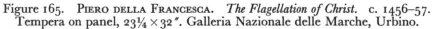

Figure 165. PIERO DELLA FRANCESCA. *The Flagellation of Christ.* c. 1456–57. Tempera on panel, 23¼ × 32″. Galleria Nazionale delle Marche, Urbino.

Plate 21. CARAVAGGIO. *Christ at Emmaus.* c.1598. Oil on canvas, 4′7″ × 6′5½″.
The National Gallery, London (reproduced by courtesy of the Trustees).

Plate 22. PIETER BRUEGEL THE ELDER. *The Peasant Wedding*. c. 1565. Oil on panel, 3′8⅞″ × 5′4″. Kunsthistorisches Museum, Vienna.

Plate 23.   DIEGO VELÁZQUEZ. *The Water Seller of Seville.* c. 1619. Oil on canvas, 41 ½ × 31 ½".
The Wellington Museum, London (Crown copyright reserved).

Plate 24. VALENTIN DE BOULLOGNE (1591/4–1632/4). *Soldiers and Bohemians*. Oil on canvas, 3'11" × 5'2½". The John Herron Art Institute, Indianapolis.

Figure 166. Piero della Francesca. *The Resurrection of Christ*. 1460. Detached fresco. Pinacoteca, Borgo San Sepolcro.

form. His body still has material weight, as seen by the discernible pressure of his leg on the tomb's edge. The dark hollows around the eyes speak of the Passion and the Entombment. Death is treated by Piero as a form of sleep, which gives additional meaning to the dormancy of the pagan guards, as yet unenlightened by the miracle.

Piero suffuses his message throughout the painting by means of contrasts, and all the contrasts involve the figure of Christ. He divides the painting into vertical and horizontal, right and left. But, as in medieval art, these directions must be viewed from Christ's standpoint. The landscape to Christ's right is one of winter and, like the wound in his right side, indicative of death. The tree trunk nearest the banner is an alliteration of his body, as are the branches of both sets of trees to Christ's head. To the Redeemer's left is the springtime of nature, alive and verdant again through his sacrifice. Thus the landscape symbolizes the world before

and after his coming. The convergence of the trees on both sides toward the figure of Christ infers his relation to the state of the landscape. (The mound at the viewer's far left serves to balance the head of Christ and hold the focus within the frame.) Piero's Christ is the God of all that lives. In Piero's paintings showing him before death, Christ is a gentle submissive figure. Resurrected, he becomes a masculine and militant being. It is conceivable that Piero painted himself as the sleeping soldier whose head seems to rest against the edge of the tomb. If this is true, it was done to suggest a personal relation between, and a further contrast of, the human and the divine.

Today it is customary to look upon art and science as incompatible and to differentiate between artists and scientists on the basis of temperament. Their broader cultural and disciplinary unity is ignored. In fifteenth-century Italy, however, many artists contributed to the study of natural science; development of mathematical perspective, for instance, was carried out by artists. Moreover, the study of human anatomy by artists was in advance of that taught in the medical schools from inaccurate textbooks. Beginning probably with Castagno, and assuredly by the time of Pollaiuolo, artists undertook actual dissection of the human body in order to study the relation of its structure to its functioning. One of the appeals of ancient sculpture was that it provided what was thought to be accurate information concerning physiology and musculature, and furnished the artists with poses and gestures by which to increase the expressiveness and animation of their figures. Although religious personages were endowed with new and more

lifelike traits as a result of this enthusiastic scientific study, in the works of such artists as Pollaiuolo the body itself is celebrated as a model of energy, strength, and robust action.

Pollaiuolo was one of the first Italian artists to join ancient Classical form with Classical subject matter (*Hercules Crushing Antaeus*; see Fig. 426). In his *Martyrdom of St. Sebastian* (Fig. 167), fascination with the expressiveness of the same body and pose seen from multiple perspectives is clear. Forms are carefully arranged around St. Sebastian so as to overlap as little as possible. In his work the human figure completely breaks the old mold of symbolical and rhetorical gesture, and he presents the exertion of physical strength in convincing muscular action. Pollaiuolo was unable to give graceful resolution to the energies and movements of his figures, who seem overdeveloped and often static. As a sculptor, he was more successful, for in paintings he was unable to resolve the new conceptions of the body with space. He used a plateau arrangement and an elevated viewpoint for the figures that tend to flatten the foreground area. The deep landscape backdrop behind the plateau has no esthetic or dramatic ties with the foreground. The figure of St. Sebastian has a certain sentimental and soft quality, which does not permit it to dominate the scene by any means other than its elevation and centrality. In sum, Pollaiuolo's painting is impressive in its parts, but not in the whole, and for its vigorous espousal of secular values, not for a communication of exalted religious ideals.

The reasons for the lack of complete success in Pollaiuolo's *Martyrdom of St. Sebastian* and in Ghirlandaio's *Adoration of the Shepherds* (Fig. 168) lie partly in the increased complexity of secular demands which had to be synthesized with those of religion. Both paintings, particularly Ghirlandaio's, reflect the extent to which Italian art of the third quarter of the fifteenth century was filled with contradictory objectives in form and content. The *Adoration of the Shepherds* took shape from a wide variety of current public tastes. Painting a few years after the importation to Florence of van der Goes' *Adoration of the Shepherds*, Ghirlandaio drew liberally upon Flemish naturalism but not upon its symbolic meaning. By temperament and taste he could not fire his figures with the spiritual fervor that exalts the van der Goes painting. The shepherds in the Florentine paint-

Figure 167. ANTONIO POLLAIUOLO. *The Martyrdom of St. Sebastian*. 1475. Oil on panel, 9′6″ × 6′7½″. The National Gallery, London (reproduced by courtesy of the Trustees).

Figure 168. DOMENICO GHIRLANDAIO. *The Adoration of the Shepherds.* 1485.
Tempera, 5'5¾" square. Sta. Trinità, Florence.

ing seem tame in comparison with their Flemish counterparts, perhaps because they were portraits of the artist's patrons. Joseph is given a transparent theatrical gesture, and the ox and ass made innocent onlookers. The Christ Child is given more weight and ample proportions. In line with the growing interest in archaeology, the shed has been supported by pseudo-Classical piers, the manger converted to an ancient sarcophagus (symbolically not inappropriate), and a triumphal Roman arch straddles the road at the left. As a projection of Florentine social life and customs, Ghirlandaio has shown a procession winding down the hill as if coming from the city to welcome a visiting dignitary. It was known in Ghirlandaio's time that the Roman triumphal arch was the locus of ceremonies in which the ancient city honored the advent of a ruler. Like their Flemish counterparts, Ghirlandaio, Castagno, and Leonardo

Figure 169. ANDREA MANTEGNA. *St. James Led to His Execution*. c. 1455. Fresco (destroyed). Ovetari Chapel, Church of the Eremitani, Padua.

da Vinci made decorative accessories such as shields, helmets, and floats for the many pageants staged by Florentine rulers.

Florence dominated fifteenth-century Italian art, but there were important painters such as Piero della Francesca in other cities. Working in Padua, Andrea Mantegna had important contact with sculptures by Donatello in that city, and his work mingles this influence with an archaeologist's curiosity about the beauty of Roman art and its ruins and with personal researches into anatomy and psychological expression. In a fresco done at mid-century and lost during a bombing of Padua in World War II, Mantegna chose the actual viewpoint of a viewer in the chapel to depict *St. James Led to His Execution* (Fig. 169). The saint is shown pausing to bless a paralytic before Mantegna's personal and inaccurate reconstruction of a

Roman triumphal arch. This low viewpoint coupled with the strong off-center locus of the vanishing point imparts dramatic tension. Contradicting theories of the time, Mantegna brings us very close to the action, which augments our emotional involvement in the scene. As did Masaccio, Uccello, Castagno, and Piero della Francesca, Mantegna first drew his figures as nudes, so that the firmness of their bodies is revealed even through their clothing in the final fresco. He shared Donatello's interest in eccentric perspective viewpoints, and in making crowds active participants in the action. A strong undercurrent of restlessness, of potential as well as actual display of energy runs all through his work. Mantegna's characters are believable as active empire and architectural builders, soldiers and executioners, rugged saints who tramped rough terrain, unlike the contemplative population of Piero's work or the middle-class types often seen in Ghirlandaio's work.

To appreciate the changed view of nature and art that had evolved from the Middle Ages into what is referred to as the Renaissance, one need only compare the tenth-century manuscript painting of St. Valerian (Fig. 110) with Giovanni Bellini's portrayal of St. Francis, done five centuries later (Pl. 18). A holy man in approximately the same posture is common to both, but where St. Valerian turns his back, figuratively speaking, to a demonic world, St. Francis seems at first to be embracing the earth and the sky and its light. Both men were hermitic personalities, renouncing the material pleasures of the world, but the rural home of St. Francis is populated by harmless animals and a verdant private garden amid the rude rocky retreat. The gestures of both saints are symbolic. That of St. Francis indicates his miraculous reception of the Stigmata, the wounds of Christ, on his hands and feet. Unlike earlier paintings of the same subject, neither Christ nor the seraph is visible to us, and, as Millard Meiss has shown, the miracle is accomplished by means of the brilliant golden light of the sky into which the transfixed saint stares openmouthed. This same scholar argues persuasively that the event took place at night and that what at first seems in the painting to be a figure in daylight is in fact the illumination from the radiant apparition. If we are to judge by the direction of the cast shadow of the saint and orientation of his body, the source of light is relatively low and on this side of the laurel tree, which reflects and moves in the supernatural glow emanating from a source out of sight beyond the left limit of the picture. Bellini continues the theological significance of light, which goes back even earlier than the St. Valerian painter, but synthesizes it with the results of optical experience. There is a second, and this time natural, light source seen streaming through the clouds at the upper left, and it is explicable on the basis of the St. Francis literature which speaks of the nocturnal event causing an illumination comparable to the light of day.

From Flemish painting, this Venetian artist may have derived the use of some sort of oil medium that gave depth to his color and allowed overpainting. His shadows have a base layer of light blue-green which gives them volume. The meticulous reconstruction of the earth and distant cities is deceptive; while the rocky area resembles the geological formations near

the site where St. Francis received the Stigmata, Bellini has synthesized many observations from nature and, like van Eyck, has used the actual to create an imaginary place that nonetheless belongs on earth. Thus Bellini affirms that by his day the earth and men belonged to each other no matter what their origin or destiny after life.

The interest of painters and sculptors in art and literature of the ancient world, which became most important in the last quarter of the fifteenth century, was to affect profoundly the pictorial synthesis of religious and secular values. A painting of 1485 by the Florentine artist Sandro Botticelli, *The Birth of Venus* (Fig. 170), celebrates the nude pagan goddess on a large scale for the first time since Roman antiquity, while serving as a visual sermon for a fourteen-year-old boy, Lorenzo de' Medici, whose upbringing was in the hands of the most brilliant Humanist philosophers in Europe. The reconciliation of nudity and pre-Christian philosophy and art with Christianity was restricted to a small group of artists, scholars,

Figure 170.   SANDRO BOTTICELLI. *The Birth of Venus.* c. 1480. Oil on canvas, 6′7″ × 9′2″. Uffizi, Florence.

writers, and aristocratic patrons such as the Medici family. According to Marsilio Ficino, the most brilliant philosopher of the time, truth and beauty knew no distinction between pagan and Christian expression; both pagan literature and the Bible were revelations of the truth, of the same principles. The chaste beauty of Botticelli's Venus was inspired by the view that she symbolized not lust or sensual pleasure but pure intelligence or the highest attainments of the mind. Her role in the education of the young Lorenzo de' Medici was to inspire him to search for the true reality behind appearances and discover the world's hidden harmony.

The figure of Venus was patterned after a specific ancient Greek sculpture owned by the Medici, while the painting's format with its attendant figure on the shore derived from previous Christian paintings of St. John baptizing Christ. The Humanists drew analogies between the miraculous birth of Venus and Christ, between her emergence from the sea and Christ's rebirth by rising from the water of Jordan. The painting's lesson included the birth of beauty in the human soul. The zephyrs who blow her to the shore are like angels, and the seashell was occasionally used by Renaissance painters and architects as a symbol of heaven.

Botticelli's style was admirably adapted to rendering Venus in a way that would not arouse physical desire. The delicacy of his drawing and tinting of colors imparts sophisticated grace and strong pleasure to the eye and mind. Drawing was the basis of the work and deemed at the time the most appropriate for the education of the intelligence; whereas strong color was thought of as stirring base emotions. (This prejudice was to have a long history, extending into nineteenth-century art.) Botticelli was an artist ideally suited to the aristocratic intellectual tastes of his courtly patrons, but he himself underwent a deep spiritual crisis and reversion to mystical Christianity toward the end of his life, upsetting the pagan-Christian synthesis announced in this famous painting and forecasting a similar and broader cultural change at the beginning of the next century.

Though known as a man with universal interests, Leonardo da Vinci did not share Botticelli's interests in antiquity, philosophy, and literature—in short, the Humanism of his time. The direct experiences of eye and hand, which painting and drawing served best,

and the active use of the mind in their support were what Leonardo believed in; and this explains his unprecedented empirical studies from nature accompanied by innumerable drawings and voluminous notebooks. Leonardo's modernity resides in his refusal to take untested assumptions as the basis for his art. Unlike many artists before him, his dedication to representing the visual world was not exclusively in the service of religion. (The purpose of art in the Middle Ages was to illustrate the Bible, thereby increasing its understanding, and to enhance the churches.) Leonardo's few paintings deal mostly with religious subjects, but this is not the case with his drawings. On the basis of the paintings, one would surmise that Leonardo believed that through knowledge and imagination one should interpret noble themes, but with his drawings the compass of art takes in the entire earthly world for the enjoyment of the eyes. His unfinished painting of the *Adoration of the Magi* (Fig. 171) serves as an excellent example not only of his interests but also of his frequent inability to conclude his ambitious projects. The setting depends upon his observations of what might be called natural science, specifically studies of trees and geology. Fascination with geometry led him to introduce at the rear left a perspective rendering of a ruined structure that may relate to the fall of the old religious order. Lifelong interest in equestrian subjects and an inclination toward violent aggressiveness account for the combat of mounted figures in the upper right. The foreground drama was the occasion for demonstrating his experience with psychology and the expressive capacities of the entire body. Against the reverent actions of the Magi, he contrasts the manifold and strong reactions of the onlookers, thereby giving full play to his researches into different age groups regarding facial types, gestures, and the drama of bodies in movement and inspiring future artists to broaden the psychological base of painting. The incomplete state of the painting shows its method of construction from first drawing and then filling in with dark colors and moving toward lighter tones, which had not been put in. Dark backgrounds often create the lighter shapes, such as some of the heads in the center group, and this was one of many devices by which he brought to painting new tonalities and more varied moods evoked by

Figure 171. LEONARDO DA VINCI. *The Adoration of the Magi.* 1480–82.
Oil on wood, 8'7⅞" × 7'11⅝". Uffizi, Florence.

light. His light is never brilliant, but favors
that of late afternoon, thereby muting differences among the forms it illuminates. In the
Adoration, Leonardo makes tangible the elusive
existence of light amid darkness.

Leonardo purposely did not employ a single
perspective system for this painting, as he was
later to do in his *Last Supper*, but used different
perspectives for different areas, giving the whole
painting a synthetic quality. Rather than first
clearly establishing a measurable space for the

foreground figures, as Piero would have done,
he sketched their movements and volumes;
and they create their own spatial environment,
which differs from the more measurable grid-
like area at the upper left. The formal arrangement of the centralized Virgin and flanking
Magi was like many of Leonardo's ideas subsequently frozen into artistic dogma.

Leonardo's finished paintings do not give as
strong an indication of his imagination as his
sketches often do. One of the studies for the

Figure 172. LEONARDO DA VINCI. *Study for the Adoration of the Magi.* c. 1481.
Pen drawing, bistre and wash, 8¼ × 5⅞″. Uffizi, Florence.

Adoration of the Magi (Fig. 172) shows how he overlaid the perspective grid, used by artists since Brunelleschi, with rough notations of scrambling and tangled figure groups, horses bucking their naked riders, a recumbent camel, and phantomlike figures moving in the ruined palace or seated in the joists of the shedlike roof. No aspect of the story of the Magi or symbolism explains this fantasy. Man and beast move impetuously within the rational framework of space and architecture. So rich and abundant were Leonardo's ideas for the painting that seemingly he did not have the power or perhaps the time after seven months of effort to weld them together into a finished cohesive work. He had incurred difficult problems for himself by the large dark area about the Virgin (how might she have been painted finally to stand out from her surroundings), created many detached gestures and heads, established frequent scale jumps, or discrepancies and background motifs disparate from the foreground. Yet for later artists such as Raphael, the unfinished work was rich in influential ideas. History shows that many times finished paintings lose the freshness and intimacy of preliminary drawings, and Leonardo's unfinished work is all the more valuable in its frank disclosure of the powerful working of his mind and hand.

To the argument over whether men make the times or the times make men, one can point to Leonardo and the other leading artists of the fifteenth century as examples of the interaction of the two. Artists benefited from the civic pride, energy, and enthusiasm for art found in Florence; and, in turn, from art men and women gained greater understanding of their own humanity. The most lasting and creative contributions of the Italian Renaissance were not social, political, or religious, but artistic. The art that grew out of and away from the Middle Ages was influenced by the rise of science and the worldly interest of Italian tyrants and vigorous merchants who patronized their work. Leonardo stands, on the one hand, for the artist who by means of art achieves greater self-realization and intellectual freedom than his medieval and ancient predecessors, but who also served despots and enemies of Florence, for as he said, "I serve the one who pays me." Political and social freedom historically have not been the prerequisites of great art. The history of internal freedom embodied in Leonardo's thinking and inquiry is older than political and social liberty.

SUMMARY

In both Flanders and Italy of the fifteenth century, art was given an earthly stage, human scale, and natural location. Truthfulness to the visual world was the desire of Northern and Southern artists. Both achieved perspective whereby the three-dimensional world was convincingly transposed through a series of corresponding points onto a two-dimensional surface. Art was confirmed as an important means to enrich earthly life. The synthesis of the heavenly and earthly was changing and unstable, and the values of the latter were gathering into a strong ground swell at century's end. Art still guided men to the meaning of true spirituality, but also corroborated their celebration of the secular beauty and pleasures of the mortal environment. The self-confident societies of Bruges, Ghent, Antwerp, and Florence had produced artists obviously aware of their own talent, importance, and ambitions; and society's recognition of and respect for artistic genius, familiar to us today, had its foundations established.

When we turn to the differences between Flemish and Italian art, it is apparent that science and ancient art had a stronger influence in the south. The Northern painters achieved verisimilitude to continuous three-dimensional space without recourse to theories or systems and the geometry so prized by the Italians. Medieval art, which had a more lasting interest and influence in the north, came to be viewed as barbaric in the south—which gave the word "Gothic" unpleasant connotations. Geographically, historically, ethnically, ancient Roman art seemed right for emulation to Italian artists.

Beginning with Giotto and continuing through Piero della Francesca, Italian style was characterized by a compact and immediately perceivable unity through the large fluid continuity of the sculpturesque figures who dominated their environment. The ideal composition resulted from the smooth interdependent functioning of figures and environment—the easy flow of statuesque figures in metrical space. Flemish style was characterized by a less mobile, if not static, complex additive ordering of the microscopic through the telescopic, in which the setting often rivaled the human being in importance. The Italians delighted in the relation of large, distinct, and more sensual figures set against one another and in credible space. Their color was important to shaping volume. It clung to the curving surfaces and was not intended to belie its distance from the viewer. The Northern artists favored dense groupings of contrasting rich tones of color and light, and intricate linkages of the edges of shapes lying at varying depths from each other. The brilliance of their color would at times make it hover in space and not hold to the actual depth of the plane it was painted on. The Flemings valued all that was given to the senses as a sign of divine meaning, and they searched for individuality in nature. Their criterion of realistic painting was largely a quantitative one of measuring and matching the subject against the painting. With the aid of geometry, Italian artists sought what they thought were the abstract principles behind the appearance of nature, the truly harmonious and beautiful form. Flemish art arrived at convincing spatial illusion through the trial and error of observation; their space, though additive, is still expressive. The Italians first developed it empirically and then through theory and preferred the over-all lucid appearance of measured order. The Italians favored the good and pleasing appearance of the human form, with supple coordination between mind and body. The Flemish accepted the unathletic yet natural movement that often accompanies profound inner feeling.

Later, in the sixteenth century, Michelangelo illuminated the differences between the art of the two areas and revealed his own prejudices:

> Flemish painting will, generally speaking, please the devout better than any painting in Italy, which will never cause him to shed a tear, whereas that of Flanders will cause him to shed many, and that not through the vigor and goodness of the painting but owing to the goodness of the devout person.... In Flanders they paint with a view to external exactness of such things as may cheer you and of which you cannot speak ill, as for example saints and prophets. They paint stuffs and masonry, the green grass of the fields, the shadows of the trees, and rivers and bridges which they call landscape, with many figures on this side and many on that. And all this... is done without reason or art, without symmetry or proportion, without skillful choice or boldness, and finally without substance and vigor.

8

MICHELANGELO

Michelangelo Buonarroti was born in the Tuscan town of Caprese in 1475; he died in Rome in 1564, and then lay in state and was interred in Florence. At the end of the 1480s, he studied painting for a year in Florence with the brothers Domenico and Davide Ghirlandaio. He then studied sculpture with Bertoldo di Giovanni, a former pupil of Donatello, who taught in the midst of the magnificent ancient sculpture in the garden of Lorenzo de' Medici in Florence. Michelangelo's youthful work attracted the eye of Duke Lorenzo, who invited the young artist to join his household. There Michelangelo was introduced to the most brilliant group of intellectuals in Europe, and their acquaintance had a deep influence upon Michelangelo's attitude toward ancient sculpture and the intellectual purpose of art. He did not continue to see himself as a conventional craftsman. During these years in Florence, Michelangelo made drawings of the work of Giotto and Masaccio as well as of Roman and Greek sculpture; in 1492 he did dissections of corpses for anatomical study.

In 1494, just before the house of Medici fell from power, Michelangelo made the first of several flights in search of the security and tranquillity he needed for his work, but was never to find. After a short stay in Venice and more than a year in Bologna, he was able to return to Florence briefly and then, in 1496, went on to Rome, where he carved his first *Pietà* (that in St. Peter's). He next returned to Florence for four years, beginning in 1501, to work on several civic commissions, including the *David*. In 1505 Michelangelo was called to Rome by Pope Julius II, one of the first great and troublesome sponsors of Michelangelo's art. It was the sculptor's fate to be frustrated and harassed by powerful patrons who encouraged grandiose schemes and then capriciously diverted the artist from completing them. From 1508 to 1512, somewhat reluctantly, Michelangelo painted the Sistine ceiling, turning intermittently to his enormous (and preferred) project for the Pope's sepulcher, of which only the *Moses* and the series of *Bound Slaves* ultimately saw realization (1513–1516). Between 1518 and 1534, Michelangelo divided his time between Rome and Florence, and also between sculpture and architecture. For Pope Leo X, he worked on the Medici Chapel in Florence. In 1529 he served as a military engineer on the Florentine fortifications.

From 1534 until his death, Michelangelo lived in Rome, painting the *Last Judgment* (1536–1541) and the frescoes of the Pauline Chapel (1542–1550). In 1546 he became chief architect for the rebuilding of St. Peter's, a project that was to excite his remaining thought and energy. During the 1530s and 1540s he wrote many religious sonnets, dedicated to his friend Vittoria Colonna, who deeply influenced his spiritual direction. Busied with a number of architectural projects, such as the redesigning of the Capitoline Hill in Rome, in the last years of his life Michelangelo did only two uncompleted sculptures, both on the theme of Christ's death.

The history of art includes many examples of artists who brought major talents to bear upon minor subjects. Vermeer and Matisse come quickly to mind as examples of men whose greatness lay in the *way* they interpreted the commonplace, giving to it the quality of the uncommon. Michelangelo brought great art to great ideas. He was the most technically gifted artist as well as one of the great intellects of his time and place. In itself, the fact that his surroundings were Florence and Rome and that his time was the Italian Renaissance should give some idea of Michelangelo's measure. The artist was obsessed with the infinite nature and mystery of God and his creation Man. Never did Michelangelo show an interest in rendering the details of objects or landscape; his was a man- and God-centered art. Nor did he paint and carve in terms of specific living men: his aim was to depict the universal fate of humanity, and so far as is known, he made only one pencil sketch of a contemporary. Unwilling to be bound to an earthly material model, he felt impelled to work from divine inspiration in order to spiritualize his experience of reality and to achieve eternal and transcendent truth.

It would be futile, within the limits of this chapter, to attempt a full history and discussion of Michelangelo. Instead, a few examples that represent seminal ideas and lend an awareness of the scope and depth of their maker's art will be discussed.

EARLY SCULPTURES

Begun when Michelangelo was twenty-six, the *David* (Fig. 173) was carved between 1501 and 1504 in behalf of the Florentine republic, partly to commemorate the completion of a new civic constitution and partly to demonstrate the city's artistic leardership and vigor. David was

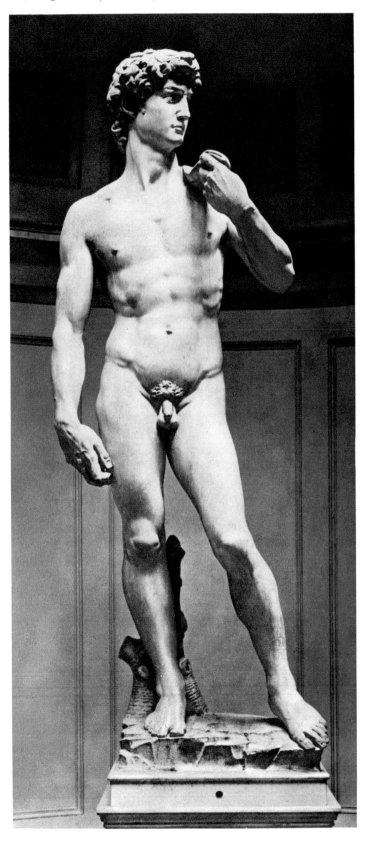

Figure 173. MICHELANGELO. *David*. 1501–04. Marble, height 18′ (incl. base). Accademia, Florence.

famous not only as the slayer of Goliath but also as a ruler, and his association with justice made him an appropriate figure to celebrate governmental reform. A decision of a committee resulted in placing the 18-foot statue before the Palazzo Vecchio, the city hall, where it quickly became an emblem of civic freedom and the virtue of its defense. In the finely muscled, alert, and somber youth, the citizens could see an embodiment of what they felt were their own virtues. Michelangelo may have shared these ideals, but he also wanted the *David* to affirm his reputation as the greatest living sculptor. In his contracts of the time, Michelangelo specified that his sculpture would be of unsurpassed beauty. Not only did he demonstrate to the satisfaction of all his knowledge of ancient Greek art and the science of anatomy, but he also gave form to a deeply personal vision of a hero. In Michelangelo's view, only a handful of men in the history of the human race qualified as heroes. These were primarily Old Testament prophets or rulers who perfectly embodied a combination of the active and the contemplative life. In his youth, when the *David* was created, Michelangelo equated truth with beauty, and to *David* he gave the body of a Greek Apollo, but not that god's temperamental equanimity. By the time of the *David*, the nude form in art had been largely divested of its medieval sinful associations, partly because of the acceptance of ancient art and thought as compatible with Christianity. Michelangelo believed that the nude male body was divine and that its ideal rendition in art would approximate the prototype conceived by God. He wrote: "And who is so barbarous as not to understand that the foot of a man is nobler than his shoe, and his skin nobler than that of the sheep with which it is clothed."

The quality of repose suggested by a front view of the youth's stance is not sustained, for there is a faint suggestion of tension in the torso muscles, which becomes more obvious in the neck and quite vehement in the angry visage. This climactic psychological element and the contrast in the states of mind and body are alien to Greek Classical ideals. There is also a decided asymmetry in the disposition of the right and left sides of the body; the figure's right side is protected by the downward-hanging arm holding the stone, whereas the upraised left arm makes that side more open and vulnerable.

Significantly, David looks to his left. From the Middle Ages there had been a tradition which associated divine protection with the right and the origin of evil with the left. It has been suggested that David is "frowning" at the sight of Goliath, assuredly the symbol of evil. Still, it would be a mistake to conceive of this work as illustrating a specific event or moment. David is, above all, a symbol of force and righteous anger, and the stone and sling signify the need for alert and courageous defense of principle. Like the pose of the *Colossus of Barletta* (Fig. 265), a late-antique imperial statue, the militant and defiant attitude of David is a warning to enemies of the good and a comfort to those he protects. The angry concentration expressed in the features may also reflect displeasure with human weakness. Michelangelo was a Christian sculptor who could satisfy his religious belief with the idea of a Hebraic hero in the body of a Greek god.

Michelangelo considered David his alterego, and he once wrote, "David with the sling, I with the bow, Michelangelo" (the bow referring to his sculptor's drill, which like the sling was his attribute and means of serving God). After the *David*, Michelangelo was asked to do statues of the Twelve Apostles, but only the unfinished *St. Matthew* was actually undertaken (Fig. 174). Unconstrained as he had been for the *David* by the thin block he inherited, which dictated the relatively flat frontal pose, Michelangelo devised for the *St. Matthew* a posture that is a tense counteraction of twisting and frontal movements. In the grip of some powerful vision that forces his head to the side, the Apostle is unmindful of his body, which in an unclassical way reacts by instinct. The strong compactness of limbs, with as little space as possible between the torso and arms, was a self-imposed restriction of the artist, who may have felt that it gave the most concentrated expression of the subject. His figure of Matthew violently twists about an imaginary vertical axis but is, in turn, inhibited by the limits of the block, which like mortal flesh is a form of confinement. The squarish shape and thick proportions of the figure, which to some degree also relate to the original block, show Michelangelo's resistance to accepted norms of the past.

The incomplete state of sculptures such as this has led to mystical, somewhat romanticized

Figure 174. MICHELANGELO. *St. Matthew* (unfinished). 1504–06. Marble, height 8'11". Accademia, Florence.

marks and vestiges of the original block make the *St. Matthew* a fine illustration for some of the artist's views on sculpture, expressed years later. Michelangelo saw his destiny in the chisel and stone. Sometime between 1536 and 1547 he wrote, "The greatest artist has no conception that a single block of marble does not potentially contain within its mass, but only a hand obedient to the mind can penetrate to this image." Elsewhere, Michelangelo defined the art of sculpture as "the taking off that puts into the rough hard stone a living figure grown most great just as the stone had grown most small." This bringing forth of life from base matter was a spiritual act for Michelangelo, one in sympathy with God's creation of life. He once referred to God as the "Divine Hammer." Great art, he believed, depended upon the artist's possessing first within himself a perfect God-given conception (the Platonic Idea), whose "first-born" was a simple clay model. The second realization of the Idea was in the "rugged living stone" and possessed "such beauty that none may confine its spirit."

No artist before Michelangelo possessed such complete mastery of the human body and exceptional ability to render its richness as a material organism as well as its emotional, spiritual, and intellectual range. Possessing natural gifts as a craftsman and observer of his subject, Michelangelo was also a great student of the art of other artists and eras. The sculpture of ancient Greece and Rome and that of his own century, all provided ideas and forms that were to be welded to his personal style. The greatest master for Michelangelo, his greatest influence as attested by the sculptor's own words, was God, the Creator. For the Greeks and certain Renaissance sculptors, beauty was achievable through fixed proportion of mathematical measure, but for Michelangelo proportion was a qualitative, not a quantitative, value. Proportion meant, for him, the extent to which his image corresponded to the "Idea" inherent in it. Furthermore, the physical beauty of his figures was not an end in itself; it was intended as a reflection of a spiritual beauty and was meant to elevate the thoughts of the beholder above material things. True beauty could not be obtained by merely copying the visible world. Michelangelo's art proceeds from the mind, through which he believed he could more truly comprehend the perfect form.

interpretations about the artist's intending to show the birth of the soul, his discontinuing once the essential idea had taken form, or his desire to reveal the material source and end of all life. It is a fact that Michelangelo enjoyed work on difficult unfinished problems; in the case of this Apostle figure, as was often to happen thereafter, demands for the sculptor's talents in Rome forced him to stop his work on it. The raw traces of tool

Michelangelo   149

Left: Figure 175. MICHELANGELO. *Moses.* 1513–16. Marble, height 8'4". S. Pietro in Vincoli, Rome.

Below: Figure 176. MICHELANGELO. *Moses,* plaster cast, seen from below and 30 degrees to the right.

Michelangelo despised Raphael's optimistic judgment of the ability of his contemporaries, such as Castiglione, to achieve grace. The sculptor felt that Raphael had a naïve and mistaken faith in simple formulas of human conduct as a means of achieving true earthly happiness and excellence. The differences between their respective attitudes can be seen in Rapahael's portrait of Baldassare Castiglione (Fig. 401; see Chapter 17) and Michelangelo's *Moses* (Fig. 175), intended for the uncompleted tomb of Julius II. To Michelangelo, Moses was a moral and physical giant, a man whose imposing physical frame was the instrument of heroic physical and spiritual acts—the leadership of his people in the Exodus. The enormous, vital head of Moses is the locus of divine visions, the fountainhead of law.

The interpretation of the *Moses* depends, literally, upon one's point of view. Until recently, although it was known that the figure was intended to be seen from below in its

place on the proposed papal tomb, all interpretations of his pose and facial expression were made on the basis of the statue's being viewed or photographed at eye level (Fig. 175). Confronting the work from this direction, scholars (including this author) tended to write of how this portrayal of Moses exemplified righteous anger or seemed as if seized by an ecstatic vision. The art historian Earl Rosenthal had the sensible idea of photographing a plaster version of the *Moses* as it was intended to be seen, raised 9 feet above the ground (Fig. 176), thereby altering our view of the prophet both literally and figuratively. The figure was carved on its side to permit the sculptor to study it from the proper angle. The intended view from below modifies the scale of what otherwise seems the disproportionately large head and beard, and it enhances the figure's composed strength. Moses appears to be gazing upward in a manner appropriate to the wise and contemplative leader of the Jews. (The Jews of Rome were particularly pleased with this sculpture, despite the fact that their religion prohibited them from having graven images of their own.) Also, barely visible from below are the hornlike forms that derive from the apocryphal tradition which had beams of light spring from Moses' forehead at the moment of his vision of the Lord. From any angle, nonetheless, the body of the seated prophet is endowed with tremendous vitality and majesty. The *Moses* helps us to understand why Michelangelo's contemporaries found in his style qualities that inspired religious awe and fear.

The spiritual antithesis of the *Moses* is Michelangelo's misnamed *Dying Slave*, or *Bound Slave* (Fig. 177). This figure, too, was intended for the tomb of Pope Julius II. Although based upon a late Greek sculpture of one of Niobe's dead children, the figure is neither a political slave nor a dying man. His real prison is the body itself, which incarcerates the spirit. If he were dying, the figure might better express a sense of joy, for his death would mean that his spirit was about to rejoin God. Backing the figure is a half-finished ape, an animal that to an educated viewer of the time would have signified the dominance of lust or the passions over reason. The human dilemma celebrated by Michelangelo is the mortal life of torment away from the Creator. The anguished fate of man is to have joined in himself a temporal body and an immortal soul, as expressed by the contemporary philosopher Marsilio Ficino, whose ideas often paralleled those of Michelangelo:

> Our mind, as long as our sublime soul is doomed to operate in a base body, is thrown up and down with permanent disquietude, and it often slumbers from exhaustion and is always insane; so that our movements, actions, and passions are nothing but the vertigos of ailing people, the dream of sleepers, and ravings of madmen.

This sculpture puts into tangible form ideas that Michelangelo was later to express in his poetry. Between 1547 and 1550, he wrote in a private

Figure 177. MICHELANGELO. *Bound Slave*, intended for the Tomb of Julius II. 1514–16. Marble, height 7'6½". Louvre, Paris.

lament to God: "For Thou not only gavest to time my divine soul, but didst imprison it in this frail body and weary flesh and must hand it over to its cruel destiny. How can I escape living thus. Without Thee."

To convey an interior state of mind, a pathetic restlessness of the soul, Michelangelo drew upon Greek principles of expressive body posturing. These principles involve avoiding the coincidence in the same plane of parts of the body having a common joint or axis. That is, joints of ankles, knees, hips, and arms must not be parallel; or if the left knee is forward, for instance, the left shoulder should be back and the right shoulder advanced. Thus, forward and backward movements are balanced in criss-cross fashion. As the eye moves upward from the feet of the slave, each direction taken by the body is countered by another immediately above, so that the whole composition is a self-adjusting mechanism in a soft, serpentine formation.

THE MEANING OF MUSCULARITY

During and after his time many artists selectively took figure types, postures, and muscular emphasis from Michelangelo's art without comprehending how rooted all these properties were in an essential life attitude. Today it is even harder for us to understand the conceptualizing that went into Michelangelo's recreation of the human body from art and life. More than painting, Michelangelo looked upon sculpture, with its sensual physical character, its mass and displacement of space, as the ideal medium through which he, as a creator second only to God, could surpass nature in composing the human body. (God was praised as a sculptor, not as a painter!) The unnatural character of his bodies derives from their being what they should be to do what he wanted them to do. Michelangelo is one of the great dramatists of the human body, whose work makes the viewer sense the full movement and force of skeleton and muscle beneath a taut leathery skin. He greatly enriched the figure's expressive repertory, yet while containing its gestures compactly within the limits of the cubic block from which they were cut.

Not since the art of ancient Greece had there been created figures so splendidly endowed to perform overwhelming physical feats. Still, this was not Michelangelo's drama. The true strength of his figures either is in their latent tension or is turned against itself. With few exceptions, his muscular figures do not use physical force against external obstacles, nor are they shown in energetic postures of work, love, war, or play. On the one hand, super-

human muscularity is for Michelangelo a prerequisite of God-like beauty, the mortal vestment of his Biblical heroes; on the other, it is fit measure for the momentous personal struggles they engage in. In this sense, his message is that great physical strength is futile against the will of God. From fragments of ancient Greek torsos he had derived the method of using muscular tension as a means of directing the beholder's thoughts to the figure's internal crises of spiritual disorder, the conflict of soul and flesh, and toward exalted moments of the spirit. No living model could serve him, nor could the instinctive or practiced gestures men make in their daily lives. Michelangelo's genius lay in making the unnatural seem natural in his art. He even invented gestures for death, such as the contorted dangling arm of the dead Christ.

THE SISTINE CEILING

In his painting of the Sistine Chapel ceiling (Fig. 178), Michelangelo executed a humanistic-religious program of all but unparalleled magnitude. The commission for the ceiling painting by Pope Julius II was accepted reluctantly by Michelangelo, who longed to devote his energies to sculpture rather than painting (particularly to the grandiose tomb project). For four years, between 1508 and 1512, Michelangelo lay on his back, covering more than seven hundred square yards of ceiling with the outpourings of a fired imagination. The strain of working while standing or lying prone on the scaffolding, under the dripping plaster, wrecked his health. At the end of his project, he wrote a poem describing his condition (*I'ho già fatto un gozzo...*) *:

I've grown a goiter by dwelling in this den—
As cats from stagnant streams in Lombardy,
Or in what other land they hap to be—
Which drives the belly close beneath the chin;
My beard turns up to heaven; my nape falls in,
Fixed on my spine; my breastbone visibly
Grows like a harp; a rich embroidery
Bedews my face from brush-drops thick and
    thin,

* *The Sonnets of Michael Angelo Buonarroti*, trans. John Addington Symonds, Crown Publishers, Inc., New York, 1948.

My loins into my paunch like levers grind;
My buttock like a crupper bears my weight;
My feet unguided wander to and fro;
In front my skin grows loose and long; behind
By bending it becomes more taut and strait;
Crosswise I strain me like a Syrian bow....

Despite his plaints and protestations, it seems likely that Michelangelo viewed this painful task as a kind of penance, in which the ardor of his creative labors was expiation for sinful guilt.

The thematic program of the Sistine Chapel ceiling is an amazing fusion of Hebrew and Christian theology with contemporary Neo-platonic ideas. In all likelihood, Michelangelo had papal assistance in formulating the extensive program; and although the Pope gave him license thereafter to do as he pleased, the project undoubtedly satisfied the spiritual and political wishes of the patron. At the time that the ceiling was being painted, the papacy was waging war against foreign troops and heretics within the faith itself. The decoration of the Sistine ceiling was touched by these contemporary events, and by means of complicated theological metaphors, the Pope had Michelangelo assert the Primate's confidence in his ultimate triumph over his enemies.

The subject of the ceiling is ostensibly that of the Old Testament God who created the world and punished man for denying his Lord. In the triangular spandrels are depicted such precursors of Christ as David, who is shown killing Goliath, and Judith, who has beheaded Holofernes. Flanking the central rectangles containing scenes from Genesis are the Sibyls and Prophets. The agitated nude figures holding garlands and large golden Eucharistic wafers are human souls, or acolytes. The secondary motives of the ceiling were to assert the theolog-ical ancestry of the Pope and to imply that he was a new messiah acting as the earthly agent of God to punish the heretics. (The Pope's family name means in English "oak tree," and there are references in the ceiling to oaks.) The spandrels depict the deliverance of the chosen people, perhaps as a prophecy of the actions of Julius II.

The principal scenes on the ceiling are depicted in rectangular frames. Their order does not follow strictly the chronology of Genesis. Above the head of the visitor upon entering the chapel are the Revilement of Noah, the Flood, the Sacrifice of Noah, and the Fall of Man. The common theme of all these episodes is God's punishment of man by means of the elements—earth, water, fire, and air. They illustrate how God chastises a world that betrays him, as well as the rejection of Christ through false offerings and the partaking of the forbidden fruit.

The fulcrum panel of the ceiling, originally situated directly above the partition that divided the chapel in half, is the scene of God's creation of Eve from the side of Adam. Eve at this time symbolized the Church; thus, in the ceiling's sequence, the Church stands as the mediator between man and God, furnishing the means of man's redemption. The second half of the ceiling is over the sacred section of the chapel, the altar. The over-all theme of the remaining four subjects (the Creation of Adam, the Separation of the Waters from the Earth, the Creation of the Sun, Moon, and Planets, and the Separation of Light from Darkness) is the creative power of the Divinity.

As in Michelangelo's earlier work, the figures are preterhuman in size and action. God is the Old Testament divinity who roars out of a whirlwind and speaks with a voice of thunder. (His visage, as seen in the Creation of

Figure 178. MICHELANGELO. Ceiling of the Sistine Chapel. 1508–12. Fresco, 45′ × 128′. The Vatican, Rome.

Adam, was strikingly similar to the bearded profile of Julius II.) The purpose of the program was to strike fear and awe into the minds of the mortals who looked upon it—awe of the Creator and the Church, and of God's earthly representatives.

The Sistine ceiling is a marvel of skill and endurance; yet the power of Michelangelo's art transcends mere virtuoso effects. There is a philosophical justification for all aspects of his style. He put his knowledge of the forms and the workings of the body into the service of spiritualizing human anguish and exaltation. The agitated, athletic figures of the Sibyls and Prophets mirror the profundity and excitement of visions inaccessible to ordinary mortals. In the scene of the Creation of Adam (Fig. 179), Michelangelo infused Adam's form with the mingled response of a body awakening with reluctance at the separation of the spirit from its Creator. Adam is not joyful at his emergence into an earthly existence; the languid attitude of his arms and torso reveals his melancholy state, and the face has an expression of ineffable longing. With great significance, Michelangelo stressed the hands of Adam and God and the slight interval between them, which represented the measureless gulf that now separated man and his Creator. Attention is drawn repeatedly to the contrasts and similarities between the bodies of Adam and God, fittingly reflecting a poem of the sculptor, possibly written during the years of work on the Sistine ceiling: "He who made the whole made every part; then from the whole chose the most beautiful, to reveal on earth, as he has done here and now in His own sublime perfections. The human figure is the particular form in which beauty is most clearly manifested."

Little indication can be given in this brief space of the intellectual wealth Michelangelo brought to the program of his ceiling. Scholars such as De Tolnay and Hartt have, in impressive and often conflicting studies, sought to unravel the many levels of meaning and alternative interpretations of its content. That such searching endeavors are appropriate to a full understanding and appreciation of Michelangelo's art is borne out in the sculptor's own views on painting:

> At its best nothing is more noble or devout, since with discreet persons nothing so calls forth and fosters devotion as the difficulty of a perfection which is based upon union with God. For good painting is nothing but a copy of the perfections of God and a recollection of His painting; it is a music and a melody which only intellect can understand, and that with great difficulty. And that is why painting of this kind is so rare that no man attains it.

THE MEDICI CHAPEL

Like the Sistine ceiling, the Medici Chapel in S. Lorenzo, Florence, on which Michelangelo worked at various times from 1520 to 1534, has been seen by some scholars not only as an artistic interpretation of a Humanistic program but also as a monumental attempt at propaganda (Fig. 180). The official purpose of the designs was commemorative, the creation of a sepulchral chapel to house the bodies of Lorenzo and Giuliano de' Medici, descendants of the fifteenth-century dukes of the same name. The date of the chapel's commencement is an important one, since it coincided with a decline

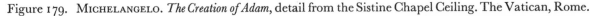

Figure 179. MICHELANGELO. *The Creation of Adam*, detail from the Sistine Chapel Ceiling. The Vatican, Rome.

Figure 180. MICHELANGELO. Tomb of Giuliano de' Medici. c. 1524–34. Marble, height of center figure 5'8". New Sacristy, S. Lorenzo, Florence.

in the power and aspirations of the house of Medici because of the death of two of its most important members. They, too, were to have been buried in the chapel (a plan subsequently discarded), which may have been intended as a grandiose allegory of princely and papal power, the Medici having produced several popes. It was to glorify the deceased occupants of the Chapel by using them as examples of ideal rulers and defenders of the Church.

Michelangelo did not himself assemble the sculptures as they are seen today. The four reclining figures on the two sepulchers were so placed by another sculptor. Below the figure of Duke Giuliano lie the figures of Night and Day; beneath the seated form of Lorenzo are the recumbent figures of Twilight and Dawn.

(That these sculptures signified time is conjectural, for Michelangelo wrote of them as mourning figures turned to stone.) As times of day, these images may signify the temporal life, which is one of ceaseless grief and restlessness. The suffering of the temporal life is given form in their ample, contorted torsos. On a sketch for the tomb over which are placed the Night and Day, Michelangelo wrote:

We have with our swift course brought to death Duke Giuliano, and it is just that he take revenge upon us thus: that we have slain him, he thus dead has taken the light from us and with closed eyes has fastened ours so that they may shine forth no more upon this earth. What would he have done with us while he lived?

Michelangelo   155

Figure 181. MICHELANGELO. *Lorenzo de' Medici*. c. 1524–34. Marble, height 5′10″. Tomb of Lorenzo, New Sacristy, S. Lorenzo, Florence.

The moral of this lament may be that in death the Duke had vanquished the temporal life and time, being now outside time. Michelangelo had also planned to insert a mouse on the tomb to symbolize the gnawing, destructive action of time.

The faces of the two dukes (Figs. 180, 181) show that Michelangelo did not create portrait likenesses of his subjects. He gave them instead a greatness and dignity that seemed to him a fitting commemoration for posterity. These seeming "portraits" are actually personifications of abstract ideals; moreover, Giuliano did not live up to the principles glorified in his sculptural effigy. The figure of Giuliano may have embodied the Neoplatonic ideal of the active life, one of vigorous physical administration, shown

by his open and commanding pose, the marshal's baton, and the coins in his hand, symbolizing a man who expends himself in outward actions. Lorenzo, his finger to his lips and his head partly in shadow, may have epitomized the contemplative life and saturnine disposition. In his meditative, introverted pose, he sits with his left elbow on a closed money box, which signified miserliness—in this case, perhaps, of the self.

Both lords look toward the Virgin and suckling Christ placed at the end of the chapel (Fig. 182). She is an incarnation of the Church, which took to its bosom the exiled house of Medici when formerly it had been expelled from Florence. She is also the prophetic mother who gives her breast to the Child but at the

Figure 182. MICHELANGELO. *The Medici Virgin*. c. 1524–34. Marble, height 7′5⅜″. New Sacristy, S. Lorenzo, Florence.

same time draws back with the premonition of his sacrifice. The Medici dukes are clad in Roman armor, recalling their election by the Pope as militant defenders of the Church. According to Frederick Hartt, these sculptured ducal effigies were in a sense a call to the leaders of Italy to rally to the defense of the Church in her time of need.

Standing in the Medici Chapel, the visitor has the curious impression of being an intruder. Michelangelo's architecture is scaled to the heroic sculpture, not to the human being. The light entering from high up in the ceiling falls onto cold marble surfaces. The room itself is of exaggerated height and gives the impression of a deep, well-like space, unearthly and congenial only to the sculptured effigies. In 1534 Michelangelo voluntarily exiled himself from his beloved Florence for the rest of his life. Ostensibly he was working in Rome, and sentimental considerations were involved as well; but it is known that he hated the tyrannical Medici, who had gained an absolute rule and were responsible for the destruction of the Florentine republic. Michelangelo's bust of

Figure 183. MICHELANGELO. *Brutus.* c. 1542. Marble, height 29 ½″ (without socle). Museo Nazionale, Florence.

Brutus (Fig. 183) was commissioned by another political exile from Florence, and this celebration of the slayer of Caesar is explained by the esteem in which men like the sculptor and his patron held the murderers of tyrants. Presented somewhat in the style of Roman busts, no model sat for Michelangelo's portrait of the noble Roman, and the artist alone conceived the features and expression appropriate to Brutus' character.

THE LAST JUDGMENT

Michelangelo's astonishing fresco *The Last Judgment* (Fig. 184) should be viewed as part of the program of the Sistine Chapel, only two-thirds of which was actually carried out. It was proposed that Michelangelo execute a great fresco over the chapel doorway, having as its subject the fall of the rebel angels. The *Last Judgment* fresco over the altar of the chapel was to terminate this cycle. It is said, perhaps apocryphally, that when the Pope first saw the finished fresco he fell on his knees in prayer. Michelangelo's painted vision is an awesome sight, calculated not to console the viewer with the promise of ultimate justice and mercy but to make him pause and reflect upon the adequacy and profundity of his personal faith. Michelangelo never intended his style to captivate the eye; he aspired instead to devotional images that would move those with little devotion to sincere meditation and tears, to reverence and fear. The subject presented in the dramatic fresco is the moments before the judgment. Some of the Biblical sources, according to De Tolnay, who has made one of the most thorough and satisfying analyses, were the books of Matthew (24:30–46), Revelations (1:7, 20:12), Daniel (7:13–14), John (3:19), Isaiah (13:6–9), and Ezekiel (37:1–9).

The seething masses of figures that comprise the great fresco do not fall into easily definable compartments or classifications; and in the absence of clothing or signs of rank, there is some doubt at first as to who are the angels or citizens of heaven, the damned, and the saved. Beginning with the Resurrection scene in the lower segment, directly above the altar of the chapel, the agitated and turbulent tone of the final day is established. The dead are literally wrenched from the tombs. There is a persistent element of tension, or rebellious strength, in the bodies of those to be judged and a fierce determination by the damned to resist their fate. Michelangelo sees man as an independent spirit capable of defying God and universal laws even in the last hour. Christ the Judge responds to the feeling of the moment in a militant, almost wrathful gesture, as he vigorously enacts his role as supreme arbiter. The position of his right hand recalls that of ancient statues of Zeus and Roman emperors, or of generals riding triumphantly in the hunt or in battle as depicted on old sarcophagi. With his left hand, he gently beckons the saved. There is no mitigating the sentence or the stern mood of Christ. The Virgin turns away, almost as if acknowledging her inability to sway her son. Around Christ are numerous figures of martyrs, brandishing the instruments of their martyrdom as if demanding justice. Soaring in the heavens are the

Figure 184. MICHELANGELO. *The Last Judgment.* 1536–41. Fresco, 48′ × 44′. The Sistine Chapel, the Vatican, Rome.

wingless angels who transport the symbols of Christ's own martyrdom, as recorded in the Book of Revelations according to St. John.

Late in the century, the Counter Reformation was to look askance at Michelangelo's daring in depicting the angels with no visible means of support, and much of the nudity of the figures was painted over. For Michelangelo, the angels and the saved rose in the heavens because of their faith, without the assistance of wings or a divine stairway. The ascent to heaven is a difficult process for the elect, and a figure being hauled up by a rosary suggests that it is prayer and intense faith which achieve the final reward. In sympathy with reformers within the Church itself who questioned the indiscriminate sale of indulgences, Michelangelo felt that ardent faith, more than good works or the intervention of celestial advocates, was responsible for man's salvation. The composition of the whole has a rotary movement of energetic figure clusters about the form of Christ. The over-all circular layout may have conveyed for Michelangelo a symbolism related to that of the rose window of the Gothic cathedral — solar or cosmic symbolism, the Wheel of Fortune, eternity, and judgment.

The damned plummet or are dragged forcibly toward the depths and Charon's bark. In the lower right corner stands Minos, the underworld judge of Dante's *Inferno* (Fig. 185). Michelangelo does not, as Dante did, depict Minos as half man and half minotaur; he is given the head and body of a man and the tail of a serpent, which winds around his body, perhaps as a sign of the depths of hell to which sinners are consigned. (The face of Minos is a portrait of a Vatican official who criticized the fresco. When he complained to the Pope, the Pontiff replied that he was powerless to redeem the official from hell.) Michelangelo indicated the area of the damned not only by its location to the left of Christ but also by the powerful downward glance of God as he peers directly into its depths. Just below Christ, and to his left, kneels St. Bartholomew, holding in his left hand the skin of a man whose features are unmistakably those of Michelangelo (Fig. 186). The head of the saint is that of Pietro Aretino, one of Michelangelo's most severe critics. The *Last Judgment* provided an opportunity for Michelangelo to profess his own strong sense of unworthiness and guilt.

Above: Figure 185. MICHELANGELO. *Minos, Prince of Hell,* detail from *The Last Judgment.* The Sistine Chapel, the Vatican, Rome.

Below: Figure 186. MICHELANGELO. Self-Portrait (skin of St. Bartholomew), detail from *The Last Judgment.* The Sistine Chapel, the Vatican, Rome.

Michelangelo   159

Figure 187. MICHELANGELO. *The Crucifixion with the Virgin and St. John.* 1550–56. Black chalk drawing, 16¼″ × 11″. The British Museum, London.

CHRIST'S DEATH

During the last thirty years of his life, Michelangelo experienced a deep spiritual and artistic change. He grew dissatisfied with physical beauty, pagan subjects, philosophic truths, and even with art itself: "Thus I know how fraught with error was the fond imagination which made art my idol and my king." Art now seemed vain to him, and it distracted his thoughts from contemplation of God. His last drawings and sculptures were all of the same theme, the dead Christ. The reason for this concentration lay in Michelangelo's belief that faith and salvation were dependent upon one's attitude toward the sacrifice of Christ— that the soul's grace came only through a complete faith in the meaning of Christ's death on the Cross. "No brush, no chisel will quiet the soul once it is turned to the divine love of Him who upon the cross, outstretches His arms to take us to Himself."

In perhaps his last drawing, he showed Christ on the Cross (Fig. 187), flanked by the mourning figures of Mary and St. John. The encompassing spread of Christ's arms is emphasized by the contraction of the two figures at the base of the Cross. The multiple outlines of the forms impart a tremulous appearance to the group. Many years before, Michelangelo had given up the hard, incisive sculpturesque edge in his drawings, in search of means to convey the inner life of his subjects. Light and shadow began to replace contorted musculature as the agents of pathos and of Michelangelo's spiritual sentiments. The more deeply felt the content, the more frugal became the artist's means.

The paradox of Michelangelo's late life and last sculptures is that he seemed to reject what had taken a lifetime to gain. Having mastered his craft, the old artist then submitted completely to private inspiration, with no self-consciousness about beauty or his art's appeal for others. Despising his own flesh and obsessed with the life of the spirit, whose future in heaven depended on Christ's broken body, Michelangelo began at the end of his life to search for a new art that, more directly than studies of muscle and bone, brought spiritual meaning to the surface.

Until the time of his death in 1564, Michelangelo worked intermittently on the *Rondanini Pietà* (Fig. 188), begun in 1550. Carved from what may have been an old Roman column, the vertical form of the Virgin supports the sagging body of the dead Christ, just removed from the Cross. Michelangelo apparently knocked off the original head and started another. Incomplete as the work is, the late style of the *Pietà* obviously scorned the supple, muscular, high-finish surface of the early sculpture. In its place were coarse textures and harsh junctures or angular interlocking of the limbs. Michelangelo sought to draw the beholder's attention away from surface qualities and toward a contemplation of the inner meaning of the subject. His vibrant late forms seem as if built from the inside out, affirming the importance of what the eye cannot see—the life of the soul and the Virgin's final spiritual communion with Christ. The earlier authority of gestures gave way to successive changes during the carving, as if the artist sought symbolically to fuse the two figures. As part of his conversion to a medieval mysticism, Michelangelo turned away from Renaissance achievements of depict-

Below: Figure 188. MICHELANGELO. *The Rondanini Pietà.* 1550–64. Marble, height 6'4¾". Castello Sforzesco, Milan.

Right: Figure 189. MICHELANGELO. Head of Joseph of Arimathaea, detail from *Deposition.* 1548–55. Marble, height of entire sculpture 7'5". The Cathedral, Florence.

ing a vigorous, healthy, and beautiful body in the Classical manner. It was not for lack of inspiration that Michelangelo struggled at the end. Though solemn in form and theme, Michelangelo's last work expresses the spiritual joy he felt in the meaning of his subject. Reputedly his last words to a friend were, "Remember the death of Christ." In accordance with these preoccupations, a detail from a *Deposition* carved earlier, the figure of Joseph of Arimathaea supporting the dead Christ, is thought to be a self-portrait (Fig. 189).

MICHELANGELO'S ARCHITECTURE

Michelangelo was not trained as an architect, and as was the case with his painting, he came to the designing of walls with the outlook of a figure sculptor who thought in terms of relief compositions, skeletal armatures, systems of muscles and tendons, and tautly stretched skins. When he came to design the Laurentian

Above: Figure 190. MICHELANGELO. Vestibule of the Laurentian Library. c. 1524–26 (stairway designed in 1558–59, completed by Ammanati and Vasari, 1559). Florence.

Left: Figure 191. MICHELANGELO. Vestibule of the Laurentian Library, looking into the Reading Room. c. 1524–26. Florence.

Library (Figs. 190, 191) for the Medici, he no more accepted Renaissance conventions of flat wall arrangements than he had the proportional systems of other painters and sculptors. The entrance hall of the library, like the space of the Medici Chapel, taller than it is wide, is a deep well that immediately casts us into an unfamiliar space and experience of proportions. Cascading into the relatively small room is the great tripartite stairway, its division being more for grandeur than for purposes of traffic. The effect of passivity or repose, so common in the architecture and art of his contemporaries, was anathema to Michelangelo, whether in carving his statues or molding a flight of steps. The central stair is like a current whose force is irresistible either in ascent or descent. The contrast of grey stone components and white stucco walls is one of the most dramatic in architecture. The doubling of columns in the wall niches served no structural purpose but, like his constricted figures, imparted a feeling of contained energy. (The wall's ambiguity lies in which is the container and which the contained.) The vocabulary of his design came both from ancient and fifteenth-century architecture, but Michelangelo devised his own grammar: the great wall brackets, for example, are for purely expressive purposes. Michelangelo, like no previous architect, could bring a building to life and endow it with a kind of harnessed power.

Michelangelo's architectural commissions were for major structures which shared that special quality of his elevated subjects in sculpture. For the west exterior wall of St. Peter's (Fig. 192), he used gigantic stepped pilasters that rise through two stories to support a massive hori-zontal entablature whose proportions justify those of its support. Not since the Gothic cathedrals had an architect given such expressive stress to the structural elements of a building (though at St. Peter's the whole wall actually does absorb load and stress). His strong and active articulation of walls is the equivalent of muscular interaction in his sculptured bodies. Windows were transformed by Michelangelo from neutral openings to emphatic projections whose sculptural frames push forward and to the sides as if resisting constriction by the other elements.

Michelangelo was attracted to gigantic projects in architecture as well as in his painting and sculpture. In his day the center of the world was thought to be the deteriorating Capitoline Hill, where an ancient temple of Jupiter had

Figure 192. MICHELANGELO. St. Peter's, apse from the west. 1546–64 (dome completed by Giacomo della Porta, 1590). The Vatican, Rome.

163

Figure 193. ETIENNE DUPÉRAC. Engraving of 1569 after Michelangelo's plan for the Capitoline Hill (Campidoglio), Rome. The Metropolitan Museum of Art, New York (Dick Fund, 1941).

stood and where the medieval city hall of Rome was located. The Pope approved Michelangelo's plans to redesign the crown of the hill, and the result was his great trapezoidal open square approached by a long inclined stairway (Fig. 193). At the end of the square stands the Palazzo dei Senatori, and on either side the paired Palazzi dei Conservatori. This open-air plaza was intended as the stage for important public functions, including the ceremonial reception of chiefs of state. Symbolically it was to link ancient pagan and modern Catholic Rome, and all the sculpture adorning it had been preserved from antiquity. Rather than commission a new sculpture, Pope Paul III had the statue of Marcus Aurelius brought to the square, because of the aura of imperial symbolism with which this work was vested. Michelangelo designed the oval pedestal for the image and raised it on a gentle mound, over which was laid out a large oval inlaid with a curvilinear grid dividing the area into twelve compartments. James Ackerman, in his fine study of Michelangelo's architecture, has shown that the mound

and its zodiac design relate to Roman Imperial shields and that the curving lines emanating from the statue's base derive from the ancient symbols of sun rays which radiated from Imperial armored portraits.

To the façades of the Palazzi dei Conservatori (Fig. 194), Michelangelo brought new architectural associations and symbols of authority. In these flanking palaces he joined one-story columns with colossal piers, and the powerful vertical thrusts and continuity of these members balanced the horizontal elements of the low rectangular façade. More than in St. Peter's, in these palaces Michelangelo fuses the organization of wall surfaces and the functions of load and support so that, as in his human figures, a sense of drama comes from the powerful countermovements and a constant adjusting of opposing forces. The device of the pyramidal double stairway before the Palazzo dei Senatori, used here for the first time in palace design, served at the same time to frame like a pediment the sculptures of the reclining river gods and the goddess Roma, to permit access to the main floor (the ground floor was a prison and so marked by heavier masonry), and to provide an elevated platform for the appearance of nobility. Stairways, plazas, and framed vistas all excited Michelangelo because they demanded movement by the viewer rather than his passive inspection, as in earlier Renaissance architecture. The patterned oval pavement and central statue force one to circulate about the plaza. Unlike a simple square plan, the trapezoid encouraged a funneling action toward the central palace, or it directed one's view from atop the Campidoglio stairway across Rome and straight toward the new St. Peter's on which Michelangelo himself was working, planning the great dome he did not live to see built. Thus the two great monuments to Church and state in Rome took significant shape under his hands, and in the process he brought the sculpture and architecture of antiquity into the service of a new and noble art for his own time.

The most gifted artist of his age, Michelangelo was also the most tormented. The image his writings give are of a man subject to depression, a man who thought he was mad and sinful. He could be timid, vengeful, and mistrustful of those about him, often with good cause. With all his endless fascination for the mysteries of creation, redemption, and salvation, he was strongly conscious of human frailty and fallibility. In short, Michelangelo's affliction was to possess magnificent visions that he felt achieved only a pale and inadequate expression in his art: his fate lay in a quest to grasp the infinite while well knowing his own finite and material limits. His visionary attempt took the form of brilliant and daring paintings, sculpture, and architecture that continue to inspire awe and wonder in the modern world. The tragic irony is that Michelangelo felt he was a failure. By 1550 he had given up painting, and afterward his last sculptures were left unfinished. At the end, he turned to architecture, the most abstract of the visual arts, to seek fulfillment of his lifetime need for a union with the Creator. What makes Michelangelo in some respects a modern personality is the extent to which his personal growth and change, his moods and his ego, were mirrored in his art. His drawing, sculpture, and painting reflect magnificent bursts of inspiration, upheavals of superhuman energy, and the weight of his disillusionment. No other artist before or during his time exhibited so intimate a bond between his personality and art. No artist before him so fiercely insisted on maintaining his individuality.

Figure 194. MICHELANGELO. Palazzo dei Conservatori. Designed c. 1546. Capitoline Hill, Rome.

9

THE SYNTHESIS
OF HEAVEN AND EARTH
IN SIXTEENTH- AND
SEVENTEENTH-CENTURY ART

In our day it is the mass communications media that convey messages to the public. In the sixteenth and seventeenth centuries, painting, sculpture, and architecture were the great message bearers of the Church. In those centuries the purpose of religious art was still to illustrate or vivify the Bible and theology, as it had been in the past, but also to engage in the war for mankind's spiritual allegiance being fought between religious factions throughout Europe. The word "propaganda" has come to have unpleasant connotations because of the recent history of its political use for distortion of truth, but in past eras a crucial purpose of art was that of disseminating information and opinion (or propaganda). The war of ideas that engaged many of Europe's greatest artists encompassed art itself, for art that by its form and content disseminated outdated, incorrect, or contradictory views had to be counteracted as much as heretical literature. For these reasons, changes in styles as well as themes during the sixteenth and seventeenth centuries must be viewed in a militant context. Although the art of Leonardo, Michelangelo, and Raphael was highly acceptable to the Church in their day, subsequent changes in Church policy and leadership, response to the Protestant Reforma-

tion, and demands for greater emphasis on piety and mystical faith subsequently caused extreme reactions and new alternatives to the work of these three great artists.

In this light, the Spanish Catholic painter El Greco's *Christ Driving the Money Changers from the Temple* can be meaningfully compared with Raphael's *School of Athens*, both works painted in the sixteenth century (Figs. 195, 196). Raphael's fresco was located in the Vatican in a room where the papal signature was affixed to important documents. Despite this location in a place of great importance to Christianity, the subject of the fresco is a portrayal of the great philosophers of antiquity, with the central focus upon Plato and Aristotle. Raphael was demonstrating the Humanistic belief in the compatibility of pre-Christian thought with Church views in his own time. He has created a series of imagined but intensely lifelike portraits of many philosophers, situating them in an equally imaginary but dignified architectural structure inspired by the work of Bramante, a contemporary architect who strongly influenced Raphael.

El Greco chose as his subject the one event in Christ's life when he employed violence. This may have been interpreted at the time as

166

Figure 195. EL GRECO. *Christ Driving the Money Changers from the Temple.* c. 1570–75. Oil on canvas, 3′10″ × 5′9″. The Minneapolis Institute of Arts, Minnesota (The Dunwoody Fund).

Figure 196. RAPHAEL. *The School of Athens.* 1510–11. Fresco. Stanza della Segnatura, the Vatican, Rome.

Figure 197. DOMENICHINO (DOMENICO ZAMPIERI).
The Last Communion of St. Jerome. 1614. Oil on
canvas, 13′8″ × 8′4″. Musei Vaticani, Rome.

support for the strenuous measures taken by
the Church to rid itself of heresy, which had
come to include acceptance of pagan philosophy
and art. In a very real sense, El Greco's Christ
drives not only the money changers but also
the earlier Humanists from the Church.
Through the archway above Christ's head,
El Greco has painted a reference to the city
of Rome, thus specifying the target of his
commentary. The spacious grandeur of Raphael's setting, the equanimity and grace of the
animated philosophers so beautifully thought
out and achieved in drawing, color, and composition, is intentionally counteracted by El

Greco. The earlier artist's delight in lucid,
metrical space, in the fluid composure of groups,
and in an orderly alignment of figures and
architecture in recessive zones parallel to the
surface is countered with congestion, angular
disconnected passages, and dissonant color.
Rather than soothe the eye, El Greco sought
painting that irritated the complacent feelings
and minds which took balm from reason.

In the war with Protestantism, the Church
called on its artists to affirm the sacraments,
and that of the Eucharist in particular. When
the Italian painter Domenichino depicted
St. Jerome, unlike van Eyck it was not to
celebrate his thoughtful character and scholar-
snip but rather to eulogize the powerful will
that helped him rise from his deathbed to
partake for the last time of the wine and wafer
(Fig. 197). The technical devices and knowledge accumulated by fifteenth-century painters
to bring art down to earth and to glorify that
marvelous organism which is the human body
were put by Domenichino into the service of
showing the struggle of the dying body to
participate in the sacred mystery of Communion. The task that Domenichino and so many
contemporary painters faced was to divert men's
thoughts from earthly concerns and redirect
them toward heaven, while at the same time
drawing from the legacy of earlier art which had
done so much to humanize and secularize art.

Because the sixteenth-century Protestants
condemned the Catholic Church's employment
of art as idolatrous, there was created no art
explicitly illustrating Lutheranism in the way
that the *Spiritual Exercises* of St. Ignatius of
Loyola found so many interpreters among
painters. But in the art of the Flemish painter
Pieter Bruegel—whose religious affiliation, if
any, is unknown to us—is to be found a mind
that saw the Bible and religious controversy in a
different perspective from that of his orthodox
Catholic contemporaries. For this reason, his
works are interspersed in this chapter. His
Blind Leading the Blind (Fig. 198), based on
Matthew (15: 12–19), could well have been a
commentary on the caliber of religious leadership (equated with the Pharisees) manifested in
the theological disputes rampant in Europe at
the time. The church fully visible behind the
blind men who pull each other and stumble into
a ditch seems a pointed reference. Painting
for a select clientele, Bruegel could count on a

Plate 25. Jan Vermeer. *The Artist in His Studio*. c. 1665–70.
Oil on canvas, 4′4″ × 3′8″. Kunsthistorisches Museum, Vienna.

Plate 26.   REMBRANDT VAN RIJN. *The Slaughtered Ox.* 1665.
Oil on panel, 37 × 26⅜″ Louvre, Paris.

Plate 27.   REMBRANDT VAN RIJN. *Christ at Emmaus*. 1648.
Oil on panel, 26¾×25⅝″. Louvre, Paris.

Plate 28.   REMBRANDT VAN RIJN. *Portrait of Jan Six*. 1654.
Oil on canvas, 44 × 40″. Verzameling der Six-Stichting, Amsterdam.

sophisticated audience, which included devout churchmen, to recognize certain absurdities in the affairs of men. For him, art served the mind and was the means by which to illustrate knowledge and wisdom detached from the customary partisan causes fought for by his fellow artists here represented. Unlike Leonardo da Vinci, Bruegel was interested in broad, even generic, human relationships, and our physical remoteness from his figures reflects the kind of intellectual detachment he assumed toward his subject.

To maintain that artists in the sixteenth century acted and thought only at the bidding of the Church is to overlook the individual initiative and personal feelings and fantasies of many of the greatest painters. Pontormo, a contemporary of Michelangelo, was famous in his time for his art and for his eccentricity, which took the form of fanatical isolation and hypochondria. Pontormo gave example to the sixteenth-century concept of the lonely genius. His painting of *The Deposition* (Fig. 199) is a deeply personal and disturbing meditation on the meaning of Christ's death, couched in a language that by comparison with that of Raphael and Leonardo seems an alien tongue. The eye is at first jolted by apple greens, metallic greys, and shrill pinks and yellows— not the anodyne palette of Raphael, with its soft reds, blues, and flesh tones. The distortions of Pontormo's figures ultimately depend upon correct anatomical knowledge, but the demands for an expressive or emotional composition

Left: Figure 198. PIETER BRUEGEL THE ELDER. *The Blind Leading the Blind.* 1568. Oil on canvas, 2′10″ × 5′1½″. Museo di Capodimonte, Naples.

Above: Figure 199. PONTORMO (JACOPO CARUCCI). *Deposition.* 1525–28. Oil on panel, 10′3″ × 6′3½″. Sta. Felicità, Florence.

impelled the distention or abbreviation of limbs, dislocation of shoulders, and the elongated, boneless torsos. His figures are of a type, a strange family whose faces betray intense shock. The laws of spatial logic, and hence reason, are decisively put aside, as the entwined figures appear to be stacked vertically in some unreal place and moment. Unlike the rationale of a fifteenth-century painting, it is impossible to conceive of what these figures will do next or where they will go, any more than one can visualize the painting's space without them. It is the unnatural occasioned by mystical attitudes and themes that nurtured Pontormo's style. As for Michelangelo, an inner, personal vision, not nature, was his model.

The Church did not always accept the license taken by an artist in the name of individuality; fearful of a corruption of its message, the Church evolved an official artistic program in the second half of the sixteenth century, and this reached fruition during the seventeenth. This program was intended to counteract the Protestant Reformation and its assaults not only upon the doctrine and practices of the Holy Roman Catholic Church but also on its art. The Council of Trent, which sat in the north Italian town of Trento from 1545 to 1563, was an arm of the Inquisition instrumental in crystallizing Church policy with regard to internal reform, as well as in plotting strategy against the northern Protestant heretics. In the last year of its meeting, the Council promulgated its views on art. In essence, this program reaffirmed the Church's belief in the importance of art, reiterated the opposition to idolatry, espoused the didactic purpose of art and its provision of an ethical model for the faithful, decried indecency in religious painting and sculpture, and insisted upon decorum, respect, and accuracy in interpreting theological or spiritual subject matter. The implications of the Council of Trent's view included an anti-Humanistic attitude, a kind of Counter Renaissance that favored an appeal to the emotions of the believer in the manner of Loyola's *Spiritual Exercises*. (These exercises involved a self-induced ecstatic trance or meditation, comparable to yoga, in which the individual lost all self-consciousness and through visions identified himself with the feelings or state of his object of worship. Ignatius felt the Stigmata of Christ during one of his trances.) Another implication

of the Council's views was a stress on the supernatural, or a suspension of the rational, thus giving rise to numerous works of art dealing with miraculous themes. Placing of theological truth before beauty and the strengthening of existing Church doctrines through visual artistic proof were essential outgrowths of this action by the Church.

To ensure the carrying out of their decrees, the Council instituted a censorship of art by agents of the Inquisition. The most famous case brought before these agents, the Holy Tribunal sitting in Venice on July 18, 1573, was that of the Venetian painter Paolo Veronese, who had painted a questionable version of the Last Supper (Fig. 200). The transcript of the trial illustrates, among other things, the uneasy synthesis of the spiritual and the secular in the minds of the judges as well as the painter. When questioned about his profession, Veronese answered as follows *:

A. I paint and compose figures.
Q. Do you know the reason why you have been summoned?
A. No, Sir.
Q. Can you imagine it?
A. I can well imagine.
Q. Say what you think the reason is.
A. According to what the Reverend Father, the Prior of the Convent of SS. Giovanni e Paolo, whose name I do not know, told me, he had been here and Your Lordships had ordered him to have painted [in the picture] a Magdalen in place of a dog. I answered him by saying I would gladly do everything necessary for my honor and for that of my painting, but that I did not understand how a figure of Magdalen would be suitable there for many reasons which I will give at any time, provided I am given an opportunity.
Q. What picture is this of which you have spoken?
A. This is a picture of the Last Supper that Jesus Christ took with His Apostles in the house of Simon. . . .
Q. At this Supper of Our Lord you painted other figures?
A. Yes, milords.
Q. Tell us how many people and describe the gestures of each.

* Elizabeth G. Holt, *A Documentary History of Art*, Vol. 2, Doubleday Anchor Books, New York, 1958, p. 66ff.

Figure 200. PAOLO VERONESE. *Christ in the House of Levi.* 1573. Oil on canvas, 18′2″ × 42′. Academia, Venice.

A. There is the owner of the inn, Simon; besides this figure I have made a steward, who, I imagined, had come there for his own pleasure to see how the things were going at the table. There are many figures there which I cannot recall, as I painted the picture some time ago....

Q. In this Supper which you made for SS. Giovanni e Paolo what is the significance of the man whose nose is bleeding?

A. I intended to represent a servant whose nose was bleeding because of some accident.

Q. What is the significance of those armed men, dressed as Germans, each with a halberd in his hand?

A. This requires that I say twenty words!

Q. Say them.

A. We painters take the same license the poets and the jesters take and I have represented these two halberdiers, one drinking and the other eating nearby on the stairs. They are placed there so that they might be of service because it seemed to me fitting, according to what I have been told, that the master of the house, who was great and rich, should have such servants.

Q. And that man dressed as a buffoon with a parrot on his wrist, for what purpose did you paint him on that canvas?

A. For ornament, as is customary....

Q. Did anyone commission you to paint Germans, buffoons, and similar things in that picture?

A. No, milords, but I received the commission to decorate the picture as I saw fit. It is large and, it seemed to me, it could hold many figures.

Q. Are not the decorations which you painters are accustomed to add to paintings or pictures supposed to be suitable and proper to the subject and the principal figures or are they for pleasure—simply what comes to your imagination without any discretion or judiciousness?

A. I paint pictures as I see fit and as well as my talent permits.

Q. Does it seem fitting at the Last Supper of the Lord to paint buffoons, drunkards, Germans, dwarfs, and similar vulgarities?

A. No, milords.

Q. Do you not know that in Germany and in other places infected with heresy it is customary with various pictures full of scurrilousness and similar inventions to mock, vituperate, and scorn the things of the Holy Catholic Church in order to teach bad doctrines to foolish and ignorant people?...

A. Illustrious Lords, I do not want to defend it, but I thought I was doing right. I did not consider so many things and I did not intend to confuse anyone, the more so as those figures of buffoons are outside of the place in a picture where Our Lord is represented.

After these things had been said, the judges announced that the above named Paolo would be obliged to improve and change his painting within a period of three months from the

Figure 201. LEONARDO DA VINCI. *The Last Supper.* c. 1494. Fresco, 15′1⅛″ × 28′10½″.
Refectory of Sta. Maria delle Grazie, Milan.

day of the admonition and that according to the opinion and decision of the Holy Tribunal all the corrections should be made at the expense of the painter, and that if he did not correct the picture he would be liable to the penalties imposed by the Holy Tribunal.

Veronese's answers give a sixteenth-century definition of painting based on the composition of figures which were to be "read," that is, which were to convey a message and be interpreted. Like a dramatist, the artist had to envision why each figure was present and what he would logically be doing. When it came to filling a large space with ornament and enrichment, Veronese claimed for the painter the same license given to poets. He had to resort to stories and information outside the Bible to bring the past event to life in terms of his own time. His criteria were his ability and personal judgment of fitness, fortified by what he had seen in great art of the past. The great scale of his painting and the sumptuous setting and elaborate social milieu were reflections of Veronese's personal delight in contemporary Venetian customs.

A fellow Venetian, Tintoretto, though not insensitive to the secular life around him, was able to paint religious images fully in keeping with the ideals of the Counter Reformation. Against the Protestant theology, the Roman Catholic Church affirmed that to participate in the Eucharistic rite was to partake mystically of the body and blood of Christ. This belief impelled Tintoretto to depict the Last Supper in such a way as to emphasize the miraculous meaning and origin of this event, and of the Eucharastic doctrine.

Tintoretto's art also exemplifies a Counter Renaissance attitude that looked upon the style as well as the content of such painters as Leonardo as too worldly in orientation. Comparison of Leonardo's and Tintoretto's versions of the Last Supper (Figs. 201, 202), a century apart in date, reveals the ideological and esthetic gulf that separated the two men and their periods. Preoccupied with the study of interior human motivation. Leonardo chose to portray the moment when Christ foretold his betrayal. This permitted a virtuoso display of his findings on how expression was conveyed by face and gestures and how different personalities reacted to the stimulus of shock. The supper takes place in an austere room, illusionistically treated as a continuation of the refectory in which it was located—a setting that permitted a display of Leonardo's mastery of the science of spatial organization and the effects of certain lighting conditions. Tintoretto's setting is a more rustic inn, and the animated meal is less like the formal banquet or social occasion seen in the earlier painting. The inn's illumination is almost melodramatic, to accord with the mystical sacramental moment chosen by Tintoretto. To devise his effects, Tintoretto made small sculptural figures, set them into an open-ended box, and then moved different lighting over the model.

Leonardo's composition is closed, or completely contained within the limits of the picture area. The vanishing points and figural action lie either at the center of the painting or firmly within its borders. Tintoretto's arrangement is open in that the space, light, shadow, and action seem to extend out of the frame at several points. Leonardo organizes his figures and the banquet table in such a way that they seem to exist in an imaginary plane parallel to the picture surface, holding the viewer off from the action. Tintoretto's figures and banquet table exist on a strongly thrusting diagonal to the picture surface and, thus, are recessional in character. It is easier to isolate individual figures, objects, or units within the Leonardo scheme than in the Tintoretto. Leonardo's work shows a multiple unity, as opposed to Classical unity. The potential isolability of Leonardo's figures derives from the clear edge that bounds each form and the relative evenness of the light, that is, a clarity of shape and illumination. The more inextricable relationship of Tintoretto's figures is a result of the overlapping shadows and of the construction of

figures through color as well as with light and shade. Tintoretto's composition is marked by the qualities of obscurity and painterly construction. Leonardo's range of light and dark exists primarily in a middle register, avoiding strong contrasts over large areas. The dramatic and mystical effects of Tintoretto's composition are realized through strong value contrasts in major areas. Leonardo, in the manner of other Renaissance painters, avoided clashing colors placed close together; Tintoretto used strong disparities between colors to enhance the visual excitement of his pictures. He also employed multiple and irrational light sources, as opposed to Leonardo's more natural and even distribution of light. Tintoretto designed space so as to pull the viewer into the picture with a swift rush, then balanced this inward thrust with the large foreground groups and the angels hovering overhead, which draw the eye forward again. Leonardo used the edges and the perspective focus of the architecture to lead the viewer into depth and then, with the head of Christ in the foreground, to draw him back into an area near the picture plane. There is a meaningful focus on Christ in both paintings. Tintoretto set Christ's head in a mystical radiance, the most intense light of the painting. In the work of Tintoretto, therefore, light replaced perspective or geometry as the principal instrument of religious significance.

Figure 202. TINTORETTO. *The Last Supper*. 1594. Oil on canvas, 12′ × 18′8″. S. Giorgio Maggiore, Venice.

It was sixteenth-century Venetians such as Veronese, Tintoretto, and Titian who gave new implications to the verb "to paint." In the preceding century, artists filled in colored areas already described by linear drawing; for this reason their work, even when seen in black and white, has a distinct, easily grasped series of contours. A black-and-white photograph of Titian's *Christ Crowned with Thorns* (Fig. 203), however, gives the misleading impression of a somewhat murky indistinctness. The relative coarseness and fusion of silhouettes with the light and space around them results from Titian's building of his figures by means of brush drawing in color. Even his pen-and-ink or charcoal drawings have a sketchy airiness that keeps attention from being drawn to distinct, continuous edges. Titian thought in terms of color as his prime means of expression

Figure 203. TITIAN. *Christ Crowned with Thorns.* c. 1565. Oil on canvas, 9′2″ × 6′. Alte Pinakothek, Munich.

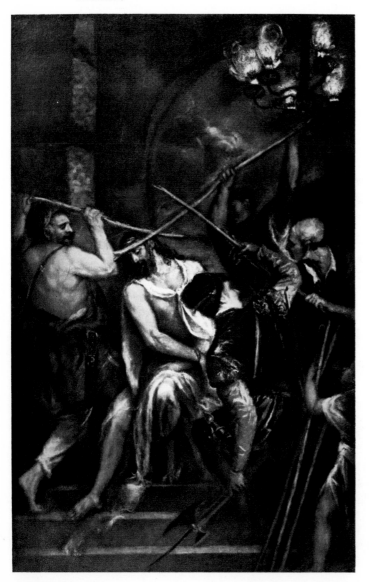

and method of construction. His personal vision was one of color seen not in a vacuum but under conditions of natural or artificial light filtered through a palpable atmosphere, as in this nocturnal scene of Christ's humiliation.

Titian and Tintoretto particularly responded to the physical sensations of brushing color onto a canvas surface, savoring the weight, texture, and pliability of the pigment and, simultaneously, how even a single stroke could give definition to a shape, degree of light, modeling, and exact color tone. The hairs of the pigment-filled brush could be spread apart by pressure from the hand, allowing previously applied color to radiate through and vibrate with the overpainting. As an old man, Titian came to realize the great economy and expressive power possible in the judicious selection of a few colored strokes; but his contemporaries, prejudiced toward his virtuoso earlier work, felt that paintings such as *Christ Crowned with Thorns* resulted from failing vision, a trembling hand, and senility. From a fellow painter and sometime collaborator, Palma Giovane, comes a description of how the elderly Titian worked:

Titian began his pictures with a mass of color which served as a bed or foundation for what he wished to express. I myself have seen such vigorously applied underpainting in pure red ochre, which was meant to give the half-tone, or in white lead. With the same brush, which he dipped in red, black or yellow, he created the modeling effect of the lighter portions. With four strokes he was capable of indicating a magnificent figure.... After he had thus applied this important foundation, he turned the pictures to the wall and left them... sometimes for months. When he afterwards returned to them, he scanned them with a concentration as severe as if they had been his mortal enemies, in order to find faults in them; and if he found something which was not in accord with his intentions, he went to work like a surgeon.... Thus by repeated revision, he brought the skeleton of his figures to the highest degree of perfection and, while one picture was drying, he turned to another. This quintessence of a composition he then covered over with many layers of living flesh, until the figure seemed to lack only breath. He never painted a figure *alla prima* [spontaneously], and was wont to say that he who improvises can never fashion a perfect line of poetry. He gave the last touch to his pictures

Figure 204. PIETER BRUEGEL THE ELDER. *The Carrying of the Cross.* 1564. Oil on panel, 4′7⅞″ × 5′6⅞″. Kunsthistorisches Museum, Vienna.

by adjusting with his fingers a spot of black in one corner or heightening with a dab of red, like a drop of blood, the liveliness of the surface.... In the last stages of the work, he painted more with his fingers than with the brush....

Just as he reworked a single painting, so did Titian reinterpret certain themes and earlier compositions, not just for his many clients but, in later years, largely for himself. In his *Christ Crowned with Thorns*, he subdued the earlier strong facial reactions, obstructed focus upon hands, and generally suffused the entire scene with a drama of light and strongly textured color. To a certain extent, late works such as this were the painter's private devotional paintings, and in a secular sense they marked passionate devotion to painting itself.

In comparison with Titian's painting, Pieter Bruegel's *Carrying of the Cross* (Fig. 204), done some years earlier, is a radical departure in

Biblical illustration, yet conservative in terms of the relation of color to drawing. The pathos resulting from Titian's intimate focus upon Christ's ordeal is matched by an equally strong ethos arising from the viewer's remoteness from the figure of Christ, struggling under the weight of his Cross. The way to Calvary is plotted along a broad curving plane, and Christ is accompanied by a crowd that takes little notice of him but is diverted by all sorts of byplay. In the foreground are the weeping Marys and St. John, and nearby is seen an elevated wheel used for the torture execution of criminals in Bruegel's time. In a double sense, Bruegel gives us the long view of Christ's ordeal. In this treatment, we see the Saviour in the broad context of a time and place, as a man among men, who like many before and after is unjustly put to death, providing the crowd with still another morbid spectacle. It is possible that the curving arc of the plain and the numerous references to circles would have suggested to

Bruegel's limited but knowledgeable audience the continual recurrence of injustice. Some historians have seen in this painting the artist's bitter commentary on the brutality of Spanish rule over the Netherlands, or an oblique reference to the sadism of the Inquisition; but if this were true, it somehow escaped the notice of the Spanish Catholic royalty, who admired his painting. Bruegel's inverted focus (from that of Titian) inhibits concentration on the personal and theological implications of Christ's Passion, but it also increases the breadth of the artist's

Figure 205. EL GRECO. *The Resurrection of Christ.* 1600–05. Oil on canvas, 9′ 1/4″ × 4′ 5″. Prado, Madrid.

statement about history and human nature to what was till then an unrivaled scale.

The most mystical of the Counter Reformation painters was El Greco, who believed in the irrational basis of Christian dogma and the necessity of a uniquely personal style to embody his private visions. The events in his paintings are not depicted in fifteenth-century Europe, according to the rational perception of a detached observer, but are emanations of an ecstatic visionary who sought to show in one explosive moment things that defy intellectual comprehension. For this reason, his *Resurrection of Christ* (Fig. 205) seems antidotal to that by Piero della Francesca. El Greco presents the mystical levitation of Christ's body rising from the invisible tomb. The position of Christ's feet assist in this feeling of ascent and also recall the posture of his Crucifixion.

El Greco was concerned more with the metaphysical than with the psychological. The cold, eerie light of the scene originates from Christ's transfigured person. His effortless upward movement contrasts with the forceful effects of the awesome mystical light, which has upset the sleeping tomb guards, dazzled those who have awakened, and exalted those present who comprehend the transformation. Through gestures at once rhetorical and symbolical, El Greco demonstrated the forceful process of spiritual enlightenment and the significance of the Resurrection. The gesture of Christ's right hand is a sign of the completion of what had been ordained, while its counterpart in the large figure at the lower right is one of simultaneous recognition and supplication. The extreme luminosity, the exaggerated elongation, and the inconstant silhouette of Christ's body reduce its corporeality and eliminate the suggestion of militancy seen in Piero della Francesca's God. All that was tangible and substantial in the work of Piero has been made elusive and immaterial by El Greco. The stability of Piero's composition—its implied triangle of verticals resting on solid horizontals, all locked within a square format—has been replaced by an unstable irregular lozenge design in a vertical format. Just as the mystical nature of El Greco's Christ was freed from the logic of matter, so is the event abstracted from a specific earthly place and time.

The strength of El Greco's religious message did not weaken his inspired inventiveness as a

Above: Figure 206. EL GRECO. *The Legend of St. Maurice.* 1581–84. Oil on canvas, 14'8⅓" × 9'10½". Escorial.

Above right: Figure 207. EL GRECO. *The Legend of St. Maurice,* detail from Fig. 206.

painter. Great artists of the past and his own time had early taught him lessons in drawing, color, and composition. As his art became more introspective, however, he posed for himself unprecedented artistic problems; and the success of their solution could not be judged by the work of others. To the viewer of today, El Greco's *Legend of St. Maurice* (Fig. 206) appears as a beautiful accomplished fact. The rightness of his solution of its problems obscures their original difficulty. Before summarizing the subject that raised these problems, one might usefully recall that the didactic message of Counter Reformation art often took the guise of instructing the faithful in the merits of dying for their beliefs. The Protestants were critical of the Church's veneration of its numerous

martyrs. To affirm the sacred act of the martyr and to encourage world-wide missionary work, Roman Catholic artists were enjoined to recount the historical sacrifices of the martyrs. The story chosen by El Greco is that of the wholesale execution of a Roman legion which, with its commander St. Maurice, had been converted to Christianity. Refusing the emperor's ultimatum to renounce their faith, every man in the legion was beheaded at the site of what is today Saint-Maurice, Switzerland. El Greco stressed the moment of decision when the legion officers surrounding St. Maurice considered the imperial ultimatum. Accordingly, almost a third of the painting's surface is devoted to this small group in the foreground. The upper part discloses angels who descend from heaven holding the crowns of martyrdom. To the smallest, most restricted area at the left is consigned the execution of the entire contingent (Fig. 207).

El Greco boldly juxtaposed the largest and smallest figures in the entire painting. By means of the medium-sized angels placed at the upper left and the large standard at the right, he set the eccentric composition solidly within the frame. The sculptural firmness of the foreground officers is replaced as the eye moves rapidly into depth by the diaphanous character of the tiny figures in the distance, who are less tangible than the clouds.

Essential to the style of these paintings by El Greco is the total absence of straight edge, evenly illuminated surfaces, continuous closed silhouettes, repose, and measurable space. Every shape seems in the process of change; rarely is the eye permitted to rest. Figures and clouds swell from tapered points, and rocks and pennants are edged in writhing contours. It is possible to follow the action of the painter's hand in the irregular cloud and flag forms. His thinking was focused on the particular objects he was painting as well as on the adjacent areas, so that rarely is a figure or object seen in isolation. No dominant sustained vertical or horizontal axis structures the composition. Unity is finally the result of a close fitting together of oscillating or irregular parts, often at obtuse angles to each other or else in parallel series.

El Greco has been called insane, and more recently misguided attempts have been made to suggest that he suffered from astigmatism. Neither was the case. His unique art was the product of years of development and lucid calculation and passionate religious conviction. El Greco might have declared that his physical vision was normal but that it was his "inner eye" which was abnormal.

Ironically the age of the Counter Reformation, which saw restoration and increase of the Church's power, was also the lustiest and most perverse in its artistic celebration of sex. Sixteenth- and seventeenth-century art, ostensibly in the noble service of defending or expounding the true faith, was in fact the frequent outlet for erotic and sadistic interests of the artist, his ecclesiastical patrons, and his audience. Church scholars chronicled all forms of gruesome martyrdom, and in a Roman college for the training of missionaries walls were lined with horrifying images of "successful alumni" who died as martyrs all over the world. Rather than discouraging, such images fired the zeal of the young. Stradanus' engraving of *The Martyrdom of Saint Agatha* exemplifies the

public's fascination with sexual violence enacted upon feminine martyrs (Fig. 208). Ugliness and beauty are blatantly contrasted as symbols of sin and saintliness. Ironically, it was the Holy Inquisition, with its well-known methods of torture, that fed the public taste for sadism. The synthesis of heavenly and earthly values at the time of the *Merode Altarpiece* had already begun to encounter the possibilities and problems of absorbing sexual life, and in the period here considered there was an increasing frankness and exposure of this subject, which often tried the credibility of a synthesis.

That there was no homogeneous Counter Reformation style can be seen by the fact that, along with El Greco's paintings, those of Peter Paul Rubens were highly acceptable to the Church. The Cretan-born and Flemish artists were opposites in temperament and style. Rubens was able to reconcile a vital love of the flesh with a love of the spirit. His mythological pagan types, kings, peasants, and religious personages are interchangeable, sharing a common robust virility, effulgent healthiness, and appetite for living. The deeply introverted El

Figure 208. STRADANUS (JAN VAN DER STRAET). *The Martyrdom of St. Agatha.* 16th century. Engraving.

Greco distrusted the carnality of the body with a medieval fervor, whereas Rubens seems to have been fulfilled through the sensuous painting of the flesh. The energy in El Greco's painting is mystical; that in Rubens' work is muscular.

When Rubens painted his *Descent from the Cross* (Pl. 19), he involved his subjects in the arduous mechanics of lowering Christ's heavy body. The figure at the upper left having both hands engaged holds the death shroud in his teeth (Pl. 20). Despite the cumbersome process, the mourners are given grace of movement. The tenderness with which the body is received is intended to contrast with the brutality of the execution. From close up, the painting of Christ's blood seems excessively lurid, but it must be remembered that this huge painting was for a large church and was to be seen by the whole congregation. Color helps us to realize how fully Rubens met the Counter Reformation ideals of encouraging the faithful to identify with Christ's Passion. The flesh of the living has layers of color touched with the key red, which makes it glow with warmth and vitality. That of Christ has the grey of death and is contrasted with the ruddy-complexioned arms, the whiteness of the shroud, and the brilliant reds of his blood and the garment of St. John. The strongest and richest contrasts are thus grouped at the center around the broken figure, and the darker tones tend to merge with the deep blue-green of the sky. By focusing the light in the central area, away from the edges, the scene would thus appear to be more illusionistic in the darkened space of the church itself.

El Greco evokes unshed tears of anguish and disdains the materiality of this earth. Rubens induces the sweat of exertion and rejoices in the sensuality of worldly stuffs. What El Greco shows lying beyond touch, Rubens addresses to our finger tips. While St. Maurice and his captains tread lightly on the earth, Rubens' race of giants grows from it. Rubens' Christ has known heroic physical exertion, that of El Greco only spiritual exercise.

Comparison with El Greco may mislead the reader into doubting Rubens' religious sincerity. Mystical asceticism has not been the only producer of great religious art. Rubens was passionately devoted to the Roman Catholic faith and spent a lifetime enriching the splendor

Figure 209. PETER PAUL RUBENS. *St. Ignatius Exorcising Demons from the Church.* 1619. Oil on canvas, 17′6½″ × 12′11½″. Kunsthistorisches Museum, Vienna.

of the altar with his paintings. Like the fifteenth-century Flemish artists before him, Rubens saw no contradictions in his response to the attractiveness of the material world or the mythological past. He had optimistic confidence in himself and in the right and power of the Church. Like the Roman Catholic rulers and ecclesiastical patrons who paid for his secular art, he saw no sin in the healthy enjoyment of what lay without dogma. When he painted religious subjects, such as *St. Ignatius Exorcising Demons from the Church* (Fig. 209), he was attentive to the spirit of his theme. Just as St. Ignatius had recommended projecting oneself into the state of the subject of worship, Rubens' painting draws the viewer into the church to

Figure 210. PETER PAUL RUBENS. *The Last Judgment*. c. 1615. Oil on wood, 5′11⅝″ × 3′11¼″. Alte Pinakothek, Munich.

The vigorous movement and sensual appearance of Rubens' figures are born in the rhythms of his brush and the creamy substance of his paint. To enjoy El Greco's color is to appreciate rare admixtures of tones, predominantly cool colors under a sometimes shrill light, restraint in the build up of heavily pigmented areas, and, by comparison with Rubens, a less obtrusive trace of the brush. Showing warm light and lush sequences of opacity and transparency, Rubens' colors and glazes create the impression of pulse and blood lying just beneath the flesh. Rubens' brush was swept with bravura across a form or was delicately touched to a tiny area demanding a highlight. The viewer looking at a Rubens painting can sense the physical as well as esthetic pleasure that the artist enjoyed as he worked. It is not difficult to comprehend Rubens' full involvement in the materiality of the medium that permitted him to re-create the sensuous world he loved.

When Rubens painted *The Last Judgment* (Fig. 210), he depicted the most sensual sinners in history. The damned flood downward from the seat of judgment and overwhelm the picture space, leaving the smaller and more remote upper regions for the elect. How paradoxical it seems that in this painting Rubens would acknowledge the sinfulness of voluptuous flesh, and then proceed for the rest of his lifetime to glorify the beautiful bodies of mythological heroes alongside of similarly endowed saints and royalty. Just as so many artists before him, it is the spectacle of Hell rather than Heaven that calls forth his most inspired painting. Punishment rather than judgment, the provocative contortions and violent intertwining of condemned bodies rather than the composed bliss of the elect predictably appealed to audiences drawn to depravity. Despite the diminished emphasis upon heaven and imbalance between the saved and the damned, Rubens' pessimistic view of the fate of most of humanity is good Counter Reformation propaganda.

Pieter Bruegel's *Triumph of Death* (Fig. 211), painted half a century before, seems to take a cynical attitude toward any efforts to buffer mankind from the facts of death. Unlike its medieval *memento mori* prototypes, Bruegel's version of the encounter of the living and the dead is catholic only in the sense of universality. Eyewitness to plagues and wars in the southern Netherlands, Bruegel could draw from personal

share the excitement of the miracle and the new hope of the sick who have been cleansed of the devil. Such projection is difficult if not impossible in the construction of El Greco's paintings. In Rubens' work, the foreground brilliance and posturing of the nearest figure draw us upward to the saint and back down into depth at the left where the devil quits the church. The diagonal in depth was a consistent stylistic device by which Rubens told a story, achieved dramatic and visual climax, and held his composition in forceful resolution.

experience concerning human vanity in the face of such disasters. Rubens championed the theological view of a Last Judgment and life in the hereafter. Bruegel, whose religious convictions are not known to us, chose to show life stopping at the entrance to the coffin, with no assurance of an ultimate justice, heaven or hell. There is no indication that the skeletal hordes dispatching the living or herding them into the open end of a gigantic coffin are the emissaries of Christ or the Devil. Instead of the Arch Angel with his valence, there is a skeleton beating a drum above the coffin, providing the insistent rhythm of death. Churches have been overrun by skeletons who perform irreverent services. The traditional figure of Death riding a pale horse is seen drawing a wagon load of

skulls while nearby a king and a cardinal are in the grips of skeletons. At the far right is the cavalier who dares death with his sword, the lovers oblivious to all and the fool who crawls under the table. The *Triumph of Death* is so sweeping in its cataloguing of all forms of destruction on land and sea that it suggests the end of the world.

Cataclysmic visions were fewer in the Counter Reformation period than those of heaven. So important was the Counter Reformation concept of the religious vision that an increasing number of Roman churches in the seventeenth century had their vaults illusionistically painted in grandiose compositions that permitted the faithful to look directly upward into heaven. One of the most powerful and biggest vault

Figure 211. PIETER BRUEGEL THE ELDER. *The Triumph of Death.* c. 1562. Oil on panel, 3′10″ × 5′3⅞″. Prado, Madrid.

Figure 212. ANDREA POZZO. *The Triumph of St. Ignatius Loyola (Allegory of the Missionary Work of the Jesuits).* 1691–94. Fresco on nave ceiling, S. Ignazio, Rome.

paintings was Fra Andrea Pozzo's *Allegory of the Missionary Work of the Jesuits* (Fig. 212). It celebrated the work and sacrifice of this order on all of the continents and demonstrated the reception in heaven of its leader and martyrs. Pozzo transformed the vault to give the impression that the church soars upwards an additional two stories and is without any ceiling. Against the illusion of massive stable architectural elements, columns and arches, Pozzo floated clusters of figures in a remarkable series of foreshortenings, so that no matter from what point the observer looks, the scene is in perspective. The entire scene is suffused with

radiance, accelerating the eye upward with no prolonged restraint. The message of the painting is that to the faithful heaven is directly accessible.

The virtuoso seventeenth-century artists achieved illusions in a wide variety of media of a staggering range of subjects. The most gifted sculptor of the century and most ardent in his devotion to the aims of the Church was the Italian Gianlorenzo Bernini. Among his other talents were playwriting, stage design, painting, caricature, and architecture. His most spectacular production in sculpture is the *Ecstasy of St. Theresa* (Fig. 213). St. Theresa was a sixteenth-century saint who recorded her visions. One of these, available to Bernini, describes the event portrayed in the sculpture:

> I saw an angel close to me, on my left side, in bodily form. This I am accustomed to see but very rarely. Though I have visions of angels frequently, yet I see them only by an intellectual vision, such as I have spoken of before. It is our Lord's will that in this vision I should see the angel in this wise. He was not large, but small of stature and most beautiful—his face burning as if he were one of the highest angels who seem to be all of fire.... I saw in his hand a long spear of gold, and at the iron's point there seemed to be a little fire. He appeared to me to be thrusting it at times into my heart, and to pierce my very entrails: When he drew it out, he seemed to draw them all out also and to leave me all on fire with a great love of God. The pain was so great that I cried out, but at the same time the sweetness which that violent pain gave me was so excessive that I could not wish to be rid of it.

Bernini chose the moment between thrusts of the spear with the saint writhing in paroxysms of pleasure and pain. The erotic nature of both the vision and the sculpture is patent, but in keeping with the religious purpose of making the situation as vivid as possible. Bernini practiced the *Spiritual Exercises* of St. Ignatius of Loyola in order to absorb himself as deeply and accurately as possible into his subject. The nature of the vision excited his interest, particularly the coexistence of conflicting psychological states, imaged on the face of the saint with consummate virtuosity. Treating stone as if it were the wax of the models from which he worked, Bernini created the illusion of clouds, cloth, and flesh. The marble was warmed by light which entered from a concealed yellow glass window. There was no previous sculptural parallel to Bernini's deliberate and controlled use of light as both form and mystic symbol in his composition. The sculptural group is set behind a proscenium arch, and in the background golden shafts serve as radiant backdrops. Sacred sculpture and painted altarpieces, such as that by Rogier van der Weyden, had served as religious theater before. Bernini transformed the chapel where the sculpture was

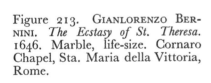

Figure 213. GIANLORENZO BERNINI. *The Ecstasy of St. Theresa.* 1646. Marble, life-size. Cornaro Chapel, Sta. Maria della Vittoria, Rome.

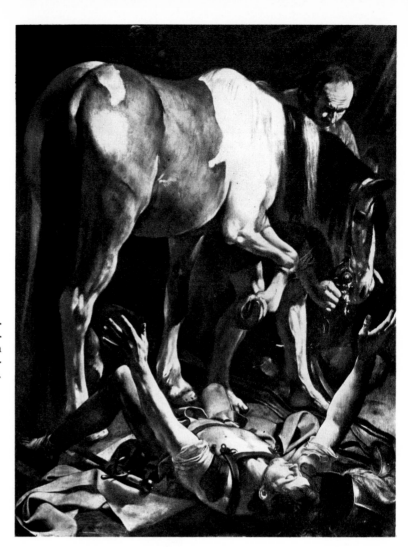

Figure 214. CARAVAGGIO (MI-
CHELANGELO MERISI). *The Conversion of St. Paul.* 1601–02. Oil on
canvas, 7′6½″ × 5′9″. Cerasi Chapel, Sta. Maria del Popolo, Rome.

housed into a sphere in which the differences between art and reality were suspended.

The single most influential painter of the seventeenth century was Michelangelo Merisi da Caravaggio, whose history of wild escapades and attraction to violence contradicts the view that only pious men can paint great religious pictures. Dedicated to making art that would meet the needs of the masses, Caravaggio was a failure, for the people, conditioned by more aristocratic images of insincere piety, distrusted the stark reality of his types and the brutal realism with which the Bible was interpreted. It was with connoisseurs and artists that the recognition of his talent was achieved. When Caravaggio undertook the theme of religious revelation in his *Conversion of St. Paul* (Fig. 214), a painting intended for a darkened chapel, he startled parishoners by showing the rider flat on his back, partially under his horse and with his head towards the viewer. Whether he wants

to or not, the beholder is the vicarious witness to Saul's conversion to Paul, for he is made to feel as if the miracle takes place at arm's length. Cold brilliant penetrating light is the only evidence of God's presence, for Caravaggio could not bring himself to depict the supernatural as later Bernini and Pozzo were to do. Always he sought credibility in terms of the experience available to those of lowest estate or the uneducated. The action of the attendant who steadies the horse while contemplating the event is natural under the circumstances. The usefulness of the old man's gesture contrasts with that of the outflung arms of Paul by which the spiritual drama is revealed. Both gestures are instinctive and good theater. The indelibility of the conception is founded in body surfaces made to seem more firm than those in life (or Bernini's later carving in marble) and the pure translucent light polarized against measure-less shadows. Later artists such as Rembrandt were to learn from Caravaggio the dramatist that eyes or faces need not be highlighted or made focal points, but that light and shadow could compound the mystery of crucial events.

Still amazing is that Caravaggio worked directly on his paintings without recourse to preliminary drawings. Ironically Caravaggio's paintings of religious subjects had a strong influence on secular or genre painting of the seventeenth century. The painting of *Christ at Emmaus* (Pl. 21) was intended for the guest room of a convent. It shows the two disciples Cleophas and Peter Simon seated with Christ, whom they had taken for a fellow pilgrim and invited to eat with them. The cockleshell on the disciple's tunic signifies that the men were pilgrims, like those who frequently used the convent's guest rooms. Caravaggio shows the moment when Christ reveals himself by his blessing and breaking of the bread. Coupled with the revealing gesture of Christ is the clarifying action of the strong light that poetically embodies the illumination of the minds of the disciples. Their reaction is violent, in contrast to the darkened face of the uncomprehending innkeeper. Caravaggio's message was simple, intended for the least sophisticated and humblest viewer: The common man may have direct knowledge of his God. The miraculous can occur without angels, halos, or opening of the skies. Christ's epiphany takes place in the heart of the faithful. The modest dress and table fare were obvious means by which to remind the faithful of Christ's humility. Not unlike the Flemish painters of the fifteenth century, Caravaggio detailed every surface evidence provided by his subjects, from the contrasting complexions of the figures to the worm holes in the fruit. Caravaggio attached mystical feelings to the most tangible items. Unlike the Flemings, Caravaggio placed the action against a plain background and spotlighted only the figures and table. He involved the viewer more intimately in the scene through the violent foreshortening of the gestures and precarious balance of the fruit on the near edge of the table. The disciple at the left is so turned as to draw the eye immediately to the hand of Christ and thence to His face, the table, and the figure at the right. The strenuous extended gesture of the latter, which seems to push into our space, is paralleled by the angle of the table before him, thus harnessing the number of strong movements that otherwise would mitigate each other. Caravaggio has demonstrated the expressiveness of which the profile is capable. Often using models taken into his studio from the street, the painter was at his most forceful in painting rugged or picturesque types and most disconcerting to the public when he attempted the head of Christ.

Many Church officials, and it would seem the general public, found Caravaggio's painting vulgar or lacking in decorum and unnecessarily impoverishing the holy personages. He was criticized for painting distracting objects, such as the still-life arrangement of the table, which undermined the drama of the moment. Because he avoided elaborate and traditional didacticism, Caravaggio's work was also condemned for not being self-explanatory. To those unacquainted with the story, the supper may have seemed like a secular event. And in fact, the seventeenth century was to see a further obscuring of the lines that separated religious from secular painting.

Having begun this chapter with examples from Renaissance and Counter Reformation painting, we should now look briefly at what happened in religious architecture. Bramante's Tempietto (Fig. 215) was designed to mark the spot in Rome of St. Peter's crucifixion. It is openly based upon ancient Roman circular temple architecture in plan, use of columns and dome. This small chapel was intended to be set within a different courtyard than exists today, but the surrounding pavement still bears inlaid concentric circles which converge or radiate from the center of the building, affirming the cosmic significance of the site. This domical centralized plan, which was also indebted to Leonardo, had celestial symbolism. The dome had an ancient ancestry of symbolizing heaven. The authority and centrality of Rome and the Church are further manifested by this formal hieratic design. The formality of the repetitive architectural elements, steps, columns, balustrade, and niches, facilitate its reading, and their obvious harmony was intended to infuse the visitor with an awareness of divine order in the universe. Just as the Tempietto is one of the landmarks of Renaissance architecture, so is Francesco Borromini's small church of S. Carlo alle Quattro Fontane (Fig. 216) one of the great achievements of seventeenth-century architecture. Bor-

Figure 215. DONATO BRAMANTE. The Tempietto, 1502. S. Pietro in Montorio, Rome.

Figure 216. FRANCESCO BORROMINI. S. Carlo alle Quattro Fontane (S. Carlino), Rome. Begun 1638; façade 1665–67.

romini rejected Renaissance and ancient Roman architectural vocabulary and grammar and equally resisted design such as Bramante's based on human proportion. The curving inflections of his façade and dramatic jumps in the scale of his columns as well as the reception of light and dark discourage reasoned analysis and create a more exciting visual effect. As with Counter Reformation painting, Borromini wanted to dramatize the Church. Unlike Bramante and most of his own contemporaries in architecture such as Bernini, he integrated sculpture with architecture. Strongly influenced by Michelangelo, he gives his columns, walls, and horizontal dividing elements a sensual or sculptural quality. Rather than the predictability of Bramante's design, Borromini opts for the unexpected, such as breaking the upper cornice line or placing a convex window above the doorway. Borromini's church seems alive to pulls and pressures (thus responding to the undulating oval interior plan), unlike the more passive dignified Renaissance structure. In painting the comparable differences would be between a figure by Piero della Francesca and one by Caravaggio, or Raphael's vision of the *School of Athens* and Pozzo's explosive heaven.

Sixteenth- and seventeenth-century art was filled with vitality, and religious art nourished within itself even broader secular human interest than before. Simple lines of over-all development do not exist, and in each period there are divergent and contradictory styles. Energy, affluence, recognition of individuality, great issues, and powerful patrons and institutions all combined for enormous productivity, which was as uneven in quality as it was in styles and viewpoints. Along with sincere and passionately inspired personal statements of faith, Counter Reformation art also laid the foundations for banal, insincere commercial religious art which afflicts too many churches today. Side by side with the continued emergence of many artists of genius, bad religious art came into being on an unprecedented scale. The means for making a convincing representation of a lovely pious Virgin and adorable Christ child were henceforth easily available to any painter who would trade on the sentiment for an undiscriminating congregation and clergy.

10

THE TABLE
IN BAROQUE SECULAR ART

More than in the preceding centuries, seventeenth-century European painting broadened its base to include varied and intimate secular subjects. Simultaneously with the great religious art produced in this century, art that responded to the curiosity of artist and patron about the daily living of the peasant and middle classes increased in the Roman Catholic countries as well as in Protestant Holland. Building upon sixteenth-century secular art, the seventeenth century derived important secular art not only from the more customary intellectual sources such as ancient literature but also from folk traditions, business, and social and domestic life, in subjects that explored the unethical, irreverent, sexual, vulgar, comical, and passive aspects of human conduct. The people chosen to populate what are called "genre" paintings were given more human dimensions than those of the imposing figures in Renaissance art. Whereas the Renaissance had discovered the means to render the actual or ideal outward appearance of men caught most often in heroic action or serious contemplative attitudes, during the Baroque period the painter's knowledge of and concern for expressing vivid emotions and the workings of the mind became paramount. The full range of

human animation came much closer to realization in seventeenth-century than in fifteenth-century art. This new focus and enlivening of human activity had important consequences for the form of painting.

Genre painting resists strict categorization, for it may overlap into religious art, allegory, and historical painting. At the core of the notion of genre painting is the relinquishing of a climactic or historical moment in favor of activities that are part of the stream of daily existence. Generally, it deals with *types* of persons involved in *types* of common occurrences, but frequently a painter goes beyond this typification into portraiture to depict the participants or chooses unique moments in the life of his subjects. Early genre painting was based upon the growing tolerance of secular art, a basic optimism toward and affirmation of earthly existence, and curiosity about the way large segments of humanity pass their days. Although this art form eschews the ritual that was so much a part of religious and political imagery, nevertheless, it concerns itself with the rituals of daily life in the home and tavern, the bank house and brothel.

Partisanship or social conscience was not the motivation for depicting peasant life. The misery, oppression, and tragedies of the peasants or the lower middle classes did not find their way into seventeenth-century art. Genre art was not intended to be democratic, for it affirmed class distinctions. Favored themes were those of diversion, local or class customs, or quiet revery, which did not threaten the established social order but provided the upper classes with vicarious experiences. The middle class as well as the aristocracy bought this type of art. The relative political and religious security enjoyed by the monarchs and the Roman Catholic Church in Europe during the seventeenth century was responsible for a relaxation of demands on the painter. Roman Catholic countries witnessed the phenomenon of painters doing both official work for the Church and the courts and genre painting for prominent churchmen as well as the laity.

In Holland, specialization came into being during this century, so that most artists painted only landscapes, portraits, still lifes, or genre art, depending upon their success with the market. Genre art, which was rarely commissioned, denoted the double edge of freedom and material insecurity that accrued to the artist during the Baroque period. In Holland, by midcentury the market was overloaded, and painters were forced to take on additional jobs or give up painting altogether.

While there is much of esthetic value that we admire today in seventeenth-century genre art, the general public who bought or speculated in this art in its time was guided primarily by fidelity to appearance and cannot be considered as connoisseurs. Genre painting was not entirely uninfluenced by religious and official painting, but the genre artist did have great license in making his paintings. The format of genre art is usually smaller than that of the grandiose paintings done for the Church or the royal courts. It was intended for the more modest scale of the home and for greater intimacy of viewing. The proximity of the figures to the picture's surface and the emphasis upon costumes, accessories, locale, and facial expression or gesture compelled a close reading and quiet contemplation.

An object frequently found in Baroque genre painting as a compositional and social catalyst is the table. In religious art the table, though used occasionally to hold the books of a Church scholar or the devotional objects of a saint, was most widely identified with the themes of the Last Supper and Christ at Emmaus. Not only did the table serve as a setting for the enactment of an important sacred drama, but Renaissance painters also utilized it as a means of linking the historical past with contemporary social customs, as we have noted earlier. In genre painting the table became the natural locus of various occasions for which people gather as well as for individual activity. Genre art, with its fidelity to everyday human life, contributed to the evolution of a broadly imitative form of painting best defined as naturalism.

Such an occasion where the table serves as a meeting place for a segment of the community is the wedding feast, as presented in a painting by the Flemish artist Pieter Bruegel (Pl. 22). Though not the first, Bruegel was the most gifted genre painter of his century in depicting the daily life of the Flemish peasants. The little available biographical material indicates that he himself was not a peasant but a rather highly educated townsman, whose paintings were bought and admired by kings and many of the intellectual elite of his day. A humanist, Bruegel regarded his art as a means of recording his study of man, not in terms of ancient writers and philosophers or the coordinate system of the Church, but in the light of advanced contemporary secular theories and his own empirical experience. Bruegel's art reflects his astuteness as an observer, not criticism of nor compassion for the peasantry. He saw the peasant not as the symbol of a basic natural wisdom but as an unreasoning creature who passively submitted to forces greater than himself. The peasants are always involved in some hereditary activity—the dominant note in their work, customs, and traditions. Bruegel's figures are motivated by simple, uncomplicated drives and enact their existence automatically, often with great vigor if not with great cheer. (Smiling peasants are rare in his paintings.)

Bruegel's subjects, whether Biblical or genre, share the phenomenon of recurrence, as if the artist had sought and set down certain eternal constants in life. Not content with social reportage, Bruegel brought to art a gift of lucid analysis and a genius for storytelling that elevates his *Peasant Wedding* from a prosaic event to good theater. The earth was Bruegel's stage and those upon it his characters. In this painting the set is a grain-filled barn after the harvest.

An overflow of guests comes to celebrate the personal harvest of the farmer's daughter, who sits both coyly and smugly beneath a symbolic crown hung on a green cloth. The full grain stacks and the ripe bride are meaningfully associated, as are the groom and the fertility symbol of the crossed sheaves hanging before his eyes. Art historians were unable to agree on identification of the groom, but the literary historian Gilbert Highet found him in the dark-clad, intoxicated figure in the center, just to the left of the rear figure holding the door being used as a serving tray. The ill-mannered groom and his glaring parents seated opposite are wealthy townspeople, and as Highet points out, Bruegel encourages our speculations on both the wedding night and the married life of the bridal couple—though the painting's evidence makes the future quite clear.

A few of the subthemes in the nuptial drama are the friar's earnest pleas for subsidy from the obdurate landlord at the far right, who seems to enjoy the occasion less than does his dog; the longing gaze of the bagpiper at the distant food; and the contrast between the bride's brother filling a jug at the left and the little girl cleaning her plate. The activity of the former figure recalls Christ's changing of the water into wine at the Marriage of Cana. In fact, the diagonal composition of the long table and triangular grouping in the left foreground can be found in sixteenth-century paintings of the Last Supper, as was seen in the painting by Tintoretto (Fig. 202). These objects also assist in maintaining the viewer's detachment from the action. The ample figures are hard edged in their firm outlines, so that the pile of round jugs in the basket invites an ironic comparison with the peasants who emptied them and with the piled-up figures in the doorway at the upper left who also wait to be filled.

The broad secularization of painting in the seventeenth century and its sociology of the table introduced themes involving satisfaction of the senses. In particular, painters and their audiences delighted in the concerns of the mouth, the appetite for food and beverage, and the gratification of the palate. Eating and drinking are fundamental to life, and Baroque painters recorded all forms of table manners and dietary preference, in a way and with a gusto that is unmatched by the photographic illustrations in a modern cookbook. The young

Caravaggio painted a well-fed, contemplative boy in the guise of Bacchus (Fig. 217). (There is debate as to whether or not this is a self-portrait.) The wine god's attributes afforded the painter the objects of a still-life study, just as the model's features lent themselves to portraiture rather than Classical idealization. (This type of painting is called a "portrait situation.") As was evident in his later *Christ at Emmaus* (Pl. 21), Caravaggio was taken with the possibilities of half-length figures, which forced the viewer's focus upon the subject. Along with being a catalogue of the effects of light upon varied textures, the painting is a study in many types of balance, from the way the elegant glass is held to the disposition of fruit and the wine carafe on the table, and even in the languorous position of the semi-reclining body. Curiously, the most immediate and seemingly stable shape is that of the glass supported by three fingers—which would suggest an unusually sober god of the grape. Later in the seventeenth century, artists were to show in extravagant ways the stronger effects and imbalance caused by alcohol, a tone that Caravaggio avoided in his restrained make-believe Bacchus.

Figure 217. CARAVAGGIO (MICHELANGELO MERISI). *Bacchus.* c. 1590. Oil, 38½″ × 33½″. Uffizi, Florence.

Above: Figure 218. ANNIBALE CARRACCI. *The Bean Eater.* c. 1585. Oil on canvas, 22⅜″ × 26¾″. Galleria Colonna, Rome.

Below: Figure 219. JACOB JORDAENS. *The Satyr and the Peasant Family.* c. 1612–18. Oil on canvas, 6′3½″ × 6′8″. Musées Royaux des Beaux-Arts, Brussels.

A contemporary of Caravaggio, Annibale Carracci, for the first time in history centered a painting on a man eating (Fig. 218); a rugged anonymous peasant fills his mouth with beans while clutching a roll. The great polarity of Baroque painting is shown by Domenichino's depiction of St. Jerome receiving the Eucharistic wafer and Carracci's *Bean Eater.* The former eats to partake of Christ's body and so ensure his future in heaven, while the latter figure is concerned with satisfying his stomach and staying alive. The association of the human mouth with both sacred and secular rituals has an interesting mythological analogy in a painting by the Flemish artist Jacob Jordaens, who shows a satyr at a table with a peasant family (Fig. 219). Jordaens was illustrating a fable of Aesop in which peasants who had given shelter to a cold and hungry satyr invited him to their table. The satyr saw the man blowing on his hands, and was told this was to warm them; then he watched the peasant blow on his soup, and was told this was to cool it. The satyr thereupon left the table, for he wisely distrusted those who blow hot and cold with the same breath. Jordaens enjoyed painting the heavy peasant types right down to their bare feet.

Figure 220. JACOB JORDAENS. *The King Drinks*. 1638. Oil on canvas, 8′7½″ × 9′4⅝″.
Musées Royaux des Beaux-Arts, Brussels.

In this instance, the wisdom of the proverb had to compete with the artist's succulent rendering of flesh.

In Jordaens' *The King Drinks* (Fig. 220), the occasion, which comes from Flemish folklore, is the feast celebrating the day of Epiphany, during which the entire clan assembles for feasting and drinking. Shortly before Epiphany, "King's tickets" were sold in Antwerp. The old man in Jordaens' painting, having made the lucky draw among the tickets at the table, becomes reigning monarch. His drinking signals an explosion of festivity. To each relative he has assigned a mock title for his "court"—the "Singer," the "Cock," the "Doctor," and the "Spinster." Jordaens epitomizes that aspect of Baroque art which delighted in situations where the individual, consciously or not, lost control and abandoned himself to feeling. In paintings such as this, the seventeenth century introduces raucous, laughing figures; before this time,

only angels or the Madonna smiled decorously as a sign of divine grace. The stimulant for laughter in *The King Drinks* and many other Baroque paintings is alcohol, and the dominant mood is one of abandon. The family table has become the setting for an orgy of the senses. In the Renaissance and the sixteenth century, mythical figures such as satyrs and nymphs might be shown having a riotous picnic in an ancient wood, but with the seventeenth century such themes were brought directly into home or tavern.

Both in form and content, this is a painting concerned with the five senses. The figures make or respond to noise, catch the eye with exaggerated or grotesque expressions, fondle objects sensuously, inhale a variety of odors, and taste and savor a staggering array of food and drink. In a way, this painting is also a study of cycles, distinguishing the flesh of young and old, presenting a broad range of

Figure 221. ADRIAEN BROUWER. *The Smokers.*
c. 1630. Oil on canvas, 18⅛" × 14⅜". The
Metropolitan Museum of Art, New York (The
Michael Friedsam Collection).

expressions from anticipation to satiation, and
so on. Jordaens displays great virtuosity in
demonstrating the number of ways people may
be portrayed with their mouths open. Faces
have a great mobility, which at times borders
on caricature. The artist's insight into the
ritual rather than spontaneous character of the
event is manifested in the forced quality of
some of the jeering expressions.

The painting itself is an assault on the senses
and tastes of the viewer. Strongly flavored
with reds, blues, and yellows, its silhouettes
seem to weave back and forth and defy equilibrium. The dark jacket and relative stability
of the musician standing to the "king's" left
serves as foil and anchorage for the agitated
goings on. The costumes and flesh of the
figures are painted so as to stress their appeal to
the touch as well as to the eye. Depicting a
scene at once hilarious and vulgar, the artist
reserves good taste for the actual mechanics of
painting, for color and design rather than sub-

ject matter. Above the "king" are the words,
"It is sweet to be admitted to a friendly table."

Such a proverb written above Adriaen
Brouwer's *The Smokers* (Fig. 221) would constitute a fine irony. A Flemish painter active in
Holland, Brouwer was preoccupied with the
boisterous life around the tavern table. His small
paintings catalogue drinking bouts, brawls,
cooking, eating, gossiping, gambling, tooth-
pulling, and painful operations on feet and, in
one instance, on his own back. His sitters appear
to be fellow artists rather than peasants.
Daringly, he devoted entire paintings to gross
types with bulbous inflamed noses and gaping
mouths, or to sleeping drunks with deluded
notions of exalted status. His self-portraits show
discoloration and deterioration in his own face
due to alcohol. Brouwer's *The Smokers*, probably
done in the 1630s, is a personal avowal of
manliness and the ethic of being oneself.
The artist can drink and smoke with the best,
take practical jokes, withstand pain, and not
give a damn for whoever looks at his painting.
Naturally disdainful of contemporary theories
on composition and drawing, Brouwer sketched
coarsely, but his characters and his painting
convey the disorder of a tavern atmosphere,
with its stale smells and murky lighting. The
paint is applied ruggedly and with gusto, the
technique also affirming his distaste for the
effeminate and precious. His strokes and tones
convincingly render the garments and flesh that
belong to those poor in pocket but rich in their
enjoyment of earthly pleasures.

MORALIZING
AND ALLEGORY

From Holland in the early seventeenth century
came the morbid association of food with human
vanity or life's brevity. In a large painting of an
interrupted banquet attributed to the French
artist Jean Le Clerc (Fig. 222), a skeleton
dramatically intrudes, implying the second
and more obvious meaning of the *memento mori.*
(Catholics feared a death too sudden to permit
the last rites.) The festive costumes and the
highlighting of the man and woman to the
right suggest that this may have been a marriage
supper and that it is the bridegroom whom
Death calls. The painter pulls out all dramatic

stops in contrasting the vehement reactions of the revelers to Death's apparition. Rather than terror or awe, the sybaritic guests at the left seem to register dismay and displeasure at the meal's interruption. The broad stagey character of the gestures and the extremes of light and shadow unmistakably place the artist among Caravaggio's following.

To understand the meaning of a handsome couple seated at a table on which is a book, flowers, and fruit requires knowing that Marten de Vos was interpreting one of the four humors, which in the past were thought to characterize human physiology and explain temperament. The four humors or fluids that mingled in varying proportions in the body were blood, phlegm, and yellow and black bile, and the preponderance of one or another led to a personality that was sanguine, phlegmatic, choleric, or melancholy. De Vos did drawings for a series of four prints, of which that on the sanguine temperament is illustrated (Fig. 223). How well the artist embodied the characteristics of this type can be seen in the fact that those having a large proportion of blood were thought to be well knit in body, ruddy of complexion,

Above: Figure 222. JEAN LE CLERC. *Memento Mori.* 1615–20. Oil on canvas, 3′11½″ × 5′8½″. The Isaac Delgado Museum of Art, New Orleans (Gift of Mrs. William Helis, Sr.).

Below: Figure 223. MARTEN DE VOS (1532–1603). *The Sanguine Temperament.* Engraving, 7½″ × 8½″. Private collection.

The Table in Baroque Secular Art   193

sociable, generous, and possessing talents of all descriptions. They were supposed to have a weakness for wine, good food, and love. De Vos shows dancing, feats of archery, and episodes of courtship in the background, while the two principals in the foreground are shown as gentle, thoughtful people of discriminating taste and intellectual interest. Enjoyment of music signified a harmonious nature. Such healthy solid types as conceived by De Vos were to bear strong influence on Rubens' art. (Incidentally, prints were not framed and set under glass as in current practice; they were originally kept in folios and taken out by their owners for moments of quiet and intimate perusal as well as esthetic enjoyment.)

BUSINESS AT THE TABLE

Secular paintings of genre subjects involving the table go back to the early sixteenth century, and one of the earliest of these introduces the theme of business. In *A Money Changer and His Wife* (Fig. 224), the Flemish painter Quentin Massys showed the couple receiving a call from a client, who is visible in the small convex mirror on the table. The painting served as a double portrait honoring the husband's profession and

Figure 224. QUENTIN MASSYS (MATSYS, METSYS). *A Money Changer and His Wife.* 1514. Oil, 28″ × 27″. Louvre, Paris.

his wife's piety. Unlike the painting of St. Eligius by Petrus Christus (Fig. 142), in which secular objects help identify a holy man, in Massys' work a holy book is the pious attribute of the businessman's spouse. The possible significance of her dividing her attention between the prayer book and the scales—a touch that might at first glance seem purely sardonic—was to certify the honesty of their business. In a figurative sense, the convex glass reflects the delight of the Flemish painters in mirroring the actual world. Its small curved surface allowed the tour de force of simulating greater space than that in which the couple actually sits. Paintings and prints such as this found their way to Rome and were known to Caravaggio, who probably was strongly influenced by their format and crisp, lifelike style.

The table appears in the Spanish artist Diego Velázquez' *Water Seller of Seville* (Pl. 23) as an adjunct to business, furnishing a base for an earthenware water jug. A painter of Spanish royalty, Velázquez did not spare his brilliant talent in portraying a street vendor named El Corzo, his young clients, and the modest objects of his trade. The mundane act of selling water has been solemnized by the painter into an almost sacramental event, and it is not improbable that Velázquez had the sacrament of the Eucharist in mind. There is no intimation of the noise and jostling of the streets. The boy drinking is in shadow, while in strong illumination the vendor and another boy receiving a glass seem to share silently in a meditative union. Both in content and in form Velázquez has changed small coin into gold. The strongly individual qualities of El Corzo, the youth holding the glass (containing a fig to keep the water fresh), and even the jugs rise above typicality and are impressed on the memory. The still tractable face of the youth contrasts with the traces of hard use in the face of the older man and the jug upon which his hand rests. There is no overt attempt at pathos. The large objects and three-quarter figures, presented close to the viewer, have a restrained dignity and give a powerful affirmation of their worth. Immobility adds to their eloquence. The effect is obtained through a formal closure of shapes, holding the eye within the frame. A rough ovular form is created by the placement and linkage of the large jug with the shadow of the smaller and the hand of the man, the small jug's tangency with the boy's wrist, the glass and the boy's right arm leading to the head and those of the other two figures, and then the smock's curvature, which returns the eye to the large jug and anchors the oval to the frame at the right. A few tones—chiefly grey, terra cotta, white, and flesh color—are applied over large areas with deft nuance; reserved for the glass and droplets of moisture on the jug are the most brilliant highlights. The lucid lighting and the firm drawing of the forms are countered by the subtle painterly manner in which the pigment has been applied.

Although possessing an ancient history as a profession, prostitution was not introduced as a theme for printmaking and painting until the sixteenth century. Mary Magdalene had been shown much earlier in religious paintings, but always as a penitent or closed in a convent. A painting known as *The Procuress* that is probably, but not certainly, by Vermeer is one of many done by Netherlandish artists on the theme of commercial love (Fig. 225). Unlike predecessors who often dwelled on the ugliness of lechers, whores, and madams, Vermeer shows two well-dressed, handsome young men clearly able to afford their pleasure with an attractive professional. The gay drinker at the left smiles in our direction as an indication of his mood, but also as a way of welcoming the viewer as an accomplice. Unusual for Vermeer is the involved range of expressions and interchange between his subjects. As was frequently done by other Dutch artists, his placement of the richly patterned rug over the table of the foreground afforded painterly enrichment. Vermeer's later paintings involving men and women are more circumspect descriptions of restrained, socially acceptable courtship.

GAMES AND MUSIC AT TABLE

The pastime of gaming, with its elements of chance and cheating, delighted an age in which high morality was so vigorously championed by the powerful force of the churches. Although not the first card game painted in history (the theme had entered painting from the North earlier in the sixteenth century), Caravaggio's *Card Sharps* (Fig. 226) was the most influential.

Figure 225. JAN VERMEER(?). *The Procuress.* 1656. Oil on canvas, 4'8¼ × 4'3¼". Gemäldegalerie, Dresden.

Figure 226. CARAVAGGIO (MICHELANGELO MERISI). *Card Sharps.* c. 1593. Oil on canvas, 3'3"×4'6". Formerly Sciarra Collection, Rome.

The Table in Baroque Secular Art   195

It survives only in photographs and numerous copies but, like so many of his other works, was definitely seen by foreign artists visiting Rome. Despite the acute characterizations and delineation of the figures, this was not a painting simply extracted from some scene in a contemporary Roman tavern. The players, dressed in costumes of a fanciful character, are seen against a background which is so bare as to eliminate conjecture as to locale but which serves to throw the actors into brilliant relief. Artful arrangement of the poses allows one to see all phases of the deception and results in movement toward the picture's center from both sides. Caravaggio's skill at showing a person doing two different things at once deeply impressed his contemporaries. Within the self-imposed restrictions of depicting a few figures in a tight space seen from close up, Caravaggio demonstrated that he could tell a good story with great vigor. One of many challenges he laid down for later artists was the ingenuity with which he could render the human head three times in close proximity and from different viewpoints, at the same time strengthening the plausibility of the narrative. Ironically, in view of the previous symbolism of light, the profile of the card sharp at the right is given fullest illumination. Unquestionably, Caravaggio's interest in games was personal, and as a result of a violent scoring dispute in a tennis match, he fatally stabbed his partner in the groin. Despite his personal notoriety, his paintings were sought after by both the aristocracy and clergy. The *Card Sharps* was, in fact, purchased by a cardinal—in itself a commentary on the inconsistent moral conservatism of the Counter Reformation.

A Dutch painter who worked in Rome from 1604 to 1616 and who consciously took whole compositional and stylistic ideas from Caravaggio was Hendrick Terbrugghen. It is a euphemism of painters and art historians to say that one artist "borrows" from another, for there is no historical evidence that this was a two-way arrangement. The strongly centralized focus, the intense concentration of animated figures in a seemingly airless space, and the clear hard light that Caravaggio made possible for painters deeply appealed to the Dutchman. As lifelike as Terbrugghen's *Three Men Playing Dice* (Fig. 227) may seem, it is a reminder that, throughout the history of art, artists have painted pictures from other pictures or, in other words, that art comes from life *and* art. Seventeenth-century painters not only studied the faces and movements of their models but also looked to notable painters such as Caravaggio for means of achieving firm volumes, expressive gestures, effective lighting, and placement of half-length figures within a limited rectangular area. The merit of any pictorial synthesis lies in the extent to which an artist can unobtrusively integrate with his own what he has

Figure 228. GEORGES DE LA TOUR. *The Cheat*, c. 1630. Oil on canvas, 3'5¾" × 4'11½". Collection Pierre Landry, Paris.

stolen, and thus impress his audience that he has gone beyond his predecessor, for instance, by making better use of modeling under clear light or in contrasting the expressive properties of hands and faces. Caravaggio's great reputation resides not only in the fertility of his ideas but also in how fresh and inventive his conceptions continue to appear when compared with most of those who had the opportunity to improve upon them. On the other hand, this is not the case when Caravaggio's work is matched with that of his own predecessors. Although Terbrugghen's effort produced a good, vivid painting having perhaps more vibrant and sensuous color and fuller and firmer surfaces than its Italian source, it nonetheless stands in the same relation to the *Card Sharps* as a colonizer to a pioneer.

In *The Cheat* (Fig. 228), painted by the French artist Georges de la Tour about 1630, the table is again the setting for intrigue, deceit, and downfall. La Tour's use of this theme followed a stay in Rome, where he may have encountered the pictorial idea. The subject may be related to the story of the Prodigal Son, favored by the Roman Catholic authorities in support of the sacrament of penance against the Protestants. Both the painting and the card game are highly contrived. The players are outfitted in what for the time were outlandish costumes. The deck is stacked against the young man in such a way that if the aces don't get his money,

wine and the courtesan at the table will. The cheat has an affected air of nonchalance, encouraging the unsuspecting youth to look at his cards as the wily opponent reaches for an ace in his belt. The eyes and hands alone are sufficient to tell the story. All the hand movements have a suave boneless ease that serves to enact the deception and also to tie the figures together visually. The shadowing of the cheat's face recalls that of Judas in earlier versions of the Last Supper. This dark deed, however, is performed in daylight, which coolly illuminates the firm, smooth volumes of the bodies and the sparkle of the shiny accessories. The airless milieu makes possible a meticulous clarity of detail in presenting types who themselves seem all surface and no depth.

Caravaggio's influence was often passed on through Italian followers, who in turn taught painters such as the Frenchman Valentin de Boullogne. Such genre paintings as his *Soldiers and Bohemians* (Pl. 24) are important historically because they show the growing separation of painting not only from religious symbolism but also from secular allegory or moralizing. Earlier we have seen how ancient ruins were used in conjunction with Christian subjects, as in Ghirlandaio's *Adoration of the Shepherds* (Fig. 168). Here Valentin uses a Roman architectural fragment for an inn table. In the sixteenth century, musical instruments often symbolized Christian virtues, godlike attributes, or intellectual and poetic gifts, but in this work they are instead the natural means of pleasure for low social types. The pocket-picking incident at the left was one of the ordinary hazards of frequenting public inns. Without the powerful concentration of Caravaggio's *Card Sharps*, Valentin has disposed his figures more casually in depth around the table, which is now set on a diagonal. The color is comparably softened, with a simple triad of reds, yellows, and blues played off harmoniously against one another and against the colder greys and the dark browns of the costumes and setting, in what is a more painterly style than that of Caravaggio. Instead of striving to create the illusion of actual textures, Valentin adapts the movement and weight of his brush and pigment to suggest a change of surfaces and stuffs—the hard sheen of metal, for example. The relaxed mood of the entire painting arises from the effortless way that each figure twists in a different direction, turning in and out of the light, free to move in a more generous orbit than Caravaggio provided his gamblers. The common device of the interlocutor between the viewer and the action that was first used in the fifteenth century (here seen in the soldier at the left who looks over his shoulder in our direction) is made less obvious by casting much of the face in shadow and giving greater prominence to the foreshortened blue sleeve. Less tightly composed than Caravaggio's scenes, Valentin's compositions introduced a relaxed air into French painting.

The indistinguishability of genre and religious themes of the seventeenth century is demonstrated in a superb engraving by the French artist Jacques Callot entitled *The Card Players* (Fig. 229). Some scholars see it as a variation on the

Figure 229. JACQUES CALLOT. *The Card Players*. 1628. Etching, 8½″ × 11″. The Metropolitan Museum of Art, New York (Dick Fund).

theme of the Prodigal Son, identified with the figure who sits in the center assisting the woman with her cards. (The music of the harp would have contributed to his seduction.) But the theme of cavaliers and courtesans making love, enjoying music, or gaming at a table was already widespread before this print. Callot sets the scene at night, so that the players are seen by candlelight. Engraving lent itself to abrupt contrasts between brilliant illumination and darkness, as well as to silhouetting and incisive modeling. Rather than using flat blacks, Callot crosshatched the dark areas so that they vibrate against the white patches. A superb draftsman and printmaker, whose work is all of small size, Callot is an example of a truly major artist who did not make his reputation as a painter or sculptor. His talent was not as a subtle analyst of the human face, for he was more interested in the psychology of gesture and costume. Characterization derived from the entire clothed figure and the movement of all its joints.

The table, a natural place for the family to assemble, was often used for a portrait situation. One of the earliest family portraits utilizing still life and the table was done by the Flemish artist Maerten van Heemskerck (Fig. 230). The prosperous-looking family is rather self-consciously arranged, with the figures posed not unlike the clear separation of objects on the table, and their silhouettes are sharply delineated against the sky. Outdoor eating was not altogether unusual in the Netherlands, as can be seen by Jan Steen's painting in the next century; yet van Heemskerck's work has the contrived air of having been done in the studio, with a natural backdrop painted in later. The pose of the naked child and its mother may have been intended to recall paintings of the Madonna and child—an association that would not be impious in the kind of well-to-do and proper family represented. Van Heemskerck, perhaps aware of the previous lack of easy interrelationships between figures in Flemish art, seems to have tried to infuse his work with the graceful movement of the Italian art he admired. Although the result is a rather stilted synthesis, the painter's over-all richness of observation keeps a certain compelling attraction.

The table as identified with the unity and humility of the family can be seen in Louis Le Nain's *Peasants at Supper* (Fig. 231), painted

Figure 230. MAERTEN VAN HEEMSKERCK. *Family Portrait.* c. 1530. Oil on panel, 3′10½″ × 4′7″. Staatliche Kunstsammlungen, Kassel.

Figure 231. LOUIS LE NAIN. *Peasants at Supper.* 1645–48. Oil on canvas, 3′8½″ × 5′2½″. Louvre, Paris.

Figure 232. JAN STEEN. *The Inn Garden*. Oil on canvas, 26¾ × 22⅞″. Staatliche Museen, Berlin.

between 1645 and 1648. The table is the means by which the family comes together each day and shares the quiet pleasures of home, hearth, and board. Absent from the painting, however, are the noise, movement, and disorder that one would expect to find during or even after the evening meal. There is no overt rapport between the figures: those in the foreground look toward the viewer, those in the shadows gaze into the fire. Le Nain, perhaps seeking to extol the probity of the peasant, cast him in an artificial mold, and each figure is very consciously posed. The child in the lower right corner, like the objects carefully distributed near him, serves as a visual stabilizer for the composition. Each person is carefully turned so as to counterbalance another figure, eliminating any impression of volition or spontaneity. The general air of decorum in the peasant hut is shared with official painting of French royalty. Le Nain stressed the peasant's reflective capacity and graceful composure, rather than his life of arduous labor or moments of energetic diversion. The painting's strength lies largely in the realization of the materiality of figures,

objects, and setting. The hard reality of the bodies and garments is heightened by soft gradients of shadow and the way the light rebounds from surfaces. Le Nain displays and elicits a certain detachment, a refusal to become deeply and emotionally involved with the subjects; yet he holds them aloof with obvious respect.

The Dutch painter Jan Steen's *The Inn Garden* (Fig. 232) has more of the familiar casualness or disarray of a family outing than the two preceding family paintings. Seventeenth-century Dutch painting of the family stressed mutual good feeling and the enjoyment of food and congenial surroundings; any disquieting notes are absent. Sociologically, and like its dining table, Steen's family is different from that of Heemskerck, and the former is not so self-consciously concerned with projecting a staid public image for posterity. Such pleasant views of the family had strong appeal in the Dutch art market, widely supported by people such as those portrayed. Such painting flattered their pride in and increased their enjoyment of national customs, games, social events, and creation of convivial surroundings for peaceful diversion. It may be said that Steen, who had a good eye for relaxed postures and situations (and this chapter has already given a sampling of the impressive number of ways that people can sit at a table)—rather than Rembrandt—was a typical Dutch painter of the era.

While for some Dutch artists, influenced greatly by Caravaggio, the table signified the opportunity for melodramatic enactment of debauchery or perverse conduct, Pieter de Hooch satisfied his countrymen's middle-class taste by showing tables in settings of propriety and quiet sociability. His paintings frequently show tables in arbors, intimate courtyards, or neat interiors around which are gathered well-bred gentlemen who play an honest game of cards, imbibe with discretion, or converse wittily with pleasant hostesses. One of de Hooch's finest paintings is *The Mother at the Cradle* (Fig. 233). Here the table, although set off to the side, is identified with domesticity, the care and vigilance of the wife for the children and the home. This ideal of insulated, constant security is measured out not alone in the relation of the mother to the cradle but also in the cool geometrical rightness and sun-warmed atmosphere of the rooms. Everything is in its correct

Plate 29. REMBRANDT VAN RIJN. *The Jewish Bride*. 1668. Oil on canvas, 3′10⅜″ × 5′4½″. Rijksmuseum, Amsterdam.

Plate 30.   *Emperor on Horseback*, leaf of the so-called *Barberini Diptych* (or *Ivory*). c. 500.
Ivory, 13⅜ × 10″. Louvre, Paris.

Plate 31.   JEAN CLOUET. *Francis I.* c. 1525–30. Oil on panel, 37¾ × 29″. Louvre, Paris.

Plate 32. ANTHONY VAN DYCK. *Charles I.* c. 1635. Oil on canvas, 8′11″ × 6′11 ½″. Louvre, Paris.

place to make up an ideal home and a beautifully arranged painting. Even the dog has turned his body at a right angle to the floor tiles and is tangent to the door frame, taking the eye both into the vestibule beyond and toward the mother. Through the door and windows comes not a suggestion of the sounds and sights of Holland's political anguish but only a dreamlike stillness, the reassuring heat of the sun and the fragrance of well-tended gardens.

THE TABLE AND SELF-PREOCCUPATION

We have seen how in many ways sixteenth- and seventeenth-century art moved into new areas of life, and eventually painting invaded the bedroom as tastes developed for the intimate and erotic. (Previously art showed only the Virgin's bedroom for the Annunciation or her death.) A mid-sixteenth-century painting by an unknown artist working at the French palace of Fontainebleau, *Lady at Her Toilette* (Fig. 234),

Figure 235. JAN VERMEER. *A Woman Weighing Gold.* c. 1660. Oil on canvas, 16½″ × 13¾″. The National Gallery of Art, Washington, D.C. (Widener Collection).

introduces the theme of what might be called "self-preoccupation." Venetian artists such as Titian depicted similar mythological subjects, for example, Venus at her toilette, but in this case it is certain that the nearly naked woman was readily identifiable at the French court. Similar paintings were done of the mistresses of French kings, and these became so popular as to be copied. The young woman is shown before her dressing table, with one hand touching her necklace, the other holding a ring. (This double gesture descended from Greek sculptures of Venus and from Renaissance Madonnas.) The action of holding the ring has been interpreted as an erotic sign or as her indication of a desire for marriage. As in Venetian paintings of Venus in her bedroom, a maidservant is shown in the background, and here too a mirror reflects the young woman's face. Conceivably she was being presented in the guise of Venus. In the sophisticated society of the

time, the meaning of the various objects and the mirror decoration would undoubtedly have been explicit. (For instance, we do not know for certain whether there is a veiled moralizing reference to vanity.) Courtly taste, as much as artistic style, influenced the elegant and restrained sensuousness of the naked torso. Art such as this had a cool, even detached attitude toward the presentation of nakedness, unlike the sensuous flesh that was to melt under the brush of later artists such as Rubens. In the painter's focus upon jewels and fine materials, as well as in the attitude toward sex, there is an unmistakable preciosity.

Toward the third quarter of the seventeenth century in Holland, Jan Vermeer helped restore a quiet decorum to the theme of the table. Constants in his art are sunlit corners of elegant whitewashed rooms with carefully disposed tables, paintings, chairs, and handsome women of calm composure. Vermeer's young women, who seem to exemplify Dutch culture shortly before the disastrous wars of the 1670s, are shown standing near or seated at sturdy tables, making lace, reading, writing, engaged in animated conversation with military suitors, admiring themselves, or sleeping. They are comforting images of sedentary feminine diversion. *A Woman Weighing Gold* (Fig. 235), painted in the 1660s, juxtaposes a painting of the Last Judgment with the figure of a girl holding a balance. A devout Catholic convert, Vermeer may have given symbolic weight to the painting and its placement in relation to the girl; it is possible that the idea is of the religious conscience of the girl, who is faithfully fulfilling her responsibility. She stands below the figure of Christ in the position that the Archangel Michael would assume as he weighed the souls of the resurrected. The violence and terror of the Day of Judgment and of the painting make an ironic contrast with the stilled life in the room. (It is interesting historically to see a religious painting no longer over an altar but hung in a private home.) Balance is not only the theme of the painting but the key to Vermeer's compositional ideas. Not unsympathetically, the woman is arranged in the setting, like the other objects, so that her hand and the scale must be grasped along with the picture frame behind them, then seen in relation to the open box and her left hand. The casually arranged cloth on the table serves to draw us to both the source of light and the girl. The tangible rigid armature formed by the right angle of the table against the wall and the alignment of the woman with the painting further, in some measure, the movement of the light and its refusal to be shaped into clearly defined patterns. With only a very restricted segment of the visible world, Vermeer was able to reveal the poetic potential of life.

THE ARTIST'S TABLE

Vermeer's private life belied the tranquillity of his paintings. Before his death in 1675 he suffered financial setbacks, and his widow filed for bankruptcy. With great difficulty she succeeded in regaining possession of the painting known as *The Artist in His Studio* (Pl. 25), which shows what appears to be an artist's workshop, a frequent genre subject of the time. A seated artist is painting a young model who holds a book and trumpet, symbols of fame. In this room the table appears in connection with art. On it are a cast and sketchbook, objects that may symbolize the arts. Scholars have shown that the wall map is of the Netherlands in the sixteenth century, before Holland achieved its independence. The artist's elegant costume is also of that century, suggesting that this is not an actual self-portrait. The half-drawn drape, also, is an old device by which to suggest revelation of a past event. The painting is thus not directly about Vermeer's studio and his own life time, but it is a nostalgic evocation of the more affluent and ideal working conditions enjoyed by Dutch artists a century before. The painting of the studio model in the guise of Fame may have been an ironic personal statement by the artist, skeptical about the future reception of his own work and aware of the artificial nature of fame itself.

To realize this wishful image of an ideal, Vermeer gave the totality of his gifts as an artist. From this painting, one can begin to comprehend the imagination and inspired effort of the artist, which went much beyond his amazing technical achievement of simulating appearances. The fact that the viewpoint, angle of light, and placement of objects were all minutely calculated before brush met canvas does not detract from Vermeer's creative excellence, for these preliminary decisions were esthetic judgments in the fullest sense of the word—the room arranged in terms of art. The eye moves into the painting slowly and logically from the large foreground shapes at the left to the artist at the right, and then to the model, with each area clearly apparent in its distance from other objects and the viewer. The careful, but not obvious, avoidance of simple alignment by means of parallel edges or right angles enriches the visual design and impels us to see each object in relation to another. Contrasts stress the idiosyncrasies of each shape, yet do not destroy the feeling of inner rapport between everything within the painting. There are several strong rhythmic sequences, such as the ceiling beams, the brass chandelier curves culminating in the Hapsburg eagles, the horizontal vignettes of Dutch cities on the sides of the map, the black-and-white striping of the artist's blouse, and the alternating floor tiles. Against these sequences can be seen the random sparkle of upholstery nails on the chairs and the highlights in the fabric of the drapery. The drape holds all the painting's colors in less concentrated hues, with the exception of a small patch of blue that exactly matches the color of the model's dress; its dense, saturate pattern contrasts with the airy brightness and spaciousness of the room itself. Shadows never obliterate, but rather lead us to new revelations of tones and shapes. The composition is anchored at the left by the half-lighted drape seen against the most brilliant light on the wall behind it, and at the right by the judicious alignment of the edge of the map, the chair, the right easel leg, and the segmented black tiles that lead into the painting. Like the seated artist himself, the viewer is expected to weigh in his mind the rightness of each stroke in terms of the stuffs, luminosity, and hue of the object brought into being. The mahlstick held by the artist is an aid to steady his hand, and Vermeer's art is a brilliant demonstration of wrist painting.

In the manner of van Eyck, Vermeer reconstructed his world in terms of the smallest ray of light and the fragment upon which it fell. Unlike those of van Eyck, however, Vermeer's subjects and compositions were free of the hierarchical demands of religious convention, so that he could bring to arrangement as well as to detail a full and unbounded revelation of his aspirations.

11

REMBRANDT

Rembrandt Harmensz. van Rijn was born in Leiden in 1606 and died in Amsterdam in 1669. His father was a prosperous miller who wanted his son to be a scholar and sent the boy to a Humanist school from his seventh to fourteenth years. For a short time, Rembrandt was enrolled at the University of Leiden, and his early contact with great literature was to influence his later art. In 1620, he entered the studio of an unimportant Leiden artist and remained there for three years. At eighteen, he went to Amsterdam, where he studied for half a year with a well-known artist, Pieter Lastman. About 1632, he moved permanently to Amsterdam, where he began to have success as a portrait painter. In 1634 he married the wealthy Saskia van Uylenburgh. In quick succession they had four children, all of whom subsequently died; only his son Titus, born in 1641, reached maturity. Saskia died shortly after Titus' birth. By 1649, Hendrickje Stoffels was living with Rembrandt. Her willingness to become the painter's common-law wife brought her social hardship and actual persecution at the hands of a rigidly Calvinist society—a fact that makes Rembrandt's repeated interpretations of the theme of Christ and the woman taken in adultery all the more poignant. She

stayed with Rembrandt through increasing financial difficulties, brought on by his omnivorous appetite for antiques and other *objets d'art*, many of which he used as props in his paintings. By 1657, Rembrandt was bankrupt and had lost his house and collection; two years later his graphic art was dispersed to satisfy his creditors. Contrary to the popular notion that Rembrandt was then reduced to a life of terrible poverty and neglect, he continued to receive good commissions and to devote himself to problems that interested him. He worked for the art firm of Hendrickje and Titus. In 1663 Hendrickje died, and in 1668 Rembrandt lost Titus.

In his personal and artistic life, Rembrandt defied convention. For most of his life he recognized none of the accepted canons of social conduct, monetary management, adherence to the state Calvinist religion, flattery of potentially wealthy and influential clients, and most of all, what and how a Dutch painter should paint. He was an "un-Dutch" artist by his refusal to specialize or to show the merrymaking, material comforts, or daily ritual of the middle class who controlled a buyer's art market. This buying public puzzled at his avoidance of the then fashionable momentary views in favor of more enduring notions of time and subject matter in his thoughtful figure paintings. From documentary evidence, it appears that Rembrandt considered himself a revolutionary in art because he did not acknowledge academic rules and followed only the nature and art of his own choosing. When Rembrandt was at work, as one historian has declared, he would not have stopped for a king.

His lifelong quest for personal freedom prevented Rembrandt from affiliating with any orthodox religion or political party. Unlike many painters of his time, he cannot be catalogued as a painter of portraits, genre, or religious subjects. No other artist of his time was identified simultaneously with the different media of painting, etching, and drawing. He drew freely from older art, literature, history, and subjects before his insatiable eye. Though he relied heavily upon the written word for inspiration, he distrusted writing about art, and the vast corpus of his work manifests a displeasure with artistic theory. His varied sources entered into a search for the ties that bound humanity throughout history. Compelled to individualize every subject in his art, Rembrandt somehow never lost sight of mankind for its men and saw life as a historical continuum from cradle to grave. With his view of the continuity of all life, travel was unnecessary, and Amsterdam became for him the microcosm of history. Rebel that he was in certain senses, Rembrandt accepted the role of the artist that had emerged

in the Middle Ages—to move, delight, and instruct.

In his own lifetime, Rembrandt's biographers commented on the secret techniques by which he enriched etching and on the unusual thickness and odor of his oil portraits, which were built up with an impasto so thick that one critic wrote they could be lifted by the sitter's nose. All that went into the making of art absorbed Rembrandt, and for the cookery of painting and printmaking he concocted his own recipes. The early biographers were impressed with his success as a teacher, for from the age of twenty-two he had many pupils, whose tuition and income from sales of their work allowed him to live well and to buy art. The students worked in upstairs rooms of his large Amsterdam house, drawing from casts, prints, and drawings and often from the nude model. Among his many drawings are several on the subject of the studio (Fig. 236), illustrating his favorite lesson, which was to work not from knowledge of theories but from a visual experience of life. In one sketch, the young apprentices themselves become the master's model. Such drawings, which the students may have been asked to copy, exemplified his teaching with regard to achieving strong relief by building from dark to light—contrasting shaded, recessive areas with the lightness of figures whose definition resulted from a rapid notation of directions made by their postures and clothing. To enhance the unity of the whole, which the subject alone could not

Figure 236. REMBRANDT. *Studio of the Artist.* c. 1635. Drawing, pen and wash, 6 7/8 × 9 1/4″. Louvre, Paris.

205

Figure 237. REMBRANDT. *The Presentation in the Temple.* 1631. Oil on panel, 24 × 18 7/8". Mauritshuis, The Hague.

give, Rembrandt would often impose shadows over his drawing. Their frequent arbitrariness shows how essential was imaginative intuition, and this irrational gift could not be taught, for none of the pupils rivaled his tutor. Although he learned much from his studies of other artists, Rembrandt's development of a highly personal style was founded in the main upon continuous work, which in over forty years yielded roughly 650 paintings, 280 etchings, and 1400 drawings.

The Presentation in the Temple (Fig. 237) is in many respects typical of Rembrandt's early paintings of religious subjects. This is not, it should be noted, religious painting, for it was not intended for use in a church. Rembrandt was a founder of what might be called private (i.e., nonecclesiastical) devotional painting. These paintings were small in format and intended for intimate contemplation in the home. He did not illustrate dogma nor propagandize organized religion. Though Rembrandt

was nominally Calvinist (a religion that looked with disfavor on paintings of religious subjects), his was in truth a private religion without theology, but his paintings, drawings, and prints constituted a spiritual art. From his Roman Catholic mother, Rembrandt had derived his love and knowledge of the Bible, and his interpretations of Biblical stories have the freshness of personal discovery. The style that produced *The Presentation in the Temple* was doubtless influenced by the Scriptures, particularly by the frequent references to the symbolism of light. Against the looming backdrop of the impressive synagogue architecture, Simeon kneels with the Christ child and his parents before Anna, standing with outstretched arms. The small group is illuminated by a strong shaft of natural light. The faces of the child and the "just and devout" old Simeon are most strongly lit, recalling the passage from the Psalms, "God is the light of their countenance." Simeon, who knew that he could die in peace with the coming of the Messiah, appears to be looking beyond the head of Anna and saying, "O Lord... mine eyes have seen Thy salvation, which Thou hast prepared before the face of all peoples; a light of revelation to the gentiles, and a glory for Thy people Israel" (Luke 2:22–34).

Rembrandt knew the chief rabbis in the Jewish quarter of Amsterdam and had visited the synagogues. In his ardor to re-create the true image of the Scriptures, he ignored the archaeology of the Italians and his Dutch contemporaries and drew inspiration from his immediate surroundings. The small painting is filled with observations of types, costumes, gestures, and poses, as well as contrast between the intense concentration of the central group and the rather indifferent presence of bystanders on the stairs to the right. The figures and architecture are so disposed in depth as to make the viewer, too, a bystander off to one side in the shadows. The darkened areas were made luminous by Rembrandt's device of underpainting his canvas with warm bright colors and then scratching through the darker overpainting of the architecture to these high-keyed layers. The whole painting has a theatrical aspect, with the principals dramatically subordinated to the great space and strident contrast of light and dark. The faces as yet do not reveal Rembrandt's later deep understanding of human motivation.

What we see is a drama of place rather than of persons.

Rembrandt's development as an individual and as a painter is reflected in a single painting that he began early in his career but felt compelled to rework as he grew older. His oil sketch *John the Baptist Preaching* (Fig. 238), begun about 1636 or 1637, was worked over intermittently until 1650. In this sketch, the ostensible subject is Biblical, but the theme is really that of an inspired individual addressing a group. At the time of this sketch's conception, Rembrandt was sympathetic to the Mennonites, a sect that decried a formal organized church and the ritual and sacraments of the Roman Catholics. Its ministers were laymen who preached not dogma but the virtues of mercy and charity, humility and obedience. Stress was laid upon the impulses of the heart, deeply felt silent prayer, and simple, warm spirituality. The Mennonites sought to return to the essential truths of the Bible instead of using it as the basis for an elaborate theology. They championed respect for the poor in spirit and love of one's brethren in Christ. It is their sentiments which may have influenced this conception of John the Baptist.

In loose array, all strata of society are gathered to hear John speak, with zeal and from the heart, of salvation. Rembrandt may have portrayed himself in one of the faces at John's feet. Rembrandt's later reworking of the sketch tended to concentrate the light upon John and those closest to him. As in the painting of Simeon, the illumination is appropriate not only for reasons of style, but also for the moment when the ascetic Baptist prophesied the Messiah as light coming into the world. John further spoke of the importance of fellowhip, the need for brotherly love. Like the word of Christ, John's word is as a light to the path of the faithful. Rembrandt depicted a crowd divided in its attention, atomized into those who hear, are moved, and understand, those who daydream or doze, and those who bicker or content themselves with trivial diversions. The various ethnic types and exotic costumes suggest the universal scope of John's message. In the center foreground, to the left of the obelisk crowned with Caesar's effigy, stand three Pharisees in partial shadow, who have turned their backs on John and dispute among themselves. Rembrandt did not resort to the obvious device of illuminating only those who are the

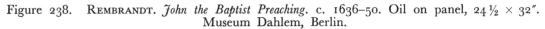

Figure 238.   REMBRANDT. *John the Baptist Preaching*. c. 1636–50. Oil on panel, 24½ × 32". Museum Dahlem, Berlin.

Figure 239. REMBRANDT. *The Three Crosses*. 1653. Etching, third state, 15 ¼ × 17 ¾". The British Museum, London.

enlightened participants, for signs of vanity and folly can be found in both the light and the dark areas of the crowd. In the bright sections can be seen his earlier style of figure construction, with more opaque faces, a heavy reliance on drawing, and attention to picturesque detail. The later style treated figures and costumes in broader, less precise strokes and with fewer, more somber tones.

Rembrandt never traveled as did other famous Northern European artists of his century; yet his imagination and taste for remote lands and peoples filled his works with archaeological monuments, rugged panoramas unlike those around Amsterdam, and opulent and exotic accessories such as turbans, ornate bridles, monkeys, and camels. This small panel is charged with almost an overabundance of ideas and esthetic means; the later alterations were in the direction of greater clarity and stability.

Rembrandt's continual restlessness and relentless self-criticism are also apparent in two states of his etching *The Three Crosses* (Figs. 239, 240). These etchings also show a great divergence from the early style of *John the Baptist Preaching*, a style that had brought him commercial and critical success. Each painting, drawing, and print seemed to open up new possibilities for the artist, who set personal goals of artistic perfection and inquiry above financial gain.

In itself, the third state of *The Three Crosses* seems to have a moving completeness. It is a readable drama whose religious subject is the Passion of Christ and whose universal theme is the loss of a man. In centrifugal fashion, Rembrandt detailed the several reactions to the execution, ranging from the indifference of the mounted troops and the satisfaction of the Pharisees at the lower left to the anguish of Christ's followers and the conversion of the centurion. The harsh barrenness of Golgotha is intruded into the scene in the rocks and scrub vegetation. The tortured bodies of the thieves flank Christ, and the descending light divides its focus among the three crosses. This division of interest and diffuse action impelled Rembrandt to make the fourth state. The successive states are like a chronology of the last hours of Christ on the Cross. The final etching shows the world in near-darkness, except for the torrential shaft of light above Christ's head. As in Genesis, the quite abrupt separation of light and dark suggests the creation of new life. The solemn centurion is the principal subordinate figure, stressing the significance of conversion and a comprehension of the meaning of Christ's death. The mood is altered not only by the inaction and rigidification of the few accessory figures still perceivable but also by the rugged, stiff outlines of their bodies and their reduction almost to obscure presences floating in a sea of darkness. Black was felt and savored by Rembrandt as a tangible substance. Etching ink and the crosshatching and close striations of the etcher's needle imparted the special qualities of a soft, absorbent black that he could not reproduce in his paintings. Its appeal may also have been that it permitted emphasis on the contrast between the polarities of light and darkness, with their implication of life and death.

Rembrandt's conception of Christ is notable. Hanging from the Cross is the taut but meager body of an ordinary human being, with no attempt by the artist to achieve sublimity in an exceptional musculature. Christ's extraordinary strength and spirit issue from a strikingly erect posture, from the head and the radiance about it. More than Michelangelo, Rembrandt was drawn to the testimony of flesh to affirm Christ's suffering manhood.

Rembrandt had avoided the more obvious evidence of pathetic struggle in the figure of Christ. In *The Slaughtered Ox* (Pl. 26), a small secular painting done two years after the Crucifixion series, however, Rembrandt evoked the violence of brutal execution. In the early Middle Ages, the ox symbolic of St. Luke was thought to prefigure the sacrifice of Christ. It is not impossible that, with the Crucifixion theme so much in his mind during the time of this painting, the emotional associations of the

two subjects may have overlapped. Further, Rembrandt's famous paintings of anatomy dissections, in which dead bodies are cut open and examined, may also have influenced his selection and treatment of the theme. The painting shows the spread-eagled carcass of the ox hanging from a rude wooden frame. The gutted animal seems self-illuminated with an almost phosphorescent glow. Massing his pigment in thick viscous patches, Rembrandt created a painterly equivalent of the moist, greasy, rich substance of the animal's muscle, fat, and bone. He showed with wonder the partially hollow interior of the flayed animal, formed of complex substance and color. Allowing it to dominate its gloomy setting and the timid woman peering around the corner, Rembrandt transfigured and heroicized the slaughtered ox and reiterated his fascination with the mystery of life and death.

To juxtapose an etching of the Crucifixion with a scene from an Amsterdam butcher shop is to bring together the poles of Rembrandt's broad interests. The past and present, the imaginary and the real, all of these alternate and interweave throughout his art. Rembrandt was a rebellious Dutchman who could not follow his fellow artists in meticulously documenting and praising their particular time and place. With grandiose projects half-formed in his head, he would still take the time to draw

Figure 240. REMBRANDT. *The Three Crosses.* 1653. Etching, fourth state, 15 ¼ × 17 ¾″. The British Museum, London.

Figure 241. REMBRANDT. *Christ at the Column.* c. 1657. Oil on canvas, 13 × 10″. Wallraf-Richartz Museum, Cologne.

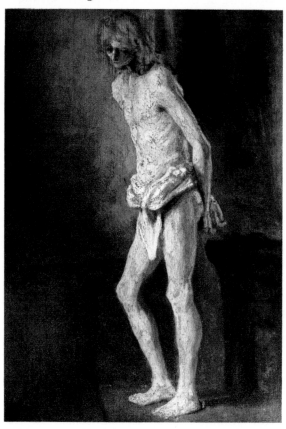

Figure 242. REMBRANDT, *Bathsheba.* 1654. Oil on canvas, 4′10⅞″ × 4′7⅞″. Louvre, Paris (Anc. Coll. Vizzavona-Druet, Musées Nationaux).

whatever immediately attracted his eye in the street or along the canals.

Michelangelo made his art in terms of Man, and Rembrandt in terms of men. No two artists in history had more antithetical views of art and humanity. The Dutch artist could not think or paint in terms of philosophical abstractions; instead, it was the real and verifiable that kindled his imagination. For Michelangelo, Christ had to be shown as endowed with a sublime body to signify his divinity. When Rembrandt painted his *Christ at the Column* (Fig. 241), he showed the Saviour as an imperfect physical specimen whose flesh hung on a bony frame. Unlike Michelangelo's ennobled conception of an impersonal and flawless skin, Rembrandt's small painting is dedicated to re-creating the particulars and material substance of the flesh belonging to a single man. The selection of a model (perhaps his son Titus) of such meager proportions and his arrangement in a slack posture that speaks of exhaustion of body and spirit dismayed Rembrandt's critics, and would undoubtedly have been scorned by Michelangelo.

It was such problems as this which the artist must have posed for his students, for the painting suggests a studio study from a live model, and there is actually no column visible. It is likely that drawing from life provided Rembrandt with the inspiration to paint subjects from the Bible, which, when realized, often retained much of the character of their secular origin. Such a painting is a later version of *Bathsheba* (Fig. 242), although none of the preliminary drawings exist. Possibly Hendrickje, who was the model for many drawings, posed for Bathsheba. Her pose may have been inspired by Rembrandt's encountering, through seventeenth-century engravings, of classical Roman sculptures that showed seated women, such as Venus, in profile. Recall Michelangelo's synthesis of David; that of Rembrandt was to take a Protestant Dutch housewife and pose her in the manner of a Roman goddess to re-create the character of a tragic Hebrew woman.

In his later years, during the period when this painting was done, Rembrandt painted fewer crowd scenes and preferred to treat isolated individuals. He tended to immobilize his subjects, placing emphasis upon their inner rather than outer reactions to events. The great mysteries for Rembrandt were not those of theology

Figure 243. REMBRANDT.
Danaë. 1636. Oil on canvas,
6′ ½″ × 6′8″. The Hermitage, Leningrad.

but those of humanity. His painting of Bathsheba shows the wife of Uriah, chosen by David for himself, in a moment of troubled reflection. The theme is typical of Rembrandt, for it reveals the individual's passive submission to fate. He has depicted the moment of recognition, crucial to classical drama. Bathsheba is attended by a servant or David's messenger, who prepares her for the fateful meeting with the king. In Bathsheba's hand is the note that incites the tragedy. The expression on her face, the limpness of the arm holding the letter, the unthinking compliance with the actions of the maid, all compose the story of an individual caught in a web of circumstance over which she has no control, though she is aware of its eventual outcome. Moved by the vulnerability of people and their unwitting involvement in tragedy, Rembrandt reconstructed the Bible in human terms. While the painting gives an initial impression of factual account, Rembrandt added an aura of elusive, lyrical revery. Julius Held characterized this type of painting as Rembrandt's formula "of making his models appear both physically present and psychically remote."

Rembrandt's nudes were not in the Italian Renaissance tradition, for they lack its classical proportions, cosmetic perfection, and litheness. More in the Northern tradition, they are naked rather than nude, and the revelation of the body becomes almost an invasion of privacy. With his intense empiricism, Rembrandt could not submit the naked body to the norms imposed by other styles and cultures. His nudes are not generalized types; each body seems shaped by the character of its possessor. His naked bodies seem still to show the impress of clothes, the effects of diet, and a relatively sedentary rather than athletic existence. Gravity of mind and the pressure of conscience are sustained in these heavy bodies.

In an earlier painting, Rembrandt celebrated the beauty of a naked woman in amorous and more joyful circumstances (Fig. 243). On an elaborately ornamented bed, Danaë awaits the coming of the god Zeus, whose presence just beyond the curtain is announced by a golden light. The anguished, constrained cupid above Danaë symbolizes the chastity enforced upon her because her father the king had been

Rembrandt   211

warned of his own murder by a future grandson. In paintings of this subject by other artists, Zeus transforms himself into a rain of golden coins and thereby gains access to Danaë's bed. Rembrandt uses the old symbol of divine luminosity, which allows him to bathe the woman's pliant body in a warm glow. His Danaë is not the passive and statuesque recumbent figure of the Italian Venus type, but in her gesture and radiant expression she exhibits a warm-blooded anticipation.

Few of Rembrandt's paintings deal with miracles, for he saw the Bible in terms of men and women with distinct personalities, problems, and hopes not unlike those daily encountered in Amsterdam. When he painted *Christ at Emmaus* (Pl. 27), he set the scene in an austere high-ceilinged stone room that dominated the figures by its scale. Only the radiance emanating from Christ immediately distinguishes the painting from genre art. To evoke the apparition of Christ, Rembrandt set him directly before a sizable hollow niche, which looms like a dark void recalling his miraculous emergence from the tomb. The niche also ties together the figures and encloses the area of dramatic, but underplayed action. By temperament unsympathetic toward Catholic theology and its association with the formal centrality of Renaissance compositions, Rembrandt shifted the focus of the painting to the left of center. Unlike Leonardo, also, Rembrandt bathed the room in deep but transparent shadow and a powerful warm light that the figures seem to absorb with varying intensity. He gave to Christ an unaristocratic personality, stressing his gentleness, capacity for love, and ability to be at home with the humble. No painter before Rembrandt came so close to fathoming the Jesus of the Gospels or the historical Jesus (see Chapter 3, "Images of Gods"). Rembrandt did portraitlike studies of Christ, probably based on a bearded youth from the Jewish quarter near his home. In the Emmaus scene, the bearded Christ retains the soft, gentle qualities with which Rembrandt endowed him in scenes showing his earthly ministry. Only the sad expression of the eyes suggests the suffering and fatigue of the Passion. Significantly, one of the disciples seems to study Christ's face for signs of the miracle, rather than follow his gesture of breaking the bread. Deliberately avoiding Caravaggio's rhetoric

of gestures and accessory objects, Rembrandt himself said that he sought to convey the greatest inner emotion.

Another subject relating to an epiphany is the drawing of God announcing his covenant to Abraham (Fig. 244), done after *Christ at Emmaus*, in the mid-1650s. As recounted in Genesis (15, 17), God promised to give the ninety-nine-year-old Abraham a son and to make him the father of nations. Both themes had a deep attraction for Rembrandt, who was preoccupied with the family all his life and believed that the Jews were the chosen people. Rembrandt saw in the community an extension of the family unit; and in rituals such as Christ's presentation in the temple, a linking of the two groups.

In the Bible it is written that at God's appearance Abraham fell flat on his face. This was a sign of fear and an indication of his unworthiness to look upon the face of the Lord. Rough as the sketch is, Rembrandt gave enough attention to the face of the Lord to evoke his kindly admonition, "Fear not, Abram, I am thy protector." Rembrandt did not look upon Jehovah as the wrathful force of Michelangelo but, instead, gave the Old Testament God the same benevolent aspect as his images of Christ. He flanked the Lord with two angels and above his head drew the dove of the Holy Ghost, thus introducing the trinitarian symbolism that recurs when the three men appear to Abraham and Sarah, and the Lord once again promises them a son.

The rhythms of Rembrandt's hand as it moved over the grainy white paper, holding the reed pen, presented an intimate revelation. *God and Abraham* was not done from posed models, but the information and shorthand acquired from long study served him when he drew from imagination. The strokes that establish the broad gestures and the limits of movement for the figures of the angels do not form continuous constrictive outlines, but they overlap or leave gaps in the silhouette that suggest the fusion of the body with the surrounding atmosphere. In the prostrate figure of Abraham, several of the lines begin or end within the body's outline and have a hooked termination. With a single flourish of the pen, Rembrandt established where a limb was joined to the body and where and to what extent it projected from the body. The body

Left: Figure 244. REM-BRANDT. *God Announces His Covenant to Abraham.* c. 1656. Drawing, pen and bistre, 7¾ × 10½″. Kupferstich-kabinett, Dresden.

Below: Figure 245. REM-BRANDT. *Tobias Healing Tobit's Blindness.* c. 1649–50. Drawing, pen and bistre, wash, 6⁹/₁₀ × 5¼″. Kupfer-stichkabinett, Staatliche Museen, Berlin.

and its clothing were conceived in terms of directional lines and weights. Observe, for example, the area of the Lord's head and shoulders, the slashing silhouettes of the angels, and the weighted outline of Abraham's back. With the paper as a source of light, a few expert touches of dark establish the mood and detail of the Lord's face. To define such accessory elements as the clouds and the space, Rembrandt's hand swept over the surface in quick series of parallel lines.

The more that is learned about Rembrandt, the more it is realized how his preoccupation with certain themes satisfied many different personal interests and needs. His drawing of *Tobias Healing Tobit's Blindness* (Fig. 245) is but one of some fifty-five interpretations the artist made from the Book of Tobit. This Old Testament story of God's compassion toward men, with its emphasis on family unity and loyalty, appealed to Rembrandt, who not only had strong feelings of love and concern for his son Titus but also an abiding love for his own father, who had died blind. The drawing shows the subjects near an open window and Tobias examining the sightless eyes of his father before curing them with the gall of a fish held in a bowl

by Tobit's wife. The archangel Raphael, who revealed the means of cure to Tobias, stands behind the father and son like a guardian angel or an attending physician. (It has been shown that, in this and similar drawings, Rembrandt has correctly depicted the medical procedure for cataract operations then being performed in Amsterdam.) Rembrandt depicted many themes in which sight or blindness are important elements—understandable because of the artist's concern with vision as it related to his profession and as the noblest means for making possible all forms of revelation. The drawing possesses a weighted stillness and a concentrated attention on the part of the participants; Rembrandt also extended his characterization to the whole bodies of the parents, so that many of the strong accents of the drawing occur in their garments and give an expressive balance to the whole composition.

Rembrandt's etching of *The Sacrifice of Isaac* (Fig. 246) reverses the roles of Tobias and Tobit, for Abraham tenderly covers the eyes of his beloved son as he is about to deprive him of life. So intense is Abraham's grief in complying with God's command that even the intercession of the angel, who physically stays the sacrifice, does not affect at once the anguished facial expression of the father. In this last version of the subject, Rembrandt compressed the action in the close contact of the three figures, and the ass and servants were relegated to insignificant roles. The deep black cavities framing the sacrifice suggest the tragic mood of the moments preceding it and the symbolic conversion of darkness to light by the angel's miraculous appearance.

One of Rembrandt's last paintings is the *Return of the Prodigal Son* (Fig. 247). Perhaps because of his own close ties with Titus, Rembrandt repeatedly interpreted the theme of father and son. In this picture, the wordless but profound reaction of all to the homecoming signifies the indivisible ties of the family. The sons who remained with the father display no jealousy or recrimination but are sympathetic witnesses to a sacred moment. Just as Rembrandt understated the drama, his frugal means add to the force of the painting. There is no emphatic action or elaborate interweaving of figures and background. The individual forms are somewhat rectangular and blocklike. This suggestion of regularity and self-containment is offset by

the dissolution of the edges of the forms and their fusion with the luminous ambient. There is a simple scale of emphasis, with the greatest wealth of color lavished on the rags of the son. With the reduction of the figures to a static condition, Rembrandt solemnized the human being and achieved a supreme drama of persons. This image of forgiveness and pity is a form of self-revelation that may reflect the artist's own resolution of conflicts with the world.

From about 1640 to 1656, Rembrandt did a number of drawings, prints, and paintings of landscape, which earlier had appeared solely as a backdrop for figural subjects. Many of his landscapes are of the flat plains, picturesque thatched peasant cottages, and canals in and near Amsterdam. Dutch artists were known to make drawings from nature on the spot, but their paintings were completed in the studio and were often composites of different views. In his etching *Three Trees* (Fig. 248), Rembrandt shows the tiny figure of an artist sketching on a hilltop at the far right. Unlike in his more numerous figure compositions, where humans dominate their setting or claim most of our attention, in his landscapes Rembrandt was able to contrast their small scale and quiet routine activities with the grand sweep and endless variety of nature. By alternating zones of dark and light, Rembrandt suggested the depth and continuity of the earth's surface and dramatized the rugged trio of trees against the

brightness of the clearing sky. A shaft of sunlight illuminates the fisherman and his wife at the left, while above them on the horizon is the silhouette of a city. From the rich sensuous blacks of the foreground shadows emerge the highlighted traces of bushes. Just as he could draw our attention to and dignify the rags of a beggar, so he provokes our curiosity and pleasure in even the meanest vegetative scrub in his prints. The etching *The Omval at the River Amster* (Fig. 249) repeats Rembrandt's habit of combining large and small elements, a suggestive

Figure 250. REMBRANDT. *The Anatomy Lesson of Dr. Deijman.* c. 1656. Drawing, 4⅓ × 5¼″. Rijksmuseum, Amsterdam.

detailing of the near and far. Secret places in nature such as caves or the shadowed copse seen at the left of the print enhance pictorial interest. To keep his compositions from disintegrating under accumulations of detail, Rembrandt graded the density and definition of areas and left as contrast large untouched spaces. The tangled wooded area at the left is built up from the inside out, whereas the houses and mill across the canal have more pronounced silhouettes and spare linear definition within. At no point does nature seem finite and arrested, but it is captured as if in a perpetual transitory condition of illumination and growth, or of what it reveals and conceals. Rembrandt imposes an emotional character on the nonhuman, for as with his figures he virtually draws out the biographies of his buildings and trees.

Rembrandt's insistence on personal discovery parallels developments in Western European science and the empirical attitude reflected in the great anatomist Vesalius' opinion that the proper study of mankind is man. Whether searching a landscape or the naked body, Rembrandt relied upon the practiced coordination of his eyes and hands, and occasionally he even had recourse to the advice of famous Dutch doctors. The coincidence of the discoveries of

advanced Dutch science with those of Rembrandt is most apparent in his painting *The Anatomy Lesson of Doctor Deijman* (Fig. 250). Only a sketch preserves for us the painting's original format; fire reduced it to a fragment, which shows us the foreshortened view of the corpse and presumably Doctor Deijman or his assistant standing next to it and holding the top of the skull which has been removed. Commissioned to make a group portrait of the doctor and his assistants or students, Rembrandt chose to depict a public dissection such as occurred in the Amsterdam medical amphitheater. In an excellent book, William Heckscher has shown that, while it constitutes a tribute to the triumph of modern science over superstition and ignorance, the painting also combines the old moralizing ideas of a *memento mori* and "the wages of sin are death." The corpse was that of a hanged thief, and this was in a sense a punitive dissection comparable to that shown earlier by Gerard David (Fig. 145). Like Doctor Deijman, Rembrandt was heir to the Renaissance admiration of the body not only as an object of beauty but as the key to understanding life. The foreshortened cadaver has precedents in such works as Mantegna's *Dead Christ*, and the dissection scene also has analogies with the segment of Michelangelo's Last Judgment where men are divested of their skins. (Fig. 184). (A copy of Michelangelo's masterpiece hung in the Leiden medical amphitheater.)

Rembrandt's early prominence, even before his arrival in Amsterdam in 1632, was based on his talents as a portrait painter. Like his fellow Dutch painters, he responded to the demand of the well-to-do middle class for portraits. Personal friends—writers and doctors —and interesting-looking individuals he pulled in from the streets of Amsterdam also sat for their likenesses. In later years, Rembrandt experienced difficulties with clients who claimed that their portraits were not good likenesses, since they were accustomed to the slick, extroverted, and often smug images the fashionable painters achieved. After his bankruptcy, Rembrandt continued to receive important portrait commissions, one of which, from the governing board of the drapers' guild, resulted in the group painting known as *The Syndics* (Fig. 251).

One of Rembrandt's important contributions to group portraiture lay in his successful solution of the problem of achieving an informal, unself-conscious, and convincing union of all the sitters. Since portraits were paid for on the basis of the amount of the figure shown, it was essential that all of the faces be clearly in evidence and that priority be given to the guild president. Rembrandt chose a moment during a meeting of the board with its stockholders, immediately after a query had been made from the floor. Within the painting, the figures are subtly united in their relationship to the president, who is rising to respond. The interlocked groupings and the positions of the bodies give a sense of this official relationship. The device of directing all attention outside the picture, in the direction of the viewer, unites the figures at some external focus. The sobriety and similarity of their apparel and the warm heavy atmosphere of the room, suffused with rich brown and gold tones on the walls and the near edge of the table covering, further the painting's harmony.

As in the best of Rembrandt's work, there is in *The Syndics* an underlying conflict between the apparent and the real. The subjects were, in fact, men of status and solid achievement who, on the occasion of the board meeting, presented an image of unshakable probity and solidarity. To the far right, however, is set into the wall paneling a painting of a burning city, which in Rembrandt's time, as De Tolnay has shown, signified the ephemerality of worldly power. It was a commentary on vanity and a warning to those of wealth not to be proud. The faces of the men betray their inherent individuality and those human qualities which do not always accord with official roles. Rembrandt did not caricature these men; nor can their faces be read merely as units in a group program. But to begin to dwell on the subtleties of each face is to remove oneself from the room and matters at hand, for in this discerning record the private history of each figure cannot be masked by the occasion. As prosaic an event as a business meeting, as astutely viewed by Rembrandt, has been transformed into a work of art and a probing psychological study of the price and nature of power.

In 1662, the same year that he painted *The Syndics*, Rembrandt worked on a painting for the Amsterdam town hall. Its subject was the ancient conspiracy of the Batavians, ancestors of the Dutch, who rebelled against Roman rule. Untypical for the Dutch artist of his time was the painting of a past event not actually witnessed by the painter. It is an ambitious example of Rembrandt's yielding to the urge to make a painting out of his head. In its original

Figure 251. REMBRANDT. *The Syndics*. 1662. Oil on canvas, 6′7⅞″ × 8′11⅞″. Rijksmuseum, Amsterdam.

Figure 252.   REMBRANDT. *The Conspiracy of Julius Civilis*. 1661–62. Oil on canvas, 6′5⅛″×10′1⅝″. Nationalmuseum, Stockholm.

state, *The Conspiracy of Julius Civilis* (Fig. 252) was probably the largest painting Rembrandt ever undertook. When it was rejected, he removed it from the town hall and cut it down to the area he liked most, which made a work of marketable size. The nearly concurrent date of its painting makes the contrast between the group portrait of *The Syndics* and this historical work all the more interesting. Rembrandt's visionary inclination came forth to the fullest in the midnight meeting of the conspirators. He was inspired by the swearing of allegiance until death upon the sword of Julius Civilis—an ironic contrast to the mundane dispute in the stockholders' meeting. The confident reserve of the fiscally wise guild president makes an equally interesting comparison with the heroic presence of the one-eyed Julius Civilis, who was to challenge the legions of the Roman Empire. The quiescent sunlight of the board room, with its connotations of security and permanence, gives way to the brilliant, inconsistent, and concealed radiance emanating from the conspirators' table, a strange light that transfigures their varied, rugged features and then fades into the surrounding gloom. The faces of the

conspirators belong with their costumes and roles of the moment; the intriguing double life of the syndics is absent. Each figure has freedom of movement within a restricted space, preserving his individuality without weakening his relation to the group. Layers of glazes build up the surface into thick crusts; no color area is composed of pure single tones, and the colors seem suspended within a tangible atmosphere. Characteristic of Rembrandt's late style, as the paint became richer and more mobile, the outward action of the figures even in such a histrionic episode was reduced, and they became more submerged within themselves.

Linked in spirit with the *Julius Civilis*, and likewise an imaginative portrait, is Rembrandt's misnamed *Polish Rider* (Fig. 253). The proud and alert horseman is based upon Eastern European light cavalrymen, whose heroic exploits in defending Christian Europe against the Turks were legendary even in Amsterdam. Their service as mercenaries in Western Europe would have accounted for Rembrandt's encounter with his subject, since he shows the full military equipment of this type of soldier without specifying his Polish or Hungarian nationality or personal identity. The darkened background throws into relief the rider's manly beauty and the inspired painting of the horse and military costume, based on a triad of red, white, and gold. A clue to the portrait's meaning lies in the painting itself, in which the warrior rides his gaunt horse through an inhospitable landscape dominated by a massive fortress. The self-assured pose and unnatural radiance enveloping the horse and rider is perhaps suggestive of his symbolic role as a Christian knight errant in a world of peril. Descendant of Titian's equestrian portrait of Charles V (Fig. 281), Rembrandt's work makes horse and rider a more unified organism and gives the animal greater character. (Rembrandt had had the opportunity to study the skeleton of a horse in one of the medical amphitheaters.) Although without royal patronage for his theme, he combined the regal and triumphal associations of the equestrian motif with an idealized portrait, and at the same time reflected Europe's concern over the Moslem threat and his own private hopes that resided in youth.

Rembrandt knew Raphael's portrait of Castiglione and made a drawing of it. The *Portrait of Jan Six* (Pl. 28) epitomizes Rembrandt's ideals—dignified masculinity, a certain quality of cool correctness mingled with an irrepressible human warmth. Rembrandt en-

dowed the living subject of his art with traits of an active and a contemplative life, for in reality Jan Six was both a successful poet and a politician. Significantly, Rembrandt did not portray the great contemporary Dutch political and military heroes. The most compatible subjects in his later life were men such as Jan Six who, like the painter himself, fully indulged both their worldly and intellectual appetites and ambitions. Personal rather than civic accomplishment seems most to have impressed Rembrandt. Such admiration for men who lived by strong individual codes was natural for a painter who resisted the formulas of painting. Jan Six stands to the right of center, takes no notice of the viewer, and does not assume a stable pose in the disposition of his limbs. With part of his face concealed in shadow, he is decidedly not represented as the extroverted affable or the prim type favored at the time.

The *Portrait of Jan Six*, like Rembrandt's most inspired work of any period, is a summing up of all that the artist had learned about his craft and the nature of men. By 1654, when the portrait was done, Rembrandt could produce painting that was both elegant and profound, in which with economical means he achieved great expressive power. The painting of Jan Six is in a sense a double portrait, a blend of studied contrasts that gives simultaneous insight

Figure 253. REMBRANDT. *The Polish Rider.* c. 1655. Oil on canvas, 3′10″ × 4′5⅛″. The Frick Collection, New York (Copyright).

into the public and the private identity of Jan Six. The automatic gesture of putting on a glove prefaces his going out into the streets; the tan gloves, scarlet cape, green-grey coat, and black hat are part of the gentleman's public identity. The actual public face has not as yet been "put on" or arranged, but the subject's features are relaxed in a momentary unawareness of others as his mind is absorbed in gentle reverie. The collar and row of buttons have a firm, tangible appearance that restores the viewer to the external man. Rembrandt did not try to dazzle with the virtuosity of his brush. He used a studied casualness in the single strokes of the gold braid and the vertical streaking of shadows in the cloak. Within the critical areas of focus, such as the hands and head, the strokes are accented and more strongly directed, grouped firmly together to suggest the rough and modulated substance of flesh against smooth cloth.

Rembrandt's ability to tell a story and to widen the narrative beyond its literal meaning was not restricted to group scenes, for it can also be seen in a painting with but two figures: *The Jewish Bride* (Pl. 29), which he did in 1668. Though the work was possibly based on the

Figure 254. REMBRANDT. *Studies for a Self-Portrait and Beggars.* 1632. Etching, 4 × 5⅜". Rijksmuseum, Amsterdam.

Biblical story of Rebecca and Isaac, its essential theme was marital concord, and the models were probably Titus and his wife. Into this painting the artist projected his sentiments of family and erotic love. It proposes a frank, sensual attitude, one of sharing, that is unlike any found in Renaissance paintings of the family. The story unfolded in delicate and subtle gestures can be compared to the marriage portraits by van Eyck and Kokoschka. (Pls. 52, 53). The gestures of the man suggest love and possession, while the attitude of the bride convey submission and encouragement. A gamut of affectionate feeling finds expression in this one painting. Its economy and restrained style make the slightest movement count. Colors emerge from shadow, with the strongest tones reserved for the area in most intense light. This highlight, significantly, does not fall on the faces but on the man's sleeve. The lightest parts are most thickly painted, so that in some places the pigment actually forms a relief which catches shadow and light from the room where the painting hangs.

As we have seen, Michelangelo's humor in art could be bitingly vengeful, whereas Rembrandt's art has many amusing moments that are often at his own expense. Early self-portraits show the artist clowning or making preposterous faces at the viewer—not unlike some created by Adriaen Brouwer, whose work he admired. He liked to draw or etch himself as a young country ruffian or a dashing romantic type. The mobility of his own face was endlessly fascinating. He could be unsparing toward his large, almost shapeless nose and scrutinize himself with the same unflattering candor he reserved for the ragged forms of street beggars (Fig. 254). Nonetheless, some of his human vanity show, through when he dresses in exotic costumes includes himself in a mythological or Biblical painting, or romantically shades portions of the face without lessening the intensity of his gaze, as in the etching illustrated. No artist has left a more intimate history of changes in his face, fortune, and family, with the result that much of his work constitutes a private artistic chronicle.

A portrait of himself and his first wife Saskia, done about 1635 (Fig. 255), shows what was then Rembrandt's ideal of a man and a successful artist. This ideal includes woman and wine in hand, fine clothes, with a suggestion of the bold cavalier, and a fine table and

Figure 255. REMBRANDT. *Self-Portrait with Saskia.* c. 1635. Oil on canvas, 5'4" × 4'4". Gemäldegalerie, Dresden.

surroundings. The format he used was one employed by other Dutch artists for brothel scenes. Rembrandt shows himself as a sociable extrovert, proud of his material possessions and willing to be liberal with them. The carefree attitude seen in this painting helps to explain his later bankruptcy, and it also records his conversion from a coarse miller's son to an elegant Amsterdam gentleman. It provides a personal inventory, giving a visual richness to the sword hilt and glass that rivals the rendering

of his own face. The painting mirrors a type of materialistic preoccupation that precludes any serious human revelation.

Rembrandt's self-portraits after 1650 reflect a succession of personal crises and show a more critical and perceptive self-appraisal. Where the early self-portraits were based in part upon his own availability as a model, his ostentation and wholesome self-esteem, the later portraits demonstrate an increasing desire to know himself. A self-portrait from the 1660s summarizes

Figure 256. REMBRANDT. *Self-Portrait.* c. 1660. Oil on panel, 13¾ × 9½". The Museum, Aix-en-Provence.

these late alter images (Fig. 256). There is no setting or elaborate costume, and for this painting Rembrandt chose not to play a role. There is a total self-consciousness (in the literal sense of the word). Although his life had been marred with suffering and bitterness, there is no mood of resentment or self-pity in this portrait. It is a calm and supremely comprehending study of the evidence with which age invests the flesh—the flesh has become a human poem. For Rembrandt, man is ultimately a solitary being. The world is found in his brain; the eyes now mirror introspection rather than outward alertness of the early portraits. Moreover, greatness of intellect is unrelated to exterior beauty. While no one knew better than Rembrandt the insecurity of existence, the artist's last portraits still show wonder and enthusiasm for life.

The principal means by which Rembrandt expressed his human consciousness was light. Early in his career, he used light as a device to organize his paintings, to achieve melodramatic effects, and to convey a transparent symbolism. As he grew older, he became aware of its more profound potential. The luminosity in his later paintings was no longer the convincing illumination of the room in which the viewer stands; nor was it subject to national theories of the particular relation of solids to voids. The light in his mature works is a mysterious and enveloping radiance, tangible yet independent of local colors. Its qualities proceed from the nature of the subject. Rembrandt used light to play upon the polarity of inner and outer worlds, and he used a rich incrustation of paint with a materiality previously unknown. By doing so, he achieved an astonishing range of substances as well as infinite gradations of light and shadow. A profound synthesis in Rembrandt's art is that of a basic materiality and a spiritualization of forms.

Rembrandt has not always been acclaimed as a great artist. He was "rediscovered" in the nineteenth century, but it was not until our own century that the magnitude of his achievement was realized. Today it is acknowledged that no other painter surpassed Rembrandt in his sensibility to paint and his ability to develop its expressive potential. His ideas and feelings about man rank him with the finest Humanists. His art is one of human beings, whose destiny he saw through the body. In Rembrandt's paintings and graphic works, man appears in both historic and private moments, as hero and victim. To the protagonists of the Bible, legend, myth, and history, remote from the artist's sight, he gave a personality and humanity unprecedented in the history of art. He showed rulers in their fallibility, Biblical heroes and businessmen in their frailty, and the King of Kings as a gentle human being. Moral expression, for Rembrandt, took precedence over physical beauty.

12

IMAGES OF AUTHORITY

In this country as elsewhere, for the last hundred years or more—since the invention of photography and the growth of the mass media—the leaders of government have no longer called upon their finest artists for official portraiture. This separation of the best and most advanced art from the uses of political authority is historically a recent development. The informality possible in the photograph, as opposed to the official state portrait, better accords with modern sovereigns' and politicians' views of the tastes of their subjects or the electorate. More than written chronicles, however, it is the great portraits of past rulers that bring them to life even today, continuing to satisfy human curiosity about the appearance of famous men. In this chapter we shall see how historically art has served the ruler in many vital areas, particularly as a means of projecting for its time, and ultimately for the future, effective concepts of authority more than individual human personalities.

In the ancient world, art was one of the most important means of making concrete for the public the abstract concepts of kingship. The average man in antiquity usually knew his ruler through art rather than through the king's physical presence. The burden of creating an embodiment of the divinity or omnipotence of the king fell to the artist, who relied not only on a likeness of his subject but also on certain prescribed and traditional devices to interpret attributes in a way that would be clearly decipherable by the people. In the mind of the populace, the symbolism of authority was also extended to architecture that related to the residence, appearance or epiphany, and ceremonies in honor of the ruler. The historical recurrence of Egyptian hieratic symbolism elsewhere in the Mediterranean world, as well as that of antiquity during the Middle Ages, was not motivated simply by its design appeal in painting, sculpture, and architecture. Symbols and devices were assimilated by succeeding cultures to inform their own art intended to glorify the kingship of an earthly or heavenly monarch.

THE KING A DEITY

The Egyptian pharaoh was regarded as divine, for he was the descendant and heir of the sun god, the ruler of the sky. An Old Kingdom statue of Khafre (Fig. 257) seated on a throne includes the carved symbol of the hawk-headed god Horus, who is lord of the rising

Figure 257. *The Pharaoh Khafre*, from Giza. c. 2560 B.C. Diorite, height 5'6". The Egyptian Museum, Cairo.

sun, directly behind the head of the Pharaoh. The hawk's wings encircle the ruler's headdress, symbolic of his origin and divine protection. The Pharaoh is shown rigidly frontal, a timeless pose which was repeated without deviation for over three thousand years of Egyptian history and which was ancestor to the twelfth-century enthroned Christ at Chartres. The transcendence of the Pharaoh over mortality is revealed through his aloof and immutable posture. There is no suggestion of bodily movement or facial expression. The stiffness and immobility of the human body and countenance were the means by which the sculptor, working with human anatomy, indicated the distinction of his king from mortals. In short, pharaonic imagery, dealing with a cosmic kingship,

sought deliberately to be as unnatural as possible. The only variation in the position of pharaoh statues is from the elbows down; the ruler is sometimes shown holding a staff of office or the crook and flail, the attributes of authority held by the lord of the underworld and afterlife, Osiris. His tasks were to be shepherd and judge of his people. The sacerdotal nature of pharaonic imagery parallels the ceremonious nature of Egyptian court life and the extreme formality of the kings' public appearances.

One of the oldest and most persistent devices for showing absolute authority and divinity of a ruler is that of centralized composition, which meant setting him between two flanking figures whose lesser stature is shown literally in their smaller scale or by subservient gestures. The pharaoh Mycerinus had himself portrayed erect and rigidly frontal between two goddesses, signifying not only his divine descent but also, for political reasons, demonstrating his acceptance by the local goddess of a province (nome) in his kingdom (Fig. 258).

Whether or not elements of naturalism and such techniques as bronze casting, as well as Egyptian symbols of kingship, penetrated westward into Negro Africa or were themselves influenced by older Negro cultures is a problem that still occupies anthropologists and archaeologists. The West African civilization of Benin had a highly organized central government and a concept of sacred kingship analogous to that of European countries in the sixteenth and seventeenth centuries. A bronze relief plaque, dating perhaps from the seventeenth century, shows a seated Benin king (or Oba) flanked by two kneeling attendants (Fig. 259). His immobile posture and ritual gesture, larger scale, frontality, and possession of a hammer were all symbolic of authority. Both in Egypt and Benin, certain materials were royal prerogatives or monopolies for use in art. Both kings adorned their palaces with their own effigies. (Plaques such as the one illustrated lined the halls of the Oba's palace.) Both rulers were thought to be descended from dead kings and to be of divine nature. Elaborate ceremonies attended their public appearances. In certain African tribal societies, the ruler and important personages wore clothing (a warrior's surcoat, for instance), and nakedness was a mark of inferior social status. Egyptian pharaonic ima-

Figure 258. *The Pharaoh Mycerinus Between Two Goddesses.* c. 2500 B.C. Green slate, height 38½". The Egyptian Museum, Cairo.

Figure 259. *Benin King (Oba) and Attendants,* from Nigeria. 17th century(?). Bronze, 16¾" × 15¼". The British Museum, London.

gery allowed some facial likeness; that of Benin, however, insisted on a stereotype, so that the imperial image was representative of an abstract principle.

WARRIOR KINGS

For three thousand years, pharaohs were presented in paintings and relief sculpture that proclaimed their godlike character and protection of the people. Shown in battle, at the hunt, in the company of other deities, and officiating at state ceremonies, the pharaoh's effigy was placed on the walls of tombs, palaces, and temples. One of the greatest of Egypt's rulers, Ramses III, who lived in the twelfth century B.C., followed an established tradition by using the pylon of a great temple as a political billboard. In a relief decoration, he had himself shown hunting wild bulls (Fig. 260). This was not meant as a secular scene of frivolous sport, for all activities engaged in by a pharaoh were religious, symbolic of his fight against evil. Wild beasts as well as enemy tribes were viewed as the partisans of Set, an evil underworld deity. While the benevolent hawk god Horus flies above him, the Pharaoh coolly dispatches the fleeing animals with his spear. The reins tied to Ramses' waist seem unnecessary because of the perfect discipline and unison demonstrated by the chariot's horses.

Figure 260. *Ramses III Hunting Wild Bulls* (detail of a pylon relief), from Medinet Abu. c. 1180 B.C. Sandstone. The Oriental Institute, University of Chicago.

Images of Authority   225

Above: Figure 261. *Ashurnasirpal II Killing Lions,* from Nimrud. c. 850 B.C. Limestone relief, 3′3″ × 8′4″. The British Museum, London.

Right: Figure 262. *King Hormuzd II Hunting Lions.* from Iran. 302–309 A.D. Sassanian silver plate, engraved and partially gilded, with applied cast relief, diameter 8¼″. The Cleveland Museum of Art (John L. Severance Fund).

The symbolically small-scale troops also seem superfluous, for the divine ruler's victory was inevitable. The raised and extended front legs of the horses were a victory symbol throughout the ancient Near and Far East. The fallen thrashing animal beneath the horses is interchangeable with bodies of dead warriors in battle reliefs. So effective was this combination of gallop and fallen prey that it persisted in imperial imagery into the nineteenth century and recurred with new connotations in Picasso's *Guernica* (see Fig. 466). This relief of the hunt also demonstrates a fine synthesis of naturalistic observation (in fishes, reeds, and bulls) and the stylized or schematic formula with which Ramses and his retinue are depicted. The intrusion of pictographic writing extolling the Pharaoh demonstrates that the event and art transcended unities of time and space and possessed instead a higher reality.

A hunting relief from a ninth-century B.C. Assyrian palace shows King Ashurnasirpal II aiming at a lion poised on the rear of the royal chariot (Fig. 261). Assyrian palaces abounded in symbolically repetitive reliefs of imperial warfare, hunting, and religious ceremonies. The great size and number of reliefs were intended to impress visiting emissaries with the king's might. Assyrian kings were not deified; they were mortals who demonstrated their right to rule through physical prowess, actually jeopardizing their lives in stalking their prey or in hand-to-hand combat with their foes. The king's acclaim depended in part upon acknowledging the courage of his opponent, who was given an opportunity to attack. The Assyrian relief shown here indicates the type of hunt the king might conduct, utilizing captured lions that, if recalcitrant, could be goaded into fighting by the noise of cymbals and irritating wounds. Deliberate in his aim despite the beast's proximity, the king is about to release the fatal arrow. The muscular character of Assyrian kingship is reflected in the strong relief modeling, in contrast to the flatter Egyptian forms, which seem to lack bone and sinew.

The overlapping of figures and objects in depth and their abundant detail, schematized as it is, show a more earthbound orientation in Assyrian art than they do in Egyptian royal art. The profile view was favored in antiquity for its ready identification, clarity of exposition, and usefulness in rendering animals and figures in movement.

Ancient Persian rulers continued the motif of showing themselves combating wild animals. At the court of Sassanid kings such as Hormuzd II, the tableware included silver drinking bowls bearing reliefs of the hunting triumph (Fig. 262). The use of this subject was a royal prerogative, and the bowls were made in palace workshops. Shown astride a horse in full gallop, Hormuzd II effortlessly pivots his body and is about to kill a wild lion rearing up on its hind legs. This movement shows to good advantage his horsemanship and profile. The ritualistic rather than realistic depiction required that the artist employ certain conventions such as showing a dead animal under the horse to balance the one still alive, and riding with his back to the horse's head, the ruler is shown wearing his crown. To preserve the purity of and focus on the royal profile, the artist willingly compromises reality by depicting the king's garment as being blown in the same direction as he is riding. The metal sculptor first hammered out his design from the back (known as *repoussé* work) and then used a burin to render the elegant trappings of horse and king with a jeweler's precision. Just as admirable is the adapting of the composition to the concave circular field of the bowl, and when we consider this aspect of the artist's problem, his contractions of distance and placement of subjects make excellent artistic logic. It was in antiquity that the idea developed that artists should not show the ruler as he was, but as he ought to be. So successful were Persian artists that their work, often transportable wares such as drinking bowls and textiles, exerted a powerful influence throughout the Mediterranean world into the Middle Ages.

The richest legacy of imperial imagery is that found in Roman art. The transformation of Rome from a republic into an empire is reflected in two statues of Roman rulers: the first, of Emperor Augustus, was made in the late first century B.C. (Figs. 263, 264); the second, which dates from the late Imperial era, is probably to

Above: Figure 263. *Prima Porta Augustus.* c. 19 B.C. Marble, height 6'8". Musei Vaticani, Rome.

Below: Figure 264. *Prima Porta Augustus*, detail of Fig. 263.

Left: Figure 265. So-called *Colossus of Barletta* (Emperor Marcian?; reigned 450–57 A.D.). Bronze, height 16′9″. Outside Church of Sto. Sepolcro, Barletta.

Above: Figure 266. *Colossus of Barletta*, detail of Fig. 265.

be identified with Emperor Marcian (Figs. 265, 266). The statue of Augustus, found at his wife's villa outside Rome, is known as the *Prima Porta Augustus*; the bronze cast of Marcian is usually referred to as the *Colossus of Barletta*, from the Italian town on the Adriatic coast where it is located. Augustus is shown in military uniform, as befitted the Imperator. His gesture is that of the commander-in-chief exhorting his troops. On his breastplate beneath the approving figure of Jupiter is the scene of a Parthian chieftain voluntarily returning cap-

tured eagle standards from Roman legions, a historic diplomatic feat of Augustus, signifying his peaceful rule. The figure below symbolizes Magna Mater, and the overflowing cornucopias attest to the material prosperity under Augustus' rule. The dolphin by his leg alludes to the belief in the divine origins of the Emperor's family, and the Cupid astride it alludes to Venus and fertility. Thus, brought together on the breastplate are an actual historical event, divinities, and allegories that demonstrate the universal Pax Romana for which Augustus was famed. Although deified by some of the provinces he conquered, in Rome itself Augustus chose to remain its first citizen, or princeps, nominally subservient to the senate in nonmilitary matters. His effigy is that of a handsome and athletic, dignified but humane ruler, given to clemency as well as to war. His weight is gracefully balanced in a manner reminiscent of the Greek *Spear Carrier* (Fig. 418), and the poised figure seems capable of easy movement.

Like a second, bronze version of the *Augustus*, the Barletta statue also stood in a public place. It is a rare survival of the full-length imperial statues of the time. Unlike that of Augustus, which was only slightly larger than human scale, Marcian's effigy towered impressively over the crowd, more than two and one-half times life size. No longer mortal and responsible to an earthly power, Marcian is deified in aspect and wears a crown. Both emperors were military figures, but Marcian's statue is the more militant. The quality of human mercy exemplified in Augustus is replaced by the severity of the later divine, uncompromising guardian of the Empire. In the original state, Marcian probably held a sword (now he holds up a cross), his martial spirit giving comfort to his many non-Christian followers and evoking fear in his enemies. As symbols of his power and accomplishment, the sword and the orb replaced the complex allegorical program of Augustus' armor. The relaxed fluidity of Augustus' movements gave way to a more firm stance and a rigid arrangement of the limbs and body. The sensuous softness of Augustus' form was succeeded by a tough, unyielding surface, as well as a more stiff and masculine treatment of the drapery.

Both sculptures are portraits of the rulers. The head of Augustus echoes Classical Greek tastes, displaying physical beauty, controlled and slightly softened treatment of the hair and the features, and an air of composure. The bronze head of Marcian has a geometric, blocklike form and axial symmetry enhanced by the charismatic fixity of the enlarged irises. Augustus' more relaxed portrait does not belie an ability to speak eloquently and to extemporize. Marcian's tight-set mouth reminds us that on public occasions the post-Diocletian emperors spoke in formulas or communicated with prescribed signs, avoiding spontaneity and the trivial gestures that might have marred their godlike impersonality.

Between the Barletta and Prima Porta figures in date are two other works of Imperial art that reflect political and artistic changes. The equestrian statue of Marcus Aurelius (Fig. 267), made between 161 and 180 A.D., survived medieval destruction of Roman Imperial statuary because it was mistakenly believed to depict the first Christian emperor, Constantine. Originally, a fallen barbarian lay beneath the horse, and Aurelius' gesture is one of clemency to his foes. In his left hand he held the orb. Free-standing sculptures of mounted figures were in that era the prerogative of the emperor. So esteemed were this and other imperial effigies that laws were written concerning human conduct prohibited in their vicinity; violation meant severe punishment. Public executions were performed before the monument, and a prisoner on trial could touch the statue, claiming sanctuary and the right of appeal to the emperor.

Aurelius' horse is rendered in meticulous detail, so that the bronze cast reveals strongly the modeled veins and creases in the flesh. The head of the Emperor is less detailed, however. To accommodate the beholder's gaze from below and at a distance, the hair portions are deeply drilled and the planes of the face are broadly modeled. There is an over-all lessening of particularized features and portrait quality, making the figure and its gesture into more an

Figure 267. *Equestrian Statue of Marcus Aurelius.* c. 161–180 A.D. Bronze, over life-size. Piazza del Campidoglio, Rome.

ideal embodiment of the near-deific status of the living Emperor.

Toward the end of the second century A.D. the gladiator-trained emperor Commodus had himself depicted as Hercules (Fig. 268), thus proclaiming himself immortal. Nero had assumed the role of a living god in the first century, beginning a long tradition that centuries later in America produced Horatio Greenough's sculpture of George Washington in the manner of Zeus and Lincoln's enthronement in a Roman temple. The statue of Commodus reflects the vanity that caused this soldier-emperor to shoot five hippopotami with a bow and arrow from his box at the Colosseum before a cheering multitude. It also gives some indication of the caliber of ruler resulting from the choice of the army in its growing power over the senate in electing and sustaining an emperor. Nonetheless, Commodus' bloody murder after a short and turbulent reign did not diminish the drive to deify the ruling authority of Rome.

Figure 268. *Commodus as Hercules.* c. 185 A.D. Marble, height 43 ½". Palazzo dei Conservatori, Rome.

IMPERIAL PORTRAITS AND RELIEFS

Like their Assyrian predecessors, Roman emperors were shown in a wide variety of reliefs and paintings of battles, hunts, and ceremonial functions. One of the most beautiful and impressive reliefs of the Augustan age is the Ara Pacis (Altar of Peace), constructed and carved between 14 and 9 B.C. Built on the Field of Mars, a military parade ground then outside Rome, it was intended to publicize the Emperor's foreign and domestic policy. The Emperor and his family are shown on one of the exterior sides joining in a procession led by the priests either at the founding or completion of the altar. Only a detail of the relief is shown here (Fig. 269), but it demonstrates the conscious informality of the groupings and the indistinguishability of Augustus (probably the figure at the left, the left half of whose body has been lost) from the other august personages. Like other members of his family, the Emperor wears a laurel crown, but neither in posture, gesture, or position is his preeminence stressed. The image Augustus sought to project was that of a ruler anxious to restore sincere religious observance and the unity of the family. Dilatory temple attendance and juvenile delinquency were not unknown already in Augustus' time.

Over three hundred years later, a great triumphal arch was erected near the Colosseum and Forum to commemorate the victory of Constantine over Maxentius. It was adorned with new sculpture and with reliefs taken from older monuments. Two of the new reliefs (Fig. 270) showed Constantine receiving homage from the senate and distributing gifts, according to tradition. In strong contrast to the more naturalistic figures of the Augustan relief, those of the Arch of Constantine jar the eye with their stunted bodies, large heads, repetitive gestures, geometric alignment, and total loss of individuality. The figures are flattened out and have lost all sensual appeal. The reliefs were relatively small and were not intended to fulfill the same function as, for example, the more than 60-foot full-length statue of Constantine that was placed in his basilica. Although the best talent available at the time evidently did not work on the relief, it still has a certain force and succeeds in conveying the court ideals

Left: Figure 269. *Procession of the Augusti*, portion of the frieze of the Ara Pacis. c. 14–9 B.C. Marble, height 5'3". Rome.

Below: Figure 270. *Constantine Receiving Homage from the Senate and Distributing Gifts*, frieze on the Arch of Constantine. Early 4th century A.D. Marble, height 41⅜". Rome.

of the time. In the Emperor's presence all activity was conducted according to a strict ritual. The importance of these reliefs lies in their culmination of the tendency toward a centripetal mode of composition, with total focus upon the strictly frontal and centralized figure of the Emperor. No previous ancient culture had realized so completely the artistic devices in the service of authority. Official taste of this epoch was indifferent to the organic qualities of flesh and blood. Expression of ideas superseded emphasis upon outward form, and the sensual life of the body glorified in Greece and early Rome passed into eclipse. A new and positive esthetic evolved in accord with hieratic and spiritual ideals that would have been

Images of Authority   231

Figure 271. *Narmer Votive Palette*, from Hieraconpolis. c. 3000 B.C. Schist, heigh 25″. The Egyptian Museum, Cairo.

outraged by such an interpretation as that of the Ara Pacis. A sophisticated, predominantly urban taste produced the Arch of Constantine statuary and the Barletta figure, and this provided the basis for such medieval Christian imagery as the Ravenna apse mosaic of Christ (Pl. 5).

The eastern portion of the Roman Empire, known as Byzantium, was founded by Constantine in 330 A.D., with its capital city named for the founder, Constantinople. Earlier Roman imperial devices for imbuing art with the majesty and deeds of the ruler were continued and refined in the Eastern Empire in the centuries that followed. Art workshops were part of the Great Palace of the Emperors in Constantinople, erected during the reign of Theodosius. The ruler, who held a monopoly on many luxury materials such as purple dyes, sought to ensure that imperial art would continue to remind his people of perpetual victory and divinely sanctioned rule. Coins, public statues, ivory reliefs on boxes, consular credentials, textiles, paintings, mosaics, army standards, and such precious objects as silver disks presented the imperial effigy for a thousand years. The emperor was always shown as a majestic

authority, whether in battle, hunting, officiating at public ceremonies, or attending the games in the hippodrome. The so-called *Barberini Ivory* (Pl. 30) is an outstanding example of the image of the early Byzantine ruler. A semiprecious medium imported from India and Africa, ivory had the advantage of softness for delicate and detailed carving, combined with durability and the capacity to take paint. Made about the turn of the sixth century, the Barberini panel was probably part of a series commemorating military and diplomatic triumphs of Emperor Anastasius I. The tripartite organization is a design scheme that can be traced back to Egyptian imperial imagery of the first dynasty, notably in the votive palette of King Narmer (Fig. 271).

In both objects, the top zone is symmetrical, its uncompromising formality being reserved for images of a supreme deity. Flanking Egyptian gods represented in the form of bulls precede their later anthropomorphic treatment. On the ivory, a frontal bust of Christ appears in a medallion held by angels. The Christians had simply replaced earlier pagan Roman images of the emperor with those of their God

232   Purposes of Art

Plate 33. ANTOINE JEAN GROS. *Napoleon Visiting the Pest House at Jaffa.* 1804. Oil on canvas, 17′5″ × 23′7″. Louvre, Paris.

Plate 34. EUGÈNE DELACROIX. *Liberty on the Barricades.* 1830. Oil on canvas, 8'6½" × 10'8". Louvre, Paris.

Plate 35. EDOUARD MANET. *A Bar at the Folies-Bergère.* 1881–82. Oil on canvas, 3'1½" × 4'3". The Courtauld Collection, London.

Plate 36.   CLAUDE MONET. *Fourteenth of July, Rue Montorgeuil.* 1878.
Oil on canvas, 24½ × 13″. Musée des Beaux-Arts, Rouen.

and preserved the hieratic format. The second zone of the ivory shows the Byzantine Emperor on horseback, his standard largely obscuring the figure of an Asiatic chieftain. His stirrup is supported by an allegorical figure of Earth, and a flanking official presents him with a statue of Victory. On the palette, King Narmer is shown in a ritualistic gesture, with mace in hand, about to destroy his adversary with a single stroke. (Reflecting Christianizing influence, by the time of the *Barberini Ivory* Byzantine emperors had reduced the number of battlefield images and those involving cruelty.) While subordinate to their respective gods, both rulers assert their importance through their great scale within the zones they occupy. Anastasius is shown in not quite frontal pose so that he tactfully does not compete with Christ; he is relatively central within his field, but one flanking official is missing. In the lowest, most inferior register, both pieces have the greatest mobility and, symbolically significant, their least ordered portion. The enemies of Narmer flee or are dead, their disarray contrasting with the King's composed solemnity. Below Anastasius, at the left, are barbarians bringing tribute and, on the right, emissaries from India bearing gifts that include ivory. The relief carving in both works is of the highest quality—precise, clear, and adept in shaping compositional demands to political ones. The art of intervening centuries is testified to in the Byzantine relief, with its greater sensuousness, variety of movement, and body perspectives.

To someone unfamiliar with Byzantine art, it may appear stiff, repetitious, and unfeeling; there is no display of human warmth in the imperial images, no dialogue between the figures. Accustomed to no alternatives, Egyptian, Roman, and Byzantine artists accepted their assigned roles and succeeded in creating inspired art within officially imposed strict limitations. Much of the power of Byzantine art, like that of earlier Rome, derives from its complete realization of political and religious ideals. Like many other works, the *Barberini Ivory* and the silver *Disk of Theodosius* (Fig. 272), made at the end of the fourth century, show the possibilities of excellence in art that is not created in a republican society. Wearing the imperial diadem, Theodosius is enthroned in the center of a gabled and arcaded structure that may have symbolized a façade of his

Figure 272. *Disk of Theodosius.* c. 390 A.D. Silver, diameter 29 ⅛". Academy of History, Madrid.

palace. To the left and right of him are his sons, the princes Honorius and Arcadius, holding orbs symbolic of temporal rule. Flanking the whole are pairs of imperial guardsmen. An official kneels to receive a gift or investiture of power from the Emperor. According to court ritual, no one looks at the official. His hands are cloaked, showing his unworthiness to touch the divine person of the Emperor. In the area below is the earth goddess with the cornucopia symbolizing abundance under Byzantine rule; at this time, Christian emperors were not averse to using pagan symbolism. The Emperor's omnipotence is shown in hieratic fashion by his great scale, his centrality, and his location beneath an arch symbolic of heaven. These attributes are more important than the individual personality or features of the ruler, hence the essential impersonality of the image. Again, the artist is depicting an abstract idea. An eyewitness description of an audience held with a Byzantine emperor by Liudprand of Cremona in the tenth century illuminates the environment that the artist was expressing, but not literally describing. Having been led into the audience chamber of the Emperor, Liudprand wrote:

Before the seat stood a tree made of bronze, gilded over, whose branches were filled with birds, also made of gilded bronze, which uttered different cries, each according to its various species. The throne itself was so marvelously fashioned that at one moment it seemed a low structure and at another it rose into the air. It was of immense size and was guarded by lions, made either of bronze or of wood covered over with gold, who beat the ground with their tails and gave a dreadful roar with open mouth and quivering tongue. Leaning on the shoulders of two eunuchs I was brought into the emperor's presence. At my approach the lions began to roar and the birds cry out…. I lifted my head and behold, the man whom I had just before seen sitting on a moderately elevated seat had now changed his position and was sitting on the level of the ceiling.

Unfortunately, no images of this marvelous throne and audience hall have survived. The imaginative genius that contrived the tree and lions lives on only in Liudprand's words.

The influence of Byzantine imperial imagery was felt all through the Middle Ages. One of its strongest manifestations is in tenth- and eleventh-century Ottonian manuscript art depicting the Germanic emperors. An Ottonian emperor had married a Byzantine princess who brought to her husband's court works of art, and possibly artists, which helps to account for Eastern influence in Western Europe. The Emperor Otto II had himself portrayed in a manner reminiscent of Theodosius (Fig. 273). Allegorical figures of four nations bring gifts to the impassive ruler sitting beneath an architectural canopy, itself a celestial symbol. The perspective of the canopy is rudimentary and inconsistent. To preserve the ruler's hieratic centrality within the arc of the canopy, the artist arbitrarily omitted the fourth column. To have rendered the depth of the painting consistently from the viewpoint of a spectator outside the picture would have meant subordinating the ruler to an external system governed by the viewer. Hieratic conventions or schemes were used without concern for fidelity to natural appearance, only for reasons of suitability to the theme.

The Ottonian portrait shares certain traits with a Japanese portrait of the great Shogun Minamoto Yoritomo, by Fujiwara no Takanobu (Fig. 274). Both were iconic representations of power. Takanobu, however, combined the impersonal symbols and stiff forms of the

Figure 273. *Emperor Otto II*, from the *Registrum Gregorii*. Trier. Manuscript illumination. c. 985. Musée Condé, Chantilly.

Figure 274. FUJIWARA NO TAKANOBU. *Portrait of Minamoto Yoritomo*. c. 1185. Painting on silk. Jingoji, Japan.

commander's ceremonial costume with a noticeable facial likeness of his subject. The Shogun is seated on a cushion throne, as he would be seen in the place of honor during a formal ceremony in the audience hall of his palace. This imposing portrait on silk was painted shortly after 1185, when Yoritomo overthrew the pleasure-loving Fujiwara regents and the Emperor retired from active rule. Yoritomo brought the samurai, the warrior caste, into power and created the military regime (Baku-Fu) that lasted in Japan until the nineteenth century.

Takanobu's painting inaugurated a portrait tradition in Japanese art. The style, a continuation from earlier periods, comprised large crisp silhouettes, clear ornamental surface patterns, a flat-toned, textureless flesh rendering, and an austere, seemingly airless surrounding. Mineral colors were mixed with glue to give opaque, unmodeled surfaces. By Western standards, the lines may at first seem uniformly drawn, but on closer inspection they reveal occasional deft changes in value while preserving a flowing, wirelike quality. The Shogun's individuality resides in the small, immobile shapes of the eyes, nose, and mouth. The position of the head and the hair style are traditional, as are the symbols of his office and power, the sword and scepter. Nevertheless, the injection of some of Yoritomo's distinctive features is evidence of an encroachment of the samurai taste for naturalism, as opposed to the abstract facial types characteristic of previous periods.

In Yoritomo's shogunate the code of Bushido came into ascendance. Yoritomo's portrait is therefore representative of a Japanese feudal ideal of the perfect knight, a code that Takanobu seems to have illustrated in many respects. The samurai was disciplined in the strict course of rational conduct: "Rectitude is the bone that gives firmness and stature...without rectitude neither talent nor learning can make of a human frame a samurai." He would at all times exhibit stoic composure and presence of mind. ("A truly brave man is ever serene.") The absence of animation in the portrait expresses the samurai view that it was unmanly to show emotion in the face and that truly strong character was possessed by him "who shows no sign of joy or anger." An appreciation of culture was also part of his training. The samurai esteemed, and might even spare, an opponent who in the heat of battle maintained

Figure 275. ANDREA DEL VERROCHIO. *Lorenzo de' Medici.* c. 1478. Painted terra cotta, life-size. The National Gallery of Art, Washington, D. C. (Samuel H. Kress Collection).

the presence of mind to compose or recall an appropriate couplet.

Yoritomo's portrait, which hung in a palace, may have been intended for worship. More likely it was a memorial to his military and administrative genius, to be venerated as an ideal by later generations of samurai. Thus, the concept of a ruler's portrait serving as an ethical example was shared by East and West.

STATE PORTRAITS

The finest sculptural portrait of a fifteenth-century Italian Renaissance ruler is that of Lorenzo de' Medici, done by Andrea del Verrocchio about 1478 (Fig. 275). This painted terra-cotta bust bears impressive witness to the Duke's power and excellence. The extent to which Florentine style was able to impart ideals of authority is further demonstrated when the bust is studied along with Machiavelli's statements in *The Prince*, written in 1513 and first published in 1532. Although Lorenzo the Magnificent died some twenty years before their writing, these precepts were influenced by Machiavelli's knowledge of his career and the tradition out of which he came. Their relevance to art can be seen in the importance the writer has placed upon appearances:

Images of Authority   235

Figure 276. PIERO DELLA FRANCESCA. *Battista Sforza, Duchess of Urbino*. c. 1465–72. Oil on panel, 18½″ × 13″. Uffizi, Florence.

Figure 277. PIERO DELLA FRANCESCA. *Federigo da Montefeltro, Duke of Urbino*. c. 1465–72. Oil on panel, 18½″ × 13″. Uffizi, Florence.

We...encourage such Princes to fortify and guard their own capital city.... The Prince ought to go in person and perform the office of a commander...have no other aim, nor thought, nor take anything else for his proper art, but war. It is necessary for a Prince, desiring to preserve himself, to be able to make use of that honesty, and to lay it aside again as need shall require. Wherefore a Prince ought not to regard the infamy of cruelty, for to hold his subjects united and faithful...a Prince (ought) to serve himself of the conditions of the Fox and the Lion...and let him seem to him that sees and hear him, all pity, all faith, all integrity, all humanity, all religion...for all men in general judge thereof, rather by sight than touch, for every man may come to the sight of him, few come to the touch and feeling of him. A Prince ought to endeavor in all his actions to spread abroad a name of his magnificence and worthiness. He ought in the fit times of the year entertain people with Feasts and Masks.

Verrocchio's bust gives Lorenzo a tough, sober, but contemplative appearance. Subtle exaggerations in the face gave the subject a some-

what leonine appearance. Like his palace, to be discussed in Chapter 13, Lorenzo's bust has a solid, even militant appearance owing to its firm roundness, unostentatious dress, and the strong forward thrust of the nose, framed by the cornicelike cap and severe hairdo. Every zone is distinclty separate in a composition built on a frame of verticals and horizontals.

Skilled in the arts of war and politics, Lorenzo was also a man of culture, who gathered in his court a brilliant circle of philosophers, men of letters, and artists, such as the young Michelangelo. On a more modest scale than had the Roman emperors, the Medici also staged public pageants for the city of Florence.

Italian portraits of nobility in the fifteenth century, like the design of their palace façades, were strongly influenced by ideas from ancient Rome. Piero della Francesca's double portrait of the Duke and Duchess of Urbino poses the subjects in profile, emulating coin and medallion effigies of Roman emperors (Figs. 276, 277). The profile view also served to conceal the Duke's damaged right eye, for while a fair degree of portrait likeness was considered desirable in this period, that which seemed ugly or deformed, along with conspicuous emotion, was to be concealed. The striking broken bridge of the ducal nose adds to the impressiveness of his birdlike profile. Un-Roman, on the contrary, was Piero's use of a landscape backdrop for the portrait. Artful placement of the heads above the horizon line perhaps implies that the Duke is, literally and figuratively, lord over the land he surveys. The couple's elevated viewpoint suggests that they are depicted on a balcony of their palace; the Roman tradition of the ruler's association with a loggia or "window of appearances" is also discussed in Chapter 13. On the reverse of the portrait panels (Figs. 278, 279), Piero painted the Duke and Duchess sitting on triumphal carriages; Federigo is shown being crowned by Fame, and personifications of virtues accompany both husband and wife. The fifteenth, sixteenth, and seventeenth centuries witnessed the revival of triumphal processions and pageants of the nobility. In the Baroque period, the simplicity of Piero's carts gave way to more elaborate and complex ceremonial floats.

State portraits of the past have little popularity or relevance today because of their extreme formality, their lack of warmth and individuality. These were portraits of concepts as well as of persons, and it is the alien character of absolutist political ideals that contributes to present-day public indifference or dislike. The formulas for the state portrait that originated in exceptional painting of the sixteenth and seventeenth centuries encouraged mechanical repetition in the hands of uninspired technicians that continues even today in trustee portraits on our campuses or in corporative board rooms. With the rise of the state in the sixteenth and seventeenth centuries, it became the task of the portraitist to give material form to the immaterial entity of the state. The historian Garrett Mattingly, in his fine book *The Defeat of the Spanish Armada*, describes the climate in which state portraits emerged:

> The deepest longing of the troubled and divided sixteenth century was for unity and peace, and the only effective symbol men could find for the social order they craved was the person of the monarch. So the life of even the wickedest prince, most preachers taught, was sacred, and the duty of obedience was explicit no matter what the character of the

ruler. Gradually that ultimate allegiance once given to the universal church was being transferred to secular sovereigns, in preparation for its further transference to an abstraction called the national state when men should think of it. The blasphemous doctrine of the divinity of kings was beginning to be in the air...everywhere in Europe. The sixteenth century belonged to the monarchs.

Above: Figure 278. PIERO DELLA FRANCESCA *Triumph of the Duke of Urbino,* reverse side of the portrait panel (Fig. 277).

Below: Figure 279. PIERO DELLA FRANCESCA. *Triumph of the Duchess of Urbino,* reverse side of the portrait panel (Fig. 276).

Early in the sixteenth century Jean Clouet painted a half-length portrait of Francis I that is regal in subject and style (Pl. 31). Required to portray grandeur, and therefore restricted in the gestures he could use, Clouet shows the king with one hand symbolically on his sword and the other at rest on a cloth-covered table. Rational composure and power are thus conveyed in the hands alone. The outward swelling of the costume upward from the hands to the shoulders, culminating in the finely shaped neck, was consonant with what were thought to be ideal royal proportions, as well as with the current fashion, which meant exaggerating the breadth and masculinity of the king. Clouet gives only a subdued relief to the head, which is so disposed as to permit firm but delicate delineation of the long regal nose. The remote stare of the eyes is a fitting expression for a monarch, who was thought to exist and to govern in total isolation. Clouet's design stresses sharp contrasts of brilliant color, such as the red tapestry against the black and cream of the king's attire. Cool, nontactile surfaces add to the aloofness and unsensual character of the subject. State portraits were not supposed to be too literal or lifelike, and Clouet's almost abstract design of color, figure placement, and pose did much to create an aura that was symbolically unnatural. The style of a successful royal portraitist such as Clouet was one and the same with that of the ruler. As in antiquity, the state portraitist was enjoined to show the ruler as he should be, not as he was—just as Mattingly points out that even from the pulpit men were told to revere and obey the most unscrupulous monarch.

The ruler who dominated the sixteenth century by his will, integrity, and sense of duty, along with his political and military success in putting together a global empire, was Charles V, the last German emperor crowned by the Pope. King during the Protestant Reformation, Charles warred with the heretics in Germany, yet sent a Lutheran army that sacked Rome in 1527, was the power behind the Council of Trent, and for most of his life overcame the intrigues of rival kings such as Francis I. The demand for imperial portraits such as those of Charles I was so great throughout Europe that not only copies of paintings but also engravings were used to disseminate the royal image. Aeneas Vico, an Italian printmaker, engraved

a portrait of Charles V, based probably on a painting by Titian, in which the King's image was framed with allegorical figures of conquered territories, fame, and virtues (Fig. 280). All were set against a structure that resembled a Roman triumphal gateway or temple portico. Charles's roles as defender of the Faith, leader in war, and provider of prosperity are symbolized by the figures and garlands in the upper area of the print, while over the landscape at the left behind the structure his armies wage war. The ruins at the right refer to his conquests in Italy. The eagle above the portrait, on whose back stands the figure of Victory, is a motif from Roman triumphal arches, where it relates to the apotheosis of the emperor. Against the background activity of its frame, the Emperor's visage is serene but firm; utilizing Titian's characterization of Charles, Vico portrayed him as handsome and wise. When one reflects that it was during the reign of Charles V that great explorations were conducted in the New World and that such diverse territories as the Netherlands, Germany, Sicily, Spain, and Portugal were united, such extravagant homage from an Italian artist becomes understandable.

So successful was Titian in capturing the ideals of monarchy that Charles V ordered that no one else be allowed to paint his portrait. One

Figure 280. ENEAS VICO. *Charles V.* 1550. Engraving, 20 ¼" × 14 ¼".

of many influential state portraits that Titian
did of Charles (Fig. 281) shows the Emperor
riding on the field of Muhlberg, where he won
a great victory over two rival German rulers.
In depicting Charles at the zenith of his power,
Titian chose to adapt the old equestrian format
from sculpture to easel painting. The result was
to increase the scale and monumentality of the
ruler's image and, though in a seated pose, to
show him full length. His mastery of sixteenth-
century ideas of horsemanship was validated in
the noble bearing Titian gave him on horseback. The gold and black armor, coupled with
the aristocratic pose and the isolation of horse
and rider, would seem to locate the action not
in battle but as if on parade. The three quarter
pose of horse and rider permitted what Titian
felt was the most striking view of Charles' face
and the beauty of the rounded sash-covered
breastplate. Many scholars have pointed out
that Titian s clients favored his way of working,
which was not bound to a strict likeness of the
subject. After studying the sitter's features,
Titian would then re-create him as he felt he
ought to be. Although his painting is more
sensuous than that of Clouet, Titian's state
portrait loses none of its majestic quality.

Sixteenth- and seventeenth-century Indian
rulers included the equestrian portrait in their
artistic repertory. A painting of a Rajput ruler
on horseback impaling a lioness testifies to the
persistence of the victorious hunt motif in
Eastern art (Fig. 282). The Maharajah, who
embodied solar power, plunges the lance into
the animal with no more show of feeling or
individual reaction than was evidenced by
Hormuzd II, for he too is performing essentially
a ritual or symbolic act. How remote Indian
painting is from that of sixteenth-century
Venice is seen in many ways. The Indian painting is small, intended for an album which would
be leafed through and looked at leisurely and in
privacy. The artist was completely self-effacing
with respect to artistic personality, and he
repeated general types of hunter and hunted.
Drawing and coloring were in an impersonal
traditional style, which preserves bright surface
patterns that are delicately and cleanly edged.
Conventions of drawing explain the thin, even
rarefied, continuous outlining of the subjects and
the use of flat color areas, often filled in by a
painter rather than by the draftsman who first
set down the image.

Figure 281. TITIAN. *Charles V on Horseback*. 1548.
Oil on canvas, 10'10¾" × 9'1 ⅞". Prado, Madrid.

Figure 282. *Maharaja Kesari Singh on Horseback
Overcoming a Lioness*. c. 1715–20. Painting. Lallgarh
Palace, Rajasthan.

Figure 283. PETER PAUL
RUBENS. *Henry IV Receiving the
Portrait of Marie de' Medici.*
1622. Oil on canvas,
12′11 ⅛″×9′8 ⅛″. Louvre, Paris.

European painting of royalty in the seventeenth century was not as tradition-bound as Eastern aristocratic art, and artists of intelligence such as Anthony van Dyck had discreet freedom to innovate, as long as they suited the taste and ideal of the patron. Rather than first analyzing van Dyck's finished painting of Charles I (Pl. 32), let us consider the problem of representation as it might have been posed in the artist's mind. Charles I saw himself as a cavalier or perfect gentleman, a patron of the arts as well as the embodiment of the state's power and king by divine right. He prided himself upon his dress more than on robust and bloody physical feats. Van Dyck had available to him precedents for the ruler on horseback and the theme of the strenuous hunt, but he set these aside. How then might he show the regal qualities and sportsmanship of a dismounted monarch in a landscape? Compounding the artist's problem was the King's short stature,

just about five feet, five inches. To put him next to his horse, rendered in correct scale, could present an ungainly problem of their relative heights. Titian supplied van Dyck with a solution to this last problem in a painting where a horse stood with neck bowed, a natural gesture that in the presence of the King would have appropriate connotations. Placing the royal pages behind the horse and farther from the viewer than the King would reduce their height and obtrusiveness yet furnish the ruler with some evidence of his authority over men. Nature also is made to support and suitably frame the King. Van Dyck stations the monarch on a small rise and overhead paints the branches of a tree like a royal canopy. The low horizon line and our point of view, which allows the King to look down on us, subtly increase the King's stature. There laxation yet inaccessibility of Charles depends largely upon his pose— itself a work of art, derived from art, notably that of Rubens. Its casualness is deceptive; while seemingly at rest in an informal moment, the King is every inch the perfect gentleman and chief of state. The cane was a royal prerogative in European courts of the time, and its presence along with the sword symbolized the gentleman-king.

Just as the subtle pose depicts majesty, van Dyck's color, with its regal silver and gold, does much to impart grandeur to the painting and to achieve a sophisticated focus on the King. The red, silver, gold, and black of his costume are the most saturate and intense of the painting's colors and contrast with the darker or less intense coloring of adjacent areas. Largely from Rubens, van Dyck had learned the painterly tricks by which materials and textures could be vividly simulated, so that the eye moves with pleasure from the silvery silken sheen of the coat to the golden leather sword harness and then on to the more coarse surface of the horse, with a similar but darker combination of colors in its coat and mane. Van Dyck's state portrait is evidence that, while one may not be in sympathy with his message, the artist's virtuosity and esthetic can still be enjoyed.

The great esteem in which painters were held by royalty has already been noted in Charles V's granting of a monopoly for his portraits to Titian. Peter Paul Rubens actually served as an ambassador for royalty and was treated and lived like a member of the aristocracy. Rubens was the greatest interpreter of the Baroque rulers' claims to power and divinity, for with his broad education, which included the study of ancient imperial art, he was able to create a synthesis of pagan and Christian symbols for interpreting absolute monarchy and the divine right of kings. In 1635, for the triumphal entry of Archduke Ferdinand into Antwerp, Rubens was given a corps of artists to decorate the entire city. On another occasion, Marie de' Medici commissioned Rubens to paint a great cycle of paintings for her palace, dealing with her life as Queen of France and celebrating the achievements of her late husband, Henry IV. In his painting of *Henry IV Receiving the Portrait of Marie de' Medici* (Fig. 283), Rubens mingled fact and fantasy. It was then customary among royalty to have an important artist portray the bride-to-be for the groom, who may never have seen her. In this scene, Rubens flattered both the Queen and himself, for he portrayed the King as enraptured by the painting of his betrothed. Over the King's shoulder, the allegorical figure of France shares his admiring gaze. The two cupids that have taken charge of the King's armor signify that, for love, he had put aside thoughts of war, which was then actually being waged in Saxony—perhaps the explanation for the burning city in the distance. Above the bearers of the portrait sit Jupiter and Juno, ironically inferring that the marriage of these Catholic monarchs was made in a pagan heaven. (The eagle and peacock are attributes of these gods.) In one of the most inspired postures in state portraiture, Rubens shows the King, equipped with the militant armor of monarchy and the cane of the courtly gentleman, gracefully turning his body so that we see him full length with the royal profile directed logically toward the smiling visage of Marie. Although even in the seventeenth century such conceptions demanded a willing suspension of disbelief, Rubens carries off the artifice with vigor and persuasiveness, for his grand style and masterly staging of the action quite convinces us that such an event as this might well be verified through the senses.

The deification of Louis XIV was a full-time project for the army of artists, musicians, writers, and poets gathered at the great court of Versailles in the seventeenth century. Among this brilliant coterie was the sculptor Gianlorenzo Bernini, who in 1665 carved the magnificent bust of King Louis XIV (Fig. 284) that remains in his bedroom at Versailles.

Figure 284. GIANLORENZO BERNINI. *Louis XIV*. 1665. Marble, height 31 ¼". Palace of Versailles.

Figure 285.   HYACINTHE RIGAUD. *Louis XIV*. 1701
Oil on canvas, 9′1⅞″ × 5′10⅞″. Louvre, Paris.

portion of the body is unself-consciously posed in a three-quarter view, staring into space as if responding to some "inner light." The long wig billows and curls about the serene countenance. The highly polished marble radiates with light, reminding the spectator that Louis was the Sun King.

The most expensive portrait ever painted is reputedly that of Louis XIV by Hyacinthe Rigaud (Fig. 285), for it is believed that the artist received in excess of seventy thousand dollars for it. Borrowing liberally from van Dyck, Rigaud's work is the logical culmination of state-portrait development. An imposing full-length treatment, it abounds in references to the kingly vocation of the subject. The great column is a royal symbol that goes back to early Greece. There are yards of purple ermine-lined robe emblazoned with fleurs-de-lis. The King stands as the epitome of confidence and courtly grace, with his left hand on his hip and his right holding his cane. His shapely legs are carefully exposed, revealing their trained suitability for the dance. Although the high-heeled red shoes may strike the modern observer as effeminate, the King was nevertheless proud of his manliness and his embodiment of the etiquette that he demanded of his courtiers. The elaborate full-length portrait does not encourage a close inspection of the face but forces the viewer to dwell on the accessories and splendor of the King's office.

Napoleon was the last of the great rulers of Europe to employ the most important artists of his time. At Napoleon's request, the French artist Jacques Louis David showed the general leading his troops on a historic march across the Alps in 1800 (Fig. 286). Although Napoleon was still in the office of First Consul, this constitutes the last of the great imperial equestrian paintings. Following the orders of his subject, David showed Napoleon expertly mounted on a wildly rearing horse, pointing upward as if to the mountain peaks or heaven. (It was not such a romantic commanding gesture, however, but great staff work and soldierly fortitude that took 40,000 men five days to traverse the mountains.) Napoleon posed briefly for the rendering of his face, telling David that close resemblance was not important: "It is not the exact reflection of features, warts on the nose, that makes a likeness; it's the character and what animates the physiognomy, that

In his memoirs, Louis set down his views of the ideal Christian king:

> As he is of a rank superior to all other men, he sees things more perfectly than they do, and he ought to trust rather to the inner light than to information which reaches him from outside. . . . Occupying, so to speak, the place of God, we seem to be sharers of His knowledge as well as of His authority.

Bernini carved his ideals of kingship, which accorded perfectly with those of Louis. The bust forms an impressive contrast to Verrocchio's sculpture of Lorenzo de' Medici. Whereas the latter rests solidly on a broad base, with the eyes turned down and the entire figure geometrically organized, Bernini's King is poised in the air above a cloudlike sweep of drapery that swirls about a narrow base. The upper needs to be painted. No one inquires if the portraits of great men are likenesses. It's enough that their genius lives in them." By showing the advancing army in the middle ground, seen from under the belly of the horse, David was following tradition and rational perspective, but Napoleon himself was displeased that his men were shown so small, as if they could be crushed by the horse's hoofs. The painting, with its obviously staged quality, is indeed contradictory to fact, for Napoleon crossed the Alps not on an unstable steed but on a sure-footed mule. As stand-in for the Emperor, one of David's students posed atop a ladder, pointing his arm till it dropped. Separate studies were made of Napoleon's white charger, which was shown rearing in the manner of seventeenth-century equestrian portraits. Despite such contrivances, David was sufficiently inspired to make the painting genuinely impressive. A dark foreground, spotlighting, and the pearly grey of the mountain setting and turbulent sky throw the striking figure of Napoleon into dra-

matic relief. Reviving an ancient symbol of victory, David represents the wind at Napoleon's back, thus further agitating the area around the face, which is like the serene center of a storm. The message of the painting was that, like Hannibal and Charlemagne, whose names are inscribed with "Bonaparte" on the rock in the left foreground, the soon-to-be Emperor would lead his country to new heights of glory.

Unlike hereditary monarchs such as Charles V and Henry IV, Napoleon had to use art to help legitimize his claims to power and, in one spectacular instance, to counteract a terrible catastrophe that turned his Egyptian army violently against him and threatened his base of support in France. After the fall of the Syrian city of Jaffa, Napoleon's generals violated the terms of surrender and slaughtered the entire garrison. Shortly afterward, bubonic plague broke out and nearly decimated Napoleon's army. Many construed this as divine retribution. At great personal risk, Napoleon visited the hospital at Jaffa and passed among his suffering

Figure 286. JACQUES LOUIS DAVID. *Napoleon Crossing the Alps.* 1800. Oil on canvas. 8'10" × 7'7". Palace of Versailles.

Figure 287. EHRLER. *Der Führer*. 1939.
Oil on canvas. Whereabouts unknown.

men. Although not an eyewitness to the visit to the Jaffa pesthouse, Baron Gros, working under Napoleon's order, utilized written accounts of what had happened to produce a painting that is a fine example of counter-defamation propaganda (Pl. 33). Baron Gros shows Napoleon in the midst of the plague-stricken and, having removed a glove, calmly about to reach out and touch the bubonic boil in the armpit of one of his soldiers. This gesture was not taken from the actual account of his visit but derives from art history, from works in which Christ and saints are shown healing the sick and from the seventeenth-century imperial tradition of the king as a miracle worker, by which the royal touch was thought to effect cures. In no previous imperial image was the public made so strongly aware of death, for at the base of the large painting, at the viewer's eye level, are the faces and gangrenous bodies of the dead and dying. Baron Gros confirmed reports of the terrible casualties of the Egyptian campaign but at the same time transformed Napoleon, who was responsible for so many disasters, into a saviour-king. When, in fact, Napoleon was forced to

retreat from Acre and Jaffa, he ordered poison placed by the immobile wounded so that they could take their own lives.

Very much aware of the past history of art as powerful political propaganda, Adolph Hitler outlawed modern art and turned to technically proficient and compliant artistic mediocrities to revive the tradition of state portraiture. A formal portrait of Hitler (Fig. 287) equals in craftsmanship Rigaud's portrait of an earlier monarch. The eye level of the viewer is intentionally placed well below the figure of "Der Führer," so as to increase his unimpressive physical stature. He is in uniform, backed by a gigantic sculpture of a powerful youth holding an eagle. The setting recalls ancient pharaonic imagery with the hawk god and other portraiture showing the ruler in the presence of deities. He is shown outdoors, and in the foreground are scattered building blocks and instruments, a sign of the construction of the New Order and of Hitler's obsessive self-image as an architect. Off in the distance on a low horizon can be seen the outline of a stadium, the incubator for Nazi youth who recognized Hitler as their spiritual father. The painter gave Hitler a visionary aspect by posing him in a three-quarter view and directing his gaze upward, as if he were contemplating the future. The artist avoided the uncompromising frontality that would have brought portraiture full circle and back to the image of the pharaoh. As in the older portraiture upon which this was based, the painter was interpreting the abstract ideas of the Third Reich rather than the personality or mood of his subject. Such a painting shows how, with skilled propaganda, a legend of Hitler's strength, invincibility, and immortality could have grown up in Germany. Nothing in the handling of the figure suggests compromise, humility, or compassion.

The last portrait in this chapter is one of the late President John F. Kennedy, painted by Elaine de Kooning (Fig. 288). Not an official state portrait, it resulted from a series of sketches and paintings made by her to fulfill a commission from the Truman Library. One of the few notable modern painters who does not look upon portraiture as inhibiting imagination or self-expression, Elaine de Kooning had behind her years of doing portraits of friends, many of whom were fellow artists. She had developed a style based on quick execution in a single session, in order "to get close to the essential gesture of the sitter." The restless, informal, and energetic President by his nature could not hold still for long and collaborate with the artist for a formal portrait in the historical sense, even if she had wanted to do one and her style permitted it. Where Clouet saw the state in Francis I, Elaine de Kooning saw the following traits:

> He was not the grey, sculptural newspaper image. He was incandescent, golden. And bigger than life. Not that he was taller than the men standing around him; he just seemed to be a different dimension. Also not revealed by the newspaper image were his incredible eyes with large violet irises half-veiled by the jutting bone beneath the eyebrows.... In succeeding sessions of sketching, I was struck by the curious faceted structure of light over his face and hair—a quality of transparent

ruddiness. This play of light contributed to the extraordinary variety of expressions. His smile and frown both seem to be built into the bone. Everyone is familiar with the quick sense of humor revealed in the corners of his mouth and the laugh lines around the eyes, but what impressed me most was his compassion....

Though executed in a few hours, her portrait was built upon numerous drawings that were often made from television appearances and newspaper photographs. "I had to contend with this 'world image' created by the endless newspaper photographs." De Kooning's color keys in the portrait, unlike those used by Clouet, come from the subject's face and her strong personal feelings. Both in the way it was painted and in her portrayal of the President, the emphasis is upon her own individuality as a painter and on the subject's humanity.

Figure 288. ELAINE DE KOONING. *President John F. Kennedy.* 1962–63. Oil on canvas, 5'4" × 4'. The Truman Library, Independence, Missouri.

245

13

THE ARCHITECTURE
OF AUTHORITY

How misleading is the notion that architecture must always be an abstract art form was demonstrated earlier by the discoveries of scholars regarding the symbolism of religious buildings. Temples and churches, in turn, derived much of their symbolism or mystical associations from architecture that in ancient times had served kihgship. Over a period of centuries certain architectural features such as gateways and palace façades acquired, not just from written sources but in the mind of the masses as well as the rulers themselves, connotations of authority. When kings acted like gods, and gods were interpreted as kings, it is not surprising that the ancient architecture of palace and temple should have acquired royal and divine associations. The influence of ancient royal architecture descended through the Middle Ages and into the Renaissance and Baroque periods. In modern times, its propaganda and symbolic value was revived by Mussolini and Adolph Hitler. It is clear, then, that the history of architecture often mingles with the history of ideas and has been used as a powerful instrument by rulers to strengthen their image in the minds of their subjects. The destruction wreaked on so many palaces is a substantial tribute to the effectiveness with which monarchy has been identified with its masonry.

In their formal relations with the public, ancient rulers used specially designed architecture as a backdrop for ceremony. But even without such public rituals, the architecture, by its symbolic associations, grandeur, durability, and distinction from the homes of the common man, was, in a sense, a substitute for the ruler, a constant reminder of his power whether he was at home or abroad. Ancient coins usually bore the king's image, but often there was merely a rendering of the entrance to his palace—which for most people was all they would know in their lifetime of the royal residence. The dome over the United States Capitol, for example, is today sufficient to identify this country and evoke its form of government, though ironically the dome has anything but a republican source and history, rooted as it is in ancient symbolism of heaven and serving to proclaim the divinity of Near Eastern and Roman monarchs.

Unlike our own and other present-day governments, those of the past regularly called upon their best architectural talents to construct public buildings. As with religious architecture since the nineteenth century, the best modern architecture on the whole has developed independently of the state, under the patronage

246

Figure 289.   Funerary Temple of King Ramses III, Medinet Abu (Thebes). 20th Dynasty, 1198–1167 B.C.

Below: Figure 290.   Drawing of a Pylon from the Temple of Khons at Karnak.

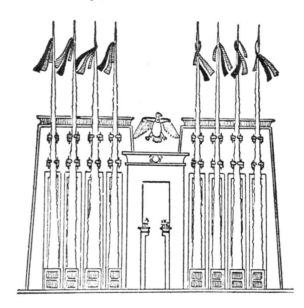

of private persons and business. For this and other reasons, it has become difficult for us to appreciate that what seem to be dead and impersonal ancient ruins once embodied so many of civilization's most important political values.

ANCIENT GATEWAYS

Ancient Egypt and Mesopotamia cradled much of human civilization and evolved important architectural symbols, notably that of the imposing gateway to a city or to a palace-temple complex. The great pylons, or gateways, to Egyptian temples such as that of Ramses III at Medinet Abu also served to front the palace when it adjoined the sacred precinct (Fig. 289). Upon the huge walls of the pylons, the pharaohs had carved and painted records of their victories and descent from the gods, with whom they were often shown in company. Roman emperors were later to do the same on their triumphal arches. Set into rectangular recesses on the face of the pylons were flagstaffs from which flew pennants signifying the god or pharaoh in residence (Fig. 290). The pylon form consists of a central zone for the great doorway, possibly surmounted by a solar disk;

both disk and doors were originally covered in lustrous metal. Completed by two taller flanking sections, the pylon ideologically represented the gateway to heaven, with its hieroglyph denoting the sun setting between two mountains. (The Egyptian pylon may, in fact, have derived its three divisions from Mesopotamian fortified gateways.) The great scale of the pylons was intended to overwhelm those who approached them frontally, along a prescribed path that was often flanked by guardian sphinxes. Their

The Architecture of Authority   247

Left: Figure 291.   The Ishtar Gate of Nebuchadnezzar II (reconstructed by Koldewey), from the Processional Way, Babylon (Iraq). c. 575 B.C. Staatliche Museen, Berlin.

Below left: Figure 292.   The Lion Gate, entrance to the citadel, Mycenae. c. 1250 B.C.

massiveness is explained in the declaration of a pharaoh who announced to his god that he had built him an august house which would endure for a million years. The act of passing through the gate was a symbolic one, for within lay the Egyptian equivalent of paradise. Although they have been destroyed, it is known that when palaces adjoined the temples (at right angles to the forecourt and central axis) provision was made for the pharaoh to appear on a balcony or at a window (the "window of appearances"), from where he could look down on his subjects and the ceremonies in the first open court behind the pylon.

In Mesopotamia, most of the prevalent mudbrick architecture has survived to a lesser extent than have the stone structures of Egypt, but the shape and meaning of its great symbolic gateways are known, and through an archaeological reconstruction one can see the famous Ishtar Gate of Babylon (Fig. 291). The simple tripartite design consists of two flanking square towers with an arched portal between. Crenellated battlements for defensive purposes crowned the gateway. The arch was a symbol of heaven, simulating its apparent curvature, and the decoration in blue enhanced the comparison. The king would often appear enthroned under the arch of the gateway to his palace or the city, and there hold public audience or administer justice. The animals modeled in ceramic tile distributed over the wall surfaces of the Ishtar Gate are spirit guardians, and the king's epiphany to his people was thus staged with tangible evidence of his support by the gods. The persistence of this type of tripartite, arcuated portal can be seen in various examples in this chapter, for not only the Egyptians but also the Romans and medieval lords found it ideal from the practical standpoint of defense as well as for its long-standing associations of kingship.

When Agamemnon marched off to rescue Helen, thus beginning the Trojan war, he passed through the Lion Gate of his citadel Mycenae, which dates probably from the mid-thirteenth century B.C. (Fig. 292). The gate is so

Figure 293.   The City Gate from Miletus (restored). c. 160 A.D. Staatliche Museen, Berlin.

named because of the heraldic lions carved in relief above the actual opening. The utilization of sculpture and symbolic figures to heighten the appearance and significance of an important entrance had analogies in the Assyrian human-headed winged bulls who guarded royal palace entries. The device of the lions flanking a single column is interpreted as an emblem of the royal house of Mycenae, for the ruler lived in the only structure fronted by columns. The column of the relief rests upon an altar, intended to signify the closeness of the royal house with the city's goddess and the descent of the royal family from Zeus. The association of the house of the ruler with columns persists down to the twentieth century, and rulers often had a column included in their portraits. While the column itself may not have had specific symbolism, early in its history it came to indicate a special place—the royal house—of king or god, and this continuing association was more important than esthetic considerations of design.

As Rome acquired dominion over the ancient world and gradually absorbed the varied cultures of the conquered peoples, her emperors adapted to their own use the imperial archi-

tectural devices of their enemies. As reminders of imperial rule, triumphal arches were built in conquered cities, and special ceremonies celebrating the emperor's visit were performed before this background. A reconstruction of the Roman city gate from Miletus (Fig. 293) has a place for the emperor's effigy in the niche above the central portal, and this was probably flanked by statues of Roman gods. The columns, niches, and porchlike design possibly derived from architectural features of the imperial palace in Rome, an edifice that no longer exists. Of interest in studying Baroque development of palace design some 1500 years later is the articulation of the Miletus gate, with its projecting flanks and focus on the center by means of the interrupted pediment above the imperial effigy. (A triangular roof line was an imperial prerogative.) Here are early architectural symbols of centralized authority achieved by a subordination of the flanking parts and by a manipulation of projection and recession that climaxes in the middle niche.

One of the best-preserved Roman palaces is that built by Emperor Diocletian at Spalato, on what is today the coast of Yugoslavia, from which at the beginning of the fourth century he

Figure 294. Reconstruction Model (after E. Hebrard) of the Palace of Diocletian at Spalato (Split, Yugoslavia). 4th century A.D.

ruled his half of the Empire. The west gate had the Mesopotamian design, but was augmented with niches for sculpture flanking the door and an open arcade above, denoting an imperial residence and calling to mind the "window of appearances." A reconstruction of the palace (Fig. 294) shows the mile-long arcaded loggia that afforded the Emperor and his court a pleasant stroll and view of the Adriatic. The broad cruciform avenues of the palace, which bisect the over-all square into four different areas, served not only ordinary traffic but also the many liturgical processions required. Immediately behind the colonnaded sea wall are the audience and ceremonial chambers, the state banquet hall, and the imperial apartments. The octagonal structure jutting out above the others around it is Diocletian's tomb. Opposite is a temple precinct. The two large atriumlike structures were residences for members of the court and the palace guard. The palace was in effect a walled city, with its own martial order of landscaping. The layout provided for many long colonnaded vistas whose dramatic focus was on imperial symbols such as ceremonial courts or some other space intended for an appearance of the ruler himself. Axial symmetry, found initially in the layout of Roman military camps, became an imperial symbol in implementing the strict organization of buildings and space on a vast scale. Nowhere is this seen more impressively than in the great ruined structures of the city of Rome itself.

ROMAN CIVIC STRUCTURES

THE ARENA

The single monument that best commemorates the imperial, and uncivil, playground is the Colosseum (Figs. 295, 296), built between 70 and 80 A.D. by Vespasian and his son Titus, on the site of an artifical lake on Nero's palatial estate. The Colosseum was inaugurated in 80 A.D. with the killing of five thousand animals in the arena. Within the three succeeding centuries, this imposing figure paled beside the expenditure of five thousand pairs of gladiators and eleven thousand animals in one day or in comparison with the bill of $2,500,000 for gladiators paid by Marcus Aurelius for a single series of games. The martyrdom of Christians was, numerically, but a minor item on the arena's bill of fare.

While many of the architectural forms and principles used by the Romans had been known earlier, no previous culture had brought so

Figure 295.   The Colosseum, Rome. 70–80 A.D.

many ideas and techniques together on such a grandiose scale. Whereas the finest styles and most perfect buildings had previously been reserved for the gods and kings, the Romans also made fine architecture available for public use. The development of the arch, buttress, barrel and groin vaults, and the masonry and concrete dome were Roman contributions utilized for the needs of the living populace, but at the same time they constituted symbols of imperial benefaction.

The Colosseum rises in several tiers above the ground, covering six acres and forming an open-air oval amphitheater with diameters of 615 and 510 feet; the arena itself is 281 by 177 feet. It probably accommodated fifty thousand spectators. The partially ruined exterior shows its three tiers of arcades, the upper two of which were filled with sculpture. Above the arcades was a wall punctuated by windows, shields, and supports for the ship's masts to which the ropes for the canvas awning shading the spectators were fastened. Sailors manned catwalks to manipulate the awning,

Figure 296.   The Colosseum (aerial view).

The Architecture of Authority   251

which was at times painted like a billboard of political propaganda. On the exterior, the 160-foot wall gained a muscular and rhythmic emphasis from the columns engaged to the piers of the arcades. Travertine marble attached with metal clamps covered the outer wall. At ground level, eighty archways gave access to the arena. The exterior had a handsome masculine simplicity in the clarity, vigor, and starkly expressive design of its serial openings and horizontal courses.

The open arena was supported on a great brick, stone, and concrete skeleton of piers, arches, vaults, and corridors. This network permitted quick entrance and exit of the masses, whose tickets—like those of a modern stadium—showed them their entrance arch and seat designation. The concentric, continuous vaulted galleries on the second and third levels permitted shaded strolling during intermissions. Beneath the arena, with its floor of sand (often covered by wooden boards), was a network of rooms, cages, ramps, and elevators run by counterweights and pulleys that brought the beasts directly onto the field. Elaborate sewers served not only for the disposal of blood and waste but also for draining water when the arena had been flooded for mock naval battles. The natural springs that had fed Nero's lake serviced the Colosseum. On a given day, the arena might in the morning contain a miniature fleet in combat, and in the afternoon hold artificial mountains and forests through which animals and hunters would stalk each other. The ingenuity, energy, and ambition of the Colosseum stage managers became taxed increasingly and drawn to perversion as the centuries went by and the public demanded new and bigger thrills from their rulers.

IMPERIAL BATHS

The Colosseum and its slaughterhouse function for purposes of public diversion are not the sole means of understanding Imperial architecture and Roman society. No other government provided its people with architectural facilities for enjoying life that were as extensive, practical, and handsome. The Roman Imperial bathing establishments, or thermae, provided recreation in a healthier sense. While Rome had hundreds of small public baths, there were eventually nine major thermae, which could serve several thousand people at a time. Roman concern with personal hygiene goes back to the city's earliest history. By the time Emperor Caracalla built his enormous bath, there was a long tradition whereby all Romans set aside at least the late afternoon to go to the thermae, there to tend both body and mind. The Imperial baths were, in truth, miniature cities. All are presently in ruins, but those of Caracalla, built in 211 A.D. and in modern times appreciably restored, are typical.

The Baths of Caracalla (Figs. 297, 298) were built upon a great walled platform, which was 1080 feet on each side and covered 270,000 square feet; outside the thermal complex were shops. Underground were furnaces for heating water and steam to warm the gigantic rooms, great hypocausts or ducts, and service corridors large enough for horse-drawn vehicles to pass through. Within the walled area were colonnades, gardens, fountains, sculpture, lecture halls, and libraries (in the east and west semicircular segments of the plan), as well as athletic fields and the great central complex of bathing halls, dressing rooms, and grand concourse. For the first time in antiquity, sports and bathing practices were brought together, permitting both athletic exercise and cleansing of the body. The cultural facilities permitted audition of new plays and of speeches, examination of art objects, and reading. Juvenal's prayer for "a healthy mind in a healthy body" could thus be realized. Further, the baths were ideal for socializing and the exchange of news and of political views. Personal reputations and political fortunes were, needless to say, both at stake during sessions of mixed bathing in the nude.

A bathing ritual began with skin-scraping and a "dry bath" of steam; then followed immersion in a domed hot pool (caldarium) to the south, passage to the central concourse (tepidarium), for cooling off and conversation, and finally a dip into the cold pool, in a chamber (frigidarium) open to the air on the north side of the complex. The warm central hall contained an estimated sixteen hundred people at one time. No previous society had provided such extensive *indoor* facilities for civic enjoyment.

This conquest, or creation, of vast internal space was made possible by engineering.

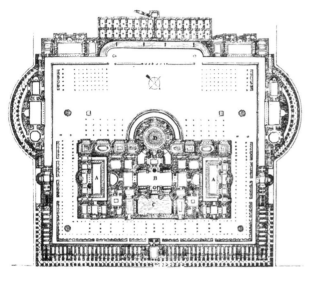

Below: Figure 297. Plan of the Baths of Caracalla, Rome. 211 A.D.

Right: Figure 298. Reconstruction of the Baths of Caracalla.

Enormous brick and concrete vaults were raised upon huge buttressed piers. The groin vault, the intersection at right angles of two barrel vaults of equal diameter, permitted support of the structural load on four piers. This in turn freed great wall areas for fenestration. The Romans were masters not only of spatial organization but also of the use of lighting. This light fell, moreover, not upon rude concrete but on marble and mosaic floors and pools, polychromed marble walls, and gilded stucco and coffered ceilings. Exteriors were often stuccoed and painted to simulate marble, for the Romans lavished their art and costlier materials on the interior. Within the baths the average Roman found delight and grandeur for the eye, endless gossip for the ear, culture for the mind, the means of making fit or pampering the body and satisfying the soul (the basement of Caracalla's baths included a shrine to the god Mithras).

The emperors built and supported admission to the baths to keep the political allegiance of the public, but it is the formal design and organization of the environment created by these buildings that put the imperial stamp on the baths as well as on all great Roman public monuments. The shaping and control of a vast impersonal interior space and its vistas, the precise ordering of the sequence of rooms according to function and scale, with the whole garbed in the costliest materials, comprise as much an image of Imperial authority as was the emperor's own effigy.

THE BASILICA

The most influential Roman Imperial structure for the subsequent history of architecture was the basilica, or public assembly hall. Its layout, with a long central hall terminating in an apse and often with flanking aisles, was a decisive influence on the form of the Early Christian basilica and, ultimately, on the Gothic cathedral. While Roman basilicas varied, they were generally rectangular and had either double-pitched wooden roofs or masonry barrel and groin vaults, as is seen in the great Basilica of

Figure 299. Reconstruction of the Basilica of Constantine, Rome (after G. Gatteschi). c. 310–320 A.D.

Constantine (Fig. 299). Basilicas served the military as drill halls, were found as separate chambers in the Imperial baths, saw use as stock exchanges, and were host to the administration of justice. What imparted an aura of royalty and divinity to the basilica was the law by which the effigy of a god or, more usually, the emperor had to be enshrined in the basilica's apse. The Christians, when they found the basic plan of the basilica adaptable to their liturgy, substituted the image of Christ for that of the emperor in the apse. Though most edifices of this kind have been destroyed, it is known that they were often sumptuously decorated in their interiors and also that some basilicas may have had small flanking towers or cupolas above the corners. The entrance façade, which along with the occasional addition of an arcade on the parapet level would have related to palatial symbolism, indicated that the basilica was the seat of royal power. The Early Christian bishops took over the contrasting plain brick exteriors and luminous colorful interiors as fitting symbols of the house of the Lord. Ancient visions of the Heavenly Jerusalem were conditioned by the most sumptuous of earthly structures, one of which was the basilica.

MEDIEVAL CASTLE AND TOWN HALL

After the breakup of the Carolingian Empire in the ninth and tenth centuries, the resulting decentralization of political power throughout Europe led to the development of the private

castle, which became the chief architectural symbol of the medieval aristocracy. In antiquity, fortified castles had served to protect cities. In the Middle Ages, the fortified castle became the residence of men of wealth, lords, princes, or kings and, with its turret-flanked gateway descended from Roman Imperial architecture, the prime symbol of feudalism. The castle wall, the design of which was dictated by military defensive strategy rather than by esthetics, signified many concepts: loyalty and service, the stronghold of the lord, for personal defense or as a base of attack, a refuge for the serfs who contracted for the lord's protection by serving his garrison. It established the political hegemony of the lord over a specific geographical area, with the promise of protection for the nearby lands. (In thirteenth-century England alone, it is estimated that there were about four hundred castles performing this function.)

It was the surviving examples of Roman military genius that in the twelfth and thirteenth centuries influenced much castle design throughout medieval Europe. The problem of protecting the defenders on the walls from undermining of the castle's foundations by attackers was solved by adopting the Roman mural tower, which not only guarded the gate, the castle's most vulnerable point, but also its corners. Better than simple square towers were those which were faceted or drum-shaped, as in the severely beautiful Castel del Monte, built in Sicily by Emperor Frederick II (Fig. 300). The trend in medieval castle design toward regularity of plan and integration of the old keep (the donjon, or inner fortified tower) and bailey (the outer circuit of walls) also attests the Roman influence in Castel del Monte. Its octagonal layout resulted in an interior plan of eight rooms of equal size on each level. The gateway is framed by a medieval version of a Roman temple façade. The window above the portal not only served practical functions but also continued the imperial symbolism of the Roman gateway complex.

In medieval Europe the cities that gained independence from the nobility announced their freedom by means of a great tower connected with the town hall. The Palazzo Comunale of Siena (Fig. 301), with its soaring tower and impressive red-brick façade, dominates a huge fan-shaped square (where the famous horse races, or Pallio, are still run). The embattled

Left: Figure 300.   Castel del Monte of Frederick II, Sicily. c. 1240.

Below: Figure 301.   Palazzo Comunale, Siena. 1288–1309.

histories of cities such as Siena explain the fortified aspect of the building, with its stepped battlements. The blind arcade that runs below the third story of the two wings flanking the center may be a vestige of the Roman Imperial use of arcades to designate the seat of authority. Characteristically medieval are the pointed arches and the mostly tripartite windows of the upper stories. The entrance of the tower, which served practical as well as symbolic purposes, was enhanced with a portico containing sculpture. The numerous doors remind one of the frequent and ubiquitous use made of these town halls in the daily life of the medieval citizenry.

PALACE FACADES

Many of the most beautiful walls in the history of architecture were those designed as palace façades. Particularly from the fifteenth century on, architects had the opportunity to give greater articulation to palace façades; and as palaces and castles gradually lost their function as fortresses both in the city and countryside, even greater flexibility of design was possible. Rather than significant engineering challenges, palaces offered the architect the best opportunity to display his talents as a designer and decorator.

The Architecture of Authority   255

Figure 302.   Ca' d'Oro, Venice. 1422–40.

Figure 303.   MICHELOZZO. Palazzo Medici-Riccardi. Begun 1444. Florence.

Throughout the history of palace design, there recurs the imperative of announcing the dignity, power, and taste of its owner. For both practical and symbolic reasons, the formal façades of palaces furnish little notion of what their interiors are like. In comparison with an often cold, austere exterior, palace interiors might be lavish and brilliant in décor. The public face of the aristocrat, according to the Renaissance code of courtiers, should not betray his inner feelings; and a cardinal rule of urban palace façades was to not betray the privacy of the inhabitants or their true natures. The architect had the problem of conforming to current social laws of the aristocracy, which meant achieving the right tone in terms of the amount of formality or sumptuousness, and these considerations influenced the degree of freedom permitted to the designer. In practical terms, this conditioned the choice and finish of stone and other materials, the proportional relation of width to height and base to upper stories, disposition of windows and doorways, number of openings, amount and kind of ornamentation, and the scale and character of horizontal dividing elements and the roof line.

How all these parts were interrelated and design focus achieved was a reflection both of taste and of changing symbols of status. To understand certain constant features of palace façade design, it is important to know that the ground floor was not used for entertaining or for living quarters by the owners but was reserved for servants, storage, and stables. Stairways came to be increasingly important after the fifteenth century, gradually becoming more than an inconspicuous means of moving between levels. The true first floor—what in the United States would be the second story—was the "piano nobile," where receptions and entertaining were conducted. Its ceilings, which were often the highest in the palace, looked down on large salons and banqueting halls. Sleeping quarters were usually on the third floor. During the Renaissance many rulers had self-enclosed small private apartments within their large palaces. Physical comfort was placed second to marks of prestige inherent in large-scale elegant structures, for the most part unheated and lacking such conveniences as plumbing. The conventional proportion of the palace was a greater width than height. Urban palaces like those of Florence and Rome frequently had inner courtyards surrounded by colonnaded loggias, and in some instances there was also a walled garden at the rear. Later drastic changes in interior décor, owing to the fact that many old palaces have continued to be used, explain why this discussion is concentrated on their exteriors.

Chronologically, the Ca' d'Oro and Palazzo Medici-Riccardi were built at about the same time, but their designs mirror the radically different environments of Venice and Florence (Figs. 302, 303). The Venetian palace, called the "House of Gold" because of the gilded ornament lavished upon its interior by a French artist, has one of the most delicately beautiful screen arcades in all architecture. The canal-level arcade is broader and simpler than those above, signifying its more prosaic function as a gondola landing from which visitors quickly mounted to the upper levels by means of a courtyard stairway. The entire left half of the façade is dematerialized into a rich pattern of light and dark. Emphasis of the piano nobile is subtly achieved in the open clover-leaf arcade terminating the lower rhythmic sequences established in the railings and colonnades. The Near Eastern and medieval flavor of the Ca' d'Oro design reflects Venice's maritime contacts with Oriental lands and also its remoteness from the significant changes in architecture then evolving in Florence.

Michelozzo's Palazzo Medici-Riccardi looks militant and solemn because of the heavy rusticated, or rough-hewn, stonework of the lower story and the barred windows. The turbulent history of the Medici in fifteenth-century Florence makes such precautions understandable. In keeping with the primarily social function of the piano nobile, the stonework changes at that level to a more finished variety. Double arcaded windows framed by a strong round arch punctuate the wall at regular intervals, maintaining the independence of the story by not aligning with the large windows of the street level. Round-arched windows were medieval carryovers, and the palace still has a fortress look. Each horizontal level is distinctly marked by a horizontal stringcourse, whose slenderness and fine-scaled rhythm contrasts with the powerful overhanging cornice of the roof. The ponderous base, the clear delineation of the upper zones, which seem to grow progressively lighter, and the dramatic termination of the cornice and roof partake of the same style as Verrocchio's bust of Lorenzo de' Medici. Both bust and palace have an aspect of solid impenetrability. The façade is quite flat, without embellishment of the doorway, accentuation of a main window, or vertical division into central body and side wings. The preponderant proportion of wall surface to openings assures a massive and compact effect.

If there was an analogy in architecture to the fifteenth-century secularization of painting, it was in the growing rivalry of churches by ambitious palace design. The architect most responsible for giving secular architecture an importance comparable to Renaissance church design was Leon Battista Alberti. His façade for the Palazzo Ruccelai (Fig. 304) has a less martial and more imperial Roman tone than Michelozzo's Palazzo Medici-Riccardi. It was the first Renaissance palace with repeated

Figure 304. LEON BATTISTA ALBERTI. Palazzo Rucellai. 1446–51. Florence.

Figure 305. ANTONIO DA SANGALLO and MICHEL-
ANGELO. Palazzo Farnese. 1530–89. Rome.

superimposed orders, like those of the Colosseum. Alberti was consciously seeking to re-create
the appearance of ancient Roman palaces, and
this aim accounts for the finely cut and more
or less uniform masonry, the flat vertically
aligned pilasters dividing the whole façade into
rhythmic rectangular bays, and the substantial
cornice, which along with the horizontal string-
courses serves to balance the verticality of the
aligned windows and pilasters. (The arched
windows are still medieval in character.)
Alberti's ideal of harmony, and hence of beauty,
rested on the proper mathematical proportioning of all parts of the structure in relation to
other parts and to the whole. For Alberti,
classical beauty meant that nothing could be
added or taken away from a perfect, ideally
based design. The pronounced flatness and
grid arrangement of the entire façade is derived
from Alberti's interest in transposing an architectural idea into linear organization on a two-
dimensional surface whose own logic could be
independent of the building's actual structure.
One of many architects without formal architectural training who practiced after the Middle
Ages, Alberti was largely responsible for making
the architect a wall decorator or arranger,
rather than a builder involved with engineering
problems and the discovery of new ways to

enclose space. With rare exceptions, the great
architectural engineers of the Middle Ages do
not again have counterparts until the advent of
the notable nineteenth- and twentieth-century
engineers. Although the right side of the façade
remained unfinished, Alberti's design for the
Palazzo Ruccelai influenced later architects in
terms of its fine balance of vertical and horizontal elements and its tendency toward a
general harmony and uniformity, with some
subtle distinctions in the two upper stories.

The over-all use of heavy stone became out-
moded in Roman palace design of the sixteenth
and seventeenth centuries and was reserved
thereafter for country villas. The Palazzo
Farnese (Fig. 305), designed largely by Antonio
da Sangallo, with the top story facing on the
interior courtyard and various other details
done by Michelangelo, reserves the use of stone
for the corners, providing a new framing device
for the façade and the main portal. The windows of the two upper stories are surrounded
with elaborate tabernaclelike combinations of
columns and pediments resting on brackets.
Alternation of curved and triangular pediments
helps to distinguish the piano nobile, and the
tabernacle forms give greater sculptural projection and emphasis against the flat stucco
walls. The main portal begins to protrude
somewhat, and is enhanced by the ornamented
and balconied window directly above. At this
window the Farnese Pope would make his
public appearances not unlike the ancient
pharaohs. (In modern times, Mussolini continued this practice from a balcony of the
Palazzo Venezia in the center of Rome.)
Michelangelo's addition to the Sangallo façade
incorporated into one expressive unit the
earlier symbolic devices of the gateway, window
of appearances, and coat of arms for the first
time in palace architecture. The site was also
modified to create a slight rise for the central
doorway.

Although Sangallo and Michelangelo succeeded in making the façade of the Palazzo
Farnese more expressive in terms of its strongly
framed windows and powerful jutting cornice,
the exterior wall was still basically a flat surface
and the palace a block in general outlines. In
the seventeenth century, more three-dimensional articulation of the exterior wall occurred
with the development of recessive or projecting
wings for urban palaces and villas. The Palazzo

Barberini in Rome (Fig. 306), begun in 1628 by Carlo Maderno and completed by Bernini, has a façade that is more openly symbolic of centralized power. This was appropriate to a family that gave so many important popes to the Church. Bernini's completed façade has qualities of dignified grandeur, lightness, and openness not seen before in palace design. His extensive use of glass partially accounts for this effect and also reflects the wealth and security enjoyed by its inhabitants. Each story had a distinctiveness, yet the over-all design is unified through harmonious scale and proportion, as well as by a rigorous vertical alignment of the bays. The top-floor windows are recessed within their architectural frames, thus animating somewhat the inherent flatness of the façade and also further emphasizing the piano nobile below. The piano nobile is made dominant by the greater size of its windows and its projecting balcony, as well as through the range of engaged columns flanking its arched windows.

The autocratic rule epitomized by the Barberini has an echo in the way in which windows and columns have lost their independence and are all subordinated to the total effect. The use of projecting wings and the narrow recessed portions flanking the middle section helps to focus attention on the central balcony. Bernini's most spectacular architectural symbol of centralized authority, which entailed thrusting extensions of the façade deep into the viewer's space, was his inspired colonnade for the huge square before St. Peter's. In his design of the Palazzo Chigi-Odescalchi (Fig. 307), Bernini's use of giant orders for the pilasters and an unbroken vertical continuation of two stories was very influential in the planning of subsequent palaces. Although poorly altered by later architects, and given more bays and entrances than Bernini himself had stipulated, this façade was perhaps as fruitful a source of ideas for Baroque symbols of nobility as Roman Imperial architecture had been.

Figure 306. CARLO MADERNO and GIANLORENZO BERNINI. Palazzo Barberini. Begun 1628. Rome.

Figure 307. GIANLORENZO BERNINI. Palazzo Chigi-Odescalchi. Begun 1664. Rome.

259

Figure 308. BALTHASAR NEUMANN. Central Staircase, the Residenz. 1719–44. Würzburg.

THE STAIRCASE

The inventiveness of architects in giving form to the tastes and station of their clients extended to the designing of great staircases. As pragmatic a problem as getting people from one floor to another was brilliantly resolved by the German Balthasar Neumann in designing the main staircase for the Residenz, the bishop's palace in Würzburg (Fig. 308). From the low-vaulted and dark vestibule, one begins his ascent of the stairs and has the exhilarating experience of moving upward, back and forth, through a dramatic space with dazzling perspectives. Neumann's grandiose conception called for an enormous two-storied room to house the stairs. His design embodies the basic components of the so-called "imperial staircase," a single flight that branches off into two parts which double back in direction.

Neumann made the ascension from the ground level an unforgettable experience, for climbing his stairway is like promenading through a museum gallery. The great width of the stairs was not intended to receive crowds or heavy traffic, but to accommodate elegant fashions and impart a regal atmosphere by an unstinting use of interior space, which necessarily supposed great expense. Each step is of slight elevation to allow an effortless ascent that encourages the visitor to look back, around, and upward rather than down at his feet. The continuous carved stone balustrade is surmounted at intervals by lanterns, decorative urns, and statuary. As one arrives at the various landings, there is a natural incentive to pause and look in all directions at the radiant surroundings. At the top of the stairs, the glistening white walls have been set back to allow a promenade around the stair well, and this inviting ambulatory permits observation of the entrance of others. In this theatrical setting, audience and actors may continually interchange or become one. Surmounting and climaxing the whole scheme is the magnificent 60-foot-wide vaulted ceiling colorfully and illusionistically decorated by Tiepolo, representing symbolically the four continents. As one moves up the stairs, it is as if he is gazing into the open area of the sky, and the allegorical figures are arranged to seem as if peering down from above the moldings, not unlike those guests who would look down over the upper balustrade. Thus, though working indoors, Neumann absorbed into his perspective design the spaciousness of the out-of-doors, but probably no external vista was ever so sumptuous. Eighteenth-century German bishops lived and acted like temporal rulers, and their palaces were not justifiably to be treated as symbols of heavenly mansions. (Skeptical of the structural reliability of the elaborate vaulted enclosure, Neumann's client yielded when the architect offered to allow a cannon to be fired inside as a test.)

THE SHAPING OF NATURE

The political symbolism of Baroque squares and boulevards is today forgotten. Few remember that public parks have a history, that they originated as private gardens for kings and nobles. Some of the most beautiful playgrounds in history were originally conceived as lavish private gardens for the exclusive use of a privileged few. No public park undertaken in more recent times has entailed the costs, the advanced technology, and the finest art that are to be found in the old palace and villa gardens of Europe and the Far East.

Though surviving in an altered and incomplete state, the gardens of the Villa d'Este at Tivoli (Fig. 309), near Rome, still reflect the magnificence of their sixteenth-century origin at the command of that period's most secular Roman Catholic prelate, Ippolito II d'Este. With the aid of architects, masons, archaeologists, sculptors, and French fountain experts, the Cardinal laid out on the sloping hill beneath his villa an elaborate geometrically designed ensemble, which comprised myriad fountains and pools, walks and stairways, grottoes, a cross-shaped pergola dividing herb and flower gardens, labyrinths, and groves of trees increasing in density as they neared the villa. (There were even secret gardens and a tennis court for the Cardinal's residence.) The axial grid layout of the paths and orderly pattern of the trees contrived an imposing artificial environment that flattered the power of its owner.

Diversion of river waters into the fountains, pools, and channels of the gardens was made possible by skilled hydraulic engineers. Archaeological excavations in the nearby ruined villa of Emperor Hadrian supplied the gardens with genuine antique statuary of pagan gods and goddesses, as well as with models for the contemporary sculptors who adorned the fountains and grottoes with nude figures expressive of anything but Counter Reformation attitudes. Likewise inconsistent with the Cardinal's vocation were concealed devices that without warning sprayed unsuspecting guests with water. More important, esthetically, were the variety and beauty of the fountains, with their appearance and sound being gauged to their situation. Parallel and quite close to the villa is the Lane of One Hundred Fountains; here, water issues from vases and boats, spraying upward or pouring down into troughs on two levels. The Fountain of the Dragon abruptly emitted jets of water sounding like cannon shots, while yet another fountain had a metal tree with singing bronze birds frightened off at the appearance of a mechanical screech owl. Fountain noises were achieved hydraulically

and were patterned after ancient treatises on pneumatics. Perhaps the most spectacular water and sound spectacle was furnished by the Fountain of the Organ (Fig. 310), described by the French writer Montaigne during a visit in 1581:

> The music of the organ, which is real music and a natural organ, though always playing the same thing, is effected by means of the water which falls with great violence into a round arched cave and agitates the air that is in there and forces it... to go through the pipes of the organ and supply it with wind. Another stream of water, driving a wheel with certain teeth on it, causes the organ keyboard to be struck in a certain order so you hear an imitation of trumpets.

Figure 309. PIRRO LIGORIO. Gardens of the Villa d'Este (engraving by Dupérac of the projected design). Tivoli. c. 1550.

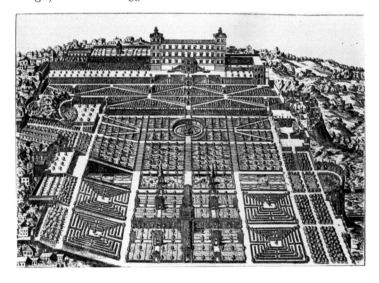

Figure 310. The Fountain of the Organ, Villa d'Este.

Figure 311. LOUIS LE VAU and JULES HAR-DOUIN-MANSART. Palace of Versailles. 1669–85.

Hearing and smell may also receive delight-ful sensations, but it was mainly to the eye that the garden was addressed. Water was harnessed in seemingly endless forms, ranging from geysers, fan shapes, and spitting torrents to bubbling cascades and gentle dribbles. In his fine history of the gardens, David Coffin points out their significance as a demonstration of man's dominance over stone, water, and verdure, and how "during the deadly hot Roman summers the gardens were to bathe all one's senses, visual, aural, and tactile, with the refreshment of water."

The Tivoli gardens were to have a widespread influence on the later courts of Europe and upon such gardens as those at Versailles. It is only in comparatively recent times that the public has been given access to such delights as the grounds at Versailles and the Tivoli in Copenhagen. It was in the French Palace of Versailles that many of the traditional archi-tectural symbols of authority were joined, refined, or elaborated upon.

Versailles symbolized the complete cen-tralization of power in one man. The palace, which was built on a malaria-infested swamp and cost the lives of thousands of men, became not only the residence of the royal court but also the seat for the entire administration of govern-ment. The main building of the palace, over 600 yards wide, was in itself a completely self-contained city. It contained living quarters, business offices, kitchens, banqueting halls, ball-rooms, rooms of state, and even its own theater. In size and splendor, there was no other palace in France or elsewhere in Europe to rival it. For members of the French court or high govern-ment officials, not to be able to live at Versailles was tantamount to exile.

Aerial views of Versailles (Fig. 311) illustrate the symbolical relationship of the palace and its environment. On one side lay the city of Versailles, which had been built up as the palace grew. From that direction, great avenues slashed through the city and converged on the main parade ground before the palace. Just as in ancient times, all roads now converged upon the capital of the world. The central road came from Paris and, like the palace, was built along the same axis as the Champs Elysées and the Louvre, over nine miles away. Geometric city design stressing long straight avenues connecting broad squares and royal buildings was a Baroque authoritarian symbol.

The public side of the palace faced the town and the people, the source of the King's finances and manpower. The funnel shape of the city plan reflects this relationship. The rear façade of the palace was addressed to many square miles of private gardens, an area of private pleasure reserved for the King and his court. Here, Louis' rule over nature was made patent

Figure 312. The Court of Honor, Versailles.

by the rigid but beautiful geometry of the gardens, planted according to the plans of Le Nôtre. The palace, which significantly stood on the highest ground, was thus the fulcrum between two worlds, public and private, the focus of man and nature.

The approach to the palace was through the traditional Court of Honor (Fig. 312). This gigantic court was recessed toward the center of the palace in a series of stages. Moving toward the main entrance, a visiting ambassador would not enter a fortified, blocklike castle, but would be gradually embraced by long elegant palace wings that reached out like hospitable arms to draw him in. In the innermost court-yard, marble busts of Roman emperors were mounted on the walls. Exactly in the center of the palace and above the main doorway, framed by double columns, was the King's bedroom, which opened onto a balcony from which Louis could make public appearances and observe military reviews. The "window of appearances" that had been developed in Egypt was here given its most resplendent setting.

Within the palace, Louis had an army of artists and artisans lavishly decorate the ceilings and walls with murals depicting events in the lives of the gods, with whom Louis felt a kinship. The famous Gobelin tapestry and ceramic industries were founded as royal monopolies to supply Versailles with miles of tapestries, carpeting, and moldings. Over one hundred and forty types of colored marbles were assembled from all over Europe for the wall and stairway decorations. Hundreds of stucco and marble sculptures of gods, nymphs, nudes, and, naturally, of French royalty were carved and set in the rooms and gardens. No expense was spared in making this the artistic center of the Western world; indeed, it became the model for all European royalty. The Palazzo Medici-Riccardi would have been as inappropriate to Louis XIV as Versailles would have been to Lorenzo de' Medici. Louis had no need for a fortified residence, since his armies ruled all of France and much of Europe. He did not need rusticated masonry walls to suggest his strength. The huge floor-to-ceiling windows and the great Venetian mirrors in the famous Hall of Mirrors were as expressive of the Sun King as the thick walls and barred windows of the Florentine palace were of the Renaissance rulers. Since Louis was the "Lord of Light," his earthly palace became a materialization of this concept.

The gardens were designed to be used by the six or seven thousand people who lived at the court. On the upper levels of the gardens, Louis held fabulous banquets, which were often accompanied by brilliant displays of fireworks. Over thirteen hundred waterspouts were built for the many fountains, each designed around a

Figure 313. Katsura Palace, Kyoto (aerial view). 17th century.

Figure 314. Katsura Palace, view from the New Palace toward the Middle Shoin.

marine motif. In shaping the water so variously, Louis showed his rule over nature, as was implied in the virtuoso clipping of hedges and trees. Long garden prospects shaped even the natural space. Great open-air stairways, whose design went back to those built by Bramante for the Vatican and by Michelangelo on the Capitoline Hill, not only carried the promenader from one level of the garden to another but also gave a sensation of leading directly to the clouds. The gardens and palace of Versailles constituted a private city that required the most advanced mathematics and skilled engineering of the time to build.

Contemporaneous with Versailles is the great Japanese princely palace of Katsura (Figs. 313–316), built near Kyoto under the direction of

Prince Toshihito and his son Prince Toshitada. The palace occupies sixteen acres, bounded by bamboo thickets and screens and adjoining the Katsura River, the waters of which were diverted into the gardens. As much as by totally different architectural traditions, Versailles and Katsura were formed by different concepts of authority and of man's relation to nature. At the time of its construction, in the seventeenth century, the imperial family was feeling the oppression of the shoguns, and Prince Toshihito had no effective political power. His palace was thus symptomatic of his retreat from the outside world, whereas the French King used his palace to symbolize the world centered in his person. Except in the temples, the Japanese builders avoided symmetry, and the approach to Katsura was carefully designed to be informal and natural and to provide by its turnings unexpected vistas of the beautiful gardens and finally of the palace itself. The accent on artifice or mastery of the elements demonstrated at Tivoli and Versailles

Plate 37.   PIERRE AUGUSTE RENOIR. *The Luncheon of the Boating Party.* 1881. Oil on canvas, 4′3″ × 5′8″. The Phillips Collection, Washington, D.C.

Plate 38. GEORGES SEURAT. *A Sunday Afternoon on the Island of La Grande Jatte.* 1884–86. Oil on canvas, 6'9¼" × 10'1¼". The Art Institute of Chicago (Helen Birch Bartlett Memorial Collection).

Plate 39. CLAUDE MONET. *Bordighera Trees*. 1884. Oil on canvas, 25 ½ × 31 ¾″. The Art Institute of Chicago (Potter Palmer Collection).

Plate 40. Nicolas Poussin. *The Funeral of Phocion*. c. 1648. Oil on canvas, 3'11" × 5'10½". Louvre, Paris.

is alien to the Japanese aristocratic attitude toward nature, which was more passive and romantic than that of the French court.

The main building at Katsura immediately reveals the absence of a strong central focus (there is no formal stairway or forceful accent on a main door); nor is there the familiar European blockish quality and self-sufficiency with regard to setting. Under the direction of the Prince, Katsura, like its predecessors, was made to appear perfectly adapted to the seemingly unplanned variety of its natural surroundings. The main building is an echelon or zigzag arrangement of three large *shoin*, or halls, consisting of some forty modest-sized rooms, few of which have designated functions. The large, slightly convex roof is the dominant design motif, and its weight is crucial for structural stability. The architecture is basically a skeletal post-and-beam construction, with paper walls that are not load-bearing as in European palaces. Many of the external and internal walls at Katsura are made to slide open, thereby allowing multiple changes in room layout and vistas into the gardens. The aristocracy stoically accepted any discomfort of climatic conditions, feeling that architecture should serve essentially the spirit rather than the body. Unlike European architects, Japanese designers based their work more on esthetic preference than on ideal geometry when it came to formulating a pro-portional system. (Only by sitting on the floors can one sense the rightness of Katsura's interior proportions.)

The building is raised off the ground by posts, both because of the sloping site and as protection against floods. (The basement is walled to keep animals out.) The uniform floor level at Katsura was also a break with the traditional aristocratic symbolism of different levels that was found in earlier imperial palaces. The modern Japanese architect Kenzo Tange, who has written a fine study of Katsura, points out that these deviations from the historical aristocratic norm reflect a new influence of the ideas and energy of the lower classes, who were responsible for the No plays, puppet theater, and the tea ceremony so vital to Japanese culture and enjoyed by the aristocracy. Prince Toshihito employed as his director of construction a garden and tea expert named Nakanuma Sakyo, who came from the newly prosperous merchant class, while the chief gardener is known to have been of low birth. Although advice was forthcoming from fellow noblemen and Zen priests, the Prince seems to have been susceptible to new ideas from outside of the court as well.

Katsura does continue most of the characteristics of Japanese imperial architecture. Its beauty depends largely upon the utmost restraint in decoration, as seen in the spareness

Left: Figure 315. Katsura Palace, Middle Shoin seen from the first room of the Old Shoin.

Above: Figure 316. Katsura Palace, the New Palace and lawn seen from the Middle Shoin.

of its rooms and the clean contrasts between vertical and horizontal elements. Japanese designers thought of space in two-dimensional terms, and the interior of the palace might be described as an additive sequence of flat patterns. Similarly, the symbolic gardens were to be viewed sequentially and with much attention given to contemplating what was underfoot. Neither within nor without the palace does one have the sense of a total integrated form, in contrast to the European palaces with their more static blocklike arrangement, planned and fixed vistas in and from the interior, and predictable over-all symmetry. The openness of Katsura becomes in itself an aristocratic symbol, for the houses of the farmers were closed against the elements. Unlike the highly finished decoration of Versailles, that of Katsura is, intentionally, often left rough or incomplete in order to harmonize or suggest analogies with nature. The Japanese brought to a high art the enclosure of space for human enjoyment.

The lesson to be learned from the garden was that of the underlying harmony of all life in the universe—not, as at Tivoli, for example, one of man's self-glorification at the expense of nature. The garden at Katsura is the loving creation of gardeners who were fine artists. Mingling ponds, mounds, beaches, and groves, the Katsura gardens are totally unpredictable on the basis of any one part. The ritual tour enjoyed by seventeenth-century royalty followed prescribed water routes or the discrete paths and stepping stones contrived to appear as integral parts of nature. Constantly changing views were unfolded to the eye, just as textures subtly changed underfoot. Except for the buildings, the gardens possess no reference to human scale or activity, so that at one moment they are recognized in their normal aspect, and in the next they may appear as endless depths, expanses of sea and mountains. Worn stones and moss and aged trees preserved the viewer's impression of being surrounded by timeless serenity. Impeccably cared for, the garden's correct informality is preserved by the elimination of mud and unsightly collections of leaves. In such an environment, men could cleanse their minds of mundane concerns.

The building most appropriate to such a setting is the teahouse (Fig. 317), where the *chanoyu*, or traditional tea ceremony, is performed. Usually a one-room structure surrounded by a small-scale garden, at Katsura the seventeenth-century tea pavilion, the Shokintei, contains additional rooms. A religious ritual practice by Zen monks before the image of Buddha, *chanoyu* later became secularized into a form of social meditation but preserved the rules and solemnity of its origin. A few invited guests assembled at the garden gate and, in prearranged order, passed leisurely through the garden, cleansing their hands in a rude stone basin and usually entering the teahouse through a low door, as a symbol of humility and the democratic nature of the ceremony. In an alcove of the austere tearoom would be placed a painting, a simple flower display, or a single beautiful object that, after thoughtful inspection by the entering guests, served as a source of discussion. Following strict ritual, the host prepared the tea with intentionally crude but handsome utensils. Simplicity and naturalness were the notes struck by the environment, the tea objects, the gestures, and the subsequent conversation, which ideally never touched on business or politics.

From the Buddhist temple the tea ceremony passed to a deceptively simple, light, wooden-framed structure topped and stabilized by a heavy thatched roof. Between the exterior wooden supports were rough, mud-covered lath walls and translucent rice-paper screens. Openings in the wall were intentionally disposed in an irregular way, both for visual effect and to

Figure 317.   Katsura Gardens and Teahouse, or Shokintei.

Figure 318. Interior of the Katsura Sho-kintei, with hearth and tree trunk used to support a partition.

guide the light properly for the tea ceremony. Painstakingly and at great cost, the owners of the teahouse constructed a building that gave the impression of austere rusticity and natural imperfection. Devoid of interior furniture, with the guests sitting on rice mats, arranged over the floor, the tearoom has an air of emptiness and contemplative space.

Arthur Drexler has explained the significance of this quality of "emptiness" according to Zen and Taoist ideas as the means of expressing the sole reality:

The purest style of tea house architecture... claimed to be concerned not with the material of the building itself, but with the emptiness within.... It was important to produce a space that would reflect the transiency of things in this world...and to this end asymmetrical compositions were preferred: only what is incomplete is still within the process of life and is therefore imperfect.

This worshipful attitude toward imperfection extended to introducing an untreated tree trunk as a partition support in the room, thus linking those within to the natural world without.

THE VILLA

Thus far, we have considered imposing palaces and the garden of a royal villa; but the country house or villa itself had great importance in the history of architecture. One of the most famous and influential was the sixteenth-century Villa Capra (Figs. 319, 320), designed by Andrea Palladio for a nobleman who served the popes. The villa, which gains its familiar name of "La Rotonda" from its domed interior, is situated atop a hill near Vicenza, Italy, and is set off starkly against its garden and surroundings so that it completely dominates the site from all directions. Palladio was the first architect to apply systematically to his villas the façade concepts of ancient Roman temples. In the Villa Capra, the basic cube of the buildings has temple façades grafted onto

Figure 319. ANDREA PALLADIO. Villa Capra ("La Rotonda"). Begun 1550. Vicenza.

Figure 320. Plan of the Villa Capra.

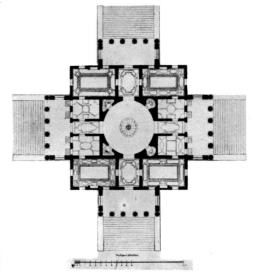

all four sides, giving the residence an imposing appearance from any direction it is viewed. Palladio's motive for this adaptation of an ancient religious structure to a secular residence was explained by him in a book on architecture:

> I have made the frontispiece (the pediment of the portico) in the main front of all the villas...because such frontispieces show the entrance of the house, and add very much to the grandeur and magnificence of the work, the front being thus made more eminent than the rest; besides they are very commodious for placing the ensigns of arms of the owners, which are commonly put in the middle of the front. The ancients also made use of them as is seen in the remains of the temples, and other public edifices and... they very probably took the invention and the principles [of them] from private buildings, i.e., from the houses [*The Four Books of Architecture*, II, 16, 1570.]

Palladio's archaeology was incorrect, for he did not actually see the façades of ancient private homes. His supposition of the origin of the temple façade is now known to be wrong. Nonetheless, it was Palladio's conviction that the temple façade had a secular origin, which explained how he might rationalize its use on a private villa. The custom of Italian aristocracy to imitate Roman nobility of the past would have accounted for the client's assent and pleasure with this unusual design for his house. The ground plan of the villa shows that it was laid out on geometric premises rather than on the basis of what one would assume to be the physical comfort or individual needs of the family. Such a geometrical straitjacket, into which one shaped his habits of living, was unquestioningly accepted in Palladio's day as appropriate to high social position; moreover, it was following the precedent of Roman palace ruins, which appeared to sanction this mode of design.

One of the most beautiful private homes in modern architecture is the Kaufmann house, or "Falling Water" (Figs. 321, 322), which Frank Lloyd Wright designed in the 1930s for Edgar Kaufmann, owner of a Pittsburgh department store. In a society which does not know the historical European class system, it is those people with money, imagination, and daring who have been able to engage the best architects to design houses comparable with Palladio's "La Rotonda." When Palladio imper-

Right: Figure 321. FRANK LLOYD WRIGHT. "Falling Water" (Kaufmann House). 1936–37. Bear Run, Pennsylvania.

Below: Figure 322. Plan of "Falling Water".

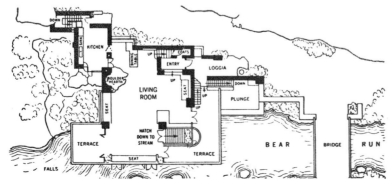

sonally wrote about his villa, it was in terms of his service to the nobility, not to a particular individual, and he commented on his use of a preexisting building type from antiquity. Here is what Wright had to say about what went into the design and building of the Kaufmann residence:

> For the first time in my practice, where residence work is concerned in recent years, reinforced concrete was actually needed to construct the cantilever system of this extension of the cliff beside the mountain stream, making living space over and above the stream upon several terraces upon which a man who loved the place sincerely, one who liked to listen to the waterfall, might well live.... In this design for living down in a glen in a deep forest, shelter took on definite masonry form while still preserving protection overhead for extensive glass surface. These deep overhangs provide the interior... with the softened diffused lighting for which the indweller is invariably grateful, I have found.... This building is a late example of the inspiration of a site, the cooperation of an intelligent appreciative client, and the use of entirely masonry materials except for an interlining of redwood and asphalt beneath all flooring. Again, by way of steel in tension this building takes its place and achieves its form.... The cantilever slabs here carry parapets and the beams. They may be seen clutching big boulders.... This structure might serve to indicate that the sense of shelter—the sense of space where used with sound structural sense—has no limitations as to form except the materials used and the methods by which they were employed.... The effects you see in this house are not superficial effects.

Wright thus reveals the importance of Mr. Kaufman's choice and love of a site that is secluded and tells how the building grows from the cliff not as an engineering tour de force but as an instrument to facilitate his client's enjoyment of nature. Materials such as prestressed steel were used for the first time in a house to solve the site problem. Unlike the stucco over brick used by Palladio for his walls, Wright championed the frank use of materials and opted for the natural stone his workmen quarried near the actual site. (Concrete does cover the steel, however.) The ground plan of one of the many levels in "Falling Water" makes

an eloquent contrast with that of Palladio's Villa Capra and allows us to see Wright's desire to integrate the interior and exterior of the house and yet allow many areas of privacy for the family and its guests. It also explains the nonblocky, unpredictable character of its appearance when seen from various viewpoints. Wright considered his materials and architectural form as sculpture and decoration in themselves—unlike Palladio, who worked with sculptors and painters to enhance his structure.

Notwithstanding the absence of historical devices for showing social prestige, by its dramatic design and obvious costliness the Kaufmann house impresses the visitor with the affluence and taste of the client as well as with the imaginative vision of the architect. To afford a house such as this by Frank Lloyd Wright required a sizable income (though Wright did design some more modest homes for other clients). As opposed to our past usage, when we speak of "Falling Water" in terms of an architecture of authority, we are referring not to the social status and political power of the owner but, in another sense, to the mastery of the architect such as Wright over his materials, site, and organization of space and light.

MODERN CIVIC ARCHITECTURE

Rare are the modern public buildings that house civil authority which can be enjoyed both for their beauty and for the way in which the particular character of governmental institutions has been embodied in the over-all design. More familiar to us in our republic are city halls and county, state, and federal buildings that mingle (or mangle) architectural motifs borrowed from the temples, churches, and palaces of ancient Rome and the Renaissance and Baroque periods. The governments that inspired the dome and giant orders were not elective; yet American federal architecture is basically indistinguishable from the products of autocracy as well as from that of the Soviet Union, Nazi Germany, and Fascist Italy. Massive bleak walls of heavy masonry, squared and monotonously aligned windows, endless flights of steps, and grandiose cornices are

Figure 323. OSCAR NIEMEYER. Palace of the Dawn (President's Palace). 1959. Brasilia.

traits that describe equally well all the foregoing styles of twentieth-century official architecture. Throughout American history, Democratic and Republican administrations alike have shared in the bad taste and the contradictory tendency toward architectural timidity and fiscal extravagance that have led to the earth crushers, such as the Senate Office Building, which typify the United States capital.

It is to newly emerged governments of the world such as those of Brazil and India that one must look for intelligent and truly contemporary solutions in public architecture. One of several buildings that Oscar Niemeyer designed for Brasilia, the new inland capital of Brazil, is the Palace of the Dawn (Fig. 323), used both as the president's residence and as the setting for state functions. Somewhat in the manner of the Ca' d'Oro, Niemeyer has fronted his long boxlike glass core with an elegant curvilinear colonnade; its free-flowing lines can be doubly enjoyed in the reflecting pool in front of the building. Behind the colonnade is a spacious veranda, where visitors and officials can meet informally. The glass façade conveys the idea that a government elected by the people should be open to observation at all times. Niemeyer took advantage of the site on a broad plateau to spread the presidential

palace and his other buildings over the landscape. The reflecting pool and wide paths invite movement toward the colonnade, which is then interrupted before the entrance. It takes little imagination to sense how out of place the gigantic columns of Bernini would be instead of the organic concrete supporting elements, which seem to push off from the ground at their pinpoint contacts as if floating, or how inappropriate a "window of appearances" in the form of a Michelangelo tabernacle would be above the main doorway. (Behind the inverted arcade are lengthy balconies that are accessible from private quarters and permit the presidential family and guests to enjoy the view without being observed by the crowds outside.)

Niemeyer received a number of his ideas from Le Corbusier, who in 1951 began to design the entire capital city of the Indian state of Punjab at Chandigarh. While associates concerned themselves with the residential areas, Le Corbusier concentrated on the design of the administrative center of the city, located at the upper end of a broad plain at the foot of the Himalayas. The Palace of Justice (Fig. 324) is a long rectangular building of unfinished concrete, topped by an imposing upswept umbrellalike roof with a wide overhang. Unlike the plan of the Roman basilica, the entrance court has no outer wall to shield it, and one enters by way of a sheltered yet open space between huge molded concrete piers. At the rear of the entrance hall are the "flying" ramps of raw concrete that connect the different levels of the building. The many courtrooms flanking the entrance hall are protected from the brilliant natural light by Le Corbusier's "sun breakers," organized into a decorative concrete grill, behind which bright color areas have been painted. The entire structure has been designed to facilitate the free circulation of air and people—essential considerations in view of the climate and the functions of the building.

Unlike the balanced treatment of Renaissance and Baroque palace façades, in his design Le Corbusier rejected rigid symmetry and overall repetition of forms. The giant piers are used for structural, not for symbolic, reasons. The entrance court is to the left of center, and motifs are repeated in different sections in a looser manner and without any hieratic connotation. Within the bare rectangular frame of the Palace of Justice, Le Corbusier has created strong sculptural effects and alternating forward and backward movement, which animate the structure and reduce the potentially heavy appearance of so much raw concrete. The dry climate is admirably suited to the use of this material. Frank use of materials and revelation of structure provide a model of architectural ethics that might well be emulated by the justices presiding within. The avoidance of any sign of luxuriousness or decorative show has a frugal rightness for a government building. The

architect felt also that sparing touches of bright color would please Indian taste and relieve the building's sober appearance.

In undertaking the design of an entire city, Le Corbusier looked upon his task not merely as an esthetic challenge but also as a powerful means to influence for the better the daily lives of hundreds of thousands of people. He recognized that his architecture could beneficially affect the attitude of the population toward its government, as well as instill pride in the administration of the state. In contrast to Renaissance and Baroque architects, many of whom were without any practical training in construction techniques, Le Corbusier, Wright, and Niemeyer have seriously involved themselves with engineering and the study of various building materials, with the technology as well as the esthetics of building. Moreover, they have sought to take into consideration the sociological, economic, and psychological backgrounds and needs of their clients. Where past architecture might be defined as primarily an art of organizing and enclosing space, the work of the conscientious modern architect like Le Corbusier takes in the art, technology, and sociology of creating a synthetic environment for human use and enjoyment. Because the contemporary architect is confronted by changing problems with each new client, Le Corbusier refused to repeat conventional architectural symbols such as those associated with political authority. When one recalls the Egyptian pylon, it becomes apparent that in his work at Chandigarh Le Corbusier developed a viable new architecture for interpreting a civil authority that is dependent on the consent of the governed.

Figure 324. LE CORBUSIER. The Palace of Justice. Begun 1951. Chandigarh, India.

14

TO BE OF ONE'S TIME: THE SYNTHESIS OF PAST AND PRESENT IN NINETEENTH-CENTURY PAINTING

Like a river changing in depth and width, receiving new springs of ideas or changing its course and leaving isolated bodies of water to dry up, art's history has continual movement that is not checked or governed by the calendar. The ineffectuality and the irrelevance of the old synthesis of "heavenly" and "worldly" values at the beginning of the nineteenth century was not a new development, but rather the result of a gradual loss of strength in the two centuries preceding. Like many other fields, art has a dialectical history in which there have often been conflicts of opposites to motivate the artist. The newer synthesis that perplexed and inspired many nineteenth-century painters centered on the ways in which, and extent to which, their art should be influenced by both past and present. Should one's style and subject imitate the past in interpreting the present? Should the artist's themes be of the moment, yet in a style that did justice to the Baroque or Renaissance masterworks in the Louvre? Or should *both* form and theme be grounded in the artist's own time?

In themselves, such questions did not pose entirely new problems only for the first time after 1800, for history had already provided examples of various alternatives. Since the

seventeenth century, for example, Dutch as well as French artists had been interested in showing their own time and place without resorting to a paraphrase of the styles of other periods and countries. Portraits, still lifes, and landscapes were modes that permitted an artist to interpret aspects of his time, while he also did mythological or historical painting in a style taken from another artist in another country from another time. Even before the nineteenth century there had been excellent alternatives to the view that the purpose of art should be to educate and ennoble its public. Genre and the foregoing types of painting of people, objects, and nature sidestepped these noble aims, and the high value given them by private collectors had established a base for a nonintellectual painting, esteemed for how it was made rather than for its subject matter.

In the nineteenth century, principally in France, a number of conditions conspired to change the answers to these questions and to produce viable new syntheses in terms of what was to happen at the beginning of the present century. Many of the leading independent artists were separated from the patronage and ideals both of church and state, as well as from formal art-school training. Progressive artists

272

after 1850 could hope for support from an increasingly large middle-class art-buying public and from the emergence of increased numbers of art dealers. For many important artists, personal study in the Louvre or other art museums came to replace academic art schools. Artists relied upon other artists and sympathetic art critics and dealers for criticism and encouragement. Independence involved substantial risks, but the ideal of contributing to culture and gaining personal fulfillment from artistic activity was a strong incentive. The heroic focus in advanced painting shifted away from saints, statesmen, and warriors to the masses, to the private citizen and the artist himself.

Some of the dramatic changes that occurred in art in the course of the nineteenth century are apparent when Jacques Louis David's large canvas *The Battle of the Romans and Sabines* is juxtaposed with Toulouse-Lautrec's lithographic poster *Moulin Rouge* (Figs. 325, 326). Purposes, sources, and styles are separated by much more than merely ninety years of time. David's painting was intended to hang in the great palace of the Louvre, which in 1800, though still serving in part as a residence, had been converted into a museum for the nation. Toulouse-Lautrec's posters were pasted on walls

Above: Figure 325. JACQUES LOUIS DAVID. *The Battle of the Romans and Sabines.* 1799. Oil on canvas, 12′8″ × 17′3¾″. Louvre, Paris.

Below: Figure 326. HENRI DE TOULOUSE-LAUTREC. *Moulin Rouge.* 1891. Color lithograph poster, 5′5″ × 3′10″. The Philadelphia Museum of Art (gift of Mr. and Mrs. R. Sturgis Ingersoll).

and kiosks around Paris as advertisements for a Montmartre dance hall. (Artists had done commercial work for businessmen even in Roman times.) David sought to unify his society by bringing together an aristocracy and a middle class become distrustful of each other as a result of the French Revolution. Toulouse-Lautrec's message was spelled out literally; his job was to bring together the general public with the virtuoso performers in a night club for purposes of business and pleasure. True to tradition at the beginning of the century, David drew upon a historical episode—that is, borrowed from the past—to make his moral point for the present. His sources for the painting were literary, Petrarch's *History of Romulus.* The incident chosen was the moment when the wife of the Roman leader interceded to stop his personal combat with Tatius, chief of the Sabines and her kinsman. David assumed an educated audience that would comprehend the idea of how women could mediate in class conflict through inter-marriage. Toulouse-Lautrec derived the subject of his poster from frequent visits to the Moulin Rouge and direct observation of such stars as La Goulue ("The Glutton") and Valentin le Désossé ("The Boneless One").

David based his style on ancient Greek and Roman art. The past thus provided him with models of pose and composition, as well as confirmation of the archaeological accuracy of details. To assure anatomical exactitude, he first drew from skeletons posed in the manner of the final painting, and then from live models similarly posed in imitation of ancient works of art. It was not David's opinion that the artist should be original, that he should innovate, but rather that he should take from the past and perfect his choices. Toulouse-Lautrec's style, though to some extent indebted to contempo-raries such as Degas, was largely formed by personal taste, visual perceptiveness, and the idiosyncrasies of his hand. Just as the dancers in his poster prided themselves on their ability to improvise and to create highly stylized, even grotesque and surprising movements, so did the artist value his talent for direct observation and spontaneous translation of their movements in a style that was equally exaggerated and individualistic. Both David and Toulouse-Lautrec were affirming the superiority of art over nature—the former by

homage to the exalted impersonal styles of the past, the latter through expressing his own temperament.

For David, as for many artists since the fifteenth century, his model for the rhetoric and arrangement of pictorial presentation was the theater and its performers on a stage. Toulouse-Lautrec's figures were inimitable in a double sense: not only were their postures uniquely unstable, but the artist's conception negated measurable three-dimensional stage space and the illusionistic devices that permitted the audience physically to identify with his per-sonages. His poster has a decided surface emphasis, whereby all the shapes and colors are flattened out, and it is the silhouettes rather than facial expression and modeling, as in David's work, that impart character and expressiveness. The segmented treatment of Valentin and the ambiguity of the yellow globular shapes at the left (probably a lamp) presuppose changes in the value of the human figure, compositional balance, and clarity from those which had obtained in David's day. Toulouse-Lautrec's art is symptomatic of the turn-of-the-century interest on the part of independent artists in capturing and developing those properties and experiences which are to be found only in the graphic medium of painting and prints, that is, which do not readily lend themselves to paraphrase in other media. David's work is discursive painting whose subject one could read and talk about without reference to how it was made. In relation to painting, the poster reflects nine-teenth-century changing attitudes toward his-tory and constitutes a form of popular social history of the moment. This democratization of history was accompanied by broad changing attitudes toward the artistic suitability of subjects drawn from daily life.

At the beginning of the last century historians and painters began to show that history involved masses of people, and accord-ingly the reactions of the common man to his fate gradually replaced those of the epic leader. In Chapter 12, "Images of Authority," we saw how David and Baron Gros interpreted history through the feats of a great military hero. Since the Romans, war had been shown in terms of kings and generals, the victors and their generosity toward the vanquished. During and after Napoleon's reign, war and the hero

Figure 327. FRANCISCO GOYA. *Execution of the Madrileños on May 3, 1808.* 1814.
Oil on canvas, 8'8¾" × 11'3¾". Prado, Madrid.

concept underwent a change in European painting. When Francisco Goya painted *The Execution of the Madrileños on May 3, 1808* (Fig. 327), he did not choose to record a battle-field scene. The French occupation general Murat, who ordered the killing of hostages in reprisal for the civilian uprising in Madrid, was not even shown. Goya had originally been sympathetic to the Napoleonic invasion of Spain, in the hope that it would bring modern ideas to his country. His painting is a manifestation of partisanship, not as an oppressed Spaniard but as a human being protesting brutality and injustice. He does not glorify war as artists had done before him, but instead shows the slaughter of defenseless civilians by a firing squad. The anonymous, doomed yet defiant Madrileños are the real protagonists and heroes, though pathetic ones; the con-

querors are machinelike in the cold precision with which they carry out the execution at brutally close range. To impress his audience with the true horror of the moment, Goya brilliantly illuminates those about to die before the volley of the shadowy troops and sprawls lifeless figures in the foreground in the unnatural contortions of violent death. Rather than histrionic pose, the hostages manifest instinctive reactions of grief, resignation, and outright defiance at the last moment, and Goya contrasts their disarray and shapeless grouping with the close formation of the soldiers, the unfeeling single-mindedness of those disciplined to carry out any order. Goya may or may not have actually witnessed the firing squads in action on the night of May 3, 1808, but he did not require the intermediary of a writer to furnish his strongly felt subject matter.

The Synthesis of Past and Present in Nineteenth-Century Painting   275

Figure 328. THÉODORE GÉRICAULT. *The Raft of the Medusa*. 1818–19.
Oil on canvas, 16′1 ⅜″ × 23′9″. Louvre, Paris.

One of the great nineteenth-century paintings (Fig. 328), which deals with a mass catastrophe having political implications, was based not on a history book but on contemporaneous newspaper reports and interviews by the artist with the survivors. The French painter Théodore Géricault had ambitions of doing a monumental painting on a noble theme that would rival great works of the past such as Rubens' *Last Judgment* (Fig. 210) and Michelangelo's awesome fresco of the same theme (Fig. 184). However, he wanted the subject to be contemporary, in order to prove that he could paint modern history on an equally heroic scale. In 1816, the wreck of the government ship *Medusa* off North Africa and the ensuing tragedy of more than a hundred persons cast adrift on a raft for several days provided Géricault with a sensational and topical subject. Shipwrecks had often been depicted in the past, but this overworked theme had never been treated with the stark immediacy and intense focus upon human suffering that Géricault brought to his huge canvas, with its emotional sincerity and imaginative staging. He had the ship's carpenter reconstruct a model of the actual raft, which he then set afloat; he studied not only the faces and bodies of those

hospitalized by their ordeal but also the heads of dead criminals and putrefying limbs from the Paris morgue. He made numerous drawings and painted sketches of various incidents of the shipwreck, but finally he passed over such dramatic moments as the mutiny in favor of showing the handful of survivors rising like a human pyramid to signal a ship in the distance.

The eye level of the viewer is at the lower part of the painting, so that one is confronted with a jumble of corpses and the old man's grief over his dead son. This device of engaging the viewer in a direct confrontation with death was learned from Baron Gros. Although Géricault worked from over a hundred preliminary drawings and studies, the final composition evolved slowly by trial and continual change. Its roughly triangular design has precedents in Renaissance painting, with hieratic implications of social and political authority; but here the compositional pyramid formed of suffering bodies has an unstable base, and the climatic figure is a Negro slave who has his back to us. Professor Lorenz Eitner has demonstrated, in his many excellent studies on this work and its period, that the figures adrift on the wind- and sea-tossed raft were a contemporary metaphor

Figure 329. JEAN-AUGUSTE DOMINIQUE INGRES. *The Apotheosis of Homer*. 1827.
Oil on canvas, 12′8″ × 16′11″. Louvre, Paris.

for the tragic condition of modern man and his soul.

The scandal of the *Medusa* episode arose over what was interpreted as the negligence or calculated cruelty of the ship's captain and officers toward the crew and passengers in cutting the lines connecting the overloaded raft with the lifeboats. This act provided ammunition for political foes of the Bourbon monarchy. Stories of mutiny and cannibalism persisted long after the event, which saw the death of most of the unfortunates on the raft. While Géricault's motives for the painting may have been in part political and humanitarian, they still afforded the opportunity to prove his great gifts as an artist.

In the first half of the nineteenth century the most significant change in art was in subject matter, and artists such as Géricault drew liberally upon the ideas and styles of older artists such as Michelangelo and Rubens. With the decline and fall of Napoleon, artists of independent convictions were confronted with the absence of an inspiring leader to celebrate in painting, and their shift of focus to humanity and its suffering and joys produced a new, humane art.

For the majority of artists working in France who sought the support of the government, there was little problem about fitting their subject matter to maintain the political, social, and cultural status quo. When the painter Ingres was commissioned to decorate a ceiling for the gallery of Charles X in the Louvre in 1827, he created a theatrical pantomime of the deification of the Greek poet Homer (Fig. 329). Before the backdrop of a Classical temple is seen the enthroned poet, who is being crowned by Fame. Before him sit personifications of his *Iliad* and *Odyssey*. The attendant figures to the left and right are famous poets, musicians, and artists who pay homage to the great epic writer. The painter Poussin, seen at the lower left, points toward the ceremony. With paintings and devices such as this, both the public and the art world were informed of the artists of the past who currently enjoyed official favor.

With what markedly different artistic effects and social connotations the pyramidal composition could be employed is attested in Géricault's and Ingres' diverse conceptions. The formal organization of the *Apotheosis* was a quotation from Raphael's work, used in the service of authoritarian ideas about painting,

The Synthesis of Past and Present in Nineteenth-Century Painting   277

culture, and society as a whole. It was Ingres who complained that Géricault's *Raft of the Medusa* was unhealthy in terms of its focus upon death and the disagreeable, which he felt would not ennoble the minds of the public. His own poised and robust figures are models of personal hygiene and control over mind and body. Color as an emotive device is severely checked, as are other expressive instruments such as dramatic light and shadow, painterly texture, and strong brushstroke. Ingres represents the nineteenth-century conservative artist who could not come to terms directly with his time, perhaps feeling that contemporary costume, customs, and events lacked the dignity and beauty of the past and that, although living individuals were suitable for portraiture, they were inappropriate for historical painting. To those few artists who sought to build upon the past yet come to grips with the present and openly express strong convictions, Ingres' view of history seemed hollow and false, and his style in large figural compositions frigidly antiquarian.

Eugène Delacroix, a contemporary and rival of Ingres, is an example of the advanced artist who was at the same time a literary painter, drawing upon the past for stylistic and thematic ideas. His *Death of Sardanapalus* (Fig. 330), also painted in 1827, was based on Lord Byron's poetic account of the last Assyrian king, who destroyed his harem and himself before capture by the Persians. Delacroix transferred the orgy of death from the battlefield to the boudoir, and his self-image and sadistic attitude toward women found release in this painting. In the nineteenth century, it is Delacroix who is the great painter of passion, who more than any other painter of his time built upon the effects of strong colors such as red, green, and black. From Rubens he learned much about rendering the figure in strenuous action and how to build his forms through color. The scene of carnage in the Assyrian king's harem afforded Delacroix the opportunity to dazzle the eye with the brilliance of exotic trappings and the rich contrasts of the flesh of the horses, slaves, and dying women.

Such vicarious reliving of romanticized past history did not always content the painter, who like certain others had strong egalitarian political views which did not accord with those of the rulers of France, and on occasion he used painting as the means of their expression. As a young artist, Delacroix had posed for one of the dead figures on Géricault's celebrated raft. From the slightly older man, Delacroix received the impetus to make a monumental history painting that would rival great Baroque compositions and yet do justice to the concerns of his day. His opportunity came during the revolution of 1830, which led to the overthrow of Charles X and his replacement by Louis-Philippe. Originally titled by the artist *The*

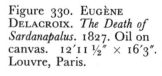

Figure 330. EUGÈNE DELACROIX. *The Death of Sardanapalus.* 1827. Oil on canvas. 12'11 ½" × 16'3". Louvre, Paris.

Events of July, the painting commonly known as *Liberty on the Barricades* (Pl. 34) was meant to express Delacroix's hopes for a more enlightened government as well as to gain the ruler's favor. Although in Paris at the time of the uprising, Delacroix like Géricault had to rely upon newspaper accounts, journalistic prints, and other visual sources, as well as on memory, for his painting of a skirmish that took place at a bridge connecting the Ile de la Cité with the Right Bank of Paris, with the insurgents successfully fighting off the government troops. The Parisian boy of the streets who bravely retrieved needed ammunition from the dead troops and planted their flag while under gunfire was included. Delacroix's stirring painting, with its swirling smoke, vigorous movement, and strident red, white, and blue tones, synthesized the old and new while capturing the momentary nature of the event. From past traditions came the allegorical half-naked feminine figure symbolizing France and liberty; from the specific moment came the excitement of the place and participants, among whom Delacroix may have placed himself as a figure in a top hat. From Géricault came the pathetic motif of the naked corpses and the dense pictorial triangle, here climaxed by the heroic Amazon. The motif of the dying revolutionary looking up to the symbolic flag-bearing woman is a translation from a Napoleonic battlefield scene by Gros, where a wounded enemy soldier gazes upward at Napoleon as if to a savior. Thus Delacroix was showing a transfer of allegiance from an individual leader to a principle or an abstract concept. This is very likely the last great painting in which an important artist frankly confessed his political activism and optimism in support of a government. Subsequent political disillusionment with Louis-Philippe also made this Delacroix's last partisan political painting.

At the cost of personal imprisonment and the official prohibition of his political caricatures, Honoré Daumier was the most outspoken critic of the French state. With his thousands of drawings and prints taken from daily life, Daumier is the first modern artist for whom the attitude "one must be of one's time" became a lifelong ideal. His lithograph *Rue Transnonain, April 15, 1834* (Fig. 331) is a stark disclosure of the murder of a worker and his family by government troops in retaliation

Figure 331. HONORÉ DAUMIER. *Rue Transnonain, April 15, 1834.* 1834. Lithograph, 17 ½ × 11 ⅞".

for labor's defiance of the state. The print's title is taken from a tenement in Paris in which all the working-class occupants had been systematically slaughtered. Daumier grimly but subtly depicted the death of three generations.

As in the work of Géricault and Delacroix, Daumier's superb draftsmanship and style were predicated upon older art. The foreshortened corpse of the father is a reworking of past images of the dead Christ, and the artist must have known that this antecedent would not be lost upon a public that still read art in terms of art. In the nineteenth century there was an increase in the practice of artists' adapting pictorial designs previously reserved for religious themes to the service of more mundane values. In one sense, this is another manifestation of the growing secularization of religion, which had begun at the end of the Middle Ages; yet it also produced a new and viable spiritual art. Whereas the great works of modern art do not celebrate the Bible and the Church (for in religion as in politics there was a "lost leader"), they do deal sincerely with the life of the human spirit. Historically, the religion of humanity comes closest to explicit realization in the art of the last century.

It is ironic that the birth of modern art should be found in connection with themes of death. One of the most crucial paintings for the emergence of modern art, Courbet's *Burial at Ornans*, deals ostensibly with a funeral ceremony

Figure 332. GUSTAVE COURBET. *Burial at Ornans.* 1849. Oil on canvas,
10'3⅞" × 21'8¾". Louvre, Paris.

near a French provincial town (Fig. 332). Gathered at the grave side are relatives and friends of the deceased, the priest and his assistants, and just entering the scene at the left the pallbearers with the draped coffin. In the foreground the grave digger kneels by the open grave. A leaden grey sky looms over the event. Such a routine daily ceremony would hardly seem to provide the basis for a painting that shocked its first Parisian audiences. In retrospect, one might say that more than just a coffin went into the open grave at Ornans. Earlier funeral paintings such as those of Christ, the saints, or historical and literary figures always answered the implicit question of who died, as well as why and how. Courbet devoted an enormous canvas with some fifty life-size portraits of his neighbors to the burial scene of a person whose identity and cause of death is unknown to history. More significant than who died is *what* died and was buried at Ornans. In his writings, Courbet gives us most of our answer:

> ...the art of painting can consist only in the representation or objects visible and tangible to the painter. An epoch can be reproduced only by its own artists. I mean by the artists who have lived in it. I hold that artists of one century are fundamentally incompetent to represent the things of a past or future century.... It is in this sense that I deny the existence of an historical art applied to the past. Historical art is by its very nature contemporary...[1861].

Figuratively speaking, one might say that Courbet cast into the grave the previous history of art, in so far as it was to be imitated in his time. To be of one's time meant for Courbet that anything he had not seen for himself was ethically impossible as a subject. It was therefore the death of everyman that he painted. There is no suggestion of a life beyond the grave, no promise of a soul or its ultimate ascent to heaven. A man now survives in the memory of those he leaves behind. The hero or protagonist becomes the enduring community. Ordinary men and women are the actors and actresses of history, and their costumes signify its change. Judged by the prevalent critical standards of art, which glowingly praised Ingres, Courbet's painting was a failure because nothing of consequence was being recorded, and there seemed to be no subject in the traditional sense and no moral. The figures seemed wooden and not gracefully modeled, there was no carefully organized composition, and the thickly painted surfaces were offensive to the eye of the public of the day.

Courbet's style did reject any overt use of older pictorial compositional devices such as the pyramid, harmonious reciprocal physical movement, neatly drawn contours, and smoothly finished surfaces. The basic color range stresses the blacks and greys of the clothing and sky, against which are set the ruddy coloring of the begrieved faces and various accessories of the clergy. The absence of conventional methods of ordering the figures resulted from Courbet's conscious desire to preserve the look of the unarranged. His subjects were not athletes, and he caught them in their unimpressive natural postures or movements. Color and an all-over dispersal of strong accents were relied upon to hold the painting together. It is incorrect to say that Courbet cut himself off completely from the previous history of art, for it is precisely the way he used the past that helps us to understand the attitude of so many modern artists on this subject:

> I have studied the art of the masters and the art of the moderns, avoiding any preconceived system and without prejudice. I have no more wanted to imitate the former than to copy the latter; nor have I thought of achieving the idle aim of art for art's sake. No! I have simply wanted to draw from a thorough knowledge of tradition the reasoned and free sense of my own individuality. To know in order to do: such has been my thought. To be able to translate the customs, ideas and appearances of my time as I see them—in a word, to create a living art—this has been my aim [1855].

Edouard Manet manifested his indebtedness to museum art as a means of discovering his individuality by making drawings and painting copies of such artists as Titian, Hals, and Velázquez; yet in the 1860s and 1870s he was recognized as the foremost painter of modern urban life. Like Courbet's, his style was distinctly personal, but inconceivable without the previous history of art. From the old masters he learned how colors worked together and the culture of the brush by which they were to be applied. His painting *Funeral in Montmartre* (Fig. 333) rejects the opportunity for sentiment in favor of a remote viewpoint, treating the scene of a burial on a cloudy day as a pure painterly problem of matching tones of greys, blacks, and creams under given lighting conditions. As a result of this approach, it is impossible to focus for any length of time on the actual funeral procession, since our attention is pulled toward the deceptively shapeless areas of color, their stroking and nuances. In no previous painting that we have considered has the actual painting process rather than the theme dominated our awareness to a comparable degree.

Manet's generation (which included Degas, Monet, Pissarro, and Renoir) was disenchanted with artistic manifestations of political partisanship, piety, and strong emotional involvement. Their ideal in painting was a detached confrontation of the world, with alert observation and wit. The act of painting was alone approached with passion by Manet. In comparison with Ingres' or Delacroix's historical or literary compositions, which were intended to be read as much as viewed, those of Manet were largely independent of the written word and were grounded in his immediate environment. The validity of his painting was to be judged in terms of artistic rightness, his handling of color and shape, and their similitude to the world of esthetic sensations.

The present-day fame of an artist such as Manet may mislead one into believing that he enjoyed similar repute in his own time or that he was representative of the art then being produced. Both in numbers and according to the gauge of public approval, it was artists such as Thomas Couture, Manet's teacher, whose work best represented the preferences of the public of their time. In the last century, academic and conservative rather than forward-looking art was the true mirror of social tastes.

Figure 333. EDOUARD MANET. *Funeral in Montmartre*. 1870. Oil on canvas. 28⅝ × 35⅝". The Metropolitan Museum of Art, New York (Wolfe Fund).

Figure 334. THOMAS COUTURE. *Romans of the Decadence*. 1847. Oil on canvas, 15′ 1″ × 25′ 4″. Louvre, Paris.

Couture's *Romans of the Decadence* (Fig. 334) was a commentary on the moral decline of modern Paris that was veiled in terms of antiquity. As long as Couture or any other artist couched sex in a dead language, he was safe from critical and public censure. Manet's *Luncheon on the Grass* (Fig. 335) was a scandalous picture largely because it was a contemporary scene and, by contrast with the animated goings-on of Couture's painting, nothing was happening between the sexes. Merely to have shown a naked woman in the woods would have been acceptable, but Manet had the effrontery to add the company of two gentlemen dressed in contemporary fashion and to show his nude unreservedly eyeing the viewer! One of the many witty inversions of what the public would have expected in the painting was his clothing of the woman bathing in the background and stripping the woman seated on the grass beside her male companions, with her clothing strewn about in the foreground. (The original title was *The Bather*.)

Manet's painting forms an important bridge between the past and present. It is essentially a studio problem in which he synthesized landscape, still life, genre, portrait situations, and the nude—at the same time making the painting appear a spontaneous encounter. Formally, he reworked and loosened the conventional triangular arrangement of figures, and from Raphael he borrowed the posture of the male figure at the right, replacing the nude river god of the Renaissance with his brother.

Notwithstanding this impressive legacy of different types of painting, Manet brought his eyes and esthetic judgment to bear on his visual allusions in welding the whole together. The richest painting in the work is in the area of the still life, not in the faces. His desire for a more immediate visual impact and convincing optical effect lead him to reduce modeling, sharpen silhouettes, and force us to discern his fine nuances of closely matched tones.

The absence of any dialogue or interaction among the figures removed a basic compositional prop, but it also enhanced the sophisticated character of the subject. With Manet, we begin to see the breakdown of psychological reciprocation, the mutual awareness or exchange between figures in close proximity that, from the time of Giotto, artists had developed and refined into a high form of pictorial rhetoric. The detached air of his figures may have seemed socially appropriate to Manet, but it was also a reflection of his own attitude toward life. It was Emile Zola who said, in writing about Manet, that when looking at his work in order to appreciate what he was doing "one had to forget a thousand things about art." Since Manet, this has been the case with most of the leading painters and new art movements, for again and again the public has had to set aside or widen its notions of what art should be in order to understand what the artist has done.

Shortly before his death, the ailing Manet brought together in one great painting a number of refractory motifs that summed up what had been the source of his pleasures as a painter. *A Bar at the Folies-Bergère* (Pl. 35) brings together a beautiful young girl, still life objects on the bar, and the mirror reflection of a world of sociability and diversion. For the first time in art a mirror occupies the entire background of a paiting. When the crowd is encountered in Manet, it is for purposes of social pleasures rather than for the enactment of fateful events. Manet's world is one in which no claims are made on those who enjoy it; is is there to delight the eye, like the barmaid and her wares. The poetic depths of his painting lie not in psychological insights but in a subtle visual counterplay, in the contrast between the world seen directly and its mirrored reflection. The head of the daydreaming barmaid is the intermediary between the tangible objects of the foreground and the elusive optical effects of the mirror behind. What is behind the viewer, that is, what reappears in the reflecting surface, tends to mingle with what is before his eyes, confounding the separation of the two spheres. Enigmatically, the reflection of a top-hatted man is caught in the mirror at the right—like a phantom image, for it is not meant to be the artist nor anyone visible on our side of the counter, and the barmaid takes no notice of him. Her reflection is of another pose.

Further, the scene reflected in the mirror requires a viewer on our side of the counter, but there is no indication of any such person. Undoubtedly aware of these visual paradoxes, Manet quite likely preserved them intentionally to spice his painting.

The unheroic, undramatic nature of his paintings has led to the mistaken view that Manet had no real interest in subject matter. For the discriminating and aristocratic eye of Manet, Paris was essential to his art—a city whose provision of worldly pleasure caused Balzac to describe it as a "great consuming eye." Manet's brush needed such an inspiring motif. Without disguising its traces, his brush re-creates the handsome wine bottles, the ripe orange color of the fruit, and the elegant cut and softness of the woman's costume. These subtle effects of color and light and texture cannot be captured in a drawing, for, like Courbet, Manet sought what was only possible in painting. The problem of distinguishing so many reflecting surfaces was one for a master painter. His attentiveness to actual perception induces him to cut off the trapeze artist at the upper left, so that only her legs are shown in the mirror. He further proves that the mirror image of the visible world as seen through human eyes can be blurred and obscure. It is in the nineteenth century that the painting as a whole most faithfully approximates the true experience of vision.

For conservative artists such as Ingres, the worth of any painting other than a portrait depended in large part on its choice of subject and its affinity with approved styles of the past; whereas for Manet, as for his Dutch predecessors in the seventeenth century, it resided in *how* any subject was painted. Ingres could not content himself with frankly painting an anonymous naked model in the studio, for

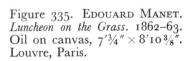
Figure 335. EDOUARD MANET. *Luncheon on the Grass.* 1862–63. Oil on canvas, 7'3¾" × 8'10⅜". Louvre, Paris.

Figure 336. JEAN-AUGUSTE DOMINIQUE INGRES. *La Source*. 1856. Oil on canvas, 5'4 ½" × 2'8 ¼". Louvre, Paris.

Figure 337. HONORÉ DAUMIER. *The Hot Bath*. 1839. Lithograph, 10⅞" × 8½".

by training he was compelled to add accessories and a title from literature or mythology to appeal to the beholder's intellect and good taste. For many, Manet's painting of a barmaid seen with wine bottles lacked the intellectual value and dignity of an Ingres nude, such as that posed holding an antique vase and titled by her creator *La Source* (or *The Spring*; Fig. 336). Ingres' passion was for purifying the silhouette of the feminine body, which accounted for his adaptation of an antique pose identified with beauty. Omitting the prop of the Classical urn would have lowered or even vulgarized the final painting in his eyes. To be of one's time meant, for Ingres, to accept the timeless beauty of ancient and Renaissance art, as acknowledged by the public and most of his fellow painters. (One might say that his ideal was, in essence, to be of another time.)

When Ingres wanted to show the naked bodies of women bathing, in the remote manner of *La Source* he garbed them with the identity of nymphs or of harem girls in the exotic Near East or North Africa. With Daumier, instead, the act of bathing was divested of its exotic and erotic associations to become a mundane act of hygiene and even of comedy. Daumier's *The Hot Bath* (Fig. 337) was inspired by the Parisian ritual of hauling boiling water up flights of stairs to one's flat, pouring it into a tub, and then immediately immersing oneself in the scalding depths to obtain the maximum thermal benefit. He shows the prudent but agonizing bourgeois stoically lowering himself into the boiling water and instinctively elevating his nose in expression of his divided instincts and notions of heaven and hell. The dramatic agony of the Christian martyr was thus humorously supplanted by the discomfort of the anonymous modern Parisian apartment dweller.

When Degas shows us a woman bathing, it is like a glimpse through a keyhole, for unlike the perspective of Ingres and Daumier, which is that of the Renaissance, his viewpoint is close to and above the bather (Fig. 338). This Degas pastel drawing is but one example of his disenchanted view of women. Our closeness to the figure, which Renaissance theorists such as Alberti warned against, tends to produce curious foreshortenings, emphasizes the body's awkwardness and angularity, and in general precludes showing all that Ingres strove to draw and paint in feminine beauty. For Degas, the act of washing was like the cleansing function performed by an animal, and he dwells upon the woman's contortions to accommodate herself to the meager basin.

Degas gave up formal art-school training after two years and, like many other independent painters, continued his education on a personal basis, by making copies in the Louvre. His desire was to honor the lessons learned from Giotto and other great artists of the past while painting the contemporary Parisian scene. Art was for him a personal fusion or resolution of contradictions, the intellectual and the sensual, and a love for drawing and color. It was in pastels that for him these last two found perfect union. While he admired fixity of pose in certain aspects of traditional art, he could not bring himself to render static postures. If Manet has preserved for us the tones of his time, Degas has captured its movement. Rejecting the academic repertory of approved body movements, he drew from both the practiced and the unthinking, routine gestures of his subjects as performed in their day-to-day existence. These gestures tended, as in his bather, to stress the purely physical activity rather than the intellectual and emotional life of his subjects, who were very often chosen from the lower classes.

The Cotton Broker's Office in New Orleans (Fig. 339), with its institutional green walls and customary business gestures of men in their black suits or shirt sleeves, exemplifies what being of one's time meant for Degas. Many of the figures are members of the New Orleans branch of the Degas family, whom he visited in 1872,

Figure 338. EDGAR DEGAS. *The Tub*. 1886. Pastel on cardboard, 23 ⅞ × 32 ⅞". Louvre, Paris.

so that the painting is a modern group portrait or genre scene whose daring informality is a nineteenth-century counterpart of Rembrandt's innovations in the *Syndics*. The spatial construction is from the viewpoint of someone actually in the brokerage office and standing in a corner, so that the room moves diagonally away from us into depth. Degas would not compromise the conditions of actual vision for the artificial frontal perspective of the Renaissance, with its location of the viewer at a greater distance from the foreground figures. Faithfulness to the idiosyncrasies of vision led to Degas' overlapping of his figures, and his disdain of the formal caused him to pose his relatives and their business associates in suit-

Figure 339. EDGAR DEGAS. *The Cotton Broker's Office in New Orleans*. 1873. Oil on canvas, 28 ⅜ × 35 ⅜". Musée des Beaux-Arts, Pau, France.

able and unself-conscious poses. With its fidelity to an American business office, Degas had hopes (unfulfilled) that the painting would be purchased by some English or American industrialist.

In the prodigious output of Degas there is an unmatched visual record of contemporary theater and ballet, rehearsal halls, café life, horse racing, modish shops, brothels, and laundries—in sum, the world of diversion and artifice, its places of performance and of preparation, and those whose professional talents made the Parisian spectacle possible. Paradoxically, professionals of the lower classes fascinated Degas, who memorized their specialized gestures, and yet he showed no sympathy or feeling toward them. Some expression of warmth occurs only in a Degas print of prostitutes celebrating the birthday of the madame. The psychological isolation of people in public is captured in Degas' painting of the *Absinthe Drinkers* (Fig. 340), which was mistakenly interpreted in Victorian England as an indictment against the debilitating effects of alcohol. Degas was not a social critic but, rather, a sharp sociological observer of his time. For the *Absinthe Drinkers* he posed an artist friend, Marcel Desboutin, and his wife. Their

Figure 340. EDGAR DEGAS. *Absinthe Drinkers.* 1876. Oil on canvas, 36 ¼ × 27″. Louvre, Paris.

divergent and distracted expressions convey the boredom that afflicts café-goers who consistently rely for enjoyment upon chance public encounters. This fidelity to visual experience meant that new compositional forms had to be evolved, and in nineteenth-century art such as that of Degas the viewpoint from which the picture is made is the most specific in the history of art. The spectator becomes a definite part of the scene, and the remoteness of the stage construction seen in David and Ingres has disappeared. The second phase of the modern revolution, occurring roughly between 1850 and 1885, was the radical change in form which accompanied that of subject matter. Degas does not place the figures at the painting's center, or even to left or right of center, as a Renaissance or Baroque portrait painter would have, but he locates them eccentrically to the upper right as if toward the periphery of our field of vision. Degas thus contributed to the devaluation of the painting's center as the prime location for a subject (and to the upgrading in visual importance of the peripheral field).

For Degas and Manet, painting continued to be figure-dominated. Degas did few landscapes and no still lifes or panoramic city views but preferred instead indoor subjects under artificial light. It was Monet, Renoir, and Pissarro, the open-air painters, who interpreted the great outdoor spectacle of Paris itself. Under Louis Napoleon, numerous boulevards were built in Paris after 1850 to let in "light, air, and infantry." When Monet painted the *Fourteenth of July* (Pl. 36), in order to depict the French Independence Day, he did not paint the storming of the Bastille during the Revolution of 1789 but a contemporary flag-bedecked Paris boulevard seen from a window. Unlike Delacroix, Monet did not deal with historical painting in terms of violent heroic military action but, rather, as the thrilling esthetic experience of sunlight playing over a city street transformed by red-white-and-blue decoration. To the public of his day, it appeared that Monet suffered from an eye disorder, for they were not accustomed to seeing in painting what they saw ordinarily from their own windows. From Monet's elevated and remote viewpoint, the street and flags dissolved into countless individual sensations of light and color. Each touch of his brush gave their equivalent, and the purpose of his discontinuous touches was to

Figure 341. CAMILLE PISSARRO. *Place du Théâtre Français.* 1898. Oil on canvas, 27¾″ × 36¼″. The Los Angeles County Museum of Art (Mr. and Mrs. George Gard De Sylva Collection).

reproduce the scene's brilliant shimmer. Figures observed in the street were reduced to disconnected spots of dark color, which were captured on the canvas by masterly single strokes. The depersonalization of the urban crowd is explicable on the basis of the remote physical perspective of the artist. By disengaging his strokes from a uniform fused mass, Monet was being visually honest—that is, seeking to convey true empirical perception—but also calling attention to the independent existence of the touch of color applied *on* the canvas. Paradoxically, there was created both an over-all illusionistic image and its opposite effect, which was a random disposition of colors over a flat surface. It is this all-over pattern and roughly equal density of the strokes which weaves the compositional fabric. The new intensity of Monet's color, born of a desire for consistency with visual appearance, was to impress later artists such as Seurat and Gauguin with its emotional, symbolic, and decorative possibilities.

Pissarro's later boulevard views capture the free and unpredictable ebb and flow of city traffic (Fig. 341). Mobility was for the Impres-

sionists a satisfying sign of modernity, and the physical transformations that did much to beautify and mobilize Paris after 1850 were joyfully celebrated rather than criticized in their paintings. The Impressionists, unlike Degas and Manet, painted directly from their subject on the spot and relied upon their thorough artistic training to compose with great rapidity a perfect painting. Pissarro makes no attempt to contain precisely or to centralize the subject, and like our field of vision the painting's borders trim the scene on all sides, so that we are made strongly aware of seeing only a segment of a larger fluctuating world. Because there is no horizon line, the street appears to parallel the painted surface, thus accentuating the ambivalence between spatial depth and the picture plane.

Renoir, who was more committed to the figure because of academic training, tended to personalize his street scenes more than Monet and Pissarro did, so that some figures retain their identity. His paintings are sometimes treated as if focused on one spot, such as a woman standing next to him, and the rest of

The Synthesis of Past and Present in Nineteenth-Century Painting   287

Above: Figure 342. PIERRE AUGUSTE RENOIR. *Place Clichy.* c. 1880. Oil on canvas, 25 ½ × 21 ⅓″. Collection the Right Honorable R.A. Buttler, Cambridge, England.

Below: Figure 343. HONORÉ DAUMIER. *The Uprising.* c. 1860. Oil on canvas, 39 ¾ × 42 ⅞″. The Phillips Collection, Washington. D.C.

the image slips into a blur that is analogous to peripheral vision. This change in social and optical focus can be appreciated by comparing Renoir's *Place Pigalle* with Daumier's *The Uprising* (Figs. 342, 343), dated about 1860, which shows rioting figures on a Paris street. The Impressionists had political convictions but kept them out of their paintings. Daumier continues the militant partisanship that characterized advanced painting of the first half of the century, and he translates the crowd at least in part into individuals—in fact a family. Although the work is unfinished, the drawing of the heads shows that Daumier intended all to be in focus. For the Impressionists, the new boulevards constructed between 1850 and 1870 were not be shown as battlegrounds or parade sites, but as the locus of the truly Impressionist experience, places where one walked casually and without destination, responding to esthetic perceptions such as the sight of beautiful women, sunlit trees, and elegant shops. From Impressionist painting such as that of Renoir, one could never glean Balzac's famous lines about Paris: "Paradise for women, Purgatory for men, Hell for horses." Moreover, Impressionist painting, unlike the large-scale historical paintings, was intended primarily for middle-class homes.

At the end of the century, Pierre Bonnard painted a beautiful screen, patterned as an object and partly in style after Japanese art, with the subject of a Paris square (Fig. 344). Influenced by the late-nineteenth-century Paris Shadow Theater performances, in which silhouettes were illuminated on a screen, as much as by Japanese prints, Bonnard presents the flattened cut-out shapes of a row of horse-drawn cabs and three cloaked women at the top of the screen and below the figures of a woman and child seen against a great empty space. The shimmering Impressionist colored mosaic had given way to large monochromatic shapes and the consequent emphasis on flat surface pattern. The third phase of the modern revolution continued with already established subjects, but these were now given new meaning through new formal ideas. Art began shifting away from imitation of nature and stressing the unnatural. By inventiveness of personal style, the artist made the familiar seem unfamiliar. The rightness or veracity of the work of art was not determined by matching it against a

Figure 344. PIERRE BONNARD. *Paris Square*. 1897. Four colored lithograph screen panels, 4′5 ⅞″ × 1′6 ⅝″ each. The Museum of Modern Art, New York (Abby Aldrich Rockefeller Fund).

specific place and moment, but by its internal coherence of color and shape and their emotive appeal. The imperative of independent artists after 1885 was to explore deliberately the expressive possibilities of the materials of art themselves, such as line, shape, color, and surface organization. The Impressionist fleck of color had been expanded to a. larger, firmly bounded flat color area; illusionism was abandoned, but representation remained. Modeling of forms, rational perspective, nuances of light and dark or value construction, natural illumination and shadows, as they were traditionally known and used to achieve illusion, all began to be ejected from progressive art. The stress was now upon artifice, on the treated surface itself. Both at the beginning and at the end of the nineteenth century, artists believed style was everything, that is, the

essence of art; but for David and Ingres this implied an imitation of Classical and Renaissance styles, whereas for Bonnard and Toulouse-Lautrec it was the expression of a highly personal style.

From what we have so far seen in the second half of the nineteenth century, one might derive the notion that advanced painting was devoted to depicting a second Eden on earth. While this was true in Impressionism, there were prophetic developments of a different, more grim nature in other countries, in art that also dealt with the motif of the modern city street.

Even in the late nineteenth century, some artists did not look to the city with sympathy and optimism. The ugly and hostile aspect of city life, never assessed by Monet, was measured out in paintings by the Belgian James Ensor

Above: Figure 345. JAMES ENSOR. *Entry of Christ into Brussels in 1889.* 1888. Oil on canvas, 8'5 ½" × 14'1 ½". Casino Communal, Knokke-le-Zoute, Belgium.

Below: Figure 346. EDVARD MUNCH. *Evening on Karl Johan Street.* c. 1892. Oil on canvas, 33 ¼ × 47 ⅝". Rasmus Mayers Samlinger, Bergen.

and the Norwegian Edvard Munch. Ensor's *Entry of Christ into Brussels in 1889* (Fig. 345) is a bitter commentary on society's perversion of a religious event into a vulgar carnival; the painting reflects the artist's personal disillusion and feeling of alienation from society. The actual events that Ensor witnessed in the streets of Ostend and Brussels, in which political

factions assailed each other verbally and physically, became the basis of a personal metaphor. The inconspicuous figure of Christ at the painting's center is drowned in waves of grimacing masks and commercial slogans. The airy openness of Monet's boulevard has been replaced by a claustrophobic crowding of the street. The subtly inflected touch of Monet's brush contrasts with Ensor's assaults on the painting surface, his violent twisting and streaking of thick pigments. Ensor brought to his paintings sharp insights into the psychology of crowd behavior under conditions of extreme stimulation and with the resulting loss of inhibition. The masks become intimate revelations of the depravity inherent in their wearers. Ensor compulsively jammed every inch of the painting with distasteful, hostile figures, thereby weakening the total composition. The painting is important mostly for the arresting qualities and expressive power of its details, as the means by which Ensor brought to art a frank self-realization in his harsh themes and brushwork.

In Munch's painting of *Evening on Karl Johan Street* (Fig. 346), the crowd is divested of its individual identity and given no attributes of human warmth. Through magnification of psychological overtones the faces have become dehumanized, presenting less expression than the blank windows, which are given an exaggerated treatment that makes them seem to pulsate. While the street pulls the eye strongly into depth, physical passage is actually blocked by the phalanx of the crowd. This is a painting whose true subject is anxiety over one's place in a world that is inhospitable and menacing. Munch imparted to his paintings psychotic distortions of the color and shape of familiar objects—faces, trees, the rooftops, the sharp recession of the street. In previous art, the distressed individual was seen within the painting as if perceived by a rational onlooker; with Munch, however, the total environment of the painting was colored and shaped by the subjective state of the artist. Although influenced by Scandinavian writers of the time such as Strindberg, Munch's insights, like those of Ensor, derived in large part from personal crises. In no previous period had the artist's personal uneasiness in his society been so frankly painted.

The themes of sociability so prevalent in nineteenth-century painting were not new to the history of art, as was evidenced in Chapter 10, dealing with the table in art of the sixteenth and seventeenth centuries. Common and crucial to Baroque table paintings was the demonstration by the subjects of their awareness of others, and pictorial composition was supported by connecting figures through their gestures and facial expressions. Renoir's *Luncheon of the Boating Party* (Pl. 37) continues, and brings to a glorious culmination, this theme and its sophisticated rhetorical devices. The last of the conversation paintings, its subject and form strongly depend upon people clearly manifesting their mutual awareness. Thereafter, when shown together by other artists, the figures revealed a diminishing (or nonexistent) sense of mutuality or personal interaction. Renoir, who was cognizant of older art, once again brought the table to life and depicted his friends enjoying the delights of good food and drink, the countryside, and one another's company. The painter's bride-to-be is seen at the lower left, playfully occupied with her dog. Across the table is the artist Caillebotte, whose posture of sitting on a chair that is turned backward and whose sportsman's shirt did not accord with conservative notions of decorum either in public or in art. As in seventeenth-century Dutch and French paintings, Renoir gives us a history of the commonplace. The moral of his painting, which was that of Impressionism on the whole, was to be yourself.

The painting's colors are mostly red, white, and blue for festive rather than for patriotic reasons. It is worth the viewer's attention to examine how each color is varied throughout the composition, thereby tying objects, figures, and setting into a radiant harmonious whole. Just as the subjects manifest complete relaxation, so is the beholder enjoined to savor at leisure such beautiful passages of the painting as the still life on the table or, as Renoir had learned from Rubens, the delights of contrasting colors and textures in a beautiful woman's dress, hat, and flesh. Within a few years, Renoir was to abandon such themes of informal diversion and the Impressionist style in favor of conventional subjects involving nudes, treated with a tighter surface finish and firmer modeling—a mode that he felt brought him closer to the more disciplined and enduring painting of the past.

When Vincent van Gogh painted his *Potato Eaters* (Fig. 347), he was living in one of the poorest areas in Europe, where he found his subjects in Dutch peasants. His dark tones matched the character and mood of his grim environment. In this painting he showed his reverence for those who lived by what they could retrieve from the reluctant soil of Brabante. The solemnity of the figures around the simple table and its humble fare evokes memories of religious paintings of Christ and the disciples or the partaking of Communion,

Figure 347. VINCENT VAN GOGH. *The Potato Eaters.* 1885. Oil on canvas, 32 ¼ × 44 ⅞″. Collection V.W. van Gogh, Larne, The Netherlands.

and this analogy may well have been in van Gogh's mind. The cheap religious print hanging on the wall is like an attribute of their piety. Living more poorly than his parish during this missionary period in his life, van Gogh had failed to win their respect as a preacher, and it was only with difficulty that his subjects were persuaded to pose individually for him. Self-trained as an artist, he had not learned how to interweave gracefully the glances and movements of his figures in the manner of even the most mediocre academic student, let alone with the skill of Renoir. Van Gogh fiercely asserted the individual identity of each peasant in his portraiture and captured that sense of angular movement conditioned by hard physical labor, but he also achieved a feeling of their sharing in the fruits of common toil. The glow of the oil lamp served to illuminate their faces, but also to endow them with a sympathetic radiance. Van Gogh had become disillusioned with the orthodox church, and he came to believe that those deserving of reverence were not the saints of the past but the humble plowmen, "all those who wear the stigmata of a whole life of struggle, borne without ever flinching." Distrustful of his memory and of painting pictures of unseen subjects, he believed that the Bible could best be illustrated in the guise of the men and women of his own time and place. Once again the secular subject of figures at a table acquired religious overtones.

Edvard Munch was in some ways a Norwegian van Gogh, and he created a "Frieze of Life" that dealt, in paintings and prints, with ordinary men and women and the crises with which they were continually confronted in life. It was patterned after the great painting cycles of the past that recorded the life of Christ, the Virgin, or saints. Like van Gogh, Munch endured great personal suffering and sought to transform himself through art. The anguish of others became a metaphor of his own. In his *Death Chamber* (Fig. 348), the theme of tragedy and death that was so prevalent at the century's beginning returns, but now it strikes nameless victims and is presented in a homely setting. (It was based on his own sister's death.) The print is like a modern version of the medieval *memento mori*, except that Munch's focus is now upon the great grief that each of the living must bear within himself. The stark use of black and white and the strong outlining of silhouettes sharpens the sense of sorrow's containment and the unbridgeable isolation of every man in such moments of crisis. For Munch, Impressionism was too superficial an art, an attitude that failed to deal meaningfully with feeling and the suffering in life. Like van Gogh, it was his desire to give to men and women that quality of holiness formerly imparted by the halo and to induce the viewer to remove his hat before such paintings as if he were in church. Both artists continued, and carried even further, a tradition of more than four hundred years' standing, that of humanizing the sacred and saintly. Unlike more financially successful conservative artists who repetitiously exploited the formats and devices of older religous art, Munch and van Gogh created inspired paintings and prints out of their strong, genuine feelings for their fellow men, hoping thereby to unify mankind as was once done by the organized church.

The abstract, idealized art of the nineteenth century was not provided by its progressive painters but by artists such as Puvis de Chavannes who championed conservative values of history and culture. Admired as the most important painter of his time by artists of widely different convictions and tastes, Puvis continued the tradition of making paintings intended as symbols of an entire cultural epoch and civilization. He did not consider nineteenth-century society as worthy of or appropriate for such treatment in painting. When he was commissioned to decorate the museum in Lyon,

Figure 348. EDVARD MUNCH. *The Death Chamber*. 1896. Lithograph, 15 ½ × 21 ½". Munch Museum, Oslo.

Puvis chose to interpret abstract concepts of what Lyon meant in antiquity, for him the golden age in that city's history. His *Vision Antique* (Fig. 349) was to decorate a museum room filled with ancient Greek and Roman works of art. The painting was not based on actual history, and unlike David, Puvis was unconcerned with action. Instead, it is his imaginative evocation of the beauty and serenity of the region's countryside and population. In effect, he was painting life as it ought to have been and should be. The viewer was expected to ponder the intellectual premises of the painting. Each figure is distinctly isolated and is shown in a reflective mood, in a landscape setting that itself encourages meditation. A dominant tone of cool grey establishes the remoteness of the scene and reflects the painter's disdain for the strong color and taste for out-door immediacy found in Impressionism. Puvis' painting illustrates art governed by rational notions of what art ought to be, and the artist's divided personality is shown by the fact that he produced the most gruesome and sadistic private drawings in French nineteenth-century art.

When Georges Seurat undertook a large painting in the same years that Puvis was working on his mural, he too dealt with an eternal, idyllic life, but it was that of the weekly holiday outing enjoyed by the working classes, not as portrayed in an imagined Greek setting but on an island in the Seine in northern Paris. In his *Sunday Afternoon on the Grande Jatte* (Pl. 38), Seurat's personal vision transformed a prosaic event into a poetic occasion. What seems at first to be a gathering of familiar persons in a mundane setting becomes the source of a haunting paradox. While out-wardly appearing to share in the enjoyment of the place and moment, the figures do not com-municate. The gaiety of the moment derives essentially from the warmth and brightness of the colors, not from expressive traits of the figures themselves. Ignoring the potential for movement, Seurat chose to present what might be termed still*ed* life. Seurat believed that monumental painting such as that of Piero della Francesca required keeping gesture and movement to a minimum and, moreover, that composition could be achieved without conventional psychological and emotional rhetoric.

Figure 349. PUVIS DE CHAVANNES. *Vision Antique.* 1885. Oil on canvas. Musée de Lyon.

The landscape is painted from a single view-point, but each figure within it is rendered from an individual perspective, as if the artist were directly opposite each of his subjects. Seurat restored to advanced painting the monumental size and impressive volume of the figure that Impressionist painting gradually destroyed. The shadows cast by the sun do not accord with a single light source. Convincing as is the intensity of sunlight, the painting was done in the studio by artificial light, for unlike the Impressionists Seurat had explicitly avowed a theoretical basis of working. He distrusted the intuitive and spontaneous. Despite the appar-ently informal dispersal of the figures, none can be shifted from its position. A taut com-positional scheme is contrived by the relation of silhouettes and aligned shapes that link fore-ground, middle distance, and background. The whole painting has the fresh appearance of instantaneous execution, but each silhouette was meditated upon in extensive preliminary studies and purged of the superfluous. For his purposes, Seurat's edges are more expressive than his faces. The large, solemnly static figures are, ironically, constituted of minute, volatile touches of color. A strict systemization of Impressionist color style, Seurat's esthetic of meticulously divided strokes of color ensured each color's brilliance by adjoining it with its

Figure 350. PAUL GAUGUIN. *Day of the God (Mahana no Atua)*. 1894. Oil on canvas, 27⅜″ × 35⅝″.
The Art Institute of Chicago (Helen Birch Bartlett Memorial Collection).

optical complement—yellow with violet, red with green, and so on. His stroke varied in size and direction, depending on the shape he was painting and the scale of his canvas. By contrast with the work of Munch, Seurat's distortions were objective and were grounded in consciously formulated esthetic theory. Seurat achieved an air of the casual through minute calculation. From the recurrent, uneventful moments in the life of mundane city dwellers, he created an impression of the eternalized and heroic.

The most famous independent artist of his day, who found that he could better be of his time in Polynesia rather than Paris, was Paul Gauguin. In previous centuries, artists frequently left their own countries and traveled for purposes of study (often to Rome, as has been pointed out), but in most cases they eventually returned to their home country.

Gauguin left Paris for the South Pacific for the first time in 1890 for varied reasons, one of which was economic. Also, Paris seemed to him to suffer from an excess of civilization (and an inadequate appreciation of his gifts). Among the Polynesian natives he sought the simple evidence of the true meaning of life and religion, but nonetheless he looked at his subjects through the eyes of a sophisticated and Christian European artist who sought to sell his works in France. Much of what he painted was dependent upon visual encounters, on remembrances of Parisian painting such as that of Seurat or Puvis, and on his own amateur studies in religion and in ancient and primitive art. He was critical of Impressionism as being too imitative and for lacking in imagination, qualities of the mysterious and spiritual, and the capacity to arouse strong feeling. Yet, his painting *Day of the God* (Fig. 350) is unthinkable without the work of the Impressionists that Gauguin had emulated in the early 1880s and without the innovations of Seurat's *Grande Jatte*. In place of Parisians enjoying the pleasures of the open air and the beach, Gauguin painted South Sea natives in their vaguely distinguished secular and sacred rituals, ranged about his own version of a Polynesian deity. Their postures are in part paraphrases of Egyptian art, in part natural movements. The positioning of the foreground figures is of his own invention, perhaps to symbolize the powers of creation possessed by the idol behind them.

Gauguin's form of symbolism was unsystematic and largely intuitive. His imagination led him to gestures, shapes, and colors that he believed would have an instinctive universal meaning. Gauguin is the prototype of the modern artist who, while discrediting the form, premises, and values of conservative or academic art, strives to continue its unifying social function and utopian imagery on his own terms. By personalizing past influences and means of conveying meaning, unlike conservative artists who drew from an official public iconography, Gauguin helped to open the gulf between artist and public, with respect to understanding art, which has not since been closed. Even more influential for later art than his symbolic programs and treatment of the figure, however, are the brightly colored amorphous shapes in the water in the foreground, which resist definition but create a strong visual and emotional experience.

Unlike Monet, Gauguin did not paint directly the source of his feeling in nature; rather, he sought equivalents in shape and color for conveying the feeling itself. To define an object precisely was to eliminate its mystery. Thus, he alone could judge the rightness of what he painted—a premise that introduces the dilemma and risks of the modern critic and audience. Whereas the Impressionist might argue in defense of his painting, "This is how I see it," Gauguin would very likely argue that he was painting the look of emotion, or that

"This is how I feel it." Gauguin summarizes the problems and possibilities of the modern artist at the end of the nineteenth century. As was already noted, he yearned for the universal role that art had played in the days of the great allegorical and religious paintings, when artists could subscribe to public values or symbols and interpret a theology in which they believed and by which they could be genuinely inspired. But Gauguin was also heir to new ideas of personal expression that mitigated against public painting such as illustrative or dogmatic art. Like his progressive contemporaries, he had a horror of literature as providing the basis of art. The expressive power of his means, drawing and color, which he had learned in France from fellow artists, musicians, and poets, defied verbal translation. The artist was thus obliged to communicate feeling in terms which were possible only in painting.

Much of advanced nineteenth-century art was based on ordinary worldly encounters, which did not need interpretation in the sense of the involved subject matter of previous centuries, and instead it surrendered its meaning to direct experience of the painting. The public has been slow to comprehend this attitude or approve. Gauguin vacillated in his conviction of purpose and sometimes wrote out programs for his work, or he compromised his flat abstract surface patterns with modeled figures. It remained for artists in the twentieth century to develop Gauguin's legacy further and more consistently. The nineteenth century witnessed the logical culmination of tendencies in art since the end of the Middle Ages, which was devoted to simulating the world of appearances. At the century's end came the beginnings of a deliberate fidelity to the world of feeling, and of positing art itself as the subject of art and the basis for valid abstraction. One of the great ethical bases of modern art had been established, namely, that of working directly from private empirical experience in an individual style, personally acquired, as a more direct means of realizing true self-expression.

15

THEMES FROM NATURE

There is no continuous history of landscape painting ranging from ancient times down to the present. The first true landscapes did not appear until the first century B.C., in Roman art, and subsequently in Western art there was a thousand-year interruption of this theme from the end of antiquity to the fourteenth century. Landscapes reappeared first in the margins and background of religious art, and it was not until the seventeenth century that they became a central concern in the European artist's focus in significant numbers. The absence of landscape painting in past periods of history does not imply that men were totally unaware of or uninterested in nature. The lack of incentives and the artistic means by which to render nature in art largely accounts for this protracted absence.

The painting of nature has seldom been done by those who lived closest to the land. It was not peasants, but educated and inquisitive townsmen, who evolved the sophisticated coding systems by which mountains, trees, earth, and water found their equivalent on the painted surface. Topographical recording and the ideal of literal imitation of specific natural locations have a shorter art history than do many other purposes of landscape art. Indeed, many ideals

embodied at various times in past painting of nature would have found its accurate surface imitation inimical to their fulfillment.

In the first century B.C. the Romans developed the first true landscapes in painting. These are to be found painted on the walls of private houses, notably those in Pompeii which were preserved following upon the eruption of Mount Vesuvius in 79 A.D. The owners of urban villas commissioned artists to disguise the walls with illusionistic fresco painting, so that they appeared to be views into depth of architecture or the countryside. These landscapes were not re-creations of specific locales but were imaginative, mysterious places that present-day scholars believe may have had sacred and idyllic connotations. The Pompeiian landscape illustrated (Fig. 351) suggests such ties with religion by the presence of a shrine (next to the tree). The Egyptian goddess Isis had a strong following among the Romans, who looked upon her as a nature deity, and it is possible that this shrine relates to her worship. The dominant bluish tone of the fresco adds to its unreal or enchanted mood. To have such a painting in his home gave a Roman the prestige of being an educated as well as religious man of good taste. Much Roman painting was

Plate 41. PAUL CÉZANNE. *Mont Sainte-Victoire*. 1885–87. Oil on canvas, 26³⁄₈ × 36¹⁄₄″. The Courtauld Institute, London.

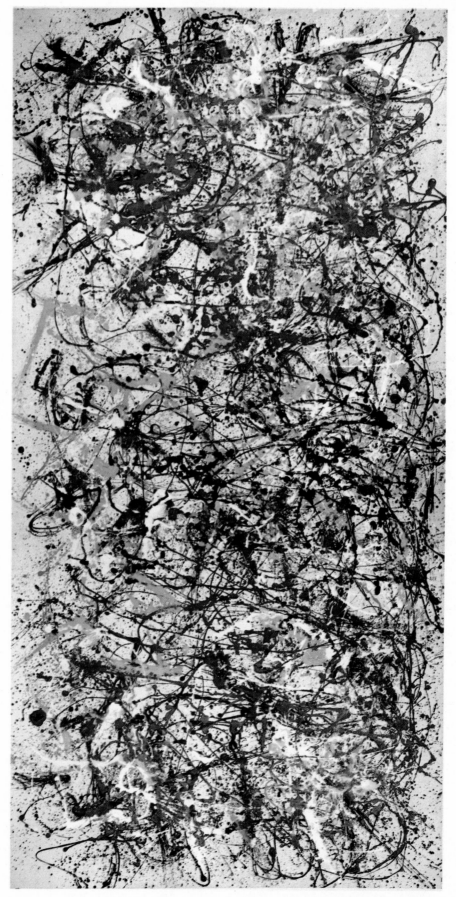

Plate 42. JACKSON POLLOCK. *Autumn Rhythm.* 1950. Oil on canvas, 8′9″ × 17′3″.
The Metropolitan Museum of Art (George A. Hearn Fund).

Plate 43.   Pieter Claesz. *Still Life*. 1643. Oil on panel, 29½ × 35″. The Minneapolis Institute of Arts.

Plate 44. Jean-Baptiste Siméon Chardin. *Still Life*. c. 1732.
Oil on canvas, 15⅞ × 12⅜″. The Los Angeles County Museum.

based on Greek art, and paintings containing architectural elements may have been derived from lost Greek painted scenery for stage plays. Unlike the Romans, however, the Greeks never developed the illusion of natural prospects extending laterally and in depth, with a horizon line, beyond the borders of the painting. The Romans, like other ancient peoples, never developed the unified geometric perspective system of the Renaissance, but they did create an art that related convincingly to empirical visual experience. Thus, the artist may not have systematically converged all his receding lines on a single vanishing point (thereby suggesting a fixed viewpoint from which the scene is observed), but he was alert to the appearance of objects, trees, hills, and the land and achieved depth through atmospheric coloring, overlapping of shapes, and the diminution of figures and landscape elements as they receded from the viewer. The prime Roman device for conveying depth in nature was the use of the elevated viewpoint. (We have already seen how this was done in landscape after the Middle Ages when systematic perspective was not yet known.)

For the Roman urban dweller, these landscapes afforded spiritual comfort and escape from the annoyances of his everyday environment. He was brought into contact with the beauties of the countryside by painting just as the reading of Vergil removed his thoughts to the idyllic pastoral life. (Today the travel poster is perhaps the most familiar means by which we indulge in such imaginative displacement.) The emergence of landscape art in China a few centuries after its appearance in Rome is similarly based on religious purposes, literary analogies, and the escapist desires of its collectors.

A landscape painting by Hsu Tao-ning (Figs. 352, 353) indicates that by the year 1000 A.D. Chinese art possessed a consistent, integrated world view with a focus on nature, not man. Landscape painting had developed from beginnings in about the fourth century A.D. in magical funerary functions and animistic beliefs and afterward passed into the service of Confucianism and then Taoism. Chinese pictorial writing was the source of painting, and all artists were first trained in calligraphic brushwork. Artists were frequently scholars, poets, and philosophers, and their painting was

Figure 351. *Sacred Landscape*, fresco from Pompeii. Museo Nazionale, Naples.

intended for an audience of these groups, constituting therefore an elite or aristocratic rather than a public art. Although its esthetic values were appreciated, landscape painting remained closely tied with mysticism and a function of facilitating the beholder's communion with the reality of the universe. It demonstrated the belief that all things in nature, no matter what their size, were of worth.

Although Hsu Tao-ning's painting is not the literal recording of a specific mountain site, it shares many qualities with the mist-shrouded, jagged, soaring peaks of northern China. Its subject, fishing a mountain stream, is an activity as timeless as it is universal in that country. Never in Chinese and Japanese painting was the artist enjoined to imitate surface appearance; literal imitation was thought to be vulgar, an impediment to true insight and the genuine spiritual and esthetic experience of nature through art. The sign of a great painter was his ability first to fathom the meaning of what he was painting and then to impart this wisdom to his art. For this reason, Chinese and Japanese painting was in great part based on copying the works of venerable masters. Nature was shaped according to conventional types, signs, and symbols in order to convey thought and feeling. The painter learned by heart the various ways to render mountains, water, and trees, the principal ingredients of landscape art. Despite typification that extended to every stroke the artist might make, the sublime

Figure 352.   HSU TAO-NING. *Fishing in a Mountain Stream.* c. 1000. Scroll painting on silk, 1′7″×6′10½″ (four panels). The William Rockhill Nelson Gallery of Art, Kansas City, Missouri.

artist—as he was regarded by those who followed—was able to transmit his unique personal reactions to a given subject. The ideal mode of painting was one that gave the appearance of being effortless (made possible in part by mastery of types and strokes), as if, figuratively, the artist allowed his landscape to paint itself. To do this, he had to be able to identify with the subject he was painting and be a part of the vital movement, the resilience or resistance of the water, trees, and mountains. Painting became a form of deep and serious communion with nature, permitting the artist and the compatible beholder to realize a sense of oneness with the perfect unity, creative energy, and essence of the natural world from its infinite space, to the mountain range, and down to the smallest pebble. The great purpose of painting was to bring joy to the soul. A city dweller who possessed a landscape painting was supplied with a source of religious experience and a release from urban cares. These paintings were to be approached with reverence, humility, and intense concentration.

The scroll painting, developed by such tenth- and eleventh-century masters as Hsu Tao-ning and probably executed at tables, is one of the great vehicles of Oriental painting and the finest format for Oriental landscape. These paintings were not meant to be viewed in their entirety and rarely by more than one or two people at a time. The scroll was to be unrolled gradually, from right to left, in reflection of the temporal progress of a traveler

through a landscape. Thus, a succession of motifs customarily is revealed in an area about two feet wide. The classic format of scroll painting initiates the scroll with a depiction of the ground near the bottom of the silk, or paper, as if inviting the viewer to enter. In the next passage, the viewer is led into the middle distance by a path or stream, and subsequently to the distant peaks, and finally back again. This sequence is repeated, with variations, throughout the whole. At any point, the viewer can look to his right, from whence he has come, or to the left, the area still before him. Ideally suited to this format, some scrolls took as their subject the course of a river from its source to its termination in the sea. There are no dramatic episodes, no climactic events, as we know them in Western painting. Man is not the measure of the universe in this art; he plays an important but small role in the unfolding of time.

The construction of a Chinese or Japanese landscape painting does not assume a fixed position of a spectator outside the painting. Oriental painting never used the Western window-frame device, which tends to separate the viewer from the scene and suggest a single viewing point. The Eastern paintings were constructed from many viewpoints. Usually the artist began at the top with the most distant forms, such as the faint outlines of mountain peaks, and then, in the manner of Chinese writing, worked downward and forward toward the bottom. The total spatial construction

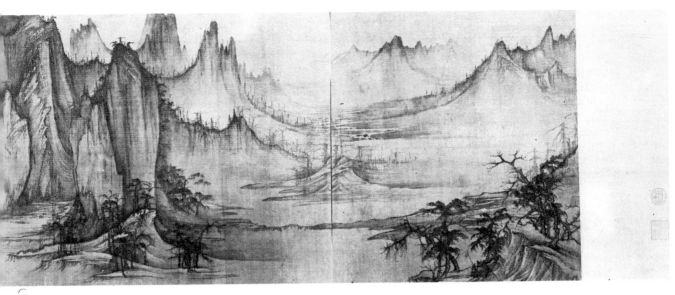

Figure 353. HSU TAO-NING. *Fishing in a Mountain Stream.* c. 1000. Scroll painting on silk. 1'7" × 6'10½" (four panels). The William Rockhill Nelson Gallery of Art, Kansas City, Missouri.

depends upon the moving focus of the traveler within the scene. The painter wanted the effect of an infinite and unmeasurable space extending beyond the limits of the frame and the eye, a space in which all things in nature lived. This space could be suggested by pale washes of ink or by entirely blank (that is, unpainted) silk or paper. The space was illuminated by no strong single source of light but rather by an over-all diffused light, concentrated more in certain areas than in others. Shadows were rarely shown.

Color was seldom used in Oriental landscape painting; ink and wash were preferred. Free of descriptive purpose and seeking to infuse their paintings with qualities not given directly to the senses, artists found an ideal instrument in the gradients achievable with ink.

In China and Japan, Zen Buddhist painters developed a technique of splashed-ink painting. During long meditation, the artist conjured up the vision of his painting in his mind and waited for the moment of perfect unity with it—in Zen terms, the moment of "enlightenment." When he achieved this instantaneous revelation, his task was to set it down as rapidly as possible in order to sustain the ecstatic vision. The ink was then literally splashed onto the surface, in conjunction with controlled brush strokes also. A Japanese master at this type of painting was the fifteenth-century artist Sesshu. In his painting *Fisherman and Woodcutter* (Fig. 354), a dozen quick strokes establish or, rather, insinuate the environment. There are

varying degrees of form definition. The relative concentration of the ink establishes what is near and far, and the traceable movements of the brush create forceful directions for the eye as well as suggest the substance of the landscape. This type of painting was not for amateurs, for it demanded firm, disciplined control of the brush, a sure sense of tonal values, and great sensitivity to solid-void relationships, with particular care to the use of empty space. Only what was caught in the web of the artist's consciousness emerges, and once the idea was fixed on paper, the brush was spared. The artist signed his name with a woodblock, and often he, a priest, or a poet might inscribe a message or line of poetry directly on the painting. Moreover, the paintings were frequently inspired by poetic passages. The place-

Figure 354. SESSHU. *Fisherman and Woodcutter.* Late 15th century.

ment and weight of the dark ink was with an emphasis on total composition. The writing and the position of the figures testifies to the sureness required of the artist in locating his forms within the space of the painting, for he had no systematic network of edges or ground lines to guide him.

There are important similarities as well as differences between the painting of nature in East and West. The sixteenth-century Flemish painter Peter Bruegel, like his Oriental counterparts, was a man of culture in close association with geographers, philosophers, and writers who shared many of his views and who most appreciated his paintings. The development of landscape art in the sixteenth century was related to other forms of exploration. There is a thesis that Chinese landscape painting also had its roots in geography. Like many of the Chinese painters, Bruegel traveled widely, storing in his memory and sketches a vast repertory of motifs. His finished paintings were not of specific locales but were attempts to present a cosmic view of the infinite extension, depth, height, timelessness, change, and order of nature. The purpose of Bruegel's art was to demonstrate his comprehension of nature and man's relation to it. Like Hsu Tao-ning, Bruegel found the world governed by laws over which man had no control and to which he passively submitted. In *The Return of the Herds* (Fig. 355), men and animals bow before the impending storm. Man loses his individuality against the overwhelming backdrop of the world in which he lives; it is the face of nature, not man, that acquires expressive power and individuality. Bruegel, again in the manner of Oriental painters, had an animistic view of the earth, which he conceived of as a great organic body, as described in the words of the fifteenth-century philosopher Nicholas of Cusa: "The earth is a great animal, the rocks are his bones, the rivers his veins, the trees his hair."

The towering mountain to the right in *Return of the Herds* has a gaping cavern in its side, like an enormous wound. Breugel often sketched cracks and fissures in rocks and the evidences of erosion and decay in nature. He was also attracted to signs of regeneration, however, and this painting was one of a cycle devoted to the seasons, which pictures the death and rebirth of the land. Before Bruegel, Oriental artists had done cyclical paintings of the same subject, but in Bruegel's painting important formal differences appeared. He painted a continuous earth surface and sky, and gave a greater sense of tangibility to space. His viewpoint was more consistently that of an external observer in a fixed position. He sustained a complex integration of the many parts of the scene and covered the entire picture surface with paint, drawn forms, and particularized textures. Like Hsu Tao-ning and Sesshu, Bruegel wished the viewer to lose himself within the painting as he searched out its smallest parts—the village at the mountain's base, the harvested fields, the gallows—and to realize that it was not the human beings that imparted important drama to the scene, to recognize that man's efforts to change the face of nature have produced little more than flyspecks.

Bruegel organized his landscape with a clear, firm, continuous foreground that falls away into the distant valley in a series of overlapping areas. Zigzag diagonals lead the eye to

Figure 355. PIETER BRUEGEL THE ELDER. *The Return of the Herds.* c. 1560. Oil on panel, 3'10¼" × 5'2⅝". Kunsthistorisches Museum, Vienna.

Figure 356. HASEGAWA TŌHAKU. *Pine Wood*. Early 17th century. Folding screen, ink on paper, height 5'1". The National Museum, Tokyo.

the greenish-blue hills below the horizon, and the dark cloud cover returns us to the foreground. The partially visible foreground trees at the right and left create a framing effect that is never found in Oriental landscape scrolls. The composition may also be read as a foreshortened, roughly ovular form beginning in the foreground with the herd, curving back at the left along the mountain range to the horizon, and then drawn back to the lower right by the large, scarred mountain and foreground tree. Not only does this design assist in holding the vista within the frame, but it also has connotations of recurrence, like the seasonal cycle of which this painting was a part. Chinese scroll landscapes of mountain ranges tend largely toward lateral orientation, with no such circular movement pivoted on the viewer as is found in Bruegel's work.

A distinguishing talent of Oriental painters was the ability to evoke the elusive qualities of a landscape seen in a mist. One of the most beautiful examples of this type of painting is a depiction of a pine wood (Fig. 356) on a folding screen by Tōhaku. His inspiration came from the early morning view of pines around Kyoto. With but three or four ink tones, and leaving broad areas of the paper untouched, he suggested the appearance of a pine forest suspended in a soft vaporous atmosphere. The one tree represented in distinct focus serves as a stable base for contemplation as well as for compositional purposes. The strokes are not intended to imitate the surface aspect of the

tree but to convey a more subjective impression of the sharp, compact, vertical clusters of needles and the asymmetrical, individual character of every tree. Each screen panel is complete in itself and yet adds to the scope and depth of the whole composition. Fugitive as thought, at one point the painting offers something tangible and solid, then lets shapes melt into the measureless void. Mingled here are the painter's delight in an everyday scene, perhaps an esteem for the pines as analogues of human dignity and endurance, and an awareness of spiritual immanence in nature.

Tōhaku died in 1630, within a few years of the time when a Dutch artist named Hercules Seghers made his etching *Mossy Larch Tree* (Fig. 357). It is possible, but not probable, that Seghers may have seen the work of Oriental artists as a result of the Dutch East India Company's contacts with the Far East. Seghers' small etching, roughly four by seven inches, bears a deceptive surface resemblance to the aged, picturesque trees in Chinese and Japanese painting. The moody isolation and morbid undertones of Seghers' print, consonant with his other etchings and paintings of wild, uninhabitable, rocky landscapes, show little analogy to the form and spirit of Oriental art. Not enough is known of Seghers' life to say definitely that this tree is a personal melancholy metaphor, but taken with the body of his work, it gives grounds for speculation that there may be some private connection between the two. Seghers was drawn to ruin and decay, and the

Figure 357. HERCULES SEGHERS. *Mossy Larch Tree.* c. 1635. Etching, 6⅝ × 3⅞". Rijksmuseum, Amsterdam.

etching medium (unknown to Oriental artists), in which the metal plate is eaten into by acid wherever it is not protected by a repellent substance, lent itself well to the exposition of his fantasies. In the *Mossy Larch Tree*, no firm armature nor solid connection with the ground exists. What can be seen of the trunk is a dense succession of discontinuous light and dark splotches resulting from the plate's corrosion by acid. Because of its semitransparent treatment and disposition of weighted branches parallel to the picture surface, the almost phantom skeletal form of the tree seems to hover within the space. The dark areas were raised above the surface during the printing process when the moistened paper was forced into the etched areas of the plate. This slight relief helps to materialize the tree's substance within its nebulous environment. The peculiar quality attainable with a sharp instrument drawing on metal appealed strongly to Seghers for delineation of the grotesque angularities of branch endings and the loose, raveled strands of moss.

The technique which underlay Tōhaku's painting and Seghers' etching is but one of many basic differences between their work and Monet's *Bordighera Trees* (Pl. 39). Monet did not select from nature properties that could be transcribed into lines or set down with clear, firm boundaries. When Monet confronted the trees, he was not concerned with hidden essence, philosophical symbols, or memory images; rather, he was concerned with sensations of sunlight and color directly experienced at the moment and place he painted. Chinese and Japanese landscapes are without—and did not seek to achieve—the brilliance of Monet's sunlight.

Tactile sense, volume, solidity, continuity, and sometimes even identity of objects are generally absent from Monet's paintings. The painting's fabric is composed of an over-all accumulation of short divided strokes of bright color. Monet's painting reveals a discontinuous edge, but a continuous touch. The spectrum of color and the mixture of tones in a square inch of his *Bordighera Trees* has no counterpart in Eastern painting. A square inch taken from the bushes at the lower right contains in dispersal many touches of green; a few flecks of red, the complementary color induced in the eye by exposure to green; yellows and whites from the sun and reflected light; violet induced by the yellow; and some oranges and blues from areas either seen through the bushes or adjacent to them. The strokes do not follow lines established in nature itself, and each seems different from the others. This technique was not acquired from a tradition but developed from Monet's earlier painting and from his immediate encounter with the landscape as he worked quickly to fix with the brush what was fleeting before his eyes. The inventiveness and energy of his painting is clear at every point on the canvas. The tree trunks, from root to branch, show no formularized pattern but express continuous discovery of the action of light upon color and form. No part of the surface is unpainted. The ground is covered with the thick tangled web of Monet's strokes, heavy-laden with oil pigment. Monet did not compose his painting by arranging his landscape like furniture; he made the whole work together through the equivalence of visual weights or densities of color in each area. In his personal study of the effects of mixed color on the eye of the beholder, Monet learned which tones expand and which contract, which advance and which recede, and how a few high-keyed areas serve to counterbalance deeper tones. It was not color in the abstract, but nature's color, that excited Monet. The landscape was not an excuse but the reason for him to paint.

In contrast to Sesshu's landscape, *Bordighera Trees* shows finite space that does not swallow up those who live within it. It is a personal space that is directly relatable to the location, viewpoint, and feelings of the man who painted near the Bordighera trees. His excitement, betrayed in his brushwork, comes from direct confrontation of the scene in nature. In a fifteenth-century landscape forming part of an altarpiece by Jan van Eyck, there is a gem-strewn earth that symbolizes the second coming of Paradise. And one might say that not until

four hundred years later, in the secular Eden of Monet's luminescent, sun-soaked landscapes, was a comparable optimism expressed.

One of the painters who influenced Monet's direct focus upon nature itself, rather than as merely a landscape backdrop for human action or for purposes of moralizing, was Gustave Courbet. His life view was that of a materialist in the most positive and dignified sense of the word. No artist in history loved more than Courbet the physical substance of nature, its closed, secret places and its vast openness. Two paintings which beautifully demonstrate these last two polarities in his art are his *Source of the Loue* and *The Waterspout* (Figs. 358, 359). From his oil pigments, using a brush and palette knife, Courbet wrested those properties which permitted re-creation of the material substances of water and rock, the varied texture of stones,

Figure 358. GUSTAVE COURBET. *The Source of the Loue.* c. 1864. Oil on canvas, 3′3½″ × 4′4″. The Albright-Knox Art Gallery, Buffalo, New York.

Figure 359. GUSTAVE COURBET. *The Waterspout.* 1866. Oil on canvas, 16½ × 25″. John G. Johnson Collection, Philadelphia.

Figure 360. SESSON SHOKEI. *Wind and Waves*. Ashikaga Period, 16th century. Hanging scroll, ink and slight color on paper, height 8¾". Formerly, Nomura Collection, Kyoto.

the filminess of rain-laden air. Beyond such technical accomplishment, moreover, Courbet's response to nature was meditative and not confined to its surfaces, for in the grotto painting the deep cavities from which the river issues lead our thoughts toward contemplation of nature's invisible depths. In *The Waterspout* the sweep of the wind is made tangible and distance is dramatically felt. In Courbet's many paintings of waves, we are given a strong sense of the hidden pressures of the sea. The grandeur of the cave painting depends upon the absence of humans, which concentrates the drama on the weathered rock and the relentless action of the river. Contrasted with this intimate confrontation of a pocket of nature is the sea painting, with its small-scaled boats set against the infinite ocean and sky. Courbet painted these works out of doors, directly from nature, and often in the space of a few hours. In subjects such as this grotto, he would first prepare his canvas with a dark color. To friends watching him paint such a subject, he once said: "It surprises you that my canvas is so dark. Nature without the sun is dark and obscure. I do as the sun does. I clarify the salient points and the picture is made." Unlike his Oriental counterparts, Courbet was not humbled by the spectacle of nature. When he first visited and painted the seacoast, he showed himself in the foreground, facing the sea with his hat in his hand and saluting nature. He wrote, "O sea! Your voice is tremendous, but it will never succeed in drowning out the voice of Fame as it shouts my name to the whole world."

Weather and water were interpreted with great effect in such Japanese painting as Sesson's *Wind and Waves* (Fig. 360). The absence of any horizontal line and the cumulative curved forms aligned in one direction instill a feeling of the wind's presence. The precarious tilt of the boat and the backward curving thrust of the foreground tree imply the unseen force. A few stylized strokes coalesce into wave forms, but it is the broad undefined area of the painting even more that suggests the magnitude of nature's power. Sesson did not attempt to emphasize the human drama by placing the boat and its tiny figures in the foreground. Chinese and Japanese artists saw in the bamboo and pine that bowed before the wind a model of ideal human conduct. They emphasized less the danger of the moment than the habitual means by which men and trees accommodate to the adversity of wind and waves and submit to cosmic forces.

Nothing in Chinese or Japanese painting is comparable, in form or subject, with Leonardo da Vinci's series of drawings depicting cataclysms. Where Sesson showed a convincing natural tempest, Leonardo created a vision of the world's destruction in a roaring convulsion. Leonardo's religious paintings reflect his admiration of order and the harmonious existence of man with nature; but his notebooks and drawings reveal a preoccupation with disorder and a belief that the world was a precarious balance of powerful forces. Were these forces unleashed, he believed, the obliteration of all life would be accomplished with greater violence than had occurred in the Deluge.

Leonardo made scientific studies of a wide variety of phenomena, such as the flow of water and rock formation, in order to comprehend all of nature. He used theory and empirical observation to interpret his experience. The scope of Leonardo's interest was so broad that there existed no complete models of drawing for him to imitate even if he had so desired. The cataclysm drawing reproduced here (Fig. 361) shows Leonardo's own devices for tracing the movements of water, wind, and dust clouds. A mountain undermined by the action of water is disintegrating, and its surface, scoured by powerful winds, reveals the ancient marks of earthquakes on its sides. As the mountain peels away and collapses, clouds of dust-filled air and waves move outward in a centrifugal pattern.

Accompanying the sketch were long, vivid, and precise written statements detailing the sequence of destruction, the violent and psychological physical reactions of men and animals to disaster, and the "pitiless slaughter made of the human race by the wrath of God." These statements and drawings show that Leonardo was haunted by visions which may have been induced by widespread prophecies that the world would be destroyed at the end of the century. Into these visions there entered the artist's misanthropy, pessimism about a natural harmonious order, and deep personal disquiet.

The seventeenth-century French landscape artist Nicolas Poussin restored nature to a noble and orderly setting for the enactment of grandiose classical tragedies. Moreover, its mood is directly determined by the human drama enacted within it. The subject of *The Funeral of Phocion* (Pl. 40) is drawn from Plutarch and concerns the Athenian general Phocion, unjustly executed by the state he had loyally served. At his request, Phocion's body was carried from Athens to his native city to be cremated, and his ashes were scattered on the earth. The solemnity of the return of Phocion's body is to be read in the mien of the litter bearers and in the gravity of the landscape itself. Basing his ideas on principles of Greek and Roman rhetoric and of music, Poussin conceived of painting in terms of "modes" by which one could interpret happy, calm, or sad events. To control the effect of his art, he did not allow his own emotions to influence the act of painting, which was to be governed only by a rational adherence to these modes. Nature

and art were thus constrained by Poussin's intellect. He felt it to be the painter's task to impose his will on nature and art, to study carefully everything within the painting, to avoid the spontaneous and the trivial, and to make each stroke a controlled expression of his will. He believed, as did the philosopher Descartes, that the faculty of reason could determine the true nature of physical order. Nature appears in Poussin's painting as an unopposed harmony, not unlike an aspect of a mechanistic universe. Nature's order was the model upon which Poussin based his painting, showing ancient Classical architecture juxtaposed with precisely formed trees and mountains. The calm stability of the landscape is further stressed and perfected in the walls, columns, and pediments of the city.

Much of the scene's tranquil atmosphere comes from the soft late-afternoon light falling over the landscape from the left. This lighting, which was partially a device to suggest that the event took place in the remote past, illuminates the critical passages of the story and creates successive light zones that gently alternate with soft shadows and lead the eye into depth. Poussin insisted that extreme values of light and dark be smoothly modulated by intermediate ones; thus he provided a measurable and logical transition from the darkened foreground to the most brilliantly illuminated area on the distant horizon. The dark foreground areas hold the viewer apart from the scene, in order to elicit a detached, sustained awareness of the action and the painting's well-thought-out structure. Furthermore, the painter avoided rough edges,

Figure 361. LEONARDO DA VINCI. *Cataclysm.* c. 1516. Chalk and ink on paper, 6⅜ × 8″. Windsor Castle (reproduced by gracious permission of Her Majesty Queen Elizabeth II).

jarring angles, or disturbing color combinations to effect an easy, graceful flow from one area to another. His colors were mostly dark browns, greens, and greys, with the strongest colors, the reds and whites, reserved for small areas in which they were essential to identifying the figures. The large trees at the right and left and the clouds were used as subtle coordinates of and containment for the action, providing within the picture frame a second, natural framework for the scene. In the right foreground are some stone ruins which provide visual anchorage for that portion of the canvas; but these also serve to remind us that Poussin meticulously constructed his entire painting as if using building blocks, with each shape and shadow and tone having an unalterable position in the whole.

Poussin's definition of art was "an imitation made on a surface with lines and colors of everything that one sees under the sun. Its end is to please." His work did not truly embody this definition, however, for his painting is based on literature and is a conceit, or a conception of the mind, not a scene as directly encountered. He favored drawing over color in the construction of form; nor did he reveal colors as they actually appear under sunlight. His vision was highly selective, and his painting was strongly addressed to the intellect.

Poussin's definition of art was more closely realized in the nineteenth century by Cézanne, who admired the older painter. This admiration was directed principally toward Poussin's logical method, his systematic means of setting down his thoughts. Unlike Poussin, Cézanne was firmly committed to reproducing strong sensations of color, light, and air, the lessons he had learned from the Impressionists. In *Mont Sainte-Victoire* (Pl. 41), he painted what he saw; he emphasized consistently the lines and colors of surfaces; and he directed the whole toward delighting the senses. Cézanne made no demands upon literary erudition. By the 1880s, he had given up somber, figural dramas in landscape settings, and the mountain became a personal obsession and the climactic focus of his paintings from nature. Meyer Schapiro defines this attraction on the basis that the mountain externalized Cézanne's "striving and exaltation and desire for repose." No single form, but an idealized nature as a whole, may have held somewhat the same appeal for Poussin. The mountain in the *Funeral of Phocion* was for Poussin, as for the Chinese, the dwelling place of public gods.

Cézanne's landscape painting involved more of a struggle than that of Poussin in putting nature in order, for Cézanne's harmony involves a difficult and arduous balancing of unlike forces—stability and instability, energy and repose. Poussin made careful plans for a painting and could foretell precisely how it would look upon completion. Each shape such as a tree or a building was probably carried to its completed state before the over-all composition was finished. Cézanne's method was more empirical and relied upon momentary intuitions and judgments. He repeatedly worked over the whole painting and would alter what he had already painted or what he saw if it did not fit into the total esthetic organization. Unlike a composition of Poussin, Cézanne's landscape cannot be separated into definable parts or tidy zones. Cézanne's building blocks are simultaneously color and drawing, and these means constantly fuse, overlap, or grow out of each other. In the fields, for example, he used a line segment to give firmness to a section that would otherwise have been spatially ambiguous or without some sense of direction. He was at once intentionally concerned with presenting a stabilized view of nature in depth and with achieving a coherent surface pattern. The left-hand area between the pine trunk and the frame shows this concern. In isolation, lacking any specific object reference, the section appears to be a succession of colored patches that alternately move forward and backward, but with consistent reference to the surface. Put back into its original context, it falls in place and contributes to the valley's recession. Cézanne coordinated the foreground shape of the tree trunk in its edge, color, and axis with the adjacent areas. Just above the horizon line, he painted sections of pine branches whose agitation heightens the mountain's massive immobility. Appropriately, the mountain is the only object seen in its entirety. The branches also bring the viewer's eye back to the foreground plane.

Unlike Poussin, Cézanne tolerated sharp juxtapositions of warm and cool colors, saturate and dilute tones, such as those found in the area of the sky. The brush stroke directions of Cézanne's brush are in actuality more essential to the painting's structure than to the imitation of textures in the landscape. They indicate the direction in which a solid moves into depth, such as the foothills of the mountain, vitalize a large area such as the sky, and accelerate or decelerate the eye's movement through the painting, as in the zone of the fields. Cézanne sought an equilibrium between emotional and intellectual response to nature and painting, but never did the modern master domesticate the natural world to the extent that Poussin did. Cézanne preserved the irregularity, energy, and contradictions he found and admired in nature, and his emotional excitement with the scene comes through clearly in the final painting.

Landscape painting underwent great changes in the works of the two French artists we have discussed; two Dutch painters presented striking developments as well. Jacob van Ruisdael, a contemporary of Poussin, shows a divergent attitude toward nature in his *Wheatfields* (Fig. 362). The only importance assigned to literary subject matter and the human figure in van Ruisdael's work is to contrast their insignificance in relation to the immensity of nature. The landscape is not conceived as the projection of the moods of men within the painting; indeed, nature's indifference to man seems somehow a comfort to the Dutch painter. He shows wheatfields, human attempts to cultivate nature, but he accentuates the wild scrub along the road, the eccentric positions of the trees, and the shifting shapes of enormous cloud formations that defy human alteration. The rough silhouette and tangled mass of vegetation are characteristic of van Ruisdael's style.

In *Wheatfields* the road is brought almost to the viewer's feet to lead him more directly and

quickly into the landscape. Poussin avoided the emotional involvement that van Ruisdael felt was so essential. By alternating zones of shadow and golden light, van Ruisdael controlled the pace at which the eye moves through the landscape. The forward roll of the clouds seems to counter the inward thrust of the earth, so that the composition assumes a foreshortened wedge shape in depth as opposed to Poussin's arrangement of successive zones largely parallel to the picture surface.

Van Ruisdael gave to his painting a vivid sense of nature in movement—its processes of growth and decay, the shifting light as the sky changes, and the violent force of winds that propel the clouds and contort the trees. He was stirred by the wars within nature herself, between the natural forces of life and death and man's ultimately feeble attempts to conquer land and sea. A solitary individual himself, van Ruisdael sought in his painting to come to terms with a great impersonal, indomitable force outside himself.

The painting of nature was an even more deeply personal instrument for Vincent van Gogh—so much so that his *Plowed Fields* (Fig. 363) may belie the painter's stated intent. Writing from St-Remy to the painter Emile Bernard in December, 1889, van Gogh described a painting that is probably the one reproduced here:

> The sun rising over a field of young wheat, lines fleeting away, furrows running up high into the picture toward a wall and a row of lilac hills. The field is violet and yellow green. The white sun is surrounded by a great yellow halo. Here... I have tried to express calmness, a great peace.

Figure 362. JACOB VAN RUISDAEL. *Wheatfields*. c. 1650. Oil on canvas, 3′4½″ × 4′3½″. The Metropolitan Museum of Art, New York (bequest of Benjamin Altman).

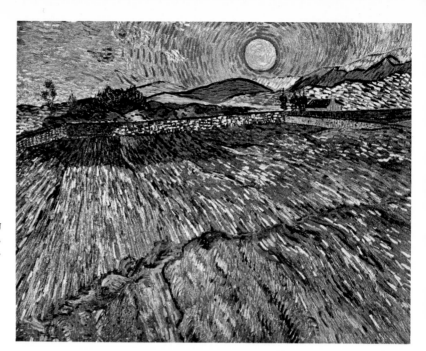

Figure 363. VINCENT VAN GOGH. *The Plowed Fields*. 1889. Oil on canvas, 28 × 35 ⅝". Private Collection.

What a shock the last sentence is! The viewer is pulled immediately and violently by the arrow-like flight of the fields into the painting's depth, but not to another and prime focus of the scene—the sun. Compounding the painting's tension between perspective and spiritual focus is the leftward tilt of the land, which also competes with the pull of the sun. The sun is the only stable form in the entire work, but it is placed at the right and the very top of the painting, the most difficult point of access. No previous landscape painter had looked at and painted the actual sun so directly. This act of van Gogh was as startling as that of the medieval artist at Daphne who painted the powerful face of his god. For van Gogh it was from the sun's force and brilliance that nature, art, and he himself gathered vigor and life. In his last years, the basis of his being lay in attaching himself, through the hard work of his art, to man, the soil, and the heavens. He wrote of "plowing on my canvases as they do in their fields." The striving for impossible goals of perfection and possession and the accompanying purge of great feeling perhaps explain why van Gogh could write of the finished work as being calm.

Van Gogh wrote to his brother and friends that his paintings should be framed in white and hung in white kitchens or against plain backgrounds. This was both a sign of his humility and a realization of how his paintings could be shown to best advantage. They can be seen in the strongest sunlight, unlike those of van Ruisdael or Poussin, and still surpass the intensity of the actual scene. Van Gogh wanted not simply an equivalent of nature but a more intense re-creation of it. He wanted his drawing and color to smell of the earth. The fields that van Gogh painted are in a sense disappointing. He made them exciting in the way that they were coded in his strong pure tones, boldly set against one another in a torrent of staccato touches. We are always conscious of the life of the painter's hand, its obvious power, trained responsiveness, yet inexplicable individuality. The painter himself wrote, "What a queer thing *touch* is, the stroke of the brush." Perhaps van Gogh's wonder and uncertainty stemmed from his use of the brush as a direct and spontaneous extension of his internal state of being. He used the touch to decipher the inner character of what he felt was the true soil of Provence. Wherever he went, van Gogh absorbed through painting the sights and effects that alone could give him peace.

A common theme from nature is the close-up of a small cluster of plant life in which the artist searches for the individuality of the part. With botanical accuracy, the German artist Albrecht Dürer in his *Study of Plants* (Fig. 364) depicted the flora in a tiny area of marsh. This was more than a purely secular scientific investigation, for in his natural subject Dürer sought the minute and multiform evidence of God's creativity. Dürer's quantitative surface reproduction would have been anathema to Chinese and Japanese artists, who felt that optical fidelity concealed rather than disclosed the essential quality of nature. Dürer, however, found challenge and meaning in the multitude of shapes, colors, textures, and the precise proportions and inclination which described each plant form. The clustered natural forms demanded different and less strict compositional solutions than his large religious and figural paintings had involved. He did not impose an obvious stilted ordering on the plants but carefully preserved the appearance of a casual, overlapping disarray, while unobtrusively contrasting and harmonizing the stalks and leaves with one another. In his own words, "Art, however, is in nature, and whoever can draw it out, he possesses it."

To enact his fantasies of nature in such paintings as *Botanical Theater* (Fig. 365), the modern Swiss painter Paul Klee staked out a small uncontested territory of his own, one inaccessible to such optical aids as Dürer's perspective or the modern microscope. Klee searched for a totally new and poetical approach to lend familiarity to obscure and minute aspects of nature, such as the intimacy of the night world of plants. His viewpoint is not that of a detached scientific investigator, but a conception that evolves in the mind when the eyes are closed. Through his meditations, Klee's art became a fusion of the interior and exterior world in a way never previously seen in Oriental or Western art. His oil and watercolor *Botanical Theater* seems disarmingly famil-

iar at first. There is no horizon line or sky, no definable light source or measurable distance between the viewer and the plants. No means exist to compare the space and the scale of the painting with oneself or a real landscape. There is no botanical guide to catalogue the plant life. Klee's world seemingly has its own laws of size, light, growth, and species. He believed in the interrelation of all phenomena, and his objects have a dual character, being part vegetal and part animal. Identical dispositions are shared by plants and humans. The pungent color that floats over and permeates the shapes, and the prickly textures in and around the plants recall experiences of sight, smell, taste, hearing, and touch. The artist's fantasies are derived from personal sensory responses to varied stimuli. It is as if Klee were able to project himself into the subhuman night world and perceive the scene through the senses of its occupants.

Klee's drawing method was to some degree automatic; he let his pen and brush explore the surface as if guided by impulse and the feel of the materials. The creative act sprang from inner watchfulness and listening and from an uninhibited response to the free associations induced by imagination as he worked. When a spiral was begun, for instance, it might emerge as a snail, or two leaves might change into a pair of eyes. He once wrote, "Art is a simile of the Creation.... Today we reveal the reality that is behind visible things,

Left: Figure 364. ALBRECHT DÜRER. *Study of Plants.* 1503. Drawing, 16⅛ × 12⅜". Albertina, Vienna.

Below: Figure 365. PAUL KLEE. *Botanical Theatre.* 1934. Oil and watercolor, 19⅝ × 26⅜". Paul Klee Foundation, Berne.

thus expressing the belief that the visible world is merely an isolated case in relation to the universe and that there are many more other, latent realities." Klee felt that his art would comfort his viewers by reminding them that the mind itself is not confined to earthly potentialities.

Klee strove for union with what he called the "heart of creation... in the womb of nature... where the secret key to the universe is safely kept." His paintings were small—done, one might say, within the radius of his elbow and the action of his wrist. This modest size encourages intimate and prolonged discourse between viewer and subject. The miniature scale is essential to his style, and again in Klee's words, "style is the ego."

The art of Paul Klee may be termed "imagistic," for it took form from his imagination, and the root of the word "imagination" is "image." Imagistic painting gives form to that which is unattainable for the outward senses. Klee felt that the artist's moral imperative was to search his inner being for inspiration and "to render visible those impressions and conceptions not in themselves visible." Another modern painter who responded to inner sensations and created private images to some extent related to nature is the Chilean-born artist Matta (Echaurren). His large work *The Earth Is a Man* (Fig. 366) is an "inscape," or a landscape of the mind, a transformation of his experience of the volcanic landscape of Mexico. Matta's tropical palette of yellows, reds, and blues and his vague retention of a horizon line, with its contingent major divisions of sky and earth, preserve some of the qualities of the Mexican

landscape. The painter's transformations are elaborated, however, into a visionary fusion of genesis and apocalypse, of coalescence and dissolution. Unlike Leonardo's visionary cataclysms, those of Matta are not susceptible to literary programing, nor are they based on scientific geological and climatic studies. Matta's turbulent imagery may reflect the anxiety of the times (World War II), as Leonardo's drawings reflected the disturbed conditions of his day.

In his painting Matta created an untraversable and uninhabitable world in constant flux. There is fantasizing upon flora, primeval birds, molten eruptive geology, and a solar eclipse. In the upper area is the eclipse, which surprisingly intensifies the light permeating the entire painting. Every shape and area is in the process of changing, and outlines are smooth, undulant, and unstable. Matta gave his shapes an insubstantial and elusive quality by wiping the paint on with a cloth at certain points, thereby dissolving one color area into another and obliterating sustained reference to the pigment and its materiality. The poetic ambiguity of his space comes from soft transparencies of shapes, avoidance of logical recession, and unpredictable areas of phosphorescent brilliance or absorbent darkness. There is an ambivalence of direction in the composition, so that lateral and vertical movements are reversible, thus enhancing the cyclical nature of the theme. Putting Matta's work into historical perspective, William Rubin wrote, "Whereas the rationalist Greeks had used the external image of man (microcosm) to represent the order, logic, and finite mechanical perfection

Figure 366. MATTA. *The Earth Is a Man.* 1940–1942. Oil on canvas, 6′11 ⅝″ × 7′11 ⅝″. Collection Mr. and Mrs. Joseph Shapiro, Oak Park, Illinois.

of the universe (macrocosm), Matta invokes a vision of galaxies to suggest the infinity and mystery within man."

NATURE AND ABSTRACT PAINTING

At the beginning of this century the artist's decision to move away from illusionistic painting of nature frequently entailed important concerns and commitments that extended beyond the world of the studio. The implications of the way a man paints reach into his psychological and emotional make-up, and style is part of the artist's world view. Furthermore, the artist will often preserve in his nonillusionistic work a certain residue of his earlier imagery based upon his perception of nature. This can be seen by juxtaposing works from both styles of a single painter.

As a young painter in Holland at the turn of the century, Piet Mondrian was inclined toward passive depictions of the Dutch countryside without action or figures. As in his painting of a windmill (Fig. 367), Mondrian searched for solitary prospects, small segments within the vast panorama of nature that reflected an inherently stable and tranquil world. Mondrian selected a viewpoint that allowed him to align principal axes within the scene, those of the bridge and windmill, with those of the picture frame, thus permitting stable pictorial construction. The reflections in the placid water echo and reinforce the directions of the mill and bridge, and a grid pattern is recurrent. Many brush strokes, such as those at the left and in the pond, are unrelated to literal observation of nature but serve to strengthen the design armature of the whole composition. The artist's viewpoint, with the large foreground area given over to the reflecting surface of the water, has contributed to a perceptible flattening of the space, which, coupled with the pronounced use of repeated motifs, gives a strong surface rhythm and pattern to the painting. During Mondrian's subsequent growth as an artist, as well as in his writings, his obsession with the possibilities of rhythm became patent. Rhythm was a critical link by which Mondrian hoped to unite "the individual with the universal."

Hundreds of paintings intervened in Mondrian's career from the *Landscape with Mill*

Figure 367. PIET MONDRIAN. *Landscape with Mill.* c. 1900. Oil on canvas, mounted on cardboard, 11 ⅞ × 15″. The Museum of Modern Art, New York (Purchase).

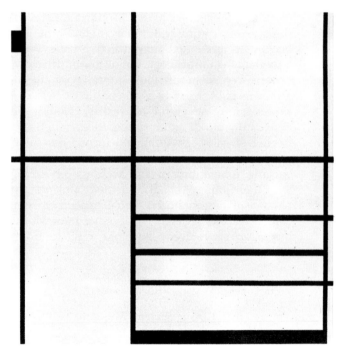

Figure 368. PIET MONDRIAN. *Composition in White, Black, and Red.* 1936. Oil on canvas, 40¼ × 41″. The Museum of Modern Art, New York (gift of the Advisory Committee).

to the *Composition in White, Black, and Red* (Fig. 368) of 1936, but in mood and design the latter work is a condensation of the former. Though it gave up representation of the specific in nature, his later art preserved the ideal of manifesting the underlying harmonious order of nature in its broadest sense. The structural components of the later work, straight lines meeting in a rectilinear grid, were present in the mill painting. Junctures now become crisp right angles, and all the rectangular shapes and pure colors lie completely at the surface. Irregularities traceable to the hand of the artist are absent. Crucial to the continuity of form and meaning between the two paintings is the relation of the asymmetrical composition to the frame, treated as if what is within its borders were an incomplete, fragmented view of a greater order. The irregular quadrature of the later painting is controlled not by directly perceived shapes in nature but by the artist's intuition of balance between black lines and small red and large white rectangles. Mondrian's compositional reflexes had been conditioned by his paintings of land, sky, water, and trees. The painting's title accurately describes what is *on*, not *in*, the picture plane. Mondrian believed this type of painting was important for humanity because it presented in purified artistic form a model of equilibrium, a condition imperfectly experienced in nature but eternally sought in all forms of life. Seeing as the painter's task the expression of a vision of reality, Mondrian desired the purest expression of life through the freeing of color, rhythm, and form from their particularized appearance in nature. In the varying dimensions of the rectangular areas, with their impeccable arrangement and perfect balance of tension, he felt such artistic liberation could be accomplished. ("Space becomes white, black or gray; form becomes red, blue or yellow.")

Figure 369. WASSILY KANDINSKY. *Landscape with Factory Chimney*. 1910. Oil on canvas, 26 × 31½". The Solomon R. Guggenheim Museum, New York.

Another pioneer of abstraction after 1900 was the Russian painter Wassily Kandinsky. His early art shows a strong attraction to the countryside. By 1910, when he painted his *Landscape with Factory Chimney* (Fig. 369), Kandinsky had proceeded to a point where it was increasingly difficult to match his painting with an actual landscape. He had reduced distinctions between land and sky, trees, hills, and buildings, between space near and far; his paintings coalesced into strong arbitrary color harmonies that were less and less governed by perceived sequences of hues. Kandinsky did not seek a stable viewpoint or a geometrically based order, but instead he presented a turbulent heaving earth. Against the broad sweeping curves of the hills are ragged and diffuse color patches, which produce intense color sensations and contribute greatly to the excited mood of the whole. Unlike the Impressionist painter, Kandinsky did not paint the mood induced in him by contact with nature but, rather, superimposed upon the landscape an already existing emotional state. Kandinsky's predilection was for wild, hilly terrain laced with precipitous diagonals—the kind of landscape that might provide an adequate carrier of his feelings. These qualities flood over into a later painting, *Picture with White Edge, No. 173* (Fig. 370). Although not consciously intended as a landscape, it shows that his mind and the movements of his hand could not expunge his earlier experience, for within this seeming abstraction there remains a pictorial sign language of wavelike hills and jagged series of peaks and trees.

Taken as a whole, the *White Edge* has an apocalyptic mood. Dating from the eve of World War I, it may have been indirectly inspired by Kandinsky's response to the tense atmosphere in Germany, where he was working. Its brilliant color evokes a sensation of clashing sounds. Kandinsky believed that sensory experiences overlapped and that each color had its equivalence in sound, so that painting became an orchestration of elements having inherent expressive associations with which the painter could strike chords in the soul of the viewer. Framing the dense and saturate color mass in the painting is an irregular white edge, a color that Kandinsky wrote of as a "pregnant stillness." Like Balzac's Frenhofer, Kandinsky sought a perfect fusion of drawing and color

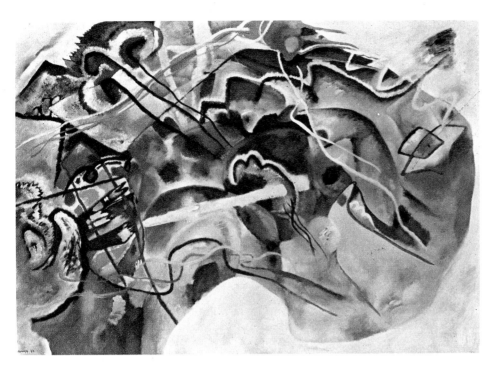

Figure 370. WASSILY KANDIN-SKY. *Picture with White Edge, No. 173.* 1913. Oil on canvas, 4'7¾" × 6'7". The Solomon R. Guggenheim Museum, New York.

and, like the fictional painter, achieved an exquisite but nonetheless controlled chaos.

Kandinsky's departure from illusionism was gradual, hesitant, backsliding, and rarely complete in the years between 1910 and 1914. His writings show a deep awareness of and misgivings about a possible important loss to art in abandoning the familiar and nature as a frame of reference. What impelled him in the direction of the *White Edge* was a growing distrust of modern materialism, science, organized religion, and illusionistic art, all of which he came to regard as impediments to free expression of the human spirit. Inner freedom was for Kandinsky the sole criterion for both ethics and esthetics. The creative process ideally meant a suspension of consciousness and a purely spontaneous and intuitive activity; however, Kandinsky did in fact impose some critical judgment:

I have painted rather subconsciously in a state of strong inner tension. So intensely do I feel the necessity of some of the forms that I remember having given loud-voiced directions to myself, for instance, "But the corners must be heavy." The observer must learn to look at the picture as a graphic representation of a mood and not as a representation of objects.

The American Jackson Pollock's early *Seascape* (Fig. 371) is a moody image of a storm-tossed boat seen against a disquieting sky. The canvas is filled with dense pigmentation, rough shapes, and strong movement. The subject was appropriate to the strong and aggressive temperament of the young artist. From his first works, Pollock asserted his rebellious nature and a need to impose his will and muscular energies on both nature and art. The small format and the limits of the canvas are strained to contain the violence of his painting.

Figure 371. JACKSON POLLOCK. *Seascape.* 1934. Oil on canvas, 12 × 16". Collection Lee Krasner Pollock, New York.

Themes from Nature   313

Created sixteen years and hundreds of paintings and drawings later, Pollock's *Autumn Rhythm* (Pl. 42) continues, refines, adds to, and subtracts from the seminal qualities of *Seascape*. From the scale of the conventional easel painting Pollock had gravitated toward what might be called a "portable canvas mural," a huge work roughly 8½ by 17 feet. In 1947 the painter wrote:

> I prefer to tack the unstretched canvas to the hard wall or floor. I need the resistance of a hard surface. On the floor I am more at ease. I feel nearer, more a part of the painting, since this way I can walk around it, work from the four sides and literally be *in* the painting.

Vermeer's painting of the artist in his studio demonstrated a system ideal for wrist painting; the artist's subject was reduced to the scale of a traditional easel format. In Pollock's work of the late 1940s, scale was not strongly predetermined but resulted from the interaction of the artist and his evolving image, which set the finished size of the painting. Further, Pollock was impelled to arm as well as wrist painting; the rhythm and energy of his whole body found outlet in the creative act. For both technical and esthetic reasons, he gave up oil for enamel paints. In this way, he was freed of oil paint's historical associations, and the more viscous enamel medium also permitted a continuous spinning out of the linear fabric, the heart of Pollock's mature style. The dripping and spattering of paint as Pollock walked around and over the horizontal canvas was a technique thoughtfully and deliberately arrived at as the inevitable means by which to impose his visions and feelings on the painting's surface and the viewer's eye.

Accidents and chance were encouraged, but controlled and corrected. "I *can* control the flow of paint: there is no accident, just as there is no beginning and no end." The automatism of Kandinsky continued in Pollock's colored drawing, but with less disposition to repeat obvious landscape and object forms. Pollock literally wished to be *in* his painting, more deeply involved in its creation than had ever been physically or psychologically possible.

> When I am *in* my painting, I'm not aware of what I'm doing. It is only after a sort of "get acquainted" period that I see what I have been about. I have no fears about making changes, destroying the image, etc., because

the painting has a life of its own. . . . It is only when I lose contact with the painting that the result is a mess. Otherwise it is pure harmony, an easy give and take, and the painting comes out well. . . . I want to express my feelings rather than illustrate them.

The expression rather than illustration of feeling is therefore the content-form of *Autumn Rhythm*.

Just as Pollock felt that he must not lose contact with the painting, so must the beholder give it full and sustained attention, and not look for an image of leaves and clouds. Seen in its own terms, *Autumn Rhythm* constitutes a new, physically impenetrable, and unstable environment. Its tangled web or netlike configuration possesses inconstant densities, suspended in ambiguous relation to the surface. The eye is permitted to look through the web as if into a tinted void that is given atmospheric properties by the spattered color. This web is woven by the intimate calligraphy of the artist into a composition punctuated by nodes of coagulated color, congested tangles, and open and airy passages. Like a graph, the surface is a record of the artist's hand responding to his internal state as he works over the entire surface, its fluid lines serving as traces of impulse and decision. There is neither beginning nor end, but at the four sides the configuration tends to turn back in upon itself as if signifying the limits of the nucleus. The parts and their relation are unpredictable, and no segment is duplicated. The key to the color harmony of the painting is the predominance of black, against which are browns and whites in lesser quantity, and the pervasive color of the canvas itself, which has become a positive element in the artist's conception. The title was supplied after the painting was done, perhaps when Pollock found some correspondence of qualities or mood between the two. He placed his finished works outside his barn in a field, not to appraise their similarity to nature but to decide whether or not they held their own as autonomous objects.

SCULPTURE OF NATURE

Until the twentieth century, sculptural themes from nature were usually decorative foliate motifs for architecture, synoptic landscape backgrounds for figures in reliefs, or personifications

Figure 372. JEAN (HANS) ARP. *Growth*. 1938. Bronze, height 31½". The Philadelphia Museum of Art.

of the seasons, fertility, and the like. Two among many modern sculptors for whom nature has supplied significant themes and a central focus for art are the Alsatian Jean (Hans) Arp and the American Seymour Lipton. Arp's *Growth* (Fig. 372) is but a single example of a lifetime of work dealing with the unseen forces and processes shaping life. In this small bronze sculpture, Arp has evoked the internal fluid pressure of life's force in the soft serpentine ascension of the form and its multiple protuberances. Although the theme is generic, the form suggests associations with various plant and human shapes. Movement is achieved through the flowing surface continuity, the absence of clearly delimited parts, and the smooth finish that permits unobstructed play of light and shadow. The sculpture gives an impression of pulsation, enlargement, and upward striving. Arp has treated the lower area in a way that suggests it continues below the level of sight into a root.

To his abstract sculpture Arp gave a sensuality and grace as great as, or greater than, a Greek sculptor might have bestowed on the figure of Venus. Like Klee's, Arp's purpose was to show the importance and relatedness of common, recurrent phenomena in nature and to recompense for a human vanity that viewed

the world as man-centered. A witness to wars and revolutions, Arp wanted an art to counter both human bestiality and society's adulation of the rational and technological. In affirming the peaceful, the handmade, and the irrationally conceived, he longed for man's return to a more simple existence and "an elemental, natural healthy art" that would release men from material cares and self-consciousness. "Works of art should remain as anonymous in the great workshop of nature as the clouds, the mountains, the seas, the animals and man himself. Yes! Man should once again become part of nature."

Lipton's *Earth Forge No. 2* (Fig. 373) is a kind of sculptural emblem of nature's processes in the hidden areas where life is made. The sculpture's effect is that of a horizontal casing emerging from and enveloping a spiral core. The artist sought a form that held the promise of a gradual, inevitable unfolding. He meant the work to convey a sense of what goes on in the bowels of the earth during the winter period of gestation. The regenerative process as viewed by Lipton is accompanied by great force and tensions, unlike Arp's view of growth as a tranquil and unopposed natural pressure. Their sculptural styles and biological preferences are accordingly different. Arp's forms seem as if shaped by cellular multiplication and, when they are not vegetal, are invertebrate. Moreover, Arp's surfaces are smoothly continuous and closed, showing only the external aspect of his growths. Lipton's sculpture shows the internal and external aspects of his subjects simultaneously. His conceptions are of relentless

Figure 373. SEYMOUR LIPTON. *Earth Forge No. 2*. 1955. Monel metal, height 31⅛"; length 52⅝". The Brooklyn Museum.

conflicting drives, like outward and inward thrusts, uncoiling and recoiling motions. His shapes and silhouettes are crisper than those of Arp, and his curving, roughened surfaces envelop clearly defined spaces. Existence and art signify for Lipton a continuous dialectic, or a coexistence of contraries in uneasy relationships. Through his art, Lipton seeks to give this tension an intelligible esthetic form and to encourage men to accept and live with the difficult character of existence.

Like Arp and Klee, Lipton has relied on mental association, and the process of transferring insights and reflexes into sculpture evokes reminiscenses of widely disparate objects. *Earth Forge No. 2*, which mingles mechanical, botanical, and sexual symbols, is an example of the *compound image* frequently found in modern art. This type of imagery is greater than the sum of its parts and is unpredictable on the basis of any or all of its components. It requires a logic of form and an illogic of events, such as combining in one work plant and machine forms. The parts give up certain aspects of their individual identity and share qualities or fuse with the other motifs to create a unique total image. This compound image does not originate in conscious written or verbal programs but is an irrational and intuitive creation. The

beholder is not expected to try to break down the whole into its parts but to expose himself to it in a free and unprejudiced way and to sense whether or not the generic theme has been given effective artistic form.

The American sculptor David Smith, who died in 1965, forged, twisted, and welded steel into his *Hudson River Landscape* (Fig. 374). While riding on a train back and forth between Albany and New York, he drew several ink sketches of impressions the moving landscape made upon him. Smith's sculpture has a unique quality of drawing in space, and its steel configuration appears to have been lifted from a flat surface. (When seen from the side, the sculpture does have more projection and recession than appears in the full-front photograph.) Smith was not representing any specific locale or particular landscape feature, for he himself said this could be any landscape; but he found the flow, contrast, and rhythm of the Hudson River Valley appropriate to his way of making sculpture. The sculptor liked to view his work outdoors, with the countryside seen through it, particularly in winter, with the snow forming additional and complementary shapes on the twisted steel form. The use of steel is not anachronistic, for only in the tensile properties of this material could he achieve the

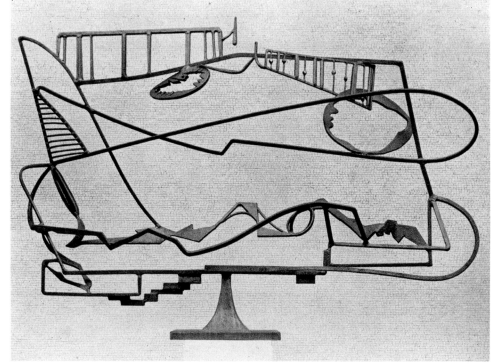

Figure 374. DAVID SMITH. *Hudson River Landscape.* 1951. Steel, length 6'3". The Whitney Museum of American Art, New York.

highly personal style that conveys his private vision of nature.

Another American sculptor who has found his mode of expression in steel is Theodore Roszak. His *Recollections of the Southwest* (Fig. 375) derives its harsh, pitted, and belligerent surfaces and shapes from the action of the oxyacetylene torch and acids on steel. His shapes seem to derive from the century plant and cactus, from the weathered bones and perhaps the disused farm implements that evoke the deadly toll of the desert. Ubiquitous crescent forms splay outward in all directions, making the sculpture seem like a menacing object. Smith's sculpture has a lyrical sweep to it, whereas Roszak's work seems a somber meditation on violence and the struggle for survival of plant life. Until this century sculptors, maintaining tradition longer than painters, utilized the human figure to personify nature. It is within the last fifty years that modern sculptors have achieved personal metaphors for their physical environment. The works shown in this chapter have tended—with the exception of Arp—to deal with the harsh realities of biological and botanical nature rather than with idyllic or ingratiating natural motifs. Lipton and Roszak believe that art should encourage us to face up to the grim dialectic of life and death that has continued throughout history and is outside considerations of good and evil.

Art, like science, is a record of man's interaction with nature. Landscape art is not important because it gives geographical information about China, Holland, or southern France; it has value because of the way these places were seen, felt, and thought of and then given esthetic form by its makers. For artists such as Bruegel, Dürer, and Leonardo, art did have some cartographic function, but this was not its sole or primary purpose. Inherent in all the art discussed in this chapter has been the artist's desire to know about creation, his gods, and the nature of reality—where he and other men stood in relation to the universe. The act of painting and making sculpture from nature has in itself been as important perhaps as the knowledge imparted by the finished works of art, for it is during the art process that the artist feels most strongly his communion with nature. For some, painting from nature helped the artist to fathom its essential order and to re-experience its genesis, but for others it was

Figure 375. THEODORE J. ROSZAK. *Recollections of the Southwest.* 1948. Steel, brazed with nickel-silver, 32 × 48″. The Pierre Matisse Gallery, New York.

the occasion for putting nature into a more perfect and personal order while preserving its violent aspects.

Artists have derived from nature the means or motifs to externalize their feelings or images of themselves; an awareness of life not given to the eye, the reconstruction of an ideal past, understanding of the present, and even a prediction of the future; escape from the difficulties of daily existence, or terms on which to meet reality; satisfaction of a need for objective knowledge, or the stimulation of fantasy.

The impossibility of the artist's producing an exact and objective record of nature is explained in a statement by Klee, in which he makes an analogy between the artist and a tree:

He is like the trunk of the tree. Afflicted and moved by the forces of the stream he conveys what he has perceived into his work. The treetop expands in all directions and becomes visible in time and space and all the same things happen with his work.... It would never occur to anyone to demand of the tree that its top be shaped just like the roots. Everyone knows that what is above ground cannot be just a reflection of what is below.... The artist, like the trunk of the tree, is really doing nothing else than accumulating what comes from the depth and passes it on. He neither serves nor commands; he is an intermediary.... Beauty has merely passed through him.

16

PAINTING AND OBJECTS

To understand the appeal that the painting of objects has had for centuries, it helps to remember that we are not neutral toward objects. Aside from the specific practical function for which objects have been made, their human use and the mind's tendency to make analogies have throughout history invested objects with multiple and important associations or symbolical purposes. In the Middle Ages, for example, the relics or objects used by saints and kings had great value, as if some of the holiness or power of these revered figures had rubbed off on what they had handled. Even today the personal effects of a dead man have special meaning to his family; or a common ice pick, hammer, or rope can assume great importance for the jury in a murder trial. To witness the public's fascination with the late President Kennedy's rocking chair, or the spirited bidding for hotel bed sheets used by the Beatles is a reminder that people still invest inanimate objects with irrational meaning and value.

We also tend to forget that paintings themselves are objects. They are wood panels or canvases stretched over rectangular wooden frames on which color has been applied. Throughout most of art's history, this fun-

damentally static character has been disguised by illusionistic painting and the depiction of movement. As will be shown in this chapter, artists have long had the ability to look searchingly at objects and invent many possible relations with the framed surface. The artist can create an unfamiliar context for objects by using his frame like a camera lens, forcing the spectator to focus upon objects while severely limiting their environment. The small size of most objects chosen for painting allows the preservation of their exact scale, a condition that can vivify a painting. Since the objects are painted imitations, they cannot be touched or used, and we are therefore obliged to experience them in a new way, to appreciate them solely with our eyes. Thus, probably for the first time, we become aware of an object's color, shape, volume, texture, and surface reflection of light—the esthetic properties that commonly unite the interest of artist and viewer.

Like the physical circumstance of the painting itself, objects lack movement, and many artists have been fascinated with their fixity, their quality of just being there. The combination of picture and objects has often been used to produce a restful visual experience satisfying the need of artist and viewer to see things put

318

in order. Placing two or more objects next to one another can establish a "dialogue" for the painter. Painting has stressed various forms of interchange or reciprocation between objects, creating types of order or harmony that have metaphorically been models for human existence. Changes in composition as well as in choice of objects often parallel important shifts not just in styles but broad developments outside the sphere of art. This type of painting is important in the sociology and psychology of art. It is the one form of painting in which the artist has generally been superior to his subject and could dispose of it when he was finished. Beginning in the seventeenth century, it was the one form of painting in which, to begin with, the subject was not considered superior to the painting itself. Many beautiful paintings have been created from the most modest or unlikely subject objects. Before the nineteenth century, it was perhaps still-life painting that most readily allowed the discriminating viewer to contemplate and appraise the judgment and coordination of the artist's eye and hand. Even the most illusionistic rendering of objects does not require total self-effacement on the part of the artist. We can come to recognize many still-life painters by their choice of objects, by their arrangement and lighting. There are endless ways in which a round wine bottle can be convincingly transposed to the flat surface of a painting. Throughout the history of art, men have delighted in the challenge of reworking the same subject and even repainting the same picture.

The largest surviving pre-Roman body of painting concerning itself with objects is that found in Egyptian tombs. The pictures of foodstuffs and vessels in Egyptian reliefs and wall paintings do not constitute pure still-life painting, or rendering of inanimate objects for their esthetic value alone. They are accompanied by representations of the deceased whom these objects were to serve in the afterlife, of workers who were to make and gather the objects in the service of the dead man, or of the gods who were to receive the objects as offerings. Their purpose in Egyptian art was thus utilitarian. As long as ancient art was god-centered and deeply rooted in magic and religion, no legitimate tradition of still-life painting could develop. But, by the fourth century B.C., ancient literary sources recount, urban Greek

artists had achieved highly illusionistic techniques of representing objects in stage sets and on portable panel paintings and frescoes for homes and shops. Though none of this Hellenistic art has survived, its emergence in the fifth and fourth centuries B.C. accompanied an increasing secularization of artistic subject matter in both painting and sculpture. It was part of a public taste for enjoying and capturing the immediate material existence, as well as of a growing religious and political relativism. Much of the still-life art produced by Greek artists dealt with food and the vessels and plates with which meals were served, reflecting the tastes and social customs of the artist's patron and his guests and the delight of city dwellers in the products of the country. The Greek imitation of the fruits of nature, with its connotations of sociability and connoisseurship, had later parallels and influence in Roman painting and mosaic, many examples of which have survived.

One such mosaic, representing the floor of a Roman dining room, is known as *The Unswept Room* (Fig. 376). Dating from the second century, it is probably a copy by Heraclitus of a lost work from the Greek city of Pergamum. It was not uncommon for guests at a fashionable banquet to litter the floor with bits of food. The scattered objects in the *Unswept Room* mosaic are table discards, the refuse of a discriminating, ritually ordered banquet such as would be held in the triclinium, or dining room. The mosaic consists of small, roughly squared cubes of white and colored stone set into a cement base. The color range and intensity of the stones, or

Figure 376. HERACLITUS. *The Unswept Room*, copy of a lost mosaic from Pergamum (?). 2nd century A.D. Lateran Museum, Rome.

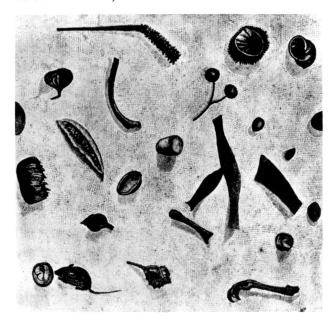

tesserae, used by Roman mosaicists surpassed the palette of the fresco and panel painters in antiquity. The minute size in which the stones could be cut permitted subtle tonal gradations and intricate curves, so that the artist's medium did not inhibit his choice of objects or illusionistic intent. Not only the shape and color of the objects but also the relief effect from cast shadows and the naturalistic mouse in the lower left corner would cause an unsuspecting guest to tread carefully in the rooms and would doubtless provide conversational diversion between the courses. Study of this seemingly random composition reveals the brilliant calculation and sensitivity to complex balance exercised by the artist. Objects do not overlap or touch; nor are shadows tangent at any point. There is no single organizing axis or consistent light source. The mosaic is rendered in perspective, so to speak, from any point in the dining room. The careful spacing between shapes and shadows and the over-all density established in each large quarter of the floor results in a harmonious ordering of a highly sophisticated type. Comparison of this mosaic with Egyptian paintings of objects illuminates the changes that had taken place in the relationship between man and his environment—from a sense of fear and a deep need for security in the next world to an attitude of relaxed pleasure and confidence.

From the fourth through the fourteenth and fifteenth centuries in Western art, the achievements of the Romans in the naturalistic rendering of secular objects and their making of them the complete subjects of works of art were apparently forgotten or ignored. The life of the objects in art underwent significant transformation. For about a thousand years in painting, mosaics, and sculpture, objects served in the main as attributes, symbols, or accessories for Christian heroes. The throne, for instance, occupies an important place in Early Christian imagery. While the Bible narrates the magnificence of Solomon's throne, Christian imagery was influenced by the thrones of Roman emperors that the artists had before their eyes. Use of the throne as a venerated object and imperial substitute in art and life also derived from pagan traditions. (We have also referred to such use in connection with the Buddha.) During the important Council of Ephesus in the fourth century, a throne, empty except for the Gospels placed upon it, had the place of honor as a sign that Christ chaired the conclave.

A fifth-century mosaic (Fig. 377) from a church in Rome illustrates how an object could, thus, replace the image of Christ himself. The regal, authoritarian tone of the mosaic is attributable not only to the sumptuousness of the throne, with its inlaid precious stones, elegant drapery, and brilliantly colored cushion beneath the scroll of sacred Scripture, but also to the formality of the object's placement. Not unlike the arrangement in mosaic images showing Christ in Glory (Pl. 5), the throne is frontal, placed centrally between symbols of the Evangelists John and Luke, and dominates the whole ensemble in its size. The central axis of the throne is shared by the Scriptures and the dove of the Holy Ghost, which reveals to the eyes of the enlightened beholder the source and omnipotence of Christian law. In contrast to the whites, greys, subdued and pastel tones of the *Unswept Room* mosaic, by the fifth century, Christian mosaics had acquired a more consistently rich, dark, and luminous color and surface quality. The decorative border of the mosaic also displays less caprice or spontaneity in design than did the decorative motifs in earlier Roman art, symptomatic of the formality

Figure 377. *Throne with Scroll and Symbols of the Evangelists Luke and John.* 5th century. Mosaic. Rome.

320

Figure 378. VINCENT VAN GOGH. *The Artist's Chair*. 1888. Oil on canvas, 35½×28″. The Tate Gallery, London (by courtesy of the Trustees).

and stylization that developed in Christian art along with the codification of Church dogma and power.

Whereas the Christian mosaic of the throne was valued in its time for the exalted nature of its subject and the preciousness of the medium, van Gogh's late-nineteenth-century painting of his own chair (Fig. 378) has come to be valued for its artistic merit and powerful revelation of the artist's feeling about himself and his relation to others. It is questionable whether van Gogh was conscious of the earlier tradition of the subject as a symbol of a human presence or of a god. Largely through instinct and an urgent need to attach himself to others, he came to endow objects—his own shoes, pipe and tobacco, books, gloves, and flowers—with human associations. The objects that moved him were modest, and their appearance was shaped by use. A companion painting to that of his own chair was one of Gauguin's chair, bought by van Gogh when the former moved in for an ill-fated stay at Arles. Gauguin's chair was characteristically the better-made, set on a carpet in a carefully decorated room, and it bore the candle and book that Gauguin used for reading late at night. Both the gift of the painting to Gauguin and

the expense of procuring the better furniture would seem poignant testimonies to friendship.

Although the subject is inanimate, van Gogh's painting of his empty chair can nonetheless induce disquiet in the viewer. The heavy dark outline of the chair aggressively asserts its object character, as does the substance of the thick, strong yellow pigment re-creating the wood and straw. Unlike the impressive frontal throne of Christ, seen from slightly below and eternally stabilized against the backdrop of heaven, van Gogh painted the chair from above and turned it at a severe angle to the floor tiles and the corner of the room. He made no attempt to align the objects into a simple deliberate pattern. To hold the chair visually within the frame, van Gogh joined its left front leg to the door frame and brought the chair close to the picture's top and bottom edges. The taut equilibrium of the composition makes it impossible to visualize the chair in any other position. Each part of the whole vigorously appeals to the eye, prohibiting tranquil inspection, and in this way the chair's magnetism as an object and a visual form is brought home to us—for it is to it that we must constantly return our gaze. Whereas the throne in Christian art helped to relate man to his god, to orient him to the universe, van Gogh's chair was the artist's link with sanity and human love. The thirst to possess what he painted, whether objects, people, or trees and wheat fields, may have been increased by his awareness that attacks of epilepsy could be forestalled through the concentrated effort of painting.

The storytelling capacity of objects was recognized more than five and a half centuries ago by a Spanish artist, possibly Domingo Crespi, who decorated a private book of religious lessons and prayers for King Martin of Aragon. The section dealing with the events leading up to Easter includes a large painting filled with an assortment of objects whose conjunction would be incomprehensible to anyone unfamiliar with the details of Christ's Passion (Fig. 379). As recounted in the Bible and the apocryphal gospels, the devout reader of the royal breviary can single out an object and put it into the context of the events leading to Christ's death. But this ability to reconstruct the religious drama owes much to previous painting. Even in the Middle Ages, with its emphasis on textual interpretation, artists took the license of filling in details omitted by Scripture (for instance, the insertion

Figure 379. DOMINGO CRESPI (?). *The Instruments of the Passion,* from *The Breviary of King Martin of Aragon.* 1395–1410. Bibliothèque Nationale, Paris.

of medieval tongs or pliers, by which the nails were removed from Christ's hands and feet). Purposes of clarity and ready identification influenced the even dispersal of the objects, each carrying with it poignant associations. The mystical nature of the painting allows the painter to suspend objects and fragmentary heads and hands in space.

It was from the medieval tradition of objects as attributes of Christ, the Virgin, and the saints that their independent secular painting emerged in the fifteenth century. A German painting dating from 1470–1480 by an unknown artist, *Cupboard with Bottles and Books* (Fig. 380), has been interpreted as a pharmacist's sign, perhaps from a hospital. (The tag on the flask says, "For toothaches.") The lower half of the composition is a neatly distributed but static display of objects hanging on a wall or standing upon a shelf. Within this recessed niche, the objects are susceptible to varying intensity of light and shadow. The cupboard above is shown with one of its doors partly open, as if it had pivoted into the viewer's space. Paintings that astonish the eye by illusionistically moving away from or toward us had a tradition as far back as ancient times, and their reappearance in the fifteenth century, both in Northern Europe and in Italy, is thought by some scholars to be a conscious revival of this ancient practice.

There is a strong possibility that this German advertisement may have been inspired by compositions of polychrome inlaid wood, called intarsia, which were developed in Italy before the middle of the fifteenth century and for which such major artists as Piero della Francesca and Uccello willingly supplied drawings. Because of its associations with Roman nobility, Italian rulers such as the Duke of Urbino commissioned intarsia or inlay artists to decorate entire rooms of their palaces with this type of illusionistic art. Fra Vincenzo da Verona was active in designing optically deceptive inlaid decoration for the Church of Modena about 1480. Showing his mastery of complex perspective problems, in the panel illustrated (Fig. 381), Fra Vincenzo simulated a partially opened cupboard, whose latticed shutters angle toward the viewer with such convincing effect as to arouse the impulse to open them further or close them. Piled on the lower shelf are liturgical objects such as a cross and a censer, while the hourglass and skull above symbolize, as they had since antiquity, the theme of mortality and human vanity. Instead of depicting living and dead figures, the artist employed objects for his *memento mori.* The French art historian Charles Sterling, in his excellent history of still life, points out that inlay artists

Figure 380. UNKNOWN GERMAN ARTIST. *Cupboard with Bottles and Books.* 1470–80. Oil on wood, 41¾×31⅞". The Geib Collection, Rochester, New York.

utilized the most advanced techniques of perspective developed by fifteenth-century painters and geometers and that, ironically, their inlaid work in turn began to influence sixteenth-century painters to try their hand at illusionistic compositions which seem to advance toward the viewer.

Heir to the foregoing illusionistic tradition and subject matter that went back to ancient Roman mosaics, Caravaggio painted a solitary basket of fruit (Fig. 382) that, like the vivid relief of his figure paintings, was to have a substantial impact on seventeenth-century painting. This lowliest of subject matter, by artistic standards of the time, was boldly centered in

Figure 382. CARAVAGGIO. *Basket of Fruit.* c. 1596. Oil on canvas, 18⅛ × 25⅜". Galleria Ambrosiana, Milan.

Figure 381. VINCENZO DA VERONA. *Cupboard and Niche with Objects.* c. 1480. Wood inlay. Louvre, Paris.

the painting, preempting the customary place of a noble figure. Within this strong formal emphasis, the artist preserved the informal disarray of the fruit spilling over the basket and out of the picture. Rather than perfectly formed and fresh clean fruit, he showed fruit that was dust-covered and deteriorating from worms and the long interval required by the painting. Caravaggio was not appealing to the sensation of taste, nor was he moralizing by using the fruit to signify the transiency of life. Rather, he was giving a lesson in seeing, compelling his audience to look long and hard at what they ordinarily took for granted. That he finds the basket of fruit worthy of comparison with figure subjects may be supported not only by the time which must have been required for patient detailing of its properties but also by the fact of its illumination with the same kind of hard lucid light.

Caravaggio and the Spanish Carthusian friar Juan Sanchez Cotán furnish persuasive evidence that the serious painting of fruits and vegetables can satisfy both worldly and pious temperaments. Shortly before taking monastic vows, when he was about forty years of age, Cotán did a series of still-life paintings, and their sober profundity far exceeds in quality his sentimental religious figure paintings (Fig. 383). Like a second frame, he employs a stone window casement in which a quince and cabbage are hung near a melon and cucumber resting on

Figure 383. JUAN SANCHEZ COTÁN. *Quince, Cabbage, Melon, and Cucumber.* c. 1630. Oil on canvas, 25¾×32″. The Fine Arts Society of San Diego, California.

the ledge. The carefully staggered disposition of the objects suggests musical notation, but whether or not this was his inspiration, Cotán hit upon an ingeniously simple device to separate and dramatize the individual objects and their relationship. It is known that Cotán was interested in geometry, and this painting may have resulted from personal meditations on contrasts between shapes conceived in nature and the human mind. By cutting open the melon and using a niche which interrupts the strong cold light, he expands the variety of ways in which we can know his subject. The gradual advance of the objects from left to right culminates in the cucumber precariously balanced on the edge of the sill, so that the artist counteracts the impression of a monotonous horizontal alignment and seems to make a partial loan of one of the objects to the viewer's space. Caravaggio's testimony to the

worth of such a theme and the intriguing potential of emphatic side lighting must have encouraged Cotán to digress from his customary pious subject matter.

The seventeenth-century Spanish artist Francisco de Zurbarán, a contemporary of Cotán, exhibited a duality of interests that produced official religious and royal imagery as well as meditative still lifes. His art as a whole reflects the painter's existence at court and in the cloister, and it captures the domestic environment of objects. That Zurbarán carried over attitudes from one mode of life to another can be seen in his *Still Life with Four Vessels* (Fig. 384). Four beautifully made, variously shaped, but relatively modest objects are disposed along a stone ledge, like a litany, in a line parallel to the picture plane. This arrangement suggests an array of offerings placed before the altar in a Spanish cathedral of the time. The mood of the whole echoes, in inanimate fashion, that of Zurbarán's images of humble monks. Unlike Dutch paintings involving objects, this picture gives no suggestion of casual use or sociable situations. They are presented for serious contemplation, not unlike the monk's practice of meditating at length upon a single passage of Scripture. The symmetrical placement of the four vessels is deceptive, for Zurbarán was deeply aware of the individuality and worth of each object and elicited a range of contrasts far beyond the number and superficial appearance of the objects.

Oriental painting does not include the Western category of still life. Despite the fact that Chinese artists produced magnificent objects with a history of important religious and esthetic use in temple, tomb, and home, they never created entire paintings devoted to inanimate objects. Closest to Western still lifes of fruit detached from the tree is *Six Persimmons* (Fig. 385), by the Chinese artist Mu-Ch'i, who

Figure 384. FRANCISCO DE ZURBARÁN. *Still Life with Vessels.* 1633–40. Oil on canvas, 18⅛×33″. Prado, Madrid.

324

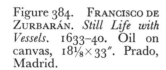

Figure 385. MU-CH'I. *Six Persimmons.* Southern Sung Dynasty, late 12th century. Ink on paper, width 14½″. Daitoku-ji, Kyoto.

painted in the late twelfth and early thirteenth centuries. Mu-Ch'i's six pieces of fruit, painted in ink on paper, are divorced from any setting or support; they hover in an undefined space as if suspended in the viewer's consciousness. It is only their proximity to the lower edge of the hanging that suggests a normal relation to a table or the ground, or at least an acknowledgment of the pull of gravity. (Because the painting has been cut, it is impossible to comment on the relation of the objects to the total field.)

The spiritual speculations of the artist are suggested by the fact that the persimmons are rendered in various stages of their life cycle. (For this reason alone, the French term for still life, *nature morte*, or "dead nature," would seem inappropriate.) The Chinese painter dealt only with living things, and he found the life cycle of the persimmon as important as that of man. Each fruit has a singular shape, tone, weight, density, and relation to the adjacent fruit. Unlike Zurbarán's regular spacing, the deployment of Mu-Ch'i's persimmons seems naturally informal. They are related by overlap, tangency,

and discrete intervals, yet these objects do not share even an invisible ground line. No two stems are the same, nor are their proportions and direction predictable. To alter any of the foregoing subtle relationships would be to disrupt their internal harmony in the eyes of a sensitive viewer. The many esthetic judgments made by Mu-Ch'i in his study of the persimmons resulted from sustained concentration and final revelation. Zurbarán's vessels and Mu-Ch'i's persimmons remind us that an artist's attitudes toward life may be manifested through the smallest, most modest subjects.

In the seventeenth century, painters of objects began to depart from the rigorous "inventory" style of alignment and to dispose them in more informal ways and with a greater sense of depth. A French painter named Bauguin, who derived much from Caravaggio, constructed a painting of objects that to his contemporary audience evoked the pleasures of the table as well as the gratifications of all the senses (Fig. 386). Their seemingly casual disarray implied recent use, and in a continuance of the illusionistic tradition of visual tricks, the mandolin seems to jut out toward the viewer's reach. In painting such as this, it is not the meaning or purpose of the objects that dictates their locations. Not trusting to gambler's luck, Bauguin invites us to discover his reasoned decisions for pairing and juxtaposing

Figure 386. BAUGUIN. *The Five Senses.* c. 1630. Oil on panel, 21⅝×28¾″. Louvre, Paris.

different objects, such as the repetition of fluted edges in the mandolin and purse, the geometric order of the gaming board and the disorder of the adjoining table area, the shape of a flower against the octagon of the mirror, the pure geometry of the glass versus the natural irregularity of the melon. Sophisticated audiences in the seventeenth century shared the artist's enthusiasm for visual perception and the exercise of intellect and would have appreciated the correct shadings of the mandolin calculated on the basis of the light source and varying surface angles and would have admired the mental calculation that produced musical and pictorial harmonies.

The object became central to painting in the late fifteenth and sixteenth centuries. In seventeenth-century Holland, still lifes were an art form of esthetic as well as symbolic significance. In contrast to the situation in Roman Catholic countries, the Dutch Protestant Church was not an important sponsor of art, and still-life paintings were developed to satisfy the needs and taste of a secular, largely middle-class clientele. These paintings were modest objects, intended for hanging in the home among other prized domestic possessions. Still lifes were also purchased as financial speculations, so that the Dutch artist, anticipating his modern counterpart, did not always know his future buyer. The esthetic subject matter and passive quality of the Dutch still lifes, in accord with the insulated atmosphere of the middle-class Dutch home, recall the tranquilizing effect of the pleasant objects and rural scenes painted inside urban dwellings of ancient Rome. It was from Dutch paintings after 1620 which described partially eaten meals, with their consequent suggestion of physical deterioration, that still another evocation of the themes of *vanitas* and death emerged. The Dutch love of finely painted objects testifies to a distaste for the passions of epic and dramatic images, which did not suitably reflect the secure and complacent character of Dutch culture and prosperity in the seventeenth century. The still-life paintings record Holland's acquisition of material wealth and an extensive overseas trade that returned to the home country exotic objects, foods, and wines. The fact that most Dutch still life refers to meals also makes of these paintings emblems of the Dutch pride in hospitality. They are fit companion paintings to portraits of affable Dutchmen who invite us to share their wine and company. There was a wide range of still-life painting, involving different types of meals and degrees of opulence or modesty, depending upon such factors as the different cities where they originated and their date. Toward the end of the seventeenth century, the still lifes were composed of more precious, exotic objects and began to display more complex arrangements and a more feminine air.

The Dutch enjoyed seeing inanimate objects organized in stable compositions. Objects were placed close to the viewer, as if soliciting him to share intimately the knowledge and experience of the artist. Both the painstaking creation and the appreciative seeing of the art was best accomplished while seated. Absorbing the satisfactions of a Dutch still-life painting demands the same kind of savoring as is required in doing justice to a finely prepared meal. As illustrated in a work by Pieter Claesz (Pl. 43), the Dutch artist and his patrons delighted in a calculated chaos that was very much unlike the pristine neatness of Cotán and Zurbarán. The objects are represented in disarray, as they might be seen after a meal by someone who had just pushed back from the table. A suggestion of the meal's original order and the timepiece at the left impart a slightly morbid touch of temporality. Before undertaking the painting, the artist spends a great deal of time thoughtfully arranging the objects in search of shapes that "rhymed," means of linking disparate forms and easing the eye's course through the painting, and an angle of illumination that offered a maximal range of values to set off both the materials and the shapes of the objects. Just as the highlight of the meal might often derive from a single tang, such as that obtained from a lemon peel, so was the painter's cuisine dependent upon perhaps a touch of brilliant color against a prevalent monochrome or within a narrow range of subdued tints. The transition from vertical to horizontal forms, from near to distant items, was accomplished through careful adjustment of objects and lighting. The drama ultimately became one of light, illuminating and annealing the multiple shapes and textures.

Originated in Northern Europe were both the theme of a meal spread on the table and its artificial illumination by a light source within the painting, such as a candle. In the seven-

Figure 387. GOTTHARDT DE WEDIG. *Still Life by Candlelight*. c. 1630. Oil on panel, 13½ × 10⅝″. Hessisches Landesmuseum, Darmstadt.

teenth century, meals for all times of day and all manner of cookery became subjects for painting. We can partially reconstruct gastronomic history and the art of table setting on the basis of still-life paintings. Just as they dazzle the eye and assault the salivary glands in painting, so the recipes for some great festive meals boggle the mind, and very likely stop the fainthearted with the first line: "Bleed two pigeons from the pigeon run . . ."; "Bone and stuff the blackbirds with juniper-flavored game . . ."; "Singe and scrape the head of a boar carefully, then bone it completely, taking care not to tear the skin. . . ."

Out of consideration for the novice chef, we shall offer a more modest repast, painted by the German artist Gotthard de Wedig (Fig. 387). His depiction of the single-edged cutting knife (which gradually supplanted the dagger) and wooden plate accurately reflect contemporaneous table setting, for the knife, fork, and spoon were not customary table equipment in Europe until the middle of the eighteenth century. Metal and porcelain plates such as shown by Claesz were slow to replace the wooden trencher of de Wedig's painting. Glassmaking, which originated in Italy, passed from Venice to Northern Europe, where local styles developed. The German artist shows off

a fine local wineglass with a sensible utilitarian base for those venturing beyond one drink. The fascination that objects held for still-life painters was comparable to that found in the human anatomy by figure painters. De Wedig wants us to see how a hinged top works, the differences between the two sides of a single-edged knife, the distinct ways that light passes through wax, an eggshell, and a yellow-tinted wineglass. As salt flavors the egg, so the painter complements the various related round forms with the crisscrossed bread and knife. Without the inherent mysticism of Cotán's work, Northern still life has a more robust sensual character.

By means of elegant objects, the French painter Pierre Subleyras fashioned an alter image of Francis I, Duke of Este and one-time commander of the French army in Italy (Fig. 388). The objects are indicative both of the attributes of the Duke and of the early-eighteenth-century ideal of a ruler. Francis I is visibly represented by a handsome marble bust carved by Bernini in 1651–1652. Ironically, the bust itself was made from its subject's portrayal in two paintings, so that we see the Duke ultimately through the eyes of four artists. The white gloves and red carnations

Figure 388. PIERRE SUBLEYRAS. *Still Life with Bust of Francis I, Duke of Este*. 1730–45. Oil on canvas, 4′5¼″ × 3′4″. The Minneapolis Institute of Arts.

resting on a finely embossed silver platter announce his courtly mien. The body of the exotic plumed bird refers both to his participation in the aristocratic pursuit of the hunt and to his taste for gourmet food. The armor and the astrolabe suggest his interest and prowess in military and astronomical science. The bronze sculpture of Hercules supporting the world reminds the viewer of Francis' ethical guide. The frightened woman and children in the painted background may signify the terrors of war and the threat to life against which the Duke stood as protector.

Subleyras' casual display of objects seems as if intended as an informal contrast to the highly ordered court life submitted to by the ruler on official occasions. Bernini's bust, moreover, shows a subtle combination of loosely flowing forms with the firm self-assured pose of the ruler himself. Both the painting and the bust epitomize the eighteenth-century aristocratic ideal of intermingled formality and informality—seeming one thing, but in fact being another.

The beauty of Subleyras' painting was in certain respects assured before the work was undertaken by the intrinsic quality of the objects chosen. This was art about art. In another eighteenth-century still life, however, a superior work of art was made of inferior objects. The French painter Chardin found in simple household utensils a source of wonder and matter for life-long exploration (Pl. 44). Even more than could specifically religious or political accessories, the objects chosen by Chardin reveal the strong morality of the painter. The sturdy basin or pitcher, worn and recolored from daily use, was for Chardin silent evidence of frugality, temperance, and constancy. It served his passionate interest in the mysterious effects of light upon material substance—in other words, reality as given to the eyes.

Like Zurbarán, Chardin aligned his objects on a shelf beyond reach and set out for visual research. Unlike the cool, dry, and hard surfaces of Zurbarán, Caravaggio, and Cotán, Chardin's warm and elusive equivalences of his subjects took shape not from firm outlines but from manipulation of light values and the viscous properties of his medium. The durable was created by the inconstant. With the exception of the works of Rembrandt, nowhere in the Dutch still-life painting that Chardin admired are we as conscious of the physical nature of the oil medium, the touches of the brush, and the sheer material substance of the painting's surface. From a few pigments, Chardin coaxed a rich gamut of tones such as those in the copper basin. When closely studied, these variegated tones contradict the initial impression of the basin's solidity and simplicity. Working without preliminary drawings, Chardin established each tone in response to minute sensations of light and dark given directly to the eye, as seen, for example, in the ladle at the left. The artist also expressed the forceful contrast between the pitcher's bulge and the concavity of the basin, the irregular edge of the cloth against the regular contour of the pitcher, and a rhythmic continuity by means of tangencies among the handle, basin, lid, and pitcher. The artist used the pyramidal climactic composition favored by academic painters of the time for exalted figure paintings. Instead of mounting a goddess or king at the apex of the whole, Chardin ironically gave this important place to a succulent side of meat hanging from a hook.

Subleyras and Chardin exemplify the distinction between "picture makers" and "painters." Picture makers, such as Subleyras, wish us to experience the object in a literal manner, to observe their success in closely matching the distinctive properties of objects in a seemingly airless space. It is as if one might reach out and pluck a flower from within the picture frame and thereby perfume the air. Neither the oil medium nor the hand of the artist intrudes upon the viewer's awareness of the illusion before his eyes. Painters such as Rembrandt and Chardin, while they create plausible illusions of objects, also impart to them visible evidence of artifice, the traces of oil and brush, and make it impossible to separate the object from its unique painterly environment.

Edouard Manet was a painter, not a picture maker. To enjoy his painting is to savor nuances of color and the subtle matching of tones, the tasteful dispersal of color accents over the field of the canvas, the bold application of shapes to the painting's surface. His paintings of objects were not intended as inventories or as incentives to philosophizing. Manet's constructions of broad, strongly edged, and relatively flat areas of closely linked tones appeal more quickly to the eye than do any of the previously considered paintings. The painted

Plate 45.   EDOUARD MANET. *Still Life with Carp*. 1864. Oil on canvas, 287/8 × 361/4″. The Art Institute of Chicago.

Plate 46.   JUAN GRIS. *Guitar and Flowers*. 1912. Oil on canvas, 44 1/8 × 27 5/8".
The Museum of Modern Art, New York (bequest of Anna Erickson Levene
in memory of her husband, Dr. Phoebus Aaron Theodor Levene).

Plate 47. ROBERT RAUSCHENBERG. *Broadcast.* 1959. Combine painting, 5′2″ × 6′4″. Private Collection, Milan.

Plate 48.   AGNOLO BRONZINO. *Portrait of a Young Man* c. 1535–40. Oil on panel, 37⅝ × 29½″.
The Metropolitan Museum of Art, New York (H. O. Havemeyer Collection).

fabric of Manet's objects and background is more apparent and more loosely woven than that of Chardin and the Dutch still-life masters. There is a more consistent awareness of the flat picture surface; breadth, direction, and twists of his brushwork call attention to the surface as well as to the object. Manet reserved the most brilliant tone for the small patch of the lemon off to one side. Less brilliant hues such as coppery brown and pinks occur more frequently than the yellow, but less frequently than the greys. Manet gave to the greys and whites, which fill the largest part of his painting, the greatest range of nuance. *Still Life with Carp* (Pl. 45) was painted for the cultured vision of a sophisticated, but at the time a limited, audience. The objects included were important not only because they set up challenging tonal problems, but also because in themselves their qualities created a discriminating and pleasurable esthetic experience.

Whereas Manet was content to accept the generally perceived shape, if not the tone, of objects, Cézanne insisted upon reexamining all properties of what he painted as if he were seeing the object for the first time. Cézanne could not unquestioningly repeat anything that was given to the senses, but instead he was impelled to re-form, recolor, and reorganize whatever entered within the boundaries of his canvas. Zurbarán and the Dutch could admire the craftsman's art in making handsome objects, but Cézanne felt no allegiance to the glass-maker, the ceramicist, or even to the farmer whose apples he painted (Fig. 389). His reconstruction of objects was motivated by a desire to search out their essence, to increase their visual interest, and to meet the particular compositional and expressive demands of the painting. Neither perversity nor ignorance of perspective techniques led him to reshape the compote into an asymmetrical, flattened oval; rather, his main consideration was the pictorial need of added coordination with the frame to increase the stability and visual weight of the composition. High-keyed tones at the upper left balanced the cloth at the lower right, and the dislocation of the base of the compote was necessary to harmonize with the assembled apples and glass. This meant stretching the basin of the compote.

Each successive decision made in the painting solved some esthetic or compositional problem raised in a preceding stage of the canvas rather than satisfied a concern with fidelity to the appearance of the object. Previous painters had allowed the objects to compose their paintings; Cézanne relied upon the criteria of painting to compose the objects chosen. The apples illustrate this point, for Cézanne realized them in paint both from the outside edge inward and from the inside out. The direction of their stroke-faceted surfaces was coordinated with, and must be seen against, the directions of the knife, the cloth, and the pile of fruit itself, and ultimately of all other movements in the painting. Each daub of the brush on an apple was calculated to fix the light value, hue, curve or flatness, warmth or coolness of a particular area of sensation. Any part of Cézanne's painting yields to the pull of adjacent areas because of the thoroughness with which all have been fitted together. Cézanne devised such blunted shapes as those in the mouth of the glass and the compote and used the ingenious connection of objects and touches of bright color to achieve an ambivalent relationship between the picture's surface and the objects in depth. Cézanne repeated the objects, but never his mode of painting them. The importance of Cézanne's contribution and the value of his art has been succinctly expressed by Meyer Schapiro:

> At the threshold of our century stands the art of Cézanne, which imposes on us the conviction that in rendering the simplest objects, bare of ideal meanings, a series of colored patches can be a summit of perfection showing the concentrated qualities and powers of a great mind.

Figure 389. PAUL CÉZANNE. *Still Life with Compote.* 1879–82. Oil on canvas, 18⅛ × 21⅝". Collection René Lecomte, Paris.

Fortified by Cézanne's assertion of the artist's obligation to restructure the visual world, the Cubist break with the imitation of the object as seen in nature was a relatively quiet revolution. Picasso, Braque, Léger, and Gris did not select radically new subject matter or issue violent manifestoes attacking those who represented the literal form of the object as perceived in three-dimensional space. At no time during Cubism's most important years (1909–1914) did these artists completely renounce the object. Their objects, however, were derived from a restricted and immediate area of their environment. More specifically, the objects were associated with a favored café, the studio, and the artist's home, the latter two frequently being one and the same. Old photographs of Braque and Picasso in their studios, made between 1910 and 1916, show walls, tables, and floor covered with randomly juxtaposed objects, and the object character of Braque's paintings themselves is stressed by their being on the floor (Fig. 390). The objects found in their paintings are not costly or rare possessions, but were prized for esthetic or personal reasons and were utilized in daily activities, often conveying an intimate sense of conviviality. Death, moralizing, personal crisis, world events, and so on were all excluded from Cubist paintings in favor of themes of simple, mostly domestic pleasure. Although the objects conveyed human sentiments, they were rendered in a way that showed the artists' unsentimental attitude toward the older tradition of still lifes. Nor did the Cubists ever arrange objects in the prosaic sequence of their original setting.

If we compare Bauguin's still life, *The Five Senses* (Fig. 386), with Juan Gris' *Guitar and Flowers* (Pl. 46), the significance of the Cubist revolution in form may become clearer. Bauguin follows the shapes, textures, and colors of the objects quite literally, whereas Gris asserts his right to rework all the objects in his painting. Gris has destroyed the closure and autonomy of objects, so that they fuse with other shapes or are joined in complex patterns on the painting's surface that have no natural counterpart. Color is not confined within distinctly bounded areas but is disposed in broader zones. The artist's brush strokes are similarly independent of the objects and are used to create decided directions, textures, and visual patterns that are

essential to the painting's structure. There is no manipulation of light and dark according to a fixed light source, as found in Bauguin's work, but an effect of flickering light and shadow is maintained within new rules laid down by the artist. It is difficult to look beyond (that is, to ignore) the surface of Gris' painting into a spatial volume as is possible with the seventeenth-century work. With the modern painting, one is very conscious of the artist's inventiveness in imposing a new structure upon objects (such as the guitar) that otherwise had remained unchanged for hundreds of years. Gris wants the viewer to be very aware of the constructed aspect of his work, in which no area is neutral or merely "fill." Space and object both become part of an intricate pictorial scaffolding that holds the composition tautly suspended within the frame. Bauguin could conceivably have finished the painting of each object separately, always keeping in mind their final appearance and arrangement. With Juan Gris and other Cubists, the artist began without such assurance, without such a fixed conception of the finished work, and while thus improvising moved back and forth over the whole picture surface at all stages of the painting's development. He continuously adjusted every element in the painting to its adjacent areas and the over-all design. It is this approach which requires that the spectator judge for

Figure 390. Georges Braque in His Studio. Maeght Gallery (LIFE Magazine © 1949 Time, Inc. All rights reserved).

esthetic rightness rather than for fidelity to the appearance of objects arrayed under light on a studio table.

By drawing our attention to the physical aspect of artistic creation, to the painting's pigment and strokes, Gris is also affirming the object character of the painting. Although he simulates some movement into depth and forward, we are conscious primarily of the painting's surface. The tangency of compositional elements with the edges of the canvas at various points and the many vertical and horizontal accents reiterate the physical dimensions of the painting. Gris does not depend upon the intrinsic or preexisting beauty of objects, but wrests esthetic value from each touch and from the firm and lucid total design he has invented. To appreciate his achievement demands not that the viewer try to reconstruct each object from seemingly scattered components in the painting, as if it were a jigsaw puzzle, but that he should savor the pleasures of the work in its painted parts and in the harmony of the whole. Gris' discipline and method may be compared to those of the musician, whose improvisations are governed by a profound knowledge of musical structure.

Georges Braque assembled pieces of a newspaper *(Le Courrier)*, a cigarette package with its government seal, and simulated woodtextured paper and pasted them to each other and to the paper surface over which he drew with charcoal (Fig. 391). Thus he chose not to simulate in painting materials that were flat in nature and susceptible of incorporation in his compositions. There were wit and playfulness in Cubist collage (pasted paper); here, for instance, Braque cut out a heart from a newspaper article about Italy and alliances. Use of daily newspapers helps to date these compositions and makes them quite literally of their time. The assembled objects were common and readily identifiable, linking the composite artistic image to the world of familiar activities. Unlike older illusionistic painting, Braque actually built his composition outward from the surface toward the spectator. With charcoal drawing he integrated the pasted paper segments with each other and with the white background, introducing shading for purposes of compositional accent without reference to a consistent light source as was seen in the Bauguin. Thus, even light and shade were now

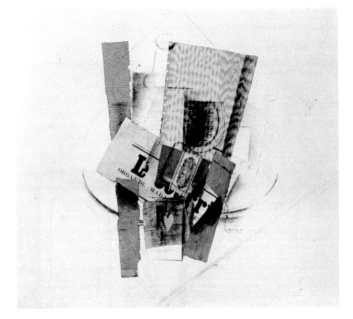

Figure 391. GEORGES BRAQUE. *Le Courrier*. 1913. Collage, 20 × 22½″. The Philadelphia Museum of Art.

Figure 392. HENRI MATISSE. *Gourds*. 1916. Oil on canvas, 25⅝ × 31⅞″. The Museum of Modern Art, New York (Mrs. Simon Guggenheim Fund).

made subject to the artist's will. It was the Cubists such as Braque, Picasso, and Gris who gave to modern art a declaration of independence—a freedom to choose what are the materials of art and how they may be used, without adherence to conventions about what was noble or faithful to the world of appearances.

It is unnecessary to refer to the original objects in order to evaluate and enjoy Matisse's *Gourds* (Fig. 392). Line, color, and composition, though influenced to a degree by his contact

Figure 393. GIORGIO DE CHIRICO. *Grand Metaphysical Interior*. 1917. Oil on canvas, 37 × 27″. Collection James Thrall Soby, Farmington, Connecticut.

with the visual world, became primarily personal inventions. The standards of control and quality in his art were supplied by Matisse's exceptionally good taste and dependence upon artistic intuition. *Gourds* gives itself immediately and fully to the eye as a fresh sensory experience, the viewer being affected before any reasoning process occurs. The choice, limited number, and forceful rendering of objects eliminates questions of their meaning. Their clarity of contour and careful dispersal without overlap emphasizes their familiarity and durability. The objects' internal coherence within the frame and the broad, flat areas of pure bright color quickly establish for the eye the rightness and importance of the total harmony.

Matisse "dreamed" of an art having "balance, purity and serenity." His imagery endures beyond the first moments of contact because of the range and provocativeness of his contrasts.

His shapes and colors possess a tenuous tie with the visual world. Painting from memory rather than from direct perception, Matisse liberated drawing and color from the specific properties of objects so that they in turn could release his feelings of joy and serve his views of expression in art. In 1908, the artist wrote:

What I am after, above all, is expressiveness. Expression to my way of thinking does not consist of the passion mirrored upon a human face or betrayed by violent gesture. The whole arrangement of my pictures is expressive. The place occupied by figures or objects, the empty spaces around them, the proportions, everything plays a part.

As with the term *espressivo* in music, we do not ask "expressive of what?" Matisse's drawing is expressive because behind its execution there clearly lie not only skill and taste but also strong will.

The irregularity of objects in *Gourds*, though also occasioned by the subtle demands of the painting's surface structure, does not extend to the extremes of the Cubist's manipulations. Matisse delighted in the formal completeness of objects as well as in the entire painting. Instead of the linear framework of the Cubists, he set up a seemingly loose dispersal of shapes on a strong asymmetrically divided blue-black background, achieving a daring balance of his few objects against their ground. The painting makes very effective use of intervals as well as of linear correspondences, and plays upon the visual weight of a color when seen in areas of varying size and in different contexts. New color chords, such as blue–black–reddish brown, were sounded in *Gourds*. These chords did not originate in established sequences before Matisse's eyes but came to him instinctively as he responded with pleasure to a particular tone he had set down. "I cannot copy nature in a servile way; I must interpret nature and submit it to the spirit of the picture. When I have found the relationship of all the tones, the result must be a living harmony of tones."

The Italian painter Giorgio de Chirico could not, in another sense, accept the visual world as a basis for expressing his views of reality. In de Chirico's *Grand Metaphysical Interior* (Fig. 393), the painting of objects involved fanciful images that were not imitated from what is given directly to the senses. The stimulus of external sensations was replaced by the artist's inner attentiveness to "strange sensations." The objects of de Chirico's painting can for the most part be inventoried and identified, but their context and connection elude definition. Indeed, what is crucial for the painter is that they *are* enigmatic. The objects are set in an interior which is not a room in the sense that it knows human presence. It is an interior because behind a window shade suspended at the right is not a blue sky, but a green exterior. Within this interior is a naturalistic painting of an Italian villa; the familiar exterior world is thus displaced, consigned to a picture frame to become one more inexplicable object. Painted with equal illusionistic precision in an adjacent framed panel are various normally unrelated objects. The framed panels are supported by a network of drafting instruments, ordinarily to be associated with rational design. De Chirico endowed these tools with obscure meanings that we can perhaps sense but cannot fix in precise terms. They have been used as part of a calculated irrationality. The light and shadow in the room and its spatial construction are also independent of traditional usage or the position of the viewer. Shadows, shapes, space, and the pervasive stillness make an uncanny ambient that is all the more compelling because of the convincing exactness of its rendering.

The word "metaphysical" in the title refers to de Chirico's belief that the artist should paint a higher reality than that of the senses. He therefore sought to restore mystery to art and to paint the obsessive hallucinatory images which he felt mirrored the state of his soul. He became alienated from the empiricism and pictorial rationale of previous artists. De Chirico's world is that seen when the eyes are closed— a cool, dry, inert, and uninhabitable environment meant to be traversed only by the eye. The intimate personal nature of his choice of objects is in contrast to the social and hedonistic connotations of those used in Cubism or in Matisse's work. ("I fill up the empty spaces in my canvas as the structure of the picture requires with a body or an object according to my humor.") Objects in older still lifes exhibited some unity of origin and use, involved some shared frame of reference. Perhaps influenced by Cubism and its collage technique, de Chirico's irrational dislocation and juxtaposition of objects from the everyday world he

distrusted were important in loosing the inhibitions and fantasy of later artists who felt that "to be true to oneself" in art demanded response to the fringes of consciousness and the deepest recesses of the self.

For Marcel Duchamp the meaning and value of a work of art depended on its interpretation in the viewer's mind. "The spectator brings the works in contact with the external world by deciphering and interpreting its inner qualifications and thus adds his contributions to the creative act." The painter of *The Bride Stripped Bare by Her Bachelors, Even* (Fig. 394) was against traditional notions of meaning, whereby the painting illustrates the title and is fully

Figure 394. MARCEL DUCHAMP. *The Bride Stripped Bare by Her Bachelors, Even.* 1915–23. Oil and lead wire on glass, 9′1¼″×5′9⅛″. The Philadelphia Museum of Art (Louise and Walter Arensberg Collection).

understandable on the basis of a preexisting common knowledge. *The Bride*, instead, was intended as a cynical commentary on art, the machine, reason, sentimentality, and sex. Duchamp's intentionally dry, academically precise painting of objects was meant to discourage praise of the virtuosity of his hand. He baffled attempts to trace the origin and meaning of his objects and deflated technology by producing irrational machines that do not produce. For those who may be seeking the sentiment suggested by its nominal subject, there is little likelihood of empathy with Duchamp's *Bride* or her "bachelors." Done during a period of personal crisis, *The Bride* is a complex metaphor or private myth, modern in its obscure personal origin, incompleteness, and ambiguity. Duchamp used his metaphor with wit in order to mechanize love and humanize the machine, to depersonalize art but

Figure 395. JASPER JOHNS. *Target*. 1958. Encaustic and newsprint on canvas, with plaster casts and wood, 4'3" × 3'8". Collection Leo Castelli, New York.

personalize the act of *viewing* art. Duchamp was giving form to what he called a "world of unknown quantity," of which the visible world is only a shadow. Art should be made, he felt, only by intuition and revelation. "The artist acts like a mediumistic being who, from the labyrinth beyond time and space, seeks his way out to a clearing."

The Bride consists of two glass panels mounted in an aluminum frame measuring roughly 6 by 9 feet. The shapes were applied to the glass with paint, varnish, and lead wire. (The cracks, of which the artist approved, resulted from an accident in shipment.) Technically, the work is marvelously made. Objects are not represented on the glass surface; they exist on the glass, as if knowing no other habitat. From Duchamp's notes, it appears that the top panel is the "bride," and the lower one the "bachelors." The "bride" herself, at the upper left corners, consists of intricate and suggestive plumbing forms. To the right is a perforated cloud shape. At the lower left are nine objects recalling those used in dry-cleaning plants; Duchamp called these his "malic molds," or "bachelor machine." Below them is "the slide," or waterwheel, on which one looked into an idealized extension of space. Duchamp painted his objects on the window so that, in looking through the glass, we see our own world, not one imagined by the artist. Within an object-filled room, the forms of *The Bride* seem to hover and move, existing in ever-changing contexts when viewed from different angles.

The art of de Chirico transposed familiar objects into unfamiliar situations. Duchamp invented objects that insolently parodied objects, human situations, and the body itself. *Target* (Fig. 395), a work by the young American artist Jasper Johns, is *itself* the painted object. There is no illusionism, and the painting has no reference to anything outside itself. The subject is a two-dimensional target coincident with the painted papered surface on which it exists. When the artist wished to introduce three-dimensional objects, he made plaster casts and closeted them in a row of boxes with movable lids set above the principal motif. He presents us with no riddle and asks only that his work be taken at its face value. Johns removed two-dimensional objects—in this case a target, elsewhere the American flag or stenciled numbers—from their accustomed surroundings and connotations. He did not, however, put them into de Chirico's uncanny and enigmatic settings. Johns exaggerated the vividness of the object through increased or intensified size, color, and texture. In short, he wished the viewer to have "a direct painting experience." Johns' position reflects the current view of art as an empirical experience for the viewer, with the work of art regarded as an independent object of entirely surface importance and brought into being by any means the artist may choose.

This permissive notion of means is illustrated in Robert Rauschenberg's *Broadcast* of 1959 (Pl. 47). From his New York environment the artist culled a host of objects that he brought together into "combines." The objects have a general character of personal souvenirs, like entries in a diary of the artist and the city. There is no illusionism of objects involved. As such, they have been used before in their everyday existence, and are used directly again in the combines. According to Rauschenberg, "A pair of socks is no less suitable to make a painting with than wood, nails, turpentine, oil and fabric." He combined a stuffed angora goat with an automobile tire, a stepladder with a thermometer, scraps from billboards with photographs of celebrities, mirrors, baseball bats, Coca Cola bottles, and, in one instance, live grass. His selection of objects was not indiscriminate but involved careful judgments of the eye. In *Broadcast* he mounted two working radios and adjusted them so that each can be tuned to only one station. One transmits news and sports, the other music. Near the radios are appropriate photographs of racing, police beating a rioter, and the word "Help." The improvisation of parts and the over-all structural effect of the paint produce a jazz quality in harmony with the sounds transmitted by the second radio. *Broadcast* is thus environment painting in a broader sense than we have heretofore encountered. Rauschenberg's combines are like fanciful time capsules, bearing witness for the future to his life and times. Rauschenberg has included smells and sounds along with sights, and the pathetic, comic, vulgar, and exuberant means by which modern society has expressed itself as brashly as the artist.

We began and now approach the end of this chapter with art made from discards—from the table, from the life of a city, and from a super-

Figure 396. ANDY WARHOL. *Campbell Soup Can.* 1962. Magna on canvas, 5′10″×4′6″. Leo Castelli Gallery, New York.

market. The first two share random and sophisticated composition while at the same time preserving the flavor of their sources. Both Heraclitus and Rauschenberg have given society's leavings a second, more durable life through art. The young American painter Andy Warhol's recent painting *Campbell Soup Can* (Fig. 396) infuriated not only the public but many critics and artists as well. Traditionally, artists have been their own worst critics. One is reminded of what Zola said about Manet, and if one is to enjoy Warhol's work, to be sure, it is necessary to forget a thousand things about painting, but there are some things from the past worth remembering on his behalf. The strongest criticism leveled against the work is that, aside from its magnified scale, the painting presents no imaginative transformation of the subject, no apparent exercise of artistic judgment. Such fidelity to the object has already been seen in seventeenth-century still life, however. And, while perhaps not of a high order, imagination was involved in both cases.

Warhol flattens out the can (which appears bent as is often the case when it has been opened), but in this respect his flatness of style belongs to this century and is characteristic of commercial as well as noncommercial art. (One might indeed argue that any painting put up for sale is an object of commerce.) In selecting a soup can, Warhol was doing much the same as Gotthard de Wedig when he selected an egg. The beautiful handmade objects of German and Dutch painting were of their time, and by selecting a mass-produced product and its container, Warhol continues such expression of his own era. If the artist continues to be free to choose any subject today, Warhol certainly has the right to draw inspiration from advertising or the supermarket. To the charge that painting such as this is all subject matter and shows no stylistic individuality on the artist's part, the answer is, historically, that in past centuries subject was often most important to the public and the artists themselves, and after the intial shock—or repulsion—toward the new subject matter has worn off, one can judge the painting on its esthetic merits or demerits alone. Furthermore, Warhol does not believe in individuality of style, and his calculated self-effacement before his subject is as old as the most naturalistic still-life picture making. The great irony is that for much of this century the public has cried out for art that it can understand and that clearly relates to its experience; yet when artists such as Warhol deliver what the public seems to have been clamoring for, this same public is outraged. Fortunately for Warhol, he has had more success than the Ford Motor Company had with its Edsel model, which was designed exclusively from exhaustive market research of the public's wants.

This introduction to the artist as a painter of objects has suggested the range of his performance, from imitator to creator to selector of objects; from fabricator of illusionistic familiar surroundings to inventor of new environments. He has ranged from playful deception through storytelling, personification, moralizing and philosophizing, metaphor and emblem making, esthetic contemplation, and meaninglessness. The painting of objects reflects great changes not only in style but also in man's attitude toward his environment— whether it be one of fear, reverence, wonder, curiosity, pride, dependence, distaste, or pleasure.

17

THE PORTRAIT IN PAINTING AND SCULPTURE

The artist knows the face in a way that differs from our knowledge of it. He must be conscious of how it is made, how features merge, taper, or swell, how colors work up through the skin's surface. He thinks in terms of distances and proportions, and how these change from area to area. Although modern psychology has taught us to be wary of physiognomic analysis in determining a person's character, the study of how an individual's features reflect his soul, spirit, or personality is an old concern of artists. Adherents of this "science" assume that the habitual set of the features, the angle at which the head is usually held, bodily posture, formation and gestures of the hands, and even clothing can be meaningful. The way a man sits or wears his coat has been an important consideration in artists' studies of personality or social status. In this century photography has preempted the portrait function, and many modern artists avoid portraiture because of demands for likeness and some degree of imitation that conflict with their personal esthetic. In the past, however, imitation had an honorable history and infused many powerful portraits without weakening their individuality of style.

If all that remained of ancient Rome was the sculptural portraiture of its citizenry, we should still have a significant record of that civilization. No people before or since the Romans indulged themselves so extensively in carved and painted portraits. Worship of and fidelity to one's ancestors and a healthy strain of egotism accounted for countless death masks and portraits for Roman home, tomb, palace, and forum. A *Portrait of a Man* (Fig. 397), from the Republican epoch, may have been a marble copy from a death mask, for the subject's cheeks are sunken and the flesh is pulled back in the mouth area as might be seen on the head of a dead man. Except for official effigies of their leaders, the Romans of the Republican period made no attempt to flatter themselves

Figure 397. *Portrait of a Roman.* 1st century B.C. (Republican). Marble, height 14½". Musei Vaticani, Rome.

and preferred to portray the stark, harsh evidence that living left upon the face. Since so much has remained of Roman culture, the weight that Romans placed on their values may be balanced against the testimony of the many surviving portraits. In theory, the citizens of the Republic and early Empire valued honesty and frugality, self-reliance, simplicity, firmness of purpose, and a gravity that revealed a sense of what was important. They believed in toughness and discipline, organization and a pragmatic approach to daily life. Roman literature reveals many and spectacular exceptions to these values, but the Roman conquest of the ancient world and the *Pax Romana* furnish much evidence that during the Republic and the early Empire many Romans did live by these elevated standards. The attitude of the sculptor toward his subject in the portrait here illustrated shows an honest and tough-minded desire to record the man's individuality, from the dented skull to his sagging jowls. The simulation of flesh and bone is a compelling achievement, there for us to touch. The natural discrepancies between the two sides of the man's face have been retained. Even with the eyes painted in, as they were in the original state, there would not appear to be any discrepancy between the shrewd gaze and the experience-worn features of the inner and outer man.

The third and fourth centuries of the Christian era witnessed the decline of the Roman Empire. It was in these centuries that sculptors and painters gave to the human face a sense of crisis which was at once individual and public. No comparably large body of portraiture from any single era exists in the history of art. The late-third-century portrait of a Roman (Fig. 398), perhaps a senator, was done at a time when the old material and religious values had fallen into disrepute and there was a search for new ideals in life and art. Portraits of men, women, and children conserved from a wide geographical area of the Empire reflect this climate of change. The artist and patron of this era show less regard for sensuous or material likeness. No longer is the surface supple and highly finished. Hair is synoptically treated by deep drilling and shallow cuts. The axis of the head has become rigidly geometric, and its structure lacks the flexibility or idiosyncrasy of earlier work. The face has lost

Figure 398. *Head of a Roman.* c. 265–285 A.D. (Imperial). Marble, height 15½″. The Museum of Fine Arts, Boston.

the traces or potential of mobility except for a single feature—the enlarged eyes, which animate these sculptures and reveal the formal change that underlined an attitude new to the ancient world. The eyes are set in conflict with the axis and disposition of the rest of the face. For Roman philosophers, the eyes were the gateway of the soul, and through their expression the sculptor could capture inner qualities and focus upon the spiritual life. No longer were men confident in their mastery of the physical world. There became apparent a conflict between the spirit and the body, the present and future life, not only in Christians but in non-Christians as well. In art, esthetic emphasis on physical attractiveness was reduced in order to impart metaphysical ideas more forcibly.

For almost a thousand years, from the end of antiquity to the end of the Middle Ages, the portrait conceived as a realistic likeness of a specific individual was not to be found in European art. Its return in the fourteenth and fifteenth centuries coincided with the emergence of naturalism in the secular art commissioned by royalty and a powerful, prosperous merchant and banking class in northern and southern Europe. There are no surviving paintings from antiquity that equal or surpass in anatomical exactness those of the Flemish painters in the fifteenth century. The modern writer Eric Ambler once wrote:

A man's features, the bone structure and the tissue which covers it, are the product of a biological process; but his face he creates for himself. It is a statement of his habitual emotional attitude; the attitude which his desires need for their fulfillment and which his fears demand for their protection from prying eyes. He wears it like a devil mask; a device to evoke in others the emotions complementary to his own. If he is afraid, then he must be feared; if he desires, then he must be desired. It is a screen to his mind's nakedness. Only a few men, painters, have been able to see the mind through the face.

Jan van Eyck, one of the earliest and finest portraitists in European art, was such a painter, capable of grasping the difference between the biological and the psychological in the human face. In his portraits of the 1430s, which number among the earliest easel portraits in art history, there is an amazing coincidence of technical virtuosity and powers of observation. In his portrait of Balduyn Delannox, known also as *The Knight of the Golden Fleece* (Fig. 399), no physiognomic detail escapes the painter's eye. Even the capillaries of the eyes are rendered. This face is not unlike a map in which all the inflections of the terrain have been microscopically recorded.

Van Eyck displayed great sensitivity to the mass of the head, which he accentuated by lighting most intensely that part of the face farthest from the viewer, with the near portion rendered in half-lights. Both the lighting and treatment of flesh reveal the painter's empirical study of the head structure, skeletal as well as muscular. The vivid and telling quality of the flesh is a result of extremely subtle tonalities, achievable in part because of the use of oil glazes, which both capture and repel the light.

Despite the impassive set of the sitter's face, there is drama generated in the visual intimacy achieved by van Eyck with the flesh and its unique biography. The subject's individuality is not proclaimed by specific action or setting;

rather, his dress, pose, undifferentiated background, and even the sparse props all suggest that he conforms to an aristocratic ideal of composure and dignity. His face is a silent residue of a life of action. It is as if van Eyck believed that the accumulation of an infinite number of details would provide the circumstantial evidence to identify the character as well as the physical aspect of his subject.

Four hundred years after van Eyck's painting, the French artist Géricault portrayed a number of insane patients of his friend Doctor Georget. This series was a project to demonstrate Georget's belief that insanity proceeded from physiological rather than psychological causes, and that pathological evidence could be obtained by close study of the face. The same discerning scrutiny with which van Eyck approached his sitter was thus employed for clinical purposes. The patients knew they were being painted, and they were allowed to dress and act as normally as possible. Nothing in the background, dress, or general pose of the portraits reveals that the subjects had been hospitalized. Géricault's task was to study and record the mask into which the face had been set, but also to mirror the grinding impulses behind it. In his portrait of a man afflicted with a monomania for theft (Fig. 400), Géricault brought to bear all his sensibility to subtle

Figure 399. JAN VAN EYCK. *The Knight of the Golden Fleece, Balduyn Delannox.* 1430–35. Oil on panel, 10¼×8″. Staatliche Museen, Berlin.

Figure 400. THÉODORE GÉRICAULT. *Portrait of a Kleptomaniac.* 1821–24. Oil on canvas, 23¼×19⅝". Musée des Beaux-Arts, Ghent.

color and surface inflections, thereby creating a painting of considerable esthetic as well as psychological value. The most obvious symptoms of the man's malady lie in his eyes and the sense of tension in his facial muscles.

Géricault's style, temperament, and interests were ideally suited for this project. His focus was often on subjects without external anchorage, figures who by force of circumstance were thrown back upon their own resources—men portrayed in action or in a state of tense inaction, an oscillation mirroring the severe political and social changes occurring after Napoleon's fall.

Géricault painted portraits of those who were, in a sense, victims of modern society; the Renaissance artist Raphael painted portraits of those comprising the elite society that flourished in the early sixteenth century. (Raphael was himself admitted into this society, marking the artist's increased social stature at that time.) The Raphael that best epitomizes the Renaissance social ideal both in style and subject is that of Baldassare Castiglione (Fig. 401). In a manner of speaking, the picture was made before Raphael took up his brush. The pose, which largely determined the composition, was probably a joint decision of the

sitter and the painter. Castiglione's treatise *The Courtier* set forth the requirements for the ideal Renaissance man—his skills, conduct, and objectives. Castiglione could have served as a model for his own book, since he was a poet, a brilliant scholar, and an outstanding ambassador and courtier. In the book, Castiglione comments as follows on his ideal: "besides nobleness of birth, I would that he have not only a wit, and a comely shape of person and countenance, but also a certain grace which shall make him at first sight acceptable and loving unto whosoever beholdeth him." The perfect courtier was also expected to be capable of feats of arms and hardihood, to have ingenuity and loyalty, and to be pleasant to every man, always witty and discreet. Everything that he did was to be accomplished with grace. On the clothing of the perfect courtier, Castiglione wrote:

A black color has a better grace in garment than any other color...and this I mean for his ordinary apparel....He ought to determine with himself what he will appear to be and so to apparel himself, and make his garments help him to be counted such a one, even of them that hear him not speak, nor see him do any manner of thing....Our Courtier ought not to profess to be a glutton nor drunkard, nor riotous and inordinate in any ill condition, nor filthy and unclean in his living.

Figure 401. RAPHAEL. *Baldassare Castiglione.* 1510. Oil on canvas, 32⅜×26½". Louvre, Paris.

Not only did Raphael faithfully record Castiglione's appearance and manner, but he also enhanced the man's grace and bearing by subtle plays of shadow and light. The pyramidal shape formed by the figure and locked within the frame ensures its stability. The figure's advancing left arm forms a gentle barrier between him and the viewer, a suggestion that is balanced by the more frontal face, which promotes a certain impression of cordiality without excessive intimacy. The careful, yet easy and unostentatious, placement of the hands further exteriorizes the man's inner grace—a matter of mind as well as of physique.

One of the great painters of sixteenth-century courtly life was Agnolo Bronzino, whose style, like that of Jean Clouet in France, was perfectly attuned to the tastes of his aristocratic Florentine clientele. His *Portrait of a Young Man* (Pl. 48) is the refined embodiment of Castiglione's ideal courtier, a comely man, discreetly elegant in dress, superbly in control of his body and feelings, and a gentleman of letters whose learning included art and architecture. In comparison with Castiglione's portrait, Bronzino's youth has a decidedly cool and more detached air, which seems to indicate the premium placed upon the social remoteness and exalted self-imagery of his elite group. Full comprehension of this portrait at the time of its creation presupposed as sophisticated a beholder as the subject himself.

The three-quarter format allowed more ample display of a manly figure and at the same time established the viewer at a greater distance than the bust-length portrait. It also permitted Bronzino to contrive a striking design involving the body, accessories, and architecture. The architectural backdrop underscores the youth's erectness, and its olive tones complement those of the flesh and costume. The purple tones of the table and chair, like those of the wall behind, are unnatural accents that reflect a taste for artifice. The entire painting is an ultrarefined study in contrasts, indicative of the fact that there is more here than meets the untrained eye. The youth's body is treated like an abstraction, its contours alternately smooth and irregular, the spine rigid and the wrists supple. The aristocratic attitude of the elbow posture has had added to it an affected spread of the fingers against the hip. The complex, even perverse interests of this society are suggested by the contrasts be-

Figure 402. PHILIPPE DE CHAMPAIGNE. *Portrait of a Man.* 1650. Oil on canvas, 35½×27⅜". Louvre, Paris.

tween the perfectly formed beauty of the subject's face and the grotesque carved heads of the table and chair arm. That such extremes of beauty and ugliness could derive from the same imagination intrigued Bronzino and his clients. An austere or ascetic appearance often masked highly sophisticated erotic imagination and indulgence in Florentine courts. The youth's costume, for example, has such features as a tight-fitting, constricting cut to the coat and an exaggerated codpiece.

Over a hundred years after Bronzino's portrait, the French artist Philippe de Champaigne painted his *Portrait of a Man* (Fig. 402), possibly the Huguenot leader Arnauld d'Andilly, with a conception totally lacking in courtly rigidity or subtle allusions. While making it a formal portrait, into his figure centralized within a simulated window casement Champaigne has introduced ideas that add naturalness without compromising the dignity of the subject. The man gracefully leans forward slightly beyond the casement and looks thoughtfully away from us, as if sharing in our space and light, yet discreetly held apart. Like still-life painters such as Cotán, Champaigne was interested in optical tricks, and he clearly meditated upon the light's revelation of the oval volume of the head just as the former might have studied a cabbage. The portrait's life-giving tension depends upon the suggestion that at any moment the man's lips will part in speech, his eyelids blink, or his relaxed fingers move lightly. The effect is as if the man has paused to reflect while conversing with the beholder. Champaigne's taste and dramatic skill caused him to make extensive use of cold greys and satiny blacks to prepare for the pleasurable surprise of the warm, sensual painting of the flesh. Unlike Bronzino's ageless and unmarked faces, Champaigne's portrait is built upon the evidence of vigorous use of the facial muscles, so that his subjects always convey the potential for great mobility of the features. The beauty of his discriminating brushwork in the man's robe is calculated not to compete with but to augment that which colors and shapes the features of the face.

An entirely different ethic of manliness and painting resulted in the seventeenth-century Dutch *Portrait of a Man* by Frans Hals (Pl. 49). Quiet reserve has given way to a warm and frank affability, a shared intimacy between viewer and subject. Calculated or affected composure is superseded by an appearance of good-natured

Figure 403. JEAN-AUGUSTE DOMINIQUE INGRES. *Monsieur Louis Bertin.* 1832. Oil on canvas, 3′10″ × 3′1½″. Louvre, Paris.

spontaneity. The Dutchman's dress, unkempt hair, casual pose, and complexion ruddied by excesses make him not a perfect courtier but the ideal male companion for his time and place.

Raphael's and Bronzino's smooth, immaculate picture surfaces, so in keeping with their subjects, has analogies only in the underpainting of Hals' portrait style. After painstakingly detailing his subject in a relatively tight surface treatment, Hals rapidly painted over the entire work in slashing strokes and ragged patches of color. Moreover, it is possible that by this late stage in his career Hals had dispensed with the underpainting. Raphael may be judged a superb picture maker, Hals a consummate painter. In contributing to the total effect, the material substance of Hals' pigment is as vivid as are the man's physical qualities themselves. Making no effort to fuse or disguise the touches of his brush, Hals set down a few brilliant highlights, rawly exposed. Against these key values, he scaled his other lights and darks. Unlike Raphael, he created strong esthetic accents that draw the eye away from the man's face—random touches that contribute, however, to the stability of the whole painting. No large, single-color area is unrelieved by traces of vigorous brush manipulation. The painter's gusto is apparent in the way he has avoided the staid architectural posture used by Raphael and instead twisted the hat, face, and body into angles opposed to those of the frame. Raphael's composition directly relates Castiglione to an impersonal ethical coordinate system. Hals' sitter seems to provide his own moral and esthetic axis.

In the nineteenth century, portraitists loosened the conventions of the genre and permitted their subjects to assume more personal poses. Portraits by Ingres and Manet show how a seated pose can be indicative of divergent personalities (Figs. 403, 404). Ingres had struggled unsuccessfully through many sittings to find the right pose to manifest the strong character of Louis-François Bertin, a newspaper owner. During a conversation with a friend, Bertin unconsciously assumed an attitude that caught the painter's eye, and even before a single stroke had been painted Ingres informed his client that the portrait "was done." The resulting portrait has the suggestion of some great predatory bird. The disarrayed hair, the attenuated nose, and the talonlike hands are not disguised but, rather, are accentuated. The man's ample girth is stressed, and Bertin quite overwhelms his chair. Even the wrinkled suit magnifies his energy. Ingres was at his painterly best not in the mythological or narrative scenes discussed elsewhere, in the chapter on nineteenth-century painting, but when he was face to face with a unique and strong-willed human being who inspired him.

One of the most relaxed and informal portraits in the history of art resulted from a visit by the poet Stéphane Mallarmé to the studio of a friend, the painter Manet. As they talked together, the artist decided to jot down in color the distinguishing gestures of his friend. With only a small piece of canvas at hand, he nevertheless had completed the portrait in a few hours by painting directly what he saw. No attempt was made to fit Mallarmé into a conventional portrait pose or an attitude of social correctness. The horizontal format, unusual in portraiture, derived from the situation. The poet is shown slouched in his chair and cross-legged, with one hand in his pocket and the other holding a cigar and resting on some papers. (Mallarmé believed that it was a good idea to put a little smoke between oneself and the world once in a while.) In his preliminary drawings, as well as in the final painting, Ingres wrestled for a month with every detail of his subject's face and clothing. Manet drew with his brush, and his rapid strokes established the color and direction of every surface. He did not graduate visual interest to a climactic point in the sitter' expression, and the painting of the poet's right hand is as eloquent as the entire face. Manet made no probing attempt to define the character of his gentlemanly subject beyond what was given readily to the eye. Frans Hals' impulsive way of laying on color and contenting himself with broad surface appearance had strong appeal for Manet.

The history of portraiture includes images not only of the living but also of the dead. The Spanish painter El Greco portrayed St. Jerome (Fig. 405) over a thousand years after the saint had died. El Greco's portrait is also the personification of an ethic, but a spiritual rather than a secular one. El Greco removed his figure from any specific setting, and as painted by the artist, the saint embodies the qualities of asceticism and inner vision. The aura of

Figure 404. EDOUARD MANET. *Portrait of Mallarmé.* 1876. Oil on canvas, 10¼×13¼". Louvre, Paris.

coolness that characterizes the painting is due both to the stark whitish light pervading it and to the artist's concentration on the other-worldly reflections of the saint, who seems to pause as if contemplating what he has written. The attenuated head and body exteriorize El Greco's concept of spiritual enlightenment.

Figure 405. EL GRECO. *St. Jerome.* c. 1600. Oil on canvas, 43⅝×37⅝". The Frick Collection, New York (copyright).

Figure 406. Vincent van Gogh. *Patience Escalier*. 1889. Oil on canvas, 27¾ × 22¾". Collection Chester Beatty, London.

The portrait is an exhortation to pursue the contemplative life that ignores physical comfort. The head and hands of the saint are like magnetic poles, and El Greco does not let the eye tarry over what intervenes. Despite the figure's quiescent attitude, the painting is veined with tension rather than repose. The activity of the light on the cardinal's robe, the angle of the beard in relation to the head, and even the suggestion of the body beneath in relation to the garment all give a taut feeling to the whole.

Van Gogh's painting of an old French peasant, *Patience Escalier* (Fig. 406), forms an interesting modern counterpart to El Greco's saintly image. Van Gogh wrote of this painting:

> Instead of trying to reproduce exactly what I have before my eyes, I use color more arbitrarily so as to express myself more forcibly.... I think of the man I have to paint, terrible in the furnace of the full harvest, the full South. Hence the strong orange shades, vivid as a red-hot iron, and hence the luminous tones of old gold in the shadows.

Van Gogh could never have painted a person or thing he could not see before him. He did not paint the saints of Church history but, instead, made holy the ordinary people he painted. The area behind the old man's head has the color not of the sky but of the soil of Provence. This venerable peasant has been beatified through his lifelong contact with the earth. The arbitrary local colors introduced into the face convey van Gogh's love for the man, and the identity of every feature is fiercely insisted upon through drawing as well as color. The brush strokes in the face are directed like a magnetic field, pulling the viewer's gaze toward the man's expressive eyes, which give eloquent testimony of his humanity. The worn hands further testify to a life of travail, marked by infinite patience and endurance of suffering. The painting is over life-size, which in itself might be construed as a gesture of love and friendship by the artist. Unlike El Greco's distant and unapproachable *Saint Jerome*, the old peasant absorbs the viewer in his human personality and warmth. Van Gogh gave to a man on the lowest rung of the social ladder charismatic properties that in the Middle Ages had been reserved for images of Christ and the saints.

For the sculptor Auguste Rodin, the making of a portrait demanded an all-encompassing knowledge of his subject. Every inflection of the head had to be searched out, felt as well as seen. When he began to work, an exhaustive study was made of every view of the head, even as seen from above. When these successive views were joined, he had an accurate physical resemblance. But what gives Rodin's superb modeling its final power is the revelation of character. In his head of the poet Baudelaire (Fig. 407), there is more than just a precise rendition of skin and skull; there is an unbearable intensity of expression in the taut mouth and transfixed eyes. The unformed lumps on the forehead were a final, sculptural touch, unrelated to real anatomy, yet crucial to bringing the effigy to life. Unusual in the whole history of portraiture is the deliberate severance of the head from both the neck and the chest; but Rodin sought to create a portrait of a poet who lived completely the life of the intellect. The head is tilted upward as if the poet's gaze were directed toward some invisible horizon of his own thought. Paradoxically, Rodin, who could only model from living examples, made a compelling spiritual portrait of a man he had never seen and who had been dead for some thirty years when this bronze head was cast. He had found a young artist who resembled Baudelaire and had resorted to photographs of the poet for guidance. But

Rodin also knew the poet's life and work by heart, which gave him insight into his subject's complex personality. His own description of the portrait reflects a strongly psychological interpretation of facial features:

It is not Baudelaire...but it is a head that resembles Baudelaire. There are a series of characteristics that...preserve the cerebral conformation that one calls the type; this bust is of a draftsman named Malteste who shows all the characteristics of the Baudelairean mask. See the enormous forehead, swollen at the temples, dented, tormented, handsome nevertheless, the face described at length by Claudel; the eyes have the look of disdain; the mouth is sarcastic, bitter in its sinuous line, but the swelling of the muscles, a little fat, announces the voluptuous appetites. In short, it is Baudelaire.

The finest art of the twentieth century has included relatively little portraiture. The best portraits that have been done have been intimate and probing studies of unstable individuals. Twentieth-century artists have generally turned away from portraiture because of traditional demands of fidelity to the subject and have chosen instead subjects or areas that fulfill their personal notions of what art should be. The Swiss-born sculptor Alberto Giacometti was an exception to this avoidance of portraiture. From his earliest works, he carefully studied the human face, almost exclusively that of his young brother Diego (Fig. 408). Giacometti wrote:

Sculpture, painting, and drawing have always been for me the means by which I render to myself an account of my vision of the outer world and particularly of the face....It is utterly impossible for me to model, paint, or draw a head... as I see it, and still, this is the only thing I am attempting to do. All that I will be able to make will be only a pale image of what I see.

From this statement we learn that his sculpture was meant to satisfy Giacometti alone. His dilemma and inspiration lay in a fascination with his elusive vision of the external. He was not trying to penetrate the surface and to reveal a man's character. For Giacometti, the problem was that when he focused on a detail, he tended to lose sight of the whole, and when he looked away from the live model to the clay he was shaping, he struggled to remember what he had seen. Given his portrait of Diego, the complexity and precariousness of Giacometti's art is manifest. *Diego* has an almost Egyptian remoteness, like an order of being unto itself. The fixity of this state is paradoxically achieved through an inconstant surface; the more closely we examine the head, the more remote it seems to become, for no part is a literal match

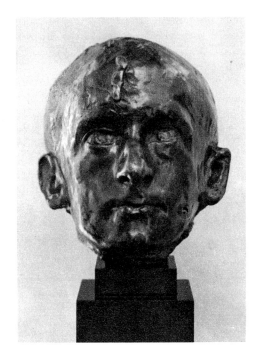

Far left: Figure 407. AUGUSTE RODIN. *Head of Baudelaire.* 1892. Bronze, height 8". Indiana University, Bloomington (gift of Mrs. Julian Bobbs).

Left: Figure 408. ALBERTO GIACOMETTI. *Diego.* c. 1955. Bronze, height 15½". The Walker Art Center, Minneapolis, Minnesota.

for the surface or features of the actual face portrayed. For Giacometti, each face has a dual existence: the first is the face he observes; the second is the face which he sees in his imagination and which constantly eludes him. Therefore, to him, the finished sculpture is invariably an unhappy compromise.

PORTRAITS OF WOMEN

Until the last quarter of the fifteenth century, Italian portraits of men and women tended to be in profile, because the nobility of that era preferred to have only half the face committed to posterity. This preference for the profile portrait was influenced by ancient coins and medallions that bore profile effigies of rulers. The significance of antiquity's attraction for Renaissance society is shrewdly put by Johan Huizinga in his book *Homo Ludens: A Study of the Play Element in Culture:*

> If ever an elite, fully conscious of its own merits, sought to segregate itself from the vulgar herd and live life as a game of artistic perfection, that elite was the circle of choice Renaissance spirits....The game of living in imitation of Antiquity was pursued in holy earnest....The whole mental attitude of the Renaissance was one of play....This striving...for beauty and nobility of form is an instance of culture at play. The splendours of the Renaissance are nothing but a gorgeous and solemn masquerade in the accoutrements of an idealized past.

This elite segregation and search for beauty and nobility of form is manifest in the design of fifteenth-century Florentine palaces as well as in profile portraits. Renaissance palace designs were inaccurate attempts to revive the principles of ancient Roman palaces. Both art forms may be conceived of as the public, social façades of their owners. Neither encourages a feeling of intimacy with the viewer. The relevance of such a comparison is apparent in Alberti's Palazzo Rucellai (Fig. 304) and Piero Pollaiuolo's *Portrait of a Young Lady* (Fig. 409). In the profile portrait the sitter is caught in an attitude that is permanently aloof and detached. A background of blue sky serves to elevate the figure beyond earthly reference. The careful setting of the head within the picture area and the broad-based tapering form created by the pose add to the stability and dignity desired by the patron. While the profile pose eliminates the possibilities of a searching psychological study of the face, it encourages a stress on the esthetic grace of the subject. Renaissance costumes and tastes share a certain cool, reserved surface elegance. The woman's tight-fitting bodice, upswept hairdo, and plucked eyebrows create a pronounced rhythmic sequence and a continuous graceful silhouette. There is no strong accent, modeling, or coloring of the face within its contours, so that emphasis remains upon the edges. The cosmetic fashion favored an artificiality that disguised the natural potential of the flesh. In her grooming and costume the woman has herself altered nature, and it might be said that the artist continues in this spirit.

Rubens' ideal woman, as seen in his portrait of Susanna Fourment (Pl. 50), enhanced her natural endowments with graceful and revealing clothes whose sensual textures flattered those of her flesh. She neither affected an imitative role nor held herself aloof, but was desirable in personality and body. To give fullest expression to the charms that delighted his eye, Rubens used a three-quarter frontal pose, which was at once modest and alluring. The vitality of the woman and her outgoing personality are set off with a turbulent sky and a splendid hat, which it has been suggested was perhaps a

Left: Figure 409. PIERO POLLAIUOLO. *Portrait of a Young Lady.* c. 1475. Tempera on panel, 19¼× 13⅞". The Metropolitan Museum of Art, New York (bequest of Edward S. Harkness).

Figure 410. PIERRE AUGUSTE RENOIR. *Madame Henriot*. 1877. Oil on canvas, 27⅝ × 21⅝". The National Gallery of Art, Washington, D.C. (gift of the Adele R. Levy Fund, Inc., 1961).

He is also the first portraitist to paint the face as we actually tend to see it. Because, in focusing upon the whole area of the face and body at one time, whatever is not central in our range of vision is less sharply defined, Renoir does not paint the woman's hands with the same definition as the eyes and nose, which are the focal points from which the portrait was done. This softening of peripheral areas, of the woman's outline, serves also to heighten her charm. The fine nuances of delicate color evoke associations with perfume or cosmetics and the attractive effects of these small sensations of sight and smell.

Cézanne's portrait of his wife seems at first to lack the outgoing qualities and warmth of the other portraits we have considered (Fig. 411). Many have compared, unfavorably, his depiction of women to his painting of bottles, saying that he displayed no more feeling for the one than for the other. Cézanne was not without feeling toward his human subjects,

flattering recollection of the umbrellas or canopies under which royalty was accustomed to stand. It is possible for the viewer to enter into a private dialogue with Rubens' sitter. This, unlike Pollaiuolo's portrait, was a very personal painting, portraying a close friend whose younger sister Rubens was later to marry.

Rubens formed his subject of rich color, tempered or heightened by soft shadows and brilliant highlights. The astonishing range of his brushwork is revealed in the broad treatment of the sky and large areas of the sleeves, the more tightly executed forms of the feathers and hair, the subtly graded strokes in the flesh, and the deft touches that created highlights in the earrings and eyes. Both the outpouring and restraint of feeling in the completed painting would seem to reflect the mood of the woman portrayed.

Rubens' passionate portraits found a nineteenth-century counterpart in Renoir's sympathetic painting of beautiful women such as Madame Henriot (Fig. 410). The gifted portraitist can convince us that he is at once painting an individual and a type. Renoir presents us with a woman who is French in such a way as to create an ideal of the French woman.

FIGURE 411. PAUL CÉZANNE. *Madame Cézanne in the Conservatory*. c. 1890. Oil on canvas, 36¼ × 28¾". The Metropolitan Museum of Art, New York (bequest of Stephen C. Clark, 1960).

however. In portraits he presents them as introverted, passive types, seemingly with infinite patience. (The endless hours they were required to sit for the artist would require such forbearance.) Accurate or flattering likeness was not enough for the painter, and he struggled with adjusting his figure to her surroundings. The tilt of the head and broad directions of Madame Cézanne's body are picked up in the tree and wall behind her, thus effecting a total harmony of the woman and her place. In this unfinished painting, the stages of its construction are still evident; the artist proceeded from a sketchy outlining and thin filling of color areas to a deepening and saturation of color as seen in the area of the shoulders. Even the angles of the brush strokes reiterate the major axes of the body.

The joyous hedonism of Rubens and Renoir was shared by Henri Matisse, as attested in a portrait of Madame Matisse, commonly known as *Woman with the Hat* (Pl. 51). Like Susanna Fourment, Madame Matisse wears a glorious hat piled high with flowers. Matisse did not insist upon a climactic facial focus, as did Rubens. It is not the flesh nor a mood of enticement that Matisse celebrates in this painting of his wife. He has painted her as a warm esthetic delight. Her face is handsome and sympathetic, a strong, quiet foil for the riot of color and movement around her. Matisse painted ecstatically and unfettered color from previous obligations to modeling and texture. Rubens accentuated and modulated his bright colors by placing them next to subdued hues or by setting them in partial shadow. The flat areas of bright color in Matisse's painting are modulated only by degrees of saturation; they range from pastel greens and pinks to full-bodied orange-reds and purples. The large color patches of the background complement others within the figure and serve as blocks to stabilize the form within the frame. Setting aside the finesse of brushwork of which he was capable, Matisse applied his paint with a raw haste, scrubbing and striping to effect the immediate release of his exuberant feelings. He dispersed his color accents according to the needs of esthetic structure—thus making the painting, like Madame Matisse's hat, a beautiful bouquet of color sensations.

Sculpture as well as painting has recorded many faces of women, with some of the finest portraits dating from as early as Egyptian times. From the ruined workshop of an Egyptian sculptor who lived in the fourteenth century B.C. has come an unfinished head of Queen Nefertiti (Fig. 412), the wife of Akhenaten (Amenhotep IV), the pharaoh who broke with the religious traditions of Egypt and acknowledged only one divinity, that of the sun. He also broke with tradition in demanding that the artists humanize himself and his family in their work. Consequently, this sculpture is an image both of a queen and of a handsome woman. The upper portion of the sculpture was to have been fitted with a crown that would have continued the diagonal line of the tilted face. Marks on the stone indicate that the eyes and eyebrows were to be painted in and also that the artist produced the face in perfect symmetry by dividing it exactly in half. Completed Egyptian stone sculpture portraits were usually fully painted. Despite his recourse to stylizations such as that of the eye, the artist gave to the

Right: Figure 412. *Queen Nefertiti.* 14th century B.C. Limestone, height 13″. The Egyptian Museum, Cairo.

Far right: Figure 413. GIANLORENZO BERNINI. *Costanza Buonarelli.* 1636–39. Marble, life size. Museo Nazionale, Florence.

obdurate surface of the stone sensitive undulations that imply direct observation of the Queen. A quiet sensuousness accompanies the serene dignity of the Queen. Whether seen full face or in profile, the portrait has an immutable self-containment and permanence of mood, in fulfillment of Egyptian art's purpose of assuring the subject a tranquil eternal life.

Very different from Nefertiti's portrait is Bernini's bust of his mistress Costanza Buonarelli, done in the seventeenth century (Fig. 413). The visage of Nefertiti transcends the temporal world; Bernini's woman is decidedly of the moment. She is rendered in movement, as if on the verge of speaking. Bernini re-created her as an impressionable, vital person. In removing the extraneous stone, he also lifted off all that masks the private, unguarded, and impulsive facets of woman's conduct. The intimate emotional nature of the relationship between the sculptor and the woman is hinted in her rather disheveled garment and hair, which seem to be extensions of an internal excitement. As a sculptural form, the bust knows no symmetrical blocklike confines but boldly twists into the space about it. The silhouette is irregular and agitated yet carefully controlled to return the eye to what lies within it. The iris of the eye is incised to complete the surface reception of light. Bernini's figures presuppose some unseen presence outside themselves to receive the outpouring of their feeling and action.

Constantin Brancusi worked through what he considered layers of superficial appearance in order to find essential, seminal forms, such as the ovoid of the egg, by which to prove his private belief in the underlying unity of living forms and to realize an absolute beauty characterized by simplicity, purity, and equity of existence. He used reduction in facial detail and arbitrary redesigning of the features in his bronze portrait of Mlle. Pogany (Fig. 414). He stripped away those very characteristics and idiosyncrasies of the woman's face which so delighted Bernini; and by rearranging his subject, he created an impeccable clarity and continuity of rhythm and shape. The head has been contracted into a simple egg shape. Trained in a Budapest art academy, Brancusi abjured its surface virtuosity and naturalistic fidelity that produced what he called "beefsteak" art. He insisted upon the hard, smooth,

Figure 414. CONSTANTIN BRANCUSI. *Mademoiselle Pogany*. 1913. Bronze, height 17¼". The Museum of Modern Art, New York (Lillie P. Bliss Bequest).

closed, reflective surface inherent in metal, which alienated the work of sculpture from the Baroque ideal of intermingling art and visible reality.

The expressiveness of the head lies not in animation of the features and flesh but in its total gesture, in the constantly changing reflections on the polished bronze surface, and in the evocative power of the design. The self-containment of the composition harmonizes with the quiet, introspective withdrawal of the woman. The sculpture retains a quality of "likeness," but its measure has become that of the work of art against the spirit of the woman and Brancusi's personal ideal of beauty.

MARRIAGE PORTRAITS

The double portrait, already known in Egyptian and Roman times, has occurred quite often since the fourteenth century. The type of double portrait to be considered here is the marriage portrait.

Giovanni Arnolfini and His Bride (Pl. 52) was painted in 1434 by Jan van Eyck. The painting depicts a private wedding ceremony that took place in the bedroom of the bride of a wealthy Italian banker living in Flanders. The presence of witnesses is inferred, one of whom was the painter himself, indicated by the inscription above the mirror, "Jan van Eyck was here." Until the sixteenth century, two people by mutual consent could contract a legitimate marriage outside the rites of the Church. Van Eyck's painting is more than a superficial document of the occasion; quite literally, there is more than meets the eye in this portrait. It exteriorizes all the implications of the union of man and woman; in order to accomplish this, van Eyck used a setting filled with objects whose symbolic connotations were well known to members of his society.

The bride and groom are shown full-length, standing in the center of the room with hands joined. To show the entire figure in a portrait requires a greater interval between viewer and subject; consequently, less area is devoted to the face. Despite this diminished area, the facial characterizations are strong. Van Eyck did not attempt to flatter the groom, whose morbid sensuality and equine resemblance come through strongly. The man is shown as the dominating figure by his frontal pose and solemnity, while the bride turns toward him in deference. Some have mistaken the proportions of the bride for signs of pregnancy, but in actuality she is holding the folds of her voluminous long skirt up to her waist.

The choice of the bedroom as the setting for the event and the painting was symbolic, for it was sanctioned by a long religious tradition as a nuptial chamber. Northern medieval painting usually showed the Annunciation to Mary as occurring in her bedroom. The lighted candle in the chandelier relates not only to a masculine symbol but also to its use in marriage rites and its implications of divine light. The dog is a sign of fidelity and, possibly, of passion. (On medieval tombs, a dog was placed at the feet of its master to serve him in death.) The light filtering through the window may have alluded to the purity of the bride. The mirror directly above the joined hands of the newlyweds was a symbol of the all-seeing eye of God, and its presence is like a celestial notary seal. Within the convex mirror are seen in miniature more of the contents of the room than are evident in the rest of the painting. Its spotless reflection of reality made the mirror a symbol of truth. This use of the reflected objects permitted a second wedding, that of the visible with the invisible. Poetic extensions of the figures themselves, the objects serve to identify the locale and to symbolize the hidden spiritual and sexual relationships.

Oskar Kokoschka's portrait of the newly wed Hans Tietze and his bride Erica (Pl. 53), painted early in this century, does not depend upon elaborate symbols, setting, witnesses, or prescribed gestures to show the bond that exists between man and wife. The picture is given no specific locale; the figures are seen as if in terms of their self-awareness. The painter's intuitive expression of their feelings resulted in the absorbent, measureless space around them, the warm ephemeral colors, and the wiry, scribbled lines etched into the paint surface about the figures by the hard end of his brush.

The hand gestures suggest a bridge between the man and woman, but it is an incomplete span, since, significantly, the hands do not touch. Kokoschka seems to have sensed an unbreachable gulf between the two, their essential isolation. In contrast to Giovanni Arnolfini, Hans Tietze is the more dependent member of the couple. His profile pose, slightly shorter height, lack of his wife's relative self-containment, all seem to bring to the surface certain private weaknesses. This was not a posed portrait; Kokoschka studied the movements and character of his subjects, as he searched for the moment that permitted him to pierce the social veneer. He valued the awkward gestures impelled by inner forces, as tangible surface evidence of the existence and power of the subconscious. What he presents is even more private and less decipherable than what would find outlet in his subjects' diaries. Kokoschka suggested, but never circumscribed, the ultimate complex depths within individuals in their relation to themselves and to others. Working in Vienna while Freud was teaching there, Kokoschka's findings were made in his own, visual terms and furnished yet another instance of modern artists' attainments in the study of man, independent of contemporary science.

SELF-PORTRAITS

Having seen examples of the portrait artist's purpose to serve others, we may conclude with the artist's study of himself. At sixty, Leonardo da Vinci approached the drawing of his own countenance with the same curiosity and discernment that he brought to his observation of nature. In many respects, his drawing (Fig. 415) is an objective likeness, but Leonardo accentuated his eyes as the focal point of the work. The eye was an endlessly fascinating organism for Leonardo, who was amazed that within its small dimensions the whole external world could be perceived. In the drawing there is a graduated focus from the cursory outline of the top of the head and the broad undulant treatment of the beard through the darkening and increased detailing of the brows, mouth, and nose and culminating in the deeply recessed and shaded eyes. The head is a summary of studies of bone and muscle structure, as well as of the painter's curiosity about the operation of the mind behind the face. The beard recalls the new modes of drawing Leonardo developed to capture flow of water and the upheaval of dust clouds. Just as he made painstaking studies of the action of weather on the earth's surface, so also Leonardo set down in closely matched sequences of thin parallel lines the effects of age upon his face. He made no attempt to elicit sympathy or to further a personal inter-

Figure 415. LEONARDO DA VINCI. *Self-portrait.* 1510–13. Red chalk. Biblioteca Reale, Turin.

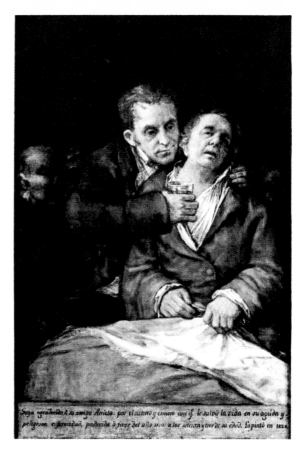

Figure 416. FRANCISCO GOYA. *Self-portrait with Dr. Arrieta.* 1820. Oil on canvas, 45½×31″. The Minneapolis Institute of Art, Minnesota.

change between himself and the viewer. Significantly, he omitted reference to his hands and the upper part of his body. He drew attention exclusively to the fountainhead of his extraordinary ideas and visions.

The Spanish painter Goya has left perhaps the most poignant self-portrait of any artist, which is at the same time a moving portrait of a man practicing his profession (Fig. 416). As a young man he had often depicted himself as a gentleman artist, a dashing and romantic figure. After the age of forty, when he was beset with such personal afflictions as deafness, his self-portraits changed and became searching examinations of his face for signs of insanity. In 1810 he became gravely ill and would have died but for the skillful ministrations of his doctor. Art history is filled with works commissioned as ex-votos, or offerings of thanks from the cured to their patron saints, Christ, or the Virgin. Goya dedicated this painting to his physician, inscribing it with the following words: "Goya thanks his friend Arrieta for the sureness and care with which he saved his life from the serious and dangerous illness suffered

351

at the end of the year 1819 at the age of seventy-three. Painted in 1820." In this amazing self-study, Goya shows his own total helplessness and vulnerability to death. The doctor tenderly supports him with one arm and with the other hand offers the dying man a glass of medicine. In the background at the left are a priest and possibly Goya's housekeeper. The wild head at the far right barely visible in the darkness at Goya's shoulder may symbolize Death or one of the apparitions of the artist's fevered mind. By honoring the doctor with his portrait as a man who thoughtfully and humanely practiced his profession, Goya brought to art the first image of the artist's private emotional turmoil, at a time when like other men his mind and body had broken down and he was at death's door.

Another Spanish painter, Joan Miró, has left an intimate self-portrait of a different nature (Fig. 417). Goya had rendered himself as someone else would have seen him during his crisis. Miró drew directly his part intuitive, part mental self-image at a time when because of poverty and hunger he suffered hallucinations. Drawing partially from a reflection in a convex mirror, he gave free play to fantasies induced by irritability at the sight of his own features. Miró could not be neutral toward any part of the head, and he found in each feature of his face deeply personal as well as playful associations expressible only in his unique pictorial language. He did not superpose his invented forms on the face but made them an integral part of its new structure. He exaggerated the asymmetry not only of the face, but of each pair of features. Weight, texture, shape, and tangibility have been consistently reworked,

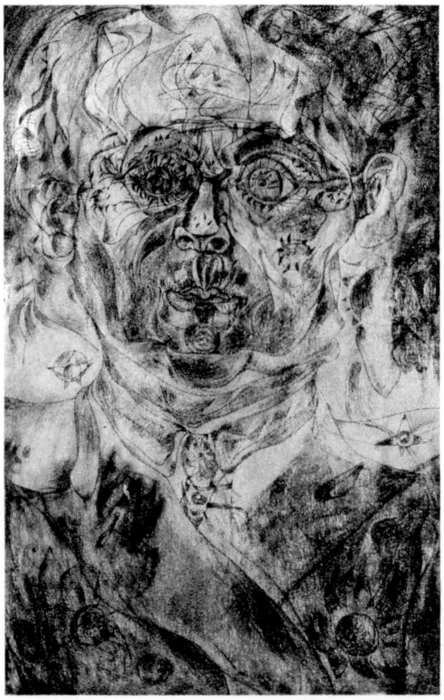

and the artist inverted or parodied functions. He was drawn to openings in the head and accented their existence, as in the mouth, also suggesting their relatedness to other parts of the body. Lines such as found in the hair and eyelashes caught his interest and were transformed into knifelike projections. Miró used the facial muscles as a point of departure for self-involved, fanciful configurations. The forehead erupts into flamelike conformations that destroy any sense of the head's closure. The head itself seems unable to hold the wealth of sensations and ideas induced therein, and textures and shapes are shared by the areas both within and outside the face.

Miró permitted his hand to move automatically across the surface, responding to impulse as if he were in a trance. His previous habits of drawing and typical shapes come through, nevertheless, for much in this portrait is traceable to his earlier art. The self-portraits of Leonardo and Goya in their own way were affirmations of the control of art by the intellect in combination with perception. Miró celebrated the irrational and emotional basis of art and life. His rendering of the eyes transformed their function as receivers of sensations from the external world into that of objects of internal sensation.

Portraits fulfill myriad functions. The rendering in painting and sculpture of the human face has been linked with religion and the need to secure ties between the living and their dead ancestors, as in Roman and certain primitive cultures. For Egyptian royalty, the portrait was assurance of immortality by providing an eternal abode for the soul in an effigy. Status in an exalted political or social sphere could claim the right to portraiture in many societies. The likeness and pose of an important figure could serve to perpetuate an ethic of ideal social conduct. Concepts of manliness and femininity found important interpretation in Renaissance and Baroque portraits. Inquiry into human nature and conduct as expressed through the physiognomic traits and psychological evidence of the face was another function of portraiture. The desire to convey intimate personal sentiments motivated many artists, whereas the problem of finding a mystical human essence joined with the quest for personal absolutes of beauty and perfection attracted others. A major function of portraiture was thus that of building a bridge between the artist and his natural and human environment.

FIGURE 417. JOAN MIRÓ. *Self-portrait.* 1937–38. Oil, crayon, and pencil on canvas, 4′9½″×3′2¼″. The Museum of Modern Art, New York (Collection James Thrall Soby).

18

THE FIGURE IN SCULPTURE

The elasticity of the human body in art has not been limited by its anatomy but, rather, by the sculptor's skills, incentives, and imagination. While some objective knowledge of the physical aspects of the body was possessed by all the artists discussed in this chapter, the absence of a continuing historical norm for its appearance in sculpture testifies to the repeated intrusion of strong social, religious, intellectual, emotional, and esthetic ideals in its representation. The celebration of the body for its intrinsic anatomical interest, with no ulterior purpose, is a surprisingly infrequent phenomenon compared with the many instances over the centuries in which it was used to personify abstract concepts involving man or nature. Ideology rather than biology has been more often served in the history of the human body in art.

THE FIGURE IN OLDER SCULPTURE

The appearance and development of the nude in Greek art, from the seventh century B.C. down to the Classical period of the fifth century B.C., constitutes one of the finest legacies of Greek civilization. Its development implies a civilizing process not encountered earlier in the ancient world. It signifies an overcoming of the duality between man and the world, a gradual subsiding and mastery of man's fear, or cosmic dread.

Particular needs, associations, experiences, and ideals went into the formation of the nude, making of it a collective expression of an important aspect of Greek culture. The *Spear Carrier* (Fig. 418) shows that the relation of man to the world had become one of self-confidence. This statue, which has come down to us only through Roman copies and in a reconstruction by a German archaeologist, was made by Polyclitus the Elder in the fifth century B.C. The identity of the figure is not known with any certainty; it may represent Hermes, Achilles, a messenger of the gods, a soldier, or a hero of the gymnasium. The Classical nude represents a frank extension into art of man's own ego, and signifies its creator's concern with the here and now, not his speculation on vague, mystical subjects or death. What in Homeric times had been remote, distant, and feared was brought within man's ken and perception. The Classical nude thus reflects a man-centered world, one where man is the focus and measure of all things.

The Classical Greek figure without clothing must be termed "nude" rather than "naked." The latter term suggests shame, self-conscious-

353

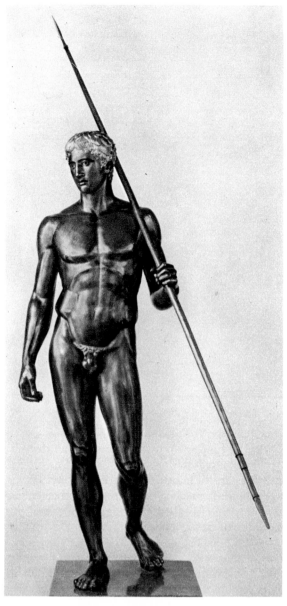

Figure 418. POLYCLITUS. *Spear Carrier (Doryphorus)*, reconstruction by Römer after an original of c. 450 B.C. Bronze, height 6′11½″. Glyptothek, Munich.

matical measure as an insurance of perfection in his art. Although it has been lost, Polyclitus is known to have recorded his perfected canon of proportion. He based his system upon a division of an ideal body, whereby each part could be expressed as a fraction of the whole, for example, the head as one-eighth or one-ninth of the body's total height. The application of mathematical proportion to the nude human figure evidenced the Greek propensity for giving tangible and sensual form to abstract concepts, for making rational abstractions into a delight to the senses. The virtues signified in the nude *Spear Carrier* were those of hygiene, courage, and a dignified self-composure.

The Classical view of beauty depended upon a subtle manipulation of opposites. The fifth-century "beauty pose" showed a condition of rest tempered by movement, a balance between perfect energy and perfect repose. (Vigorous movement and displays of energy were reserved for sculptures of the gods.) The artistic device that permits the capturing of this dualism is counterpoise; that is, for every movement in one direction, there is a countering tendency in another.

The Greeks of the fifth century believed that everything had an ideal form, of which the phenomena of ordinary existence were more or less corrupted replicas. It remained for the artist to see through this imperfection and to perfect what nature had disguised or left unfinished. Classical sculpture was not a mere juxtaposition of limbs and body parts that the artist had observed in his models. The Greek view of ideal form was a balance between functional necessity and an ideal schema. What makes Classical art so effective is the continued presence of imagination and positive design.

Large-scale stone sculpture declined after the fall of Rome, its abandonment reflecting Early Christian apprehension about carved images, and revived only after 1000 A.D. Executed more than 1500 years after the *Spear Carrier* was a Romanesque sculpture of the Old Testament prophet Isaiah, from the southern French Abbey of Souillac (Fig. 419). This relief sculpture was based on other contemporary carving and manuscript painting rather than on a living model or the long tradition of free-standing sculpture. Furthermore, the Isaiah figure is seen in connection with architecture. These factors account for the relative

ness, an unaccustomed state. The nude figure instead is one perfectly at ease without garments. For the Greeks, the ideal of nudity separated them from the barbarians. They had no sense of sin or shame in respect to the unclothed body. Through the perfectly formed nude body the Greeks expressed and re-experienced their ideals of eurhythmics. The balance and rhythm of the *Spear Carrier* signifies not only control of the body but the training of the mind and the Apolline values of moderation. This proper standard of human conduct is partly paralleled in art by the Classical sculptor's love of mathe-

flatness of the form and its orientation parallel to the wall and an invisible surface plane. Isaiah is presented in what appears to be a kind of ecstatic dance, holding at arm's length a scroll on which was originally written an excerpt from his prophecies. In form and meaning, the figure of Isaiah is the antithesis of the *Spear Carrier*; in purpose, however, the two are similar. Both were concrete realizations of human beliefs, which presented the viewer with ideal modes of being in the guise of heroes greater than himself. The Christian figure testifies to the existence and superiority of a spiritual world transcending the mundane sphere of the viewer. The Romanesque Christian sculptor, unlike Polyclitus, did not adopt a single proportional norm for an ideal figure based on constant, numerical rations. His proportions were varied according to the rank of his figure and the expressive needs of his design.

The elongated proportions of Isaiah, which deemphasize his material weight and volume,

Figure 419. *Isaiah*, from the portal of the Benedictine Abbey of Souillac, Lot. c. 1110–30.

permitted a complex countermovement in the axes of his form. The prophet's body has assumed a violent variation upon the Greek Classical ideal of tranquil counterpoise. The prophet's many joints and the lack of synchronization of his gesturing arm with the multiple directions of the rest of the body are stressed. While it is not hard to conceive of the Greek spear carrier smoothly shifting his stance, it requires a greater effort of imagination to visualize Isaiah altering his rather precarious pose. The reason is that the Greek sculptor used a strong physiological basis for the body structure, whereas the Romanesque artist used an abstract linear armature in organizing his figure, with no celebration of muscular coordination. The spear carrier is an athlete in the usual physical sense; Isaiah, an athlete of the spirit. The movement and proportion of the Isaiah was directed in its appeal less to the eye than to the mind. There is an excitement in the prophet's pose, a sort of spastic and unself-conscious total gesture that mirrors his spiritual intensity. The exaggerated crisscrossed oppositions of the Romanesque work create a more drastic self-involvement than is found in the Greek design. However, whereas the spear is an expendable design accessory, the scroll is needed to complete the balance of the prophet. This suggests the relatedness of the Christian figure to elements outside himself and his existence within a complex universal hierarchy.

To understand the appropriateness of Isaiah's costume for the figure itself and to gain further understanding of the remoteness of this Romanesque interpretation from that of Classical Greece, one may compare this sculpture to a fifth-century relief from the Acropolis, *Nike Adjusting Her Sandal* (Fig. 420). The Greek garment, the chiton, clings to the goddess' form in a revealing manner, because of the practice of oiling the body prior to donning a robe. The drapery folds are dependent on the modeled articulation of the body, and hence the veiling of the female form in no way reduces its sensual appeal. There is a flattering reciprocal relation between skin and garment that heightens the physical charms of the woman. The Romanesque drapery, like the treatment of the beard and hair, shows a taste for strong abstract linear surface design that has no organic interplay with the body. The Greek drapery carv-

ing is deep and produces strong rhythmic effects of light and shadow; the medieval French modeling is shallow, on the other hand, in keeping with the reduced sensuality of the whole.

The mid-twelfth-century jamb figures of the Royal Portal of Chartres Cathedral demonstrate another medieval ideal of the human figure (Fig. 421). It must be remembered that, simultaneously with such Old Testament figures, Gothic sculptors were called upon to represent a variety of other subjects and in so doing treated the human form in several ways. The artists demonstrated repeatedly that in certain contexts they could render the human form in movement with a surprising degree of naturalism. In other words, not all twelfth-century Gothic cathedral sculpture demonstrates the properties seen in this example. The jamb figures have been given a columnar rigidity and vertical emphasis, for their principal axis is bound to that of the building to which they are attached. The antithesis of such absorption in a nonhuman structural system is found in Greek caryatids (Fig. 422) from the porch of the fifth-century Erechtheum on the Athenian Acropolis. These Classical maidens, who serve as vertical supports for the roof of the porch, still display freedom of movement. One of their legs is stiffly poised, indicating that the weight is carried on this member; the other is relaxed. Each maiden is allowed a degree of mobility that demonstrates the sculptor's view of the essential autonomy and integrity of the human form. He could not even conceive of an inorganic basis for bodily construction, despite the context. The Gothic sculptor willingly foregoes this liberty in his saints in order to enhance the impression of the power and superhuman attributes of his subjects.

The expression of a spiritual ideal through the body did not mean to the Gothic artist an imitation of reality, but a reorganization and invention of nonnatural devices. The jamb figures are also dematerialized in part by their elongated proportion. In contradistinction to the caryatids, who stand confidently on a base or ground, the Gothic saints are poised on

their toes, almost as if suspended, in a way that announces their transcendence of corporeality. The jamb figures manifest no awareness of each other; moreover, each is shut off from the material world. The rational attitude and sensory experience of the Greek artist, with which he animated his optimistic figures, was alien to or untenable for his Gothic counterparts. The bodies of the Gothic saints comprise refuges from the uncertainties, tensions, and anxieties of the natural world. There is no appearance or hint of the repose and relaxation emblematic of man's concord with himself, with his society or the world. The Gothic world could not accept the outlook of the Greeks.

The art of India, too, reflected a world outlook closer to the Greek than to the Gothic. The warm, ripe Indian tree goddess (Fig. 423), or Yakshi, who entwines herself with a tree on a gate of the Great Stupa at Sanchi has no place in the medieval Christian constellation of sacred personages. Her generous, curving body with its globular breasts belongs with the hemispherical stupa (burial mound) rather than amid the pointed arches and rectilinear towers of Chartres. With nothing of the columnar associations or constriction of the Greek maidens, the abandon of the Yakhis's posture accentuates the sensuality of her form and recalls her role as fertility goddess. No apparent internal skeleton impedes the suggestive torsion of her inflated "Subtle Body." The Yakshi was symbolic in both Buddhism

Above: Figure 422. *Caryatids,* from the porch of the Erechtheum. c. 420 B.C. The Acropolis, Athens.

Below: Figure 423. *Yakshi* (Indian Tree Goddess), from the East Gate of the Great Stupa, Sanchi. Bracket figure. Early Andhra Period, 1st century B.C.

The Figure in Sculpture   357

and Hinduism, which in their teachings and art convert the human erotic instinct to higher purposes than merely being an end in itself. The exaggeration of the Yakshi's sexual parts had a religious motivation and was intended to arouse those who looked upon her to initiate their spiritual communion with the gods. The proportions, sequences of curves, and shaping of the parts did not proceed from a system based directly on the actual human body but shared some of the arbitrariness of later Romanesque design. More so than painting, the three-dimensional and tactile potential of sculpture successfully embodied the spiritual eroticism of Indian artists.

To turn from the Sanchi Yakshi to Donatello's *Mary Magdalen* (Fig. 424) creates an interesting juxtaposition. Although Donatello is referred to as a Renaissance sculptor, his life-sized, painted wooden image of the Magdalen remains the expression of an essentially medieval Christian attitude toward the incompatibility of body and soul. Although Donatello often carved healthful and cosmetically attractive figures in an age that admired physical beauty, he retained much of the penitential spirit of the late Middle Ages. Intended for the Baptistery of Florence, his sculpture is a merciless study of the body made less than human, first through self-indulgence and then through a self-denying asceticism. He renewed the late medieval dichotomy between inner truth and surface beauty. The Magdalen has become a living corpse, like a medieval reminder of death and the wages of sin. Only the zeal of the convert animates the leathery flesh of this skeletal figure, holding out the same hope as baptism. The spiritual intensity imparted to the sculpture by Donatello transcends its physical repellence and makes the work esthetically compelling. The slight gap between the hands creates a life-giving tension that complements the psychological force emanating from the head. Essential to this focus is the rigidity of the body, which differs from that of the Chartres jamb figures in that here it is self-imposed. No sculpture in Western art is further from the Greek Classical ideal of eurythmy; yet Donatello did make sculptures

of the body which share certain Classical ideals.

It was Donatello who created, in his *David* (Fig. 425), the first life-sized nude figure since the end of antiquity. The work was probably commissioned by a private patron for his home. In 1430 the sculptor's society was not yet prepared to see a Biblical hero such as David

Right: Figure 424. DONATELLO. *Mary Magdalen.* c. 1454–55. Polychromed wood, height 6'2". Baptistery, Florence.

an early-fifteenth-century Florentine aristocratic ideal of youthful masculine beauty and intelligence, with the latter faculty triumphant over the brute strength of Goliath.

About a half century later, the scientific curiosity of another Florentine sculptor and the heroic connotations of strenuous physical action produced an important departure from Donatello's ideal of passive beauty. The full enactment and revelation of the human body's considerable strength, rather than its potential force, is what separates Pollaiuolo's small bronze sculpture of *Hercules Crushing Antaeus* (Fig. 426) from the struggling figures in ancient Greek art. The Greeks would temporize the full or extreme manifestation of muscular tension in order to ensure conformity of the body's design with an ideal of fluid grace. Pollaiuolo, who had the opportunity to dissect corpses, was breaking new ground for sculpture and was excited by the discovery of means of convincingly embodying the human energy demanded in gestures of violent pushing and pulling. The more angular and active silhouettes of his figures, in comparison with those of the Greeks, resulted from direct observation of how, for instance, the shoulder bones of the human form (e.g., Hercules) are pushed outward as the arm muscles are stretched and tighten. Unlike in Donatello's *David*, the skeletal-muscular systems of the body thus clearly operate in the Pollaiuolo statue and are to be traced in its construction right down to the feet of Hercules.

Interest in depicting human psychology through the body reached a climax in the work of the Baroque sculptor Bernini. His *David*

Above: Figure 425. DONATELLO. *David with the Head of Goliath.* c. 1430–32. Bronze, height 5'2¼". Museo Nazionale, Florence.

Right: Figure 426. ANTONIO POLLAIUOLO. *Hercules Crushing Antaeus.* c. 1475. Bronze, height 18″ (with base). Museo Nazionale, Florence.

commemorated in an unclothed representation. For unknown reasons, Donatello chose to show the vanquisher of Goliath wearing a hat and boots, accouterments unthinkable for Classical Greek sculptors. The contrapposto beauty pose of the body was borrowed from ancient statuary. Donatello's figure is a synthesis of postural derivation and personal observation of the body. His youthful model lacks the fluid contours and joints and the pronounced articulation of body structure, such as the joining of the legs and torso, found in ancient athlete figures. The *David* nonetheless furnishes

Figure 427. GIANLORENZO BERNINI. *David.* 1622–24. Marble, life size. Galleria Borghese, Rome.

(Fig. 427), worked on from 1622 to 1624, shows a mature male body in a mobile position—in contrast to the Donatello figure, which satisfied the ideal of a free-standing figure in repose. Like Renaissance sculpture, however, Bernini's *David* had one viewpoint from which it was most effectively seen in terms of disclosing the full, uninterrupted sweep of the gesture. The body is coiled, spiraling in space, as David prepares to loose the stone against Goliath. The momentary stance, contraction of the muscles, and set of the face establish the figure's mood and purpose. It is impossible to question Bernini's understanding of anatomy and the movement of the body, for he was heir to the great achievements of the Renaissance and Michelangelo.

Dissatisfied with the static, self-contained, and aloof aspect of most Renaissance figures, nevertheless, Bernini disposed the body in corkscrew fashion. The viewer is thus induced to move about the statue. Bernini sought to unite the work of art with the space of the beholder. His *David* was the culmination of a long tradition in which the artist celebrated the physiology and psychology of the human body in terms of its ideal external appearance. Not until Rodin, in the nineteenth century, was there further significant change in the sculptural imagery of the body.

FIGURE TRANSFORMATIONS IN MODERN SCULPTURE

In the sculpture of Auguste Rodin, which ranges from 1863 to 1917 in date, there was a culmination of ancient traditions and the beginnings of the modern revolution in sculpture of the human form. Rodin brought to sculpture of the body a fresh and exciting naturalism while at the same time preserving the broad conventions of imitating its external appearance. His *Crouching Woman* (Fig. 428) dismisses the studio pose and the making of art from the art of others by presenting his model in a condition of physical and emotional contraction brought on by fatigue. Where for centuries sculptors had generally worked from a conventional repertory of poses and easily apprehended rhetorical gestures, Rodin sought the instinctive movement inspired by the body's natural response to the spirit. To reproduce the mirroring of the spirit in the flesh, and not just a surface manifestation of bone and muscle, Rodin built up his sculptural bodies from thousands of touches based on actual search of the living form by his eyes and fingers, and as a result of long meditation upon how the clay and bronze had to be conditioned to receive the light that would bring it to life. No previous sculptor had probed so many movements so extensively with so many different models, in order to bring to sculpture the endless manifestations of being alive. For Rodin, the great practical consideration in basing sculpture on the human form was the fact that both consisted of surfaces and silhouettes, mass and volume, and the perfect joining of many parts to express the life force that animated them.

Plate 49.   FRANS HALS. *Portrait of a Man*. c. 1661–64. Oil on canvas, 31 ⅛ × 25 ⅝″. Staatliche Kunstsammlungen, Kassel.

Plate 50.   PETER PAUL RUBENS. *Susanna Fourment*. 1620. Oil on panel, 31 × 21 ½".
The National Gallery, London (reproduced by courtesy of the Trustees).

Plate 51.   HENRI MATISSE. *Woman with the Hat.* 1905. Oil on canvas, $32 \times 32\frac{1}{2}''$.
Collection Mr. and Mrs. Walter A. Haas, San Francisco.

Plate 52.   JAN VAN EYCK. *Giovanni Arnolfini and His Bride.* 1434. Oil on panel, 32¼ × 23½".
The National Gallery, London (reproduced by courtesy of the Trustees).

When all these things worked well together as in the soundly functioning body, good sculpture could result.

Rodin's lifelong ideal of imitating the live model rather than the ideals of past ages did not involve mechanical duplication, for he relied on his eye and allowed feeling or inspiration to express themselves through the mastery of his hands. To preserve the look of the natural meant both drawing from and suppressing his knowledge of past styles. To study the surface of his *Crouching Woman* is like exploring unknown territory. We know the body in narrow or specialized ways such as the pre-occupations of the doctor, fashion designer, athlete, or lover. Each of these forms of knowl-edge focuses on and rejects various properties of the body. Rodin instead ignored nothing and sought out everything. Our eyes and hands are not accustomed to the intensity of modeling, the revelations of his sculptural surfaces which, derived from our most familiar possession, must be felt as well as seen.

The broad range of human gesture in Rodin's work is partially related in such figures as the *Crouching Woman* and his *John the Baptist Preaching* (Fig. 429). In the former, the body is seen in its maximal contraction; the figure of a woman could not be compressed into a smaller area. But Rodin did not set out to solve this as an abstract problem. What makes his art convincing to us is that his figures assume postures which appear to have been genuinely motivated by feeling. The figure of the Baptist tends toward the other extreme in a body that is briskly moving and expanding. Resting firmly on a base, the body is re-created as a continuously enclosed, solid articulated mass. Structure and movement are dictated by anatomy and physiology; expres-sion derives from the artist's psychological observations, and the theme comes from a literary source. The prophet's gestures toward heaven and earth are within the conventions of sculptural rhetoric. The human form was modeled by Rodin as it was given to his eye and hand, and as his mind comprehended its inner structure. But the sculptor also passion-ately loved the body as a marvelously expressive organism of balance and counterbalance. To make his sculpture lifelike, he gave it the appearance of being a résumé of successive motions. In his view, man, not the saints, was

Figure 428. AUGUSTE RODIN. *Crouching Woman.* 1880–82. Bronze, height 33". The Rodin Museum, Philadelphia (cour-tesy the Commissioners of Fairmont Park and the Philadelphia Museum of Art).

Figure 429. AUGUSTE RODIN. *John the Baptist Preaching.* 1878. Bronze, height 6'6¾". The Museum of Modern Art, New York (Mrs. Simon Guggenheim Fund).

holy, and the body was the temple of the spirit. It was not the Baptist's message nor what he symbolized that moved Rodin so much as the model's instinctive urge to express himself and his resulting bodily tension.

The vigor of the figure's stance and gesture was matched by the energy of the sculptor's fingers as he built up the surface to suggest organic growth and animation. The body was realized from Rodin's studies of thousands of figures perceived from all points of view, a technique he claimed to have derived from the study of Greek sculpture. The reception and rejection of light by the surface gives a pulse to the bronze, making the flesh responsive to the figure's psychological condition. The bold attitude and thrust of the arms bring the sculpture into our space and remove it decisively from the cold realm of academic sculpture. In his best work, Rodin created intimate presences that intrude disturbingly into the world of the viewer.

Few modern sculptors have shared Rodin's psychological interests and generous use of dramatic gestures. One sculptor who sought to extend, but not to imitate, Rodin's naturalism and bodily rhetoric was the German sculptor Wilhelm Lehmbruck. In his search for a modern heroic style before World War I, he drew from Rodin's celebration of the living (other than those with themes from the past). Part of Rodin's positive legacy to Lehmbruck was the vision of the heroic in human suffering. Lehmbruck's solemn consecration of the body in his *Standing Youth* (Fig. 430) proceeded from equating an exaggeratedly human figure with the spiritual. The body is given monumentality through meticulous measure, without loss of a sense of its organic development. The youth is not posed in the assertive stride of Rodin's *John the Baptist* but is fixed in an erect stance which, in conjunction with the elongated proportions, accentuates his qualities of elevation.

The sculpture's visual force comes from its lack of physical movement and the necessary implied strain. The willful reduction of the body conveys Lehmbruck's concern with the tense striving of the human spirit. It is not a trained, lithe body that permits Lehmbruck's figure to survive; the body of this naked youth has been shaped by his individual character. In the manner of Isaiah, he is an athlete of the spirit, not of the flesh. Lacking the more obvious rhetoric of Rodin's art, the meditative

Figure 430. WILHELM LEHMBRUCK. *Standing Youth.* 1913. Cast stone, height 7′8″. The Museum of Modern Art, New York (gift of Mrs. John D. Rockefeller, Jr.).

gestures seem to turn back in upon the figure, suggesting his essential isolation and a need to know and master himself. The difficult course of his life is suggested by the abrupt thrusts and changes of direction in the silhouette of the body. Done on the eve of World War I, this statue perhaps expresses Lehmbruck's hopes for youth. In Lehmbruck's sculpture done during and after the war, the body seems to break down, quite likely reflecting the artist's loss of confidence in man's mastery of his fate. Lehmbruck is one of the few modern sculptors who, along with Rodin, achieved pathos in portraying the human body.

One of Rodin's most dramatic contributions historically was his demonstration that parts of the body were dispensable in a finished sculpture. In 1900 he exhibited publicly for the first time a small headless and armless study made for his *John the Baptist*. Some years later he enlarged this work and gave it the title *Walking Man* (Fig. 431). Inspired by his study of the fragmented figures of antiquity in museums, Rodin became convinced that a complete work of art did not presuppose an entire figure. He cited the example of portrait busts and pointed out that in Greek fragments we can appreciate perfect beauty (a premise to which the Greeks themselves would have objected). When Rodin eliminated the head and arms from his sculpture, he also removed its identity and the traditional means for rhetorical expression. As pedestrian a subject as a man walking now took on the aspect of universal drama, and for the first time biological man became the central artistic concern. From certain angles the *Walking Man*, in full stride and with the upper part of his torso tilted forward and to the right, appears about to topple over. The powerful legs suggest a pushing off from the back foot and a receiving of weight and downward pressure on the front foot—a simultaneous condition that is impossible in life yet believable in Rodin's sculpture. (The left leg is slightly longer than the right to accommodate the shifting of weight and allow for the extended stride.) Like Michelangelo, Rodin was willing to adjust anatomy in the interest of artistic plausibility. When asked why he had left off his figure's arms and head, Rodin replied, "A man walks on his feet."

Another drastic departure in this exciting sculpture by Rodin was his retention of the raw marks of its fashioning, the gouges of his fingers and the ragged separation of the shoulder from the omitted arms. His dedication to creating an art that had the complete look of the natural would seem at first to have been compromised by this action, until we recognize that Rodin was retaining by deliberate esthetic choice the natural evidence of sculpture making.

Great naturalistic sculpture of the human body has waned in this century, for with few exceptions during and after Rodin's lifetime the best sculptors have found new possibilities for the figure. Two exceptions who were able to extend Rodin's ideas and their own without loss of integrity or strength were Aristide Maillol and Gaston Lachaise.

At the turn of the century, Maillol had evolved his own way of celebrating the human form in its external appearance. With few exceptions, Maillol confined himself to the female body, always choosing models whose temperaments and proportions met his personal ideal of perfect healthful beauty and equanimity. Maillol's sculpture was an alternative to the powerful but more nervous surfaces of Rodin's art. Rodin brought a new shiver of excitement to sculpture; Maillol established a new serenity. The former's precedent of establishing the validity of the partial figure resolved certain problems for the younger sculptor. "Arms are my Calvary," Maillol was known to say, and he would often divest his figures of their arms or of their head and legs. For Maillol, through a refinement of its volume, the torso of a woman in itself held all the

Figure 431. AUGUSTE RODIN. *Walking Man*. 1878–80. Bronze, height 33¹/₈″. The National Gallery of Art, Washington, D.C. (gift of Mrs. John W. Simpson).

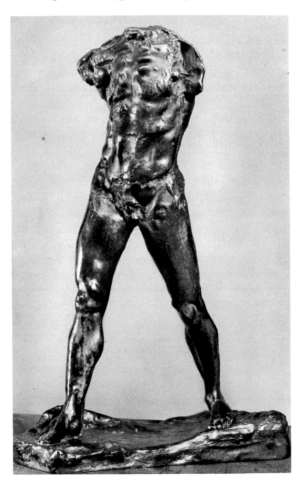

Left: Figure 432. ARISTIDE MAILLOL. *Chained Action (Torso, Monument to Blanqui).* c. 1905 (cast in bronze 1929). Height 47". The Metropolitan Museum of Art, New York (Fletcher Fund).

Above: Figure 433. GASTON LACHAISE. *Torso.* 1932 (cast in bronze 1963). Height 9½". The Estate of Isabel Lachaise (courtesy, the Felix Landan Gallery, Los Angeles, and the Robert Schoelkopf Gallery, New York).

essential ingredients for harmony. His *Chained Action* (Fig. 432), a striding female figure, is a personal reworking of Rodin's *Walking Man.* Maillol recognized that the male body could be more dramatic, but like many sculptors and painters before him, he was convinced that a woman's body, with its smoother surfaces and firm sensual volumes, was the basis for the most perfect beauty.

Lachaise made many robust, full-blown sculptures of his wife which recall statues of prehistoric fertility goddesses and which contributed to modern sculpture an honesty of attitude toward sex. His bronze torso of his wife (Fig. 433) drew heavily upon her natural endowments, but its proportions and shaping also were indebted to the legacy of the partial figure. Unlike the proportions of Classical or Indian art, those of Lachaise's work were not dictated by abstract numerical relationships but were frank, direct expression of strong sensual feelings. In selecting only the torso, Lachaise created a strong and personal image of woman as the source of life, which invited the kind of generous reformation illustrated.

Rodin's art both attracted and repelled

young artists at the beginning of the century. To some, it seemed melodramatic and deficient in formal strength. In a statement made in 1908, Matisse spelled out this criticism without reference specifically to Rodin: "What I am after, above all is expression.... [which] does not consist of the passion mirrored upon a human face or betrayed by a violent gesture. The whole arrangement of my picture is expressive." For the word "picture," Matisse could have substituted "sculpture."

Matisse made important contributions to sculpture, and his statement was prophesied by his own work *The Serf* (Fig. 434), done between 1900 and 1903. The lower arms of the clay version of *The Serf* had fallen off before casting, and perhaps inspired by Rodin's partial figures Matisse did not replace them. This suited his ideas on expression, drawing our attention from what the figure is doing or can do to what Matisse has done in his working of the body's surface and mass. Although it reveals the influence of Rodin's art, it is also an outright rejection of the use of facial and gesticular expression in such works as *John the Baptist.* The surface of both sculptures received accents of modeling not wholly dictated by the outward character of the male body. Matisse's figure is even more dense and compact than the *John the Baptist*. Both sculptors at some point went beyond empirical knowledge to create expressive changes that brought to the eye new esthetic sensations. Certain shapes and kinds of surface finish are more expressive than others, as can be seen by comparing these qualities in Maillol with those of Matisse. While the model is essentially passive, the sculpture becomes dramatic through the activity of the sculptor. The total effect of *The Serf*, rather than its facial expression, makes it visually moving. Matisse had sought in both the face and body of the model evidence of a deep gravity that he felt existed in every human being. For Matisse and Rodin, the purpose of rendering the body was to convey their near religious feelings toward life, symptomatic of the replacement of "religious" by "spiritual" sculpture in modern art.

Relative inaction gave drama and dignity to Lehmbruck's and Matisse's concepts of the body, but the Italian sculptor Umberto Boccioni saw the human form only in terms of vibrant force. Reacting against academic sculpture, with its insistence on imitative modeling, sublime poses, and ennobling subject matter, Boccioni recast the body in terms of what he thought was the science and technology of his

day and with the lessons he had learned from Rodin's *Walking Man*. In his *Technical Manifesto of Futurist Sculpture*, written in 1912, he discloses this indebtedness as well as a new idea of the source for sculptural harmony:

> We proclaim that the whole visible world must fall in upon us, merging with us and creating a harmony measurable only by the creative imagination; that a leg, an arm... having no importance except as elements of plastic [sculptural] rhythm, can be abolished, not in order to imitate a Greek or Roman fragment, but to conform to the harmony the artist wishes to create. A sculptural entity... can only resemble itself, for in art the human figure...must exist apart from the logic of physiognomy.

Boccioni was obsessed with the visible and invisible movement and interpenetration of all matter. In *Unique Forms of Continuity in Space* (Fig. 435), the closed shell of the body was ripped open and forcibly penetrated by the space about it. The solid portions of the body that act upon space are not shown as taut muscles in a fixed position but, to indicate the path of their motion through space, acquire instead an undulating molten flow that heightens the fusion of the irregular silhouette with its environment. Boccioni even considered painting the edges to enhance the impression of

Figure 434. HENRI MATISSE. *The Serf.* 1900–03. Bronze, height 36¼". The Knoedler Art Galleries, New York.

Figure 435. UMBERTO BOCCIONI. *Unique Forms of Continuity in Space.* 1913. Bronze, height 43½". The Museum of Modern Art, New York (acquired through the Lillie P. Bliss Bequest).

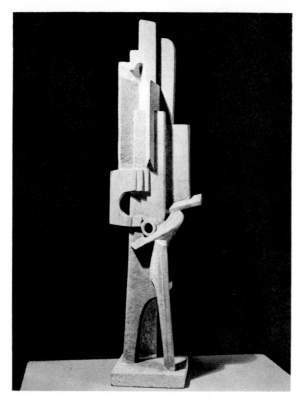

Figure 436. JACQUES LIPCHITZ. *Man with a Guitar*. 1915. Stone, height 38¼". The Museum of Modern Art, New York (Mrs. Simon Guggenheim Fund).

a continuum. Although Boccioni contributed to Futurist publications enthusiastic writings extolling the machine and its dynamism, he was earnestly committed to the human body and bronze. Where academic sculptures indicated science by having a Classical figure hold a scientific instrument, Boccioni imparted to the body itself qualities of the scientific attitude it was meant to represent.

Sculptors from the Renaissance to the present time have succeeded in transforming a studio model into a god, a general, a lover, or a virtue. While academic sculptors altered the identity of the model, Jacques Lipchitz and the Cubists acknowledged his or her identity but revolutionized the appearance. Cubist sculptors such as Lipchitz demonstrated the dispensability of surface resemblance for figural sculpture. Lipchitz' *Man with a Guitar* (Fig. 436) perhaps first impresses the viewer by those things it is not. This is not a sculpture into which the viewer can project himself or which exhorts him to be a better member of society. The body, which lacks flesh and feeling, has not been "imitated from nature" and does not correspond to the sensory experience of our eyes and hands.

The label "Cubism" is also misleading, since there are no pure cubes in the sculpture. It was the intention of Lipchitz and the Cubists to assert the sovereignty of the mind of the artist, not of "nature," over the work. In an interview, Lipchitz said, "We Cubists chose a man-made language rather than a naturalistic one, for we wanted to find a new language to adequately fit our feeling. Cubism is less attached to Mother Nature, it is more a pure invention of the human imagination." The human body has not been deformed, but *re*formed, by the artist's intellect and esthetic judgment. Anatomy and physiology, the traditional vocabulary and grammar of the sculptor, have given way to what might be called a new sign language—a language not inherited from the ages, but one which Lipchitz thought was of his time and personal invention. Flattened, mostly rectilinear segments of varying thicknesses set at various angles to one another construct an arbitrary armature for the generally vertical figure.

The body is translated into an esthetic object in Cubist art. The basic change is from the body *seen* to the body constructed. There is no separation of inside and outside. The sculpture has its own spirit and logic of organization. These properties, along with structural rightness and expressiveness, become the sculptor's criteria. The expressiveness of the sculpture resides not in dramatic gesture but in the character of the shaping and joining. In arriving at this type of art, Lipchitz did no violence to hallowed subjects; his figure is anonymous and is involved in what is itself an esthetic activity. Lipchitz detached himself from notions of heroicism and social or moral correctness. But within a few years, he began to feel that his crystalline structures were too remote from human qualities and gradually introduced more sensual and volumetric forms.

In his *Figure* (Fig. 437), done between 1926 and 1931, Lipchitz showed a new concern with art and life. This work began a new direction both in his own art and in body imagery in modern sculpture. Lipchitz created a new sculptural metaphor for a state of being. His interpretation of tension is a chainlike configuration climaxed by a concave oval in which are set two small cylinders suggesting eyes. For moments of mental crisis we have such verbal images as "my stomach is tied in knots." What Lipchitz gives us is not a view of a tormented individual, as if seen by someone else, but rather an imaginative interior image or a sculptural metaphor of tension or distress. A poetical "internal" anatomy is revealed, not the contents of an X-ray plate. Lipchitz' form suggests the stresses and unresolved forces to which a human being may be subjected and, as signified by the integrated welding of base to the link forms, the resultant immobility of spirit and body. The oval suggests an internal or introverted sense in its reversal of the normally convex head, its elimination of useless detail, and the fixity of the eye forms. (Photographs of people in a state of shock show a kindred suspension of consciousness, their entire being rigidified under some immense but invisible pressure.) Lipchitz was concerned with the effects rather than the cause of such paralysis. Man here is not a hero but a victim. Cubist painting and sculpture had brought about an interruption of older habits of seeing and rendering the human body and had

provided unlimited alternatives to the imagination by showing that *reference to the body could be achieved with forms unlike those of actual anatomy.* The primarily esthetic concerns of *Man with a Guitar* were thus enriched by the sculptor's growing involvement with the inner life and feelings of his subject, seldom if ever sought after in earlier sculpture.

The decades of the 1920s and 1930s saw the introduction into sculpture and painting of exciting fantasies on the human body. The body was conceived in terms of the artist's personal ideas and private feelings of desire or repugnance. While dreams were not the primary source of the new conceits, novel forms were often induced by the artist's irrational associations with body parts.

The Spanish sculptor Julio Gonzalez sought to restore to sculpture properties of mystery, fantasy, and even the diabolic. His *Woman Combing Her Hair* (Fig. 438) resists the old

Left: Figure 437. JACQUES LIPCHITZ. *Figure.* 1926–31. Bronze, height 7'1¼". The Museum of Modern Art, New York (Van Gogh Purchase Fund).

Below: Figure 438. JULIO GONZALEZ. *Woman Combing Her Hair.* 1936. Wrought iron, height 4'4". The Museum of Modern Art, New York (Mrs. Simon Guggenheim Fund).

criteria. There seems to be no rational principle according to which he projected into sculpture his image of woman. He evoked and re-formed the woman's body and movement with a series of contraries—open instead of closed forms, sharp as opposed to the customary rounded shapes, hard and rough versus soft and smooth surfaces. Space does not exist as something outside and around the body but becomes its intimate possession, something to be shaped and pierced and set off by what Gonzalez considered his "drawing" of strong forms. This union of solid and void is for Gonzalez equivalent to the coexistence of spirit and flesh. In the 1930s, a time when plowshares were being beaten into swords throughout Europe, Gonzalez fashioned iron into lyrical and civilized objects. In his own words, "It is time this metal ceased to be a murderer and the simple instrument of a super mechanical science. Today the door is open for this material to be, at last, forged and hammered by the peaceful hands of an artist." Iron and welding, new and exciting media for the modern sculptor, gave Gonzalez inexpensive means by which to achieve shapes, angles, and projections impossible in wood, stone, or cast metal. Under his hands, the toughness of iron yielded the most delicate as well as strenuous constructs of his imagination. Though he later returned to more naturalistic forms, Gonzalez' personal example and art created an important influence on many later sculptors using metal.

Alberto Giacometti's *Woman with Her Throat Cut* (Fig. 439) literally and figuratively takes woman off the pedestal. Instead of the languid posture of a fulsome nude, we see the body dissected and recomposed in an imaginative skeletal arrangement that presents a frankly sadistic image. Giacometti could not engage himself in rendering dispassionately a model to

Figure 439. ALBERTO GIACOMETTI. *Woman with Her Throat Cut.* 1932. Bronze, length 34½". The Museum of Modern Art, New York.

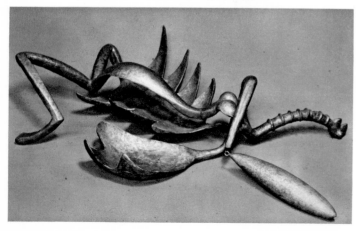

whom he was indifferent. He saw the body not in its external aspect but in the way it affected his life and moved him within. Here he created a spiky and violent configuration, antipodes to round and calm Classical forms. The figure lost all its compact and cohesive qualities, and in its skeletalizing in space became a transparent construction. The body resembles an aggressive landscape with tensions created by movement in opposing directions. The moral imperative in Giacometti's art of the 1930s was his belief in the primacy of fantasy and the conviction, shared with many other sculptors, that abstract forms are the true forms for sculpture.

Modern sculptors have been conscious of the human body in ways different from the conventional layman's view. Looked at abstractly, the human body consists of parts that differ widely in shape and proportion. Its masses are unevenly distributed, so that the rounded yet somewhat blocky form of the torso to which are attached two different pairs of roughly tubular hinged limbs is surmounted by an ovoid head joined to a cylindrical neck. The esthetic balancing of these disparate shapes poses a difficult problem, and down to the twentieth century sculptors relied heavily upon the general familiarity with and acceptance of the anatomical sequence of bodily parts and their formal disparateness. But in this century artists, no longer constrained by an ideal of fidelity to appearance (and, thanks to Rodin, being able to dispense with esthetically troublesome parts), could imaginatively reshape the body to achieve a more harmonious visual and esthetic balance. To illustrate this development, we can compare torsoes made by an ancient Greek named Apollonius, the Rumanian sculptor Constantin Brancusi, the Alsatian-born Hans Arp, and the Englishman Henry Moore.

Apollonius' sculpture known as the *Belvedere Torso* (Fig. 440) may have been of a satyr, and originally it was certainly a complete figure. The Greek ideal of beauty was grounded in wholeness, and a partial or unfinished figure would have been unthinkable in ancient times. Apollonius' statue contradicted earlier Classical ideals of moderation both in its focus upon excessive muscular development (hence, an imbalance between mind and body) and in an attention to anatomical details unbalanced by imaginative over-all design. After the torso was rediscovered in the Renaissance, it gained a

Figure 440. APOLLONIUS. *Belvedere Torso.* 2nd century B.C. Marble, height 5'½". Musei Vaticani, Rome.

new and influential existence in the work of artists from Michelangelo to Rodin. Both sculptors added heads and limbs to their versions of this torso, the former in his allegorical figures for the Medici tombs, and the latter in his well-known *Thinker.* For centuries the *Belvedere Torso* was admired for its heroic proportions and compressed energy. Michelangelo and Rodin learned from it the drama of muscular tension as an expression of the body's inner state, and also how the torso could be shown as the vital core of life.

As a young art student, Brancusi had made an anatomically exact replica of the musculature of the human body, which gave evidence of a technical and scientific knowledge equatable with that of Apollonius. (In fact, for many years Brancusi's plaster figure served as an object of study in a Budapest medical school.) But Brancusi gave up academic naturalism soon after his arrival in Paris in 1904, and he also renounced Rodin's type of modeling and naturalism. His *Torso of a Young Man,* carved in 1922 (Fig. 441), nonetheless depends on the

partial-figure concept developed by Rodin, who in turn had derived his inspiration from such ancient fragments as the *Belvedere Torso.* Brancusi stripped his body to a point where its shapes have been generalized into a few cylindrical volumes. (Despite its title, the ambiguity of its gender creates of this sculpture a kind of "impartial" figure.) Simplification to the point of absolute reductiveness was the means by which he thought his art could approach the essence, or "real sense," of things. At a certain point in the process of reductiveness, as Brancusi found, the body can become associated with other, nonhuman shapes of a botanical or technological character, depending in part upon whether the material was wood or bronze. (This piece can be exhibited successfully even if inverted, something wholly impossible in naturalistic art.) Thus a plurality of associations, which broaden the frame of sculptural reference, are possible. Brancusi had no desire to emulate what he called the "beefsteak" of the *Belvedere Torso* or the sculptures of Rodin. His final surfaces are the outcome not of modeling but of rubbing and polishing. By reducing the torso to elementary but kindred and still sensual shapes, he was able to achieve sculpture that was for him perfect in its proportions and over-all concordance.

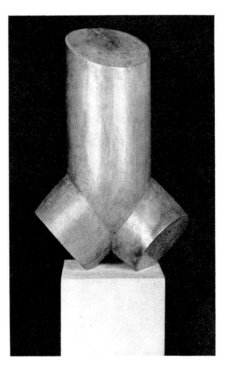

Figure 441. CONSTANTIN BRANCUSI. *Torso of a Young Man.* 1922. Wood, height 19"; marble base, height 7". The Philadelphia Museum of Art (Louise and Walter Arensberg Collection).

Figure 442. JEAN (HANS) ARP. *Human Lunar Spectral (Torso of a Giant).* 1958. Bronze, height 47¼". Collection Mr. and Mrs. Burton Tremaine, Meriden, Connecticut.

Hans Arp's *Human Lunar Spectral* (Fig. 442) has certain affinities with the *Belvedere Torso* and yet remains suggestively ambiguous. The torsion of the former recalls the flexibility of the Greek work but lacks any definite evidence of spine, pelvis, or muscle. There are also affinities in the lower portions of both; but Arp's form gives no hint of a skeletal or muscular substructure. Both Arp and Brancusi helped introduce into modern art a "sculpture without parts." Unlike Brancusi's torso, that of Arp seems capable of growth or swelling and contraction, thereby having greater reference to organic life. Rodin had defined sculpture as the art of the hole and the lump, yet as something always tied to the body's configuration. Arp gave a purer and more obvious demonstration of sculpture as a logical succession of pliant concave and convex surfaces enclosing a volume. The rightness of this sequence is measurable not against the standard of the human body but only in terms of the sculpture itself.

Sculptors since the Egyptians and Greeks had frequently used the human body to personify some aspect of nature. (The Greeks used reclining male figures as river gods.) Modern sculptors such as Arp and Henry Moore have tended to see the body in terms of nature and to fuse qualities of both into a single work, thereby suggesting the unity of all life.

Woman receives a new life and serenity in the work of Henry Moore (Fig. 443). In terms of the problem of disparate and unevenly distributed shapes referred to previously, Moore transformed the body to effect a more satisfactory sculptural balance, consistency, and continuity. When Moore reduced the size and definition of the head, eliminated the feet and hands, fused normally distinct or unconnected body parts, and introduced a great hollow in the middle of the torso, he was not motivated by a superficial desire to shock. His rephrasing of the body and investing it with a tissuelike surface created strong and fluid rhythms that for him suggest linkages of man and nature. His reclining forms of wood and stone seem shaped—that is, smoothed down—by the corrosive and abrasive action of the elements. The reclining pose had been traditionally associated with tranquillity and dignity, and these connotations were still honored. The living body possesses many openings, and Moore's use of hollows derives from mixed associations, from esthetic and sexual reveries centering on the inner cavities of the body, the womb, as well as fantasies and inspiration from caves and holes in wood and rock. His personal image exalts qualities and processes sensed, if not seen, in the body and elsewhere in nature.

Since the World War II, there have been unprecedented changes and developments in sculpture of the human figure—developments too extensive and varied to be typified summarily at the end of this chapter. The three illustrated works done since 1945 have been selected arbitrarily, because they are strong sculptures which manifest the mature efforts of exceptional sculptors and which add significantly to the history of figural sculpture. It is also possible to compare these recent works with two from the past, and thereby to reflect upon what has been gained and lost in sculpture as a result of this century's developments.

Figure 443. HENRY MOORE. *Reclining Woman*. 1946. Wood, length 76″.
The Cranbrook Academy of Art, Bloomfield Hills, Michigan.

Giacometti's *City Square* (Fig. 444) reflects his change in the early 1940s from fantastic conceptions of the body to a mode involving attempts at a personal faithfulness to observation of the human figure. Giacometti himself has pointed out that in the past sculptors rendered the figure as if they were only a few feet away from the model, so that the knowledge and experience gained from touch combined with sight to re-create the human figure. Unlike Rodin's *Walking Man*, Giacometti's striding figures are modeled as they are viewed by him from a considerable distance: extremely attenuated, lacking in definition to the extent that flesh and clothing are indistinguishable, and flattened out according to the profile they present to us. The base of the group is meant to simulate a city street, and Giacometti captures the momentary encounter of five figures who share a unity of time and place yet seem to experience no other interchange. As with Rodin's striding figure, identity or goals are irrelevant. All that is important to Giacometti is the fascinating visual phenomenon of these human bodies made elusive by their distance from one another, their motion, and his own perceptions. The sculptor disclaims any symbolical intent, avowing that he has enough trouble just in seeing and modeling the external

appearance of his subjects. Despite the differences of his forms from those of Rodin, it is the latter's example of separating the human figure from heroic or literary identity and accepting the facts of everyday existence as the basis for sculptural drama in which Giacometti's work is grounded.

Giacometti's preoccupation with the mystery of surface appearance that arises from his attempts at truth to *his* vision are not shared by Henry Moore and the American Seymour Lipton. Two militant themes executed by these men contrasted with a similar subject from the fifteenth century help us to remember the infinite possibilities available to interpretation

Figure 444. ALBERTO GIACOMETTI. *City Square*. 1948–49. Bronze, base 25×17″; height of tallest figure 8″. The Pierre Matisse Gallery, New York.

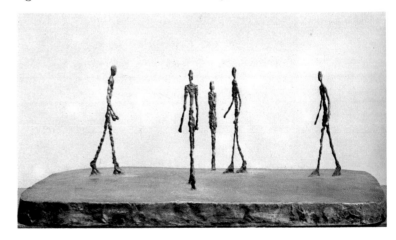

of the human figure. Donatello's *St. George* (Fig. 445) was a heroic public image with which the citizens of Florence could identify. The saintly knight was a civic symbol of manliness, strength, and courage. (Its commissioning by an armorer's guild also served a commercial interest.) The figure's humanity shines through its armor in the handsome face, the erect posture, and the palpable pressure of bodily weight against the ground.

Henry Moore's *Warrior* (Fig. 446) was done on his own initiative, possibly as a personal rememberance of the heroic and defiant stand

Figure 445. DONATELLO, *St. George*. c. 1417. Marble, height 6'8¼". Museo Nazionale, Florence.

Figure 446. HENRY MOORE. *Warrior*. 1953–54. Bronze, height 5'2". The Minneapolis Institute of Arts, Minnesota (John Cowles Foundation).

of wounded Britain in the early days of the Nazi bombings. (We have seen how in the nineteenth century the concept of the hero changed to a pathetic one.) Along with defiance and a demonic will to survival, Moore's partial figure, unlike those of Rodin, carries with it deliberately the fact of mutilation. Though more strongly naturalistic in the formation of the body than his earlier *Reclining Woman*, the head of the Moore *Warrior* has a surprising inversion in the form of a cleft where the nose should protrude. Moore has taken ideas from very early Greek art, incentives to depart from external appearance, and also has sought to evade specific ethnic or temporal reference in his figure. The warrior's body is Moore's personal mixture of anatomical knowledge and an intuitive sense of what are expressive re-formations (such as the hollow of the stomach) and good sculptural form. For Moore to have imitated Donatello's *St. George* or Apollonius' torso would have been as impossible, ethically and otherwise, as going back to late medieval warfare or worshiping the Greek gods.

One of the most powerful sculptures based on the human form since 1945 is Seymour Lipton's *Sentinel* (Fig. 447). Despite its lack of reference to the familiar external anatomy of the body, such as found in Donatello's figure, the sculpture possesses a strong human presence. *Sentinel* is in the tradition of twentieth-century imaginative metaphorical sculpture. Lipton conceived of a sculpture to signify brooding power and demonic force. His metaphor, which has internal and wider associations than the *St. George*, is compounded of reminiscences of a helmeted figure in armor, a battering ram, a fortress battlement, Chinese calligraphy, a heraldic device, and the orchestration of feelings of push and pull, human dignity, and life's mystery. Lipton's metaphor exists as part of a profound personal language and is, one might say, "open-ended." The work is not meant to be dissected nor to have its components systematically traced.

The sculpture is about 8½ feet tall, so that it is possible to approach it and stand under the arrow-visor-battlement shape at the apex. The sculpture has both an inside and an outside. It deals with fantasies on internal anatomy; it is an attempt to exteriorize the inner struggle and defiance in the life of man. Using cut-out sheets of Monel metal, brazed with nickel, silver, or bronze, Lipton carried out his conceits and created a new psychological depth and physiology for the body.

In modern sculpture the body has lost many of its previous heroic and religious functions as a vehicle for abstract thought and ethics. It has gained new forms of life and spirituality by being imaginatively turned inside out, metaphorized, and reconstituted in unnatural forms or shapes whose ambivalence has linked it with other forms of organic life—often reversing the Greek and Renaissance ideal of interpreting nature by means of man. The modern sculptor has claimed a personal and complete authority over the body, reshaping it according to private values and in sculptural, rather than theological or biological, terms. The complete physical body has come to be frequently and frankly rejected as indispensable to a perfect work of art.

Figure 447. SEYMOUR LIPTON. *Sentinel*. 1959. Monel metal, height 8'6". The Yale University Art Gallery, New Haven, Connecticut.

While the modern sculptor's vision may not be judged to be as lofty or intelligible as that of his predecessors, he nonetheless seeks to be honest in interpreting what he actually sees and feels in ways that are possible only in the means and media of sculpture, both old and new. Moreover, the modern sculptor has made us conscious of shapes and rhythm apart from representations of the body, to a degree that we can be moved by the esthetic values of older sculpture whose original meanings and cultural background are forever lost to us.

The Figure in Sculpture   373

19

PICASSO

More than any other artist, Pablo Picasso symbolizes to the general public the revolutionary aspect of modern art. A census of his subjects, however, reveals that for the most part they conform to those of older art—portraits and self-portraits, still lifes, landscapes, animals, the studio, mothers and children, lovers, illustrations of literature and myths, war and combat between men and animals, themes of pleasure and suffering, and the reinterpretation of past works of art. The extent and variety of subjects demonstrate the artist's tremendous range of interests and his sensibility to the esthetic, social, psychological, emotional, and physical make-up of life. In 1964 Picasso summed up this aspect of his work, "I have a curiously restless quality that does not reflect the self-doubt of an insecure mind, but the creative spirit of a man sure of himself." By his own assessment, "I am fundamentally an original artist in tune with the cultural discontents and attitudes of our age, but I often show a decided tendency to break away from the proved mold of modern society." Picasso is one of the few modern artists who have not specialized. This may be explained by his attitude toward what the artist is:

The artist is a receptacle for emotions that come from all over the place: from the sky, from the earth, from a scrap of paper, from a passing shape, from a spider's web.... Where things are concerned there is no class distinctions. We must pick out what is good for us where we can find it [1935].

Despite Picasso's seemingly encyclopedic interests, with but few exceptions he has not concerned himself with religious problems and Biblical themes. Picasso is close to Rembrandt in his spiritual concern with man as he exists outside the organized church and its laws. Unlike Rembrandt, however, Picasso does not attach a deep philosophical importance to flesh, light, and pigment, though his strength lies in the way he has been able to interpret the human body.

Accompanying the variety of Picasso's subject matter is an equally diversified series of styles, sometimes utilized in the same period. Again the artist's own words are relevant:

If the subjects I have wanted to express have suggested different ways of expression, I have never hesitated to adopt them.... This does not imply either evolution or progress, but an adaptation of the idea one wants to express and the means to express that idea [1923].

There is an ethical basis, then, for Picasso's modal system and his recourse to such diversified media as painting, graphics, drawing, and sculpture.

Throughout his life Picasso has returned to certain basic themes and problems, feeling that in growing older he has brought new insights to bear, as well as superior means of realization. With his pride in craft and concern with its problems and potential, there coexists a humanistic sense of inquiry and sympathy.

Merely the outlining of the statistics of Picasso's personal history, his travels, outstanding projects, and the people who have influenced him would take up an entire chapter. To begin with, however, it should be noted that there were no important and famous teachers in his youth, no sponsors of the stature of the Renaissance—a fact that casts light on the conditions under which many modern artists work. The many books on Picasso make his fascinating biography easily accessible to the interested student. Let it suffice to say here that Picasso was born in 1881 in Malaga, Spain, the son of an art teacher, with whose assistance he passed with distinction and amazing speed the entrance examinations for two Barcelona academies in 1895 and 1897.

The uneasiness that much of the public still has about Picasso's ability to draw accurately from a subject stems from an unfamiliarity with his naturalistic student drawings, such as a conte crayon rendering made from a plaster cast of a reclining figure from the Parthenon, which was given as a problem to the Barcelona art students (Fig. 448). This early exposure to making art from art deeply influenced Picasso, and years later he was to continue making drawings and paintings in which his version of ancient sculpture and its fragments would be the subject or basis of his style. What this early drawing demonstrates is the precocious control the young Picasso had over drawing as an instrument and the acuteness of his vision in preserving the proportions as well as profile of the motif before his eyes. In Barcelona, he came in contact with an important group of artists and intellectuals and with advanced European art of the day. By his third trip to Paris in 1904, he had decided to settle in that city; by this time, also, critical success was beginning to come to his work after early years of neglect and privation.

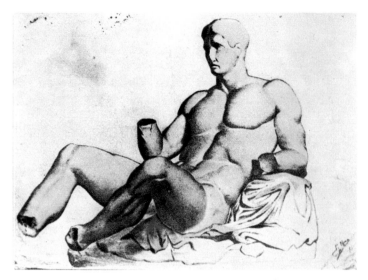

Figure 448. PABLO PICASSO. *Drawing from a Cast of the Figure of Dionysus* (East Pediment of the Parthenon). 1893–94. Conte crayon. Private collection.

Picasso's art before 1905 was filled with images of poverty, which were a sincere expression of his own economic plight and that of his Spanish and Parisian friends. His subjects were bohemians, artists, personal acquaintances, the part of society forced to live a difficult marginal existence. *The Frugal Repast* (Fig. 449) is one of Picasso's first prints, a virtuoso performance both in its technique and in its demonstration of the artist's ability to wed modes of drawing to the mood of his subjects. The seated figures, one of whom may be a self-portrait, reflect Picasso's early search for pathos in postures. Joined by the arrangement

Figure 449. PABLO PICASSO. *The Frugal Repast.* 1904. Etching, 18¼ × 14¾".

Figure 450. PABLO PICASSO. *Self-portrait*. 1906. Oil on canvas, 36×28″. The Philadelphia Museum of Art.

of their limbs, the bodies make a stable closed composition that contrasts with the apparent instability and divergence of their attention and personalities. Their bony attenuation is an expressive device that at the same time conveys privation and permits extreme and elegant figure distortion. The greys and blacks of the etching are appropriate to the morbid subject. At this time Picasso was exploring the over-all use of single tonalities (such as blue and green), with wide latitude of nuance, to set the mood of an entire work. Remarkable as is the sensitive reconstruction of the faces and hands, of even greater importance artistically is the way that Picasso interrelated the figures with the objects on the table. The structure, placement, and weight of the vessels can be felt in relation to the emaciated human bodies. The curve in the neck of the bottle is echoed in the curved shadow at the upper left and in the man's elbow. Adding to the depressing aura is the hollow of the empty bowl, seen against the declivity of the man's torso as if a visual metaphor of hunger.

In his earliest etchings, Picasso accommodated his style to the inherent potential of needle, acid, and ink. The silhouettes appear as if the etching needle were actually touching inflections of the arms; no nuance of observation is missed, and some are added. The gamut of exquisitely soft shaded tones affectingly evokes flesh, cloth over bony flesh, and bottle glass. This etching is rich in the number, disposition, and means by which Picasso used his blacks and moved through a full tone scale, from the deepest to the lightest. The over-all intensity of untouched white paper is held in check by faint touches of the needle, such as in the fan-shaped clusters of strokes on the wall behind the figures.

Two years after *The Frugal Repast*, Picasso painted a vigorous self-portrait (Fig. 450) that reveals his changed attitude toward the human body and art. Elimination of pathos and social consciousness seems to have coincided with Picasso's improved financial status and artistic success. Throughout his work, the painter's life and his art intermingle in confessional, playful, or boastful tones. In this portrait Picasso avowed a new willfulness that joined altered conceptions of what was manly and what was art. There is no melodrama or plea for sympathy. Instead, the portrait exudes frank self-confidence; Picasso keeps no secrets. His power comes from his will, eye, and hand and from the colors of the palette. Years later, Picasso was to remark that it was above all the hand which determined the painting. In this self-portrait, Picasso stripped away those details which might mitigate or be extraneous to the concentrated and immediate effect he desired. He had become aware that expressivity resides in the way in which the means of art are used, reflecting the urgent feelings and the intelligence of the artist. Picasso here reduced his means drastically from the manner of the etching. A contrast of the eyes and ears of the man in both works is revealing, but comparing their right arms is an even more effective gauge. The right arm of the man in *The Frugal Repast* is one of the most beautiful in Picasso's art. It was born from a thousand tiny openings incised in the metal plate. In the painting, by contrast, two major strokes establish the arm's shape, weight, direction, and robust strength.

What Picasso was seeking was a forceful reduction of means, not necessarily simplifica-

Plate 53.   OSKAR KOKOSCHKA. *Hans Tietze and Erica Tietze-Conrat.* 1909. Oil on canvas, 2′6⅛″ × 4′5⅝″. The Museum of Modern Art, New York (Abby Aldrich Rockefeller Fund).

Plate 54.   PABLO PICASSO. *Les Demoiselles d'Avignon.* 1906–07. Oil on canvas, 8' × 7'8".
The Museum of Modern Art, New York (acquired through the Lillie P. Bliss Bequest).

tion. This reduction may leave few strokes, colors, and shapes, yet its residual effect is not simple. The self-portrait has a strong immediate effect but reveals still more after a slow and thoughtful reading of its part-to-part construction. No arc or curve in the painting is pure geometry; each contains irregularities that come from Picasso's feeling for the nature of the shape and his need to preserve vitality and interest of line. The two lines of the arm, those of the neckline, the brows, and the contour of the face are distillations of thousands he had drawn earlier, such as those in the etching. The silhouette of the white shirt developed from the contour-probing of the tablecloth and arms in *The Frugal Repast*. Accumulated experience provided the basis for the seemingly intuitive judgment that distinguishes the bold black contour lines appearing in the shirt, for example.

Picasso admired the intensity of expression in primitive masks, but he admired more the asymmetrical constructions of symmetrical human features and objects in Cézanne's art. Also from Cézanne, Picasso received the idea of creating continuities in art where in nature there were discontinuities, and vice versa. The palette, for instance, is locked into place in the self-portrait by its close coincidence with the sleeve and bottom of the shirt. Cézanne's reduction of myriad shapes to multiples of each other found comprehension in Picasso's conjugation of ovoid forms in the head and the neckline of the shirt and the multiplicity of arcs within the same area. The young artist was learning to recognize and manipulate the emotive power of certain shapes in varied combination, and in his self-portrait he made of himself more an object of esthetic rather than psychological study.

For some reason, Picasso removed the brush from his hand in the painting, and the heaviness of the pigment's application suggests that he might just as well have worked the paint with his fingers. In these years Picasso was searching for a new feeling of what the primal nature of art was and could be. Preserving a certain rawness of means, he gave the completed work a rugged, handmade look. Picasso had even eliminated the customary use of a mirror, as shown by the placement of his right arm on the left side of the painting.

Les Demoiselles d'Avignon (Pl. 54) is one of Picasso's most notorious, but by no means most

esthetically successful, paintings. The ideas and energies unleashed in its creation as well as its failures make it important in the history of Picasso's art. The painting, which was the largest undertaken by Picasso until that time, was destined to incompletion and inconsistency because of the rapidity and excitement with which his art was changing from month to month and from painting to painting. Thus, in 1906 and 1907, both emotionally and esthetically, Picasso was incapable of producing a large, complex, and homogeneous canvas. In a single year of this phase his production of drawings and paintings equalled or exceeded the lifetime output of many artists of the past. It was not only a question of youthful energy but also of Picasso's compulsion to work out every idea and impulse as it flooded through related series of drawings and paintings which cannot be taken in isolation as they enter into his artistic development.

Les Demoiselles d'Avignon was both a battleground and a nursery for Picasso's art. On its surface he seemed to wage war with the accumulated traditions of Western painting, accepting solely the demands of pictorial order. The tearing down accomplished in this work was partially balanced by what it presented as new and fruitful alternatives, for it was to take Picasso additional thousands of drawings, canvases, and sculptures—in fact, a lifetime—to realize and fulfill all that was begun or hinted at in this one painting. The painting's theme began in sketches as an allegory: "The wages of sin is death." Prostitutes in a brothel paraded before a sailor and, in one instance, a death's head. Accompanying the departure of the skull and sailor from the successive designs was also the moralizing intent. The painting passed through numerous stages until it lost any programatic meaning and would then have been awkward to fit into the traditional category of genre. What Picasso was moving toward was painting primarily as an esthetic object intended to move and delight the beholder. This meant stripping away the conventional sentiment of the female nude as well as other conventions of drawing, color, and composition. Brutal as are its conception and execution, *Les Demoiselles d'Avignon* descends nonetheless from a long line of genteel and robust paintings of nudes. In retrospect, it seems almost a parody of suave sensuous nude studies by such Baroque painters as Rubens. Picasso's nude females elbow against the woodland nymphs, goddesses, and innocent bathers who for so many generations symbolized concord with nature and sinless fertility.

Picasso seemed undecided whether to stage the women indoors or out; the figure at the left seems to have a farm woman's tan, unlike the pink complexion of the woman next to her. Picasso's women are objects of display transformed by the instincts of the artist, which enter freely onto the canvas. The prostitutes are given a mixed ethnological background, reflecting Picasso's new-found excitement with ancient art (the central two figures) and with African tribal art (those on the sides). Picasso's primitivizing tendency adopted certain models of distortion and what he may have felt was the sexual intensity of African sculpture. These were grafted onto the Greek Classical beauty pose in the center, the rigid vertical Egyptian stance at the left, and the seated studio model at the right. In the profile figure at the left Picasso used the Egyptian frontal eye, while in the two adjacent figures he put a profile nose on a frontal face.

The green-striped face of the woman at the upper right may have derived from primitive masks showing scarification, a process echoed in Picasso's painting. Each figure is either an ethnic or esthetic hybrid, and only the still life of the fruit is finished and consistent. Left with too many fragments and ideas, he was forced to suspend his growth to complete the whole.

Within the frame of the painting, traces of Picasso's struggles to destroy and reconstruct are plainly visible, even to notations such as the rough blue outline superimposed on the leg at the lower left. Picasso had set aside tradi-

Figure 451. PABLO PICASSO. *Drawing of Head, Apple, and Box.* 1909. Collection Douglas Cooper.

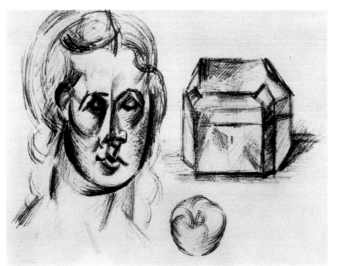

tional means of uniting a group of figures: common focus, activity, moods, viewpoint, setting, and light and shade or coordinated limb arrangement no longer met his needs. To give his canvas its own autonomy, the figures and setting had to relinquish theirs. The body contours were broken into, and parts were made almost interchangeable by their reduction to such basic shapes as the V repeated in crotch, breast, elbow, and jagged background forms. Cohesion and expressiveness of surface demanded flat rather than voluminous bodies, the obscuring of the figure's means of support, making space relationships inconsistent, and the assigning of accents and visual importance that rivaled the bodies themselves to intervals between figures. The rhythms and force set by the restructuring of the bodies spill over into the indeterminate background.

The painting's pinks, blues, whites, browns, and blacks are a tonal recapitulation of all Picasso's previous periods. The blue between the central and right figures is glacial and sharply appealing to the eye. Picasso's conflicting impulses led him to mix outline and edge, modeled and flat surfaces, and black, white, and blue silhouettes. He could not resolve so much color and so many modes into a single dominant harmony of contrasts; yet ironically, much of the painting's initial appeal derives from this very freshness of color and raw juxtapositions. Picasso probably intended a painting with shock value, to stab directly at the senses or the emotions rather than the intellect. With Matisse and others of the time, Picasso shared an ethic of the primacy of feeling in art as well as in life. His dilemma as a painter lay in possessing the instinct for lucid control and linear organization; ultimately, he was unable to liberate both color and drawing as could Matisse.

Picasso's development was rapid and extremely varied. There was no simple continuous progression toward his completely Cubist paintings, but we shall try, briefly, to illustrate this latter direction. *Head, Apple, and Box* (Fig. 451) shows a more consistent style than *Les Demoiselles d'Avignon*. It illustrates the artist's extension of the Cubist mode to objects as well as to the human form. The head's anatomical structure and the shapes of the objects do not predict the premises of Picasso's drawing. His design does not follow, say, the musculature of the face, the natural curves of the features, nor the proportions and planes of the box as generally perceived. He increased the complexity and expressiveness of the face through new angles and facets. Though passive in mood, the woman's face is activated by the energized drawing in such inventions as the peaked eyes and the arbitrary placement and increased degree of shadow. There is no dominant symmetrical vertical axis in any of the forms; the artist clearly preferred disconnected sequences. The box, with its inverted perspective and multiplication of planes, becomes a crystal form of increased weight and stability. At this stage of Cubism, Picasso was still interested in light and shadow, mass and volume, and the sensual swelling of flesh. Characteristic of his drawing was the swinging rhythm of repeated parallel movements by which he worked from light to dark, re-created the rotundity of the apple, or found a continuity between the right side of the woman's face and the arc under the chin. No large flat surface remained uninflected, no parallel lines were of the same length, and no two features were identical. Still, with all the resultant variety and richness, his means were restricted to simple straight and curved lines.

Ma Jolie (Pl. 55) was a painting of Marcelle Humbert, with whom Picasso was deeply in love and who died during World War I. "Ma Jolie" was both the epithet he gave to her and the title of a popular song. In line with his ideas of the years 1911–1912, Picasso could not paint her in the traditional portrait manner. In part he "inscribed" his love, as he put it, on the canvases devoted to her, with the words "J'aime Eva" and "Ma Jolie." Such sentiments had never before been so literally a part of the work of art. The fact that Picasso accomplished this without disrupting the integrity or logic of the painting is in itself a sign of Cubism's radical break with the past. From the Renaissance through the nineteenth century, art consisted in imitating the physical appearance of nature. With the development of Cubism, empirical verification was to be found only in the terms of the painting itself. The similitude to be appreciated is that of the final painting to the emotions of the artist who produced it. Expressed in another way, Picasso in *Ma Jolie* did not deal directly with the world of appearances, with regard for its distinctions and logic.

His drawing and color were meant as visual equivalences of his love for Eva in the same way that the words "Ma Jolie" could be equivalences of a song and a woman without really looking or sounding like either. In a sense, the pulse of warm and cool color alternation and the shimmer of countless touches of the brush give a palpable presence to the "vibrations" of her life as Picasso felt them. The diagonals and vertical massing of the planes are vestiges of the seated human figure. Still, Picasso wanted not the literal appearance of a woman but of a painting, a unified, moving, and beautiful object. On the wooden stretcher of the canvas, Picasso wrote, "Woman with a Zither," probably the original title. Part of a hand seen at the lower right is properly in position to hold the instrument. The zither's design has analogies to the painting's vocabulary of forms. While music did not supply the theory or model for Cubist painting, it was a bond by which the artist and, in this case, the woman Picasso loved were joined. Though the resulting order of the painting reflects intellectual precision, the whole was done with genuine passion. The drawing and painting of *Ma Jolie* is disciplined and of great beauty.

Some of Picasso's own statements on Cubism, made in 1923, are important in understanding the artist's conception of its nature and its relation to the past:

Cubism is...an art dealing primarily with forms, and when a form is realized, it is there to live its own life....Drawing, design and color are understood and practiced in Cubism in the same spirit and manner that they are understood and practiced in all other schools....We have kept our eyes open to our surroundings and also our brains. We give to form and color all their individual significance....The fact that for a long time Cubism has not been understood...means nothing. I do not read English, an English book is a blank book to me. This does not mean that the English language does not exist, and why should I blame anybody else but myself if I cannot understand what I know nothing about.

Picasso's inexhaustible creative energy and the fertile ideas of Cubism led him to work in sculpture in a manner as unprecedented as his painting. One of Picasso's most influential works is the wooden construction *Mandolin*

Figure 452. PABLO PICASSO. *Mandolin.* 1914. Construction in wood, height 23⅝″. Collection of the artist.

(Fig. 452). Its fabrication and appearance appear to resist the label of sculpture, for it has not been cast, modeled, or carved; it does not sit upon a base, and its subject is a musical instrument. For his materials Picasso used scraps of wood from boxes and canvas stretchers, discards that lay about his study. The wood that Picasso employed had been processed and shaped to fulfill utilitarian functions before being put to his purely esthetic purposes. His selection of these scraps was not haphazard, for he was attracted initially by the grain, size, and shapes. Some pieces may have been used without reworking; in these, the "found object" is preserved intact in the sculpture. Most of the scraps had something done to them, however, either painting or sawing. The curved white piece, like the planes in Cubist paintings, reveals the rough marks of its formation, for none of the forms was sanded. The rude finishing is essential to Picasso's ethic and esthetic sense. The sculpture has been assembled, constructed, literally manipulated; this method of joining along with the expanded tolerance of artistic materials was to have a strong effect on subsequent modern sculpture.

Picasso, like other advanced artists of the time, was rebelling against the academic conception of "noble media," such as marble and bronze, and "noble subjects," such as the human figure in heroic action. Whatever heroism is present in the *Mandolin* resides in the courage and daring of the artist's defiance of tradition; literally and figuratively, Picasso helped to remove sculpture from the pedestal of tradition. His is not relief sculpture in the old sense, for it has no rectangular frame to contain the sculpture or to balance and coordinate the shapes within. The absence of the frame also introduces the possibility of a play of irregular shadows cast onto the wall by the projecting parts, and these shadows give added depth and vibrancy to the work. There is no consistent or uniform rear plane to which successive relief planes can be referred. Even more than in Cubist painting, the planes of this sculpture advance into the space of the beholder, and yet display an inconsistent overlapping that maintains an ambivalence of inward and outward movement. Picasso painted some of the construction, reversing the trend begun with Michelangelo, one of the first major sculptors to give up painting his figures.

As an artist, Picasso has frequently indulged in playful activity, making his seriousness of purpose suspect to some. When, for example, he made the *Head of a Bull* (Fig. 453) by juxtaposing a bicycle seat and handlebars and hanging them on a wall, he was creating art from a child's toy. His earlier construction *Mandolin* had taught him the possibilities of

Figure 453. PABLO PICASSO. *Head of a Bull.* 1943. Handlebars and bicycle seat, height 16⅛″. Collection of the artist.

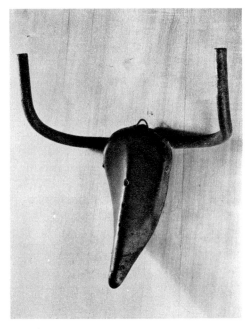

transposing and manipulating materials and already existing objects, to which his eye and mind gave a second life. Much of today's sculpture involving the rehabilitation of discarded objects, which derives its artistic value from the witty and imaginative visual plays of the sculptor rather than from manual reforming, owes a great deal to such earlier works as *Head of a Bull*. Picasso has never claimed that such playful activities as this constitute great art. He would be the first to remind us that what he has done in such works is not unlike what occurs to youthful imagination that is too soon lost as we become adults. As is true of much modern literary criticism, that of art is too often obsessed by false absolutes of greatness that may cause both critic and audience to forfeit enjoyment of much that is good or interesting.

THE ARTIST AND MODEL SERIES

As with Rembrandt, the theme of the making of art or the artist and model in the studio appears repeatedly in Picasso's work. Different versions of this theme reveal Picasso's ability to work in different modes. An etching with a subject revealing the way Picasso worked is *Painter with Model Knitting* (Fig. 454), an illustration for Balzac's *The Unknown Masterpiece*. The short story is concerned with a certain Frenhofer, a seventeenth-century painter who devoted his life to achieving a perfect balance, within a single painting, of drawing and color. In Balzac's time, Poussin and Rubens were considered rivals championing, respectively, drawing and color. The artist's final masterpiece is a chaos of drawing and color, out of which emerges a small but superb woman's foot. The old artist, recognizing his failure, destroys himself and his art.

In the etching, the artist's design bears no resemblance to the external appearance of the woman, but it does catch the spirit of Frenhofer's dictum that in drawing a hand it is not enough to show its attachment to the body, but it must also be shown as a continuation or extension of thought and feeling. The drawing on the canvas is a form of knitting, in which the woman is translated into a series of interwoven rhythmic configurations. Unlike the painting in progress in Vermeer's *Art of Painting*, the outcome of the drawing is unforeseeable on the basis of the model. In 1935, Picasso said, "A picture is not thought out and settled beforehand. While it is being done, it changes as one's thoughts change. And when it is finished it still goes on changing according to the state of mind of whoever is looking at it."

It is unwise to try to label Picasso's modes or to call the drawing of the model in his illustration "abstract." On the use of this word, Picasso said in 1935:

Figure 454. PABLO PICASSO. *Painter with Model Knitting.* 1927. Etching, $7^5/_8 \times 11^3/_8$". The Museum of Modern Art, New York (gift of Henri Church).

There is no abstract art. You must always start with something. Afterward you can remove all traces of reality. There's no danger then, anyway, because the idea of the object will have left an indelible mark. It is what started the artist off, excited his ideas, and stirred up his emotions (that) will in the end be prisoners in his work....They form an integral part of it even when their presence is no longer discernible. Whether he likes it or not, man is the instrument of nature. It forces on him its character and appearance.

In 1927 Picasso also did a painting, *The Painter and His Model* (Fig. 455), in which the artist was remade into an angular linear frame and the woman became a hybrid entity, with drastic relocation of bodily features. The period of the late 1920s was one of Picasso's most fertile in terms of body imagery and imaginative nourishment of his art. Fantasies on the body took diverse forms, and in this particular painting the model has been brutally reduced to an animallike and precariously balanced shape. Strong sexual feeling freely entered Picasso's work at all times and inspired new inventions such as those here seen for distinguishing the man and woman. What liberated Picasso's imagination still further after Cubism was the conviction that external appearances could be dispensed with in painting and that there were alternative means originating in strong feeling by which to preserve reference to human sub-

Figure 455. PABLO PICASSO. *The Painter and His Model.* 1927. Oil on canvas, 7′¼″×6′6¾″. Private collection.

jects. This independence from likeness and conventional modeling of the figure in painting was accompanied in this work by Picasso's separation of color from the limits of drawn contours, so that it is disposed in amorphous areas cutting across several of the drawn motifs.

In 1928 when Picasso again took up the theme *The Painter and his Model* (Fig. 456), color became wedded to the rigid compositional skeleton, itself a logical outgrowth of the earlier Cubist weblike structure. The entire painting surface has a continuous interlocking of distinct flat shapes that affirm the flatness of surface and the nonillusionistic, artificial character of Picasso's creation. Both painter and model have only token reference to actual bodily features, and even these are rearranged to accord with the over-all surface emphasis. The surprising element in the painting is the handsome naturalistic profile that the artist has heavily outlined upon his canvas, a reminder that for Picasso art can slip easily from the fantastic into the naturalistic.

In 1933 Picasso did a series of etchings for the dealer Ambrose Vollard that contain a rich assortment of themes and stylistic modes. Many of these plates were devoted to the theme of the sculptor in his studio. Despite their obvious reference to ancient sculpture, Picasso's own interest in this medium during these years makes these prints another kind of self-portrait. He shows the bearded sculptor, for example, reclining and contemplating a finished sculpture, the model for which lies next to him with a mask raised above her face (Fig. 457). Unlike in the previous works, Picasso draws the artist, model, and work of art in the same style, which is his personal version of classical drawing, inspired to a large extent by that of Matisse. The clean purity and unerring limning of contours in this print presuppose Picasso's academic training and consummate knowledge of the body. The strong suggestion of the body's roundness conveyed by the character of the line made shading unnecessary, thereby conserving the surface unity as well. The print is also Picasso's personal ideal of the tranquillity necessary for a creative life. He recently wrote, "I have an unquestioning faith in the expressive power of the human body, untiring devotion to the glories of the nude."

It was natural for Picasso, when he worked with etchings, to think of Rembrandt. Not

Left: Figure 456. PABLO PICASSO. *The Painter and His Model.* 1928. Oil on canvas, 4′3⅝″×5′3⅞″. Collection Mr. and Mrs. Sidney Janis, New York.

Below left: Figure 457. PABLO PICASSO. *Artist and Model with a Mask Before a Sculpture.* March 27, 1933. Etching, 10½×7⅝″. The Museum of Modern Art, New York (Purchase).

Below right: Figure 458. PABLO PICASSO. *Rembrandt with a Young Woman.* February 18, 1934. Etching, 5½×8¼″.

detailed self-portraits of the old master. He could not resist framing one of his own women's heads in the pendant worn by Rembrandt, and the model could only be Picasso's creation. What unites the two artists, besides their prolific artistic production, is their abjuring of systematic theories and their commitment to working from art and life, which is most graphically presented in the studio portrait situation.

Given Picasso's life-long fascination with the subject of the artist and art itself, his repainting of El Greco's *Portrait of an Artist* (Figs. 459, 460) is logical. To some this may seem like plagiarism, but we have seen how, in the history of art, artists for centuries before Picasso repainted (that is, did their own versions of) each other's pictures. Contradictory as it may seem, Picasso was thus paying his respects to a painter he greatly admires. The somber tones, the position-

only was he fascinated by the older artist's etched gradations of black, but Picasso also did several prints of Rembrandt based on the latter's self-portraits in which he dressed himself in a fur-trimmed robe and soft cap and hung a gold chain across his chest. In 1934 he etched Rembrandt (Fig. 458), with his "elephant-like eyes," as Picasso called them, contemplating a beautiful bare-chested model, appropriate in view of Rembrandt's teachings and works on the subject of life drawing. Picasso evolved his own mode of involuted lines and their dense grouping to interpret the picturesque and richly

Figure 459. PABLO PICASSO. *Portrait of an Artist* (after El Greco). 1950. Oil on wood, 39¾×31¾". Collection Mlle. Angela Rosengart, Lucerne.

Above: Figure 460. El Greco. *Portrait of an Artist (Jorge Manuel Theotocopuli).* c. 1600–05. Oil on canvas, 31⅞×22". Museo Provincial, Seville.

ing of the hands and implements, the enframing of the head by the collar, all these details appealed to Picasso's eye, and his redrawing of the artist's features was not intended as caricature. New styles can give new life to old themes, as we well know from popular musical arrangements. If the artist is truly the source of creation for art, how plausible then that Picasso should have made the artist himself the inspiration for imaginative painting.

WORK LEADING TO GUERNICA

Although Picasso's painting of the bombing of Guernica was not painted until 1937, its sources within his own art go back many years and can be found among such seemingly unrelated subjects of the 1920s as still lifes, dancing figures, and bathers and during the 1930s in his interpretation of the Crucifixion themes, bullfights, and Greek mythology.

The still life of the *Ram's Head* (Pl. 56) testifies to the viability of the Cubist style and to Picasso's alertness to new subject matter.

There is far less decomposition of objects than in *Ma Jolie*, and familiar textures and shapes facilitate reading the contents. What is new and unfamiliar in Picasso's art is the range of unpleasant sensations the objects inspire. The objects are foods in a raw inedible state, unlike the more palatable contents of earlier Cubist still lifes, with their sociable connotations and objects that appealed to the touch. Picasso contrasted the horn and hair of the ram, fish scales, and shells with sharp edges against moist, pulpy substances like the squid at the lower left. Violence is to be seen in the subjects themselves—in the severed head of the ram and the arsenal of teeth in the gaping fish mouth—consonant with the abrupt conjunctions of textures. The yellow of the blue-veined lemon to the left of the ram's head, a rectangular patch cut by the circular lemon, adds a conspicuous note of color to the dominant blues, whites, and browns of the painting. The black linear scaffolding of the paintings of the *Ma Jolie* period has disappeared; the composition includes large, free-swinging curved lines and planes that alternate and join with rectilinear passages in tight cohesion. The colors and textures lie flat upon the surface, affirming its two-dimensionality. The objects are tautly grouped and held within the frame by such inventive drawing as the free repeat of the serrated edge under the ram's head and in the spine of the fish.

Another area of sensation into which Picasso's sensibilities forcefully expanded in the mid-1920s was that of internal body imagery, seen in *Three Dancers* (Fig. 461). Traditionally, naked figures in an interior meant that the artist was studying anatomy and poses. By 1925, Picasso had become interested in the art of fantasy as exhibited by Miró and Arp. What appealed to Picasso were their bold incursions into the irrational and the unlocking of inhibitions with respect to form and content. Rather than having created a studio study of the way three naked models might look to someone else, Picasso seems to have imagined their own inner sensations as their bodies are given over to the abandon of a frenzied dance. Each dancer possesses a phantom double, a second and even a third self. This is made apparent in the black areas, which are not literal projected shadows but poetic extensions of each figure's consciousness of the body area in which the strongest feelings are localized. The figure at the left is given an extra breast, that to the right a second and larger head of different silhouette and expression. In an unclinical, intuitive way, Picasso showed how, in moments of great physical exertion and erotic stimulation, a new self-consciousness may come into being. Affected by these conditions may be the emphasis, size, weight, color, shape, location, and even orientation of the body parts. All the figures seem to be boneless, for example, and much of the distortion occurs in the most fleshy areas. Cubism's breakdown of the body as a continuous closed vessel was the foundation for this new imagery in Picasso's art. Picasso and other artists could now extend their most intimate sentiments to the complete internal as well as external reconstruction of the body in art. Picasso gave his figures a fictive transparency, so that we see simultaneously the pink of the flesh and the suggestions of internal organs.

In *Bather Seated by the Sea* (Fig. 462) of 1930, Picasso was making a reconnaissance of an idea for a huge sculpture to be located on the Mediterranean coast. The solidity of the body was broken up, and there is an intriguing

Figure 461. PABLO PICASSO. *Three Dancers*. 1925. Oil on canvas, 7⅝″×4′8¼″. The Tate Gallery, London.

FIGURE 462. PABLO PICASSO. *Bather Seated by the Sea*. 1930. Oil on canvas, 5′4½″×4′3″. The Museum of Modern Art, New York (Mrs. Simon Guggenheim Fund).

fusion of bone and flesh forms. The head of the "bather" has an astonishing and ominous pincer or viselike substitution for the jaws. The transparency of the sculpture derives from his transparent-metal sculpture constructions of two years before, which themselves grew out of his pictorial armatures. The "cross-pollinating" of Picasso's work in different media has always been strong, added to which transfers are his seemingly inexhaustible ideas for metamorphosing the body. The artist had the impulse to make heroic and monumentally scaled sculptures, feeling that there were certain artistic traditions which should not die and to which his viable art could give new life. This impulse to revitalize artistic traditions even when they seem to run counter to his own work is illustrated by his taking up of secular and religious themes that had been overworked and demeaned by insincere and uninspired handling.

CRUCIFIXION AND GUERNICA

The first painting by Picasso in which he treats a theme of explicit violence, as contrasted with his own artistic violence in painting passive subjects, is a small picture done in 1930 after many drawings, entitled *Crucifixion* (Fig. 463). This is an unusual painting for Picasso in many ways. It was the first time he had interpreted a subject drawn from literature, or the Bible, and it was a work not intended for a church or the public. We do not know what caused him to take up this theme, and its relation to his personal life or his possible reaction to a painting on the subject can only be conjectural. What seems to

Figure 463. PABLO PICASSO. *Crucifixion.* February 7, 1930. Oil on wood, 20×26". Collection of the artist.

have initially attracted him to the subject of the Crucifixion, judging by the preliminary drawings, was not Christ's agonies on the Cross but rather the passionate sufferings of Mary Magdalen and the complex and expressive interweaving of limbs and faces. With his own breakthrough in body imagery of the late 1920s, whereby the emotional state of the subject could be exteriorized by drastic changes in the appearance of the body, he could thus reinterpret in a personal and subjective way one of the great themes of art that had been given up by most modern artists. Unlike the symbolic objects in the *Breviary of King Martin of Aragon* (Fig. 379), we cannot easily interpret and relate all the parts of Picasso's painting. It is possible to identify the crucified Christ and the figure on a ladder nailing a hand to the Cross, the soldiers gambling for Christ's cloak, the mounted centurion who lances Christ's side, and at the far right the draped Magdalen figure with outstretched arms. The fantastic heads with gaping jaws seen in different parts of the painting, which spring from Picasso's previous secular imagery, may have been introduced to symbolize the animallike brutality of the event. (A crowing cock to illustrate the episode of Peter may be the creature to the left.) The painting's intensity within such a small format results from its hot red and yellow colors, which like the shapes are crowded into a restricted space. As much as the drawing, these colors convey Picasso's passionate feeling and, rather than being decorative, add to the emotional dissonance of the conception.

During the 1930s Picasso was strongly attracted to ancient Greek mythology, partly as a reaction to the futility of rational conduct in the face of the rise of fascism. There resulted in Picasso's art, notably in his etching *Minotauromachia* (Fig. 464), the formation of private myths, rather than literal interpretations of such Greek legends as Theseus and the Minotaur. In many drawings, prints, and paintings preceding this etching, Picasso had created fantasies based upon the Minotaur, the bull, and the bullfight. These, coupled with prior themes in his art, were brought together in the *Minotauromachia* with no rational plan or discernible narrative. The whole is a model of the illusionistic surrealist image built upon instinctive creation, as discussed in the next chapter. The artist responded to obsessive

themes mingling the bizarre, erotic, violent, and innocent in free association.

Both in his previous interpretations and in the *Minotauromachia,* Picasso deviated from the original story of the Minotaur. In antiquity, the Minotaur was a destructive being to whom young girls were sacrificed. In Picasso's art the Minotaur was severally shown as a pathetic victim, as a tender abductor or object of love, and as confounded with the person of Theseus. In the *Minotauromachia* the Minotaur is not a menacing figure but is shown reaching for the light held by the young girl. Just to the left of the Minotaur's legs is a white sail, instead of the black sail that in the Theseus myth was erroneously kept, resulting in the suicide of Aegeus. The horse and the woman toreador emerge from the earlier bullfight series; and as before, the woman shows evidence of violation. In her dreamlike state she menaces the gored horse with the sword rather than the Minotaur, who also has been fused with the bull in the bullfights series. The figure ascending the ladder at the left, who looks over his shoulder in the direction of the light, is Christ. The theme of Christ mounting to his death is an old one in Spanish art. Above the scene, in the niche of a blockhouse, are two young girls, who are seemingly witnesses to the scene but whose attention is upon two doves. These witness figures also derive from earlier studies of arena combat. The two birds standing before a niche occur in a painting done by Picasso's father before 1900. Much of the etching's fascination comes from the myriad references and ambiguous interrelationships of time, place, and action.

In May, 1937, Picasso began work on studies for a large canvas to commemorate the bombing of the Spanish Basque town of Guernica by Franco's German dive bombers. This was his first painting directly inspired by a specific historical event. Nevertheless, the studies and the completed painting were a logical outlet and summation of his imagery of the late 1920s and 1930s that had dealt with brutality and fantasies upon the body. One brilliant sketch (Fig. 465) shows how Picasso became deeply engrossed in the nonpolitical aspects of the project—notably the theme of the human

Figure 466. PABLO PICASSO. *Guernica*. 1937. Oil on canvas, 11'5½"×25'8¾".
Collection of the artist, on extended loan to The Museum of Modern Art, New York.

deranged by pain. The woman's head has been completely detached from the body, and each feature's response to pain is shown separately. Even the normally neutral areas of eyelashes, brows, and hair participate aggressively. The eyebrows do not lie passively on the forehead but cut into it like deep scars. The hair pulls away from the head, resembling rawly exposed nerves such as are also suggested in the lines from the right eye running down the cheek. The eyes have been pulled apart and transposed into teardrop forms filled and surrounded by splintering shapes. A large dark patch between the eyes localized another area of intense aggravation. The nostrils, one almost detached from the nose, are swollen and flared. The entire head seems divested of its cranial skeleton as it is twisted into soft and angular contortions. The climactic feature is the mouth burst open in a scream, the lips peeled back to reveal the irregular and precariously rooted teeth, the lining of the palate, the black cavity of the throat, and the rigidification of the tongue into a sharp, cutting instrument.

Grünewald's *Isenheim Altarpiece* (Pl. 6) was a source of this drawing. From children's art, Picasso took the use of crayon, and deceptively childish scribbling within the facial contours achieved a graduated series of vaguely defined irritated spots. The drawing betrays the fierce pressure with which the crayon was dug into the paper, particularly in the brow and hair.

Picasso's sadism, extended to his means as well as to his subject, is frankly manifest.

In the final painting of *Guernica* (Fig. 466), Picasso avoided specific or unmistakable political reference to the locale of the tragedy, to the fascist aggressor, or to modern warfare, focusing his attention upon the agonies of the noncombatants. No cipherable links between the figures and groups exist, and while Picasso may have had private symbols in mind, he has consistently refused to spell out his intent. At various times in Picasso's art, the bull has signified Franco and the Spanish people. To assign to the bull at the left the role of aggressor is to overlook clear indications that the bull is also a victim. In the center is the distended head of the dying horse, with its body pierced by a spear. Beneath the horse are segments of a man whose arm clutches a broken sword and a flower. In older art, the figure fallen beneath a galloping horse was a victory symbol, but this tradition was ended in the *Guernica*. From his student days in the Barcelona academy, Picasso had made drawings of figure casts and had introduced them into still lifes during the 1920s. The figure who runs in from the right is a descendant of earlier paintings of gigantesque nudes running along a beach, but now the woman's form is swollen and constricted in exaggerated exteriorization of her internal distress.

Other reminiscences of earlier work are the mother and child, and the woman who leans from the window holding the lamp, who may have vague connotations of justice. There is ambiguity as to the interior or exterior locus of the action (the people of Guernica died both indoors and outdoors) and a puzzling redundancy of light sources. *Guernica* is in part a study in panic; the two women at the right, deprived of all reason, are inexplicably drawn to rather than repelled by the center of the disaster.

The great scale of the *Guernica* was new for Picasso, and he made many drawings for the composition and ended by reducing the number of textures and colors. The use of blacks, greys, and whites not only eliminated certain color problems, but it also created suitable and dramatic accompaniment to the nightmarish theme. The stippled texture in the horse and the over-all black and white, furthermore, resemble the qualities of newsprint and journalistic photos of violence during the turbulent years before the painting. (He did not work from photographs for the *Guernica*, however.) Picasso's recourse to the Classical pyramidal composition is not out of character, for he had taken many motifs and devices from Classical art in previous years. He could not, however, accept the Classical insistence upon the pyramid's centrality, symmetry, and stability, and the climax of the pyramid is not an idealized human but a terrorized beast. (Picasso clearly knew the great paintings of war and disaster by Géricault, Delacroix, and Baron Gros in the Louvre.) The pyramid is interlocked with the

flanking areas through continuities and discontinuities of colors and shapes. The part thus tends to predict the whole, since no single figure is shown in the same tone, nor can its shape be detached from that to which it is adjacent.

It is interesting to compare Picasso's commentary on war with a painting by a Nazi artist, *Dive Bombers over England* (Fig. 467). At first, this looks like a painting of a bright cloud-filled sky over a city, but then the bombers can be seen diving out of the sun toward the brown ruins below. Concern with aerial tactics rather than with human suffering guided the Nazi painter, whose style, ironically, has some indebtedness to French Impressionism, perhaps the most pacifistic art in history. For those people who feel that a democratic, humane art must have complete legibility, Nazi paintings should give pause.

So many ideas emerged in the process of painting the *Guernica*, as evidenced by changes in the final work, that their momentum was carried over to additional studies even after the painting was exhibited.

One such postscript is a painting of the head of an agonized horse (Fig. 468). Picasso continued to build upon the ideas excited by the internal experiences of pain. To the horse's head he has added a simulation of the texture of the hairy and smooth flesh of the outside of the head and the roof of the mouth. This single head set

Figure 467. GEORG LEBRECHT. *Dive-bombers over England*. 1941. Location unknown.

Figure 468. PABLO PICASSO. *Horse's Head*, study for *Guernica*. May 2, 1937. Oil on canvas, 25½× 36¼". Collection of the artist, on extended loan to the Museum of Modern Art, New York.

Picasso   389

Right: Figure 469. PABLO PICASSO. *The Kitchen.* 1948. Oil on canvas, 5′8⅞″×8′2⅜″. Collection of the artist.

Below: Figure 470. PABLO PICASSO. *Seated Woman.* 1959. Oil on canvas, 4′9½″×3′9″. Collection Mr. and Mrs. Victor Ganz.

against a black ground is like a summation of the total anguish of the larger *Guernica*.

Since *Guernica*, Picasso seems to have become content to cultivate his own garden. Few of his later works match his earlier profundity and sustained inventiveness. He has been more playful and recreative, less self-critical. He has chosen to rework his own earlier themes and the art of the old masters and modes, particularly as they relate to his love of his own children, women, and animals.

In *The Kitchen* (Fig. 469), Picasso reworked the Cubist linear structure of his studio painting of the late 1920s by making it more pliable. The secondary color pattern that plays against the black ligatures also descends from one of the studio series. Picasso could never bring himself to remain consistently abstract in a series of paintings, always feeling the need to introduce some reference to nature or objects and thereby holding on to what he feels has been the continuing adhesive force in the history of art.

His *Seated Woman* (Fig. 470) shows how late in life Picasso could still vigorously conceive and paint uningratiating subjects in a strong style. The angularity of design and hairy armpits are a disenchanting but amusingly frank acknowledgment that this is a studio model. Within his own art, he continually reacts against his concocted delightful mythological figures and beautiful women by now and then reintroducing an earthy type. Picasso has described his own work as, "whimsical, tender, biting, garrulous, I often look at the world as a satirist...." But he added, "I often record life with profound compassion and exalt the greatness and anguish of the human situation...." [1964].

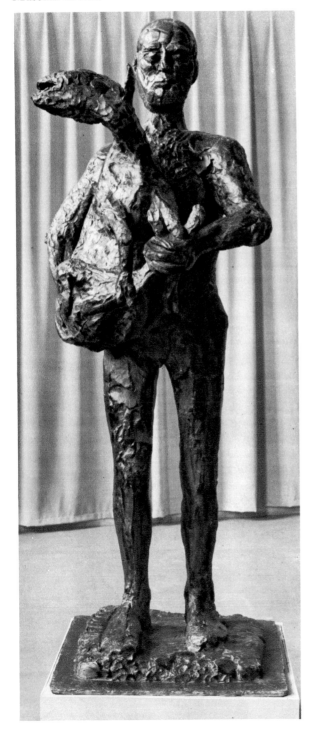

Figure 471. PABLO PICASSO. *Man with a Lamb.* 1944. Bronze, height 7'4". The Philadelphia Museum of Art.

This last aptly applies to one of Picasso's finest sculptures. Always exhibiting an awareness of his great facility, Picasso's sculpture *Man with a Lamb* (Fig. 471) is in part a suppression of this gift in order to create a sculpture that moves us not by virtuosity and surface appeal but by the simplicity and depth of its theme. Like many of his works, it was preceded by drawings and long meditation. Execution in clay was done in a single day during World War II. The shepherd's gentle cradling of the lamb is as much a part of Picasso's feelings for animals as those drawings and paintings in which they are used to destroy or are themselves destroyed. During the war a plaster cast of this work greeted those who came to the artist's Paris studio. Today a bronze cast stands in the southern French village of Vallauris where Picasso has worked for many years. Both locations indicate the strong feeling of the artist about how art images the artist and can still take its place in public to unite the community. The theme of the man with the lamb goes back to Egypt and ancient Greece, where it indicated animal sacrifice and was a votive gift to a god. Picasso once again revives and transforms an old idea, giving it relevance to himself and his age. It is Picasso's personal peace offering. This aspect of Picasso's involvement with history and his motivation to continue painting and sculpture helps us to understand what he meant when he said, "My whole life as an artist has been nothing more than a struggle against reaction and the death of art" [1937].

Since World War II Picasso has exerted less influence on the important younger painters, for new problems and possibilities have been introduced into art. Many important developments occurred in the early art of this century for which Picasso was not responsible, as will be seen. Abstract art, for example, was a peripheral interest with Picasso, whose thinking was mainly centered on the human form. The notoriety of his highly publicized private life and carefree ageless appearance, due perhaps to revitalization by incessant creation, make a serious appraisal of his recent work difficult. Few can disagree that before 1940 his protean energies, intelligence, attention to feeling, and sheer technical skill produced art of the highest quality in astonishing abundance. Not the least inspiration to Picasso at all times was his curiosity, concern, and delight with the faces of art and humanity.

Picasso   391

20

IMAGINATIVE ART

As presented so far to the reader in this book, the history of art must seem to have been largely a continuous tribute to man's reason. We have seen how art performed loyal service to church, state, and society as a whole, and how it was frequently dedicated to practical purposes. Men and gods have been respectfully and reverently depicted. Our museums and art survey books usually focus selectively upon the good and beautiful. However, art, and therefore its history, also encompasses the ugly, the irreverent, and the disrespectful. The night world of dreams and demons has seen the light of day in painting, sculpture, prints, and drawings from antiquity to the present. Under the heading of "Imaginative Art" this chapter is concerned with art that derives from sources other than the imitation of the waking, visible world. These other sources include the visionary, revelation, dreams, revery, fancy, hallucination, the realm of the bizarre, the grotesque, and the fantastic. Art produced from these origins tells us much about the social and moral histories and tastes of various cultures as well as the individual artists. The history of these subjects is still another way of clarifying for us the changes and departures from past traditions that have taken place in the art produced during the last one hundred years.

What may seem fantastic to us in older art, because it does not accord with our present frames of logical reference or with our concepts of what is rational, could originally have made sense and been intelligible to the artist and to the public of his time. Thus, ferocious African or Polynesian masks are not pure creations of their artists' imaginations; rather, they depend largely upon previous masks and the full cultural complex of tribal customs and beliefs reflecting a life view that we are only now beginning to understand even in small measure. For many years scholarship has been unraveling pictorial riddles in Western art, with the result that today we must be more cautious about using the word "fantastic." We must discern and describe different manifestations of the imaginative in art. It is not always easy to separate what was genuinely the result of a dream experience from a symbol the artist may have appropriated from a predecessor. Freudian psychology has been a valuable but risky tool of research and has led to much unhistorical interpretation of artists of the past, and to conclusions drawn without sufficient reference to case histories or knowledge of the art and social context out of which the artists' work grew. Evidence that an artist of the past

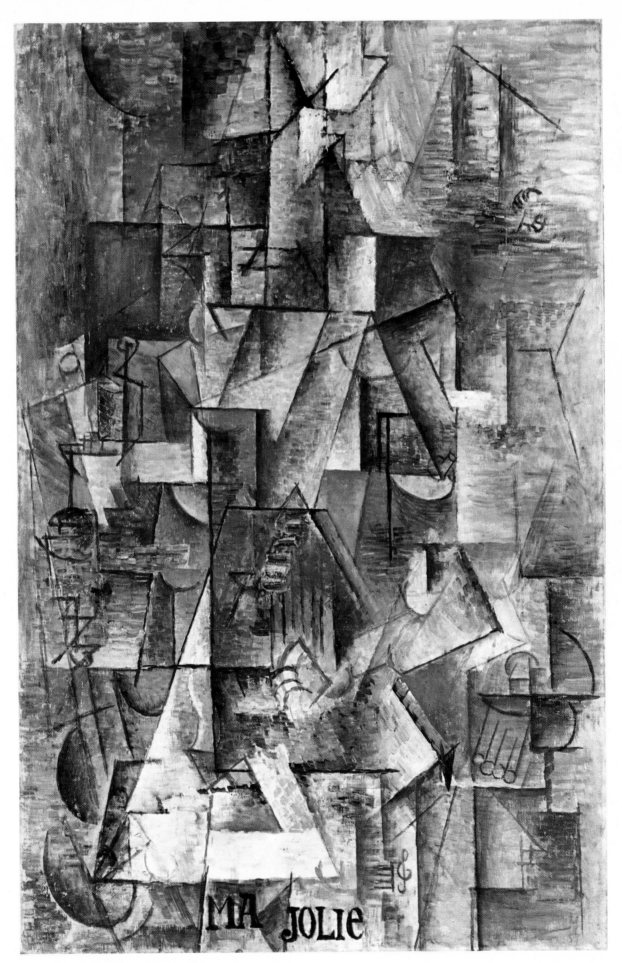

MA JOLIE

Plate 55.   PABLO PICASSO. *Ma Jolie*. 1911–12. Oil on canvas, 39⅜ × 25¾".
The Museum of Modern Art, New York (Lillie P. Bliss Bequest).

Plate 57.   MARC CHAGALL. *I and the Village.* 1911. Oil on canvas, 6′3½″ × 4′11½″.
The Museum of Modern Art, New York (Mrs. Simon Guggenheim Fund).

Plate 58. JOAN MIRÓ. *The Hunter (Catalan Landscape)*. 1923–24.
Oil on canvas, 25½ × 39½″. The Museum of Modern Art, New York (Purchase).

was not completely creative or entirely inventive in the formation of his symbols does not in itself detract from the potential importance of that artist, for he may have sought to preserve a sign language that was familiar to his audience while demonstrating considerable skill and imagination in reinterpreting his acquired symbol. By the same token, the fact that an artist has originated a symbol or created purely out of his own fantasy has not been a guarantee of excellence in art. For the reader discomfited by the imaginative art he sees being created around him today, the first part of this chapter, concerning a protest written eight centuries ago against the meaninglessness of imaginative art, may be welcome.

LITERARY AND ARTISTIC SOURCES FOR IMAGINATIVE ART OF THE PAST

The great Western tradition of fantastic art has its roots in antiquity, but the subsequent Middle Ages experienced a more significant and influential expansion and development of painting and sculpture concerned with the demonic, the infernal, the unnatural, and the bizarre. From the twelfth through the fifteenth centuries, in manuscripts and the sculptural decoration of architecture, this type of art remained literally and figuratively marginal to the central focus of the religious imagery of Christ, the saints, and the Bible. In Chapter 5, "The Sacred Book," it was pointed out that in initials and margins of medieval manuscripts,

artists introduced monsters and hybrids of the human and of animals unrelated to the text itself (Fig. 472). On the great cathedrals and in the cloisters, sculptors imaginatively adorned column capitals, water spouts or gargoyles, the underside of choir seats, and many other places of importance secondary to the location of significant religious subjects, such as the framing areas of the great doorways. When the medieval artist was called upon to give a presence to the devil or to hell, or to moralize about vices, he had license to indulge his imagination as well as to reinterpret earlier art which dealt with the same subjects. Medieval imaginative art is largely related to the war of the Church on sin, and the propagation of its views on the hereafter. As with the making of religious painting and sculpture of a beatific character, the conception of the monstrous and grotesque was tied to prototypes in art. The "Hell Mouth," seen as a leviathan's open jaws in a twelfth-century manuscript (Fig. 473), has many precedents in medieval sculptural renderings of the Last Judgment. But to conclude that all of medieval fantastic art located in religious buildings was intelligible to and rationally justified by those who looked upon it is to ignore a most important witness against such argument. In the twelfth century a great churchman, St. Bernard of Clairvaux, who devoted his life to ecclesiastical reform, wrote a letter to an abbot in which he complained about what he saw in the cloisters:

But in the cloister, under the eyes of the Brethren who read there, what profit is there in those ridiculous monsters, in that marvelous

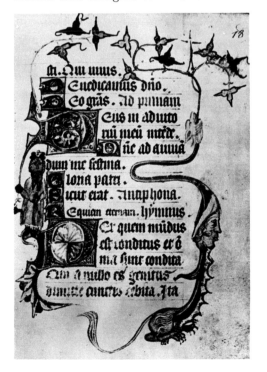

Far left: Figure 472. Drolleries, from *Les Heures et Recueil de Prières.* Avignon. c. 1360. Manuscript illumination. Bibliothèque Nationale, Paris.

Left: Figure 473. *Mouth of Hell,* from the *Psalter of Winchester.* Before 1161. Manuscript illumination. The British Museum, London.

and deformed comeliness, that comely deformity? To what purpose are those unclean apes, those fierce lions, those monstrous centaurs, those half men, those striped tigers, those fighting knights, those hunters winding their horns? Many bodies are there seen under one head, or again, many heads to a single body. Here is a four-footed beast with a serpent's tail; there a fish with a beast's head. Here again the forepart of a horse trails half a goat behind it, or a horned beast bears the hinder quarters of a horse. In short, so many and so marvelous are the varieties of divers shapes on every hand, that we are more tempted to read in the marble than in our books, and to spend the whole day in wondering at these things rather than in meditating the law of God. For God's sake, if men are not ashamed of these follies, why at least do they not shrink from the expense.

While we do not know exactly which sculptures St. Bernard had looked upon, a sufficient number of examples have survived to give us an idea of their appearance (Fig. 474). But, ironically, St. Bernard, who protests their existence, gives us a marvelously vivid and exact description of these sculptures, showing how long he had observed so many, and making convincing his closing lament about distraction. It is also evident that the artists and the patrons who commissioned them were not ashamed of "follies." The sources for the sculptures St. Bernard described are to be found in both the sculpture and the painting of an earlier time, some of which survived from antiquity in "bestiaries," or books on animals.

THE HELL OF HIERONYMUS BOSCH

The belief that the terrible underworld of hell was a near reality and that living man was surrounded by numberless demons persisted

Figure 474. Capital, from the crypt of the church of St-Eutrope, Saintes, France. 1081–96.

into the fifteenth and sixteenth centuries. Demonographers since the twelfth and thirteenth centuries had catalogued the types and symbols of demons, and the sixteenth century saw ingenius census-taking of the devil's agents as well as estimates of hell's physical dimensions. The artist who first made demons and hell the consistent central focus of high painting was the Netherlandish painter Hieronymus Bosch. His rendering of "Hell," from a three-panel painting entitled *The Garden of Earthly Delights* (Fig. 475), has impressed many as being a premonition of modern fantastic art. No rational explanation or analogies to modern life are available to the viewer today to permit him to "read" the meaning of Bosch's hell, hence the conclusion that this was a work of pure fantasy or dream experienced by the artist. Serious study by many art historians has shown, however, that Bosch drew heavily upon literary and pictorial sources in his inspired work, and that it is possible to compile an encyclopedia of meanings for his various symbols. During, and long before, Bosch's lifetime, the Church taught men that all that one saw in the world was symbolic of the invisible, whether godly or demonic. Bosch drew from the rich sources on this subject found in folklore, popular sayings, allegorical treatises, and Christian and Jewish religious literature, including medieval encyclopedias, as well as from astrology and writings on alchemy. Despite his preoccupation with sin and his belief that one could attain divine truth through sincere and deep prayer and contemplation, Bosch did not work in the service of the Church. He seems to have been a skeptic in his attitude toward both reason and the divine saving grace promised by the Church. Like many pessimists of his time, Bosch viewed the preponderance of immoral activity and folly about him as proof positive that the devil had conquered the earth. His painting had a moralizing function, the exposure of man's susceptibility to vice and the devil's temptations. By art he gave visible form to the nature of evil. Bosch's hero was St. Anthony, whose strength of soul alone permitted him to triumph over evil.

While Bosch had available to him the achievements of advanced Flemish painting of the fifteenth century in, for example, perspective, he seems to have consciously chosen an archaic, or pre-van Eyck style, as being more appropriate to what he had to say. Thus in his panel of "Hell," the elevated viewpoint permits him to lay out in a vertical format a vast cross section of hell, climaxed at the top by the vision of burning cities. (Bruegel was later to take many pictorial and symbolic ideas from Bosch, such as the burning cities he appropriated for his *Triumph of Death* [Fig. 211], but not the moralizing, the pessimism, and the view of folly as evil held by his predecessor.) While historians cannot unanimously agree on the

Figure 475. HIERONYMUS BOSCH. *Hell*, side panel from *The Garden of Earthly Delights*. 1480–1505. Oil on panel, height 6'5". Prado, Madrid.

exact meaning or implication of each of the symbols and allegorical images of the various episodes, they can re-create the intellectual atmosphere of Bosch's time which inspired his creations and re-creations of hell. Prominent in Bosch's hell is the compound heretical symbol made up of a human-headed, eggshell-bodied, and barren-tree-stump-legged figure. Within the shell, alchemists, wizards, or intellectuals are served by satanic innkeepers. (Alchemists used eggshells in their recipes.) The bagpipe on a platter above the head signified carnal love, and obscenity, thus making a type of signboard for this infernal inn. Those crucified on or tied to the harp and lute represent remorse, for these musical instruments were identified with praise of the Lord. Sexual references abound, presumably in the form of the knife, key, vases, and lanterns. The severed ears may derive from the Biblical reference to those who do not hear the word of the Lord. The rabbit devouring a man may have related to both sins of excess and the fear of death.

Charles De Tolnay, whose major study of Bosch has made this painter's work more intelligible to us, believes that the figure of a man leaning over the sides of the great broken eggshell is Bosch himself, and that the artist has shown himself daydreaming as if the scene before us originated or was contained within his mind. This would not be the first time that in art we have seen the dreamer and the dreamed, for Hugo van der Goes earlier depicted the vision of the descending Christ available only to the dead Virgin and not to the disciples (Fig. 140).

REVELATION AND DREAM IN DÜRER'S ART

Throughout Europe at the end of the fifteenth century there was widespread fear that the end of the world was coming. Bosch was not alone in giving form to his premonitions of a world-wide catastrophe. The great German artist Albrecht Dürer published in 1498 the complete text and fourteen large woodcut illustrations of the Apocalypse. (This was the first illustrated book made and paid for by a single artist.) St. John's Revelations concerning the end of the world had a long history of previous illustration, but no artist had been either as

Imaginative Art   395

Figure 476. ALBRECHT DÜRER. *Seven Trumpets*, illustration of Revelations 8 and 9 from the Apocalypse. 1498. Woodcut, 15½ × 11¼. The Lilly Library, Indiana University, Bloomington.

literal or as extensive in depicting the wrath of the vengeful God. Dürer was thus able to find in the Bible the perfect expression of his fears for man and, at the same time, to bring to bear upon his engravings all the skill and learning of an artist and educated man. In the woodcut chosen for illustration (Fig. 476), Dürer was interpreting Chapters 8 and 9 of Revelations, thereby compacting into a single but large composition a succession of catastrophic events. Taking excerpts from the Biblical account serves best to explain the action, but only a study of previous apocalyptic illustrations, here impossible, can bring home to the reader the inventiveness and imagination employed by Dürer in treating subjects not undertaken before, or in making them more vivid and plausible for the culture of his time. After. the seventh seal has been opened, and its subsequent half-hour silence, St. John writes:

And I saw the seven angels which stood before God; and to them were given seven trumpets. And another angel came and stood at the altar, having a golden censer; and there was given unto him much incense that he should offer it with the prayers of all saints upon the

golden altar which was before the throne. And the smoke of the incense... ascended up before God out of the angel's hand. And the angel took the censer and filled it with fire of the altar, and cast it into the earth; and there were voices, and thunderings, and lightnings and an earthquake.... The first angel sounded, and there followed hail and fire mingled with blood, and they were cast upon the earth; and the third part of trees was burnt up, and all green grass was burnt up. And the second angel sounded, and as it were a great mountain burning with fire was cast into the sea.... And the third angel sounded, and there fell a great star from heaven burning as it were a lamp.... And the fourth angel sounded, and the third part of the sun was smitten, and the third part of the moon, and the third part of the stars; so as the third part of them was darkened.... And I beheld, and heard an angel flying through the midst of heaven, saying with a loud voice, Woe, Woe, Woe, to the inhabiters of the earth....

Dürer showed an eagle, instead of an angel, crying "Woe, Woe, Woe." Because the eagle is the evangelical symbol of St. John, the substitution and message were appropriate.

In contrast with Dürer's interpretation of St. John's revelation of the end of the world is his own depiction in a water color of a dream that he had in 1525 (Fig. 477), which is probably the oldest example of an artist attempting to transcribe such a personal experience. When he painted his dream he also wrote below it a lengthy description:

In the night between Wednesday and Thursday after Whitsunday, I saw this appearance in my sleep—how many great waters fell from heaven. The first struck the earth about four miles away from me with terrific force and tremendous noise, and it broke up and drowned the whole land. I was so sore afraid that I awoke from it. Then the other waters fell, and as they fell they were very powerful and there were many of them, some further away, some nearer. And they came down from so great a height that they all seemed to fall with an equal slowness. But when the first water that touched the earth had very nearly reached it, it fell with such swiftness, with wind and roaring, and I was so sore afraid that when I awoke my whole body trembled and for a long while I could not recover myself. So when I arose in the morning I painted it above here as I saw it. God turned all things to the best.

What interests us about Dürer's dream is that he felt compelled to write about it, immediately translating his irrational experience into a rational and public language. He was also careful to comment on such things as distances and velocities, and record his own thoughtful, waking observations of nature. The water color itself does not have the look or style of the work in which Dürer treated another man's vision, but he did paint the earth as a landscape, introducing trees and houses to give scale to his nightmare. Although he did not show figures, or the image of the Lord, at the end of his statement he implied that God was the cause of what he had seen and of his well-being thereafter.

THE TEMPTATION OF ST. ANTHONY

Exemplifying the encouragement of the grotesque and bizarre by the Church are the many works of art which from the Middle Ages to the seventeenth century take as their subject the holy man attacked by the devil and his demons. This is often shown in the "temptation" theme, not just of Christ but of a saint. In the thirteenth century, the artist of a manuscript showed St. Guthlac being literally lifted above a church by the devil's agents (Fig. 478). In medieval Christianity beauty was equated with God, ugliness with the devil, and the artist of the St. Guthlac kidnaping and torture was encour-

aged to let his imagination concoct the most gruesome forms he could. Since antiquity, artists had used a hybrid of the human and animal or bird (or all three) to convey what was unnatural. To inspire his imagination, the manuscript artist had available to him demons in medieval sculpture, as well as other manuscripts, so that not only was he interpreting the experience of another man, but also drawing extensively upon the art of other men.

Two and a half centuries after the St. Guthlac drawing, a brilliant German printmaker, Martin Schongauer, converted the identity of this saint to that of St. Anthony, but preserved the motif of the aerial kidnaping (Fig. 479). Fortified by the great developments in naturalism of the fifteenth century, in the work of such artists as van Eyck and Rogier van der Weyden, Schongauer was able to engrave a more extensive inventory of the unattractive properties of monsters. He dwelt at greater length on the pointed and prickly, equipping the demons with a larger arsenal of dangerous weapons and more repulsive bodies. As with St. Guthlac, St. Anthony's quiet face, expressive of his stoic resignation and inner strength, contrasts with the extreme pugnaciousness, the stupidity, and the vocal assaults of his tormentors. Schongauer's gift was to make this unnatural event plausible to his audiences, such that if his monsters could actually be seen, walk abroad, or fly, they would have all the necessary anatomy or equipment to do so.

Left: Figure 477. ALBRECHT DÜRER. *Landscape Flooded with Waters from Heaven (Dream Vision).* 1525. Pen and water color. Kunsthistorisches Museum, Vienna.

Below: Figure 478. *Kidnaping of St. Guthlac,* from the *Harley Roll.* c. 1230. Manuscript illumination. The British Museum, London.

Left: Figure 479. MARTIN SCHONGAUER. *The Temptation of St. Anthony.* c. 1480–90. Engraving, 12⅜×9⅛". The National Gallery of Art, Washington, D.C. (Rosenwald Collection).

Below: Figure 480. MATTHIAS GRÜNEWALD. *The Temptation of St. Anthony*, from the *Isenheim Altarpiece.* 1512–15. Oil on panel, 8′8⅜″×4′6¾″. Musée d'Unterlinden, Colmar, France.

Perhaps the most inspired and persuasive of the Temptations of St. Anthony was that of Matthias Grünewald (Fig. 480). His painting is one of the panels of the *Isenheim Altarpiece* (Pl. 6), whose "Crucifixion" panel was discussed in Chapter 3, "Images of Gods." Grünewald showed St. Anthony crying out against the attacks of the demons. On a piece of paper in the lower right-hand corner, Grünewald wrote: "Where are you, good Jesus, where were you? And why did you not come and dress my wounds?" This plaint could well be that of the beleaguered saint, but also that of the rotting human corpse in the lower left-hand corner. Dermatologists have identified its sores as syphilitic, a diagnosis that relates the content of this picture to the skin afflictions of the patients who were brought to the altar painting to begin their therapy. Grünewald went beyond Bosch and Schongauer in depicting the surfaces of his monsters as symptoms of their various forms of corruption. Not content with showing the lurid, scaly, feathered, or fleshy covering of the foreground demons, he carried over into the ruined house of the hermit saint the jagged silhouettes and elusive forms of the devil's legion. Unperceived by the hermit, but significantly apparent to the patient who looked at first with dismay upon the painting, the Lord can be seen looking down on the trials of the saint. Emerging from the brilliant radiance about the Lord's throne are luminous armed angels who will disperse the devils of darkness. With the resources of painting Grünewald was inspired to re-create the transparencies of heavenly light and gangrenous flesh, the opaqueness of dark, demonic bodies, the shine of reptilian scales, and mucous dripping from the nose. Many things in Grünewald's painting and Schongauer's engraving are partially traceable both to previous art and to the written text of the "Life of St. Anthony" in Jacobus de Voragine's *Golden Legend*, which dates from the thirteenth century. The painter probably read the following:

... he went into a hole or cave to hide himself, and anon he found there a great multitude of devils, that so much beat him that his servant bore him upon his shoulders into his house as if he had been dead. When the other hermits were assembled and wept his death, and would have done his service, suddenly St. Anthony revived and made his servants to bear him into the pit again where the devils had so evil beaten him, and began to summon the devils again...to battles. And they came in forms of diverse beasts wild and savage, of whom that one howled, another sniffled, and another cried, and another brayed and assailed St. Anthony, that one with the horns, the others with their teeth, and the others with their paws and claws, and... to rent his body that he supposed well to die. Then came a clear brightness and all the beasts fled away.

The great seventeenth-century French artist Jacques Callot, shortly before the death he knew was coming, made a drawing for a *Temptation of St. Anthony* which was engraved by Israel in 1635 (Figs. 481, 482). Here the temptation theme was completely recast in terms of its focus, setting, and characters. Probably inspired by Italian popular theater and the theatrical productions put on in the courts of the Florentine nobility, Callot staged the temptation on an epic scale. Literally stagelike is the device of the framing of the scene by rocky cliffs on either side, the ruins of a tall arcaded stone building at the right, and the cast of thousands that sweeps onto the broad

plain of the stage. Overhead the enormous figure of the devil, chained to the rocks, spews demons and fire into what is now a scene in hell. Callot joined together infernal scenes with those of the temptation, but the effect is more comic than frightening. The devils make war on themselves more than on the saint who is seen at the right, ringed by other devils, a naked woman, and a fire-belching monster. Perhaps caricaturing the extravagant weapons of war sponsored by the nobility, Callot transformed monsters into canons, or the reverse. An irreverent religious service is conducted just above St. Anthony, and throughout the print obscene "services" are rendered by the demons to one another. As pointed out

Above:
Figure 481. JACQUES CALLOT. *The Temptation of St. Anthony.* 1635. Etching (by Israel), 14 × 18¼". The Museum of Art, Indiana University, Bloomington.

Left:
Figure 482. JACQUES CALLOT. Detail of Fig. 481.

Imaginative Art   399

earlier in this book, by the seventeenth century there was frequently a recession of the heroic or saintly focus, and Callot seems to have taken the trials of St. Anthony as the occasion for delivering a commentary, obscure as it may be to us today, on worldly institutions and human practices.

ARCIMBOLDO AND DOUBLE IMAGERY

The art of the Middle Ages and that of the sixteenth century provide abundant evidence that religious and secular fantasies could coexist in art. In 1563, the same year that the Council of Trent was preparing a statement on art as part of its war on the Reformation and secularism, an Italian artist, Giuseppe Arcimboldo, painted a series of heads composed entirely of nonhuman subjects. In the painting illustrated (Fig. 483) we can see with what ingenuity Arcimboldo found a form of marine life that in a certain position and context, and from a distance, evoked some aspect of the human head and shoulders. Without repeating himself, the painter was able to assemble an astonishing repertory of crustacean and invertebrate forms, so that the head dissects into a shark, a ray, a starfish, eels, a walrus, and so

Figure 483. GIUSEPPE ARCIMBOLDO. *Water.* 1563. Oil on canvas, 26⅜×20⅜″. Kunsthistorisches Museum, Vienna.

on. It is a far-from-pleasant assemblage, and at first it suggests a nightmarish experience or aggressive gesture toward human dignity. But Arcimboldo was a famous court painter who did this and other pictures for the Emperor Maximilian II in Vienna. There he served not only as a painter but as a decorator for pageants and set designer for the theater. The first Italian painter to make the grotesque more than a marginal or decorative element, without the sin-consciousness of Bosch, Arcimboldo focused his entire image upon the bizarre. There is a rational explanation for what he did, which does not detract from the artist's skill and cleverness in the way he painted this work. The title, *Water*, relates to his series on the elements, and identifies the source from which Arcimboldo drew all of his motifs. The precedent for relating non human life to the human body existed in literature, notably philosophical and scientific speculation on the relation of man to nature, and nature to man. The comparison of the earth to a great organism had been made in the previous century and was known to Bruegel, which was pointed out in Chapter 15, "Themes from Nature." Man was looked upon by many European intellectuals in the sixteenth century as the world in miniature, "Man—the little world." Cartographers equated land forms with figure types. Previously, artists had used human forms to symbolize nature and its seasons. Arcimboldo was using natural forms to symbolize man and, at the same time, was catering to his society's taste for metamorphosis. The sixteenth century produced a curious blending of science and myth; there was inquiry into facts, but also tolerance of fantasy. It was a time of half-science. Particularly in the courts, among intellectuals, the medieval taste for allegories, or symbols of all aspects of knowledge, persisted. The accuracy of Arcimboldo's renderings of water denizens, coupled with their substitution for facial features, thus epitomizes the duality of thought in his own age.

CARICATURE, ANATOMY, AND THE BIZARRE

What seems to us to be fantastic transformations of the human figure in sixteenth- and seventeenth-century prints and drawings can be shown, as in the case of Arcimboldo, to have proceeded from rational systems or motives. Martin

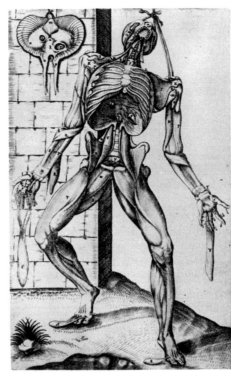

Luther, for example, created a figure that was part human, part animal, and part bird (Fig. 484). The pennant with the crossed keys in the background and Luther's famous antagonism to Rome explain that this was a caricature of what was known at the time as the *Veau-Moine* or "Calf-Monk." Its various features were to be read as manifestations of such characteristics as confusion, lust, heretical obstinacy, and hypocrisy among the Catholic clergy. The connection between the meaning and the caricatural form was in the written and verbal language of the time.

An illustration from Valverde's treatise *The Composition of the Human Body* of 1556 shows us an animated but skeletonized figure from whose frame muscles dangle (Fig. 485). Not content with a simple, stationary dissection, the artist felt impelled paradoxically to bring the corpse to life and put his figure into dramatic movement while showing its head jerked backwards by a rope drawn through the skull.

Almost seventy years later, a Genoese artist named Braccelli, who specialized in the bizarre, did a suite of prints in which the human figure was composed not of muscle and bone, but of a variety of nonorganic motifs. In the print illustrated (Fig. 486), two warriors are "skeletonized" into open frames serially connected and inflected where the joints would be. Life is thus suggested by its antithesis. Long before Braccelli, artists such as Dürer and Leonardo had utilized geo-

metry to illustrate ideal human proportions, and in the art of the former and others thereafter, geometry was used to demonstrate the ideal construction, and even movement, of the human. Braccelli was continuing a tradition of showing the triumph of human intelligence over nature and of reinterpreting the body by means of motifs that were entirely of human invention.

THE IMPORTANCE OF THE SELF IN MODERN IMAGINATIVE ART

After Callot, the next major artist to devote a considerable number of drawings, prints, and paintings to the imaginative was the Spanish

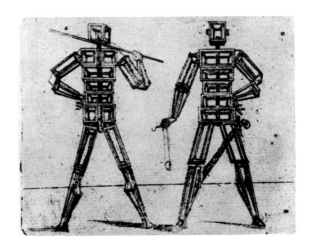

court painter Don Francisco Goya. In 1799 he published a series of prints entitled *Los Caprichos*, which, though not in separate sequences, divided roughly into areas of subject matter: examples of human folly, or stupidity, and dishonesty; donkeys enacting the roles of humans; witchcraft and markedly fantastic beings. Unusual in *Los Caprichos*, which means caprices, fantastic notions, fancy, or whim, is that the titles of the etchings and their inscriptions were added after the works were finished; they do not predate the artist's conceptions. In the work of Dürer, Bosch, Grünewald, and Callot, the title or subject existed before the work of art, which was its illustration. Goya's conceptions often first appeared in his own art, and then seem to have suggested associations with, for example, popular sayings. The artist was very much aware of folklore and demonology, and scholars of Spanish art and culture like Professor José López-Rey believe that there are many veiled references to individuals, customs, and institutions in the *Caprices* which time has obscured for the modern audience. Fortunately, Goya published in a newspaper article on February 6, 1799, an announcement of his series of etchings that was accompanied by a statement of purpose:

A Collection of Prints of Capricious Subjects, Invented and Etched by Don Francisco Goya. Since the artist is convinced that the censure of human errors and vices (though they may seem to be the province of Eloquence and Poetry) may also be the object of Painting, he has chosen as subjects adequate for his work, from the multitude of follies and blunders common in every civil society, as well as from the vulgar prejudices and lies authorized by custom, ignorance, or interest, those that he has thought most suitable for ridicule as well as for exercising the artificer's fancy.

Since the majority of the objects represented in this work are ideal, it may not be too daring to expect that their defects will perhaps meet with forgiveness on the part of the connoisseurs as they will realize that the artist has neither followed the examples of others, nor been able to copy from nature. And if imitating Nature is as difficult as it is admirable when one succeeds in doing so, some esteem must be shown toward him who, holding aloof from her, has had to put before the eyes forms and attitudes that so far have existed only in the human mind, obscured and confused by lack of illustration, or excited by the unruliness of passion.

One would be assuming too much ignorance of the fine arts, if one were to warn the public that in none of the compositions which form this series has the artist had in mind any one individual, in order to ridicule particular defects. For truly, to say so would mean narrowing overmuch the boundaries of talent, and mistaking the methods used by the arts of imitation in producing perfect works.

Painting (like Poetry) chooses from the universal what it considers suitable to its own ends: it reunites in a single fantastic personage circumstances and characteristics that nature has divided among many. From such a combination, ingeniously arranged, results the kind of successful imitation for which a good artificer deserves the title of inventor and not that of a servile copyist. [*Diario de Madrid*, translation © by Professor José López-Rey.]

For many reasons, this statement is interesting, and in the context of the imaginative art it is important because the artist disclaims recourse to the art of others and claims for himself the gift of invention. Living in the Age of Enlightenment, he professes to expose the night world of human conduct and imagination to the clear light of reason. One of the most famous of the plates in the series is that in which the artist has shown himself sleeping at his writing table (Fig. 487). Behind and from out of the darkness, presumably of his subconscious, comes a flight of owls and bats. Written on the desk is, "The sleep of reason produces monsters." In the ink drawing for this etching Goya wrote: "Universal Language. Drawn and Etched by Francisco de Goya. Year 1797." The word "Dream" was also written on the upper part, and below the drawing was added: "The artist dreaming. His only purpose is to banish harmful, vulgar beliefs, and to perpetuate in this work of caprices the solid testimony of truth." Beneath the etching Goya noted: "Imagination deserted by reason, begets impossible monsters. United with reason, she is the mother of all arts, and the source of their wonders." Despite these writings by the artist, the intention of the *Caprices* is still open to conjecture. The great number, strength, and inventiveness of these many etchings show not only the artist's fascination but also his obsession with the power of dreams, hallucinations, and visions of superstition, with human subservience to passions, response to impulses, and indulgence in folly. Goya was tormented by deafness and concern over his own mental equilibrium, and we can only speculate on how much of the *Caprices* are personal fantasies. His own mind may have been at times disordered by sickness and anxiety.

The choice of etching, a medium of blacks, greys, and whites, was appropriate for this invisible world. When Goya showed humans, they often acted like monsters. In his etching *They Pair Their Own Nails* (Fig. 488) monsters act with the vanity of humans. The grim and the ludicrous intermingle in this conception of foul creatures preoccupied with what may strike us as hygiene. (The inscription reads, "Long nails are so harmful that they are forbidden even among the witches.") Goya's hybrids, beings that are part human, part animal, and part bird, lack the decipherability into intelligible symbols of those in the work of such an artist as Bosch. The vague separation between human and animal in the faces of the witches reflects the artist's interest in the old studies of correspondences between certain types of human and animal physiognomy, and the belief that physical ugliness was proof of the soul's corruption. Goya's etchings were based on his own drawings, but often the print is stronger in taking a motif, such as the witch's nail that is about to be cut, and using it as a menacing shape elsewhere, as in the scissors and wings. The many textural gradients he extracted from the etching process made possible the evocation of convincing textures for wings and flesh, as well as the dark mysterious depths and spaces in which these monsters thrived. Whether or not

he was in the grip of a vision when he did these drawings and prints, we don't know. Their careful working and reworking in large and small areas shows the artist's persistent consciousness of the necessity of converting the conception into a work of art.

REDON AND THE LOGIC OF THE INVISIBLE

After his death Goya was greatly admired in France during the nineteenth century, but only in the work of one artist were there comparably imaginative prints. Odilon Redon, though less well known today than such of his contemporaries as Monet, Seurat, and Gauguin, was the great nineteenth-century French artist of fantasy. His reputation is based on the many charcoal drawings, lithographs, and pastels that he did, works that have no resemblance to the art of the nineteenth century discussed in Chapter 14. From the late 1860s through the first part of the twentieth century, Redon refused to direct his vision toward the external world and the production of pleasing subjects after the manner of the Impressionists. He wrote in 1868 that the concerns of Manet and the Impressionists constituted a restricted and paltry research and that while true artists...

recognize the necessity for a basis of *seen* reality, to them true art lies in a reality that is *felt*....We must remember that we have other things than the eyes to satisfy, that we carry in ourselves... troubles, joys, or pains to which the great artist knows how to address himself.

Far left: Figure 487. FRANCISCO GOYA. *The Sleep of Reason Produces Monsters,* from *Los Caprichos.* 1796–98 (announced for sale, 1799). Etching, 8½ × 6″. The Metropolitan Museum of Art, New New York (gift of M. Knoedler & Co.).

Left: Figure 488. FRANCISCO GOYA. *They Pare Their Own Nails.* 1797. Etching, 8½ × 6″. The Metropolitan Museum of Art, New York (Rogers Fund).

One can understand Redon's imaginative alternatives to Impressionism by comparing his lithograph which shows a window (Fig. 489) with any of the nineteenth-century window views in Chapter 14 or in the final chapter, "The Death of the Window and Life of the Square: Abstraction." For Monet, Pissarro, Caillebotte, or Bonnard, the window looked out upon the real world of the city. In Caillebotte's painting, which shows a street view framed by a window in a room (Fig. 505), what lies on this side of the window is of the same order of reality as what is seen without. Redon shows us a segment of brightly illuminated tree through his window. But as we focus on our side of the window we see that this is no ordinary room, and that vague, softly luminous shapes hover in the darkness. It is as if Redon were metaphorically showing us the mysterious dark world that exists behind the human eye. What we see through the window we can describe, but what lies in front of it has been only *suggested*, not defined, and this is the goal of his poetic thought. Of his drawings he wrote that they "inspire yet cannot be defined. They do not determine anything. Like music, they transport us into the ambiguous world of the undetermined."

Redon deliberately cultivated his subconscious as a source for his imagery; he also relied upon the stimulation he received from working in charcoal and lithography. In a letter of 1898, describing how he worked, Redon confessed:

A sheet of white paper horrifies me. It impresses me disagreeably to the point of making me sterile, of depriving me of the taste for work.... I am forced as soon as it is on an easel, to scrawl on it with charcoal, with crayon or any other material, and this operation brings it to life. I believe that suggestive art owes much to the stimulus which the material itself exerts on the artist....

Redon went on to describe how he abandoned himself to fantasy:

Fantasy is also the messenger of the "unconscious," ...nothing in art is achieved by will alone. Everything is done by docilely submitting to the arrival of the "unconscious." The analytical spirit must be quick when it appears, but afterwards it is of little importance to remember it....

The fantastic world created by Redon was not intended, as Goya's probably was, to make comment on the people and behavior of his time. It is a private world of immeasurable spaces and, often, of infinitesimal beings. Of great influence on Redon was the work of a gifted French biologist named Armand Clavaud, who introduced the artist to the world of the microscope, of natural history, and, especially, of botany. Redon was obsessed throughout his life with finding a logical structure for his imaginary beings that would parallel the newly discovered laws of biological life. His *Swamp Flower, a Sad and Human Face* (Fig. 490) was part of a series of lithographs that he dedicated to Goya. Rising from an endless expanse of water, beneath an infinite black sky, is Redon's imaginary growth, which blossoms into a radiant but lugubrious head, the likes of which cannot be found in the paintings of any other artist. This is no revival of a medieval drollery, but a new and fantastic organism whose head has a seriousness and mystery for which medieval artists had neither the means, the models, nor the training to render. Redon's

Left: Figure 489. ODILON REDON. *The Light of Day,* from the *Dreams* series. 1891. Lithograph, 8¼×6⅛″. Bibliothèque Nationale, Paris.

Right: Figure 490. ODILON REDON. *Swamp Flower, a Sad and Human Face,* from *Hommage à Goya.* 1885. Lithograph, 10⅜×8″. Bibliothèque Nationale, Paris.

fantasies on the head involved its separation from the body and either conjunction with another form of life or suspension in space. In many instances features would be omitted, or a single feature, such as the eye, would be detached and given a life of its own. Often these heads were childhood recollections: "I owe to my country those sorrowful faces... which I have drawn because I have seen them and because my eyes, as a child, had preserved them for the intimate echoes of my soul." Redon's modernity as a fantast thus lies in his cultivation of his own experiences, the creation of a private, undecipherable, but lonely world; he was an artist stimulated by the creative process whose intent was not to criticize or reform his public. His interest was to involve the spectator "by means of a sudden attraction, in all the allure of the uncertain." Of great importance for artists who followed him in spirit, among them André Masson, were such statements by Redon as, "My originality consists in bringing to life, in a human way, improbable beings and making them live according to the laws of probability, but putting—as far as possible—the logic of the visible at the service of the invisible." Writing at a time in 1880 when Monet and his contemporaries were intent on capturing the painterly equivalences of natural light and on abandoning the human-figure landscape, Redon wrote prophetically of himself, as well as many others to follow: "Man is a thinking being. Man will always be there; whatever the role played by light, it won't be able to turn him aside. To the contrary, the future belongs to the subjective world."

DE CHIRICO AND ENIGMA

Down to the twentieth century, much of fantastic art was obviously involved with the creation of the monstrous, in the form of unnatural hybrids, and of strange inaccessible places existing only in the imagination. While this continued in the work of certain modern artists, the sources and character of fantastic art have changed considerably in our time. More and more after 1900, artists followed the precedent, whether consciously or not, of Redon and departed from literature, previous art, and moralizing as a source for their

Figure 491. GIORGIO DE CHIRICO. *The Mystery and Melancholy of a Street.* 1914. Oil on canvas, 34⅜× 28½". Collection Mr. and Mrs. Stanley R. Resor, New Canaan, Connecticut.

imagery. In Chapter 16, "Painting and Objects," the art of Giorgio de Chirico was introduced in the form of his imaginative handling of objects. In his *Mystery and Melancholy of a Street* (Fig. 491), we again meet this new type of imaginative art in terms of a person and a place. Everything in the painting is recognizable or familiar—the arcades, the open, old-fashioned railroad van, the child rolling a hoop, the projecting shadows. What gives to de Chirico's painting the quality of the uncanny is his intentional divorce of such things as light, shadow, space, and silence from their previous rational associations in pictorial construction. They are transformed into enigmas, or unexpected inversions of what they ought to be. As if through a window or from a balcony, we look down on a scene that is unfolding before us. Things are not as they first seem. Perspective lines of the buildings do not recede to a common vanishing point; the angles of the shadows are inconsistent with a single light source; the sky is green. In the painting's context we tend to read the child against the van, which while open is so stationed as to conceal part of its interior. De

Chirico is a painter who poses but does not answer questions. He gives us no program notes or literary sources to transcribe his image. His poetic gift is to be haunted by irrational situations, and when he paints these images he does not eradicate but preserves their irrationality. The spaces of Goya, Callot, Grünewald, and Dürer are still formed according to perspective devices employed by them in the depiction of rational subjects. De Chirico's illusionistic world is constructed on the basis of an intuitive or irrational use of devices originally evolved for the rationalization of sight. In his memory de Chirico distilled certain physical, cultural characteristics of his native Italy, and while living in Paris between 1911 and 1914, he painted not a world remembered literally, but one which became a backdrop for mysterious relationships and unexpected encounters. Silence for de Chirico, which he sought to evoke in painting, had different characteristics, depending upon whether, for example, it existed before or after a catastrophe. Except for Redon, in the previous art of fantasy noise was assumed or suggested. A personal art became for de Chirico a refuge or alternative to the waking world of reality, an art of great personal consolation despite its disturbing qualities. In the same year he did the painting illustrated de Chirico wrote:

> To become truly immortal a work of art must escape all human limits: logic and common sense will only interfere. But once these barriers are broken, it will enter the regions of childhood vision and dream. Profound statements must be drawn by the artist from the most secret recesses of his being.... What I hear is valueless; only what I see is living, and when I close my eyes my vision is even more powerful. It is more important that we should rid art of all that it has contained of recognizable material to date; all familiar subjects, all traditional ideas, all popular symbols must be banished forthwith.... We must hold enormous faith in ourselves; it is essential that the revelation we receive... which has no sense in itself, which has not subject, which means *absolutely nothing* from the logical point of view....

How personal was this world and how reflective of his temperament can be seen when the foregoing painting is compared with one done by a Russian-born artist working in Paris at the same time.

CHAGALL AND THE REALITY OF THE INTERIOR WORLD

The imaginative private world of Marc Chagall, which he painted in *I and the Village* (Pl. 57) while living in Paris in 1911, differs from that of de Chirico by its abundant qualities of joyfulness, warm sensuality, fragrance, and delightful vertigo. In his private souvenir of a childhood in Vitebsk, Chagall painted a green-faced boy holding a sprig of blossoms and confronted by the transparent head of a donkey. Surface and depth, right side up and upside down freely interchange, as Chagall's picture of loving, pleasurable memories resists translation into the normal language and syntax of rational painting. Both Chagall and de Chirico bring to modern painting the practice of free association whereby the selection and conjunction of objects or motifs are irrationally suggested to the artist during his conception or execution of the work. Chagall felt, however, that these associations had also to work in terms of the structural needs of his painting. The circle and X forms in the lower center of the painting may have had some private symbolism for the artist, but they also serve to unite disparate formal motifs on a common surface. De Chirico restored to painting the dramatic power of deep, clear space, whereas Chagall created an immeasurable, untraversable environment in which one cannot write of solids and voids, or the consistent diminution of size related to a fixed viewpoint. Scale, color, and solidity, or transparency, of figures and houses are not the function of a detached or objective observer from whose physical vantage point the scene is constructed. Rather these properties reflect the weight and impulse of feeling and fantasy in the painter. Older artists interpreted another person's vision in pictorial terms that, like the literature in which dream experiences were recorded, served to codify the means of dealing with the irrational. Chagall, de Chirico, and the artists that follow their example fight codification or intelligibility on a public level. Years after his painting of *I and the Village* Chagall wrote:

> There is nothing anecdotal in my pictures— no fairy tales—no literature in the sense of folk legend associations.... For me a picture is a plane surface covered with representations of objects—beasts, birds, or humans—in a certain order in which anecdotal illustrational logic

has no importance. The visual effectiveness of the painted composition comes first....I am against the terms "fantasy" and "symbolism" in themselves. All our interior world is reality...perhaps more so than our apparent world. To call everything that appears illogical, "fantasy," fairy tale, or chimera would be practically to admit not understanding nature....The fact that I made use of cows, milkmaids, roosters and provincial Russian architecture as my source forms is because they are part of the environment from which I spring and which undoubtedly left the deepest impression on my visual memory of any experiences I have known. Every painter is born somewhere...a certain essence—a certain "aroma" of his birthplace clings to his work. But do not misunderstand me: the important thing here is not "subject" in the sense pictorial "subjects" were painted by the old academicians. The vital mark these early influences leave is, as it were, on the handwriting of the artist.

Both de Chirico and Chagall would have been very different and less effective painters if they had not come to Paris while still very young. At the turn of this century the exciting art environment of Paris acted as a liberating force on the imagination as well as on the styles of many young painters. Cubism, for example, was the artist's declaration of independence from the world of appearances. Both de Chirico and Chagall were influenced by it, despite the fact that they could not content themselves with imitating the forms of Picasso and Braque, nor be wholly satisfied with its dark colors and conventional subjects of still life and the figure. When the Cubists broke up the closed character of objects and destroyed rational, measurable space, this was a crucial breakthrough of old boundaries for painters who by inclination believed that the world one sees with the eyes closed should preserve its imaginative qualities in painting.

It is in the twentieth century, beginning with such artists as Chagall, that *originality* becomes a conscious aim for the artist. Following the Middle Ages artists sought individuality, but Chagall wanted an art which did not look like anything that had come before or that could be seen at the time. Goya claimed for himself the title of inventor, but his drawings and prints are at times closer in spirit or form to those of Rembrandt and Callot than are Chagall's paint-

ings to the work of any other artist. This imperative of originality derives largely from the nineteenth-century ethic of faithfulness to one's own experience in a style personally acquired.

INSIDE *THE BRIDE*

In the same years before World War I during which there were so many formal and psychological breakthroughs in modern art, one of the most important innovations was that of the artist imaginatively interpreting the internal nature of the human body by denying its surface appearance. More famous for his *Nude Descending a Staircase* of 1912, Marcel Duchamp painted in the same year his *Bride* (Fig. 492). The former painting was described somewhat pejoratively by President Theodore Roosevelt as resembling "an explosion in a shingle factory." *The Bride* in turn avoids all that is sentimentally associated with the title—something old, something new, something borrowed, and something blue—in favor of showing woman as consisting of a complicated pumping and filter plant. The painting is at once an imaginative dissection of both the body and public taste. With the detached attitude of an anatomist, Duchamp ironically

Figure 492. MARCEL DUCHAMP. *The Bride (Le Passage de la Vierge à la Mariée)*. 1912. Oil on canvas, 23⅜×21¼". The Museum of Modern Art, New York (Purchase).

reconstructs the inner organs in terms of mechanical and quasi-organic forms, a network of pipes and filters, painted in a brownish color, with a slick, even slippery, type of surface that, more than the individual objects, conveys a visceral quality to the whole. In the chapter "Painting and Objects," Duchamp's *Bride Stripped Bare by Her Bachelors, Even* of 1923 (Fig. 394) was discussed, and in the earlier work, *The Bride*, we can see the beginnings of this artist's fantasies upon sex and science. Unlike the moralizing of Bosch, whose cynical views of man led him to receive and invent human-animal-mechanical hybrids, Duchamp's conception is divorced from this larger frame of reference and derives from personal reflections on the nature and purposes of art. He later wrote, "A painting that doesn't shock isn't worth painting."

Right: Figure 493. MAX ERNST. *The Invention*, from *Repetitions*. 1922. Collage.

Below: Figure 494. MAX ERNST. *Oedipus Rex*. 1921. Oil on canvas, 35×45¾″. Collection Claude Hersaint, Paris.

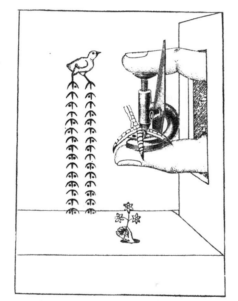

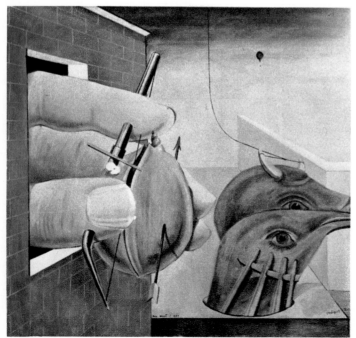

MAX ERNST AND "NO-SENSE" ART

During and after World War I, artists of many nationalities continued to explore the possibilities of art based upon free association, intuition, or the logic of the illogical. Between about 1915 and 1922 there was a loose international confederation of artists who called themselves Dadaists, the word "Dada" supposedly having been picked by chance from a Larousse dictionary. It was a movement dedicated to art that made no sense, one that championed irreverence and irrationality and disclaimed all system or esthetic pretentions (which in itself required a system). It was the first movement in art history openly to seek originality and a complete break with the past. Painterly technique and questions of style were damned by most of the group, who sought a directness in their imaginative images, thereby opposing what they felt was the cult of painterly virtuosity or individuality. Their appeal to the public was intended to be on the instinctive rather than conscious or verbal level. Dada believed that the unexpected was as much a part of life as was the predictable, and infinitely more stimulating to creativity and audience response. One of the most imaginative and productive of the Dadaists was the German-born Max Ernst. In his desire to move away from Western technical traditions he developed collage, or pasted paper, beyond what the Cubists had done and elevated it from a means to a principle of organization. (Composition was the one rule from the past observed by the Dadaists.) In his collage *The Invention* (Fig. 493), Ernst cut out nineteenth-century wood engravings of objects and pasted them into a new context. The title may refer to the process of assembling the picture, for Ernst captioned his works after they were done according to the ideas suggested to him by the finished pieces. He transferred to painting the principle of irrational juxtaposition of familiar objects in unexpected situations or locations. Ernst liked to repeat Lautréamont's phrase, "Beautiful, like the chance meeting on a dissecting table of an umbrella and sewing machine." Ernst's painting *Oedipus Rex* (Fig. 494) seems to have been based upon *The Invention*, but now the artist added a new and unpleasant simulation—while extended through the window the fingers are penetrated by the object they hold. More

Plate 59.   ARSHILE GORKY. *The Liver Is the Cock's Comb.* 1944. Oil on canvas, 6′ × 8′2″. Albright-Knox Art Gallery, Buffalo, New York.

Plate 60.   WILLEM DE KOONING. *Woman and Bicycle*. 1952–53.
Oil on canvas, 6′4½″×4′1″. The Whitney Museum of American Art, New York.

Figure 495. SALVADOR DALI. *The Persistence of Memory*. 1931. Oil on canvas, 9½×13". The Museum of Modern Art, New York.

than the collage, the painting was done with methods that were almost academic or reactionary in their rendering of objects and space. This reflects Ernst's reaction against the earlier revolutionary styles of Cubism and was his appeal to the good taste of such artists as Matisse. By these reactionary means Ernst was able to achieve the total illusion of his subject without imposing on the spectator's consciousness evidence of his hand and brush. In this alone is Ernst like Bosch, for the Dadaists did not set good against evil. The absurd was a fact of life for them, and art was to accept this condition and act accordingly.

DALI'S HALLUCINATIONS

Since the 1920s imaginative art has polarized around two essentially different modes of expression. One of these modes has, since the appearance of Ernst's *Oedipus Rex*, been expressed by artists creating illusionistic irrational images in paintings whose deep, three-dimensional space approximates, in many respects, that of older illusionistic art. The objects filling these spaces are often, either by themselves or in their components, based upon what is available to us in the external world. For the Surrealists and their satellites, from 1923, the aim of painting was to cull scientifically from the subconscious. The "inner world" was thought to be of a higher reality than the external world. They adopted the Dadaists' device of working from free association and with the unpredictable juxtaposition of the familiar.

The artist whose work epitomizes the illusionistic, imagistic, "hand-painted" dream picture of Surrealism is Salvador Dali. He created his most inspired and sincere works during the late twenties and early thirties. One of these, *The Persistence of Memory* (Fig. 495), contains subjective, obsessional features such as the rocky coast of Spain, the arid plain, and the startling confrontation of "melted" watches with a fetal form and a dead tree positioned on a blocklike object. Frequently Dali would paint a picture in parts, working on individual areas and objects as they appeared to him in hallucinations often induced by the austere act of staring at the blank canvas. The limpid timepieces may have been punning references to the artist's conceit over bending time to his will, or perhaps to childhood regressions in which Dali compared the exposure of his soft tongue to the molten watches. (The French word for watch is *montre*, as is the personal imperative of the verb *montrer* used by a doctor asking a sick child to expose his tongue.) Dali drew freely upon his own extraordinary and disturbed past for ideas that his professional training and mastery of academic drawing enabled him to render with dazzling precision.

The enactment of Dali's psychologically inspired dramas usually takes place in a profound, lucid space. The paradox he loved was this exact transcription of what seemed to make no sense: the juxtaposition or fusion of unrelated objects; inversions of the familiar or of expected properties of the animate and inanimate; double images like those of his own head, but images that resist the programatic trans-

Figure 496. RENÉ MAGRITTE. *The Six Elements.* c. 1928. Oil on canvas, 28⅞ × 39¼″. The Philadelphia Museum of Art (Arensberg Collection).

lation of those in Arcimboldo's work; the mingling of animal, vegetable, and mineral motifs into a molten hybrid.

Many Surrealists did not look upon their work as art, but as scientific documents in the systematic exploration of their own subconsciousness. They sought to liberate creativity from mechanistic materialism; but, paradoxically, instead of freeing the mind, they established new and strict limits for creativity. Reason was denied any function (which disqualified the Surrealists as scientists), and, in the words of Herbert Muller, "the studio in the psyche became an underground dungeon."

Like many movements in modern art, Surrealism was not homogeneous, and there were many artists who accepted only certain aspects of its program. Its great value was in demonstrating the possibilities of instinctive creation and in opening up new sources of imagery, thereby widening to a generous new dimension the *possibilities* available to artists.

MAGRITTE'S DISLOCATIONS

The difficulty with a word like "surrealism," as with many art labels, is that it does not describe, illustrate, or explain what the artists identified with it have done. There is little agreement in style, subject, or intent among the various Surrealists, beyond what they will *not* show—the external world in terms of its familiar logic of appearance. The Belgian artist René Magritte gives us paintings which are exact transcrip-

tions of what he sees as the "unexpected" in the visible world. His *Six Elements* (Fig. 496), for example, shows six framed segments of subjects that in themselves are describable, but once we have made this simple, rational observation, it is possible to go no further in explaining why these subjects and scenes are where they are. Magritte used the device of a window frame (or picture frame), with which we normally associate views of the familiar, external world. But in imaginative painting of the twentieth century, and that dating back to Redon, the window is no longer associated with conscious experience. Even Magritte's framing device is out of joint, inflected or bent in a way that is comparable to the dislocation he has made in the expected sequence of his subjects. Writing about his intentions, Magritte has said:

The art of painting, as I conceive of it, consists in representing through pictorial technique the *unforeseen* images that might appear to me at certain moments whether my eyes are open or shut....I readily avoid explaining the things I love...we get no enrichment from a thing explained. In effect, the thing explained drops out of sight in favor of the practical explanation itself or a more or less intelligent hypothesis....

As defined in the discussion of Paul Klee's work in Chapter 15, "Themes from Nature," Magritte is what might be called an "imagist," one who paints conceptions that are unavailable to the external senses of his audience (until he paints them), but conceptions that he is able, after long meditation on objects, to conjure first in his mind and then fix in painting:

Certain images are the models for the paintings that I like to paint. In my opinion nothing other than images should be represented in painting. I have no desire, therefore, to express ideas or sentiments through painting, even if they seem to me extraordinary.... The titles of my paintings accompany them in the way that names correspond to objects, without either illustrating or explaining them.

Magritte thus plays against our natural inclination to rationalize what we see. He wants to evoke the mysterious and the unpredictable in the most commonplace subjects that we see and accept every day without second thought. *What* he paints is paramount, but Magritte takes little pleasure from the act of painting. Because for this artist painting is the most effective instrument for realizing his revelations, he does not want his work to be viewed primarily for its esthetic quality. This explains why Magritte's style is cooly precise and dry; it is a style to enforce the identity of the subject, while making the pictorial means as unobtrusive as possible. Magritte even displays boredom and disgust toward the painting process. If there is a precedent for Magritte's attitude in older art, it may be in the work of such artists as Bosch, who scorned new techniques or painterly devices and minimized their own hand to give maximum stress to their image.

At the same time, the possibilities of painting private fantasies have attracted men who feel passionately about painting itself and who pride themselves on the inventiveness of their forms and color, and on the power of their art to move the viewer esthetically as well as through thought and feeling. Such an artist was Max Beckmann, whose paintings, while not Surrealist, reveal his involvement with some of the major problems confronting the modern artist committed to the exploration and use of his own imagination for new and experimental artistic purposes.

BECKMANN'S *DEPARTURE*

By adhering to the morality of being true to one's own experiences and needs, many of the most creative artists of this century have, without question, produced works that are largely unintelligible to the general public. Frequently, when the artist has wanted to express something of importance to mankind, the very nature of his meaning, which like his form is partly derived from intuition, has been incompletely or inconsistently understood by the layman. It is not at all unusual for the meaning of a complex painting to change for the artist while he works on it, and even subsequent to the work's completion. One of the most powerful personal statements by a modern painter, expressing the complex of his responses to himself, to his times, and to the history of the human race is Max Beckmann's three-panel painting entitled *Departure* (Fig. 497). It was painted in Berlin in 1932 and 1933, following Beckmann's dismissal by the Nazis from his directorship of an art school. Fearing confiscation of his painting, the artist wrote on the back of the canvas, "Scenes from Shakespeare's Tempest." The panels were not, however, the illustration of a literary source.

Figure 497.   MAX BECKMANN. *Departure*. 1932–35. Oil on canvas, center 7′¾″×3′9⅜″; sides 7′¾″×3′3¼″. The Museum of Modern Art, New York.

Beckmann's hope was that the sympathetic viewer would meditate upon all three panels at once. He felt that their visual interrelationships would reveal his intentions. Historically, such three-panel paintings had precedents in Christian altarpieces, and it is possible that Beckmann intentionally revived this format, with its religious connotations, as the vehicle for his reflections on human spiritual history. The two flanking panels are narrower, darker, and more congested than the central one, and both are filled with unpleasant images of torture, noise, and nightmarish situations. By its greater size, its bright spaciousness, and the freedom of movement available to its characters, the center panel immediately establishes a different, more hopeful, but solemn mood and implication. Thus, even before we examine individual figures or speculate on the significance of gestures, we can sense the importance of these fundamental and readily apparent major contrasts. (T. S. Eliot believed that an artist begins to communicate before he is understood.) Like the work of other modern artists who attach symbolic significance to objects and gestures, Beckmann's previous art does not give us the basis for interpreting his imagery, for the German painter has not been consistent from painting to painting in the associations or values assigned to the same contents. Each object must be related to its particular context. The brutality in the left panel may possibly relate to Nazi tortures, of which Beckmann was all too well aware. This, however, is not made explicit, and the artist would have considered a more direct statement a limit to the scope of this painting's potential reference. While inventorying the indignities and violence to which the human body has been subjected, not unlike Goya in his *Disasters of War* and the *Caprices*, Beckmann surprises us by not introducing a plausible weapon or instrument for violence. We cannot even be sure that the stripe-shirted figure is an executioner. The settings of the framing panels are a curious mixture of references to a columned room and a stage. They are of an ambiguity that makes it impossible to localize the action. There is also an intriguing mixture of clothing that ranges from the uniform of a bellhop and the drummer's ermine collar to the ancient draperies and crown of the central figures. This should remind us that Beckmann does not want to specify the who, when, where, what, and why

of *Departure*. In a letter to a friend he set down his thoughts on the painting:

> The center is the end of the tragedy, but the meaning can only be understood by the three parts together. Life is what you see right and left. Life is torture, pain of every kind—physical and mental—men and women are subjected to it equally. On the right wing you can see yourself trying to find your way in the darkness, lighting the halls and stair-cases with a miserable lamp, dragging along tied to you as a part of yourself, the corpse of your memories, of your wrongs and failures, the murder everyone commits at some time of his life—you can never free yourself of your past, you have to carry that corpse while life plays the drum. In the center, the King and Queen have freed themselves, freed themselves of the tortures of life. They have overcome them. The Queen carries the greatest treasure—Freedom—as her child on her lap. Freedom is the one thing that matters—it is the departure, the new start.

On another occasion Beckmann said, "Departure, yes departure, from the illusion of life toward the essential realities that lie hidden beyond." It is as if he is commenting on the timelessness of oppression, but also on the capacity of the human spirit to overstride evil and to renew itself. But it is tribute to the poetic power of Beckmann's painting that once he has described so eloquently what he feels about its meaning, we can return to the work with still more questions, or the feeling that its ramifications are even deeper and more complex. Where Beckmann's *Departure* and Picasso's *Guernica* share a common ground is in their mingling of myth with the contemporaneous Fascist movement of the 1930s. It is in the artists' interpretation of a subject that was topical yet timeless, in the reaction they both felt against the forces of inhumanity and for the survival of the spirit.

AUTOMATISM AND IMAGINATIVE PAINTING

So far in this chapter all the imaginative art illustrated has had an illusionistic character, its subjects exhibited as if in a three-dimensional world existing behind the surface of the painting or print. Further, it has been possible to relate and identify objects and figures, entities physically complete despite their often hybrid make-up. Shortly after World War I, at about the time the work of the Alsatian artist Hans Arp began to appear (see Chapter 21), and during the early 1920s, there evolved an immensely fruitful and influential device for the creation of works of art, one that was employed by artists expressing a wide range of temperaments and styles. This was the device known as "automatism," and it has been adopted in a nonillusionistic context emphasizing the surfaceness of the drawing or painting by such artists as Masson, Miró, Gorky, and Pollock, who have produced much of the best art to appear between the two wars. Automatism has had continued, widespread use since 1945, and it is the second of the two major modes that have engaged the interest of artists whose works explore the imagination.

The earliest and most important definition of automatism was given by the French writer André Breton, who became the leader, high priest, and chief impresario of Surrealism. Writing in the *First Surrealist Manifesto* of 1924, Breton said: "SURREALISM. Pure psychic automatism by which one seeks to express, be it verbally, in writing or in any other manner, the real workings of the mind. Dictated by the unconscious, in the absence of any control exercized by reason and free from aesthetic or moral preoccupations." The use of the principle of automatism in literature and music would be what was known as "stream of consciousness" and jazz improvisation. For the layman, automatism is practiced in "doodling," or saying the first thing that comes into one's head. Many of the artists employing automatism did not live up to its literal definition, or to Breton's injunction not to let reason enter into the creative process at all. The artists' previous training and commitment to composition, as well as their taste, undoubtedly played some part in what they did. The historical emergence of automatism was related to the concern of many artists with the problem of how to be truly creative in a mechanistic world, and the belief that reason did not tap all of the potential source of important imagery in an artist's make-up. Automatism was thought to be essential to the "liberation" of the subconscious.

The automatist drawings and sand paintings produced by André Masson between 1924 and 1929 illustrate perhaps the purest utilization of this artistic device. He approached the sheet of paper, or canvas, with no preconceived image in mind. To stimulate or irritate his imagination he sometimes fixed sand to the canvas but, again, with no predetermined or definite configuration (Fig. 498). As if in a trance, Masson let his pen or brush move across the surface until he began to see possible images emerging. Thus, his "painting" began abstractly and then, with the introduction of certain instantaneous judgments, moved in the direction of a human configuration.

> I begin without an image or plan in mind, but just draw or paint rapidly according to my impulses. Gradually, in the marks I make, I see suggestions of figures or objects. I encourage these to emerge, trying to bring out their implications even as I consciously try to give order to the composition.

These decisions did not interrupt the continual movement of his hand, however. When the possibilities of a certain image became apparent, Masson made them more articulate, but he never took his drawing or painting to the stage that it became literal. During the process of evoking the final configuration, the artist was both creator and spectator, observing what resulted from his unconsciously controlled hand movements. Masson and other artists in the mid-20s considered what they were doing as "beyond painting," but they were not anti-art. Like much that has happened in this century, the history of Masson's work is that after it was made the word "art" was stretched to encompass it. ("Art" is probably the most elastic word ever invented by man.)

Figure 498. ANDRÉ MASSON. *Battle of Fishes.* 1927. Pencil, oil, and sand on canvas, 14¼ × 28¾". The Museum of Modern Art, New York (Purchase).

413

A second artist, who like Masson produced many of his most important paintings in the 1920s and worked "automatically," was the Spaniard Joan Miró. We can see the consequences of Miró's assimilation of the automatic method and how it radically altered the look and meaning of his art in two paintings. The first, entitled *The Farm* (Fig. 499), was done in 1921–1922, while the artist was at his home in Montroig, Spain, and then in Paris. For the picture he used souvenirs of his beloved homeland. The intense particularization of all objects in an airless space contributes to their charm and eventual ambiguity. Simultaneously, we are given the diversity and unity of a staggering number of objects, so that we become aware of a conjugated series, of visual puns based on holes and circular patches, scalloped and peaked shapes, radial spoke forms in the trees and grass, parallel diagonals and horizontals in roof and earth. The vividness and interest of the painting come from the relatively even distribution and the avoidance of overlap in a wide range of shapes, from the tiny pebbles through the buildings and trees to the infinity of the sky.

The fantasy incipient in *The Farm* was unchecked in Miró's *The Hunter (Catalan Landscape)* (Pl. 58). Suspended upon a flat surface of yellow above and pink below is an aggregate of lines and shapes derived from the earlier painting. Now, however, the drawing has suggested the object, so the undulating line lives an ubiquitous life as a mustache, the horizon, an animal body, waves, and birds.

Figure 499. JOAN MIRÓ. *The Farm*. 1921–22. Oil on canvas, 4'1½"×4'7¼". Collection Mrs. Ernest Hemingway, on extended loan to the Museum of Modern Art, New York.

Certain shapes and lines obsessive to Miró are now disassociated from the objects that generated them. There is a playful mocking of geometry in the use of the ruled line and the triangle. First, the triangle appears in its more familiar state at the lower left, but then it becomes part of the rabbit's tail just to the right and, above, the hunter's head. The pipe-smoking hunter has a large ear, not inappropriate for the chase, an exposed heart, and a scraggly beard whose mossy shapes appear on the wall of the farmhouse in the earlier painting. The dotted trail that he follows meanders playfully against the lines of his body and arms. Influenced by his contact with Cubism, Miró detached a large eye from a head and introduced the letters S A R D, perhaps from the Spanish word *sardana*, a Catalan folk dance. The earlier disposition of elements has become more random and whimsical. The range from minute to large is retained from the earlier work, but here Miró has magnified and reconstituted certain objects, such as the rabbit and insect forms, in a much more arbitrary way, according to the weight of the objects in his general awareness of them and the dictates of fantasy. While vestiges of a scene or a subject remain, they are accompanied by less decipherable elements, and the painting's poetry is more obvious in its rhymes, more arcane in its meaning. There is no longer the intent to follow the logic of nature's appearance. Miró's creatures live only on the painting's surface. The artist's full conversion to an art based not upon the restraint of reason but upon the encouraged, instinctive, or automatic outpouring of fantasy was a moral one.

The great stylistic divergence possible in art induced partly by the practice of automatism can be seen in a comparison of Miró's painting with one by the Armenian-born American artist Arshile Gorky, entitled *The Liver Is the Cock's Comb* (Pl. 59). Miró's motifs are cleanly drawn, and they float in an airless, imaginary, and seemingly limited space or on the painting's surface. Gorky's configurations are still more illegible and difficult to decipher, being tortured twistings that fuse or separate from one another in an intensely congested environment. Color ranges from deep earth tones to hot patches, and none of the color is related to the linear outlines. The artist's technical range in manipulating his paint is far greater and more subtle than Miró's. Gorky derived his imaginative composition from a drawing, or, as he thought of it, a blueprint, where he mingled fantasies upon things directly observed in nature, visions of internal human organs, recollections of art he had seen, and a consciousness of the need for composing his creations so that they made sense in terms of the painting's form. The title of the work is in no way related to the painting's inception and provides no clue to its interpretation. Often Gorky's titles were suggested, at his invitation, by friends. He was not the first artist to rebel against the "tyranny of the title." Gorky demanded an audience that would pay continued attention to his painting, not to the words by which it was labeled. With Surrealism, as Gorky's biographer Ethel Schwabacher has written, "art entered into man," which implies that artists were exteriorizing through art, as directly as possible, the inner world of their own feelings and imagination. Gorky, in turn, wanted his painting to enter, through sympathetic eyes, into the consciousness and subconsciousness of his audience. With time, one becomes aware not only of the implied violence of the motifs and strong sexual references in Gorky's work, but also of the beauty of its drawing, the painter's intimate handwriting, with its delicate or vehement passages, the careful adjustment of colors to each other, and the shape they share with the linear fabric of the composition. To content oneself with a game of hide-and-seek, or a few conclusions about what a specific passage is or might be, is to deny the occasion for seeing and feeling the conception of a Gorky painting as a whole, with its abundance of interrelationships that resist exhaustion throughout a long and continuous association.

It is indeed true that much of modern imaginative art deals with the unpleasant, and that for many people its form poses a parallel problem in being contrary to conventional taste. But even our abbreviated or synoptic sampling of older art derived from irrational experience has shown us that there is a precedent for art's contradiction of the polite, the prudish, and the pleasing. Tradition and familiarity make Goya and Bosch acceptable to those who rankle at Gorky or the French artist Jean Dubuffet. One cannot guess how many times, during exhibitions, the images in Dubuffet's *Corps de Dame* series (Fig. 500) have been likened to a naked woman run over by a steam roller on a newly paved street. Second in

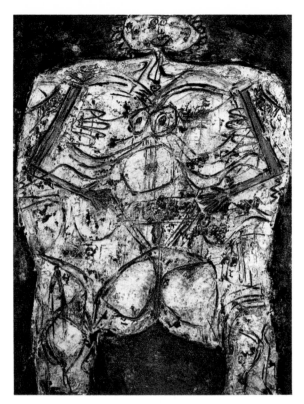

Figure 500. JEAN DUBUFFET. *Corps de Dame, Sanguine et Grenat.* 1950. Oil on canvas, 45⅝×35". Collection Alfonso A. Ossorio, East Hampton, N.Y.

frequency might be the comment that it looks like something scrawled on a wall in a public rest room. While Gorky paid homage to the "cookery" of brush painting, Dubuffet literally concocted his own recipes for paint and other substances in order to achieve a medium that in itself would stimulate his imagination. By incising his lines with the end of a paintbrush or a stick, he has invited comparison with defacement of walls; in fact, Dubuffet, a middle-class former wine merchant, has spent many years in the study of *l'art brut*—the "raw art" or "unschooled, unadulterated art" made by psychotics, children, and the "self-taught" draftsmen who leave their mark in public places. What he finds interesting is the direct, frank character of this type of art, its expression of another, invisible, or repressed side of men and women.

The *Corps de Dame* series (which Dubuffet followed with a comparable treatment of men, indicating no favoritism) submitted the body to brutal handling, not by someone in the painting, as in paintings of anatomy dissections or martyrdoms, but by the artist himself. Ugly women are to be found in Leonardo's drawings from deformed subjects, in Goya's *Caprices* as symbols of vanity and evil, and in countless

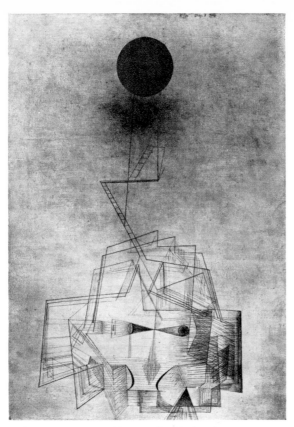

Figure 501. PAUL KLEE. *The Limits of Reason*. 1927. Oil and water color, 21⅝ × 16⅛″. Private collection.

caricatures, but Dubuffet's predecessors in Western, post-Renaissance painting located their gruesome subjects in a world of space and light and sought to make them appear as life-like as possible. Dubuffet has said that in doing the series he was working with "a general concept," which prevents our assuming he was motivated toward moralizing caricature or scientific investigation. Dubuffet's women exist in what the artist has referred to as "a state of immateriality"; they are made of and live in the substance of the medium used. One can only conjecture whether Dubuffet's conception is a personal antidote to the popular notion of "woman" created in France by the mass media. His known habits of work—which are not to illustrate a mental image but to respond to stimulations offered by his matrix as it is brushed, troweled, or scraped on the surface—still allow for the expression of strong and deep feelings about the final subject.

In the same year that Dubuffet was doing his *Corps de Dame* pictures in Paris, the Dutch-born American painter Willem de Kooning began in New York a series called *Woman*, which continued for the next three years and intermittently thereafter to the present time. Despite the coin-

cidence of dates, there was no conscious exchange of influence between the two painters. De Kooning's *Woman* series grew out of paintings he had done in the 1940s involving both the subject of the feminine form and abstraction. Sometimes referred to as Abstract Surrealism, de Kooning's work depends in part upon automatism, and the spontaneous release of ideas. In it, however, the ideas are continually subjected to destruction and reconstruction during vigorous painting operations so that there is no point at which the image is completely or irrevocably finished. The painting grows or fades according to the artist's life at the moment he confronts it or is involved with it. His series and subsequent abstractions are really one continuous painting tied to his own changing moods like a personal diary of partially eradicated entries. As with Dubuffet, the violence of de Kooning's art lies not in any action depicted, but in the action of making and remaking the painting by means of assaults on the canvas. In *Woman and Bicycle* (Pl. 60), the subject seems all eyes, teeth, and breasts, and sits passively on her conveyance. Her form materializes from and is threatened by the painter's slashing applications of paint to the surface. She does not intentionally symbolize, allegorize, or allude specifically to any one person or public concept. She belongs to the reality of a painted surface and is a recurring hallucination for the painter. The artist has described his obsessional image and suggested the intervention of his inner feelings and subconscious during its realization: "I always started out with the idea of a young person, a beautiful woman. I noticed them change. Somebody would step out—a middle-aged woman. I didn't mean to make them such monsters." On another occasion he said: "Women irritate me sometimes. I painted that irritation in the *Woman* series, that's all." De Kooning is a reactive artist, potentially irritated by a wide variety of sensations and visual suggestions from all over. In one sense his painting is antidotal to the disease of emotional insincerity in society and its public glorification of women within the context of cleanliness, motherhood, happiness, youthfulness, and sex. De Kooning's method of working on *Woman and Bicycle*, and the other pictures in the series, was to build up an unpremeditated image from scraps of his earlier drawings, cutouts from newspapers or photographs, freehand drawings of letters, and the dictates of emotion, lacing it all with technical preoccupations relating to his craft. Like Frankenstein's monster, *Woman and Bicycle* is a synthetic concoction of used parts. "Whatever I see becomes my shapes and my condition. The recognizable form people sometimes see in the pictures after they are painted I see myself, but whether they got there accidentally or not, who knows?"

THE LIMITS OF REASON

Although he died in 1940, it is fitting to conclude this chapter with a work by Paul Klee, the most gifted and consistently excellent creator of imaginative art in this century. In Chapter 15, "Themes from Nature," the reader was introduced to some of Klee's ideas regarding creation. An artist endowed with the ability to express both whimsy and wisdom, who worked with facts, fables, and fantasy, Klee devoted his art to the rendering of the world seen with closed eyes. His hundreds of paintings reveal how he could preserve the special qualities of images of the mind. Klee invented his own modes of drawing, charted new spaces, and enacted fresh artistic laws for light and gravity. In his contacts with the external world, with what he saw, heard, and read, Klee continually and consistently nourished the sources of his imagination. Science, philosophy, and art fuse in his images. Klee could reinterpret an old idea, one which had a verbal or established visual history, and give it new dimensions marked with his personal touch. Consider his *Limits of Reason* (Fig. 501) and a late nineteenth-century wood engraving by E. J. Sullivan from Thomas Carlyle's *Sartor Resartus* (Fig. 502). Sullivan shows that man ascends the heights of knowledge on a mountain of books. The path to enlightenment is paved with the written word. One could read this description and in the absence of Sullivan's print still conjure the image in one's mind. But how difficult to evoke through words Klee's conception! The linear contraption at the bottom of his picture broadly suggests modern technological inventions, the means by which man aspires to reach what Klee shows to be ultimately unattainable via the ladders of reason. In Bruegel's time, and even earlier in the Middle Ages, the analogous commentary on folly was the depiction of the building of the Tower of Babel. Though made in 1927, Klee's conception prophetically suggests present-day devices by which we seek to explore the unknown spaces of the universe.

In the study of art, it is one thing to become aware of its possibilities, and another its impossibilities. This book has been very much concerned for the former. With regard to imaginative art, we can learn that it is impossible for us to understand completely the meaning and intention of paintings by Redon, de Chirico, Magritte, and Beckmann, for example. Just as there is no objective way to prove good and bad values for art, so is it in many cases impossible even for the artist to verify the meaning of his work. Meyer Schapiro admirably summed up the situation for many modern painters when he wrote:

> The artist does not wish to create a work in which he transmits an already prepared and complete message to a relatively indifferent and impersonal receiver. The painter aims rather at such a quality of the whole that, unless you achieve the proper set of mind and feeling towards it, you will not experience anything of it at all.

Max Beckmann realized that there were many in his audience who could not understand his work. He hoped that viewers would employ what he referred to as their own inner "creative sympathy" when looking at his paintings: "I can only speak to people who, consciously or unconsciously, already carry within them a similar metaphysical code." Contrary to what the public and many art educators may wish, art is not for every man, just as every man is not for art. Both creating and communing with art involve the experience and training of imagination.

Figure 502. E. J. SULLIVAN. *Sartor Resartus.* 1898. Wood engraving.

21

THE DEATH OF THE WINDOW AND LIFE OF THE SQUARE: ABSTRACTION

The emergence of abstract painting after 1909 constituted one of the great revolutions in the history of art. The *picture window* concept of illusionistic painting which had evolved in the fifteenth century and thrived unchallenged for over five hundred years was rejected by several artists before, during, and after World War I in favor of a nonillusionistic and in many cases nonrepresentational art. "Abstract" is not an adequate or correct word to describe this new painting but, like the terms "Baroque" and "Gothic," it is used for convenience. The reader will not generally be burdened with explanations of the terms used to describe various movements or with attempts to fit paintings into tidy verbal compartments, for, in the words of artist Harry Holtzman, "Hardening of the categories produces art disease."

The title of this chapter is *not* intended to apply to all painting of the last sixty years, since many painters continue to paint illusionistically; rather it relates to those artists who since 1910 for ethical, philosophical, and esthetic reasons have found illusionism no longer meaningful as a way of painting. For these artists the seemingly transparent picture surface with its simulation of the three-dimensional visual world was dead. Independence from likeness in art did not come over-

night or without its problems. The pioneer abstractionists moved into uncharted territory and were faced with creating their own shapes and composition to replace those provided by nature and tradition in art. This chapter outlines a few of the crucial steps taken toward abstraction, adopting the motif of the square to suggest the variety in nonrepresentational and the way it has satisfied many artists of differing temperaments and tastes.

The Window View of Art. A woodcut by Albrecht Dürer, *Draftsman Drawing a Portrait* (Fig. 503), from his treatise on perspective, helps us to understand the old window theory of illusionistic painting. Dürer has shown the artist stationed behind a table looking through an eyepiece set at a certain height, thereby giving a fixed viewpoint. Looking through the sight, the painter sees the seated model through a framed piece of glass that intercepts his line of vision. The pane of glass is like a window and is the actual surface on which he is painting. By painting what he sees upon the glass the artist thus transfers the model to a two-dimensional surface. Earlier in the fifteenth century, with regard to the painting's surface, Alberti had instructed the artist "to present the forms of the objects on this surface as if it were a transparent pane of glass" [1435]. Alberti's definition of painting is likewise illustrated in Dürer's print: "Painting, then, is nothing other than a cross section of a visual pyramid upon a certain surface, artificially represented with lines and color at a given distance, with a central stance established and lights arranged...." How many painters actually employed Dürer's device would be hard to estimate, but the translation of the three-dimensional world onto the painted surface, regardless of device used, was more than just a mechanical operation. It took centuries to develop an extensive repertory of illusionistic devices, such as modeling and atmospheric effects achieved by light and shadow, overlap, recession of lines, and diminishing scale of subjects. These techniques did not all vanish immediately from painting at the end of the nineteenth century, but as we saw in Chapter 14, "The Synthesis of Past and Present in Nineteenth-Century Art," they were gradually set aside as painters found new means to interpret a reality that was not confined to the visible world.

The Renaissance window theory of painting had implications that went beyond the making of pictures. In the Renaissance, systematic perspective was used to create an ideal world, the model of harmonious social and natural order. Pieter de Hooch's seventeenth-century painting *Interior of a Dutch House* (Fig. 504) is a model of polite sociability set in a neat, comfortable interior that is illuminated by means of numerous windows. Like the glass in the windows, we look through the painting's surface, aided by the receding black and white tiled floor

that also serves as a device by means of which we can measure our distance from all of the figures and objects in the room. The rectangles of the rafters, the squared shapes of the map, painting, and fireplace, and the window frames and flooring establish a clear metrical shape and rhythmic order that would make an interesting painting without the figures. Within his spatial box the Dutch painter could maneuver his figures, adjusting them to the setting, but relying more on the fixed relationships of the latter than on those of the figures. The map, the architecture, and the tidiness of the room help us to understand how much the middle-class Dutch loved to see things put into order and well made. Because of its varied repetition and frequency of occurrence, to modern eyes conditioned by abstract art it is almost as if the artist is paying homage to the square. At the same time, while the seventeenth-century Dutch knew the principles of geometry, they could not conceive of painting denuded of people, places, and things. More than two centuries of naturalistic painting had to pass before a number of circumstances permitted artists to feel that the time was right for giving up illusionism.

Closing the Window. The window approach to painting reached its culmination and denial in nineteenth-century Impressionism. A painting by Caillebotte, a friend of the Impressionists and a wealthy boat builder, art collector, and painter, of a man standing in front of an open window epitomizes the Impressionists' approach to life

Below: Figure 503. ALBRECHT DÜRER. *Draftsman Drawing a Portrait.* 1525. Woodcut, $5\frac{1}{8} \times 6$". The Metropolitan Museum of Art, New York (gift of Henry Walters).

Right: Figure 504. PIETER DE HOOCH. *Interior of a Dutch House.* 1658. Oil on canvas, 29×25". The National Gallery, London.

Left: Figure 505. GUSTAVE CAILLEBOTTE. *Man at a Window.* c. 1875. Oil on canvas, 46×32½". Private collection, Paris.

he described the window as it is encountered in paintings such as those of Caillebotte, Monet, and, later, Pissarro:

> From within, it is through the window that we communicate with the outside; the window is still a frame which accompanies us without cease, lasting while we are in the house, and this time is considerable. The frame of the window, according to whether we are far from it or near it, whether we are seated or standing, cuts off the outside scene in the most unexpected, the most changing manner, procuring for us the eternal variety, the spontaneity which is one of the great zests of reality [1876].

Monet's painting of the *Fourteenth of July* (Pl. 36) is a view from a window of the flag-bedecked street, and in some of his boulevard paintings Monet showed top-hatted figures leaning out of windows looking at the crowds below. Caillebotte, Pissarro, and Monet did not use the window as a framing device for a centralized focus upon a few figures in static situations; rather, they preserved the quality of traffic flow in and out of our frame of vision. The tilting of the street makes the picture's depth difficult to read and serves as a device for presenting the unarranged and ambiguous experiences of seeing the city from an elevated window.

Shortly before 1900, while in London, Monet painted *Leicester Square* (Fig. 506) seen on a rainy night. It is as if the artist was viewing the city not from an open window but through the rain-spattered glass which caused the

and art (Fig. 505). The man is not restricted in his view by the mechanical sighting device of Dürer, but casually stands at an angle to the window, hands in his pockets, looking out on the scene below. An impressionable person, he is quietly enjoying the esthetic moments of seeing the life of the street without himself being seen. Around the time of Caillebotte's painting, Edmond Duranty, a writer sympathetic to Impressionism, wrote an essay entitled "The New Painting," in which

Left: Figure 506. CLAUDE MONET. *Leicester Square.* 1899-1904. Oil on canvas, 32 × 25". Collection Michel Monet.

Right: Figure 507. PIERRE BONNARD. *House on a Court.* 1895. Color lithograph, 13⅝ ×10¼". The Museum of Modern Art, New York (Larry Aldrich Fund).

colors and lights to run together. In making us aware of the closed window, or semitransparency of the viewing surface, Monet also makes us more conscious of the painting's actual physical surface.

Pierre Bonnard's color lithograph *House on a Court* (Fig. 507) of 1895 comes close to illustrating Duranty's comments on the window, and he actually includes its frame. The potentially prosaic view of portions of two ordinary adjacent apartment houses is enlivened by the segmenting action of the window frame and the way the alignment of the windows, roof lines, and chimney pots across the court establish a counterpoint to the rectilinear, continuous window frame. This is a far different view from that seen through the window of Joseph's workroom in the *Merode Altarpiece* (Pl. 13). The fifteenth-century Flemings looked upon the window as a means of providing a slice of the life of the outside world, and they took pains to include in their paintings interesting vistas of figures, buildings, and landscapes. Bonnard contented himself with an ordinary Parisian tenement. By reducing detail and textural differentiation, as well as alignment, Bonnard diminished the illusionistic nature of the window, thereby collapsing both the portion of the painting we know to be in depth and the intervening space. As we saw in his screen painting (Fig. 344), Bonnard introduced a pronounced surfaceness to the window motif, affirming the identity of his subject while at the same time reinforcing our awareness that it is seen in a lithograph. In both Renaissance and Impressionist painting the artist had in mind a definite distance from which his painting would be seen, so that its full illusion could be apprecia-

Left: Figure 508. HENRI MATISSE. *Dinner Table.* 1897. Oil on canvas, 3′3½″×4′3½″. Private collection, New York.

Right: Figure 509. HENRI MATISSE. *Harmony in Red.* 1908–09. Oil on canvas, 5′9¾″×7′1⅞″. The Hermitage, Leningrad (Copyright Éditions du Cercle d'Art, Paris).

ted. Bonnard's lithograph, whether seen from close up or at a distance, maintains more consistently the surface orientation of the composition.

Henri Matisse is the modern painter who, along with Picasso, has been the most influential in preserving representation while denying traditional illusionism. His evolution toward a surface style after 1900 can be summarized by comparing two paintings of the same subject done about ten years apart. In the *Dinner Table* of 1897 (Fig. 508) Matisse was presenting to the public his masterpiece, in which he was showing in a large painting all that he had mastered up to that time. Characteristically for Matisse, the subject is an esthetic one—the maid in arranging the flowers on the table is herself performing an artistic activity. (For Matisse good living always met the requirements of art.) In displaying his skill as a painter he showed the light source coming through a curtained window in the background, so that most of the picture is not seen in full or direct light. Yet, he caught the sparkle of light on the glassware. Having previously copied the old masters, Matisse knew the great tradition of table paintings, still lifes, and genre scenes, and with this work he was claiming his right to be compared with them. Alberti's requirements for painting, that it consist of circumscribing objects, their composition, and the showing of their reception of light, still obtain.

In 1908, Matisse painted two versions of the subject of the dinner table, *Harmony in Red* (Fig. 509) and *Harmony in Blue*. Now painting had to be defined in terms of the harmonious and expressive arrangement of lines and colors upon a surface independently of the subject. There is no simulation of relief or the depth Alberti wanted achieved by the use of geometry. Consonant with this new two-dimensional world was the absence of a natural or artificial light source, there being no air or space for light to pass through. The colors themselves give off luminosity and create depth. Color and drawing replace the subtle textural distinctions of earlier paintings as the means for separating objects. In place of the earlier transparent window, Matisse has placed on the wall what is either a window or a painting, the latter, of course, being comparably flat and arbitrary in color. Sensibility to distance and light, so important to de Hooch, is replaced by Matisse's sensibility to the interaction of color. Social or human relationships that dramatized Western painting since the Renaissance have given way to esthetic relationships. Matisse too wanted his painting to evoke recollections of pleasurable experiences in the home, but now on new terms, which make of painting a decorative object. The viewer cannot mentally project himself into this painting. The artist imposes his vision by forcing us to visually absorb the effects of the painting as a whole, not to read it serially, as in the de Hooch. The character of windows, mirrors, and paintings seen in older art is leveled out in Matisse. Wallpaper has the same characteristics, or lack of them, as trees or the human figure.

As with Picasso's print of the *Painter and Model Knitting* (Fig. 454), there is no projection principle such as Dürer demonstrated by which we could predict what Matisse would have put on the surface of his painting. His decisions are governed by the need for colors to accord with the dominant tone he has chosen, and the shapes must animate the surface and ensure that the entire painting be equally expressive. He was painting to delight the eye, to surrender its total effect more fully and immediately than did the paintings in the style of 1897.

The eye, the window, the mirror, and the camera lens, all have been identified with reproduction of the visible world and what for most people is reality. By contrasting Vermeer's *View of Delft* (Fig. 510) with Fernand Léger's *The City* (Pl. 61), we can see how the same motif has been interpreted using all and none of these devices. The researches of scholars such as Swillens and Seymour have confirmed that when Vermeer depicted his native city he worked near a window in a darkened room of a house across the river from the main port of Delft. Professor Seymour has presented a good argument for Vermeer's having used a *camera obscura*, or boxlike viewing device much like the modern camera, similar to the one reproduced in an old print (Fig. 511). By means of this device (which contained a mirror to right the inverted lens image) Vermeer would have been able to see the city reflected onto a flat surface, thus facilitating its reproduction and merging of the refracted image with his painting surface. The crucial evidence for this argument is the tiny unfocused areas of light in the painting which correspond to those produced by a camera lens that cannot quite correct or sharpen focus for highlighted areas. Vermeer was thus able to patiently reconstruct detail by detail the panorama of the city seen four hundred feet away across the Schie River at about noon on a summer day when the wind was blowing from the southwest. The character of the architecture of Delft and the slow pace of the city's life lent themselves to this type of sedentary contemplation. Delft's countless

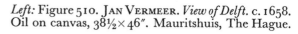

Left: Figure 510. JAN VERMEER. *View of Delft.* c. 1658. Oil on canvas, 38½ × 46". Mauritshuis, The Hague.

Below: Figure 511. ANONYMOUS. *Camera Obscura.* 17th century. Woodcut.

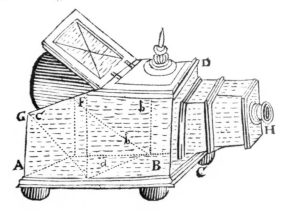

delightful prospects and details revealed themselves only to the unhurried, discriminating eye.

For Léger, the modern city was too big and too complex to be seen from a window or caught in a camera lens. He passionately loved the machines and the engineering that produced the new metropolis and could only condone a style that captured these new urban characteristics. He did not see himself as an eye reflecting the visual world, but as a painter-engineer who constructed his image with the same intellectual precision and multiplicity of viewpoints as city builders did their blueprints. Cubism provided Léger with a new syntax for presenting as pictorially connected objects that appear to be disconnected. His colors, unlike those of Vermeer, are the strong, pure hues of commercial advertising, or those of metal and cement. The textured patterns were inspired by railings, iron stairways, the Eiffel Tower, segments of mass-produced, stenciled letters, and billboard figures—anything that might suggest the handmade or traditionally picturesque. The smooth surfaces and hard edges were painted impersonally. Robotlike figures on stairs are the ideal inhabitants of Léger's mechanized metropolis. Natural light, so important in lending poetry to the urban painting of Vermeer and the Impressionists, plays no part in *The City*. As with the painting of Matisse, the shapes are self-illuminating, rarely tempered by shadings. They are always clear, clean, and hard, unnatural in their edges and juncture. Vermeer and Monet delighted in painting soft clouds; Léger mechanized smoke into a globular sequence above the stairway figures. Smoke for him was a symbol of civilization, and his use of hard lines to harness it was an affirmation of his own masculine command.

In giving up illusionism, however, Léger preserved some of its characteristics, notably the importance of contrasts. The visual spice of his painting comes from unpredictable contrasts such as bright and dull colors, a round column against flat shapes. Contrast of scale depends upon the single tall column that stands against so many medium and small shapes. In moving away from the natural, Léger's shapes tend toward the geometrically curved and angular, but unlike the abstract artists to be discussed subsequently, he could not restrict himself solely to the rectilinear. (This would have contradicted his ideal of contrast as a life and artistic ethic.) For Léger, faithfulness to perception, to the eye

Figure 512. ROBERT DELAUNAY. *The City*. 1910. Oil on canvas, 4′9½″ × 3′8″. Musée National d'Art Moderne, Paris.

as a window, mirror, or camera lens, had to be replaced by art as a conception—resulting from the intellect and feeling.

The window as an imaginative rather than rational frame for viewing the city became the subject of a series of paintings begun in 1910 by the Parisian painter Robert Delaunay, which culminated in 1915 in abstraction. In an early version of his *Fenêtre*, or *Window*, series (Fig. 512), Delaunay gives us a view from an imaginary curtain-framed window overlooking Paris in the direction of the Eiffel Tower, which can be made out at the top. Delaunay loved the Eiffel Tower and the knowledge and skill that were required for its construction. Like Léger, Delaunay wanted to bring to painting the inquisitiveness and objectivity of the scientist. Although lacking the systematic and consistent method of the latter, he sought to inquire into the possibilities of light and color and the dissolving effects of their interaction upon solid forms as perceived by the eye. He was also conscious of Cubism's liberation from likeness in these years and the possibilities of constructing painterly compositions that diminished emphasis upon illusionism and that stressed the components of painting, notably its

Figure 513. ROBERT DELAUNAY. *First Simultaneous Window*. 1911. Oil on canvas; 15¾ × 18⅛". Collection Jean Cassou, Paris.

color and surfaceness. In his 1910 *Fenêtre* he superimposed a checkerboard pattern of color over parts of the composition in order to link what seemed distant with the surface plane and to activate the contrasts of color throughout. In a 1911 version of his *Fenêtre* (Fig. 513), reference to a window and distance beyond has been eliminated, as have distinct buildings. What has been preserved are certain segmented curves that recall perhaps the profile of the Eiffel Tower. Color is laid down in large patches that softly vibrate in the viewer's eye. It is as if color is seen through a prism. Delaunay was moving in the direction of making color interaction the sole subject of his work. As with Matisse, but more removed from the world of objects, Delaunay wanted formal relationships to be the purpose of his art and the source of its enjoyment. Unlike the physicist, who relies on science for his color studies, Delaunay depended finally upon taste or esthetic sensibility in the selection and juxtaposition of colors, which include reds, blues, and oranges. Drawing, shading, perspective, textures, and strong value contrasts of light and dark, the prerequisites of illusionism, were no longer the basis for his painting. He extended his color contrasts beyond the canvas on to the border of the painting itself, thus denying even to the picture frame its traditional enhancement of illusion. We tend to take the picture frame for granted, and for many people it is a surprise

to see abstract painting lacking frames or simply bordered with thin strips of wood. The Impressionists were the first, in the early 1880s, to frame their paintings in simple white borders, thereby reinforcing the intensity of their colors. Seurat painted inner frames with colors that were the complementaries of those in adjacent areas of the canvas, which ensured the brilliance of the latter. The traditional black frame of the Dutch or the elaborate carved gold frames of the past, familiar in every museum, had been thought not only to establish the worth of the painting and dignify it but also to enforce its illusionism or window character. The death of illusionism in modern art was also the demise of the elaborate picture frame as the setting for the new painting.

More than Four Sides to the Square. Up until abstraction evolved in the twentieth century we know that shapes such as triangles, circles, and squares had a long history of symbolizing concepts and values. All three of these shapes, for example, have stood for God. The Roman philosopher Philo compared God to an infinite circle whose center was everywhere and whose perimeter nowhere. The Chinese spoke of infinity as a square without angles. The circle has stood for eternity, resurrection, the earth and heaven, the ideal city, perfection, and so on. Pythagoras referred to the triangle as symbolizing human knowledge. In Christianity the shape has stood for the Trinity, and it has signified hieratic social systems. Walt Whitman extolled God in his poem "Chanting the Square Deific." Egyptian priests symbolized man as a square. In a drawing Leonardo da Vinci used a square and circle to illustrate how these shapes could contain a perfectly proportioned figure (Fig. 514). Squares have been associated with talismans against plague, mystical architectural ground plans, games, and puzzles. The square has variously symbolized the four seasons, the elements, the points of the compass, the earth, and the sun. Our language has many idioms that utilize shapes such as the square as metaphors to denote variously a social conservative, honesty, true relationships, or the straightening of accounts. Behind the symbolism of the square in history and in current vernacular language is the fact that its meanings had a public currency. None of the past public associations with the square, including those of the geometer, have been drawn upon by

Plate 61. Fernand Léger. *The City.* 1919. Oil on canvas, 7'7" × 9'9½". The Philadelphia Museum of Art (A. E. Gallatin Collection).

Plate 62.   HENRI MATISSE. *The Snail*. 1953. Gouache on cut-and-pasted paper, 9′4″ ×9′5″.
The Tate Gallery, London (by courtesy of the Trustees).

Plate 63.   MARK ROTHKO. *Tan and Black on Red.* 1957. Oil on canvas, 5'9⅜" × 4'5⅜".
Collection Mr. and Mrs. I. Donald Grossman, New York.

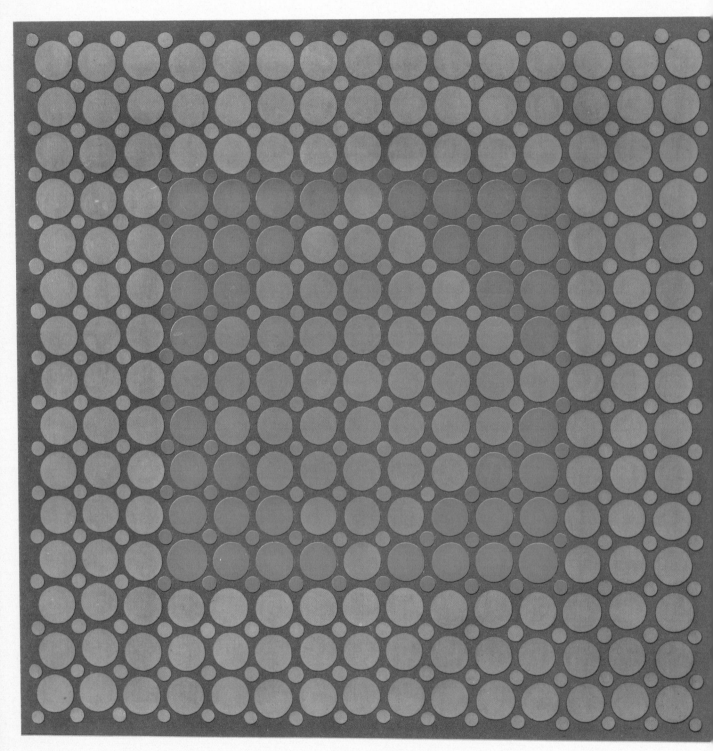

Plate 64.   RICHARD ANUSZKIEWICZ. *Injured by Green*. 1963. Liquitex on board, 36 × 36″.
Collection Mrs. Janet S. Fleisher, Elkins Park, Pennsylvania.

abstract artists, despite the fact that they intended their art to move the viewer with sympathy. Beginning in 1913, when the shape first appeared in modern art, like Walt Whitman each artist has found by reason, feeling, or intuition his own values in the square. The physical appearance of the square—its size, means of delineation and relative distinctiveness, color, weight, texture, disposition within the field of the painting, and relation to other shapes or the canvas edges—while unimportant to a geometer or to its previous symbolic effectiveness, has been paramount for many painters. Artists have given a changing face to the square similar to the change seen in the rendering of Christ through the history of art. The shape has been made a personal extension of the artist, so that we would not confuse a square by Mondrian with one by Rothko. In another sense, being closed or bounded by an edge, a square belongs to the broad class of objects. Its theme and variation in modern art are like those of the bottle, glass, or apple in the history of still-life painting. As with these objects, when set into the personal history and intentions of the artist, the square acquires new dimensions of meaning, but unlike previous meanings of objects, those for the square are often not discursive or verbal.

The Life of the Square. The entrance of the square into modern art coincides with political upheaval and revolution in Europe. Naturalism and many pre-1914 avant-garde movements such as Cubism and Futurism came to be viewed in the eyes of political and artistic revolutionaries as the products of social systems responsible for the tragic catastrophe of World War I. In Russia, Holland, Switzerland, and Germany during and after the war abstraction took hold, and artists linked their efforts with the emergence of new social and political systems. Individuality was viewed by these revolutionaries as inimical to a new society founded upon collective cooperation among all men and upon maximum utilization of the new technology. In view of present-day Soviet Communism's criticism of abstract art and its insistence upon a socially conscious naturalism in painting and sculpture, it is hard for us to imagine that during and immediately after the Russian Revolution abstraction was looked upon as the true expression of the new Communist society. (By 1920 there were more museums of modern art

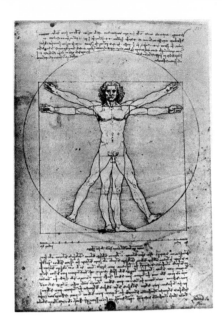

Figure 514. LEONARDO DA VINCI. *Study of Human Proportions According to Vitruvius.* c. 1485–90. Pen and ink, 13½×9¾". Accademia, Venice.

and abstract artists in Russia than in any other country.) Kandinsky was the first of the Russian abstract artists. The second was Kasimir Malevich, who in 1913 began a series of pencil drawings that departed from his paintings of peasants and Cubist assemblages. One drawing in his abstract series was of a pair of black squares meticulously placed within the white of the paper (Fig. 515). In essays begun in 1915 and published in 1927, *The Non-Objective World*, Malevich reconstructed the circumstances in which he created an art of pure feeling, the feeling of "objectlessness":

Figure 515. KAZIMIR MALEVICH. *Suprematist Elements: Two Squares.* 1913. Pencil, 6¾×11¼", ruled margins; 19¾×14½", sheet. The Museum of Modern Art, New York.

When in the year 1913, in my desperate attempt to free art from the ballast of objectivity, I took refuge in the square form and exhibited a picture which consisted of nothing more than a black square on a white field, the critics and, along with them, the public sighed, "Everything which we loved is lost. We are in a desert.... Before us is nothing but a black square on a white background!" But this desert is filled with the spirit of non-objective sensation which pervades everything. Even I was gripped by a kind of timidity bordering on fear when it came to leaving "the world of will and idea," in which I had lived and worked, in the reality of which I believed. But a blissful sense of liberating non-objectivity drew me forth into the "desert" where nothing is real except feeling...and so feeling became the substance of my life. This was no "empty square" which I had exhibited but rather the feeling of non-objectivity.... The black square on the white field was the first form in which non-objective feeling came to be expressed. The square = feeling, the white field = the void beyond this feeling.

The moving life experiences that Malevich was referring to, in which we do not encounter objects and seem to confront infinity, include those on the sea, the desert, and in the air. Malevich wanted a mystical art that captured feeling induced by the absence of objects and what lay beyond sight. It was an art that did not imitate the appearance of nature, but that resulted from the inventiveness of the human mind: "Is it not my brain which is the true factory, from which the new iron-transformed world runs....I wish to be the maker of the new signs of my inner movements....I do not wish to copy and spoil the movement of an object and other varieties and forms of nature." In 1918 he did a painting which it would seem brought millenniums of art to a conclusion or dead end. In his *Suprematist Composition: White on White* (Fig. 516), a white square is seen against or within a white background. The artist wrote, "The blue color of clouds is overcome in the Suprematist system, ruptured and enters white as the true, real representation of infinity, and is therefore freed from the coloured background of the sky." This painting is historically the first one-color conception, achieving its only contrast, tension, or drama by the acute angle at which the inner square is set in relation to its field, as opposed to its

Figure 516. KAZIMIR MALEVICH. *Suprematist Composition: White on White*. c. 1918. Oil on canvas, 31¼×31¼". The Museum of Modern Art, New York.

symmetrical disposition in the 1913 drawing. Malevich gave up painting for a number of years after this work, and when he returned to it his style was no longer abstract. The power of the Russian army and desire of political leaders such as Stalin to placate this force brought an end to Communist support of abstraction such as that of Malevich. Ironically, present-day Communist art has its basis in styles evolved during the nineteenth century in cultures that Communism condemns on ideologic, economic, and social grounds.

In 1917, a small group of artists led by Theo van Doesburg and Mondrian formed a movement in Holland called *De Stijl* (The Style). Similar to Malevich's Suprematist movement in Russia, De Stijl was intended as a positive, utopian alternative to previous artistic and social systems. Naturalism and individuality were to be sacrificed for the spiritual and artistic rehabilitation of art and society, and a new universal language of art, design, architecture, and poetry was to be formed. In addition to the publications of De Stijl, van Doesburg toured Europe giving lectures on the aims of this art, using as illustration his esthetic transformations of a cow (Fig. 517). Both van Doesburg's and Mondrian's paintings can here serve as means of visualizing the aims of De Stijl. Sentiment or subjectivity and subject matter were to be eliminated. The curve signified the former, the cow the latter. The style of De Stijl meant rhythmical relationships of rectilinear conjunctions of lines and primary-colored rectangles seen against white. The task set by these artists was to make visible what they felt were the laws of nature. "The living beauty of nature cannot be copied: it can only be expressed," wrote Mondrian. The reasoned structure of things, not their appearance, was what led Mondrian and van Doesburg to straight lines joining at right angles. They felt that the right angle is the perfect objective expression of dynamic relationships in nature and that the rectangle resolves all tensions.

Primary colors plus white and straight black lines were the necessary elementary means of expressing a content that the De Stijl artists felt had to be universal. Van Doesburg and Mondrian sought to "set the world right according to pure aesthetical principles with the aid of...discords and...consonants of color and form....By being aesthetically affected by a purely visual work of art, the contemplator immediately sets himself right" [van Doesburg, 1918]. Painting such as van Doesburg's and Mondrian's was intended to present the public with a vision of true harmony and beauty otherwise unavailable to them, thereby bringing spiritual peace. It was performing a function analogous to that of de Hooch and seventeenth-century Dutch painters.

Looking at the transformations of van Doesburg's cow, the reader must wonder what the artist felt was his final subject matter. Van Doesburg wrote: "The modern work of art indeed lacks subject-matter. But it does not lack a subject. This subject is of a pictorial nature, it is aesthetical balance, unity, harmony in a higher sense."

Van Doesburg characterized his work as "peripheric composition." This we can see in the later version of the cow.

Figure 517.   THEO VAN DOESBURG (C. E. M. KUPPER). *Left: The Cow*. Three studies from a series of eight drawings. Undated. *Above right: Composition (The Cow)*. 1916. Gouache, 15⅝×23¾″. *Below right: Composition (The Cow)*. 1916–17. Oil on canvas, 14¾×25″. All, the Museum of Modern Art, New York (Purchase).

In the course of time the symmetrical composition (Christ, Mary, Cross, Guitar, Bottle, etc.) has "pressed" itself more and more towards the center...to such a degree, that the composition is entirely pivotshaped and the periphery of the canvas remains blank and therefore gives an impression of emptiness.... Very important is the essential renewal of the method of composition. Gradual abolition of the center and all passive emptiness. The composition develops itself...instead of towards the center, towards the extreme periphery of the canvas, it even appears...to continue beyond it....

By its pictorial transformations the cow lost its specific identity, but the De Stijl artists argued that it thus became part of the universal form of nature. While the philosophy of De Stijl was not always shared by artists influenced by the movement, its emphasis upon the total expressive design of the painting and devaluation of a previously climactic area, such as the center, was of enormous consequence.

So strongly did Mondrian believe in the purity and rightness of the right angle as an expression of the individual's relation to the universe that when van Doesburg introduced a diagonal into his art around 1925, the two men broke their friendship. (Van Doesburg felt the diagonal was a dynamic symbol, whereas for Mondrian it was a neutral form.) Mondrian was the most imaginative and gifted artist of the De Stijl group, and he found innumerable ways to vary his compositions without compromising his basic beliefs. For example, rather than introduce a diagonal into the field of his composition, he turned the painting forty-five degrees so that its four sides

Left: Figure 518. PIET MONDRIAN. *Composition with Blue.* 1926. Oil on canvas, 23½ × 23½". The Philadelphia Museum of Art (A. E. Gallatin Collection.)

made a diamond shape within which his lines remained vertical and horizontal in relation to the viewer. In his *Composition with Blue* (Fig. 518), with but two straight lines he created four shapes (three white and one blue) having at least one right angle but varying in scale and length of sides. Mondrian demonstrated how much could be achieved with so little, and his considerable influence on American painting since 1945 has been predicated upon the belief that "less is more." His art has an elegance determined by the high ratio of output, to input, or minimum means achieving maximum contrast.

Mondrian had also been an important pioneer in what is referred to as "relational painting." His last completed work, *Broadway Boogie Woogie* (Fig. 519), depends upon our seeing and sensing the rightness of its relationships of color and the proportions of these colored areas to each other. Despite its impersonal appearance, the making of paintings such as this involved not mathematical calculations but endless hours of trial in which Mondrian judged each effect visually and intellectually. Although his art has the look and "feel" of geometry, its origin is based upon a balance of thought and intuition, and execution by hand, not by machine.

Broadway Boogie Woogie gave form to Mondrian's love of American music and the rhythms of New York, where he spent the last years of his life. The entire composition is made up of elementary units, variations upon a rectangle, orchestrated to achieve a maximum of richness and variety. Set against a white ground, the

Figure 519. PIET MONDRIAN. *Broadway Boogie Woogie.* 1942–43. Oil on canvas, 4'2" × 4'2". The Museum of Modern Art, New York.

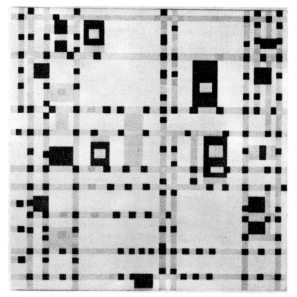

Left: Figure 520. J E A N (H A N S) A R P. *Squares Arranged According to the Laws of Chance.* 1916–17. Collage of colored papers, 19⅛ × 13⅝″. The Museum of Modern Art, New York.

Right: Figure 521. J E A N (H A N S) A R P. *Duo Collage.* 1918. Collage of colored papers on cardboard, 33⅛ × 26″. Collection Mr. and Mrs. Burton Tremaine, Meriden, Connecticut.

colors are pure tones of red, yellow, grey, and black. There is precision but also unpredictability in Mondrian's structural analogue of jazz, with its discipline and improvisation. His intentions were set forth in writing: "The art of the past established rhythm...veiled by subject matter and particular forms....In our time, rhythm is more and more accentuated, not only in art, but in mechanized reality and in the whole life." The feel and visual concept of music were important to Mondrian, not the imaging of musicians, instruments, and dancers. Privately he admired the city's youth and the sensual manifestations of the city's vitality. His writings show that he conceived of the city as the basis for a new style of art:

> The genuinely modern artist sees the metropolis as abstract living converted into form: it is nearer to him than nature....In the metropolis the natural has already been stiffened up, ordered by the human spirit. The proportion and the rhythm of patch and line in architecture will speak a more direct language to him than the capriciousness of nature. In the metropolis beauty expresses itself more mathematically.

During World War I a number of artists and writers fled to Switzerland to escape the fighting. The Alsatian artist Hans Arp was sought by both the French and German armies for conscription. Feigning mental incompetence, he escaped recruitment in causes for which he had no sympathy and went to Zurich where he found a sympathetic atmosphere for the creation of a new art. A group of avant-garde artists, poets, and writers, the Dadaists, as they named them-

selves, were against rationalism, nationalism, and militarism, which they felt were destroying Europe in a senseless holocaust. The prewar art of Germany, France, and Italy was identified with the corruption of civilization and the alienation of the artist not only from society but also from the true creative sources of art. Arp and others wanted to free thought and feeling from previous conventions such as illusionism and to restore vitality to art by affirming the artistic importance and validity of working from instinct and the irrational. While the Dadaists were against all previous art, Arp was convinced of the continued need for art—but a human art. His vision of art was not one in which humanity was the subject but one that would appeal to the spirit and imagination, uniting men on a subconscious level. Isolated from Holland and Russia, Arp and the Dadaists did not know the extent to which their aims were in accord.

During and after the war years Arp gradually gave up painting in oil and worked in wood, paper, and string. *Squares Arranged According to the Laws of Chance* (Fig. 520) and *Duo Collage* (Fig. 521) were reactions against the traditional notions of oil as the most noble medium for painting, beauty based upon sentiment or repetition of formula, and the virtuosity of the hand or "the brush stroke of genius." In the first "architectural formation," as he called these paste ups, rough squares were made by tearing dark-colored paper and pasting them on a grey sheet of paper. The random composition was achieved by letting the paper squares fall upon a flat surface. In the second paste up, Arp collaborated with his wife, Sophie Taeuber-Arp, to develop a uniform grid structure composed of paper squares cut probably on a paper cutter. The act of ordering by chance or calculation was a gesture against what Arp called the "earthly confusion, disorder, futility and stupidity" that he saw and sensed in the world around him. The impersonality with which the parts were made and arranged and the fact of collaboration were Arp's answer to prewar ndividualistic art, which he felt was morally wrong and was responsible for separating the artist from his audience. He preferred the square and grid forms in these compositions because of their unnatural appearance and because of his desire to avoid producing an art that imitates nature. Arp commented, "Our works are constructions of lines, surfaces, forms, colors. They attempt to approach reality. They hate artifice, vanity, imitation, tightrope walking.... Art should lead to spirituality, to a mystical reality." Thus the square and squared compositional armature appealed to many artists in the early days of abstraction as one of the first and most fruitful alternatives to representational art while conveying mystical, emotional, or philosophical associations.

With drawing, color, and composition no longer in the service of description, artists such as Kandinsky and the Swiss-born Paul Klee devoted themselves in art as well as in writing and teaching to exploring what could be done with these elements on a flat surface. Abstractionists believe that there are certain distinct but numberless inherent properties of color and line that can be activated depending upon their context in the work of art, properties that give them as inexhaustible a variety of form as naturalism. Arp's two collages demonstrate basically different types of compositions, one static and the other dynamic, adjectives that describe the relative action or inaction of the components. What lent a sense of excitement and discovery to early abstraction, as well as to writing on the subject, was the feeling that a whole new world of art had been opened up.

Unlike Klee's small paintings which deal with the minute and his inductive construction built upon individual elements (Figs. 365, 501), Matisse's art often embraces a large scale, even when it alludes to a subject that is minute. In *The Snail* (Pl. 62), one of his most abstract paintings, done a year before his death, Matisse assembled, cut, and pasted paper on a scale nine feet by nine feet. By means of diversely shaped rectangles, allusion to the snail is restricted to their roughly spiral placement. Paradoxically, none of the curving structure of the snail's shell is literally referred to. Not satisfied with commercial colored papers, Matisse mixed his own colors, painted sheets of paper, and then cut out his shapes with scissors. The colors are bright shades of red, blue, orange, green, and lavender, with the white of the paper showing through in large areas. His early development of self-luminosity of color, or color light, continues. He varied the transparency or density of his colors, but neutralized their surfaces with respect to texture and brush mark to facilitate the viewer's absorption of the whole. The fresh, cheerful combination of colors comes from a lifetime of taste and disciplined control of drawing and composing, as well as a conviction that colors should be decorative and "have also the inherent power of affecting the feelings of those who look at them.... A blue, for instance, accompanied by the shimmer of its complementaries, acts upon the inner sensibility like the sudden stroke of a gong. The same with red and yellow; the artist must be able to strike them when he needs to." Working in cut-out papers originated from Matisse's desire to get a quick idea of certain effects in planning large compositions. Illness, which limited his use of his hands, also led him to this medium. That this way of working still preserved his cherished values of draftsmanship and of realizing a work entirely in terms of color is supported by his statement: "Cutting colored papers permits me to draw in the color. For me it is a matter of simplification. Instead of establishing a contour, and then filling it with color—the one modifying the other—I draw directly in color.... This guarantees a precise union of the two processes; they become one."

All that Matisse and European art stood for were alien to the American painter Franz Kline. Matisse never countenanced consistent abstraction, claiming that he always began with an object and moved toward the abstract. He wanted his color, shapes, and compositions to be referred to the world of objects and people. Kline's big black-and-white paintings of the early 1950s allude to nothing, and they have a rawness and tough strength remote from the grace, finesse, and ingratiating character of

Figure 522. FRANZ KLINE. *Painting Number 7.* 1952. Oil on canvas, 4′9½″ × 6′9¾″. The Solomon R. Guggenheim Museum, New York.

Matisse's work. The traces of Kline's creative gestures are explicit and emphatic. With a housepainter's brush he enlarged small sketches onto big surfaces, preserving or enhancing the tensions and competition of his blacks and whites, a renunciation of colors rare in European painting. Confident of his capacity to constantly create new configurations, Kline refused to draw upon a repertory of shapes. The square seen in *Painting Number 7* (Fig. 522) is unusual in his work. But his square has qualities we have not seen before. It is formed as if by pressures from within and without, and the white and black seem to eat into one another around the edges. The white is as important as the black, for Kline believed that the two should be seen and felt simultaneously. Absent in Kline's painterly gestures are the clean joining of the corners and the trued or faired edges of Mondrian's and Malevich's squares, as well as the sharp scissor cut of Matisse's cutouts. Kline's visual drama lies in blatant contrasts and the taut suspension of shapes against the edges of the painting.

For many years Kline was a representational painter committed to painting the specific characteristics of a given place. When he turned to abstraction in 1950 it was to free his art from description in favor of expressing strong feelings that resulted from a variety of visual experiences. Abstract painting became for Kline a more direct expression of what he felt was emotionally true. Kline's was arm painting, not the wrist painting of European art. To achieve the big black swaths across his canvas meant working with sweeping motions that involved the entire body. Analogies with oriental calligraphy are deceptive, for Kline's pictorial writing is his own, not imitated, and not intended to be deciphered.

Long before the twentieth century, painters such as Poussin and Delacroix wrote and dreamed of an art whose sole purpose would be to delight the eye. Their painting, however, was always connected with literature and with ideas. It was not until this century, with art such as that of Matisse, that their vision of art was realized. Mondrian's relational painting was directed toward sensitive viewers whose esthetic reaction to his work would bring them inner peace. The German-born artist Josef Albers, who taught at the Bauhaus with Klee and Kandinsky and who for many years has been an influential teacher at Yale University, fell in love with color and has devoted his life to its study. He has not established a system or rules in his teaching, but rather has encouraged serious students of art to study color, to learn its many properties and inexhaustible combinations. For more than fifteen years, in his series of over one hundred paintings called *Homage to the Square* (Fig. 523), Albers has in a sense painted the same picture. He has found an ideal reproducible format by which to show endless color relationships. The paintings are approximately the same size, and the basic format is a series of concentric squares (which include the paintings's four edges) with the smallest and innermost square being generally located toward the bottom of the canvas. These squares have a common central axis, but they vary in proportion and size. The greatest

The Death of the Window and Life of the Square: Abstraction   431 variation in Albers' series is séen in his use of color. For him any combination of colors is possible. His preferred format allows him to make "colors do something they don't do by themselves" and to study the various properties of colors displayed when they interact and depend upon each other. Painting such as this allows us to see color in ways other than it appears in advertisements, for example, where the color is subordinate to the commercial message. Albers has written: "In visual perception a color is almost never seen as it really is—as it physically is. This fact makes color the most relative medium in art." The rich variety in his *Homage to the Square* series further depends upon where the colors are located in relation to each other, their amount or measure, their number, their quality—that is, their intensity of light or brightness of hue—and the means by which they are separated. "Colors present themselves in a continuous flux, constantly related to changing neighbors and changing conditions." The same size square in two different paintings will, depending upon its color, appear different in size, weight, distance from the viewer, and in degree of transparency and stability. Like the Impressionists and Seurat, Albers is aware that certain colors produce after images, or complementaries of their own color, so that to stare at violet and then to look upon white will suggest yellow to the viewer. In composing his color chords Albers takes this property along with many others into account. He seeks to show that there is no such thing as an "ugly" color, and that our normal prejudices against certain hues can be dissolved within the context of his use of colors. Albers finds the composition of color exciting and filled with potential new discoveries. Experimenting with color is for him a constant renewal of visual experience, and since the eye is part of the mind, Albers believes in the high significance of what he is doing.

In order to focus attention on the physical character of color, Albers has eliminated the distraction of facture and his paintings show no paint texture. This effect is achieved by applying the medium with a palette knife. Instead of drawing lines around the squares, he arrives at their edges from the inside. This way of pronouncing an area is crucial to the type of effect that two color areas have on each other. By situating the central square below the center,

Albers varies the intervals of different colors at the top and bottom, a technique that results in different vibrating relationships.

Since the late 1940s one of the most significant developments in painting in the United States has been emphasis on the effects of color, surface, and scale. This focus has led to large-scale paintings in which one, two, or three colors spread out and occupy most if not all of the surface. While brush stroke is unobtrusive, it can be employed to create subtle directions. Usually no attempt is made to call attention to textures or the physical substance of the medium, and there is no insistence upon arranging a number of different shapes. Color in the work of Barnett Newman and Mark Rothko occupies areas that roughly accord with the rectangular shape of the canvas. Scale is crucial to the painting's effect and is in large part a coefficient of the color chosen. In the past the scale of a painting might have been determined by a wall, subject, or conventions of public exhibitions and commerce. Newman, Rothko, and others, however, judge scale in relation to themselves—standing in front of the painting as it evolves. Newman's paintings often have a vertical or horizontal interval, a pause or tension, depending upon the individual painting, between rectangular areas of a single color (Fig. 524). Geometry is not even thought of as governing the shape of the color area. Newman has written: "It is precisely this death image, the grip of geometry, that has to be confronted. . . . Unless we face up to it and discover a new image based on new principles, there is no hope of freedom. . ." [1958]. In his final painting, Newman worked out its size, measure between intervals, and the location of these

Figure 523. JOSEF ALBERS. *Homage to the Square: Silent Hall.* 1961. Oil on composition board, 40×40". The Museum of Modern Art, New York (Dr. and Mrs. Frank Stanton Fund).

intervals as he painted over the surface, responding to the energy of the color with which he worked and to his personal associations with it. While it is tempting to think of his large paintings as decorative, they are not intended as background music nor to be seen out of the corner of one's eye. Their scale, intensity, and phrasing can compel attention in those who will let the painting work on them. For Newman, color by itself as well as completed paintings convey strong feelings that have to do with earthly and sublime experiences. "The rich tones of orange to the lowest octave of dark brown," he has written, can express "the majestic strength of our ties with the earth." Many of his titles are Biblical, for example, *Adam*, *Genesis*, and *The Beginning*, or, like *Ulysses* and *Prometheus*, allude to the epic and the heroic. These titles stem from the artist's personal associations with his paintings and are not illustrative in the sense of older figural art. Few artists have been as terse as Newman in explaining why they paint: "An artist paints so that he will have something to look at." More specifically, Newman looks upon the rectangle of his painting as "a living thing, a vehicle for an abstract thought-complex, a carrier of awesome feelings."

Mark Rothko's painting can be characterized as silent and almost immobile, and it might be described as art based on color sensation. Color and scale are the two basic ingredients of such canvases as *Tan and Black on Red* (Pl. 63). The large size of Rothko's surfaces is necessary to the power of his color sensations. Used in a smaller area, tan, black, and red do not evoke the same emotional responses as they do on the large scale that Rothko employed. The great size allows the beholder to become absorbed in the painting. Rothko, like Newman, is not as dispassionate or liberal in selecting his colors as is Albers. He takes over a color and makes it his own, after the color has proved right for his feeling. His paintings as a group seem less like color demonstrations or exercises than those of Albers, and they attain greater gravity. There are no allusive elements in the painting, only soft, vaporous-edged, rectangular patches hovering against and in front of one another. Color is unconstrained by drawn or hard boundaries; it breathes and finds its own shape. Often the colors are so close in value as to make their reproduction in black and white meaningless. Rothko soaked or stained the canvas in addition to brushing on the color,

Figure 524. BARNETT NEWMAN. *Adam.* 1951–52. Oil on canvas, 7′11⅝″×6′7⅝″. Collection Mr. and Mrs. Ben Heller, New York.

so that the final effect is not opaque color lying *upon* a surface, but rather the indefinite suspension of absorbent color. For Rothko, color is form and content, the sole carrier of his idea, which varies from painting to painting and which, to oversimplify, may be described as a mood, perhaps, of tragedy, exhilaration, or withdrawal. In the painter's words, he wanted "the elimination of all obstacles between the painter and the ideas, and between the idea and the observer." Objects, forms, marks of the artist's hand would be "obstacles." The variety and drama in Rothko's art comes from the way large color areas interact, so that, for example, redness and blackness induce anguish without being translated into a specific situation.

With much of modern painting, we may be assured of the artist's sincerity. The burden of sincerity often rests with the beholder and the way he chooses to receive the painting. There is an ethic to viewing a painting as well as to making it, and the observer must adapt himself to the new experiences this art affords. Just as for the artist, there must be decisions, openness, and risks taken by the viewer. Rothko expressed his feelings about the life of a painting: "A picture lives by companionship, expanding and quickening in the eyes of the sensitive observer. It dies by the same token." In this connection the paintings illustrated in this chapter require that

Figure 525. AD REINHARDT. *Abstract Painting.*
1960–61. Oil on canvas, 5′×5′. The Museum of
Modern Art, New York.

the viewer achieve a communion with what is
directly given to the eye.

When painters such as Newman, Rothko, and
Ad Reinhardt talk or write about their work,
much of what they say concerns what their painting is not. This is to offset misinterpretation, but
it also reflects how much of the history of art
they have rejected in their work and how
strongly and uncompromisingly they paint for
themselves. Reinhardt epitomizes the exclusivist
or purist view and has approached invisible
painting: "The one thing to say about art is that
it is one thing. Art is art-as-art and everything
else is everything else." He has given the best
description of what he has done and not done:

> A clearly defined object, independent and
> separate from all other objects and circum-
> stances, in which we cannot see whatever we
> choose or make of it anything we want, whose
> meaning is not detachable or translatable,
> where nothing can be added and nothing can
> be taken away. A free, unmanipulated and
> unmanipulatable, useless, unmarketable, irre-
> ducible, unphotographable, unreproducible,
> inexplicable icon. A non-entertainment, not
> for art-commerce or mass-art-publics, non-
> expressionnist, not for oneself [1955].

The difficulties of reproducing Reinhardt's
Abstract Painting (Fig. 525) are apparent and
derive from the fact that it is all black. (The
artist discourages its reproduction.) When we
read his statement of 1961 we are reminded of
Zola's comment about Manet—looking at
Reinhardt's painting with sympathy demands

forgetting a thousand things about art. (All of
the artists in this last section want you to look
at, not into, their painting.)

> A square (neutral, shapeless) canvas, five feet
> wide, five feet high, as high as a man, as wide
> as a man's outstretched arms (not large, not
> small, sizeless) trisected (no composition), one
> horizontal form negating one vertical form
> (formless, no top, no bottom, directionless),
> three (more or less) dark (lightless) non-
> contrasting (colorless) colors, brushwork
> brushed out to remove brushwork, a man,
> flat,‛ free hand painted surface (glossless,
> textureless, non-linear, no hard edge, no soft
> edge) which does not reflect its surroundings—
> a pure, abstract, non-objective timeless, space-
> less, changeless, relationless, disinterested
> painting—an object that is self-conscious (no
> consciousness) ideal, transcendant, aware of
> no thing but Art (absolutely no anti-art).

Unlike Malevich, Reinhardt has not given up
painting, but after his own logic he continues to
paint essentially the same black painting.

A younger generation of painters includes
those who have accepted many of the artistic
premises of the four artists just discussed, but
who have extended earlier ideas and developed
their own view of painting. Frank Stella, a
graduate of Princeton University, is representative of an increasing number of American
painters who received their training in liberal
arts colleges rather than in art schools. Stella
has challenged one of the basic constants in the
history of art, the rectangular format for a
painting. In his *Ileana Sonnabend* (Fig. 526),
named after a noted Paris art dealer who
supports certain young American artists, Stella
has painted what looks like a rhomboidal
picture frame enclosing empty space. For
several years Stella has been painting colored
stripes about two and a half inches wide
separated by a slightly irregular interval of
exposed canvas. These stripes consistently
follow the axes of the canvas and produce
concentric squares or concentric right angles
radiating in four directions from the center.
Stella's variables have been his choice of
colors—among them black and metallic paints
—and his selection for the shape of the canvas
itself. Mondrian had made the first and, for
him, only move in this direction by turning the
square canvas on edge. Stella has worked with
a number of different shapes, including X and U

shapes. Where illusionistic painting simulated the enclosure of space, Stella's *Ileana Sonnabend* literally frames space. Imperceptible in reproduction is the reflecting action of the metal paint and the delicately inconstant interval between the stripes. Stella continues the inquiry of earlier twentieth-century artists concerning the minimum conditions necessary for making a successful painting. For some, this pursuit has only the historical value of demonstration, or suggests the painter painting himself into a corner. But there is no evidence that the end of the way has been found. For younger painters like Stella, this type of reductivism still has many unexplored possibilities.

The last three artists represent a type of recent international painting that has been named Op Art by the critics and public, and Perceptual Abstraction by William Seitz, who has written most knowledgeably on the subject and who organized *The Responsive Eye* exhibition at the Museum of Modern Art in 1965. The basic premise of Perceptual Abstraction is that it does not induce associations with the visual world or symbolize ideas independent of the painting itself. The artists' concern is with the way the eye and mind respond to certain visual phenomena achievable in art. The paintings are generally characterized by a tight uniform network, often symmetrical, of small and/or repeated units. There are usually no climactic shapes, single focus, or significant variations in the scale of shapes that permit us to isolate them with ease, as in Matisse's art. This is not painting that soothes; rather, it attacks the eye and the mind. Its effects depend upon induced or after images and our tendency to fuse what is separate. Instead of being depicted by the artist, movement occurs in the eye and mind of the viewer.

Seitz summarized the historical position of Perceptual Abstraction in his catalogue for *The Responsive Eye* exhibition:

Before the advent of abstract art a picture was a window through which an illusion of the real world could be viewed, and a statue was a replica. Non-objective painting and sculpture defined a work of art as an independent object as real as a chair or a table. Perceptual abstraction—its existence as an object de-emphasized or nullified by uniform surface treatment, reflective or transparent materials, and a battery of optical devices—exists primarily for its impact on perception rather than for conceptual examination. Ideological focus has moved from the outside world, passed through the work as an object, and entered the incompleted explored region area between the cornea and the brain.

The Impressionists and Seurat mingled experiences of seeing the visible world with the optical effects of strong unmixed colors in close juxtaposition. These artists gave a vibrancy or shimmer to their paintings that was intended to reproduce a quality of the visible world. Delaunay was one of the first to build a painting entirely upon color interaction in the eye and mind of the viewer, relying upon taste as much as science in selecting his colors. But by comparison with the work of these last three artists, Delaunay's paintings are soothing because of the large areas of soft, luminous color and their selection to please. Mondrian invites the viewer to consider the rightness of the proportions and subtle placement of his segmented black grid, and his abundant use of white provides visual relief from the vibrating passages in *Broadway Boogie Woogie*. The Perceptual Abstractionists are not interested in balm for the eye or a symbolic form for universal order but intend the new experience of seeing unrelieved intensities and dissonances of colors and shapes. They believe that our eye can adjust to this type of viewing, just as we adjust our vision in examining the minute intricacies of medieval manuscript initial illumination or

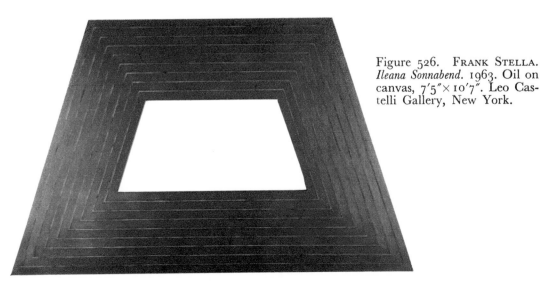

Figure 526. FRANK STELLA. *Ileana Sonnabend.* 1963. Oil on canvas, 7'5" × 10'7". Leo Castelli Gallery, New York.

in looking at a small van Eyck that is densely filled with almost microscopic detail. After the initial irritation—a reaction similar, perhaps, to one's first smoke or plane ride—the artist feels that the viewer will enter into a new type of experience that can be emotionally strong.

Much of Perceptual Abstraction has evolved from studies in optics, psychology, and design, thereby reuniting art and science. It should be remembered that Renaissance perspective and body imagery came from discoveries of Florentine mathematicians and from anatomical study and that for centuries artists have taken ideas from a wide variety of sources both inside and outside the world of art. (Illustrative art is a good example.) The importance of perceptual abstraction in the future will in part be determined by what it leads to or influences as well as what it has already achieved.

As with De Stijl, much of the interest that Perceptual Abstraction has generated among young European artists is due to the possibilities for anonymity and objective calculation provided by this kind of art. Single works have been produced by teams in Italy, Spain, France, and Germany and exhibited under the authorship of Group 57, from Spain, or Group N, from Italy. This practice results from a desire on the part of the artists for anonymity of identity and nationality and is reminiscent of collaborative efforts undertaken in medieval art. The ideals of De Stijl and other early-twentieth-century abstract groups thus continue. But many Op artists want individuality. An impeccable technique, as well as calculation, are essential for this type of art to insure purity of response in the viewer. Thus, the idea that since the Renaissance art has been moving

toward complete individuality is contradicted throughout the world. Also challenged is the view that art should please the eye, shown by the fact that many artists are interested in discovering the total range of visual responses.

The square has been a frequently used motif by Perceptual Abstractionists because it lends itself to repetition and coordination with the axes of the painting surface.

In *Straight Curve* (Fig. 527), the young British artist Bridget Riley worked from a single unit that she found susceptible to serial repetition. (It is of interest to note that this artist employs technicians to finish her works.) The unit used is a rectangle subdivided into two equal black-and-white triangles. The artist kept constant the subdivision as well as the four straight sides of the rectangle, but she varied the proportion of the height and width of the rectangles. In each vertical or horizontal stratum uniformity of these units is avoided. What creates the illusion of curving lines, where there is not a single curved line in the entire composition, is the changing of proportions from one layer to the next. Unlike Mondrian's *Broadway Boogie Woogie*, so densely grouped are the rectangles in *Straight Curve* that it is difficult to isolate them, and we are forced to look upon them in larger areas, which causes the shapes to seem blurred. Riley has varied different zones to give the composition

Left: Figure 527. BRIDGET RILEY. *Straight Curve.* 1963. Emulsion on board, 28×24½". Collection Victor Musgrove.

Right: Figure 528. BENJAMIN CUNNINGHAM. *Equivocation.* 1964. Synthetic polymer paint on composition board, 26×26". The Museum of Modern Art, New York (Larry Aldrich Fund).

a pulse or change of pace. This variation also helps to create the impression of lines curving back and forth in depth. To look at *Straight Curve* for a long time or to look at it at different times is to induce different responses in terms of the direction and character of movement. Our eyes are forced to move over the painting's surface because it is impossible to take in the whole all at once. To preserve the purity of the illusions created in the eye rather than by the painter on her surface, as in traditional illusionistic art, texture and evidence of drawing have been eliminated. Another characteristic of *Straight Curve* is the lack of distinction between the square and the background. The basic motif occupies the entire area of the surface.

In Benjamin Cunningham's *Equivocation* (Fig. 528) an over-all checkerboard pattern is so manipulated as to suggest an abstract configuration existing as a relief in a concave depression whose outer edges curve back into simulated depth. In the fifteenth century Paolo Uccello made perspective studies that divided objects into grids (Fig. 529). This technique is evident also in the ring about the neck of one of the struggling figures of his fresco *The Flood* (Fig. 157). While Uccello, Leonardo, and other Renaissance artists used a perspective grid as the basis for establishing the space of an entire painting, it became overlaid or concealed by figures and objects, thus existing partially revealed or as an implicit substructure. Delaunay had experimented with a checkerboard pattern applied over parts of his early *Fenêtre* series, thereby combining vestiges of illusionism (the areas seen in depth behind the pattern) with vibrating surface interaction. Cunningham, who is much older than Stella and Riley, figuratively takes the alternating light and dark pattern loved by Dutch artists for the floors of their paintings and makes an entire picture out of it. Alternating sizes of the squares, the angle of their setting, or muting the shades of white, he was able to evoke movement forward and backward, round and flat surfaces.

One reason that it is difficult to look at a Perceptual Abstraction painting for the first time is that colors having a maximum intensity are used repetitively. In his *Injured by Green* (Pl. 64) Richard Anuszkiewicz, a former student of Albers, restricted his colors to red, green, and blue, with the last two consistently applied in

Figure 529. PAOLO UCCELLO (1397–1475). *Perspective Drawing of a Chalice*. Pen and ink, 11⅜×9⅝″. Uffizi, Gabinetto dei Disegni e Stampe, Florence.

circles seen against a uniform red background. Anuszkiewicz is aware that the eye tends to blend separate colors when they are seen simultaneously. The result is a compromise color: thus the same red appears different when seen against green and blue circles. The eye also tends to alter focal lengths when it is exposed to red, blue, and green. Without using a single straight line, Anuszkiewicz achieved the illusion of three squares, with the innermost green one appearing to be set at a forty-five-degree angle to the others. He thus achieved the suggestion of a shape by its antithesis:

My work is of an experimental nature and has centered on an investigation into the effects of complementary colors of full intensity when juxtaposed and the optical changes that occur as a result. Also, a study of the dynamic effect of the whole under changing conditions of light, and the effect of light on the color [1963].

The light effects that Anuszkiewicz refers to are those of the room in which his paintings hang, not simulated light in the painting itself, a characteristic of illusionistic painting. As the light becomes brighter or darker on the painting the various interrelationships of the colors and of the suggested squares change.

Historically, Seurat is the pioneer whose lead Riley and Anuszkiewicz have followed. Seurat's systematic studies of color with respect to achieving the greatest intensity by placing complementary colors adjacent to each other as well as his reliance upon systematic study of optical phenomena make *Injured by Green* a descendant of *La Grande Jatte* (Pl. 38). *La Grande Jatte* in turn depends upon the work of Impressionists such as Monet, who brought a new brilliance to painting, the equivalent of sunlight and flicker, by the use of small areas of pure colors. And Monet and the Impressionists had been influenced by Delacroix, among others, who was convinced of the emotive power of strong pure color. Delacroix in turn learned much from Rubens. We could keep tracing influences in this way back through the Renaissance, the Middle Ages, and into antiquity, with side excursions into Near Eastern and Far Eastern art. This is art history, and while Anuszkiewicz' *Injured by Green* may not look like any painting before it, it presupposes the history of art. Art is more than selection, it is also rejection, and all abstract painters made decisions, historical as well as personal, when they decided not to paint in a certain way.

After 1900, when certain artists gave up illusionism and representation, it would seem that they had left to them only the rectangular, white, flat surface of the canvas. All that remained of the window was its shape. The only object was the sheet of paper or canvas itself stretched on a wooden frame. Not nature or previous art but the inventiveness of the artist was to fill the new surface. In Chapter 15, "Themes from Nature," it was pointed out that artists like Mondrian, Kandinsky, and Pollock did not come unarmed to this task, but worked logically out of their early illusionistic and representational style. Habits of composition, derived from naturalistic painting, for example, could still manifest themselves in abstraction. In the work of almost all of the artists in this last section there is a gradual development that prepares the dramatic situations or beginnings described above. The denial of illusionism did not come easily to any of the pioneer abstractionists, and many felt impelled to write thousands of words explaining the motives behind their decision. It was not photography, the exhaustion of the naturalistic tradition, or desire for novelty that caused these artists to evolve a new art. Positive attitudes toward what was reality, or the true nature of nature, and the purpose and character of art itself in this century gave the first generation of abstract artists the incentive, courage, and momentum to make this historic break. Artists encouraged as well as severely criticized each other. To the nonartist, the world of art is identified with museums, auctions, galleries, loft studios on 10th Street in New York, *New Yorker* cartoons, cocktail parties, critics, dealers, and crowded opening nights. To the serious artist, it is artists and every work of art that has ever been made, the sense of the historical continuity of formal ideas which he accepts or rejects, and moments of exhilaration and anguish when in his studio he has the chance to continue the history of art. Abstract art has a context with which we must familiarize ourselves if we are to view it with understanding, whether or not it pleases us. Abstract art, like religion, presupposes faith, and one either acquires it or one does not. To the layman, abstraction is always somehow less than what he wants. To see a painting with only a colored square in it makes many people feel that they have been cheated. Execution is favored over conception, possibly a symptom of the old gospel of labor. There is no tangible evidence of labor, no moral or symbol that can be seen or talked about, nothing with which the layman can identify or escape into as he can with television or illusionistic painting. He feels that the painter has given him too little or nothing. While this is possible, in some cases it is also highly probable that the layman has given nothing to the painting and the artist in terms of sensitivity, exposure to art, and an open mind. Painting, like music, poetry, or baseball, comes to life for a knowledgeable, experienced, and sympathetic audience. Unlike Baroque painting, whose rich interpretations of figures at a table drew upon many experiences, abstraction provides its audience with experiences that are artistic in origin. That abstraction does not touch much that is important in our lives is readily acknowledged by the artists themselves. But as these artists have ethically defined what art is for them (and it is the artist today who decides what is art), it is not possible or desirable for them to paint anything other than what they have painted, that which is most important in their lives. As a whole, the staggering variety of painting done in this century does touch many aspects of our lives and a wide variety of tastes. To urge that artists make concessions in their art for the sake of communication is to ask a dilution of their freedom and individuality. In art as well as in civilization's history, freedom has been achieved only after a long struggle, and it is a precious right to preserve for the health of all society.

CODA

THE ARTIST TODAY

Until quite recent times we have seen that the artist's role in his culture and his service to a patron (whether tribal chief, bishop, prince, or commune) was clearly established. His art was an instrument of political and religious rule and ritual, of myth making and moralizing, of philosophizing and pageantry. He was expected to gratify his patron and the community by his celebration of their heroes and values, to educate the unlettered, and delight the intellectual and connoisseur. At various times in history he has served as magician and scientist, propagandist and ambassador, decorator and entertainer. For the most part, the artist sought to present the world as others would have it.

Since the end of the last century, Western artists have had possibilities or options open to them that are unprecedented in range and character. Their education, for example, can be continued in art schools or, for the first time in history, in universities; or they may be self-taught. The young artist still looks, for the most part, to training in schools to learn his craft, to receive criticism, and to be stimulated by the company of other young artists. Formal education, often quite varied, he views as preparation for future self-sufficiency, not as a preliminary for service to institutions or the state.

In no previous era have there been as many artists as are found today. Paradoxically, however, only a small fraction of this number may be classified as professional artists who are able to support themselves entirely by their creative work. Most take on jobs in other, sometimes related fields such as teaching. While as a full-time profession art may appear to be dying or dead, its attraction continues to increase with each generation. In talking with artists, one receives many different responses to the question of the purpose of art, but there is agreement that its importance is greatest for the artist himself. The making of a painting, print, or sculpture still holds out the personal challenge of perfection and beauty—a quest that can involve the artist in wide-ranging researches and the satisfactions of invention or discovery.

The present-day possibilities of art include such disparate values as self-dramatization or, at the other extreme, a thoroughly objective detachment in order to study the properties of vision or the elements of art; it affords the opportunity to celebrate the common or the uncommon, to be reverent or irreverent, to give expression to the rational or the sensual. Art may prove to be a gesture against death or

439

an act of love. Art can mean resistance to social conformity or, instead, a more satisfying way of participating in society. Acknowledging none of the traditional symbols that in older art were used to unify the community, the modern artist often feels that he must discover or invent new signs for society, but their source must be in his own experience and values.

This plurality of motives and the art that has resulted from it over the last one hundred years have produced a reflection of ideals, tastes, and feelings that, quantitatively at least, is far greater than the encyclopedic art of the Gothic cathedrals, which are still thought by some to be the most perfect mirroring of a society. Although not the conscious purpose of painters and sculptors, art provides an important record of the encounter of the human spirit with modern life.

Both in theory and in practice, the contemporary artist has the precious right defined by Herbert Muller in his books on the history of freedom: the right to choose and pursue his purposes. Economics may force him to engage in creative activity part time, or the demands of dealers and negative opinions of critics may dissuade him from its true fulfillment, but ideally art offers the artist greater opportunities for personal freedom and possibilities for contributing to culture than are available in any other occupation.

The long history of art joins the anonymous hand at Altamira (Fig. 2) with that of Jackson Pollock (Fig. 530). For the latter to appear as it does in a painting has required that art evolve from service to the tribe, church, state, and society to a gratification of the self. Art's appearance had to move from collective public symbols, through phases of naturalism, and on to complete abstraction. Pollock had the entire history of art available to him, but personal principles demanded that he reject this legacy in order to extend art meaningfully on his own terms. How fitting it is that the last object of significant value a man can make by himself in this technological age should have been signed by Pollock with his own handprint.

Figure 530. JACKSON POLLOCK. *Number I* (detail). 1948. See Fig. 3. The Museum of Modern Art, New York.

BIBLIOGRAPHY

The following books and articles were consulted in the preparation of the text. This bibliography is by no means an attempt to list all the material available on these subjects.

SUGGESTED READINGS IN THE HISTORY OF ART

Gombrich, E. H., *The Story of Art*. New York: Phaidon, 1958. One of the most lucid and intelligent general introductions to the chronology of art history; written for English high school students, but excellent for the layman.

Gombrich, E., *Art and Illusion: A Study in the Psychology of Pictorial Representation*. New York: Pantheon, 1960. An important and interesting treatment of the subject, beautifully illustrated and intelligible to the educated layman.

Hauser, A., *The Social History of Art*, 4 vols. New York: Vintage, 1957–58. An important sociological approach to the history of art.

Janson, H. W., *The History of Art*. New York: Abrams, 1962. A beautifully illustrated and informed text covering the chronological history of art.

Lee, S., *A History of Far Eastern Art*. New York: Abrams, 1964. The best written and illustrated general history of the subject.

Millon, H. A., *Key Monuments of the History of Architecture*. New York: Abrams, 1964. A well selected photographic history of architecture.

Pevsner, N., *Academies of Art*. London: Cambridge, 1940.

Pevsner, N., *An Outline of European Architecture*, Jubilee ed. Baltimore: Penguin, 1960.

Wittkower, R. and M., *Born under Saturn*. New York: Random House, 1963. An excellent psychological study of artists from antiquity to the beginning of the nineteenth century.

THE ARTIST

Elsen, A. E., " Lively Art from a Dying Profession: The Role of the Modern Artist. " *Journal of Aesthetics and Art Criticism*, 18: 446–55, 1960.

Haskell, F., *Patrons and Painters: A Study in the Relations between Italian Art and Society in the Age of the Baroque*. New York: Knopf, 1963.

Hauser, A., *The Social History of Art*, 4 vols. New York: Vintage, 1957–58.

Pelles, G., *Art, Artists and Society: Origins of a Modern Dilemma*. Englewood Cliffs, N. J.: Prentice-Hall, 1963.

Pevsner, N., *Academies of Art*. London: Cambridge, 1940.

White, H. C. and A. C., *Canvases and Careers: Institutional Change in the French Painting World*. New York: Wiley, 1965.

Wittkower, R. and M., *Born under Saturn*. New York: Random House, 1963.

ART AS A MATTER OF LIFE AND DEATH

Adam, L., *Primitive Art*. Harmondsworth, Middlesex, Eng., 1949.

Disselhoff, H.-D., and Linné, S., *Art of Ancient America*. New York: Crown, 1961.

Elisofon, E., W. Fagg, and R. Linton, *The Sculpture of Africa*. London: Thames & Hudson, 1958.

Fagg, W., and M. Plass, *African Sculpture*. New York: Dutton, 1964.

Frankfort, H., *Art and Architecture of the Ancient Orient*. Baltimore: Penguin, 1954.

Fraser, D., *Primitive Art*. New York: Doubleday, 1962.

Groenewegen-Frankfort, H. A., *Arrest and Movement*. New York: Humanities, 1951.

Guiart, J., *The Arts of the South Pacific*. New York: Golden Press, 1963.

Hawkins, G., and J. B. White, *Stonehenge Decoded*. New York: Doubleday, 1965.

Herskovits, M. J., *The Backgrounds of African Art*. Denver Art Museum, 1946.

Laming, A., *Lascaux*. Baltimore: Penguin, 1959.

Leuzinger, E., *Africa: The Art of the Negro Peoples*. New York: McGraw-Hill, 1960.

Miki, F., *Haniwa: The Clay Sculpture of Photohistoric Japan*. Rutland, Vt.: Tuttle, 1960.

Noma, S., *Haniwa*. New York: Abrams, 1963.

Sickman, L., and A. Soper, *The Art and Architecture of China*. Baltimore: Penguin, 1956.

Sieber, R., " Masks as Agents of Social Control. " *African Studies Bulletin*, 5: 8–13, May, 1962.

Sullivan, M., *An Introduction to Chinese Art*. Berkeley: University of California Press, 1961.

Wingert, P., *Primitive Art*. New York: Oxford, 1962.

IMAGES OF GODS

Apollo

Guthrie, W. K. C., *The Greeks and Their Gods*. Boston: Beacon Press, 1955.

Hirmer, M., and R. Lullies, *Greek Sculpture* (tr. by M. Bullock). New York: Abrams, 1957.

Kitto, H. D. F., *The Greeks*. Baltimore: Penguin, 1951.
Malraux, A., *The Metamorphosis of the Gods* (tr. by S. Gilbert). New York: Doubleday, 1960.
Murray, G., *Five Stages of Greek Religion*. Boston: Beacon Press, 1952.
Richter, G. M. A., *The Sculpture and Sculptors of the Greeks*, rev. ed. New Haven, Conn.: Yale University Press, 1950.

Buddha

Bowie, T. (ed.), *The Arts of Thailand*. Bloomington: Indiana University Press, 1961.
Bowie, T. (ed.), *East-West in Art: Patterns of Cultural and Aesthetic Relationships*. Bloomington: Indiana University Press, 1966.
Coomaraswamy, A. K., *A History of Indian and Indonesian Art*. New York: Weyhe, 1927.
Coomaraswamy, A. K., *The Transformation of Nature in Art*. New York: Dover, 1957.
Kramrisch, S., *The Art of India through the Ages*. New York: Phaidon, 1954.
Lee, S., *A History of Far Eastern Art*. New York: Abrams, 1964.
Rowland, B., Jr., *The Art and Architecture of India*. Baltimore: Penguin, 1953.
Rowland, B., Jr., *Art in East and West*. Cambridge, Mass.: Harward University Press, 1955.
Rowland, B., Jr. (ed.), *The Evolution of the Buddha Image*. New York: Abrams, 1963.

Christ

Barr, A. J., Jr., *Matisse, His Art and His Public*. New York: Museum of Modern Art, 1952.
Grabar, A., *Byzantine Painting*. Geneva–New York: Skira, 1953.
Hauser, A., *The Social History of Art*, 4 vols. New York: Vintage, 1957–58.
Kayser, S. S., "Grunewald's Christianity." *Review of Religion*, 5: 3–35, November, 1940.
Mâle, E., *L'Art religieux du XIIᵉ siècle en France*. Paris: Colin, 1953.
Malraux, A., *The Metamorphosis of the Gods* (tr. by S. Gilbert). New York: Doubleday, 1960.
Muller, H. J., *Uses of the Past*. New York: Oxford, 1957.
Pevsner, N., and M. Meier (eds.), *Grunewald*. New York: Abrams, 1958.
Schapiro, M., "The Romanesque Sculpture of Moissac," Parts I and II. *Art Bulletin*, 13: 248–351, 464–531, September–December, 1931.
Thoby, P., *Le crucifix des origines au Concile de Trente*. Nantes: Bellanger, 1959.
Von Simson, O. G., *Sacred Fortress: Byzantine Art and Statecraft in Ravenna*. University of Chicago Press, 1948.

RELIGIOUS ARCHITECTURE

The Parthenon

Berve, H., and G. Gruben, *Greek Temples, Theaters and Shrines*. New York: Abrams, 1963.
Dinsmoor, W. B., *The Architecture of Ancient Greece*. London: Batsford, 1950.

Lawrence, A. W., *Greek Architecture*. Baltimore: Penguin, 1957.
Muller, H. J., *Uses of the Past*. New York: Oxford, 1957.
Scranton, R. L., *Greek Architecture*. New York: Braziller, 1962.
Scully, V. J., *The Earth, the Temple and the Gods: Greek Sacred Architecture*. New Haven, Conn.: Yale University Press, 1962.
Stevens, G. P., *Restorations of Classical Buildings*. Princeton, N.J.: American School of Classical Studies at Athens, 1958.
Yalouris, N., *Classical Greece: The Elgin Marbles*. New York Graphic Society, 1960.

The Gothic Cathedrals

Bowie, T. R. (ed.), *The Sketchbook of Villard de Honnecourt*. Bloomington: Indiana University Press, 1959.
Branner, R., *Gothic Architecture*. New York: Braziller, 1961.
Crosby, S. M., Review of Von Simson's *The Gothic Cathedral*. *Art Bulletin*, 42: 149–60, 1960.
Dow, H. J., "The Rose Window." *Journal of the Warburg and Courtauld Institutes*, 20: 248–97, July, 1957.
Frankl, P., *The Gothic*. Princeton, N.J.: Princeton University Press, 1960.
Frankl, P., *Gothic Architecture*. Baltimore: Penguin, 1963.
Gilbert, K., and H. Kuhn, *A History of Esthetics*, rev. ed. Bloomington: Indiana University Press, 1953.
Gimpel, J., *The Cathedral Builders*. New York: Grove, 1961.
Harvey, J., *The Gothic World*. London: Batsford, 1950.
Holt, E. G. (ed.), *A Documentary History of Art*, Vol. 1: *The Middle Ages and the Renaissance*. New York: Anchor, 1957.
Horn, W., and E. Born, *The Aisled Medieval Timbered Hall: A Study of Its Origins, Development and Survival*. Berkeley: University of California Press.
Hürliman, M., and J. Bony, *French Cathedrals*, rev. ed. New York: Viking, 1961.
Jantzen, H., *High Gothic*. New York: Pantheon, 1962.
Johnson, J. R., *The Radiance of Chartres*. New York: Random House, 1965.
Katzenellenbogen, A., *The Sculptural Programs of Chartres Cathedral: Christ-Mary-Ecclesia*. Baltimore: Johns Hopkins Press, 1959.
Knoop, D., and G. P. Jones, *The Medieval Mason*. Manchester, Eng.: Manchester University Press, 1933.
Krautheimer, R., "Introduction to an 'Iconography of Medieval Architecture.'" *Journal of the Warburg and Courtauld Institutes*, 5: 1–33, January, 1942.
Muller, H. J., *Uses of the Past*. New York: Oxford, 1957.
Panofsky, E. (ed.), *Abbot Suger on the Abbey Church of St-Denis and Its Art Treasures*. Princeton, N.J.: Princeton University Press, 1946.
Panofsky, E., *Gothic Architecture and Scholasticism*. New York: Meridian, 1957.
Smith, B., *Architectural Symbolism of Imperial Rome and the Middle Ages*. Princeton, N.J.: Princeton University Press, 1956.
Temko, A., *Notre Dame of Paris*. New York: Viking, 1959.
Von Simson, O., *The Gothic Cathedral*. New York: Pantheon, 1956.

Notre Dame du Haut, Ronchamp

Le Corbusier, *The Chapel at Ronchamp* (tr. by J. Cullen). New York: Praeger, 1958.

The Sacred Book

Beckwith, J., *Early Medieval Art.* New York: Praeger, 1964.

Early Medieval Illumination. Introduction by H. Swarzenski. New York: Oxford, 1951.

Goldschmidt, A., *German Illumination*, 2 vols. New York: Harcourt, 1928.

Hinks, R. P., *Carolingian Art.* London: Sidgwick & Jackson, 1935.

Metz, P., *The Golden Gospels of Echternach* (tr. by I. Schrier and P. Gorge). New York: Praeger, 1957.

Nordenfalk, C., and A. Grabar, *Early Medieval Painting* (tr. by S. Gilbert). Geneva–New York: Skira, 1957.

Nordenfalk, C., and A. Grabar, *Romanesque Painting* (tr. by S. Gilbert). Geneva–New York: Skira, 1958.

Porcher, J., *Medieval French Miniatures.* New York: Abrams, 1959.

The Synthesis of Heaven and Earth in Fifteenth-Century Art

Flemish Art

De Tolnay, C., *Hieronymous Bosch.* Bâle: Editions Holbein, 1937.

Elst, J. J. M. I. van der, *Last Flowering of the Middle Ages.* New York: Doubleday, 1944.

Flanders in the Fifteenth Century: Art and Civilization. Detroit Institute of Arts, 1960.

Freeman, M. B., " Iconography of the Mérode Altarpiece." *Bulletin of the Metropolitan Museum of Art,* ns 16: 130–39, December, 1957.

Friedländer, M. J., *From Van Eyck to Bruegel.* New York: Phaidon, 1956.

Held, J. S., Review of E. Panofsky's *Early Netherlandish Painting. Art Bulletin,* 37: 205–34, September, 1955.

Meiss, M., " Light as Form and Symbol in Some Fifteenth Century Paintings." *Art Bulletin,* 27: 175–81, September, 1945.

Oman, C. C., *Medieval Silver Nefs.* Victoria and Albert Museum, Monograph No. 15. London: H. M. Stationery Office, 1963.

Panofsky, E., *Early Netherlandish Painting*, 2 vols. Cambridge, Mass.: Harvard University Press, 1954.

Philip, L. B., " The Prado Epiphany by Jerome Bosch." *Art Bulletin,* 35: 267–93, December, 1953.

Rousseau, T., " Mérode Altarpiece." *Bulletin of the Metropolitan Museum of Art,* ns 16: 117–29, December, 1957.

Schapiro, M., " Muscipula Diaboli; The Symbolism of the Mérode Altarpiece by the Master of Flémalle." *Art Bulletin,* 27: 182–87, September, 1945.

Von Simson, O., " Compassion and Co-Redemption in Rogier van der Weyden's Descent from the Cross." *Art Bulletin,* Vol. 35, March, 1953.

Wittkower, R. and M., *Born under Saturn.* New York: Random House, 1963.

Italian Art

Bellew, P., and A. Schutz (eds.), *Masaccio: Frescoes in Florence.* Introduction by P. Hendy. New York Graphic Society, 1957.

Clark, K., *Piero della Francesca.* New York: Phaidon, 1951.

Clark, K., *Leonardo da Vinci.* New York: Macmillan, 1939.

De Wald, E. T., *Italian Painting: 1200–1600.* New York: Holt, Rinehart & Winston, 1961.

Freedberg, S., *Painting of the High Renaissance in Rome and Florence*, 2 vols. Cambridge, Mass.: Harvard University Press, 1961.

Gilbert, C., " On Subject and Non-Subject in Italian Renaissance Pictures." *Art Bulletin,* 34: 202–16, September, 1952. Reply with rejoinder: M. L. D'Ancona, 35: 329–30, December, 1953.

Horizon Magazine, editors of, *The Horizon Book of the Renaissance.* New York: American Heritage Publishing Company, 1961.

Janson, H. W., *The Sculpture of Donatello*, 2 vols. Princeton, N. J.: Princeton University Press, 1957.

Krautheimer, R., and T. H. Krautheimer, *Lorenzo Ghiberti.* Princeton, N. J.: Princeton University Press, 1956.

Meiss, M., *Giovanni Bellini's St. Francis in the Frick Collection.* Princeton, N. J.: Princeton University Press, 1964.

Muller, H. J., *Freedom in the Western World: From the Dark Ages to the Rise of Democracy.* New York: Harper & Row, 1963.

Offner, R., " Giotto, Non-Giotto." *Burlington Magazine,* 74: 258–69; 75: 96–109+, June, September, 1939.

Olschki, L., *The Genius of Italy.* Ithaca, N. Y.: Cornell University Press, 1954.

Panofsky, E., *Renaissance and Renascenses in Western Art.* Stockholm: Imqvist & Wiksell, 1960.

Pope-Hennessy, J., *The Complete Work of Paolo Uccello.* New York: Phaidon, 1950.

Tietze-Conrat, E., *Mantegna.* New York: Phaidon, 1955.

White, J., *The Birth and Rebirth of Pictorial Space.* New York: T. Yoseloff, 1958.

Michelangelo

Ackerman, J. S., *The Architecture of Michelangelo*, 2 vols. New York: Viking, 1961.

Blunt, A., *Artistic Theory in Italy, 1450–1600.* New York: Oxford, 1962.

Clark, K. M., *The Nude: A Study in Ideal Form.* New York: Pantheon, 1956.

Condivi, A., *The Life of Michelangelo* (tr. by H. P. Horne). Boston: Merrymount Press, 1904.

De Tolnay, C., *Michelangelo*, 5 vols. Princeton, N. J.: Princeton University Press, 1943–60.

De Tolnay, C., *The Art and Thought of Michelangelo.* New York: Pantheon, 1964.

Goldscheider, L. (ed.), *Michelangelo Drawings* (tr. by R. H. Boothroyd). New York: Phaidon, 1951.

Goldwater, R. J., and M. Treves (eds. and trs.), *Artists on Art.* New York: Pantheon, 1945.

Hartt, F., " The Meaning of Michelangelo's Medici Chapel." In O. Goetz (ed.), *Essays in Honor of Georg Swarzenski.* Chicago: Regnery, 1952.

Michelangelo, *Letters*, 2 vols. (ed. and tr. by E. H. Ramsden). Stanford, Calif.: Stanford University Press, 1963.

Michelangelo, *Paintings* (ed. by F. Hartt). New York: Abrams, 1965.

Olschki, L., *The Genius of Italy*. Ithaca, N. Y.: Cornell University Press, 1954.

Panofsky, E., *Studies in Iconology: Humanistic Themes in the Art of the Renaissance*. New York: Oxford, 1939.

Pope-Hennessy, J., *Introduction to Italian Sculpture*. Pt. 3: *Italian Higher Renaissance and Baroque Sculpture*, 3 pts. New York: Phaidon, 1963.

THE SYNTHESIS OF HEAVEN AND EARTH IN SIXTEENTH- AND SEVENTEENTH-CENTURY ART

Art as Religious Propaganda

Blunt, A., *Artistic Theory in Italy*, 1450–1600. New York: Oxford, 1962.

Bousquet, J., *Mannerism: The Painting and Style of the Late Renaissance* (tr. by S. W. Taylor). New York: Braziller, 1964.

Burckhardt, J., Recollections of Rubens (ed. by H. Gerson, tr. by M. Hottinger). New York: Phaidon, 1950.

De Tolnay, C., *Pieter Bruegel l'ancien*. Bruxelles: Nouvelle Société d'éditions, 1935.

Dvořák, M., "El Greco and Mannerism" (tr. by J. Coolidge). *Magazine of Art*, 46: 14–23, January, 1953.

Friedlaender, W. F., *Caravaggio Studies*. Princeton, N. J.: Princeton University Press, 1955.

Hinks, R. P., *Michelangelo Merisi da Caravaggio*. New York: Beechhurst, 1954.

Holt, E. G. (ed.), *Documentary History of Art*. Vol. 2: *Michelangelo and the Mannerists, the Baroque, and the Eighteenth Century*. New York: Anchor, 1958.

Le Siècle de Bruegel, catalogue of an exhibition. Musées Royaux des Beaux-Arts de Belgique, 1965.

Le Siècle de Rubens, catalogue of an exhibition. Musées Royaux des Beaux-Arts de Belgique, 1965.

Mâle, E., *L'Art religieux de la fin du XVIe siècle, du XVIIe siècle et du XVIIIe siècle*. Paris: Colin, 1951.

Meier-Graefe, J. A., *The Spanish Journey* (tr. by J. H. Reece). New York: Harcourt, 1927.

Wethey, H. E., *El Greco and His School*. Princeton, N. J.: Princeton University Press, 1962.

Wittkower, R., *Gian Lorenzo Bernini*. New York: Phaidon, 1955.

Wittkower, R., "El Greco's Language of Gestures." *Art News*, 56: 44–49+, March, 1957.

Wittkower, R., *Art and Architecture in Italy*, 1600–1750. Baltimore: Penguin, 1958.

Wölfflin, H., *Principles of Art History* (tr. by M. D. Hottinger). New York: Dover, 1950.

Figures at a Table in Baroque Secular Art

Blunt, A., *Art and Architecture in France*, 1500–1700. Baltimore: Penguin, 1954.

Bousquet, J., *Mannerism: The Painting and Style of the Late Renaissance* (tr. by S. W. Taylor). New York: Braziller, 1964.

De Tolnay, C., "Vermeer's 'The Artist's Studio.'" *Gazette des Beaux Arts*, s 6, 41: 265–72, 292–94, April, 1953.

Fêtes de la palette, catalogue of an exhibition. New Orleans: Isaac Delgado Museum, 1963.

Friedländer, M. J., *Landscape, Portrait, Still Life* (tr. by R. F. C. Hull). Oxford, Eng.: Cassirer, 1949.

Furness, S. M. M., *Georges de la Tour of Lorraine*, London: Routledge & Kegan Paul, 1949.

Gilbert, C., *Figures at a Table*, catalogue of an exhibition. Saratoga, Fla.: John and Mable Ringling Museum of Art, 1960.

Held, J. S., *Flemish Painting*. New York: Abrams, 1953.

Highet, G., "Bruegel's Rustic Wedding." *Magazine of Art*, 38: 274–76, November, 1945.

López-Rey, J., *Velázquez*. London: Faber, 1963.

Puyvelde, L. van, *Jordaens*. Paris, New York: Elsevier, 1953.

Swillens, P. T. A., *Johannes Vermeer* (tr. by C. M. Breuning-Williams). Utrecht, Netherlands: Spectrum, 1950.

Thuillier, J., and A. Châtelet, *French Painting, from Le Nain to Fragonard*. Geneva–New York: Skira, 1964.

IMAGES OF KINGS

Blunt, A., *Art and Architecture in France, 1500–1700*. Baltimore: Penguin, 1954.

Clark, K., *Piero della Francesca*. New York: Phaidon, 1951.

De Kooning, E., "Painting a Portrait of the President." *Art News*, Summer, 1964.

Frankfort, H., *Art and Architecture of the Ancient Orient*. Baltimore: Penguin, 1954.

Frankfort, H., *Kingship and the Gods: A Study of Ancient Near Eastern Religion as the Integration of Society and Nature*. University of Chicago Press, 1948.

Ghirshman, R., *Iran: Parthes et Sassanides*. Paris: Gallimard, 1962.

Grabar, A., *L'Empereur dans l'art byzantin*. Paris: Les Belles lettres, 1936.

Groenewegen-Frankfort, H. A., *Arrest and Movement*. New York: Humanities, 1951.

Hamberg, P. G., *Studies in Roman Imperial Art*. Copenhagen: Munksgaard, 1945.

Held, J., "*Le roi à la chasse*: Van Dyck's Portrait of Charles I." *Art Bulletin*, 40: 139–49, June, 1958.

Jenkins, M. D., *The State Portrait*. *Art Bulletin* Monograph, 1947.

Lehmann-Haupt, H., *Art under a Dictatorship*. New York: Oxford, 1954.

Lewis, W. H., *The Splendid Century; Life in the France of Louis XIV*. New York: Anchor, 1957.

Lipman, J. H., "The Florentine Profile Portrait in the Quattrocento." *Art Bulletin*, 18: 54–102, March, 1956.

Liudprandus of Cremona, *Works*. London: Routledge, 1930.

Strong, E., *Apotheosis and After Life*. London: Constable, 1915.

Titian, *Paintings and Drawings*. Introduction by H. Tietze. New York: Phaidon, 1937.

Wittkower, R., *Gian Lorenzo Bernini*. New York: Phaidon, 1955.

Yuzan, D. S., *The Beginner's Book of Bushido* (tr. by A. L. Sadler). Tokyo: Kokusai Bunka Shinkokai, 1941.

Architecture of Authority

Anderson, J., and R. P. Spiers, *The Architecture of Greece and Rome.* Vol. 2: *The Architecture of Ancient Rome* (revised and rewritten by T. Ashby). London: V. T. Batsford, 1927.

Blunt, A., *Art and Architecture in France, 1500–1700.* Baltimore: Penguin, 1954.

Brown, F. E., "Roman Architecture." *College Art Journal*, 17: 105–114, 1958.

Coffin, D. R., *The Villa d'Este at Tivoli.* Princeton, N. J.: Princeton University Press, 1960.

Drexler, A., *The Architecture of Japan.* New York: Museum of Modern Art, 1955.

Frankfort, H., *Art and Architecture of the Ancient Orient.* Baltimore: Penguin, 1954.

Gropius, W., K. Tange, and Y. Ishimoto, *Katsura: Tradition and Creation in Japanese Architecture.* New Haven, Conn.: Yale University Press, 1960.

Masson, G., *Italian Villas and Palaces.* London: Thames & Hudson, 1959.

Mylonas, G. E., *Ancient Mycenae, the Capital City of Agamemnon.* Princeton, N. J.: Princeton University Press, 1957.

Pevsner, N., *An Outline of European Architecture,* Jubilee ed. Baltimore: Penguin, 1960.

Smith, E. B., *Egyptian Architecture as Cultural Expression.* New York: Appleton-Century, 1938.

Wittkower, R., *Art and Architecture in Italy, 1600–1750.* Baltimore: Penguin, 1958.

Wölfflin, H., *Renaissance and Baroque* (tr. by K. Simon). New York: Collins, 1964.

Wright, F. L., *On Architecture; Selected Writings, 1894–1940* (ed. by F. Guttheim). New York: Grosset & Dunlop, 1959.

Wright, F. L., *Writings and Buildings* (sel. by E. Kaufmann and B. Raeburn). New York: Meridian, 1960.

Rembrandt

Benesch, O., *Rembrandt* (tr. by J. Emmons). Geneva–New York: Skira, 1957.

De Tolnay, C., "The Syndics of the Drapers' Guild by Rembrandt: An Interpretation." *Gazette des Beaux-Arts*, s 6, 23: 31–38, January, 1943.

Fromentin, E., *Masters of Past Time* (tr. by A. Boyle). New York: Dutton, 1913.

Heckscher, W. S., "Rembrandt's Anatomy of Dr. Nicolaas Tulp." New York University Press, 1958.

Held, J. S., "Rembrandt: The Self-Education of an Artist." *Art News*, 40: 10–19+, February 1, 1942.

Held, J. S., "Rembrandt's Polish Rider." *Art Bulletin*, 26: 246–65, December, 1944.

Held J. S. "Debunking Rembrandt's Legend." *Art News*, 48: 20–24, February, 1950.

Held, J. S., *Rembrandt and the Book of Tobit.* Northampton, Mass.: Gehenna Press, 1964.

Hind, A. M., *Rembrandt.* Cambridge, Mass.: Harvard University Press, 1932.

Münz, L., *Rembrandt.* New York: Abrams, 1954.

Rembrandt, H. van Rijn, *Selected Drawings,* by O. Benesch. New York: Phaidon, 1947.

Rembrandt, H. van Rijn, *Etchings* (ed. by L. Münz), 2 vols. New York: Phaidon, 1952.

Rosenberg, J., *Rembrandt.* New York: Phaidon, 1964.

Slive, S., *Rembrandt and His Critics, 1630–1730.* The Hague: Nijhoff, 1953.

White, C., *Rembrandt and His World.* London: Thames & Hudson, 1964.

The Synthesis of Past and Present in Nineteenth-Century Art

Adhémar, J., *Daumier.* London: Zwemmer, 1954.

Benesch, O., *Edvard Munch* (tr. by J. Spencer). New York: Phaidon, 1960.

Boggs, J. S., *Portraits by Degas.* Berkeley: University of California Press, 1962.

Cooper, D., *Toulouse-Lautrec.* New York: Abrams, 1956.

Deknatel, F. B., *Edvard Munch.* New York: Museum of Modern Art, 1950.

Friedlaender, W. F., *David to Delacroix* (tr. by R. Goldwater). Cambridge, Mass.: Harvard University Press, 1952.

Gauguin, P., *Gauguin* (ed. by R. Goldwater). New York: Abrams, 1957.

Hoffmann, W., *The Earthly Paradise.* New York: Braziller, 1961.

Johnson, L., *Delacroix.* New York: Norton, 1963.

Lövgren, S., *The Genesis of Modernism.* Stockholm: Almqvist & Wiksell, 1959.

Meier-Graefe, J., *Modern Art* (tr. by F. Simmonds and G. W. Chrystal), 2 vols. New York: Putnam, 1908.

Rewald, J., *Pierre Bonnard.* New York: Museum of Modern Art, 1948.

Rewald, J., *Post-Impressionism from Van Gogh to Gauguin.* New York: Museum of Modern Art, 1958.

Rewald, J., *The History of Impressionism,* rev. ed. New York: Museum of Modern Art, 1962.

Rewald, J., *Pissarro* (ed. by M. S. Fox). New York: Abrams, 1963.

Rich, D. C. (ed.), *Degas.* New York: Abrams, 1951.

Russell, J., *Seurat.* New York: Praeger, 1965.

Schapiro, M., *Vincent Van Gogh.* New York: Abrams, 1950.

Seitz, W., *Monet.* New York: Abrams, 1960.

Tannenbaum, L., *James Ensor.* New York: Museum of Modern Art, 1951.

Wildenstein, G., *Ingres.* New York: Phaidon, 1954.

Themes from Nature

Blunt, A., *Art and Architecture in France, 1500–1700.* Baltimore: Penguin, 1954.

Clark, K. M., *Leonardo da Vinci.* New York: Phaidon, 1955.

Collins, L. C., *Hercules Seghers.* University of Chicago Press, 1953.

Elsen, A., "Seymour Lipton: Odyssey of the Unquiet Metaphor." *Art International*, 5: 39–44, February, 1961.

Friedländer, M. J., *Landscape, Portrait, Still Life* (tr. by R. F. C. Hull). Oxford, Eng.: Cassirer, 1949.

Giedion-Welcker, C., *Jean Arp.* London: Thames & Hudson, 1958.

Grohmann, W., *Paul Klee*. New York: Abrams, 1954.

Haftmann, W., *The Mind and Work of Paul Klee*. London: Faber, 1954.

Lee, S., *A History of Far Eastern Art*. New York: Abrams, 1964.

Leonardo da Vinci, *Notebooks* (ed. by E. MacCurdy). New York: Braziller, 1955.

Panofsky, E., *The Life and Art of Albrecht Dürer*. Princeton, N. J.: Princeton University Press, 1955.

Rowley, G., *Principles of Chinese Painting*. Princeton, N. J.: Princeton University Press, 1947.

Rubin, W., *Matta*. New York: Museum of Modern Art, 1958.

Schapiro, M., *Vincent Van Gogh*. New York: Abrams, 1950.

Schapiro, M., *Paul Cézanne*. New York: Abrams, 1952.

Sickman, L., and A. Soper, *Art and Architecture of China*. Baltimore: Penguin, 1956.

Sirén, O., *Chinese Painting*. Pt. 1: Vol. 1. *Early Chinese Painting*; Vol. 2. *The Sung Period*. New York: Ronald, 1956.

Soper, A., "Early Chinese Landscape Painting." *Art Bulletin*, 23: 141-64, June, 1941.

Van Gogh, V., *Complete Letters* (tr. by J. van Gogh-Bouger and E. de Dood; re-ed. by Mrs. R. Amussen *et al.*), 3 vols. New York Graphic Society, 1958.

Painting and Objects

Barr, A. H., Jr., *Matisse: His Art and His Public*. New York: Museum of Modern Art, 1951.

Fêtes de la palette, catalogue of an exhibition. New Orleans: Isaac Delgado Museum, 1963.

Friedländer, M. J., *Landscape, Portrait, Still Life* (tr. by R. F. C. Hull). Oxford, Eng.: Cassirer, 1949.

Friedman, B. H. (ed.), *School of New York*. New York: Grove, 1959.

Level, R., *Marcel Duchamp* (tr. by G. H. Hamilton). New York: Grove, 1959.

Robbins, D., *Recent Still Life*. Providence: Museum of Art, Rhode Island School of Design, 1966.

Rowley, G., *Principles of Chinese Painting*. Princeton, N. J.: Princeton University Press, 1947.

Schapiro, M., *Vincent Van Gogh*. New York: Abrams, 1950.

Schapiro, M., *Paul Cézanne*. New York: Abrams, 1952.

Soby, J. T., *Giorgio de Chirico*. New York: Museum of Modern Art, 1955.

Solomon, A. R. (comp.), *Robert Rauschenberg*. New York: The Jewish Museum, 1964.

Soria, M. S. (ed.), *Francisco de Zurburan*. New York: Phaidon, 1953.

Steinberg, L., *Jasper Johns*. New York: Wittenborn, 1963.

Sterling, C., *Still Life Painting: From Antiquity to the Present Time* (tr. by J. Emmons), rev. ed. New York: Universe Books, 1959.

The Portrait in Painting and Sculpture

Ambler, E., *A Coffin for Dimitrios*. New York: Dell, 1957.

Elsen, A., "Rodin's Portrait of Baudelaire." No. 25, *A Catalogue and Collection of Essays Honoring Henry Hope*. Bloomington: Indiana University, 1966.

Friedländer, M. J., *Landscape, Portrait, Still Life* (tr. by R. F. C. Hull). Oxford, Eng.: Cassirer, 1949.

Giedion-Welcker, C. (ed.), *Constantin Brancusi*. Basel: B. Schwabe, 1958.

Held, J. (ed.), *Peter Paul Rubens*. New York: Abrams, 1953.

Hoffman, E., *Kokoschka: Life and Work*. London: Faber, 1947.

Lange, K., and M. Hirmer, *Egypt: Architecture, Sculpture, Painting in Three Thousand Years* (tr. by R. H. Boothroyd). New York: Phaidon, 1956.

Levey, M., "A Prince of Court Painters: Bronzino." *Apollo*, 76: 165–72, 1962.

Lipman, J. H., "The Florentine Profile Portrait in the Quattrocento." *Art Bulletin*, 18: 54–102, March, 1936.

Meiss, M., "Nicholas Albergati and the Chronology of Jan Van Eyck's Portraits." *Burlington Magazine*, 94: 137–46; 95: 27, May, 1952, January, 1953.

Miller, M., "Géricault's Portraits of the Insane." *Journal of the Warburg and Courtauld Institutes*, 4: 151–163, April-July, 1940–41.

Panofsky, E., *Eearly Netherlandish Painting*, 2 vols. Cambridge, Mass.: Harvard University Press, 1954.

Schapiro, M., *Vincent Van Gogh*. New York: Abrams, 1950.

Schapiro, M., *Paul Cézanne*. New York: Abrams, 1952.

Soby, J. T.. *Joan Miró*. New York: Museum of Modern Art, 1959.

Sylvester, D., *Alberto Giacometti*. Exhibition, Arts Council Gallery. London: Arts Council of Great Britain, 1955.

The Figure in Sculpture

The Figure in Older Sculpture

Clark, K. M., *The Nude: A Study in Ideal Form*. New York: Pantheon, 1956.

Janson, H. W., *The Sculpture of Donatello*, 2 vols. Princeton, N. J.: Princeton University Press, 1957.

Kramrisch, S., *The Art of India*. New York: Phaidon, 1954.

Panofsky, E., "The History of the Theory of Human Proportions as a Reflection of the History of Styles." In *Meaning in the Visual Arts*. New York: Anchor, 1955.

Schapiro, M., "The Sculptures of Souillac." In W. R. W. Koehler (ed.), *Medieval Studies in Memory of Arthur Kingsley Porter*. Cambridge, Mass.: Harvard University Press, 1939.

Wittkower, R., *Gian Lorenzo Bernini*. New York: Phaidon, 1955.

Transformations of the Figure in Modern Sculpture

Barr, A. H., Jr., *Matisse: His Art and His Public*. New York: Museum of Modern Art, 1951.

Elsen, A., "Seymour Lipton: Odyssey of the Unquiet Metaphor." *Art International*, 5: 39–44, February, 1961.

Elsen, A. E., *Rodin*. New York: Museum of Modern Art, 1963.

Grohmann, W., *The Art of Henry Moore*. New York: Abrams, 1960.

Ritchie, A. C., *Sculpture of the Twentieth Century*. New York: Museum of Modern Art, 1953.

Sylvester, D., *Alberto Giacometti*. Exhibition, Arts Council Gallery. London: Arts Council of Great Britain, 1955.

PICASSO

Barr, A. H., Jr. (ed.), *Picasso: Forty Years of His Art*. New York: Museum of Modern Art, 1939.

Blunt, A., and P. Pool, *Picasso, The Formative Years*. New York Graphic Society, 1962.

Boeck, W., and J. Sabartés, *Picasso*. New York: Abrams, 1955.

Gilot, F., and C. Lake, *Life with Picasso*. New York: Signet, 1965.

Greenberg, C., "Picasso at Seventy-five." In *Art and Culture: Critical Essays*. Boston: Beacon Press, 1961.

Kahnweiler, D. H., *The Sculptures of Picasso* (phot. by Brassaï; tr. by A. D. B. Sylvester). London: Rodney Phillips, 1949.

Penrose, R., *Picasso: His Life and Work*. New York: Harper, 1959.

Rosemblum, R., *Cubism and Twentieth-Century Art*. New York: Abrams, 1961.

IMAGINATIVE ART

General

Baltrusaitis, J., *Réveils et prodiges: Le gothique fantastique*. Paris: Colin, 1960.

Barr, A. H., Jr., *Fantastic Art, Dada, and Surrealism*. New York: Museum of Modern Art, 1936.

Bousquet, J., *Mannerism: The Painting and Style of the Late Renaissance* (tr. by S. W. Taylor). New York: Braziller, 1964.

Daniel, H., *Devils, Monsters and Nightmares*. New York: Abelard–Schuman, 1964.

Goldwater, R., and M. Treves (eds. and trs.), *Artists on Art*. New York: Pantheon, 1945.

Individual Artists

Benesch, O., *The Art of the Renaissance in Northern Europe*. (On Durer.) Hamden, Conn.: Shoe String, 1964.

Combe, J., *Jerome Bosch*. Paris: Tisné, 1957.

Dali, S., *The Secret Life of Salvador Dali*. New York: Dial, 1942.

De Tolnay, C., *Hieronymous Bosch*. Bâle: Editions Holbein, 1937.

Grohmann, W., *Paul Klee*. New York: Abrams, 1954.

Harris, T., *Goya, Engravings and Lithographs*, 2 vols. Oxford, Eng.: Cassirer, 1964.

Hess, T. B., *Willem de Kooning*. New York: Braziller, 1959.

Lebel, R., *Marcel Duchamp* (tr. by G. H. Hamilton). New York: Grove, 1959.

Lieberman, W. S. (ed.), *Max Ernst*. New York: Museum of Modern Art, 1961.

López-Rey, J., *Goya's Caprichos*, 2 vols. Princeton, N. J.: Princeton University Press, 1953.

Meyer, F. (ed.), *Marc Chagall; His Graphic Work*. New York: Abrams, 1957.

Odilon Redon, Gustave Moreau, Rudolf Bresdin, catalogue of an exhibition. New York: Museum of Modern Art, 1961.

Panofsky, E., *The Life and Art of Albrecht Dürer*. Princeton, N. J.: Princeton University Press, 1955.

Schwabacher, E. K., *Arshile Gorky*. New York: Macmillan, 1957.

Seitz, W. C., *René Magritte*. New York: Museum of Modern Art, 1965.

Selz, P., *The Work of Jean Dubuffet*. New York: Museum of Modern Art, 1962.

Selz, P., and others, *Max Beckmann*. New York: Museum of Modern Art.

Soby, J. T., *Giorgio de Chirico*. New York: Museum of Modern Art, 1955.

Tzara, T., *Bizzarie di varie figure di Giovanbatista Bracelli, pittore fiorentino*. Paris: A. Brieux, 1963.

THE DEATH OF THE WINDOW AND LIFE OF THE SQUARE: ABSTRACTION

Albers, J., *Interaction of Color*. New Haven, Conn.: Yale University Press, 1963.

Arp, H., *On My Way*. New York: Wittenborn, 1948.

De Kooning, E., in *Franz Kline Memorial Exhibition*. Washington D. C. Gallery of Modern Art, 1962.

Fried, M., *Three American Painters: Kenneth Noland, Jules Olitski, Frank Stella*. Cambridge, Mass.: Harvard University Press, 1965.

Goldwater, R. S., "Reflections on the Rothko Exhibition." *Arts*, 35: 42–45, March, 1961.

Haftmann, W., *The Mind and Work of Paul Klee*. London: Faber, 1954.

Jaffé, H. L. C., *De Stijl, 1917–1931; The Dutch Contribution to Modern Art*. Amsterdam: J. M. Meulenhoff, 1956.

Malevich, K. S., *The Non-Objective World* (tr. by H. Dearstyne). Chicago: Theobald, 1960.

Mondrian, P. C., *Plastic Art and Pure Plastic Art, 1937, and Other Essays, 1941–1943*. New York: Wittenborn, 1945.

Munari, B., *The Square*. New York: Wittenborn, 1966.

Reinhardt, A., Statements in D. C. Miller (ed.), *Americans 1963*, catalogue of an exhibition. New York: Museum of Modern Art, 1963.

Rosenberg, H., "Barnett Newman: The Living Rectangle." In *The Anxious Object*. New York: Horizon, 1964.

Schapiro, M., "The Liberating Quality of Avant Garde Art." *Art News*, 56: 36–42, June, 1957.

Schapiro, M., "On the Humanity of Abstract Painting." Blashfield Address. *Proceedings of the American Academy of Arts and Letters and the National Institute of Arts and Letters*, Ser. 2, No. 10, pp. 316–323, 1960.

Seitz, W. C., *The Responsive Eye*. New York: Museum of Modern Art, 1965.

Soby, J. T., *René Magritte*. New York: Museum of Modern Art, 1966.

Wheeler, M., *The Last Works of Henri Matisse*. New York: Museum of Modern Art, 1961.

INDEX

References are to page numbers, except for color plates, which are identified by plate numbers. Black-and-white illustrations are indicated by *italic* page numbers, and textual references by lightface numbers. The names of artists are given in CAPITALS. Titles of art are printed in *italics*; descriptive citations and titles of examples in architecture, in roman type.

PHOTOGRAPHIC SOURCES

References are to figure numbers unless indicated Pl. (plate).

Abrams, Harry, Inc., New York (363); A.C.L., Brussels (400); Aerofilms Limited, London (48); Alinari, Florence (213, 413); Anderson, Rome (270, 281, 427); Archives Photographiques, Paris (90 [below], 126, 236, 381, 401, 404, 513); Art Reference Bureau, Ancram, N.Y. (4, 5, 6, 11, 74, 75, 125, 127, 246, 258, 292, 347, 477, 489, 490); Art Reference Bureau–A.C.L. (131, 138, 140, 145, 146, 147, 148, 219, 220); Art Reference Bureau–Agraci (18, 332, 335, 338, 340, 386, 402); Art Reference Bureau–Alinari (8, 9, 73, 132, 139, 150, 154, 155, 157, 159, 164, 165, 166, 169, 170, 172, 173, 174, 175, 177, 178, 183, 185, 188, 190, 191, 196, 197, 198, 199, 201, 202, 212, 214, 215, 216, 217, 218, 224, 276, 277, 283, 294, 301, 302, 305, 307, 312, 325, 328, 329, 334, 336, 403, 425, 426, 440); Art Reference Bureau–Anderson (149, 151, 152, 153, 167, 171, 179, 184, 186, 194, 200, 211, 263, 264, 327, 382); Art Reference Bureau–Archives Photographiques (17); Art Reference Bureau–Brogi (156, 278, 279, 303, 424); Art Reference Bureau–Bruckmann (13, 137, 203, 204, 210, 225, 237, 243, 355, 483); Art Reference Bureau–Bulloz (339); Art Reference Bureau–R. B. Fleming (249); Art Reference Bureau–Fototeca Unione (306); Art Reference Bureau–Marburg (77, 232, 248, 308, 419, 480); Art Reference Bureau–Mas (207, 460, 475); Art Reference Bureau–O. Vaering (348); Baker, Oliver, New York (373, 449); Brazilian Embassy (323); Bruggmann, W., Winterthur, Switzerland (38); Burckhardt, Rudolph, New York (395); Castelli, Leo, Gallery, New York (Pl. 47); Chevojon Frères, Paris (453); The Courtauld Institute, London (342, 506); Elisofson, Eliot, New York (423); Fleming, R. B., and Co., London (85, 86); Fogg Art Museum, Harvard University, Cambridge, Mass.

(58); Fototeca Unione, Rome (61, 185, 186, 267, 296, 299, 300); Frantz, Allison, Athens (420, 422); French Embassy Press and Information Division, New York (64, 88, 94, 311, 421); French Government Tourist Office (93); Futagawa, Y. (313); Giraudon, Paris (68, 231, 234, 330); Hedrich-Blessing, Chicago (321); Hervé, Lucien, Paris (78); Hirmer Verlag, Munich (53, 62, 80, 87, 108, 257, 265, 266, 271, 289, 412, Pl. 12); Horn, Professor Walter W., University of California, Berkeley (95); India, Government of, Information Service (59, 324); Jäger Helmut (43); Janis, Sidney, Gallery, New York (Pl. 64); Kaufmann, F., Munich (418); Kidder Smith, G. E., New York (102 [above right and right]); The Kootz Gallery, New York (470); Larkin Brothers, London (60); Mas, Barcelona (134, 272); McCracken, William, New York (288); Museum of Fine Arts, Boston (Pl. 51); The Museum of Modern Art, New York (455, 469, Pl. 63); Nelson, O. E., New York (Pl. 56); Nohr, R., Munich (501); Pedroli, Gino, New York (442); Photo Meyer K. G., Vienna (Pl. 22); Photo Researchers, Inc., New York (102 [above]); Rheinisches Bildarchiv, Cologne (241); Roger-Viollet, H., Paris (180, 349); Rosenthal, Professor Earl (176); Scala, Florence (Pls. 15, 16, 17); Schiff, John D., New York (433); Shostal-Scala, New York (Pls. 5, 25, 40); Sieber, Professor Roy, Indiana University, Bloomington (26); Sollars, E. A., Winchester, England (119); Steinkopf, Walter (238); Stoedtner, Dr. Franz, Düsseldorf (298); Studly, Adolph, New York (434); Sunami, Soichi, New York (345, 367, 392, 417, 429, 430, 435, 436, 437, 438, 439, 454, 456, 457, 461, 462, 463, 468, 492, 494, 495, 497, 498, 499); Taurgo, New York (256); Trans World Airlines (79, 295 [Emit]); Ralph Morse, LIFE Magazine © Time, Inc., New York (Pl. 3); von Matt, Leonard [copyright] (192); Ward, William E. (72); Wildenstein's, London (505); Wyatt, A. J., Philadelphia (372, 391).